DISCARDED

D1267141

Handbook of
the Sociology
of Education

Handbooks of Sociology and Social Research

Series Editor:
Howard B. Kaplan, *Texas A&M University, College Station, Texas*

HANDBOOK OF THE SOCIOLOGY OF EDUCATION
Edited by Maureen T. Hallinan

HANDBOOK OF THE SOCIOLOGY OF GENDER
Edited by Janet Saltzman Chafetz

HANDBOOK OF THE SOCIOLOGY OF MENTAL HEALTH
Edited by Carol S. Aneshensel and Jo C. Phelan

A Continuation Order Plan is available for this series. A continuation order will bring delivery of each new volume immediately upon publication. Volumes are billed only upon actual shipment. For further information please contact the publisher.

Handbook of
the Sociology
of Education

Edited by

Maureen T. Hallinan

University of Notre Dame
Notre Dame, Indiana

Kluwer Academic / Plenum Publishers
New York   Boston   Dordrecht   London   Moscow

FLORIDA GULF COAST
UNIVERSITY LIBRARY

Library of Congress Cataloging-in-Publication Data

Handbook of the sociology of education / edited by Maureen T. Hallinan.
p. cm. -- (Handbooks of sociology and social research)
Includes bibliographical references and index.
ISBN 0-306-46238-9
1. Educational sociology--Handbooks, manuals, etc. I. Hallinan, Maureen T. II. Series.

LC191 .H254 2000
306.43--dc21

00-023579

ISBN: 0-306-46238-9

© 2000 Kluwer Academic / Plenum Publishers
233 Spring Street, New York, N.Y. 10013

http://www.wkap.nl/

10 9 8 7 6 5 4 3 2 1

A C.I.P. record for this book is available from the Library of Congress

All rights reserved

No part of this book may be reproduced, stored in a retrieval system, or transmitted in any form
or by any means, electronic, mechanical, photocopying, microfilming, recording, or otherwise,
without written permission from the Publisher

Printed in the United States of America

FLORIDA GULF COAST
UNIVERSITY LIBRARY

In memory of James S. Coleman
whose sociological insights profoundly influenced
twentieth-century sociology of education

Contributors

David P. Baker, College of Education, Pennsylvania State University, University Park, Pennsylvania 16802

Charles E. Bidwell, National Opinion Research Center, University of Chicago, Chicago, Illinois 60637

Elizabeth G. Cohen, School of Education, Stanford University, Stanford, California 94305-3084

Colette Chabbott, School of Education, Stanford University, Stanford, California 94305-3096; *Present address:* Board on International Comparative Studies in Education, National Academies of Science, Washington, DC 20007

Randall Collins, Department of Sociology, University of Pennsylvania, Philadelphia, Pennsylvania 19104-6299

Robert Dreeben, Department of Education, University of Chicago, Chicago, Illinois 60637

Joyce L. Epstein, Center on School, Family, and Community Partnerships, Johns Hopkins University, Baltimore, Maryland 21218

Adam Gamoran, University of Wisconsin-Madison, Madison, Wisconsin 53706

Maureen T. Hallinan, Institute for Educational Initiatives, University of Notre Dame, Notre Dame, Indiana 46556-5611

Thomas B. Hoffer, National Opinion Research Center, University of Chicago, Chicago, Illinois 60637

Stephanie Alter Jones, Institute for Policy Research, Northwestern University, Evanston, Illinois 60208

Alan C. Kerckhoff, Department of Sociology, Duke University, Durham, North Carolina 27706-0088

Helga Krüger, Department of Sociology, University of Bremen, Bremen 28359, Germany

Valerie E. Lee, School of Education, University of Michigan, Ann Arbor, Michigan 48109

Gerald K. LeTendre, College of Education, Pennsylvania State University, University Park, Pennsylvania 16802

Kathleen Lynch, Department of Equality Studies, University College Dublin, Dublin, Ireland

Cora B. Marrett, Provost's Office, University of Massachusetts, Amherst, Massachusetts 01003

Elizabeth H. McEneaney, Department of Sociology, University of Nevada-Las Vegas, Las Vegas, Nevada 89154-5033

John W. Meyer, Department of Sociology, Stanford University, Stanford, California 94305

Stephen L. Morgan, Department of Sociology, Harvard University, Cambridge, Massachusetts 02138

Jeylan T. Mortimer, Department of Sociology, University of Minnesota, Minneapolis, Minnesota 55455

Walter Müller, Department of Sociology, University of Mannheim, Mannheim D-68131, Germany

Aaron M. Pallas, Department of Counseling, Educational Psychology, and Special Education, Michigan State University, East Lansing, Michigan 48824-1034

Caroline Hodges Persell, Department of Sociology, New York University, New York, New York 10013

Francisco O. Ramirez, School of Education, Stanford University, Stanford, California 94305-3096

John G. Richardson, Department of Sociology, Western Washington University, Bellingham, Washington 98225

James E. Rosenbaum, Institute for Policy Research, Northwestern University, Evanston, Illinois 60208

Mavis G. Sanders, Center on School, Family, and Community Partnerships, Johns Hopkins University, Baltimore, Maryland 21218

Barbara Schneider, National Opinion Research Center, Chicago, Illinois 60637

Walter G. Secada, University of Wisconsin-Madison, Madison, Wisconsin 53706

Yossi Shavit, Department of Sociology and Anthropology, Tel Aviv University, Tel Aviv, Israel 69978

Aage B. Sørensen, Department of Sociology, Harvard University, Cambridge, Massachusetts 02138

David Lee Stevenson,† Office of Science and Technology Policy, Executive Office of the President, Washington, DC 20502

Pamela Barnhouse Walters, Department of Sociology, Indiana University, Bloomington, Indiana 47405

†Deceased.

Preface

The aim of the *Handbook of Sociology of Education* is to present the most theoretically grounded and empirically rigorous sociological analyses of schools to date. The authors are distinguished researchers in the field. Their contributions to the *Handbook* offer major theoretical perspectives on the schooling process and describe significant empirical studies of schools and their effects on individuals and society.

The research presented in the *Handbook* is built on three fundamental tenets of sociology. First, the authors adopt the perspective that schools are a central institution in society. An understanding of the function of schooling in social life is enhanced by viewing schools as interrelated with other societal institutions. The study of how the context of schooling influences education processes is critical to an understanding of school outcomes. Rather than being determined solely by ascribed and achieved characteristics, an individual's cognitive and social development are influenced heavily by the structures and networks in which the individual is embedded. Communities, families, schools, and social groups are critical elements in the educative process. By viewing the school as a societal institution and highlighting the interaction between context and individual behavior, the *Handbook* chapters provide a broader and deeper understanding of the determinants of learning in contemporary society.

The second sociological insight that guides the research in the *Handbook* is that the school is a social system. This focus appeared in the work of sociologists of education at the beginning of the twentieth century and continues to guide researchers today. A social system perspective was central to the theoretical and empirical work of James Coleman, whose contributions to the study of schools played a dominant role in the development of the field. The current availability of large longitudinal data sets permits researchers to analyze data from a systemic perspective, using the school as the unit of analysis. The *Handbook* chapters provide quintessential examples of systemic studies—analyses of system-level causes and consequences of schooling.

A third sociological insight on which the *Handbook* is built is that social events depend on the interaction of macrolevel and microlevel processes. Again, research in the sociology of education clearly depicts this phenomenon. Macrolevel processes link the structure and organization of schools to school-level outcomes such as communication patterns, governance structures, school climate, and social networks. Microlevel processes relate students' ascribed and achieved characteristics to their attitudes, motivation, performance, and social behavior. Linking macrolevel and microlevel processes to the transition between them is one of the most difficult conceptual challenges facing sociologists today. Several chapters in the *Handbook* make significant progress in this direction.

In the past, sociology of education was viewed by some as a narrow area, limited to the analysis of specific educational issues and problems or designed primarily to inform policy decisions about education. The *Handbook* demonstrates the fallacy of this view. Sociology of education is a field that applies the power of sociological analysis to a diverse set of important educational issues. The chapters highlight the unique and far-reaching benefits of the sociological analysis of educational issues.

The *Handbook* should serve as a valuable reference tool for social scientists and educators interested in an inclusive, scholarly analysis of schooling. The volume will be an invaluable aid to scholars interested in the field as a whole and researchers examining a particular aspect of the educational enterprise. The chapters may serve as a supplementary text or set of readings in graduate and advanced undergraduate courses in sociology or education. Finally, the breadth of perspectives and array of theoretical and conceptual linkages presented in the *Handbook* give it considerable cross-disciplinary appeal.

As *Handbook* editor, I am deeply grateful to the authors of the chapters for their seriousness of purpose, enthusiasm for the project, cooperation in the copyediting process, and gracious interactions throughout the long process of bringing this book to completion. I am also grateful to those generous colleagues who acted as anonymous reviewers of the chapters. Their insight, constructive criticisms, and attention to detail brought the work to a high level of distinction. Warren Kubitscheck acted as in-house copyediting manager and performed this tedious task with extraordinary diligence and patience. He was assisted by Valdimir Khmelkov, Elaine Li, Amy Orr, Kathryn Schiller, and Xiao-qing Wang. Sylvia Phillips provided secretarial assistance with her typical generosity and goodwill.

I am happy to acknowledge the encouragement and support of the series editor, Howard Kaplan, whose unwavering confidence in this project was a steady source of encouragement. I admit to the pleasure I experience whenever I work with Eliot Werner, Executive Editor of the Behavioral and Social Sciences Division of Kluwer Academic/Plenum Publishers. His creative wit never ceases to energize as well as entertain me, and working with him on this project was no exception. The Institute for Educational Initiatives at the University of Notre Dame deserves recognition for the research support they provided for this project. I also am deeply grateful to my family whose love makes all my professional endeavors possible.

Finally, it is with considerable pride that I dedicate the *Handbook of the Sociology of Education* to James S. Coleman. Pride stems from the fact that sociologists of education have a special claim to the scholarship of this man who was one of the most outstanding sociologists of the twentieth century. Coleman directed much of this theoretical and empirical work to the study of schools. I consider it great good fortune that his involvement in educational issues provided sociologists of education with intellectual leadership and guidance in the identification and conceptualization of important educational issues. Coleman was one of those rare prescient people who could recognize critical social problems before the rest of us. His highly heuristic, theoretical, and empirical research on critical contemporary social events influenced the scholarship of most sociologists of education over the past several decades.

Acknowledging James Coleman's contributions to sociology of education also evokes feelings of sadness that this great scholar no longer provides us with his intellectual leadership. Nevertheless, the body of scholarship that he accumulated over his lifetime is sufficient to guide research in sociology of education for many years to come. Coleman urged sociologists to engage in the comparative study of social systems. Theoretical models and empirical data available today make this goal more attainable than previously. Coleman also encouraged sociologists to analyze the transitions between macrolevel and microlevels of analysis; data on schools and students are particularly amenable to this kind of research. In accepting Coleman's direction, sociologists of education are assured of making significant progress in developing a solid and valuable body of scholarship on schools.

MAUREEN T. HALLINAN

Contents

†Deceased.

Introduction

Sociology of Education at the Threshold of the Twenty-first Century

MAUREEN T. HALLINAN

Remarkable progress has been made over the past half-century in the sociological analysis of education. At mid-century, little theoretical research on schooling was available, and few empirical studies of schools had been conducted. A large body of conceptually grounded and methodologically rigorous research has accumulated since then. Researchers have studied education from various theoretical perspectives and have analyzed complex data sets with sophisticated analytical techniques. As a result, the sociology of education has become a vital and expanding field within sociology and has made a significant contribution to our understanding of the social structures and processes that affect students' learning and social development. An overview of early theoretical and empirical contributions to the field and recent significant scholarship in the area should reveal the important role sociology of education plays in our understanding of education.

EARLY THEORETICAL CONTRIBUTIONS TO SOCIOLOGY OF EDUCATION

The early writings of Durkheim and Weber laid the conceptual foundation for the sociological analysis of schools. Durkheim was one of the first scholars to analyze education from a socio-

---

MAUREEN T. HALLINAN • Institute for Educational Initiatives, University of Notre Dame, Notre Dame, Indiana 46556-5611.

Handbook of the Sociology of Education, edited by Maureen T. Hallinan. Kluwer Academic/Plenum Publishers, New York, 2000.

logical perspective. He was concerned about the role of education in the preparation of children for their roles in adult society. In his many writings, and in particular in his important treatise *Moral Education* (1973), he discussed the importance of values in a stable society and the role of schools in teaching values to students. His work included analyses of the relationship between schools and other societal institutions, between education and social change, and between schools and the functions of a social system.

Weber's work was less directly related to education. Nevertheless, his writings on organizations, bureaucracies, leadership, and status increased understanding of the educational enterprise (see, for example, Weber, 1978). His ideal-type organization, with its division of labor, administrative hierarchy, procedural rules, formal relationships, and rational behavior, provided a model for school structure. His writings on status underscored the power of the dominant group and suggested how governing groups shape education and how power produces conflict across groups both inside and outside of schools. Weber's concept of a charismatic leader became a model for school administrators.

Other early sociologists also discussed issues directly relevant to the study of schools. Parsons (1959) analyzed the school as a social system and noted its role in the transmission of values and in the maintenance of social order and stability. Marx (1977; Marx & Engels, 1992) saw education as a system that perpetuates the existing class structure. Bowles and Gintis (1976) viewed schools as an instrument used by the dominant class to maintain the status quo, including its position of authority over the underprivileged. Waller (1932) conceptualized schools as unstable social systems in which the competing interests of administrators, teachers, parents, students, and community groups vie for power and authority. These and other sociologists contributed important insights into the nature and function of education in society.

Sociologists of education have relied on the theoretical orientations of these early writers to analyze schools as institutions and as social agents. Most of these theories describe macrolevel and microlevel mechanisms governing social behavior. The theoretical perspectives were formulated to explain social phenomena rather than to shed light on specific educational issues. Nevertheless, sociologists of education have employed tenets of these theories—including consensus theory and structural functionalism, conflict theory, and various interactionist conceptualizations—to explain schooling processes. These theoretical perspectives have provided a number of insights into schooling that have guided and enriched sociological analyses of education.

Although sociology of education has benefitted from reliance on general sociological theory to develop ideas about schooling processes, this approach is limited. One problem with depending solely on broad sociological theories to study education is that the theories are often applied to education issues without taking into account the unique environment and population of schools. As a result, the general theories have only weak explanatory and predictive power in the analyses of school processes.

A second problem associated with relying primarily on general sociological theory to study schools is that these perspectives offer little insight into the causes and consequences of interinstitutional and intrainstitutional variation in schooling processes. Although general sociological theories can explain institutional dynamics on a broad level, they cannot depict the unique interactions between schools and other societal institutions or within schools themselves. Whereas similarities exist between schools and other societal institutions, dramatic differences distinguish them from many other societal institutions. For example, schools function as partially closed institutions, have student populations that are in various stages of transition to adulthood, and include both publicly and privately owned and funded organizations. Differences exist across school sectors and across schools within sectors; also apparent are within-school differences. General sociological theories are too abstract to depict the interinstitutional and intrainstitutional interactions that are unique to schools.

In addition to relying on general sociological theories, sociologists of education have utilized theoretical concepts within subdisciplines of sociology to inform their work. For example, research on social stratification and mobility processes and in social psychology has provided useful ideas about how schools operate in society. Stratification and mobility research provides a framework to analyze the role of educational achievement and attainment in the process of occupational attainment and intergenerational mobility. Social psychological perspectives inform the study of attitudes and behaviors in school, students' motivation, student subcultures, and the development of normative systems within schools.

Although reliance on subdisciplinary research has also been helpful in developing ideas about schooling processes, it is subject to the same limitations as general sociological theory. Although many aspects of schooling can be illuminated by subdisciplinary perspectives, particularly when they are theoretically rich, the distinctive social processes that characterize schooling cannot be fully explained by these nonschool conceptual analyses. Subdisciplinary research can be most helpful to the sociology of education as a expansion of or a supplement to its own conceptual frameworks.

The heavy reliance of sociologists of education on general social theory and on ideas and models from other sociological subdisciplines to study schooling demonstrates the greatest weakness of the area. Although the sociology of education has shown remarkable progress since the 1950s in the area of empirical research, it has lagged in the development of theories about schooling. As a result, the field in general—despite its empirical accomplishments—would benefit from greater breadth, integration, and focus. A stronger theoretical foundation would guide the selection of future research studies and would insure greater progress in our understanding of schooling. Theoretical explanations that explain the social processes that occur in schools would help sociologists distinguish education from other social institutions; this would contribute to the study of societal institutions in general as well as to the study of schools in particular. Similarly, theoretical formulations that would compare and contrast social and organizational processes across and within schools would increase our understanding of specific schooling processes and of institutional processes in general.

The chapters in this handbook present a number of recent efforts by sociologists of education to develop a theory of schooling and show the progress being made in the formulation of theories of schooling. One function of the *Handbook* is to encourage continued efforts to build on and expand this incomplete theoretical base so as to increase the conceptual strength and richness of the sociology of education.

EARLY EMPIRICAL CONTRIBUTIONS
TO SOCIOLOGY OF EDUCATION

Sociologists of education have made greater advances in the analysis of empirical data than in the formulation of theoretical models of schooling processes. Three reasons account for this empirical progress. First, since the 1960s, sociologists of education have had available the analytical techniques developed in econometrics and in other applied fields to estimate statistical models of schooling processes. In particular, the formulation of the general linear model, and its many extensions, facilitated empirical studies. School data are amenable to statistical analysis because they are readily available and are conducive to categorical and continuous measurement. In the Coleman Report, arguably the most influential early empirical study in sociology of education, Coleman and associates (1966) used a production function model to examine how school and family resources (inputs) produced student outputs (achievement). Countless reanalyses of the Coleman Report were conducted and this body of work spawned related studies in the same tradition.

A second factor that promoted empirical work in sociology of education was the effort begun in the 1960s and the 1970s that has continued to the present; the collection of large, carefully designed, nationally representative surveys of schools, teachers, and students. Many of these data collection efforts were sponsored by the federal government, which overcame the obstacle of prohibitive costs. Federal agencies—such as the National Science Foundation, the National Institute of Health, and the U.S. Department of Education—provided generous support for survey research. Initially the government funded national cross-sectional surveys, and later longitudinal surveys, collecting information from large numbers of students and schools at several points in time. These data permitted analyses that traced the trajectory of students' experiences and the influences of schools on student outcomes throughout a student's career in school. The nature of the data offered researchers a choice of unit of analysis, ranging from student-level to state-level educational entities. The high quality of the data in most of these national surveys encouraged empirical studies in the sociology of education.

A third reason for the strong emphasis on empirical work in the sociology of education was that sociologists of education were becoming increasingly more aware that their empirical research could play a role in informing and shaping educational practice and policy. The federal government and state and local agencies requested social science research findings to help them make decisions about school matters such as student organization, curriculum content, and school governance. In addition, judicial officers frequently asked social scientists to act as expert witnesses to provide empirical findings that could inform actors in cases that involved educational policy. The demand for research findings that addressed contemporary political issues (such as desegregation, affirmative action, bilingual education, and mainstreaming) has grown with calls for school reform. Sociologists of education have increased the number of policy-relevant empirical studies and have disseminated their findings more widely in response to this demand for education studies.

Given that the research atmosphere since the 1960s has been particularly amenable to empirical research, sociologists of education have accumulated an impressive body of empirical studies of schools. Today the sociology of education can boast a large body of scholarship on educational issues. The empirical studies presented in the *Handbook* illustrate recent analyses that shed new light on schools and their effects on students' outcomes.

OVERVIEW OF THE HANDBOOK

The *Handbook* is divided into six sections, each representing a major area in the sociology of education. The chapters in each section present significant recent conceptualizations of schooling and identify critical issues and practical concerns about schools. The organizational scheme is meant to help the reader realize the depth and breadth of the field, identify the important research questions that define the area, and locate the chapters in the wider field of sociology of education. The following overview provides background information for each section and indicates special features of each chapter.

Part I: Theoretical and Methodological Orientations

The first section of the *Handbook* presents theoretical and methodological research that illustrates current work in these areas. Sociologists of education recognize that their research must be grounded in theory. Chapters 1 through 4 make significant advances in formulating theories of schooling. Rather than relying on general theories of society, the authors develop theoretical propositions about the social and organizational processes that unfold within schools. Chapters 5 and 6 caution the researcher that analytic models can constrain and limit the substantive issues studied in the sociology of education.

Chapters 1 and 2 present advances in the traditional conceptualizations of the school as a social system and as an organization. In Chapter 1, Bidwell presents a social psychological model of the school as an agent in socializing students for social participation in adult society. He stresses the normative dimension of schooling and its role in the development of students' social competence. His chapter offers explicit direction for researchers attempting to develop theoretical models of schooling based on social psychological orientations.

In Chapter 2, Gamoran, Secada, and Marrett provide an alternate conceptualization of the school as an organization. Anchoring their analysis in the concept of resources, the authors describe changes in the way sociologists of education have utilized organizational theory to explain the teaching/learning process. One of the major contributions of this chapter lies in the authors' insight that a school is a system of linked relationships. Their explanation of how the structure of these relationships affects teaching and learning offers a new perspective on the social organization of schools.

In Chapter 3, Hallinan attempts to relate the growing body of empirical research on race and ethnicity to work in the sociology of education. The study of race and ethnicity has been a preoccupation of sociologists for several decades. Moreover, schools have been at the center of efforts to integrate American society. Hence, it seems reasonable to expect that research on race and ethnicity would have influenced the way sociologists of education conceptualize the schooling process. However, Hallinan's analysis finds little to support this expectation. She concludes that research both on race and ethnicity and on schooling would benefit from greater theoretical and empirical connectedness. Moreover, research identifying political, social, economic, and cultural factors that affect the way schooling is conceptualized and studied would promote a better understanding of the role of schools in promoting racial and ethnic integration.

As background for her study of equity in education in Chapter 4, Lynch outlines egalitarian theory in general and critical and feminist theory in particular. She makes explicit many of the ideological and political assumptions underlying the analysis of educational equality and argues that sociology of education, as a discipline, has been more oriented to educational reform than to radical social change. Lynch calls for viewing equity from a broader perspective, taking both liberal and radical traditions into account, in order to better understand the dynamics that perpetuate social inequities in education.

In Chapter 5, Dreeben discusses the predilection of researchers for using structural effects models to analyze schools. The fact that schools are organizations makes it natural to study how the structure of a school can influence its members. Dreeben points out, however, that the strong bias of sociologists of education toward using a structural effects framework necessarily excludes the examination of other substantive issues about schools. Similarly, it constrains the use of different analytic methods that could broaden our understanding of schooling. Dreeben's analysis suggests that sociologists of education need to expand their conceptualizations of schooling and avoid the danger of allowing analytical methods to define and limit the substantive issues studied.

In Chapter 6, Sørensen and Morgan directly address the implications of the intersection of theory and analytical method. After examining the large school effects literature, the authors conclude that the primary limitations of this research are not strictly methodological. Rather, the conceptual implications of the methods used contain serious flaws. They claim that a nonlinear model of learning would better reflect the instructional process. They propose a curvilinear model of achievement and argue for its advantages over the traditional linear model.

In general, the six chapters in this section of the *Handbook* portray serious contemporary efforts to improve the theoretical foundation of the sociology of education and to harness methodology to promote theory. Greater emphasis on theory can only strengthen and improve empirical research. The creative efforts presented in these chapters make clear that the task of developing theories of schooling demands disciplined, systematic, and sustained attention. The sociological analysis of schools will make significant advances only to the extent that sociologists of education ground their research in solid substantive ideas and in clear conceptualizations of how schools promote students' cognitive and social development.

Part II: Development and Expansion of Education

Part II of the *Handbook* examines the historical development and expansion of schooling worldwide over the past century. At the beginning of the 20th century, education was limited to those privileged by geography, by class, and by religion. Today, nearly all children in developed countries receive an elementary school education and most graduate from secondary schools. Similarly, the number of students attending postsecondary institutions has increased dramatically. Though lagging behind industrialized countries, developing countries are following the same pattern of educational expansion. The four chapters in this section of the *Handbook* provide important perspectives on the growth of education and its interrelatedness with political, social, and cultural changes in society.

In Chapter 7, Chabbott and Ramirez argue that the effects of educational expansion on economic, political, and cultural advancement are more problematic than is commonly believed. They claim that whereas mass education accelerates national development, higher education plays a more ambiguous role in societal progress. Their analysis relates the effects of educational expansion to the institutionalization of schooling by nation–states. The authors conclude that arguments about the supposed effects of education on development have been used by nongovernment organizations to drive educational expansion.

McEneaney and Meyer examine two dimensions of education in Chapter 8: the role of schooling in preparing students for their responsibilities as adults and the role of mass education in preparing students to participate, as equals, in society. They discuss the tension that exists between these two goals of schools and describe their implications for curriculum content. McEneaney and Meyer argue for greater awareness of the determinants and consequences of curricular change and for a broader consideration of social context as an influence on the curriculum and, consequently, on its effects on equity issues.

Collins adopts a historical worldview of education in Chapter 9. Describing patterns in the expansion and contraction of educational systems in various countries and at various times, Collins identifies and analyzes the various societal forces that account for these evolutionary patterns. He contends that the contemporary pattern of educational expansion may be limited by societal disaffection with the bureaucratization of education and its stress on evaluation and with the financial costs of credential inflation. Collins extends his previously made arguments about credentialism (Collins, 1979) to the expansion of education at the highest level of schooling for all societies and at all times.

In Chapter 10, Walters focuses on recent educational expansion in the United States. She asks the critically important question of how educational expansion is related to equality of educational opportunity. Walters points out that most school reforms fail to reduce educational inequalities. To understand this phenomenon, she argues that it is necessary to analyze the association between educational expansion and access to educational opportunities within a school system. Walters's provocative analysis describes how school expansion promotes educational attainment for disadvantaged groups without reducing the educational advantages enjoyed by the privileged.

Besides offering a broad historical and comparative perspective on educational expansion and development, the four chapters in this section identify relationships between educational expansion and societal factors not typically studied. Their focus on the interrelationships between educational expansion and various other societal factors, rather than on causal relationships between expansion and social outcomes, provides important insights into the mechanisms that relate educational expansion and social progress.

Part III: The Study of Access to Schooling

Since the 1960s, sociologists of education have been preoccupied with the issue of equality of educational opportunity. Since the landmark Coleman Report (1966), researchers have investigated how background characteristics and school factors affect students' access to education. Of primary concern has been how learning opportunities are channeled to students. Researchers have focused on ways in which the organization of students for instruction, the content of the curriculum, students' access to the curriculum, and informal social processes within a school limit access to learning. Differential learning opportunities perpetuate societal inequalities. If students' background characteristics limit their educational opportunities, then schooling perpetuates societal inequities and violates principles of social justice. The focused attention by sociologists of education on equity issues has led to important policy-relevant research. The salience of this research to contemporary political, cultural, and social issues has given it prominence in legal and judicial proceedings, in public policy, and in educational practice.

The three chapters in Part III are examples of prominent research on educational equity. Cohen's systematic research on status differences in the classroom has long provided a strong empirical base to guide teacher practices aimed at reducing classroom inequities. Cohen builds on this body of work in Chapter 11. She identifies sources of school differences in access to learning, causes of unequal learning opportunities in the classroom, and ways to create a more equitable social system and learning environment.

In Chapter 12, Epstein and Sanders examine how family, school, and community relationships affect equality of educational opportunity. Relying on the concept of overlapping spheres of influence, they show how social capital facilitates students' learning. By framing a series of questions regarding school transitions, community ties, and students' roles, they outline the concepts that would comprise a theory of contextual effects on learning. This framework permits systematic analysis of the mechanisms that link students' background characteristics to academic outcomes. The model has the potential to reveal the fault lines in a student's learning context and to suggest ways that family, school, and community can work together to increase learning opportunities for all students.

Richardson's analysis in Chapter 13 examines two educational practices: the assignment of students to tracks and the assignment of students to special education classes and programs. He argues that the concept of educational risk has always been a central part of the discourse related to special education. However, the idea of academic risk has been less prominent in the dialogue on track placement even though disadvantaged students have been disproportionately assigned to lower tracks. Richardson traces the evolution of these two discourses and demonstrates the implications of their development for educational policy and practice.

The quite different equity issues discussed and analyzed in these chapters illustrate the breadth of research being conducted in this area. Examining educational inequalities from various perspectives yields important insights into the roots of inequity. In addition, it provides a rich background on which to build more comprehensive theories of the distribution of educational opportunities.

Part IV: The Study of School Organization

Another central interest in the sociology of education is the study of the school as an organization. This conceptual orientation has guided theoretical and empirical research on several topics including school governance structures, the content and organization of the curriculum, the assignment of students to instructional groups, and patterns of social relationships among members of the school community. Organizational analyses of schools have linked school characteristics with students' academic and social behaviors. An organizational approach to schools has attracted considerable attention both within and outside the subdiscipline. Interest in this area is due largely to the fact that research on school organization addresses issues related to access to educational opportunities and highlights ways that schools can be changed to improve equity and achievement. The study of the school as an organization and its effects on student outcomes is one of the areas in the sociology of education that contains the most systematic and rigorous research.

The four chapters in Part IV of the *Handbook* represent current scholarship on school organization and student outcomes. In Chapter 14, Lee argues that the size of a secondary school has a direct effect on students' learning, but also has an indirect effect, operating through various features of the school. Based on her interpretation of empirical findings, she contends that secondary schools should be smaller than they typically are. She also points out that decreasing size has a declining utility, that the ideal school size should not be determined by characteristics of the student population, and that small schools are particularly effective for disadvantaged students. The policy implications of Lee's arguments are of immediate importance.

In Chapter 15, Baker and LeTendre present a convincing argument for more comparative analyses of schools and their outcomes. They trace the somewhat parallel research traditions of school effects studies and cross-national comparative research and point out the general theoretical weaknesses of the few efforts to conduct comparative analyses of school outcomes. Despite the recent availability of international data that permit somewhat rigorous cross-national comparisons, the authors argue that the processes that explain students' performance have yet to be examined closely. They suggest that comparative research on school organization and outcomes has the potential to make a significant theoretical contribution to sociology by linking macrolevel and microlevel processes that govern students' achievement.

Schneider is concerned about the influence of norms on students' academic achievement. In Chapter 16, she discusses James Coleman's analysis of the emergence and influence of norms in a social system. Schneider makes explicit the relationship between Coleman's research on school effects and his lifelong fascination with norms, values, and incentives. Her analysis provides a strong foundation for further theoretical and empirical work linking normative systems within the school to students' behavior.

In Chapter 17, Persell shares Schneider's concern about schools' influences on students' behavior. Persell asks whether differences in the value systems and control mechanisms in public and private schools account for differences in students' achievement in these two school sectors. She argues that organizational characteristics of schools—including school size, client power, and financial resources–rather than school sector affect the values and control system in a school. Persell formulates a conceptual model that links school characteristics to values and control and identifies the mechanisms that relate values and control systems to students' achievement. In addition to its theoretical contribution, Persell's chapter informs the growing debate about public/private school effects on students' learning.

These four *Handbook* chapters present current conceptual approaches to the study of school organization and outcomes. Not included are chapters specifically discussing the organizational differentiation of students for instruction or the organization of the curriculum. Empirical studies on these topics are well represented in edited volumes and in sociology journals and need not be repeated here. However, the new and original conceptual work reported in this section deserves wide attention.

Part V: The Study of School Outcomes

A recent interest of sociologists of education has been the linkage between schooling and students' subsequent experiences, especially in the labor market. Studies on the transition from school to work have been increasingly motivated by a rapidly changing job market influenced by the technological advances that have altered the skills students need to compete for employment. In addition, the shrinkage of social welfare programs in the United States, and the more stringent work requirements associated with public assistance, have focused attention on the role of schools in preparing students for the labor market.

The five chapters in Part V examine the transition from school to work from a number of perspectives. In Chapter 18, Rosenbaum and Jones investigate the extent to which school officials transmit information about students to employers and the effects of this information transmittal on students' chances of obtaining employment. They compare the formal linkages that exist between school and employer in Japan and in Germany with the more informal school–employer interactions that are common in the United States. The authors conclude that by providing employers with information not only about a student's academic achievements but also about such job-related characteristics as punctuality, attendance, and responsibility, school officials facilitate students' entrance into the workforce. These school–employer communication networks are particularly useful to disadvantaged students who may have few other resources to assist them in the job market.

Shavit and Müller focus on vocational education and its effects on employment opportunities in Chapter 19. They challenge the widely held assumption that participation in vocational education limits a student's likelihood of attending college and impedes occupational attainment. The authors formulate a conceptual model that identifies the mechanisms that link various aspects of vocational education to students' job success and that specifies the contextual conditions under which these mechanisms operate. In examining student data from a comparative international survey, they conclude that observed differences in the educational and occupational attainment of students across countries are partly due to institutional characteristics of school systems.

In Chapter 20, Kerckhoff presents a comparative analysis of the transition from school to work in France, Germany, Great Britain and the United States. He argues that three dimensions of the transition process affect students' job opportunities: the degree of stratification in the educational system, the degree of standardization in the educational system, and the nature of the system's educational credentials. Like Shavit and Muller in the previous chapter, Kerckhoff concludes that at least some of the variation in the transition from school to work is due to differences in the way societies organize their educational systems.

Mortimer and Krüger focus on how formal educational pathways influence students' experiences in Chapter 21. Comparing school-to-work transitions in Germany and in the United States, they identify structural differences in the two countries such as varying connections between youths' jobs while still in school and postschooling employment. The highly structured transition from school to work found in Germany includes apprenticeships and other formal routes to adult employment. The German system contrasts with the more loosely structured, informal processes that exist in the United States where paid work while in school is viewed as a threat to students' academic achievement. The authors discuss the advantages and disadvantages of each system in the process of socioeconomic attainment.

In Chapter 22, Pallas broadens the discussion of the school-to-work transition by considering how schools prepare students for adult life in general. Pallas examines the effects of schools on several dimensions of adulthood, including family life, work, social and emotional well-being, and civic participation. His analysis underscores the role of schools in preparing students for adult responsibilities and for the importance of considering socialization experiences as well as learning opportunities when evaluating the contribution of schools to an individual's long-term well-being.

These five chapters provide convincing evidence that schools can play a major role in helping individuals obtain their first job after graduation. Schools with network ties to the labor market are particularly useful, as are schools that encourage informal ties between students, counselors, and members of the work community. Comparative analysis of the transition process across countries reveals the strengths and weaknesses of various structured and unstructured practices designed to assist students in finding meaningful employment.

Part VI: Policy Implications of Research in the Sociology of Education

The primary goal of researchers in the sociology of education is to conduct basic and applied studies that increase understanding of the role of schooling in society and the effects of schooling on individual lives. Many of these studies have implicit or explicit implications for educational policy. Basic research that explains how school characteristics and cognitive and social processes affect student outcomes can suggest policies that promote learning. Applied research that demonstrates the effects of educational practices on student outcomes can lead to improved instructional techniques and school programs. Some of the links between the sociology of education and practice and policy are stronger than others. Strong and rigorous conceptual and empirical research is expected to have the greatest impact on educational policy and school reform.

The two chapters in Part VI of the *Handbook* directly address policy implications of research in the sociology of education. In Chapter 23, Hoffer examines a major component of current school reform efforts, namely, accountability. He investigates the growth of accountability systems, the ways educational institutions implement accountability programs, and the effectiveness of these programs. Hoffer argues that because accountability policies are new and underdeveloped, sociological research can make a significant contribution to the development of effective accountability programs by identifying the kinds of information needed and how that information should be used to increase accountability.

In Chapter 24, Stevenson provides an overview of the process of policymaking and implementation and the role that sociology of education research plays in this process. Stevenson points out that policymaking has two phases: policy development and policy implementation. He claims that educational research has a significant effect on policy development but is less influential in policy implementation. He describes the role of educational research in policy initiatives related to comprehensive school reform, standards-based reform, class size reduction, and classroom technology. Stevenson argues that these and other important contributions of research to policy development have been overlooked because they are not evident in the visible and often highly partisan debates over policy implementation. At this later stage of policymaking, political considerations and compromises—rather than educational effectiveness—tend to determine which policies are enacted. Stevenson's analysis provides a strong argument for continued efforts to disseminate educational research widely and to targeted audiences.

These two chapters on policy implications of sociological research on education go beyond most work in this area by conceptualizing the process of developing and implementing policy. The chapters make explicit how research is utilized in the formation and carrying out of policy. A greater awareness of this process can suggest ways for researchers to increase the likelihood that their research influences school policy by disseminating it more effectively.

SIGNIFICANCE OF THE *HANDBOOK OF THE SOCIOLOGY OF EDUCATION*

The *Handbook of the Sociology of Education* assembles outstanding recent sociological research on schools. The theoretical frameworks, conceptual and analytical models, and rigorous statistical analyses presented in the chapters in the *Handbook* provide a firm foundation for the ongoing study of schooling. They also provide models for conceptual and empirical work on education and offer direction in the selection of future research studies.

The *Handbook* is a symbol of the dedication of contemporary sociologists of education to their self-appointed task of producing the highest quality research on schools. The existence of bodies of systematic scholarship within sociology of education, characterized by conceptual integration and steady empirical advances, is a testimonial to this dedication. Sociologists of education have made steady progress in the study of schooling both in times of plentiful research support and in times of scarcer resources. They have steadfastly pursued their research commitments without being distracted or deflected by political agendas or by cultural conflicts regarding educational issues. They have maintained their commitment to using sociological research to reveal social inequities in the delivery of education to all citizens. The result of this dedication is evident in the outstanding research presented in the *Handbook*.

The challenge that the *Handbook of the Sociology of Education* presents to contemporary researchers is to continue the tradition of vigorous scholarship that characterizes the field. Building on the conceptual and empirical studies presented in the *Handbook*, scholars need to engage in serious analyses of important educational problems and issues. Creative thinking will expand the theoretical formulations on which the field is built and rigorous empirical analyses will inform and guide theory and practice. The result of these efforts should increase understanding of the schooling process and ultimately improve the quality of education for all students. By drawing attention to distinguished research in the sociology of education and by disseminating this important body of research, the *Handbook* promises to significantly advance the field of the sociology of education in the 21st century.

REFERENCES

Bowles, S., & Gintis, H. (1976). *Schooling in capitalist America: Educational reform and the contradictions of economic life*. New York: Basic Books.

Coleman, J. S., Campbell, E. Q., Hobson, C. J., McPartland, J., Wood, A. M., Weinfield, F. D., & York, R. L. (1966). *Equality of educational opportunity*. Washington, DC: U.S. Government Printing Office.

Collins, R. (1979). *The credential society: An historical sociology of education and stratification*. New York: Academic Press.

Durkheim, É. (1973). *Moral education: A study in the theory and application of the sociology of education*. Translated by Everett K. Wilson and Herman Schnurer. New York: The Free Press.

Marx, K. (1977). *Capital: A critique of political economy*. Translated by Ben Fowkes. New York: Vintage Books.

Marx, K., & Engels, F. (1992). *The Communist manifesto*. Edited with an introduction by David McLellan. Oxford: Oxford University Press.

Parsons, T. (1959). The school class as a social system: Some of its functions in American society. *Harvard Educational Review* 29: 297–313.

Waller, W. (1932). *The sociology of teaching*. New York: Wiley.

Weber, M. (1978). *Economy and society: An outline of interpretive sociology*. Edited by Guenther Roth and Claus Wittich. Berkeley, CA: University of California Press.

PART I

THEORETICAL AND METHODOLOGICAL ORIENTATIONS

CHAPTER 1

School as Context and Construction

A Social Psychological Approach to the Study of Schooling

CHARLES E. BIDWELL

In this chapter, I use examples from a current study of high schools and a selective review of the literature on social psychology and on the sociology of education to draw out implications for a social psychology of schooling. I begin with brief descriptions of two high schools where colleagues and I have conducted fieldwork as part of a study of 13 Chicago area public and private high schools (Bidwell & Bryk, 1994).* In each of these schools, we interviewed teachers and administrators, shadowed teachers, observed them in class and elsewhere during the working day, and in a less systematic way observed the daily round of student life. This fieldwork stimulated the ideas that I outline in this chapter.

Following these introductory cases, I delineate some central, enduring problems of social psychology, attempting to show that the classic concept of the "definition of the situation" remains a valuable part of the field's theoretical armamentarium and that it can be applied productively to the study of schooling. I conclude the chapter with a discussion of implications of this theoretical approach for the analysis of schooling as socialization for social par-

* The research on which this chapter draws was supported by Grant SES-8803225 from the National Science Foundation and the National Center for Educational Statistics and a grant from the Benton Center for Curriculum and Instruction of the University of Chicago. These supporting agencies have no responsibility for the contents of this chapter. I am grateful to Alan C. Kerckhoff for trenchant comments on an early version of this chapter.

CHARLES E. BIDWELL • National Opinion Research Center, University of Chicago, Chicago, Illinois 60637

Handbook of the Sociology of Education, edited by Marueen T. Hallinan. Kluwer Academic/Plenum Publishers, New York, 2000.

ticipation, in part to illustrate how we can broaden the purview of the sociology of education beyond its current singular focus on the etiology of academic achievement.

TWO HIGH SCHOOLS

Merriwether Lewis High School is one of three high schools in a suburban district just south of Chicago. This area has been primarily industrial for many years, including most of the oil refining for the Chicago area and a good deal of the upper Middle West. This industrial base has declined since the mid- to late 1980s, and the decline has been accompanied by a change in the families the district serves. A solidly stable working class population, with an admixture of professional and managerial families, has been replaced by Appalachian in-migrants and African–American families fleeing Chicago's inner city. The district now is characterized by a high rate of unemployment and many mother-only households.

Lewis High School has been the district's flagship high school. In the early 1930s, a major oil company located its principal research laboratory adjacent to its refinery, and Lewis High was built to serve the children of a community of scientists, technicians, and research administrators who chose to live near the lab. The curriculum was almost entirely college preparatory, with an attendant array of extracurricular academic clubs and teams. From the beginning, college-going rates were high, and the colleges included a good representation of the more selective schools.

This situation remained unchanged until about 1980. Then the oil company moved its laboratory to a more bucolic setting, and virtually the entire profession that Lewis High had served moved with it. The local community had been losing population steadily over the past several years, and the less numerous new arrivals were lower middle and upper working-class families, with children who aspired to community college rather than Michigan or Stanford. To reduce overcrowding in the district's two other high schools, a consequence of in-migration to their attendance areas, the district began busing students from these areas to Lewis. Lewis High now enrolls a mixture of its new local clientele and students who, for the most part, have weak academic preparation and expectations and for high school and for the future that are very different from those to which the Lewis faculty had been accustomed.

This faculty is very senior. At Lewis, teachers have been recruited and have themselves been attracted because of the fit between their own training and pedagogical preferences and the college preparatory mission of the school. Once past the probationary period, most have stayed until retirement. By the time the student body changed, the large majority of Lewis teachers felt that they had too many sunk costs to move elsewhere and that a transfer within the district was not an option.

The transformation of the Lewis student body was a great shock to virtually the entire faculty. In interviews, in conversations with colleagues, and in more formal settings like faculty meetings, teachers consistently interpreted events in the school according to an organizational history periodized by two key events: the school's founding, which defined its mission, and the loss of its academically oriented clientele, which now made it virtually impossible to carry that mission forward. Where the students once had been highly motivated, interested in the subjects, keen, intelligent, and lively but well mannered, they were described now as unmotivated, uninterested, a good deal less smart, and either passive or boisterous. Parents, once perceived as supportive and loyal, now were seen as indifferent to their children's education and as uninvolved in school affairs. The Lewis faculty described themselves as serving out the time to retirement.

In sum, the faculty of Lewis High School had developed an interpretive account of the school. That this account was widely shared among the teachers is evidenced by its consistent, repeated, spontaneous occurrence in interaction among colleagues. The account is a schema that allows Lewis teachers to use a small number of fundamental assumptions about the school's institutional and organizational origins and about its current environment to make sense out of everyday events on the job. In this account, the foundation of the school is key because of the implications of the mission that it defined. The college prep mission specifies the principal responsibilities and qualities of faculty: subject specialization and competence; rigorous teaching; high academic and behavioral standards; and exemplification of the values of self-discipline, self-control, and civility. The mission also defines the principal responsibilities and qualities of the student, which simply put, are the counterparts to those of their teachers.

Interpreting the change of the student population as a crisis in which a formidable barrier was erected to the accomplishment of the mission is key in this account because it allows the mission itself, and the derivative faculty and student roles, to remain unchanged. The crisis is described in delimited terms as a demographic crisis rather than as a curricular or a professional one. Professional identity is bound up with the identity of Lewis High School as an academic flagship high school, and neither could be abandoned after a long, distinguished organizational history and so late in individual teachers' careers.

In effect, the Lewis faculty prior to the crisis had formed a community of fate that enjoyed the most favorable prospects. The community of fate remained, but its prospects now had drastically declined. A diagnosis was required, and the source of the crisis was singular, readily identifiable, but hard to remedy—the deterioration of the student body, to whom now were attributed motives and intellectual and moral traits diametrically opposed to those of past student cohorts. Because the mission was inviolable, so that the roles of teacher and student remained properly defined within its terms, nothing really could be done.

My observation of the Lewis High students was much less systematic, but I saw a good deal of evidence that these students for the most part were fulfilling the expectations of their teachers. In the classes that I observed, students were consistently apathetic or indifferent, and the teachers tended to be highly punitive, holding up standards of performance and conduct "from the old days," almost always finding the students wanting. In this way, the students' performance and conduct reinforced the faculty's attributions, in a cycle that no doubt gave stability to how the faculty regarded these students and how the students regarded themselves, worked, and behaved. A growing importance of athletics and cheerleading in the extracurriculum, a decline of academic clubs, and the presence of a small number of mostly middle-class achieving students with whom the majority could be unfavorably compared no doubt further confirmed the faculty's perceptions.

The story of St. Aloysius High School to a degree parallels that of Lewis High, but there is a consequential difference of faculty demography. St. Aloysius is a Roman Catholic diocesan high school. It is in a Chicago neighborhood in the shadow of a gigantic steel mill, now shut down. For many years, the mill employed the Polish and other eastern European steel workers whose sons and daughters were educated at St. Aloysius. For the most part, these families have left the community to be replaced by young Hispanic families, with aspirations for economic betterment for themselves and for their children.

Since early in the 20th century, St. Aloysius served as an educational avenue for upward mobility. Where at one time it sent the children of immigrants on toward clerical and commercial occupations, it more recently had prepared them for 4 years at one of the Chicago area's Catholic colleges or universities or, in a few cases, for one or another of the campuses of the University of Illinois. It could afford to be selective because it enjoyed a substantial subvention from the Chicago archdiocese and because its strong reputation for both academics and athletics created abundant applications. It chose its students from a set of feeder Catholic elementary schools that St. Aloysius trusted to do a good job of preparation. By all faculty accounts, this selectivity yielded hard-working, compliant students and trusting, responsible parents.

Now, faced with deficits, the archdiocese has stopped underwriting high school budgets, so that St. Aloysius, lacking an endowment, depends entirely on tuition income. The school is no longer oversubscribed, and only a small proportion of the students come from the traditional feeder schools. In fact, many come directly from elementary schooling in Mexico, often without fluent English. College preparation is still the mission, and the parents still expect it, but it is preparation for one of the city community colleges rather than DePaul or Notre Dame. The school must maintain its enrollment to survive, while the parents have become somewhat more demanding and less trustful, perhaps less deferent to a predominantly lay faculty and administrative staff than their predecessors had been to the sisters.

As at Lewis High, the St. Aloysius teachers gave a collective interpretive account of the school's foundation and its enduring mission—much like the Lewis account of its mission, although with greater emphasis on moral socialization. Again, there was the shared perception of a crisis, here attributed to the loss of diocesan funds and marked by a sudden, sharp deterioration of students' preparation for high school.

For the St. Aloysius teachers as for those at Lewis High, change in the character of the students was the key pedagogical element of the crisis, but in contrast to Lewis I found two accounts of this change. When St. Aloysius entered less prosperous times, a sizeable fraction of its teaching force moved on to other jobs. The survivors and the replacements formed two distinct faculty cohorts, with correspondingly distinct interpretations of the school's pedagogical situation. Teachers with long service at St. Aloysius saw the new crop of students as intellectually undisciplined but able enough, and therefore in need of a disciplined academic experience—in graduated doses that would culminate in readiness for four year college. The others, newly hired, saw the students as able, but not conventionally prepared for the usual academic curriculum. These teachers advocated, and then began offering, new courses intended to build on the students' prior experiences and present interests to fit them for community college.

My observations at St. Aloysius are not very informative about the students' interpretations and understanding of their role, the faculty role, or the school. But it was clear from my classroom observations that the same students, going from class to class, encountered both old guard and newcomer teachers and found themselves treated very differently from one class to another as a result—on the one hand, as unable to meet rigorous demands of a subject matter and, on the other, as privy to a world of experience of considerable value to be respected on its own terms and adapted to effective use in the urban North.

SOCIAL PSYCHOLOGY AND THE STUDY OF SCHOOLING

Social Psychology and Three Principles of the Field

In the Preface to *Social Psychology*, Morris Rosenberg and Ralph Turner (1981) review standard definitions of the field. They note that Gordon Allport (1937) had defined social psychology as an "attempt to understand how the thought, feeling, and behavior of individuals are influenced by the actual, imagined, or implied presence of others." Four decades later, the editorial statement of the *Social Psychology Quarterly* (1978) said that social psychology is the "study of the primary relations of individuals to one another or to groups, collectivities, or institutions, insofar as they substantially influence, or are substantially influenced by, social forces." Rosenberg and Turner go on to provide their own definition: "how people (and the social forces impinging on them) affect one another's thoughts, feelings, and behavior."

These definitions contain three principles that have been central to the field as it has developed in the United States: (1) a singular focus on individual psychological states and behavior, treated primarily as consequences of social influence (despite the *Quarterly's* more capacious view), (2) emphasis on primary social relationships as the immediate sources of this influence and, therefore, as mediating institutional or collective influences, and (3) by strong implication, the idea that the person's cognitive and emotional states (e.g., thought and feeling) in some way link social context and individual behavior.

The Principles and their Vicissitudes in the Study of Schooling

The considerable majority of sociologists interested in education utilize social psychology in the sense that they analyze the social organization of schooling as antecedent to individual aspiration or achievement. Those of us who have pursued this work have adhered too strictly to the first two of these principles, while often neglecting the third. Compare the work of Willard Waller with more recent social psychological models of education and educational or occupational aspiration and attainment.

WALLER ON TEACHING. Waller's (1932) classic, *The Sociology of Teaching*, was strongly influenced by W. I. Thomas's (1923) social psychology of the situation. Thomas placed the situated, volitional human actor at the theoretical center. For Thomas, individual behavior arises out of that person's own definition of the situation, which is a product in part of the person's organismic state, in part of institutionalized situational definitions, and in part of the person's self-awareness—perceptions and evaluations of possibilities for action. A major question for Thomas was the way possibilities for purposive action—behavior intended to realize some personal interest or value—are affected by differences in the unanimity and stability of individuals' definitions of situations experienced in common.

Waller envisioned the school as a social organizational whole. He made explicit a strong implication of Thomas's ideas—that the social situation that each actor confronts is created largely by the acts and, therefore, by the interests, social positions, and situational definitions of the others with whom the actor is jointly involved. In the ideal typical school that Waller analyzed, the lives of students and teachers overlap and intersect. Students must deal with a situation substantially created by teachers' efforts to impart knowledge, the form and content of which are alien to students. Teachers must deal with a situation substantially created by students' efforts to deflect teachers' demands and find alternative bases for enjoyment and accomplishment.

Both situations are constrained by firmly institutionalized curricula and by undergirding conceptions of what school is that make the school a "museum of virtue" and the teacher its curator. The students, especially the boys, enjoy the greater latitude of youth to comply or to resist. Within these institutional constraints, the members of each group, faculty and students alike, map out worlds of possibility in which the inextricable linkage of their situational definitions and corresponding conduct create inexorable conflicts between students and teachers, exemplified by a never-ending "battle of the requirements."

Waller has an essentially pessimistic view of the school, having argued that teachers become desiccated and students become disengaged as a consequence of the social organization of their common life—teachers by repeated failure to engage students in courses and in subject matters and students by both the jejune quality of school knowledge and the atmosphere of antagonism in which it is encountered.

However, neither desiccation nor disengagement arises out of passivity. For Waller, it is the ultimately overwhelming constraints of institutionalized patterns of social expectation, which define school knowledge as something distinct from practical knowledge, that ultimately defeat successive cohorts of teachers and discourage and alienate successive cohorts of students. A prospect of positive forms of conduct and participation for teachers and for students lies in the possibility of more liberating definitions of the school situation. To realize this prospect would require public expectations and values that somehow became liberal enough to let school life connect teachers and students to the educative nature of "real life" (see Cohen, 1989) .

In brief, Waller's (1932) depiction of school life is notable for its fine-grained, dynamic analysis of the school as a network of social relationships within which opportunities for individual action take shape. Individual students and teachers develop conceptions of themselves, of each other, and of the possibilities for conduct within this frame. Common situations breed common outlooks on self, on others, and on the future, and, thus, breed similar patterns of conduct. Individuals' acts, in turn, feed back to stabilize or change the social order of the school. Thus, although Waller gave prime attention to individual cognitive and emotional states as mediating situation and behavior, and to face-to-face interaction as a prime mediator of collective influence on individuals, these processes are embedded within an elaborated structural analysis of the school situation itself.

MODELING EDUCATIONAL ATTAINMENT.   More recent sociological studies have turned away from the direction of work that Waller's (1932) study exemplifies toward a more individual-centered stance. Since the late 1950s in the United States and in western Europe, imparities of educational life chances have been the defining issue of educational policy. They have been the central issue for sociologists of education as well, giving rise to a sustained line of work modeling sources of variation in students educational and occupational aspirations and attainment. William Sewell and his colleagues at the University of Wisconsin were early leaders of this effort, presenting the Wisconsin model of educational attainment explicitly as a social psychological model (Sewell, Haller, & Portes, 1969).

Compared with a work like Waller's, the Wisconsin model is striking in its inattention to the social organizational context of attainment. In this model, individuals' ultimate occupational attainments are presented as being influenced most proximately by educational attainment, each of which is a function of prior aspiration. In this way, the person's cognitive and emotional states are presented as important causes of behavior—namely, attainment in school and then in the labor market. These aspirations, in turn, are posited as affected by significant others' influence, which arises in face-to-face encounters (presumably based on a strong sentimental bond) that allow the other either to serve as a model for the individual or to communicate to him or to her expectations for behavior.

However, the model does not clearly represent the social organizational matrix within which significant others' influence arises. No identifiable social situation is represented in this model. Influence is expected to come from three principal sets of others: parents, teachers, and peer friends. However, neither family structure, school organization, nor the friendship circle appears in the Wisconsin model.

Analyzing longitudinal data from their sample of rural Wisconsin males, Sewell and colleagues (1969) presented findings that were in substantial agreement with their model and with the emerging literature on the role of educational attainment in occupational attainment (most notably Blau & Duncan, 1967). In a few years, the literature on the social psychology of educational attainment had expanded rapidly, including a series of major studies that provide a fuller specification of the student's egocentric environment (e.g., Alexander & Eckland, 1973; Kerckhoff, 1972, 1974; Rehberg & Rosenthal, 1978; Williams, 1972). However, none of the models used in these studies locates influence processes in social situations, conceived either relationally or normatively.*

It would not be hard to allow this social organizational context to enter such models, if, like Waller (1932), one regarded the student as a situated, volitional individual actor. Situating this student would require us at the minimum to take account explicitly of opportunities for the student to participate in social situations within the school (e.g., in a high school, curricular tracks or courses, extracurricular activities or athletic teams); the student's patterned interaction in each of these situations; and the incidence, strength, and normative content of the student's ties, arrayed across the situations.

Ideally, to complement these egocentric data, one also would have access to a sociocentric analysis of the social organization of the school itself, in which differences of role, beliefs, behavior, and ascription (e.g., teachers and students, high and low aspirers, high and low achievers, males and females) were mapped onto a depiction of the relational structure of the school. This sociocentric analysis would provide a picture of the school's social situations (in both structural and normative terms), in which each individual student (or teacher, for that matter) could be located and to which each could be connected (with measurable strength and directionality) using the egocentric depiction of ties to others in the school.

THE SOCIAL ORGANIZATION OF SCHOOLING. A more promising social psychology of schooling, still centered on achievement outcomes, is evident in studies of the formal organization of schools. This line of inquiry began with investigations of the organization of instruction into curricular tracks or ability groups or levels. When Sewell and his colleagues were developing their model, Sørensen (1970) published an acute theoretical argument in which he proposed that various demographic and structural aspects of curricular tracks or levels—such as degrees of homogeneity in ability composition, boundary permeability, and the location of control over a student's placement—would affect the direction and strength of students' academic motives and performance.

The mechanisms that he posited to produce these effects were similar to those adduced by Sewell and colleagues (1969) in the Wisconsin model: interpersonal comparisons, modeling, and persuasion. However, in contrast to the Wisconsin model, Sørensen's theory takes into account a school social situation—the composition and structure of either a track or ability level or a school's array of tracks or levels—and posits effects of the mechanisms that are contingent upon attributes of the situation. For example, he predicted that interpersonal influence will occur more often when track or level boundaries are strong than when they are weak because strong boundaries tend to confine students' interaction within their own tracks. Because track placement is to some degree performance based, students' motives and attainment should stabilize and converge on the track mean as a positive function of boundary strength.

---

* During this same period, a second line of work attempted to measure the normative environment of educational ambition and attainment. This effort is reviewed in detail by Dreeben in another chapter of this *Handbook*. Suffice it to note here that the models used in this research fail to specify the social mechanisms through which school norms have their effects on individual students' aspirations or attainment.

Sørensen's (1970) argument was highly promising, and subsequent work on tracking and ability grouping in part followed in train by considering tracks and ability groups as recruitment pools for the formation of social ties among students, stratified by track or group placement according to ability, performance, interests, and aspirations. Here, earlier work by Alexander, Cook, and McDill (1978) and later research by Gamoran (1987) are emblematic. (See Oakes, Gamoran, & Page [1992] for a critical evaluation of this literature.) However, none of these subsequent studies fully exploited the implications that could be drawn from the more powerful of Sørensen's insights by developing the analysis of the track or level, or a set of tracks or levels, as a social situation with its distinctive composition, pattern of social relations, and norms.

Instead, for the most part social structural aspects of tracks and groups are represented only by global scales of peer influence, like the scales used by Sewell and colleagues. Although the findings of this work suggest that social relations and, presumably, attendant social psychological mechanisms account for significant differences between tracks in students' aspirations and performance, much of the interest in tracking has turned to other aspects of curricular differentiation having to do with school policy (e.g., resource allocation) or with instructional practice (e.g., differences of subject matter coverage).

Occasional studies made interesting forays into the social organization of the school situation and the processes through which this social organization might affect students' learning. For example, Bossert (1979), studying two middle school classes of similar ability composition, was able to show that differences in the two teachers' instructional methods produced distinctive classroom social orders. In one classroom, heavy use of interindividual competition produced a stratified array of academic performance that generated a relatively wide attainment distribution. In the other, greater use of cooperative activities, like group projects, was accompanied by less stratification of performance and a narrower range of achievement.

Despite Sørensen's theoretical contribution and studies like Bossert's, it was not until Coleman and his collaborators (especially Coleman & Hoffer, 1987) applied the concept of social capital to the comparative analysis of students in public, secular private, and Roman Catholic high schools in the United States that sustained interest in the social organization of the school situation was rekindled. Coleman and Hoffer themselves were interested primarily in the school as an agent of a parental community, so their discussion deals relatively little with the internal structure of the school and more with structural linkages between the school and its external clientele.

Bryk, Lee, and Holland (1993) have made a theoretically generative foray into this terrain. Applying the community construct specifically to the internal organization of schools, they posed the same question that animated Coleman and Hoffer (1987)—how to account for differences in rates of academic achievement between public and Catholic high schools. Bryk and colleagues defined community as a constellation of distinct normative and structural variables: staff agreement about educational aims and methods and about the capacities of students (the latter reciprocated by students), a high level of student involvement in a common curriculum and in an extracurricular program, dense and strong professional and social ties among teachers, and an "extended" teacher role (i.e., high levels of teachers' time and effort denoting involvement in the school).

Bryk and colleagues (1993) provided both ethnographic and survey evidence to support their argument that these communal properties more often are found in Catholic high schools than in public ones and their further argument that, net of competing explanatory variables, these properties account for a significant portion of aggregate achievement advantages that accrue to Catholic high schools. However, they are relatively silent about mechanisms. One can imagine a variety of social psychological processes involved. For example, in the presence of a strongly supporting faculty agreement that all students in a school can master school subjects, students' self-perceptions may converge on a relatively high level of expectation. However, at least by implication, the question of mechanism is posed by Bryk and his collaborators.

SCHOOL CONTEXTS AND SOCIAL PSYCHOLOGICAL PROCESSES IN SCHOOLING

Defining Situations

The broader field of social psychology can be of help with the question of mechanism by providing further insight into ways that individuals' cognitive and emotional states mediate social contexts and individual behavior. It is striking how, over the two decades since the Rosenberg and Turner volume was published, concepts akin to Thomas's idea of the individual definition of the situation have become increasingly central to social psychology, particularly in contributions from the psychological side of the field. These concepts appear as efforts to understand the evident capacity of individuals or of small groups of individuals to comprehend events in their individual and collective lives, to invest these events with meaning, and to use the resulting interpretive accounts as guides to present and to future behavior.

Prefigured by Kelly's (1955) "personal construct," Heider's (1958) "naive psychology, and, in particular, Berger and Luckmann's (1967) "projected personal system," these approaches are notable for their attention to the emotional or affective investments that people make in their interpretations of their social surroundings. They give increasing attention to the consequent trans-situational generality and stability of these accounts as principal sources of consistent trends in individual and in group behavior.

Two examples serve, one from the literature on dyadic exchange, the other from the literature on family dynamics. Kelley and Thibaut (1978) expanded their theory of interpersonal relations to take into account the fact that people often do not interact in ways that a simple matrix of choices and outcomes would predict. Kelley and Thibaut distinguished between the "given" and the "effective" matrix. The given matrix is an individual actor's matrix of choices and outcomes that results from constraints imposed by the material environment, by institutionalized expectations or norms, and by such "personal factors" as needs and skills. The effective matrix is this actor's reinterpretation (in Kelley and Thibaut's language, the "transformation") of the given matrix. In this reinterpretation, choices and alternate outcomes are ordered by the actor according to his or her own motives, values, or preferences.

For example, the actor might forego choices that would be advantageous in the short run (e.g., profiting in a business transaction from another's financial difficulties) in order to realize a longer run outcome (e.g., building up a relationship of trust or obligation on the other's part to be drawn on later in more consequential transactions). In sum, the effective matrix is a definition of the situation that is shaped by individual purposes but also by the awareness of institutional constraints (to continue the example, such things as laws of contract) and of expected acts and responses by the other (themselves in part institutionally grounded, as in norms of specific or of generalized reciprocity).

David Reiss (1981) expanded the circle from the dyad to a small group, the nuclear family. In a clinical setting, he had been struck by families' shared understandings of their character as families and of the attendant rights, responsibilities, and styles of behavior of each member. These understandings extended to an interpretation of the world outside, of the family's place in it, and of right ways individually and collectively to investigate and deal with it. These interrelated interpretations seemingly constituted durable family "paradigms," carried over into the larger world to guide, endow with meaning, and justify the individual and collective acts of the family members. Reiss proposed that family paradigms emerge suddenly, as a consequence of events that a family experiences as a crisis—for example, the death of a spouse or a parent or a sudden, drastic loss of income.

Reiss (1981) asserted that families mobilize to deal with crises and that when they do so successfully, at least in their own eyes, this event (e.g., devising a new household economy to compensate for loss) is perceived by the whole family as a significant collective achievement. In this way, the family in subjective terms becomes a community of fate, and the mode of adapting or coping becomes the organizing paradigm that generates successive, temporally consistent, situation-specific interpretations ("constructs") that guide what the family does within its circle and beyond. For example, Elder (1974) has shown how families' success in surviving the Great Depression engendered family interpretations of the world as a world of scarcity and uncertainty, with corresponding stress on family strategies of saving and of risk-avoidance to gain security.

In Reiss's (1981) theory, unless there is an event of such novelty and magnitude that it fractures the underlying paradigm, family interaction reaffirms and reinforces the paradigm within which these situations are interpreted. Thus, the paradigm should remain intact until the family encounters another event sufficiently traumatic to break this circle of interpersonal reaffirmation. Reiss extended the idea of the definition of the situation by showing how definitions can gain stability not only on an institutional basis (that is, normative or structural similarities among situations), but also as a consequence of the persistence of group membership and of commonly interpreted experience—the degree to which by belonging to a group one has the sense of belonging to a community of fate.

Defining School Situations

In the remainder of this chapter, I outline a social psychological approach to the study of schooling that is grounded in ideas like those found in Kelley and Thibaut (1978) and in Reiss (1981). This approach leads to the proposition that in the presence of stable, collective faculty definitions of school situations, the school becomes a powerful agent of socialization that affects students' moral–judgmental capacities for social participation. I go beyond the immediate interpersonal environment that surrounds teachers and students to consider, in the manner of Thomas (1923) and Waller (1932) how formal structures of school organization affect the ways in which teachers and students define the school situation. I then draw connections between these definitions and both interpersonal and individual behavioral elements of school, moving toward implications for the analysis of schooling as socialization for social participation.

The approach that I outline clearly calls for more fine-grained data about particular schools and about their members than can be provided by large sample surveys. Detailed case studies, which may entail very systematic mapping of social relationships, patterns of thought and belief, and regularities of behavior may be required, in combination with sustained observation and the ethnographer's reliance on informants. Case studies of this kind ideally should cumulate to provide a body of material that allows for the comparative analysis of school situations. Even in less idyllic circumstances, case study findings can be used to generate propositions and measurable constructs that can bring some greater presence of the social context of the school and of the lives of teachers and students into the large-sample studies that yield generalizable results.

FACULTY DEFINITIONS: CONSISTENCY, STABILITY, AND DOMINANCE.   To begin, return to our school observations, keeping in mind that our findings for Lewis and for St. Aloysius were very similar to our findings for the full sample of 13 schools. In each of these schools, we found coherent faculty definitions of the local school situation. These definitions were widely shared within these faculties and displayed notable stability and resilience. They either were shared by entire faculties (as at Lewis High) or by distinctive faculty cohorts (as at St. Aloysius).

Thirteen is not a large number of schools. Nevertheless, one of the more striking findings of our field research was the ubiquity of faculty definitions of the school situation. Our school sample included some that were highly selective and some that had a distinctive mission, but most were perfectly ordinary comprehensive public high schools. In each we found a broadly shared account of the school's purpose, usually traced to some legitimizing aspect of the school's foundation—sometimes what was regarded as the clear intent of a founding donor, otherwise (and more often) a less dramatic but no less clear indication of some characteristic of the locality that the school was meant to express.

Often, for example, teachers told us about what the local area was like when the school had been built (a community that expected its high school youth to be prepared for business, or for the skilled trades, or for college). These accounts of school purpose were told more vividly and with more immediacy by some teachers than by others, but in none of our schools did we find either serious within-faculty or within-cohort disagreement or unawareness. Moreover, what these teachers told in interviews rarely differed, except in minor detail, from what we heard them tell one another (or from what they reported they told parents and students when they felt it necessary to justify or explain the purposes of the school's programs).

Accounts of Purpose.   Each of the observed faculty definitions of the school situation provided an account of collective purpose—at the center an organizational purpose (the school mission) and derived therefrom an account of faculty purpose that stated the chief ways in which teachers could contribute to realizing the organizational aim. These accounts did not arise *de novo* in each locality. Indeed, as Thomas (1923) had it, each was institutionally grounded in a generalized conception of what a school should be, providing a broad base of legitimacy for the specific school and faculty. This conception was specified to the distinctive founding event or circumstance, which provided local legitimacy for the school and its faculty.

In most of our cases, the core generalized depiction of mission derived from a conventional conception of an academic, college preparatory high school. The local variations had to do either with levels of higher education for which preparation was to be provided (e.g., the Ivy League in the case of a highly selective private school, or local community colleges in cases of high schools in historically working-class communities) or with the relative weight between the academic and other curricula and student clienteles (e.g., a high school that had been built to serve a community of trade and craft working-class families and that saw its mission as providing vocational education for most and a mobility route out for the few who would want to follow it).

A few of the schools had more distinctive conceptions of collective purpose—a religious mission or a mission of social service in an inner city area, for example. However, the general format was present in every case—the local application or elaboration of conventionalized, institutionalized themes. These faculty definitions of the school situation consistently went beyond accounts of purpose to describe an enduring, significant faculty contribution toward realizing the purpose—for example, Lewis High School's long record of effective college preparation and St. Aloysius' equally long record of graduates' occupational attainment. From school to school, these definitions of the school situation crossed such internal divisions as those of teaching field or department. (Compare the neoinstitutionalist analysis of sources of organizational form and process in schools, e.g., Meyer & Rowan, 1978.)

Definitions of the Faculty and the Students' Roles. From these accounts of collective purpose, the faculties we observed elaborated locally specific definitions of the faculty and the student roles. The faculty role definition allowed each faculty member to derive a specific, situated occupational identity. The student role definition allowed each faculty member to derive an array of motives, interests, and capacities attributed to the school's students. Together, these two roles as defined, each with its attendant rights and responsibilities, constituted a rough theory of pedagogy that, in the faculty's eyes, was consistent with the school's and the faculty's purpose, if not always with the current situation. In fact, this theory served as a benchmark against which the present situation could be evaluated and current faculty conduct could be justified.

These definitions of the school situation—the linked interpretations of collective school and faculty purposes and of the rights and responsibilities of teachers and of students—formed mutually reinforcing systems of meaning and understanding. The faculty's rights and responsibilities derived from the collective mission, whereas those of the student complemented the faculty's (in effect, a specification of what qualities in the students provided the appropriate materials for the faculty's work). For example, at Lewis High School, the faculty saw its mission as rigorous academic preparation, so that the responsible Lewis teacher was up-to-date in the subject and its pedagogy, with the right to demand high performance, strong motivation, and disciplined conduct from students. Within this frame, current difficulties in the school could be attributed to deficiencies of the material, not of the worker.

Emergence, Consistency, and Stability. First consider conditions for the formation of a collective faculty definition of the school situation. In every case, we found a symbolically significant event that was experienced, or at a later date was plausibly thought to have been experienced, by an entire faculty cohort and that was accompanied by successful faculty performance (e.g., Lewis High, which was built and whose faculty was formed to serve an academically select student body, with a sustained period of outstanding student attainment, and St. Aloysius, which was formed and whose faculty was recruited to train working-class students for social mobility within a securely Catholic environment, to equally good effect).

A number of our schools, like Lewis and St. Aloysius, experienced subsequent significant events. In some cases, as was true of the Lewis faculty and of the more senior of the St. Aloysius faculty, these events simply reinforced the original conception of the school's and therefore of the faculty's, purpose and the attendant role definitions, so that changed circumstance was interpreted as an adversity, to be dealt with within the frame of the school situation as already rightly defined—an effort, in effect, to reestablish the basis of faculty success.

In other cases, these events led to a transformation or a reframing of the original account of purpose. At St. Aloysius, the newly hired teachers expressed a conception of the school's and of the faculty's purpose, and definitions of their own role and of that of the student, that departed substantially from their senior colleagues' definition of the school situation. In another of our schools, which had served a small semirural town and found its student body rapidly changing by virtue of suburbanization, an essentially new faculty of academically high-powered teachers had been recruited. Whereas those of the earlier faculty still on hand spoke with wistful fondness of a school that had been communal and concerned heavily with the students' values, the new faculty saw a chance to make the school into a training ground for academically competitive and talented students, thereby validating their own individual and collective competence.

In sum, in every case, an event common to an entire faculty cohort made it possible for the cohort (in some cases an entire faculty, in other cases not) to perceive itself as a community of fate. These accounts of founding or transforming circumstance, though often constructed after the fact, have emerged as ways to endow the present with meaning, collectively and individually. (cf. Hughes 1937, on careers as unfolding perspectives on lives). When successive faculty cohorts develop distinctive definitions of the school situation, in our cases displaying the conservatism of an old guard and the innovativeness of Young Turks, the cohorts in effect become similarly distinctive faculty generations (cf. Ryder, 1965).

The faculty definitions that we observed were extraordinarily consistent from teacher to teacher and across whole faculties or faculty generations. They also were extraordinarily stable. They had changed only when changes in the objectively observed situation were accompanied by a cohort succession that allowed older definitions to be wholly or partly replaced. Both their consistency and their stability must be explained. The explanation lies in large part, though not entirely, in the formal organization of the school.

Key Organizational Attributes of Schools. Schools are organized in a way that creates strong tendencies among their faculties and their student bodies toward, in each case, a shared definition of the school situation. The greater portion of the literature on formal organizations suggests an opposite tendency in most organizations. Whether it deals with contingent relationships of organizations to actors in their environments (e.g., Lawrence & Lorsch, 1967; Pfeffer & Salancik, 1978; Thompson, 1967), the differentiation of organizations into specialized roles and subunits (e.g. Abell, 1975; Perrow, 1972), or structures that constrain flows of information (e.g., Crozier, 1964; Williamson, 1975), these analyses center on the differences of interests that correspond to a differentiated organizational structure. From these differences of interest, each of these analyses derives essentially the same proposition—that a fundamental form of behavior in organizations is the strategic use of power to serve individual or subunit interests rather than the welfare of the entire organization (e.g., Burt, 1992). Thus, the interpersonal relationships that characterize these organizations are substantially competitive and often conflictual. Organizational goals are distorted or displaced as a consequence of an overriding strategic pursuit of individual or of subunit interests.

This theoretical template does not fit schools very well, at least not the instructional core of the school. The instructional core of a school is marked by low interdependence and high structural stability. Low interdependence is the modal pattern because instruction is divided into large temporal blocks, like semesters or whole school years, whereas curricular specialization takes the form of discrete, essentially independent subunits, like the high school department. As a result, requirements for coordination are weak, and the work of one teacher in the usual case is only very loosely connected to the work of any other (Bidwell, 1965, Weick, 1976).

Structural stability arises in part from the stability of most instructional doctrines and methods, which change fitfully and often incrementally, and from their lack of specification in concrete rules and performance standards (Dreeben, 1996), so that teachers work within wide limits of technical tolerance. Structural stability also derives from schools' public or quasi-public mission and the stable revenues and student enrollments enjoyed by most public schools and most selective private schools, tending to insulate them from nonrandom environmental shocks.

As a consequence of low interdependence and high structural stability, teachers work with relatively little administrative oversight or evaluation. The chief locus of loose coupling in the Weick–Meyer–Rowan analysis (Meyer & Rowan, 1978; Weick, 1976) is the boundary between administration and instruction.

In other words, teachers work in a very substantial zone of instructional autonomy (viz. Lortie, 1969). Important lines of structural differentiation that might define distinct, keenly felt interests within the school organization are sparse and tenuous. In structural terms, and with respect to structurally grounded interests, neither teachers nor such groups of teachers as those in a subject-matter department are strongly impelled toward the strategic behavior that eventuates in either competition or conflict (nor, for that matter, are they strongly impelled to cooperate). Objectively, the entire faculty tends to be in the same organizational situation, with the consequence that their definitions of the school situation should tend to converge on the perception of a community of fate.

It was no oversight that when I described the Lewis and St. Aloysius examples, I said nothing about administrators. How these and the remaining eleven faculties defined the school situation took little cognizance of administrators or of past or present administrative policies. In fact, the administrators whom we interviewed were much more presentist in their conceptions of their schools and their jobs than their teachers, with the exception of new faculty cohorts like that at St. Aloysius. They were much more willing to adapt to what they perceived as environmental exigency. They were at best bemused, often annoyed, and sometimes angered by what some described as a lack of realism on the part of their teachers, what others described as rigidity or hidebound conservatism, and in a few instances as a lack of professionalism in the teachers' unwillingness to engage students' capacities, needs, or interests in a productive way.

Given the zone of instructional autonomy, it is not surprising that observed differences in the ways faculty members define the school situation are attributable less to structural factors than to demographic ones—differences in the ways the training, occupational socialization, and selection of successive faculty cohorts interact with local school conditions to affect their experiences and their understandings of these events.

This argument does not contradict my emphasis on individual agency on the part of either teachers or students. However, it does proceed from the assumption that immediate environmental opportunities and constraints created by school organization are sufficiently strong and pervasive so that individual psychological states (including those involved in the definition of the school situation) and corresponding patterns of interpersonal conduct in the aggregate are markedly convergent and thus have their own consistently constraining and opportunity-creating consequences for the teachers and for the students in a school.

I also should stress that of necessity I am painting with a broad brush. My discussion concerns modal characteristics of schools. I have proposed that fundamental structural attributes of schools lead to uniform faculty and student situations in a school and to consequent uniformity of faculty and student definitions of the school situation. However, there will always be variation around this central tendency.

For example, Bidwell and Quiroz (1991) proposed that the probability of competitive or cooperatively collegial relationships among teachers varies with school size and with the way power is distributed between a faculty and its student and parent clients. Bidwell, Frank, and Quiroz (1997) reported tentative, supporting evidence for this proposition, from the same sample of schools from which I have drawn the two cases for this chapter. Their argument is based on the assumption that teachers will act strategically in the pursuit of such interests of their own as the ability to offer enrollment-based elective courses rather than teach exclusively within the required curriculum. Nevertheless, my analysis of the formal organization of schools and our observations in this sample of schools has led me to conclude that such variability does indeed occur at the margins of a substantially shared definition of the school situation on the part of entire faculties and, as I try to show, consequently on the part of entire student bodies as well.

To understand the stability of faculty definitions of the school situation, consider again the zone of instructional autonomy. In this zone, teachers interact with each other and with students, forming a structure that is nested within a true loose coupling. Principals, curriculum directors, supervisors, and the like are outside this pedagogical network. School or district policies that govern instruction for the most part are interpreted by individual teachers or by groups of teachers according to their own conceptions of good teaching. These conceptions, in turn, derive from both their understandings of how to teach the subject and their understandings of their situationally defined roles. In this way, institutionalized professional understandings of what schools are like and what good teaching is have strong effects on teachers' conduct of teaching, mediated by local faculty understandings of what kinds of conduct by teachers and by students are appropriate and inappropriate in the local school situation—that is, conceptions of local possibility and constraint. This institutional basis of teachers' conceptions of school and teaching is itself an important source of the stability of faculty definitions of the school situation.

Further Stabilizing Factors. In addition, the stability of these definitions can be attributed to the symbolic salience of these situational definitions, their identity-conferring nature (both the collective identity given by the account of school and faculty purpose and the individual professional identity given by the definition of the teacher role), and the fact that they make plain the relation of each person in the school to a social and a cultural whole. These definitions of the school situation make the mundane significant and thus are not to be abandoned readily or exchanged easily. Moreover, like the family paradigms that Reiss (1981) documented, faculty definitions of the school situation are systems of meaning, so that altering any of their parts means that the whole must be altered (e.g., the implication of the faculty role by the account of faculty purpose).

Three further conditions in schools tend to reinforce extant faculty definitions of the school situation, even in the face of strong nonrandom shocks. Two are demographic and the third is structural. The first has already been implied by our high school cases. To the extent that members of a faculty are replaced incrementally, new faculty definitions become less likely to appear. The intermittent replacement of a few individuals should favor their assimilation into the existing collectivity and its beliefs. However, change in a school's objective situation provides the stuff of crisis, to which a new faculty cohort can respond in novel ways. Only then is a new faculty definition of the school situation likely to appear. This combination of events is not unlikely. As we have seen in the St. Aloysius case, a change in a school's objective circumstance can easily drive faculty away unless, as in the Lewis case, they are very senior (or otherwise have very few occupational options).

Second, the homogeneity of a faculty should stabilize its definition of the school situation because homogeneity (that is, the number of attributes that are widely shared in a faculty, such as gender, ethnicity, and seniority) reduces the number of possible differences of perception. It also reduces the number of possible new elements of belief or perception entering the situation. When the members of a faculty are similar in seniority and when they have other traits in common as well, the cohort-specific character of the faculty and the corresponding awareness of community of fate are reinforced. This outcome is no less likely when the faculty contains successive cohorts or, as I have suggested, faculty generations (e.g., new faculty recruits, a large number of whom are minorities, entering a faculty previously composed primarily of white teachers). In this case, because the cohort (generational) boundary is strengthened, the possibility that older faculty will be persuaded by their junior colleagues' understandings of the school situation and of the faculty role is likely to be remote indeed.

Third, turning to the remaining structural source of stability, students provide readily accessible scapegoats when an extant faculty definition is threatened by changed local circumstances. When events challenge the legitimacy of the faculty's self-understood mission and thereby threaten to erode the legitimacy of the faculty role and attendant local teacher identity, the subordination of students to teachers makes them natural scapegoats. Blame is readily deflected from the faculty, but in a seemingly credible way. If the teacher's craft is not at fault, then it must be the materials to which the craft is applied that cause the trouble.

STUDENTS IN THE SCHOOL SITUATION.   Although entering students may begin to form their own individual definitions of the school situation, a collective definition is likely to form very quickly. In all but exceptional circumstances, students enter schools as whole cohorts, usually according to age, and typically find themselves in the same round of activity, confronting the same opportunities for participation in the school and the same system of rewards and punishments. In other words, their objective situation leads quickly to awareness of common fate and the relative density of their interaction to the formation of a collective definition of their situation in school.

The speed with which these collective definitions form can be attributed in part to the way schools are organized formally and in part to the subordination of students to faculty. The principal formal element of school organization, in this context, is its graded (and age-graded) structure in which arrangements for instruction become increasingly differentiated and specialized, while the school comes to embrace an increasing portion of students' lives through programs of athletics and of extracurricular activities. Thus, in the earliest years of schooling, children as students find themselves for the greater part of each school day under the care of the same teacher, with the same fellow students, in a class devoted to essentially the full curriculum. As the student moves up the grades, into middle school and then into high school, courses become increasingly specialized, curricular tracks or levels appear, and opportunities to participate in athletics and in the extracurriculum become more numerous.

From the subordination of students to faculty, it follows that the faculty's definition of the school situation, including their definition of the student's role, will set a frame of meaning within which students' own definitions of the school situation emerge. That is, whatever cognitive, normative, or affective resources students bring with them when they enter a school, their own definitions of the school situation should take form primarily as reactions to the way the faculty understand, and therefore, carry out the school's work. How the faculty define the student's role and their consequent attributions of cognitive and moral traits to the students should substantially determine the incentives and disincentives that they provide for students in response to their class work and their conduct in the school.

As Parsons (1959) and Dreeben (1968) have argued, in the earliest years of school, which correspond to a period when children are strongly dependent on adults, a single classroom encompasses virtually all of the child's participation in school, so that a developmental and organizational stage is set for the child's willing compliance with what the teacher requires. This relationship between the teacher and the students in the classroom thus begins with presumption of trust on the part of the students and soon evolves into generalized goodwill. In these classrooms, the teacher's definition of the school (i.e., classroom) situation easily and naturally becomes the students' definition as well.

However, as one moves up the school grades, students gain greater autonomy of both thought and action, based on the formation of peer societies, alternate roles outside the school (such as part-time jobs), gains in social competence, and their accumulating knowledge of student lore in which teachers' reputations and the virtues and defects of their courses are depicted. Moreover, the relationship between any teacher and any student is likely to be specific to a course or a subject matter, which allows students to make firsthand comparisons among the faculty they encounter and the courses they take. Under these circumstances, grants of trust and the development of goodwill in principle should be more course-specific and teacher-specific and more variable and contingent, depending initially from year to year or term to term on teachers' reputations and on the reputations of their courses and then on the actual experience of dealing with the teacher and the course. Now students should find it possible to withhold goodwill and to suspend trust according to anticipated and realized experience—their own evaluations of multiple classroom situations.

Nevertheless, students remain in a fundamentally subordinate relationship to teachers, even though it becomes more contingent and uncertain the higher the school grade. Moreover, our high school cases suggest that a faculty's collective definition of the school situation tends to be monolithic (at least within faculty cohorts or generations), even when the division of faculty labor is intensively specialized. As a result, how the faculty define the school situation, and how they evaluate students' conduct and consequently attribute motives and capacities to them, should influence the ways these teachers conduct the school, with consequent powerful constituting effects on the objective school situation that students encounter. Moreover, the principal elements of this situation (the incentives and disincentives for performance, for example) are likely to be reproduced in each classroom and even to pervade athletics and the extracurriculum, where faculty usually remain the dominant actors. In one sense, the faculty definition of the school situation is responsive to what students do in class and elsewhere in the school, but if my analysis is accurate, this responsiveness is filtered through a screen provided by the criteria according to which faculty evaluate students' acts and, as the putative stability of faculty definitions suggests, is in most cases slow and incremental.

When the faculty definition is accompanied by an account of faculty success, this regime is likely to be benign and relatively rewarding for students. In these schools, students should be happily compliant, their compliant action thereby creating an objective situation for faculty that reinforces the faculty definition. Here, students should define the faculty role in positive terms and evaluate faculty conduct as fair and trustworthy.

However, I have asserted that when the objective situation cannot sustain a faculty's account of its success, students are likely to serve as the scapegoats that allow the faculty's definition of the school situation to survive. In these schools, our high school cases suggest, the principal faculty response is likely to be an insistence on rigorous standards to secure compliance with expected student performance, with the consequence that the students encounter an objective school situation that is much more punishing than rewarding because teachers stress disincentives for "slackness," accompanied by incentives focused on types and levels of performance that the students have great difficulty attaining.

Nevertheless, in these schools, students' subordination need not entail an inevitable compliance. Instead, as one moves up the school and age grades to the point that students have acquired the capacity for some degree of autonomous action, and on whose goodwill teachers cannot necessarily rely, we can expect that the more disparate the students' capacities, interests, motives, and behavioral styles from those depicted in the faculty definition of the student role and its attendant attributed student traits, the more likely is the student definition of the situation to center on noncompliance. Students should define the faculty role as essentially adversarial and define a student role centered on means of adapting to or resisting a regime understood as consisting of unfair and disproportionate punishment—unfair because of the lack of fit between students' conceptions of their own right conduct and the attributions made to them by their teachers and disproportionate because of the teachers' strong tendency to see their students in general as intractable.

In the absence of an alternate frame of meaning within which to define the school situation, students' noncompliance is likely to remain passive (or, for students above the school leaving age, to lead to dropping out). However, when students can employ a viable alternate frame of meaning, noncompliance is likely to take the more active forms of resistance or rebellion. Thus, in Willis's (1977) depiction of working-class "lads" in an English grammar school, the values and norms of working-class life provided a strong frame for their lives in school that was alternative to that provided by their teachers and that provided an effective buffer against teachers' demands and standards. Whether passive or more active, students' noncompliance should reinforce the tendency of faculty to impose a regime designed to secure compliance, creating schools ordered around an antagonistic faculty–student relationship.

Thus, in schools that have undergone critical events like those we found in Lewis and St. Aloysius High Schools—critical events that, in the faculty's eyes, had the potential of dislocating or undercutting the faculty's proper work—I would expect noncompliant student definitions of the situation. This student interpretation of the school situation was clearly present in Lewis High School, where, except for the handful of middle-class students, the student body consistently displayed passive resistance to the faculty's efforts.

In sum, in schools in which students willingly subordinate themselves within the frame of meaning that the faculty use to define the school situation, both the complementarity of faculty's and of students' definitions of that situation and the compliant character of the students' relationships to their teachers and, more generally, to school authority result in a self-reinforcing system of understandings and conduct. In the absence of this willing subordination, the adversarial relationship between teachers and students should become institutionalized, in an equilibrium of conflict much like that depicted by Waller (1932). Here, the adversarial character of the students' and the teachers' roles and the underlying interpretation of the school situation in terms of disjunction between faculty's expectations and students' understandings of fair and proper treatment is itself a shared system of meaning that, in a seeming paradox, can bridge the cleavage between teachers and students. Only when students find a normative basis for more truly autonomous adversarial action, more likely than not external to the school (as in the case of Willis's [1977] "lads"), is this cleavage likely to mark a relationship of overt antagonism or conflict.

SOCIALIZATION FOR SOCIAL PARTICIPATION

Finally, consider the implications of this analysis for the socialization of students. In the broadest sense, one can consider schooling as a process in which students develop capacities for social participation. Most of the research conducted since the late 1940s on schooling and its outcomes has centered on the specifically academic aspects of preparation for social participation. For the most part, we have neglected the normative elements of this process—acquiring

knowledge of and developing commitment to rules of conduct. Surely they are no less important than the more intensively studied aspects of human capital formation in the development
of an individual's social competence.

Socialization for social participation involves the acquisition of generalized understandings of the nature of distinct modes of social participation, of their appropriateness to various
kinds of social settings and circumstances, and of the attendant costs and benefits to oneself
and to others. The development of an understanding of the contingent significance and consequences of varied modes of social participation and consequent willingness under particular
circumstances to be engaged or disengaged, to compete or cooperate, to withdraw, or to resist
is a central element of socialization during childhood and youth.

In this final portion of the chapter, I focus on major normative components of an
individual's capacity for social participation. Stated succinctly, the development of this normative capacity builds on an early foundation of moral socialization in which the child acquires a generalized willingness to engage with others, with a belief in the presumptive trustworthiness of these others—that is, their benign intentions to do what is right. Later in childhood
and on into adolescence, this generalized, trustful willingness to engage must be specified in
relation to developing conceptions of fairness and of norms of reciprocity. Moreover, this
process of specification must extend not only to interpersonal relationships, but also to collective situations—for example, the development of the capacity to evaluate the fairness of conventional understandings or rules governing the distribution of rights, obligations, goods, or
recognition among friends or in a workplace.

This process in part is a process of learning to evaluate situations in relation to standards
and to do so with sufficient discrimination so that complex manifolds of benefits and costs to
oneself and to others, in areas of moral ambiguity or uncertainty, can be judged. In each case,
the child or young person is learning not only to judge, but also to determine how to respond
in a contingent fashion (in what way and how energetically) in engagement with others and in
the situation collectively. Presumably, the development of these discriminatory capacities arises
from experience in situations that differ in the content of their understandings or rules about
conduct and in the degree to which, according to some consistent standard, these normative
regimes can be evaluated relative to one another as more or less fair and, thus, as situations
calling for various degrees of engagement (e.g., positive, active involvement, withdrawal, or
opposition).

I propose that how teachers define the school situation leads them to conduct their classes
in ways that have systematic effects on students' socialization for moral judgment. This proposition rests on the assumption that teachers' definition of the school situation, in particular, the
definition of the student's role, constructs an objective school situation (especially a classroom situation), that by virtue of its consequences for students' own definition of the school
situation, gives students a distinctive kind and amount of opportunity to practice moral judgment. In the prior discussion, I considered two kinds of faculty definitions of the school situation, one casting the student in the role of the teacher's ally, the other casting the student in
the role of the teacher's scapegoat. In each case, I assumed that the faculty definition was a
matter of faculty consensus.

I consider these consensual cases first and then turn to schools in which subgroups of
teachers define the school situation in different ways. As settings for the development of contingent moral judgment, schools in which the entire faculty casts students in the scapegoat
role, so students and teachers are consistently related in antagonistic ways, should have an
adverse effect to the development of students' moral judgment. In schools where an entire
faculty defines students in positive terms, so the students tend to comply willingly with the

teacher-imposed school regime, the normatively undifferentiated character of the teacher-defined and constructed school situation provides scant opportunity for students to experience and compare distinct normative orders in ways that, I am arguing, foster mature, contingent moral judgment. So far as the school's influence is concerned, these schools should retard the development of this judgmental capacity, tending to anchor it in a generalized readiness toward trust and goodwill.

To develop capacity for discriminating moral judgment, the child and young person must become increasingly aware of distinctions between social settings that evoke differences of response—for example, the rightness of active participation that results in an equitable distribution of goods among equal participants and of resistance or withdrawal otherwise. A school generally ordered according to compliance does not provide opportunities for students to either perceive such differences or to learn the moral discrimination that these differences require. Here students' capacity for trust is likely to remain generalized rather than contingent.

However, when students are a faculty's scapegoats, the school and classroom regime tends to be a regime of consistent punishment, which students presumably cannot accept as fair because the punishment tends to be disconnected from students' levels and directions of academic effort and may also be only loosely related to their conduct in other respects. Moreover, these teachers' failure to trust their students (to do their best, to act in generally disciplined ways, and so on) is likely to be reciprocated by an unwillingness of the students to trust their teachers individually or the faculty collectively. In sum, the students' definition of the school situation is one that gives them little opportunity to realize the benefits of trust, whether given in a broadcast or a contingent fashion. Exposure to school situations of this kind are likely, then, to induce a generalized inability to trust authorities or organizations ordered according to authority. By dint of recurrently adversarial encounters, these schools should foster students' skepticism about the benefits of dealing with formal organizations and build skills and ways of thought required for lives ordered in terms of antagonism or of conflict.

The sheer fact of structural differentiation, say in middle or high schools, between curricular tracks or levels or between subject-matter fields or departments is of no help here if these structural differences do not permit an individual student to see differences in collective activities and their outcomes and to learn to evaluate them and to respond accordingly. Even if the tracks differ in faculty's and students' definitions of the situation, if they are strongly bounded, students in one may not be aware of events in the others. Moreover, if, as in our school cases, subject-matter departments differ little in the ways their members define the school situation, subject-matter specialization will have no effect on students' understanding of moral contingencies in social participation.

Differences between faculty cohorts in the definition of the school situation, like that we found in St. Aloysius High School, may have beneficial consequences for this socialization because students are likely to encounter teachers from distinct cohorts and experience their courses and classrooms. Other lines of faculty cleavage that cut across a student body should have similar effects, but our fieldwork suggests that such lines of structural difference do not often occur in the academic side of a high school. In this respect, then, athletics and the extracurriculum may have substantial socializing potential, to the extent that their faculty and student participants define the extracurricular situation and the roles of the participants in terms that are distinctive of the academic side of the school—for example, athletics that stress cooperation among teammates and an avuncular relationship between coach and players, in contrast to a more competitive and rigorously hierarchical order of academic activity.

In his classic article on the social organization of the school, Parsons (1959) described the high school extracurriculum as a setting in which embryonic managers learned managerial skills, while students headed for technical or professional occupations learned academic discipline in the classroom. The foregoing argument views the extracurriculum in different terms—as at least potentially a place where, by allowing contrasting or comparative perceptions of classroom and team or classroom and club, for example, students develop the understanding of moral contingency that is central to mature forms of social participation.

ENVOI

This chapter should be read as a call for a social psychology of schooling that will reintroduce theoretical and methodological breadth into the sociological study of schools and schooling processes. Renewed interest in the interplay of objective and subjective aspects of school situations and schooling processes is called for and with it a renewed interest in normative and affective outcomes of being in school. Exploitation of complementarities and synergies between large-sample surveys and ethnographic studies of particular school situations also is needed. Whether the promise of such efforts can be realized in an expanded and deepened understanding of the connectedness of schools and students' lives at present is an open, but, I hope, a provocative question.

REFERENCES

Abell, P. (Ed., 1975). *Organizations as bargaining and influence systems*. London: Heinemann.
Alexander, K. L., Cook, M., & McDill, E. (1978). Curriculum tracking and educational stratification. *American Sociological Review, 43*, 47–66.
Alexander, K. L., & Eckland, B. (1973). *Effects of education on the social mobility of high school sophomores fifteen years later (1955–1970)*. Chapel Hill, NC: Institute for Research in Social Science, University of North Carolina.
Allport, G. W. (1954). The historical background of modern social psychology. In G. Lindzey (Ed.), *Handbook of Social Psychology* (pp. 3–56). Cambridge, MA: Addison Wesley.
Berger, P. L., & Luckmann, T. (1967). *The social construction of reality: A treatise in the sociology of knowledge*. Garden City, NY: Doubleday.
Bidwell, C. E. (1965). The school as a formal organization. In J. G. March (Ed.), *Handbook of organizations* (pp. 972–1022). Chicago: Rand McNally.
Bidwell, C. E., & Bryk, A. S. (1994). *How teachers' work is organized: The content and consequences of the high school workplace*. Working paper OSC 94–1, Ogburn-Stouffer Center, NORC and the University of Chicago.
Bidwell, C. E., Frank, K. A., & Quiroz, P. A. (1997). Teacher types, workplace controls, and the organization of schools. *Sociology of Education, 70*, 256–284.
Bidwell, C. E., & Quiroz, P. A. (1991). Organizational control in the high school workplace: A theoretical argument. *Journal of Research on Adolescence, 1*, 211–229.
Blau, P., & Duncan, O. D. (1967). *The American occupational structure*. New York: Wiley.
Bossert, S. (1979). *Tasks and social relationships in classrooms*. London & New York: Cambridge University Press.
Bryk, A. S., Lee, V. E., & Holland, P. B. (1993). *Catholic schools and the common good*. Cambridge, MA: Harvard University Press.
Burt, R. S. (1992). *Structural holes: The social structure of competition*. Cambridge, MA: Harvard University Press.
Cohen, D. K. (1989). Willard Waller, On hating school and loving education. In D. J. Willower & W. L. Boyd (Eds.), *Willard Waller on education and schools* (pp. 79–107). Berkeley, CA: McCutchan.
Coleman, J. S., & Hoffer, T. (1987). *Public and private high schools*. New York: Basic Books.
Crozier, M. (1964). *The bureaucratic phenomenon*. Chicago: University of Chicago Press.
Dreeben, R. (1968). *On what is learned in school*. Reading, MA: Addison-Wesley.
Dreeben, R. (1996). The occupation of teaching and educational reform. *Advances in Educational Policy, 2*, 93–124.

Editorial statement. (1978). *Social Psychology Quarterly, 41,* 1.

Elder, G. H. (1974). *Children of the Great Depression.* Chicago: University of Chicago Press.

Gamoran, A. (1987). The stratification of high school learning opportunities. *Sociology of Education, 60,* 135–155.

Heider, F. (1958). *The psychology of interpersonal relations.* New York: Wiley.

Hughes, E. C. (1937). Institutional office and the person. *American Journal of Sociology, 43,* 404–413.

Kelley, H. H., & Thibaut, J. W. (1978). *Interpersonal relations: A theory of interdependence.* New York: Wiley.

Kelly, G. A. (1955). *The psychology of personal constructs.* New York: Norton.

Kerckhoff, A. (1972). *Socialization and social class.* Englewood Cliffs, NJ: Prentice-Hall.

Kerckhoff, A. (1974). *Ambition and attainment.* Washington, DC: American Sociological Association.

Lawrence, P. R., & Lorsch, J. W. (1967). *Organizations and environments: Managing differentiation and integration.* Cambridge, MA: Graduate School of Business, Harvard University.

Lortie, D. C. (1969). The balance of control and autonomy in elementary schoolteaching. In A. Etzioni (Ed.), *The semi-professions and their organization* (pp. 1–53). New York: Free Press.

Meyer, J. W., & Rowan, B. (1978). The structure of educational organizations. In M. W. Meyer (Ed.), *Environments and organizations* (pp. 78–110). San Francisco, CA: Jossey-Bass.

Oakes, J., Gamoran, A., & Page, R. (1992). Curriculum differentiation: Opportunities, outcomes, and meanings. In P. W. Jackson (Ed.), *Handbook of research on curriculum* (pp. 570–608). New York: Macmillan.

Parsons, T. (1959). The school class as a social system. *Harvard Educational Review, 29,* 297–318.

Perrow, C. (1972). *Complex organizations: A critical essay.* Glenview, IL: Scott-Foresman.

Pfeffer, J., & Salancik, G. (1978). *The external control of organizations, A resource dependence perspective.* New York: Harper.

Rehberg, R. A., & Rosenthal, E. R. (1978). *Class and merit in the American high school.* New York & London: Longman,

Reiss, D. (1981). *The family's construction of reality.* Cambridge, MA: Harvard University Press,

Rosenberg, M., & Turner, R. (Eds., 1981). *Social Psychology: Sociological Perspectives.* New York: Basic Books,

Ryder, N. (1965). The cohort as a concept in the study of social change. *American Sociological Review, 30,* 843–861.

Sewell, W. R., Haller, A. O., & Portes, A. (1969). The educational and early occupational attainment process. *American Sociological Review, 34,* 82–92.

Sørensen, A. B. (1970). Organizational differentiation of students and educational opportunity. *Sociology of Education, 43,* 355–376.

Thomas, W. I. (1923). *The unadjusted girl.* Montclair, NJ: Patterson Smith.

Thompson, J. D. (1967). *Organizations in action: Social science bases of administrative theory.* New York: McGraw-Hill.

Waller, W. (1932). *The sociology of teaching.* New York: Wiley.

Weick, K. (1976). Educational organizations as loosely coupled systems. *Administrative Science Quarterly, 21,* 1–19.

Williams, T. (1972). Educational aspirations: Longitudinal evidence on their development in Canadian youth. *Sociology of Education, 45,* 107–133.

Williamson, O. E. (1975). *Markets and hierarchies: Analysis and antitrust implications.* The New York: The Free Press.

Willis, P. E. (1977). *Learning to labour.* Farnborough, England: Saxon House.

CHAPTER 2

The Organizational Context of Teaching and Learning

Changing Theoretical Perspectives

ADAM GAMORAN

WALTER G. SECADA

CORA B. MARRETT

Sociologists have a predilection for the collective. We are centrally concerned with social facts, characteristics of collectivities that give shape and motivation to individual action. Sociological research on schooling shares this interest in the collective. School resources, composition, climate, leadership, and governance, all collective attributes of schools, are often looked to as sources of influence on the outcomes of schooling for individual students.

Yet the study of school organization is marked more by failure than by success. It is especially significant that the most important contribution by sociologists to research on schooling—the famous Coleman Report of 1966—is also the most spectacular failure to connect the collective with the individual in an educational setting. Variation in school conditions was largely unrelated to differences in student outcomes, as school-level effects were dwarfed by the powerful influence of the home environment for student learning. Though policymakers drew implications from the positive impact on learning of the proportion of White students in a school, the effect of racial composition was small compared to the great importance of individual family background factors. This pattern of results, emphasizing the individual over

ADAM GAMORAN AND WALTER G. SECADA • University of Wisconsin-Madison, Madison, Wisconsin 53706
CORA B. MARRETT • Provost's Office, University of Massachusetts, Amherst, Massachusetts 01003

Handbook of the Sociology of Education, edited by Maureen T. Hallinan. Kluwer Academic/Plenum Publishers, New York, 2000.

the collective despite the sociologist's predilection for the opposite, was only to be expected given that over 80% of the variation in student learning occurs within schools, not between schools. If most of the variation in learning is internal to schools, then schoolwide characteristics cannot explain a large proportion of the variation in learning.

Despite these limitations, efforts to study school organization and student learning persist. School climate is a popular term for the normative environment of schools, and hundreds of studies have tried to document an association between climate and student learning (Anderson, 1982). Yet findings for school climate research have been weak and inconsistent, and recent authors, pointing to substantial variation within schools in perceived climate, have questioned whether the concept is meaningful (Pallas, 1988). Studies in the effective schools tradition also emphasized collective properties of schools, such as goals, leadership, and disciplinary environment (e.g., Edmonds, 1979). Although researchers have consistently reported associations between these conditions and students' achievement, this research tradition has been challenged for a lack of rigor and systematic focus in its investigations and a lack of attention to possible mechanisms through which school characteristics are supposed to influence student learning (Barr & Dreeben, 1983; Purkey & Smith, 1983).

More recent and empirically promising studies of schools and student learning also neglect important linkages. Research that documents the achievement advantages of Catholic schools has identified students' academic course taking as a key mechanism, but it is not clear whether this mechanism operates primarily at the individual or the collective level (Bryk, Lee, & Holland, 1993; Coleman & Hoffer, 1987). A study of city high schools reported higher achievement in magnet schools than in comprehensive schools, but could not say what it was about magnet schools that led to higher achievement (Gamoran, 1996c). Research on restructured schools indicated that schoolwide restructuring may aid achievement, but many questions remain concerning what, exactly, is effective about restructuring and how school structure is linked with student learning (Lee & Smith, 1995, 1996, 1997; Newmann & Associates, 1996).

In this chapter, we respond to current limitations in the study of school organization and student learning. First, we take stock of research on school organization in greater detail. Second, we propose a new way of looking at the relation between the school's organizational context on the one hand, and the activities of teaching and learning on the other. Third, we present some different scenarios for teaching and learning activities and show how the organizational context of the school may play a different role in each case. Finally, we discuss the challenges of empirically verifying this new model of the organizational context of teaching and learning.

SCHOOL EFFECTS: FROM THE BLACK BOX TO NESTED LAYERS

Early studies of the impact of schools on student learning were exemplified by Coleman and colleagues' (1966) landmark research on equality of educational opportunity. Coleman and his colleagues estimated an economic production function in which student learning is an output that responds to various economic inputs such as expenditures, facilities, equipment, and background characteristics of teachers. In this model, the school is an unopened black box. What goes on inside the school—the production process itself—is not observed. If the production process were straightforward and predictable, the input–output production function would be a sensible way to study the impact of school resources. Yet the process of teaching and learning is complex and not fully routinized. Input–output studies do not reveal

FIGURE 2.1. The input–output model of school organization and school learning.

much about the effects of schools because so much depends on how the resources are used, and the use of resources is not included in the usual production function. Figure 2.1 provides a schematic display of the input–output model.

Scholars, educators, and politicians alike were surprised to discover that for the most part, variation in school resources bore little direct relation to variation in students' achievement, once background differences among students were taken into account (Coleman et al., 1966; Hodgson, 1975). This finding was reconfirmed in extensive reanalyses (Hanushek, 1994; Jencks et al., 1972; Mosteller & Moynihan, 1972). Most recently, a meta-analysis suggested that average resources do matter for student learning (Greenwald, Hedges, & Laine, 1996; see Hanushek, 1997, for a critique). Moreover in developing countries, where levels of resources such as trained teachers, textbooks, and facilities vary widely, the link between such resources and students' achievement tends to be stronger than it is in the United States and in other developed countries (Fuller, 1987; Fuller & Clarke, 1994; Heyneman & Loxley, 1983). In any case, it is clear that the relation between resources and outcomes is inconsistent—sometimes positive, sometimes negative, and sometimes absent—and the question of how to use resources effectively is much more important than whether average resources matter for average outcomes.

Opening the Black Box: The Nested Layers Approach

During the 1980s, sociologists of education began to open the black box of schools by studying the processes through which learning occurs. Bidwell and Kasarda (1980) distinguished between the effects of schools, the organizational context for teaching and learning, and schooling—the experiences students have in school that actually produce learning. According to this view, schools set the conditions for schooling, so that the influence of schools as organizations is always mediated by their impact on the schooling process. In this formulation, one understands the effects of schools by tracing the impact of school conditions on schooling activities and then by examining the connection between schooling activities and student learning.

Barr and Dreeben (1983) elaborated on this approach by exploring the organizational linkages among the different structural levels of school systems. In their view, outputs at one level of the organizational hierarchy (e.g., the school) become the inputs at the next level (e.g., the classroom). For example, school administrators allocate time to classroom teachers, make decisions within classrooms about how to use time, and instructional time allows teachers to cover the curriculum, which promotes student learning (Gamoran & Dreeben, 1986). This nested layers approach opened up the black box of schooling and focused attention on the

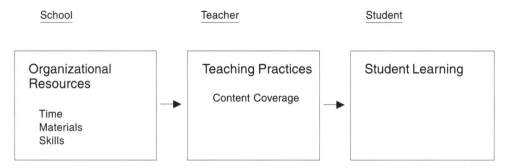

FIGURE 2.2. The nested layers model of school organization and student learning.

technology of schooling, that is, the processes of teaching and learning within classrooms. Figure 2.2 displays the nested layers model.

The theoretical foundation for the nested layers model was laid by Parsons (1963), who distinguished between the technical, managerial, and institutional levels of organization, and argued that influences tend to flow across adjacent levels. In Parsons' scheme, resource allocation was a managerial activity, and the outputs of this activity affected processes at the technical level, which in schools consists of teaching and learning. Barr and Dreeben (1983) provided concrete specification of resources allocated at the managerial level (time and materials) and activities occurring in the technical level (coverage of curricular content).

The notion of nested layers offered a valuable conceptual advance over previous work, and it has achieved some empirical success as well. Studies of the flow of resources, most notably time for instruction, show that allocations from the district and school to the classroom set constraints on teaching, which in turn influences student learning (Gamoran & Dreeben, 1986; Monk, 1992). In their analysis, Barr and Dreeben (1983) took advantage of the statistical technique of path analysis, widely known to sociologists since Blau and Duncan's (1967) seminal work on social stratification, but not previously used to examine the inner workings of school systems. Using a path model, Barr and Dreeben provided empirical documentation of the flow of resources and activities from school to classroom, from classroom to instructional group, and from group to individual student. The logic of path analysis is also evident in nested layers analyses by Alexander and Cook (1982), Rowan and Miracle (1983), Gamoran and Dreeben (1986), and others.

The nested layers model appears to have correctly identified the connections between resource allocation and the technology of teaching. However, efforts to examine a wider spectrum of school conditions have yielded inconsistent results for the nested layers model. For example, not all subjects and grade levels indicate that curricular allocations exert strong influences on student learning. Doyle (1992), summarizing the literature on the impact of curriculum on pedagogy, concluded that "curriculum is a weak force for regulating teaching" (p. 488). Although teachers tend to cover the topics reflected in the formal curriculum, they use their own discretion and may vary widely in teaching methods, in time devoted to various topics, in modes of assessment, and so on (Barr & Sadow, 1989; Freeman & Porter, 1989; Stodolsky, 1988). These findings derive from the United States, but in other countries where high-stakes tests are more closely linked to prescribed curricula, the effects of curricular allocations on teaching practices may be stronger (Stevenson & Baker, 1991; Gamoran, 1996a).

Moreover, researchers have had difficulty showing that features of schools other than resources allocated for instruction have any bearing on student learning. For example, Gamoran

(1987) examined a range of high school characteristics in an attempt to identify organizational conditions that influence learning by setting the conditions for students' instructional experiences. Although Gamoran observed strong relations between instructional experiences (e.g., coursetaking) and achievement, these associations were largely unrelated to school characteristics (e.g., student body composition, availability of academic programs). Other studies of school effects have been similarly unsuccessful in tracing the influence of organizational conditions through instructional experiences to student learning (e.g., Gahng, 1993; Gamoran, Porter, & Gahng, 1995). Researchers have uncovered important effects of different types of schools, such as Catholic schools (Bryk et al., 1993; Coleman & Hoffer, 1987) and magnet schools (Gamoran, 1996c), but the organizational conditions that mattered tended to be aggregate indicators of students' instructional experiences, such as extensive academic coursetaking and orderly classrooms. Research on school types thus supports the conclusion that instructional conditions affect student learning but offers less evidence about organizational influences on instructional conditions.

Recent studies of schools and student learning have focused less on the organizational constraints of material resources and shifted the emphasis toward organizational structures and processes such as leadership, collaboration, and efficacy among educators in a school. This literature builds on the effective schools tradition (e.g., Edmonds, 1979; Purkey & Smith, 1983) that emphasized key conditions at the school level including goal consensus, high expectations for student learning, principal leadership, emphasis on basic skills, and monitoring of students' progress. Like the effective schools tradition, several recent studies show consistent associations between organizational conditions and student learning. For example, Bryk and Driscoll (1988) observed a strong positive association between students' achievement in mathematics and an index of school community—whether teachers worked together, whether the principal supported the teachers' work, and so on. Similarly, Lee and Smith (1995, 1996) showed that students' achievement is higher in high schools in which teachers perceive a greater sense of efficacy and responsibility for student learning and in schools where educators have engaged in restructuring activities, such as team teaching, changing the grouping structure, flexible scheduling, and so on.

This body of work, from research on effective schools to studies of restructuring, is limited by ambiguity in causal mechanisms and even in causal direction. If high expectations are associated with high achievement, for example, which causes which? Research on effective schools gave little attention to the actual mechanisms through which school conditions are translated into achievement. How were expectations elevated, goal consensus achieved, and so on, and how were these conditions linked to student learning? These questions were not addressed.

Current work has implicitly adopted the nested layers view as a conceptual framework. That is, the organizational context is assumed to influence student learning by constraining conditions for classroom instruction. In this framework, social conditions such as a strong sense of community promote adherence to an academic mission among teachers, which leads to enhanced teaching and greater learning. Despite the clearer conception of mechanisms, causal ambiguity remains problematic. For example, Lee and Smith (1996) argued that students achieve more when their teachers accept collective responsibility for students' learning. Lee and Smith supported their claim by showing an association between teachers' sense of responsibility and student learning. In fact, however, the causal process could run in the opposite direction: Teachers may be more apt to accept responsibility in schools where levels of learning are high.

In a study of mathematics reform, Adajian (1995) showed that teachers who participated in schoolwide professional communities engaged in more innovative mathematics teaching, including an emphasis on problem solving and on hands-on applications. This finding is consistent with the notion that a community of teachers encourages instructional innovation, which promotes greater learning. However, it is not clear from Adajian's cross-sectional data whether the professional community led to innovative teaching, or vice versa. Similarly, Lee and Smith (1997) interpreted their analysis of national data to indicate that high levels of academic coursetaking and instructional emphases on problem solving and on inquiry accounted for the benefits of restructured schools over traditionally structured schools. Yet an alternative hypothesis—that innovative instruction may lead to both school restructuring and better learning—cannot be dismissed.

Just as Barr and Dreeben (1983) took advantage of statistical advances in path analysis, current work on the relation between school conditions and student learning has also benefited from new statistical techniques, particularly multilevel modeling (or hierarchical linear modeling). The multilevel approach distinguishes group-level and individual-level effects more accurately than earlier regression methods (Bryk & Raudenbush, 1992; Goldstein, 1995). Multilevel modeling is a particularly elegant method for examining differences between groups in individual-level effects; for example, multilevel methods provide the best evidence that the effect of socioeconomic status on student learning is weaker in Catholic schools than in public schools (Bryk et al., 1993). This finding indicates that achievement is more equitably distributed in Catholic schools. However, the multilevel approach does not address the causal ambiguities of the nested layers model, nor does it offer any special benefits in the quest to identify the mechanisms through which school conditions influence student learning. On the contrary, multilevel analysts often specify individual or classroom conditions such as coursetaking and instruction as aggregate school conditions, missing the opportunity to link school conditions to student learning through the mechanism of individual or classroom-based academic experiences (Bryk et al., 1993: Lee & Smith, 1997).

The nested layers model operates well for instructionally specific resources such as time and materials and for clearly defined teaching activities such as content coverage. It seems particularly appropriate when there are clear norms about the salience of curricular topics, such as early reading instruction. It is not clear that the perspective can be applied to a broader range of school and/or classroom conditions.

The Loose-Coupling Alternative

Whereas Bidwell and Kasarda (1980) and Barr and Dreeben (1983) responded to the failure of the input–output model by specifying more carefully the technical connections between organizational resources, teaching practices, and student learning, other writers emphasized the general absence of tight connections within the school system organization. Earlier, Bidwell (1965) had recognized the structural looseness of schools, and writers such as Weick (1976) and Meyer and Rowan (1977, 1978) expanded this notion to suggest that the structural isolation of classrooms, the autonomy of teachers, and the relative absence of formal authority means that schools are loosely coupled organizations. In a loosely coupled system, decisions occurring in one segment of the organization do not reverberate in clearly patterned ways elsewhere. Thus, what occurs in one classroom may have little impact on another, and decisions made by the principal have only modest effects on what students actually experience (Weick, 1976). According to this view, schools are tightly coupled around symbolic designations such as who gets taught by whom but are loosely coupled on matters of core technology such as what gets taught in the classroom (Meyer & Rowan, 1978). Teaching practices are a result of teacher training and on-the-job socialization and are not affected much by schoolwide conditions such as resources, plans, or administrative decisions (Weick, 1982). Student learning is primarily a response to societal expectations rather than to particular school conditions or to classroom instruction (Meyer, 1977).

The reason schools are loosely coupled, according to this perspective, is that it is difficult to judge their effectiveness using a bureaucratic model of costs and outputs (Meyer & Rowan, 1977, 1978; Weick, 1976). Teaching is an uncertain technology: cause–effect relations are not well understood, and there is no consensus on the best teaching methods. Moreover, the goals of schooling are ambiguous and often conflicting, so it is hard to determine what standards to use for judging schools. Finally, the participants in schools change over time, adding further uncertainty to the complexities of teaching and the ambiguities of goals. Consequently, schools turn away from their technical cores (teaching and learning) and emphasize their symbolic attributes such as categories and certification. In schools, structures are detached from activities, and activities are disconnected from outcomes (Meyer & Rowan, 1978). A logic of confidence allows schools to appear to work when the symbolic trappings of grade-level structures, certified teachers, students progressing from grade to grade, and so on, are present (Meyer & Rowan, 1978). In this way schools avoid inspection of their technical cores and focus on legitimation in the wider society.

Metz (1989) and Hemmings and Metz (1991) provided evidence from a study of eight high schools that is strikingly consistent with the loose-coupling perspective. Despite substantial differences among the eight schools in the characteristics of their communities, all adopted the same set of structures and routines, from the arrangement of classrooms, to the organization of the curriculum, to the allocation of time. These outward attributes articulated each school's legitimacy as a "real school." Despite the similarities, students' experiences could differ dramatically from one school to the next, because students' schooling experiences bore little relation to the symbolic structural features of their schools. Moreover, the acceptance of a real school as an organizational framework limited consideration of alternate arrangements, even when the standard structures and processes were unsuccessful in promoting pupils' progress. According to Metz (1989),

> If one looks at students' learning simply as a technical system, it is quite remarkable to see situations where a technical process (or the social structure which frames it) is clearly not effective on a massive scale, but no one in the organization calls for developing alternative technical or structural approaches. (p. 79)

On the contrary, educators in schools with the least successful students were often the most insistent that their schools reflected the societal consensus on what high schools should look like.

If schools are loosely coupled, what keeps them coupled at all? How is work coordinated in a loosely coupled organization? First, as noted previously, some aspects of schools are tightly coupled: categories such as grade levels and teacher are closely monitored and used to arrange persons and positions (though not activities). Second, according to Weick (1982), teachers' common professional socialization helps coordinate work in schools. Weick argued that "even though (educators) don't communicate much with each other, they can still coordinate their actions because each person can anticipate accurately what the other person is thinking and doing" (1982, p. 675). In fact, common socialization may be the basis for the logic of confidence, that is, unexamined assumptions about who is doing what in their classrooms. For example, fourth-grade teachers may assume that third-grade teachers are introducing concepts on which they will build when they teach the same students in the following year. Similarly, teachers teaching the same subject area in different grades share a common disciplinary socialization that yields a coherent approach to teaching despite the absence of formal mechanisms of coordination (Rowan & Miskel, 1999; Stodolsky & Grossman, 1995). Shared views of subject matter probably reflect both socialization in teacher training programs and broader social definitions of subject-matter characteristics. Several writers have noted that teachers of mathematics and of foreign languages tend to see their subjects as sequentially organized in clear hierarchies, whereas language arts and social studies teachers have more flexible views of their subject matters (Gamoran & Weinstein, 1998; Loveless, 1994; Rowan, Raudenbush, & Cheong, 1993; Stodolsky & Grossman, 1995;).

Meyer and Rowan (1978) acknowledged that loose coupling is probably more important in the United States than in many other countries because of the strong American tradition of decentralization and local control over education. Other countries typically have more centralized control over the curriculum, regulated through national testing, which results in tighter alignment between formal goals and outcomes than in the United States (Bishop, 1998). Formal inspections from central authorities, which rarely occur in the United States, may also serve to regulate the practice of teaching (Wilson, 1996). Thus, loose coupling as an explanatory framework may be more successful for the American case than elsewhere. Still, uncertainties that are inherent in teaching raise questions about the tightness of coupling even in more centralized educational systems than that of the United States (Benavot & Resh, 1998).

The loose-coupling model, displayed in Figure 2.3, offers a strong challenge to the nested layers approach. Where nested layers is correct for the narrow conditions of resources and content coverage, could loose coupling prevail for other conditions of schooling, such as leadership, relations among teachers and between teachers and students, and so on? Loose coupling would account for the weak and inconsistent impact of school climate on teaching and on learning (Anderson, 1982). It would also explain why policy interventions often fail to reach the classroom, particularly in the United States (e.g., Pressman & Wildavsky, 1979). Further, as Meyer (1977) has argued, loose coupling is consistent with the finding of little

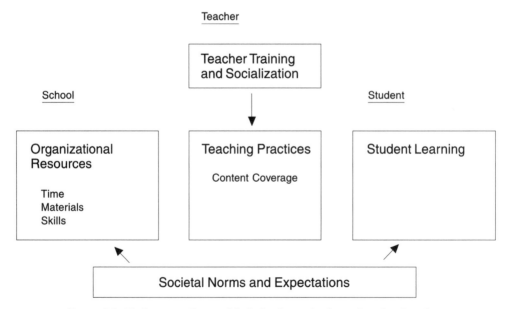

FIGURE 2.3. The loose coupling model of school organization and student learning.

variability between schools in student learning alongside substantial variability within schools. By and large, according to this view, schools operate similarly because they are focused on conformity to a common set of societal norms.

Moving beyond the nested layers model to confront the challenge of loose coupling requires a more nuanced analysis of the linkages between school conditions, teaching practices, and student learning. As a starting point, it is essential to rethink common assumptions about causal direction and change and to probe more deeply for the mechanisms that may connect the different elements of school organization.

Beyond Nested Layers

Building on the insights of Rowan (1990) and Newmann and Associates (1996), we suggest that the nested layers approach is limited by its assumption of a one-way relationship between organizational conditions and instructional practices. Rowan argued that when teaching is understood to be a complex, nonroutine activity, organizational support for innovation and success requires an organic relation between teaching practices and school organization, a connection that involves feedback and growth in both directions. The greater the recognition of the uncertainty and complexity of teaching, the more likely organic structures are to emerge. For example, teachers who recognize the complexities of teaching are more prone to form collegial networks for sharing information and mutual support. Rowan buttressed these claims with an insightful review of studies that indicated weak effects of collaboration and collegiality on teaching practices. Instead, organizational structures sometimes grew out of the demands of teaching. For example, Cohen, Deal, Meyer, & Scott (1979) observed that complex instructional tasks contributed to increased communication and teaming among teachers, but team teaching did not bring about complex instruction. Still, Rowan concluded that when collegial relations are intensive and embedded in a culture that emphasizes continuous improvement, the strength and quality of social relations among teachers may influence teaching practices. Although provocative, this conclusion was based on few cases, and Rowan found it difficult to provide evidence that relations among teachers substantially affect how they carry out their work in classrooms. In a subsequent empirical study, Rowan and his colleagues (1993) reported that the more teaching was viewed as a nonroutine activity, the greater the prevalence of organic management in the school. However, organic management did not result in greater amounts of ongoing learning among teachers.

Further support for the notion that organizational support for effective teaching may emerge from teachers' commitment to innovative instructional practices comes from Newmann and Associates' (1996) study of 24 highly restructured schools. This research began with the idea that there are levers at the school site that, when pressed, lead to better teaching and to more learning. What the investigators found, however, was more complex than a simple nested layers story. All 24 schools had innovative structural features, but few exhibited consistent evidence of exceptionally high-quality teaching and learning. The most successful schools were those in which educators were committed to intellectual quality in students' academic experiences and in which this commitment was the driving force behind organizational reforms. For example, teachers at Cibola High School were committed to disciplined inquiry and students' construction of knowledge. They used detracked classes to engage students in project work that resulted in high-quality instruction and high levels of learning. By contrast, teachers at Wallingford High School, who were also committed to detracking, had little notion of how their teaching might change in a detracked context. At Wallingford, researchers observed low-quality teaching and learning, mainly reflected in lectures and in a watered-down curriculum. Thus, detracking as a school organizational characteristic grew out of and supported a particular pedagogy in Cibola, whereas it was unrelated to instruction at Wallingford.

Similar conclusions emerged recently from another major study of school restructuring. Peterson, McCarthey, and Elmore (1996) reported that school structure had little consistent impact on teaching practices. Instead, teaching practices changed in response to teachers' learning, particularly when learning occurred in a community of educators. Teaching practices contributed to school conditions as much as the reverse. The authors concluded the following:

> Changing practice is primarily a problem of [teacher] learning, not a problem of organization. . . . School structures can provide opportunities for the learning of new teaching practices and new strategies for student learning, but structures, by themselves, do not cause learning to occur. . . . School structure follows from good practice not vice versa. (p. 149)

Our view of the organizational context of teaching and learning, displayed in Figure 2.4, is more closely related to the nested layers model than to loose coupling. As in the nested layers view, and in contrast to loose coupling, we argue that student learning responds to instruction. This notion derives from research that documents the impact of variation in teaching on student learning, ranging from coursetaking effects (Gamoran, 1987), to content coverage (Barr & Dreeben, 1983; Gamoran, Porter, Smithson, & White, 1997; Rowman & Miracle, 1983) to instructional coherence and teacher–student interaction (Gamoran, Nystrand, Berends, & LePore, 1995). Also consistent with the nested layers view, we expect that organizational resources affect student learning, but only as they are applied by teachers in classrooms. This aspect of our model has its foundation in research by Barr and Dreeben (1983; see also Gamoran & Dreeben, 1986). These studies showed that resources matter for learning when teachers apply resources in their classroom teaching. However, our model moves beyond the nested layers view in that we recognize that the relation between school conditions and classroom teaching may work in both directions and may shift over time. School conditions may respond to teaching practices, and teaching practices may be constrained or encouraged by their organizational context, as causal effects flow in both directions.

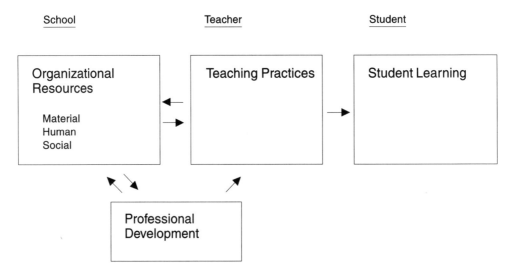

FIGURE 2.4. A dynamic, multidirectional model of school organization and student learning.

At the same time, our model draws from loose coupling the notion that teaching practices are influenced by professional socialization and training. As Peterson, McCarthey, and Elmore (1996) noted, teachers can learn to change their practice. This conclusion suggests that teachers not only respond to preservice training, as discussed by Weick (1982), but also to professional development that occurs on the job and that is a requirement for maintaining teaching certification in most states. In some cases professional development may be the sort of ritual activity that Meyer and Rowan (1978) recognized as important for legitimation but having little real significance for practice. In other cases, however, Peterson, Elmore, and McCarthey's findings suggest that professional development may result in meaningful change for teachers who participate.

ORGANIZATIONAL RESOURCES AS THE CONTEXT FOR TEACHING AND FOR LEARNING

Before elaborating on the role of professional development, we need to consider what aspects of school organization constitute salient contextual conditions for activities and outcomes. Prior research indicates that organizational resources constitute the most essential elements of the school's organizational context for teaching and for learning (Gamoran & Dreeben, 1986; Kilgore & Pendelton, 1993). We offer a broader conception of organizational resources than is found in most previous studies, as indicated in Figure 2.4 and as elaborated in the following sections. Resources emphasized by the input–output and the nested layers models are subsumed in our approach, and we also incorporate aspects of the school climate and school effectiveness traditions. Leadership, collaboration, and administrative support, as well as knowledge and skills, are all seen as types of resources that educators can draw on to improve their teaching. Hence, much of the past research on school effects is incorporated into our framework. However, our model does not include all aspects of school context. We focus on three categories of essential resources: material, human, and social. Other recent writers also point to the special salience of these conditions (Anderson, 1996; Newmann, 1998; Spillane & Thompson, 1997).

Material Resources

Despite inconsistent empirical support for the impact of expenditures on students' achievement, material resources constitute an important condition in the organizational context of teaching. Such resources include curriculum materials, equipment, and supplies; time available for teaching, planning and preparation; expenditures for personnel, particularly instructional staff; and the authority to expend funds for other purposes related to teaching and to learning. Material resources have no direct connection to learning because their impact depends on how they are used. Typically, educators at the school level have little discretion over the allocation of funds. According to the study of restructured schools, even when funding decisions are made at the school level, resources may not be used in ways that improve teaching (Newmann & Associates, 1996). However, some schools used resources in ways that improved instruction by allocating extra time for collaboration among teachers, by supporting professional development, and by providing tutoring sessions for students who needed extra help.

A variety of literatures support the conclusion that the effects of material resources are contingent on use. Resources devoted to instruction, not surprisingly, are more likely to pay off for student learning than resources directed in other ways (Newmann & Associates, 1996). Even when resources are allocated toward instructional needs, however, their benefits depend on how they are applied. Reducing class size, for example, may be the most common application of additional resources, yet a research literature consisting of hundreds of studies has yielded widely varying results. As Slavin (1989, 1990) has argued, reducing the number of students in a class is unlikely to yield any differences in student learning unless teachers are engaged in practices that are enhanced by working with fewer students at a time. When teachers carry out standard routines of lecture and recitation, it matters little whether there are 15, 20, or even 30 students in the class. Class size is likely to affect learning when instruction emphasizes more interactive involvement such as project work, extensive writing, and discussion, which may foster more intensive participation and feedback when there are fewer students at hand.

A similar argument can be made about time for instruction, another application of material resources. Generally, the research indicates that more time for teaching results in more learning for students (e.g., Brophy & Good, 1986). The implicit mechanism underlying the findings, as Barr and Dreeben (1983) explained, is a nested layers model: when teachers have more time available, they use it to cover the curriculum more extensively or in greater depth, and this yields enhanced learning for students. However, the pattern is not invariant. For example, when more time is allocated to first-grade teachers, they use it to advance their highest priority, the reading curriculum (Gamoran & Dreeben, 1986). They do not use additional time for other subjects, such as mathematics, science, or social studies (Gamoran, 1988). Thus time, a resource allocated by administrators to teachers, is an essential element in the context of first-grade reading instruction, but it has limited implications for first-grade teaching in other subjects. More generally, the impact of time as an organizational resource clearly depends on how that time is allocated by teachers within classrooms.

Because the impact of resources depends on how the resources are used, control over material resources is also an important consideration. According to one view, because teachers have the closest contact with students, they know best what resources are needed to meet students' needs. This perspective sees teachers as knowledgeable professionals and suggests that the greater teachers' control over the allocation of resources, the more effectively the resources will be used (Gamoran, Porter, & Gahng, 1995). However, research to date has found little evidence for effects of teacher control over resources on teaching or learning (Park, 1998).

Human Resources

Some perspectives on schooling assume that differences among teachers in how they have been trained or in what they know have little to do with the effects of instruction on learning. Older notions of teacher-proof curricula (see Brophy & Good, 1986) have counterparts in the most extreme view of standards-based reform, which emphasizes standardized curricula as the key to successful teaching and student testing as the means of ensuring that the curriculum is taught (see Borman, Cookson, Sadovnik, & Spade, 1996). The input–output model of schooling similarly ignores the teaching process in considering the production of learning (see Figure 2.1). These views are consistent with a highly bureaucratized model of schooling in which teachers adhere to standard procedures to maximize efficiency (e.g., Callahan, 1962).

Research evidence depicts teaching as an activity that, in some cases, is highly routinized. Jackson (1968) observed that teaching tends to be preactive, or scripted in advance, rather than reactive, or responsive to students. Many writers have documented the extent to which classroom life is dominated by teachers (e.g., Gamoran et al., 1995; Goodlad, 1984; McNeil, 1986). As loose-coupling theorists have shown, this attempted routinization has gaps—points at which teaching may or may not coincide with what students need for learning. Nonetheless, a logic of confidence allows teachers to proceed without being troubled by a mismatch between script and students (Hemmings & Metz, 1991; Meyer & Rowan, 1978).

Recent research on teaching, however, indicates that the logic of confidence does not always prevail and that teachers' knowledge makes a difference in the quality of instruction and, in particular, teachers' abilities to respond to students (Cohen, 1990). Drawing on findings from cognitive science, education researchers posit three types of knowledge that are essential for teaching: pedagogical knowledge, in which teachers know general strategies of teaching; content knowledge, what teachers know about their subject matters; and pedagogical content knowledge, the knowledge of how to teach a particular subject matter in a way that fosters students' understanding (Shulman, 1987). Following this argument, then, we propose that teachers' human resources—their knowledge, skills, and dispositions—constitute an important resource that may shape the quality of their teaching and their students' learning. Studies of teacher knowledge in specific areas of pedagogic content indicate that the implementation of a new instructional approach improves as teachers come to understand it more deeply (Tharp & Gallimore, 1988).

The emphasis on human resources implies a different model of change than that favored by a model focused on material resources. If human resources are important, then teacher development may be a central element of reform activities (Tharp & Gallimore, 1988). Given the high degree of teacher autonomy in the classroom, a perspective that emphasizes teachers' learning over material resources seems especially promising.

Principal leadership is another type of human resource found in schools. Research in the effective schools tradition emphasized leadership, but empirical corroboration for the salience of principal leadership for student learning is weak (Good & Brophy, 1986). A key limitation of this work is its failure to specify the mechanisms by which leadership may stimulate better learning. Current research on leadership emphasizes of the principal's role in creating a community with a common purpose (Newmann & Associates, 1996). Successful principals provide a vision that sets forth a particular mission for the school and galvanizes commitment from teachers and from students. At the same time, the principal may be able to select staff members who accept the school's mission. In this way, a principal's leadership may result in a schoolwide instructional emphasis on common goals.

Interestingly, this view of leadership is more compatible with the loose-coupling model than with nested layers. Rather than viewing the allocation of resources as the key mechanism for the impact of leadership, as implied by the nested layers view, this perspective on leadership emphasizes its symbolic attributes, which are central to loose-coupling theory (Meyer & Rowan, 1978). Even though selecting staff is a technical activity, it has symbolic implications when acceptance of a common vision is a chief criterion for selection. According to loose coupling, structure and technical work are weakly connected, but rituals and symbols, including those that define the school's mission in the wider society, play an important role in pulling together and legitimizing the school in its social context. Following this view, principal leadership may affect the work of teachers by shaping a purpose for the school through selection of staff and articulation of a guiding vision.

Social Resources

Our argument about social resources comes neither from loose coupling nor from the nested layers model. Both views stress the isolation and autonomy of teachers within their classrooms, differing in that nested layers studies have shown that material resources allocated to classrooms and used by teachers can affect student learning (e.g., Gamoran & Dreeben, 1986). According to these perspectives there is little to be gained from collegiality among the faculty of a school, except perhaps the pleasures of a friendlier workplace. Similarly, these widely followed theories would lead one to expect few benefits of teacher participation in collective decisions about school policies. According to loose coupling, school policies simply have little relevance for what goes on in classrooms. According to the nested layers view, policy decisions are managerial activities whose impact occurs through the allocation of resources, regardless of how allocative decisions are made. For different reasons, neither perspective supposes that relations among teachers matter for instructional practices.

In contrast, an emerging literature about the social organization of schools suggests that under certain conditions, social relations among educators may profoundly influence teachers' classroom work and thereby affect student learning. As Rowan (1990) explained, when teaching is viewed as complex and interactive, dynamic and changing as opposed to routine, an organic system of management that relies on developing commitment rather than imposing controls may lead to more successful teaching and learning. Organic management means encouraging social relationships of trust, shared responsibility, collective decision making, and common values as mechanisms for bringing about change. When these activities are focused on student learning, they may indeed matter for instruction and for achievement (Newmann & Associates, 1996). Thus, aspects of the social environment of the school, including shared values, collaboration, and collective decision making, constitute social resources on which educators may draw to bolster their teaching.

At the same time, social resources may also emerge from experiences in the practice of teaching. Teachers who refrain from regarding instruction as a standardized, routine activity are faced with the uncertainties of finding successful ways of meeting students' needs. This uncertainty is always present in teaching, but typically it is obscured by the logic of confidence that promotes following prescribed routines that avoid being deflected by students' responses. Recognition of uncertainty may lead teachers to talk with one another—breaking down the usual isolation of teaching—as they search for better solutions to the problems of teaching and learning that appear in their classrooms. These discussions about instruction may strengthen the collective ties among teachers and teachers and in turn may help address their concerns about teaching.

Although Newmann and Associates' (1996) findings are consistent with the view that social resources matter for teaching, an alternate interpretation of the evidence cannot be rejected. Even when social relations among teachers emerge out of practical experience, these social relations may have little bearing on instruction because teachers are autonomous in their classrooms. Under this scenario, social relations would be a correlate of successful teaching but not a causal factor. Research to date cannot adjudicate among the alternative interpretations.

PROFESSIONAL COMMUNITY.   One way of characterizing social resources in a school is as a professional community of educators. Several recent writers claim that a strong professional community provides the capacity for improving instruction and ultimately for enhancing student learning. Talbert and McLaughlin (1994) distinguished between professionalism and community: professionalism includes technical knowledge, an ethic of service, and commitment to the profession, and community refers to collaboration and continuous learning among teachers. Their view of professionalism is akin to our notion of human resources, except that they examine the collective, shared presence of technical knowledge, finding that teacher collaboration and learning promote a technical culture in the school. Newmann and Associates (1996) explored the contribution of professional community to authentic pedagogy, an instructional focus on disciplinary content, students' construction of knowledge, and relevance. Professional community, in their view, consists of shared purpose, a collective focus on student learning, collaboration, reflective conversations about teaching, and deprivatized practice (i.e., breaking the usual isolation of teaching by observing one another's teaching). They found more authentic pedagogy in schools with stronger professional communities. Secada and Adajian (1997), using a similar view of professional community but adding collective control over key decisions to the concept, provided a case study of an elementary school that illustrates how one schoolwide professional community helped teachers improve their teaching of mathematics.

Findings from studies of professional community are provocative, but several caveats are in order. First, the studies are based on small samples of schools. Second, particularly in the case of Newmann and Associates (1996), generalization from the evidence is difficult because the schools were selected especially for their unique features. Third, most studies of professional community have implicitly adopted the nested layers view that professional community enhances teaching and thereby improves learning; yet it is also possible that professional community is a by-product of enhanced teaching, rather than a stimulus. Secada and Adajian (1997) suggested that teachers' professional community and instructional practice may affect one another, but their empirical analysis was limited to one causal direction: the influence of professional community an instruction. Similarly, Louis, Kruse, and Marks (1996) acknowledged that the connections between social relations among teachers and classroom instruction are complex:

> [Our analysis] cannot prove that professional community causes teachers to engage in more authentic classroom practice. A skeptic could plausibly argue that teachers who are making efforts to increase authentic pedagogy are more likely to seek support for this difficult task from colleagues, thus creating professional community. (p. 184)

SOCIAL CAPITAL.   We may also think of social resources in a school as a form of social capital. Social capital in a school refers to trust, expectations, shared understandings, and a sense of obligations that may characterize networks of relationships among educators (see Coleman, 1988 for a more general definition). In contrast to schools in which teachers work in isolation, teachers in some schools form relationships with one another around academic concerns of teaching and learning. These social networks constitute resources on which teachers can draw in their efforts to improve teaching (Kilgore & Pendelton, 1993). Collaboration, collegial relations, and opportunities for reflective discussion about teaching help build social capital. In such schools, teachers are likely to work together, even in the classroom; in this way, teaching becomes deprivatized and the typical isolation of teaching is overcome. Administrative support, such as advice and consultation about teaching and school policies, also builds social resources on which teachers can draw. Coleman (1988) explained that social capital can facilitate the development of human capital. In the case of schools, social capital among teachers helps them improve their knowledge and skills (i.e., their human capital) by providing a normative environment that encourages experimentation, offers a place to discuss uncertainties, and rewards improvement. This portrait differs substantially from the standard picture of schools in which teachers' activities are largely unseen by other adults and their unique contributions are unrecognized and unacknowledged.

More broadly, it is important to recognize the potential interplay between material, human, and social resources (which may also be termed economic, human, and social capital; see Spillane & Thompson, 1997). Just as social capital may promote human capital, teachers with particular knowledge and dispositions may be more likely to forge relations of social capital in the first place. Moreover, economic capital may be essential for developing both human and social capital, as teachers' learning and collaboration require infusions of time, materials, and expertise from outside the standard worklife of a school and its staff. Perhaps most important, economic resources devoted to teachers' professional development may stimulate both human and social capital as well as their interplay. This possibility is reflected in the arrows in Figure 2.4, which run in both directions between organizational resources and professional development.

PROFESSIONAL DEVELOPMENT AS THE ENGINE OF CHANGE

What is the basis for suggesting that professional development is a key mechanism for improving teaching? Surely many teachers would react to this claim with skepticism, as professional development is often regarded as a necessary job requirement without much connection to the actual work of teaching (Sparks & Loucks-Horsley, 1989). Much professional development, it seems, fails to influence practice. Workshops are typically isolated events, often unrelated to teachers' ongoing concerns. At best, a workshop is seen as useful if it provides a new tool for a teacher's toolkit—something that can be applied in an immediate and direct way (Fullan, 1991). This type of professional development does not result in meaningful change (Goldenberg & Gallimore, 1991), nor, we suspect, does it contribute to significant variation in teaching practices among teachers.

However, current research on teaching suggests an alternate possibility. Professional development that is sustained, coherent, collaborative, and reflective may lead to real changes in practice (Darling-Hammond & McLaughlin, 1996). Lieberman (1996) proposed an expanded view of professional development including direct learning through courses, through workshops, and through other avenues, informal learning in school through peer coaching, through sharing experiences, through conducting case studies, and the like, and informal learning outside of school through opportunities such as networks, partnerships, and collaboratives. According to Lieberman, "Teachers who engage in these new professional opportunities often find themselves in an exciting and powerful cycle: The more they learn, the more they open up to new possibilities and the more they seek to learn more" (p. 189–190). Not all teachers follow this path, but those who do are profoundly influenced in their practice.

Professional development may influence organizational resources in two ways. First, it may contribute to teachers' knowledge, skills, and dispositions, that is, the human resources of a school. This is a common view of the benefits of professional development (e.g., Sparks & Loucks-Horsley, 1989), and it stands behind the regulations of many states that require teachers to participate in professional development in order to maintain their teaching licenses. Second, professional development may contribute to the social resources of a school, particularly if it is collaborative and reflective. When serious professional development is based in a school, it may help establish many of the features of a professional community, including collaboration, shared values, deprivatized practice, and reflective discussions about student learning. Thus, professional development has potential for building a school's capacity to create change in teaching and in learning (Darling-Hammond & McLaughlin, 1996; Little, 1986; Newmann & Associates, 1996; Tharp & Gallimore, 1988).

At the same time, organizational resources may affect the provision and nature of professional development. Professional development requires substantial funds, particularly if it is sustained over time and involves collaboration among teachers. Little (1986, 1990) showed that conditions for effective professional development are difficult to maintain, requiring time, leadership, and energy. Thus, the relation between organizational resources and professional development is dynamic, sometimes building momentum as noted by Lieberman (1996), but at other times faltering due to lack of resources (Little, 1990).

Not only do resources and professional development affect one another, but the impact of professional development on teaching probably depends in part on the level of resources available for implementation and for diffusion of new ideas and practices. Lotan, Cohen, and Morphew (1997) reported that teachers were more likely to engage in nonroutine behavior—a key outcome of their complex instruction professional development program—in schools where principals were more knowledgeable and supportive and where teachers obtained assistance in acquiring materials and supplies. Examining the persistence of a similar reform, Dahl (1997) found that new practices were more likely to be sustained over time when principals helped coordinate both material resources (supplies, equipment, and space) and social resources (teachers' opportunities to work together).

A key question for our formulation concerns the salience of the school's boundaries for changes in teaching and in learning. Our model assumes that resources that reach the school are of primary importance (see Figure 2.4). This assumption is clearly appropriate for material and human resources because resources applied in the classroom are filtered through the school and through teachers. It is less clear whether the school is an especially important locus of social resources. If teachers find professional communities in other types of organizations or collaboratives, how much does the school really matter for their development as successful teachers? Although much of the research literature focuses on schoolwide professional communities (e.g., Newmann & Associates, 1996), it is clear from research on high schools that departments are the key organizational units (Little, 1990; Talbert, 1995). Consequently, it may be that departments rather than whole schools should be the focus of research on professional community. Middle and elementary schools, though not typically divided into departments, may have other types of subgroups in which professional communities are embedded. In addition, teacher networks that draw participants from many different schools may serve as important professional communities for some teachers (Newmann & Associates, 1996). Hence, there is no guarantee at any level that the boundaries of the professional community are the boundaries of the school.

Professional Development and Schoolwide Transformation

In some cases, professional development serves as a stimulus to change throughout a school. Humbolt Elementary School, one of the schools included in Newmann and Associates' (1996) study, joined a national organization for school reform after a few teachers became interested in its instructional approach. In-service participation by these teachers ultimately led to the adoption of a new approach by the entire school staff. In most cases, however, the schools that exhibited exceptionally high-quality teaching and learning were not so much transformed as established as new schools from the beginning. Change, moreover, was not seen as something that took place once but was regarded as a process of continuous improvement. At Careen

Academy, an elementary school, key innovations included portfolio assessments, narrative reports on students' progress, and remaining with the same teacher for more than one year. Researchers concluded that "all three practices are works in progress, however, and teachers work continually to define and enrich them" (Newmann & Associates, 1996, p. 84). Similarly at Cibola High School, a teacher explained that ". . . every year we should get better. What we accepted as a minimum one year should be unsatisfactory the next year. It has to be that way. We have to ask for more every year. That's an ongoing thing, we'll never stop struggling over that" (Newmann & Associates, 1996, p. 131). In successful restructured schools, innovations were dynamic and adaptive, not static.

Professional development often played a key role in stimulating, supporting, and enhancing these changes. Careen Academy provides persuasive evidence of the power of professional development (Newmann & Associates, 1996). Careen teachers participate in a summer institute lasting 1 to 3 weeks every year. They also attend four Saturday workshops, as well as a variety of activities outside the school district. Newmann and Associates (1996) also discovered that teachers were participating in three voluntary study groups on an ongoing basis. These activities contributed substantially to teachers' efforts in the classroom.

Despite these cases of wholescale development and change, other evidence indicates that most often, change efforts fall short of schoolwide transformation. Drawing on recent research, we have identified three other outcomes that commonly occur, even in the face of sustained, reflective professional development involving a number of teachers in a school: Teachers who favor change may find themselves in constant conflict with other actors in the school, due to others' resistance to change; they may compromise their ideals and moderate their teaching initiatives to avoid conflict (or adapt their technological efforts to accommodate existing circumstances); or they may create alternative structures within schools in which the new teaching practices may flourish, but not expand beyond the boundary of the alternate structure (e.g., a school-within-a-school). The outcome that finally emerges depends in part on the dynamic interplay between organizational resources and teaching practices. Research on school restructuring provides illustrations for these claims and draws attention to possible mechanisms through which the various outcomes may occur.

CONSTANT CONFLICT.   In some cases, change efforts result in continual conflict within schools. Mechanisms that produce this conflict are varied. In Fremont High School, one of the highly restructured schools examined by Newmann and Associates (1996), a group of teachers attempted to eliminate low-level math classes and teach all students in mixed-ability classes within a subset of the school. These changes resulted in tension within the school, with teachers outside the group complaining that too much time was spent addressing affective needs and not enough was spent on academic concerns and arguing that students were not being prepared for upper division math courses. The same study found another example of constant conflict at Selway Middle School, a charter school led by a group of four teachers committed to authentic instruction. Although other teachers shared the ideal of authenticity, they resented the oligarchic control exercised by the four leading teachers and believed they had no voice in the policies and direction of the school.

In the first case, conflict occurred between two groups of teachers with competing ideas about the essential goals of math instruction and with differing views of the varied capabilities of students. In the second case, the conflict was also between groups of teachers, but it centered on control and governance issues rather than on a philosophy of teaching. In still other instances, conflict occurs between administrators and teachers or between teachers and parents. More generally, constant conflict seems to emerge under any one of three circumstances:

when there are philosophical differences about what constitutes real teaching and learning; when there are competing preferences for the allocation of limited resources; or when teachers resist additional work necessary for teaching reforms. Actions that foment conflict include administrators' active opposition to change, restriction of resources to leaders of change processes, sabotage by antireform forces, and educators lining up external forces to oppose the sought-after changes.

COMPROMISE AND ADAPTATION.   Efforts to avoid internal conflict may lead to a second type of outcome, in which would-be reformers moderate their innovations as an adaptation to existing conditions. In some cases this means taking on the language of change without carrying out the activities of change. Researchers observed this situation in restructured schools where teachers "talked the talk" but did not "walk the walk"—that is, teachers spoke the rhetoric of reform but did not engage in innovative instructional practices (Gamoran, 1996b; Newmann & Associates, 1996). This outcome may result from a lack of training among teachers, from an assumption that desired changes cannot succeed, or as a consequence of pressure from other sources, such as district pressure to raise standardized test scores.

One may find that the adaptation response is an incremental step on the way toward long-term change. More commonly, however, our experience suggests that limited changes do not continue incrementally over the long term. Instead, once the boundaries of change are defined, further reforms in the same area of work do not occur.

ALTERNATE STRUCTURES.   Sometimes teachers seeking change manage to avoid compromising their innovative approach to teaching and learning but are unable to diffuse their initiative to the entire school staff. In this circumstance the initiative often emerges as an alternate structure within a traditionally structured organization. An extreme example of this outcome was Island High School, in which every new idea seemingly resulted in a new structure. There were special programs for at-risk youth, for pregnant girls, for bilingual students, for low-achieving students, for technology-oriented students, and so on (Newmann & Associates, 1996). More commonly, a new initiative may result in a school-within-a-school that exists alongside and often in competition with the regular structure.

Why do innovative practices emerge through alternate structures instead of as transformations of existing institutions? Lack of organizational resources, particularly limited material and social resources, is the most likely reason. First, whereas special resources may be available for modest reforms, the new resources may be insufficient to encourage a more complete transformation. Second, teachers within schools are typically isolated from one another, separated by the boundaries of their classroom walls. They may lack opportunities to learn from one another and to teach one another. Communication among teachers around substantive issues is typically limited. Third, and probably most important, there is a strong norm of autonomy within schools, and it is considered inappropriate to criticize other teachers. Teachers are reluctant to question others' professional judgment, preferring to let others proceed as they have been and limiting the innovative practices to those who come to it on their own.

When outsiders see that reforms have been limited to alternate structures, they may take this result as a sign of the reform's failure. This perception may further inhibit growth or may lead to the reform's decline. Limitations on growth may also lead to a "circle the wagons" mentality among the leaders of change, a strong defense of a limited territory to keep the reform alive. These processes may tend to solidify the segmented character of school reforms, as Newmann and Associates (1996) observed at Island High School.

EXAMPLES OF TEACHING AND LEARNING:
APPLYING THE MODELS

Thus far we have alluded to different views of teaching, but we have not provided many details. We noted, for example, that the uncertainties of teaching are often ignored in favor of standard routines, but sometimes uncertainties are recognized by teachers who may respond by attempting to increase their own knowledge. This example suggests that differences in conceptions of teaching may have consequences for the organizational context of teaching. That is, the aspect of the organizational context that is most salient may depend on one's conception of teaching. To explore this issue more fully, we describe three different approaches to teaching that we term teaching for understanding, conventional teaching, and core knowledge teaching. Each of these approaches calls into prominence different aspects of our dynamic model of the organizational context of teaching and learning.

Teaching for Understanding

According to Carpenter and Lehrer (1999), student understanding involves five interrelated forms of mental activity: constructing relationships, extending and applying knowledge, reflecting about experiences, articulating what one knows, and making knowledge one's own. By teaching for understanding, we mean instruction designed to stimulate these mental activities. A variety of writers have described such teaching as emphasizing students' construction of meaning and discovery of knowledge through active learning (e.g., Cohen, McLaughlin, & Talbert, 1993). Newmann and Associates (1996) had a similar concept in mind when they examined authentic pedagogy, which involves disciplined inquiry, student construction of knowledge, and relevance to students' lives beyond the school.

Teaching for understanding requires teachers to confront the uncertainties of teaching. As emphasized in loose-coupling theory, teaching is an ambiguous technology. Typically, this uncertainty is managed by focusing attention on the symbolic and ritual aspects of schooling and by avoiding inspection of the technical core. In teaching for understanding, however, the logic of confidence is not sufficient for managing uncertainty. These teachers are forced to go beyond scripted routines because they are faced with pressing questions about what students do or do not understand and what activities may improve understanding for particular students at a particular point in time. Teaching for understanding requires a means of managing uncertainty that recognizes and responds to questions rather than avoiding them. In response, teachers are likely to reach out to other teachers involved in similar efforts. Colleagues may provide moral support as well as practical suggestions. They may talk with one another, plan together, visit one another's classrooms, and so on—in short, they may begin to construct a professional community. Thus, a supportive social environment may emerge from efforts to teach for understanding. To flourish, however, this environment requires material resources, particularly time for collaboration, and human resources, some level of knowledge about fostering students' understanding, which may come from professional development. We propose that the relation between teaching for understanding and social resources in a school is dynamic, as the uncertainties of instruction, once recognized, provide the content of social relationships among educators, and these relationships in turn contribute to enhanced teaching for understanding. This conception is consistent with Bidwell, Frank, and Quiroz's (1997) finding that progressivist views of teaching are more prevalent in schools in which working conditions are more collegial.

Teaching for understanding may also call for another connection not previously recognized in Figure 2.4; feedback from student learning to teaching practices. Teachers who are focusing on students' understanding must adjust their activities in response to students' progress in learning. Thus, teaching for understanding forms a nexus between two dual processes: on the one side, the dynamic relation between teaching for understanding and social relations in the school, and on the other, a feedback loop between teaching and learning.

Conventional Teaching

By conventional teaching we mean teaching organized through a set pattern of lecture, recitation, and seatwork. This is not an abstracted ideal type; rather it accurately characterizes much of the teaching in American schools, particularly after the primary grades. A variety of studies have depicted this emotionally flat, teacher-dominated process (e.g., Goodlad, 1984). Nystrand (1997) described it as "monologic instruction," meaning that classroom life is essentially a monologue—even when students recite, they are following a script that has been laid down by the teacher. The flow of questions and answers follows a well-known pattern of initiation (teacher question), response by a student, and teacher's evaluation of the student's response (Mehan, 1979). In this type of instruction, even small-group work is prescripted by teachers (Nystrand, Gamoran, & Heck, 1993).

What are the key organizational contexts for conventional teaching? Here the flow tends to be one way, not dynamic. Consistent with the nested layers model, allocations of time and curricular materials are expected to influence teachers' coverage of curricular content. In contrast to teaching for understanding, social resources would have little impact on teachers' instructional practices. In conventional teaching, teachers work in isolation from one another, and issues of potential uncertainty are submerged beneath instructional routines. Consequently, there is little impetus for reflection about the substantive problems of teaching. Of course, teachers talk every day with their colleagues about the troubles of the job. These conversations, however, typically focus on administrative issues or on problems of specific students, rather than on new instructional approaches, on content questions, or on the intellectual quality of students' work (Newmann & Associates, 1996). We propose that the predominance of conventional teaching coupled with the marginal relevance of social resources for conventional teaching accounts for the inconsistent and generally weak effects of school-level social indicators such as collegiality and collaboration. Teachers' expectations and efficacy are exceptions to the pattern of weak school effects, but these apparent effects are better explained as responses to students' success rather than as determinants. For conventional teaching and social resources, loose coupling prevails.

Core Knowledge Teaching

Core knowledge teaching refers to teachers who emphasize the transmission of subject-matter knowledge from established authoritative sources to students. According to Hirsch (1993, 1996), this transmission of knowledge is the essential function of schooling. In contrast to teaching for understanding, where students construct meaning for themselves, core knowledge views meaning as residing outside students, within the subject matter itself. Core knowledge teaching also contrasts with conventional teaching in two important ways. First, core knowledge has explicit standards for what constitutes important knowledge (Hirsch, 1996).

Second, core knowledge teaching emphasizes depth of knowledge to a much greater degree than in conventional teaching, which often introduces fragmented bits of information and ignores controversy and underlying linkages among issues (McNeil, 1986).

For core knowledge teachers, the key organizational resources are curricular materials and their own knowledge of the subject matter. Thus, material and human resources are more salient than social resources. One could imagine that core knowledge faculty might engage in substantive discussions of curricular content, and from these discussions might emerge a professional community of teachers, as in teaching for understanding. However, because the core knowledge curriculum is largely given, whereas students' understanding is highly uncertain, one would expect social relations among teachers to play a less prominent role in responding to and shaping instructional practices of core knowledge teaching as compared with teaching for understanding. Consistent with this view, Bidwell, Frank, and Quiroz (1997) reported no significant associations between the character of teachers' working relationships and their reported emphases on instructional rigor.

As in conventional teaching, we expect that student learning occurs in response to core knowledge teaching, without a meaningful feedback loop. Thus, teaching for understanding is the only case of those we have considered in which instruction responds significantly to student learning.

CONCLUSIONS: TOWARD A RESEARCH AGENDA

In this chapter, we have both simplified and added complexity to conceptions of how the school as an organization provides a context for teaching and for learning. We simplified them by arguing that organizational resources are the most essential aspects of the organizational context. We subsume most of the conditions examined in previous research under our concept of resources, including such widely diverse conditions as time, materials, class size, knowledge, leadership, and collaboration. The focus on resources allowed us to trace the development of theoretical conceptions of school organization, from input–output notions, to nested layers, to our own model. In each of these perspectives, resources are the most salient features of the context of teaching and learning.

In simplifying it, we have left out some aspects of school organization. In particular, aspects of structure that are not merely a matter of resources are not found in our model. For example, structural differentiation into tracks and ability groups is usually not a matter of economic resources, yet it figures prominently as a context for teaching (Oakes, Gamoran, & Page, 1992). Interestingly, changes in differentiation policies often fail to bring about instructional improvements (Gamoran & Weinstein, 1998). Research in this area shows that structural differentiation is not an easy policy lever because of resistance to change and insufficient knowledge about teaching under new structural conditions (Wells & Serna, 1996). Indeed, research findings about structural differentiation are consistent with the general conclusions of Peterson and associates (1996), that structural conditions may facilitate teaching improvements but they are not the primary causal factors. Further research may help to specify more fully the importance of structure as a complement to resources (Newmann, 1998).

Composition of the student body is another organizational feature that does not figure prominently in our analysis. Composition, like structure, may be associated with differences in teaching and in learning but does not appear to be a driving force (Gamoran, 1992). An important question about composition is whether it operates as a contingency for organizational resources; that is, whether different types and levels of resources are needed to bring about similar changes in schools that differ in their student bodies. For example, is professional development of a certain type or quality necessary to improve teaching when the students are especially disadvantaged? This complication may also be addressed in future research.

Although we simplified it by leaving out some aspects of organization, in other ways our model is more complex than previous visions of schools and schooling because it recognizes the possibility of dynamic, multidirectional associations between organizational resources, teaching, and learning. Such complexity may not prevail in all cases, but it likely occurs in many of the reform efforts currently underway, which focus on teaching for understanding (Cohen et al., 1993), authentic pedagogy (Newmann & Associates, 1996), and dialogic instruction (Nystrand, 1997). Research on how these dynamic associations emerge is essential for learning how to provide a supportive context for new instructional approaches. Some combination of survey and qualitative research that monitors schools and districts over time is needed to trace the connections among resources, teaching, and learning.

The relation between teaching and its organizational context depends in part on what conception of teaching prevails. The importance of particular resources may also vary among and within educational systems in response to different or to changing conceptions of governance and accountability. For example, whereas loose coupling has been especially apparent in the United States until now, new accountability standards for what teachers teach and for what students learn may change the connections between allocations and outcomes. A question for future research is whether reform that emphasize new standards will be accompanied by tighter linkages between curricular allocation and students' performance, as envisioned in the nested layers view, or whether increases in professional development for teachers, rather than the pressures of curriculum and testing, may lead to changes in teaching. Yet another alternative is that longstanding norms in American education will be maintained, and educators will successfully resist pressures for greater accountability in the context of a persistently loosely coupled system. Cross-national research, as well as research that monitors trends within education systems over time, would shed light on these issues.

Research on the allocation and impact of resources has yielded clearer conclusions for some resources than for others. For some narrowly specified aspects of time, curriculum coverage, and student learning, the nested layers view has been sustained. Human resources such as teachers' knowledge also seem closely linked to teaching when teaching practices are carefully specified. Existing research offers less confidence about the impact of other human resources, such as leadership, or about social resources, particularly the relationships among educators. Research on these conditions is inconclusive, and we have argued that a more nuanced analysis of resource flows is necessary to identify their multidirectional effects.

An organization is a system of linked relationships, not simply a collection of individuals or of isolated categories. An organizational role, such as teacher, has meaning only when thought of in connection with some other role, such as student, principal, or parent. For this reason a sociological study of an organization calls for a study of relationships, centering on how relationships become ordered, how they change, and how they influence outcomes. What may prove intriguing across organizations are differences in the character of the linkages that prevail. A focus on relationships offers greater possibilities for understanding the context of teaching and learning, and thus for supporting the reform of teaching, than does a focus on the traits of organizational participants.

ACKNOWLEDGMENTS: Support for this research was provided by the National Center for Improving Student Learning and Achievement in Mathematics and Science at the Wisconsin

Center for Education Research, University of Wisconsin, Madison, with funds from the U.S. Department of Education, Office of Educational Research and Improvement (Grant No. R305A60007). The authors are grateful for helpful comments from Andy Anderson, Charles Bidwell, Robert Dreeben, Eric Grodsky, Catherine Reimer, Brian Rowan, and Tona Williams. Findings and conclusions are those of the authors and do not necessarily reflect the views of the supporting agencies.

REFERENCES

Adajian, L. B. (1995). *Teacher's professional community and the teaching of mathematics*. Unpublished doctoral dissertation, University of Wisconsin, Madison.

Alexander, K. L., & Cook, M. A. (1982). Curricula and coursework: A surprise ending to a familiar story. *American Sociological Review, 47*, 626–640.

Anderson, C. S. (1982). The search for school climate: A review of the research. *Review of Educational Research, 52*, 368–420.

Anderson, C. W. (1996). *Reform in teacher education as building systemic capacity to support the scholarship of teaching*. Paper presented at the International Workshop on Reform Issues in Teacher Education, Taipei, Taiwan.

Barr, R., & Dreeben, R. (1983). *How schools work*. Chicago: University of Chicago Press.

Barr, R., & Sadow, M. W. (1989). Influence of basal programs on fourth-grade reading instruction. *Reading Research Quarterly, 24*, 44–71.

Benavot, A., & Resh, N. (1998). *Diversity within uniformity: Conflicting pressures in the costruction of implemented school curricula*. Paper presented at the annual meeting of the American Sociological Association, San Francisco, California.

Bidwell, C. E. (1965). The school as a formal organization. In J. G. March (Ed.), *Handbook of organizations* (pp. 922–1022). Chicago: Rand McNally.

Bidwell, C. E., Frank, K. A., & Quiroz, P. A. (1997). Teacher types, workplace controls, and the organization of schools. *Sociology of Education, 70*, 285–307.

Bidwell, C. E., & Kasarda, J. D. (1980). Conceptualizing and measuring the effects of school and schooling. *American Journal of Education, 88*, 401–430.

Bishop, J. H. (1998). The effect of curriculum-based external exit exams on student achievement. *Journal of Economic Education, 29*, 171–182.

Blau, P. M., & Duncan, O. D. (1967). *The American occupational structure*. New York: Wiley.

Borman, K., Cookson, P., Sadovnik, A., & Spade, J. Z. (Eds., 1996). *Implementing federal legislation: Sociological perspectives on policy*. Norwood, NJ: Ablex.

Brophy, J., & Good, T. L. (1986). Teacher behavior and student achievement. In M. C. Wittrock (Ed.), *Handbook of research on teaching* (3rd ed., pp. 315–375). New York: Macmillan.

Bryk, A. S., & Driscoll, M. E. (1988). *The high school as community: Contextual influences, and consequences for students and teachers*. Madison, WI: National Center on Effective Secondary Schools.

Bryk, A. S., Lee, V. E., & Holland, P. B. (1993). *Catholic schools and the common good*. Cambridge, MA: Harvard University Press.

Bryk, A. S., & Raudenbush, S. W. (1992). *Hierarchical linear models*. Newbury Park, CA: Sage.

Callahan, R. (1962). *Education and the cult of efficiency*. Chicago: University of Chicago Press.

Carpenter, T. P., & Lehrer, R. (1999). Teaching and learning mathematics with understanding. In E. Fenneman & T. A. Romberg (Eds.), *Mathematics classrooms that promote understanding* (pp. 19–32). Mahwah, NJ: Lawrence Erlbaum.

Cohen, D. K. (1990). A revolution in one classroom: The case of Mrs. Oublier. *Educational Evaluation and Policy Analysis, 12*, 311–330.

Cohen, D. K., McLaughlin, M. W., & Talbert, J. E. (1993). *Teaching for understanding*. San Francisco, CA: Jossey-Bass.

Cohen, E. G., Deal, T. E., Meyer, J. W., & Scott, W. R. (1979). Technology and teaming in the elementary school. *Sociology of Education, 52*, 20–33.

Coleman, J. S. (1988). Social capital in the creation of human capital. *American Journal of Sociology, 94*, S95–S120.

Coleman, J. S., Campbell, E., Hobson, C., McPartland, J., Mood, A., Weinfield, F., & York, R. (1966). *Equality of educational opportunity*. Washington, DC: U.S. Government Printing Office.

Coleman, J. S., & Hoffer, T. (1987). *Public and private high schools: The impact of communities*. New York: Basic Books.

Dahl, R. (1997). Organizational factors and the continuation of a complex instructional technology. In E. G. Cohen & R. A. Lotan (Eds.), *Working for equity in heterogeneous classrooms: Sociological theory in practice* (pp. 260–274). New York: Teachers College Press.

Darling Hammond, L., & McLaughlin, M. W. (1996). Policies that support professional development in an era of reform. In *Teacher learning: New policies, new practices* (pp. 202–218). New York: Teachers College Press.

Doyle, W. (1992). Curriculum and pedagogy. In P. W. Jackson (Ed.), *Handbook of research on curriculum* (pp. 486–516). New York: Macmillan.

Edmonds, R. (1979). Effective schools for the urban poor. *Educational Leadership, 37*, 15–27.

Freeman, R. J., & Porter, A. C. (1989). Do textbooks dictate the content of mathematics instruction in elementary schools? *American Educational Research Journal, 26*, 403–421.

Fullan, M. G. (1991). *The new meaning of educational change*. New York: Teachers College Press.

Fuller, B. (1987). What school factors raise achievement in the Third World? *Review of Educational Research, 57*, 255–292.

Fuller, B., & Clarke, P. (1994). Raising school effects while ignoring culture? Local conditions and the influence of classroom tools, rules, and pedagogy. *Review of Educational Research, 64*, 119–157.

Gahng, T.-J. (1993). *A further search for school effects on achievement and intervening school experiences: An analysis of the Longitudinal Study of American Youth data*. Unpublished doctoral dissertation, University of Wisconsin, Madison.

Gamoran, A. (1987). The stratification of high school learning opportunities. *Sociology of Education, 60*, 135–155.

Gamoran, A. (1988). Resource allocation and the effects of schooling: A sociological perspective. In D. W. Monk & J. Underwood (Eds.). *Microlevel school finance: Issues and implications for policy* (pp. 207–232). Ninth Annual Yearbook of the American Educational Finance Association. Cambridge, MA: Ballinger.

Gamoran, A. (1992). Social factors in education. In M. Alkin (Ed.), *Encyclopedia of Educational Research* (6th ed., pp. 1222–1229). New York: Macmillan.

Gamoran, A. (1996a). Curriculum standardization and equality of opportunity in Scottish secondary education, 1984–1990. *Sociology of Education, 29*, 1–21.

Gamoran, A. (1996b). Goals 2000 in organizational perspective: Will it make a difference for states, districts, and schools? In K. Borman, P. Cookson, A. Sadovnik, & J. Z. Spade (Eds.), *Implementing federal legislation: Sociological perspectives on policy* (pp. 429–443). Norwood, NJ: Ablex.

Gamoran, A. (1996c). Student achievement in public magnet, public comprehensive, and private city high schools. *Educational Evaluation and Policy Analysis, 18*, 1–18.

Gamoran, A., & Dreeben, R. (1986). Coupling and control in educational organizations. *Administrative Science Quarterly, 31*, 612–632.

Gamoran, A., Nystrand, M., Berends, M., & LePore, P. C. (1995). An organizational analysis of the effects of ability grouping. *American Educational Research Journal, 32*, 687–715.

Gamoran, A., Porter, A. C., & Gahng, T.-J. (1995). Teacher empowerment: A policy in search of theory and evidence. In W. J. Fowler, B. Levin, & H. J. Walberg (Eds.), *Organizational Influences on Educational Productivity, Volume 5* (pp. 175–193). Greenwich, CT: JAI Press.

Gamoran, A., Porter, A. C., Smithson, J., & White, P. A. (1997). Upgrading high school mathematics instruction: Improving learning opportunities for low-income, low-achieving youth. *Educational Evaluation and Policy Analysis. 19*, 325–338.

Gamoran, A., & Weinstein, M. (1998). Differentiation and opportunity in restructured schools. *American Journal of Education, 106*, 385–415.

Goldenberg, C., & Gallimore, R. (1991, November). Changing teaching takes more than a one-shot workshop. *Educational Leadership, 49*, 69–72.

Goldstein, H. (1995). *Multilevel statistical models*. New York: Halsted Press.

Good, T. L., & Brophy, J. E. (1986). School effects. In M. C. Wittrock (Ed.), *Handbook of research on teaching* (3rd ed., pp. 570–602). New York: Macmillan.

Goodlad, J. (1984). *A place called school*. New York: McGraw-Hill.

Greenwald, R., Hedges, L., & Laine, R. D. (1996). The effects of school resources on student achievement. *Review of Educational Research, 66*, 361–396.

Hanushek, E. (1994). *Making schools work: Improving performance and controlling costs*. Washington, DC: Brookings.

Hanushek, E. (1997). Assessing the effects of school resources on student performance: An update. *Educational Evaluation and Policy Analysis, 19,* 141–64.

Hemmings, A., & Metz, M. H. (1991). Real teaching: How high school teachers negotiate societal, local community, and student pressures when they define their work. In R. N. Page & L. Valli (Eds.), *Curriculum differentiation: Interpretive studies in U.S. secondary schools* (pp. 91–112). Albany, NY: State University of New York Press.

Heyneman, S., & Loxley, W. (1983). The effects of primary-school quality on academic achievement across twenty-nine high- and low-income countries. *American Journal of Sociology, 88,* 1162–1194.

Hirsch, E. D. (1993). The core knowledge curriculum: What's behind its success? *Educational Leadership, 50,* 23–25.

Hirsch, E. D. (1996). *The schools we need and why we don't have them.* New York: Doubleday.

Hodgson, G. (1975). Do schools make a difference? In D. M. Levine & M. J. Bane (Eds.), *The inequality controversy* (pp. 24–44). New York: Basic Books.

Jackson, P. A. (1968). *Life in classrooms.* New York: Holt, Rinehart and Winston.

Jencks, C. L., Smith, M., Acland, H, Bane, M. J., Cohen, D. K., Gintis, H., Heyns, B., & Michelson, S. (1972). *Inequality: A reassessment of the effects of family and schooling in America.* New York: Basic Books.

Kilgore, S. B., & Pendelton, W. W. (1993). The organizational context of learning: Framework for understanding the acquisition of knowledge. *Sociology of Education, 66,* 63–87.

Lee, V. E., & Smith, J. B. (1995). Effects of high school restructuring and size on early gains in achievement and engagement. *Sociology of Education, 68,* 241–270.

Lee, V. E., & Smith, J. B. (1996). Collective responsibility for learning and its effects on gains in achievement for early secondary students. *American Journal of Education, 104,* 103–147.

Lee, V. E., & Smith, J. B. (1997). How high school organization influences the equitable distribution of learning in mathematics and science. *Sociology of Education, 70,* 128–150.

Lieberman, A. (1996). Practices that support teacher development: Transforming conceptions of professional learning. In *Teacher learning: New policies, new practices* (pp. 185–201). New York: Teachers College Press.

Little, J. W. (1986). Seductive images and organizational realities in professional development. In A. Lieberman (Ed.), *Rethinking school improvement* (pp. 26–45). New York: Teachers College Press.

Little, J. W. (1990). Conditions of professional development in secondary schools. In M. W. McLaughlin, J. E. Talbert, & N. Bascia, *The contexts of teaching in secondary schools: Teachers' realities* (pp. 187–223). New York: Teachers College Press.

Lotan, R. A., Cohen, E. G., & Morphew, C C. (1997). Principals, colleagues, staff developers: The case for organizational support. In E. G. Cohen & R. A. Lotan (Eds.), *Working for equity in heterogeneous classrooms: Sociological theory in practice* (pp. 223–239). New York: Teachers College Press.

Louis, K. S., Kruse, S. D., & Marks, H. M. (1996). Schoolwide professional community. In F. M. Newmann & Associates, *Authentic achievement: Restructuring schools for intellectual quality* (pp. 179–203). San Francisco, CA: Jossey-Bass.

Loveless, T. (1994). The influence of subject areas on middle school tracking policies. *Research in Sociology of Education and Socialization, 10,* 147–175.

McNeil, L. (1986). *Contradictions of control.* New York: Routledge & Kegan Paul.

Mehan, H. (1979). *Learning lessons: Social organization in the classroom.* Cambridge, MA: Harvard University Press.

Meyer, J. W. (1977). The effects of education as an institution. *American Journal of Sociology, 83,* 55–77.

Meyer, J. W., & Rowan, B. (1977). Institutionalized organizations: Formal structure as myth and ceremony. *American Journal of Sociology, 83,* 340–363.

Meyer, J. W., & Rowan, B. (1978). The structure of educational organizations. In M. Meyer & Associates, *Environments and organizations.* San Francisco, CA: Jossey-Bass.

Metz, M. H. (1989). Real school: A universal drama amid disparate experiences. *Politics of Education Association Yearbook, 1989,* 75–91.

Monk, D. H. (1992). Education productivity research: An update and assessment of is role in education finance reform. *Educational Evaluation and Policy Analysis, 14,* 307–332.

Mosteller, F. W., & Moynihan, D. P. (1972). *On equality of educational opportunity.* New York: Random House.

Newmann, F. M. (1998). How secondary schools contribute to academic success. In K. Borman & B. Schneider (Eds.), *The adolescent years: Social influences and educational challenges.* National Society for the Study of Education Yearbook 97:1. Chicago: University of Chicago Press.

Newmann, F. M., & Associates. (1996). *Authentic achievement: Restructuring schools for intellectual quality.* San Francisco, CA: Jossey-Bass.

Nystrand, M. (1997). *Opening dialogue.* New York: Teachers College Press.

Nystrand, M., Gamoran, A., & Heck, M. J. (1993). Using small groups for response to and thinking about literature. *English Journal, 82,* 14–22.

Oakes, J., Gamoran, A., & Page, R. N. (1992). Curriculum differentiation: Opportunities, outcomes, and meanings. In P. W. Jackson (Ed.), *Handbook of research on curriculum* (pp. 570–608). New York: Macmillan.

Pallas, A. (1988). School climate in American high schools. *Teachers College Record, 89,* 541–554.

Park, B.-J. (1998). *Teacher empowerment and its effects on teachers' lives and student achievement in the U.S. high school.* Unpublished doctoral dissertation, University of Wisconsin, Madison.

Parsons, T. (1963). *Structure and process in modern societies.* Glencoe, IL: The Free Press.

Peterson, P. L., McCarthey, S. J., & Elmore, R. F. (1996). Learning from school restructuring. *American Educational Research Journal, 33,* 119–153.

Pressman, J. L., & Wildavsky, A. (1979). *Implementation* (2nd ed.). Berkeley, CA: University of California Press.

Purkey, S. C., & Smith, M. S. (1983). Effective schools: A review. *Elementary School Journal, 83,* 427–452.

Rowan, B. (1990). Commitment and control: Alternative strategies for the organizational design of schools. In C. Cazden (Ed.), *Review of Research in Education,* Vol., 16 (pp. 353–389). Washington, DC: American Educational Research Association.

Rowan, B., & Miracle, A. W., Jr. (1983). Systems of ability grouping and the stratification of achievement in elementary schools. *Sociology of Education, 56,* 133–144.

Rowan, B., & Miskel, C. (1999). Institutional theory and the study of educational organizations. In J. Murphy & K. S. Louis (Eds.), *Handbook of research in educational administration.* San Francisco, CA: Jossey-Bass.

Rowan, B., Raudenbush, S. W., & Cheong, Y. F. (1993). Teaching as a non-routine task: Implications for the management of schools. *Educational Administration Quarterly, 29,* 479–500.

Secada, W. G., & Adajian, L. B. (1997). Mathematics teachers' change in the context of their professional communities. In L. Fennema & B. S. Nelson (Eds.), *Mathematics teachers in transition* (pp. 193–219). Mahwah, NJ: Lawrence Erlbaum Associates.

Shulman, L. (1987). Knowledge and teaching: Foundations of the new reform. *Harvard Educational Review, 57,* 1–22.

Slavin, R. E. (1989). Class size and student achievement: Small effects of small classes. *Educational Psychologist, 24,* 99–109.

Slavin, R. E. (1990). Class size and student achievement: Is smaller better? *Contemporary Education, 62,* 6–12.

Sparks, D., & Loucks-Horsley, S. (1989). Five models of staff development for teachers. *Journal of Staff Development, 10,* 40–57.

Spillane, J., & Thompson, C. (1997). Reconstructing conceptions of local capacity: The local education agency's capacity for ambitious educational reform. *Educational Evaluation and Policy Analysis, 19,* 185–203.

Stevenson, D., & Baker, D. (1991). State control of the curriculum and classroom instruction. *Sociology of Education, 64,* 1–10.

Stodolsky, S. (1988). *The subject matters.* Chicago: University of Chicago Press.

Stodolsky, S., & Grossman, P. (1995). The impact of subject matter on curricular activity: An analysis of five academic subjects. *American Educational Research Journal, 32,* 227–249.

Talbert, J. E. (1995). Boundaries of teachers' professional communities in U. S. high schools: Power and precariousness of the subject department. In L. S. Siskin & J. W. Little (Eds.), *The subjects in question* (pp. 68–94). New York: Teachers College Press.

Talbert, J. E., & McLaughlin, M. W. (1994). Teacher professionalism in local school contexts. *American Journal of Education, 102,* 123–153.

Tharp, R. G., & Gallimore, R. (1988). *Rousing minds to life.* Cambridge, England: Cambridge University Press.

Weick, K. E. (1976). Educational organizations as loosely coupled systems. *Administrative Science Quarterly, 21,* 1–19.

Weick, K. E. (1982). Administering education in loosely coupled systems. *Phi Delta Kappan, 63,* 673–675.

Wells, A. S., & Serna, I. (1996). The politics of culture: Understanding local political resistance to detracking in racially mixed schools. *Harvard Educational Review, 66,* 93–118.

Wilson, T. P. (1996). *Reaching for a better standard.* New York: Teachers College Press.

CHAPTER 3

On the Linkages between Sociology of Race and Ethnicity and Sociology of Education

Maureen T. Hallinan

American sociology has made significant advances in theory and in empirical research during the 20th century. Much of this growth has led to specialization within the discipline. Indeed, specialization is so pervasive that sociology at times appears to be a set of discrete subdisciplines with little connection to each other. Evidence of this subdisciplinary independence is found in the small number of members of the American Sociological Association who belong to more than one section or who participate in the activities of sections of which they are not members.

Links among subdisciplines of sociology may be stronger than they appear at first, however. For example, examination of the development of the sociology of religion reveals a significant influence of organizational theory on the way religion and religious institutions have been conceptualized and analyzed. Similarly, tracing the roots of the sociology of gender reveals a strong influence of theories in social psychology. Recognizing the influence of other areas of thought and research on one's own sociological specialization is important in order to benefit from other intellectual heritages. This awareness broadens perspectives and encourages linkages beyond disciplinary boundaries. Making linkages across areas of specialization within a discipline should contribute to the strength and the relevance of sociology as a whole.

Given that a central focus in the sociology of education has been on issues related to race

---

Maureen T. Hallinan • Institute for Educational Initiatives, University of Notre Dame, Notre Dame, Indiana 46556-5611

Handbook of the Sociology of Education, edited by Maureen T. Hallinan. Kluwer Academic/Plenum Publishers, New York, 2000.

and to ethnicity, the question arises as to whether the sociology of race and ethnicity has influenced the sociology of education. The aim of this chapter is to examine whether sociological research on race and ethnicity has had an impact on the development of theory and on the content of empirical research in the sociology of education.

GENERAL CONTEXTUAL INFLUENCES
ON SOCIOLOGICAL THEORY AND RESEARCH

The May 1997 issue of *Contemporary Sociology* contains a dozen essays in which leading sociologists around the world describe how the field of sociology is developing in their own countries. A striking aspect of these essays is that each report illustrates how immediately the political, economic, and social conditions in a country influence the theoretical and empirical orientation of the sociology conducted in that country. For example, in Turkey, where secularism is challenged by the growing strength of Islamic fundamentalism, sociologists are concentrating on understanding the complexity of cultural and ethnic identities. Sociologists in Sweden, confronted by their country's economic crisis, by changes in the welfare system, and by internationalization, are broadening their previous interest in the welfare state to incorporate race and ethnic issues, civil and human rights, development, and culture. In Argentina, sociologists are moving beyond their preoccupation with Peronism to examine contemporary income stratification, the weakening of the middle class, and unemployment. In the aftermath of apartheid in South Africa, sociologists are moving away from a concentration on South Africa's racial divisions and the quest for democracy and toward a study of the labor market, class divisions, and internationalization.

The impact of the political, economic, and social conditions of a country on the development of sociology in that country also can be witnessed in the United States. In the past, influenced by the writings of Weber and Marx and by economic development in a newly industrialized nation, American sociologists were preoccupied with processes governing social stratification and social mobility. This focus extended to an interest in the growth of organizations, to the effects of industrialization and technology, and to the determinants and consequences of poverty. Today, in a time of unparalleled social change in America, sociologists are concerned about broad issues of culture, globalization, social norms and values, and public policy. Of considerable concern are the deeply rooted racial and ethnic tensions that characterize American society. Demographic and social changes in the United States population have deepened interest in the sociological study of conflict, the labor market, technology and communications, immigration, and individual and communal rights and responsibilities.

The contextual conditions that affect the development of the discipline of sociology also exert a strong influence on the work done in subfields of the discipline. The circumstances of a country affect the kinds of research questions that are studied, the theoretical perspectives brought to bear on these questions, and the nature of the empirical work that is conducted.

Societal issues that have preoccupied Americans over the past several decades, and that continue to be of interest, include the civil rights movement, the Black power movement, affirmative action, and multiculturalism. These concerns have motivated sociological analyses of race and of ethnicity. Many of the same societal issues, especially those concerning equal rights for students, have motivated theoretical and empirical work in the sociology of education. The question is whether sociological research on race and ethnicity has influenced the sociological study of education.

THE SOCIOLOGY OF RACE AND ETHNICITY

The object of study in the sociology of race and ethnicity is the emergence and persistence of patterns of interracial and interethnic contact and the causes and consequences of change in systems of ethnic differentiation (Barth & Noel, 1972). Sociologists of race and ethnicity aim to explain how patterns of racial and ethnic associations and interactions emerge, how the stability of these patterns is maintained, and what precipitates change in racially and ethnically diverse social systems. Their goal is to identify and describe the structural conditions and processes that account for the evolution, equilibrium, and metamorphosis of racial and ethnic associations.

A number of theorists have tried to formulate a scientific theory of race and ethnicity. Early efforts in this direction focused primarily on race, as opposed to ethnicity, and on Black–White relations in particular. The early research on race occurred in a time when sociologists were rejecting the widely held belief that Blacks were biologically or genetically inferior, but while many sociologists still accepted the assumption that Blacks were culturally inferior. During the transformation of America from an agrarian to an industrial society in the aftermath of the Industrial Revolution, Blacks were viewed as part of a premodern society, culturally backward and isolated from modern life.

Park (1950) provided one of the earliest conceptual frameworks to explain the evolution of structural patterns in systems of racial and ethnic variation. He hypothesized what became known as the race cycle. He claimed that ". . . in the relations of races there is a cycle of events which tends everywhere to repeat itself—[it] takes the form of contact, competition, accommodation and eventual assimilation [and] is apparently progressive and irreversible" (p. 150). Park believed that race and ethnic relations followed this evolutionary model in which each stage inevitably leads to the next, ultimately ending in assimilation.

Park's analysis of the race cycle reflected social and economic changes in American society in the first half of the 20th century. During this time, the modernization of American society, with its industrialization and urbanization, was beginning to displace the components of premodern society. Social scientists believed that the needs of modern society would make assimilation inevitable. Because Blacks and other minority groups were thought to be culturally inferior to Whites, sociologists presumed that assimilation would take the form of Anglo-conformity. Assimilation would remove boundaries among racial and ethnic groups by erasing cultural differences. Through much of the 20th century, sociological research on race reflected these beliefs.

Although Park's (1950) analysis of race focused on the assimilation of Blacks into White American society, his ideas were applicable to other ethnic groups as well. However, the distinctions among ethnic groups often were muted in empirical studies, as when everyone except Caucasians were classified simply as non-Whites. Only recently, with the dramatic increase in the size of various minority populations in the United States, has serious consideration been given to the different roles that various racial and ethnic groups play in society and to the distinct processes that govern their social relationships.

Until the late 1960s, it was generally believed that assimilation was the likely outcome of interracial and interethnic interactions. This belief reflected an influence of consensus theory among sociologists of race and ethnicity. Consensus theory explains how social systems operate in a state of equilibrium and how such systems respond to challenges and threats to a stable state. It depicts societal institutions as operating harmoniously. The theory is primarily one of stasis, focusing an the elements of society that produce and sustain the system through adaptation, shared goals, integration, and maintenance. To the extent that functionalists focus on dysfunctional aspects of society (e.g., Merton, 1968), they try to explain how disruptions challenge a system that eventually returns to equilibrium, rather than explain disintegrating.

The assimilation hypothesis rested on three assumptions: (1) conflict was not a likely mechanism of social change in race and ethnic relations, (2) change would be gradual, rather than disruptive and disorderly, and (3) modern social organization was irreconcilable with racial segregation. Assimilation would remove boundaries among racial and ethnic groups by erasing cultural differences. In a predominantly White society, other racial and ethnic groups were expected eventually to be incorporated into mainstream culture. Assimilation was seen as the embodiment of the democratic ideal. It would erase individual differences due to background and create a society in which all members participate on an equal basis.

Hammond (1966) argued that assimilation occurs through adaptation and described how the process occurs. He claimed that as role differentiation and specialization increased in a society, social units became more interrelated and dependent on each other. Despite possibly divergent values and desires, groups would be forced to work together to achieve their interdependent goals or risk failure. Adaptation does not imply the status quo, but it does suggest that change would occur in a slow and controlled manner.

The adaptation framework underscores interdependence as the mechanism that produces the gradual incorporation of racial and ethnic groups into a majority society. Interdependency increases awareness of the need for change, while at the same time, reducing the pressure to change. Hence the adaptation model explains gradual rather than radical social change.

The predominance of consensus theory and the widespread belief that racial and ethnic groups would become assimilated into American society deflected attention from race and ethnicity as sources of societal conflict. Neither the race cycle model nor the assimilation perspective considered race and ethnic relations to be unstable. However, the social and political events of the 1960s demonstrated that consensus theories were inadequate to account for the racial and ethnic tensions erupting in American society.

Confronted by the unrest of the 1960s, sociologists began to consider various patterns other than assimilation as possible outcomes of racial and ethnic contact. Barth and Noel (1972) suggested five potential patterns: exclusion or segregation; symbiosis, implying equal exchange among groups in different political systems; ethnic or racial stratification in a single political system; pluralism, or the integration of groups that maintain their distinct characteristics; and assimilation, or the fusion of distinct groups to form a new society. Of these patterns, symbiosis, pluralism, and assimilation are consistent with the consensus perspective that society tends to function as a stable system with various parts operating harmoniously. Patterns of segregation and stratification are based on power differences and suggest disharmony and instability. The civil unrest that began in the 1960s demonstrated these unstable patterns. As a result, sociologists of race and ethnicity turned to conflict theories to understand racial and ethnic interactions.

Conflict theory depicts society as engaged in a power-based struggle, usually stemming from class differences. The correlation of race and ethnicity with class in American society gave the application of this theory validity. Dahrendorf (1959) conceptualized a conflict relationship as one in which the interacting groups desire contradictory or mutually exclusive goals. Conflict theory views social stability as a transitory state, disrupted by the unequal distribution of societal resources and by the frustration and dissatisfaction of those with disproportionately less power and influence. Because structural incompatibilities necessarily occur in a society, conflict theory assumes that change is an inherent part of the evolution of a social system.

Sociologists of race and ethnicity explained the racial conflict during and after the civil rights era as resulting from efforts by minority groups to obtain political, economic, and social power. Blacks and ethnic minorities organized and utilized their collective power to protect their rights and further their interests. However, conflict theory has been less useful in predicting how social unrest and political struggle are resolved. Social stability has emerged in some areas, where patterns of assimilation and pluralism can be detected. However, social eruptions related to race and ethnicity continue to occur, indicating that, to a considerable extent, race and ethnic relations in America remain unstable.

The theoretical perspectives found in the sociological literature on race and ethnicity, particularly consensus and conflict theories, have contributed important insights into the role of race and ethnic relations in American society. However, these societal theories do not substitute for comprehensive middle-range theories that provide an in-depth understanding of race and ethnic relations. Consensus and conflict theories offer sociologists of race and ethnicity *post hoc* explanations of social events, but they are less useful in generating propositions about how patterns of racial and ethnic interactions are expected to evolve and how these patterns will affect specific social situations. Most sociologists view consensus theory as failing to provide an understanding of racial and ethnic tension and see conflict theory as neglecting evidence of evolving racial and ethnic accommodation into American society. A theory of race and ethnic relations that focuses on and explains the processes governing interracial and interethnic contact is needed.

Two efforts to move toward a middle-range theory of race and ethnicity are noteworthy. Blalock (1967) derived 97 propositions governing race relations. In a similar effort, Kinloch (1974) developed an axiomatic deductive theory of race relationships containing 253 propositions and theorems. These efforts in the late 1960s and early 1970s provided a useful first step toward the formulation of a theoretical framework for the analysis of race and ethnic relations. Little subsequent work built on this foundation, however.

The failure of sociologists to develop a theory of race and ethnicity is due to several factors. First, determining the meaning of the terms race and ethnicity is difficult. These terms are not abstract concepts. Rather, they are descriptions of ambiguous physical characteristics, changing cultural traits, or specific historical circumstances. A number of sociologists regard the terms as referring to variables rather than to constants. British sociologists are particularly critical of the way contemporary sociologists reify race and ethnicity. They vigorously object to the use of census categories to measure race and ethnicity, claiming that the terms have no ontological status (e.g., Solomos & Back, 1994). The ambiguity attached to the meaning of the fundamental objects of study in the sociology of race and ethnicity is a significant obstacle to the formulation of theory about these characteristics.

Another obstacle to developing a theory of race and ethnicity is that race and ethnicity are not causal agents in and of themselves. Instead, they are instances of the operation of more general, abstract, social phenomena that affect social processes. Van den Berghe (1970) argued that race and ethnicity are only special cases of larger occurrences that can be analyzed from existing theoretical perspectives. He claimed that sociologists should treat race and ethnicity as special cases of broader events and should apply general sociological theory to their analysis. Others have argued that research on race and ethnicity should take into account the total institutional or cultural context of the society studied (e.g., Park, 1950).

A third reason that sociologists find it difficult to formulate a broad theory of race and ethnicity is that few studies in this area provide a comparative analysis of race and ethnicity in different historical or cultural settings. If the meaning of race and ethnicity is culturally determined, these characteristics must be studied with an understanding of the culture in which they exist. A culture is best understood by comparing and contrasting it with other cultures. A comparative framework would reveal the critical aspects of a culture that create the meaning assigned to race and ethnicity by a particular society. Van den Berghe (1967) and Schermerhorn (1970) argued that the study of American race and ethnic issues requires a comparative context in order for American researchers to move beyond their cultural and historical biases and to recognize and analyze critical dimensions of race and ethnic relations.

A recent study by Niemonen (1997) underscores the consequences of the theoretical limitations of the study of race and ethnicity. Niemonen examined how sociologists treated race and ethnicity in articles published in leading sociological journals since the late 1960s. Most researchers include race and ethnicity among other factors in studying social psychological, demographic, and stratification processes. Much of this research is empirical rather than theoretical, and it reifies the concepts of race and ethnicity used by the U.S. Census rather than questioning their meaning or treating them as problematic.

A well-formulated theory of race and ethnicity would possess the properties that Coleman (1994) claimed are essential characteristics of a social theory. Coleman stated that social theory consists of explanations of the way social systems operate. Specifically, a theory reveals how characteristics of a social system influence the behavior of individuals in the social system. Then the theory would provide a set of rules governing the responses of the individuals to the systemic stimulus. Finally, it would explain the impact of the individuals' responses on the system. In short, a theory of race and ethnicity would explain the social processes that link societal factors to individuals and individual behavior to societal change.

In the absence of theoretical perspectives on race and ethnicity to guide empirical research, sociologists have turned to other substantive domains for conceptual frameworks for their analyses. Empirical work on race and ethnicity is often related to theories of social stratification, demography, and social psychology. Within these perspectives, however, race and ethnicity are generally treated as independent or exogenous variables rather than as key factors in some causal process.

A number of empirical studies on race and ethnicity are found in research on social stratification and on the political economy. Some studies have investigated the effects of race and ethnicity on educational and occupational attainment and on income distribution. These studies tend to highlight the role of background characteristics in social mobility processes by comparing the opportunities and attainment of Blacks, of ethnic minorities, and of Whites (Farley & Allen, 1987; Hout, 1984; Lieberson, 1980; Wilson, 1979). Other studies have shown how race and ethnicity mask social class conflicts (Cox, 1948; Wilson, 1980). Several studies have developed, refined, and tested hypotheses about the labor market, middleman minorities, and ethnic enclaves (Bonacich, 1972, 1973; Light, 1972; Portes & Manning, 1986; Sassen-Koob, 1980). A few studies have highlighted racial and ethnic factors in the study of sociohistorical forces, such as the persistence of certain ethnic groups like the Romany (Gypsies) (Alba & Chamlin, 1983; Glazer & Moynihan, 1970; Greeley, 1971; Parenti, 1967). And some studies have focused on race and ethnicity in investigations of the social, political, and economic factors affecting urban riots (e.g., Baldassare, 1994).

Demographic analyses of race and ethnicity have examined the fertility rates and marriage patterns of different groups (Lieberson & Waters, 1988). Many of these studies have paid special attention to the effects of Black migration from the rural South and the immigration patterns of various ethnic groups from Mexico, the Caribbean, Asia, and the Middle East (Kim, 1981; Portes & Bach, 1985). Some research has analyzed the effects of migration on the socioeconomic status of Whites and on minorities and has examined how these changing demographic patterns affect the labor market (Piore, 1979). Other studies have evaluated the effects of immigration rates and marriage and fertility patterns on various social institutions such as schools, medical establishments, and churches (Bouvier, 1992; Yans-McLaughlin, 1990). A number of studies have observed ethnic enclaves and have reported trends in integration, segregation, residential succession, and geographical concentrations of poverty, by race and ethnicity (Massey & Denton, 1993; Portes & Manning, 1986).

Social psychological studies of race and ethnicity tend to focus on prejudice, discrimination, and racial intolerance. Studies have shown that politically involved minority groups form in reaction to the unfair exclusion of their members from competitive processes that lead to scarce resources (e.g., Greeley, 1974). Other research has demonstrated that racial and ethnic boundaries separating groups erode in the presence of equal opportunity, economic growth, and pluralistic, political processes, leading to assimilation or to pluralism (e.g., Gordon, 1964). Researchers have compared the self-esteem of minority group members to that of majority peers in an effort to detect the basis for group differences in achievement and attainment (e.g., Rosenberg & Simmons, 1971). A number of studies have examined the roots of prejudice and have tried to identify factors that sustain bias and discrimination (e.g., Adorno, Frenkel-Brunswik, Levinson, & Nevitt, 1950). Others have looked at attitudes toward minorities and how they are revealed in overt or covert racial or ethnic hostility (e.g., Katz, Hass, & Wackenhut, 1986). The insights provided by social psychology have been helpful to race and ethnicity researchers in conceptualizing the roots of racial and ethnic tensions and the social and structural conditions that support them. Moreover, they illuminate the conditions under which racial and ethnic strains emerge into violent behavior or are resolved.

In short, a large body of empirical research on race and ethnicity is found in several subdisciplines in sociology. By being embedded in these various sociological specializations, research on race and ethnicity has become better known than if it had been limited to a single perspective. These studies have motivated sociologists from a number of subdisciplines to include race and ethnicity in analyses of social processes. Moreover, they have expanded the kinds of questions that sociologists ask about determinants and consequences of social events.

At the same time, these empirical studies do not represent sociological analyses of race and ethnicity. They merely show how social processes have a differential impact on members of various racial and ethnic groups. What is still needed is a theory of how patterns of racial and ethnic contact emerge, what the consequences of these patterns are for individual behavior and for societal institutions, and what factors are likely to disrupt these patterns and lead to new ones.

In summary, sociologists of race and ethnicity have been unsuccessful in developing a general theory of race and ethnic relations in American society. They have relied instead on consensus and conflict theories to generate general conceptions about racial and ethnic relations. Significant substantive work is needed to ground the large body of empirical research on race and ethnicity in sociological theory. Yet, even in the absence of comprehensive theory, sociologists of race and ethnicity have established this area as one of central interest and importance for social scientists. Scholars with varied interests rely on empirical studies of race and ethnicity to expand their understanding of the social processes they study. The remaining question is whether and to what extent this body of research has influenced the sociology of education.

THEORY DEVELOPMENT IN THE SOCIOLOGY OF EDUCATION

A striking feature about the sociology of education is that no overarching theory has been formulated to explain educational processes and their effects on students. Like sociology of race and ethnicity, many partial theories have been developed, with considerable explanatory and heuristic power. Among these are Bowles and Gintis' (1976) analysis of the function of schooling in stratification and mobility processes, Bidwell's (1965) model of the school as a formal organization, and Coleman's (1988) conceptualization of social networks of students, parents, school personnel, and community and their impact on academic achievement. However, these and other conceptual perspectives do not have the breadth and depth to provide a solid understanding of how schools operate in society. Moreover, these conceptualizations have not generated major propositions and hypotheses about the schooling process, nor have they integrated empirical analyses examining schools and the consequences of their organization, practices, and policies for society.

In the absence of a comprehensive theory of schooling, sociologists of education, like sociologists of race and ethnicity, have relied on consensus and conflict theories to provide explanations for various educational issues and events. Sociologists of education who rely on a consensus framework view the public school system as a social institution that prepares students to live in a democratic society. The school is seen as a place where norms and values are transmitted to students to equip them to occupy a position in adult society. Schools are viewed as institutions that promote upward social mobility by providing students with occupational knowledge and training. By preparing students for citizenship and for the labor market, schools reproduce the social structure of society (Bourdieu & Passeron, 1990; Bowles & Gintis, 1976; Meyer, 1977).

The consensus perspective sees education as promoting a meritocratic society by dissociating students' backgrounds from future social and occupational status. Schools are expected to give all students the resources needed to live in and to contribute to society, regardless of their social background. Ability, not background characteristics, is seen as the primary determinant of success (see Turner, 1960).

Sociologists studying schools from a consensus perspective paid little attention to questions about the differential preparation of students for schooling or the kind of support different students received during their schooling. The effects of background characteristics, and in particular race and ethnicity, on the potential and actual achievement of students were ignored. Moreover, school differences in students' opportunities to learn were not considered. This oversight is particularly noticeable in the absence of research on the effects of school segregation on students' performance.

Even after *Brown v Board of Education* (1954) mandated the desegregation of the public school system, sociologists working within the consensus framework did not examine school processes that channeled unequal opportunities to students with different backgrounds. The belief, promoted in race and ethnicity research, that black students would assimilate into majority white schools and would accommodate to the white culture of these schools overlooked the various ways race and ethnicity could affect students' learning. The consensus view deemphasized race and ethnic issues by arguing that schools mitigated the relationship between race, ethnicity, or other ascribed characteristics and adult social status. Consensus researchers believed that schools prepared all students for productive citizenship.

The process of desegregating the public schools was not as harmonious as consensus theorists predicted. Conflict over school desegregation, busing, and White flight mirrored racial conflict in the wider society. The civil rights movement of the 1960s strongly influenced social thinking. Sociologists in general, and sociologists of education in particular, were forced to go beyond consensus theories to develop a different perspective to explain social events. As with the study of race and ethnicity, sociologists of education turned to conflict theories to explain contemporary unrest and discord.

Scholars who adhered to the tenets of conflict theory (Bowles & Gintis, 1976; Collins, 1979) criticized schools for directing students into hierarchically ordered positions in society. They claimed that teachers prepare students for adult occupations that match their family background by teaching them selected skills and by shaping their attitudes toward work. Students are taught to play their designated roles in social institutions in order to perpetuate a capitalist economy and to sustain the existing power structure. Conflict theorists argued that schools legitimate this process by claiming that it benefits all members of society.

Notably absent in the historical development of the sociology of education were the formulation of theoretical constructions of the schooling process. Rather than formulating theories specific to schooling, sociologists of education turned to other areas in sociology for theoretical ideas about schools. This approach is similar to that employed by sociologists of race and ethnicity, who also relied on other areas for a theoretical foundation for their research. As a result, a considerable amount of research in the sociology of education rests on theoretical ideas found in social psychology, in social stratification and mobility, in the study of organizations, and in other substantive areas focusing on institutional and interpersonal processes.

The widespread interest in race and ethnicity among sociologists of education since the mid-1960s leads one to ask whether the sociology of race and ethnicity influenced the study of schooling. The reliance of both the sociology of race and ethnicity and the sociology of education on theories of consensus and of conflict provides researchers in both areas with a shared perspective, making influence more likely. Further, the dependence of the two areas on related disciplines for theoretical ideas about social processes involving race and ethnicity makes influence seem probable.

An alternate possibility is that focus on race and ethnicity in the sociology of education simply reflects widespread societal interest in race and ethnic relations. The civil rights movement, White flight, desegregation, and busing were critical societal events and movements that had a powerful impact on all social scientists. The sociology of race and ethnicity, *per se*, may have had little impact on the study of schools. Rather, general concern about issues related to race and ethnicity might have influenced research in the sociology of education. Theory has been slow to develop in the sociology of race and ethnicity. Moreover, empirical studies in this area may not have been of central interest to sociologists of education because they typically did not involve a school context. A close examination of the study of race and ethnicity in the sociology of education should provide insights into the extent to which the sociology of race and ethnicity affected intellectual developments in the study of schooling.

INFLUENCE OF RACE AND ETHNICITY RESEARCH
ON THE SOCIOLOGY OF EDUCATION

This section investigates possible connections between research on race and ethnicity and the theoretical and empirical work conducted by sociologists of education. The intent is to show whether sociological research on race and ethnicity has influenced the way sociologists of education view schools and the schooling process, the theoretical propositions they formulate to explain issues related to schooling, and the statistical models they estimate to analyze empirical data.

The sociology of education is the study of a social institution whose members are becoming increasingly more demographically diverse. The growth of racial and ethnic minorities in the United States has made elementary and secondary schools and institutions of higher education, both public and private, more racially and ethnically heterogeneous than at any earlier point in history. Sociologists of education seek to understand the impact of this dramatic change in the demographic composition of schools on the educational processes they examine and to analyze its consequences for student outcomes.

Given the interest of both sociologists of race and ethnicity and sociologists of education in the effects of race and ethnicity on individuals and on institutions, it is natural to expect that the sociology of race and ethnicity would influence theoretical and empirical developments about education. This is not to say that the sociology of race and ethnicity is the only area likely to have influenced the sociology of education, or even the most important area. Clearly, work in many subdisciplines in sociology has implications for how sociologists view education and schooling. Moreover, it would be unreasonable to presume that the sociology of race and ethnicity has had a systematic impact on the study of schooling. Areas of thought and science develop unevenly and at different rates. The particular focus of this chapter on the influence of the sociology of race and ethnicity on the sociology of education stems from the shared interest of these two areas in the effects of race and ethnicity on social behavior within societal institutions.

Stratification Research in the Sociology of Education

One area of sociology in which it would be natural to find an influence of the sociology of race and ethnicity on the sociology of education is in studies of schooling as an agent in social stratification and mobility processes. This body of research has its roots in the analysis of class, social structure, and social change. Much of the stratification research since the 1950s has examined how schools transmit the effects of background to educational and to occupational attainment. Sociologists of education have been interested in whether stratification processes differ across students who vary in ascribed and achieved characteristics.

One of the earliest longitudinal, empirical analyses of stratification and mobility processes in America was the Wisconsin Longitudinal Study of Income and Occupational Attainment (e.g., Sewell, Haller, & Portes, 1969; Sewell & Hauser, 1975). Conducted in the 1960s, the Wisconsin study aimed to identify the determinants of occupational status and income. Many of the analyses focused on schools as a major agent in the status attainment process, examining the extent to which schooling transmitted status from one generation to the next.

A noteworthy feature of the Wisconsin study is that the first questionnaires given to the students in the sample did not ask for information about race or ethnicity. Interestingly, researchers showed little concern about this omission. At the time the study was conducted, blacks and ethnic groups were expected to follow the same status attainment trajectory as whites, and for the same reasons. Failing to identify race and ethnicity in a study of intergenerational mobility did not seem to cause concern.

The failure to examine the effects of race and ethnicity in the original Wisconsin study and in other early studies of mobility processes might have been avoided if sociologists of race and ethnicity had broadened their research beyond the study of patterns of interracial and interethnic contact. The research on race and ethnicity did little to suggest that the processes that governed mobility for whites did not apply to other racial and ethnic groups as well. Hence, this research did not sensitize sociologists of education to analyze how race and ethnicity affected educational and occupational attainment.

In the 1970s and 1980s, sociologists of education focused directly on the role of race and ethnicity in the status attainment process and examined whether attainment processes differed fundamentally for students from different racial and ethnic groups. Several replications of the Wisconsin study were performed. This research consistently showed that race and ethnicity, along with socioeconomic status, were significant determinants of educational and occupational success. Some of these studies indicated that stratification processes worked differently for students from various backgrounds. They also uncovered school practices and policies that acted as agents in perpetuating the stratifying effects of demographic characteristics on social status and on occupational attainment. Other studies showed that schools depressed the relationship between background and occupational attainment by providing more equal access to educational resources and training within schools. These and similar findings led to the widespread implementation of federally funded compensatory education programs to assist disadvantaged and minority students in the learning process.

Although much of this later research on the role of schooling in stratification processes highlighted race and ethnicity as critical factors in educational and occupational attainment, this focus did not necessarily reflect an influence of the sociology of race and ethnicity. The empirical research in the sociology of education that fell within the stratification genre typically included race and ethnicity as exogenous variables in analytic models of stratification processes. Researchers controlled for race and ethnicity, rather than theorizing about how these background characteristics interacted with school characteristics to produce unequal outcomes. Similarly, sociologists of education did not model how schooling, as an agent in the stratification process, might change patterns of racial and ethnic contact of students when they reached adulthood.

The status attainment research has shown that, in some ways, the attainment process differs significantly by the race and ethnicity of the individual. However, many questions remain unanswered. Although the research describes how race and ethnicity affect achievement and attainment, it does not explain why (cf. Campbell, 1983). For example, why does a society that advocates meritocratic selection tolerate a wide distribution of status and wealth? Why do talented students from disadvantaged families attain only a high school diploma? Why does the status attainment process differ by the race and ethnicity of the individual? If theoretical research on race and ethnicity had been available to support status attainment studies, this body of work in the sociology of education might have been theoretically richer.

Research on Equality of Educational Opportunity

A second area where one might expect to find an influence of the sociology of race and ethnicity is the study of equality of educational opportunity or school effects studies. In examining how schools foster students' learning, sociologists of education have tried to determine how variation in school characteristics produce variation in student outcomes. They have focused on school resources, composition, and climate as predictors of students' achievement. Researchers have examined how variation across schools in these factors has created unequal opportunities to students who vary by race and by ethnicity.

The idea of equal educational opportunities for all students had its genesis in the concept of the common school. In arguing for universal education for the American citizenry, Mann (1832) stipulated that public schools should be supported by general tax revenues. By not charging tuition, public schools aimed to eliminate a primary source of inequality of opportunity.

Another provision of the common school ideal was that all students should be exposed to a single, classical curriculum. A common curriculum was assumed to remove the effects of social background on opportunities for educational and occupational advancement. Little consideration was given to the possibility that by failing to teach occupational skills beyond basic literacy and numeracy, schools might deprive certain students of critical occupational opportunities.

The common school model became the ideal type of the American public school system and was widely accepted for several decades. However, the political and social upheaval of the 1960s raised questions about whether public schools actually were providing all students with equal educational opportunities. In particular, the concern was raised that minority students were receiving fewer opportunities to learn than white students, not only in segregated schools but also in desegregated schools.

In response to this concern, the U.S. Department of Education commissioned the landmark *Equality of Educational Opportunity* (EEO) (Coleman et al., 1966), a national study to determine the effects of school segregation on students' achievement. Despite the widespread acceptance of functionalist assumptions about the meritocratic nature of schools, the suspicion was growing that schools were depriving minority students of educational opportunities through the mechanism of school segregation.

In an attempt to clarify the various meanings of equality of educational opportunity, Coleman (1968) provided five different definitions of the concept: equal inputs to students in the form of school resources; equal outputs, or achievement, for students with similar ability; equal achievement for students with different backgrounds (requiring the school to play a compensatory role for underprivileged students); racial integration, under the assumption that segregated schools are inherently unequal; and equal contexts, as measured by school climate and school quality. The EEO focused on equality of educational inputs, school racial composition, and school outcomes.

A major finding of the EEO research was that family background had a significant effect on students' achievement. Students whose parents had higher socioeconomic and educational attainment had higher academic achievement. A more politically volatile result was that schools played a role in creating and sustaining student differences in achievement. This finding intensified public concern about the negative effects of segregated schools on the achievement of black students. Along with the earlier *Brown v Board of Education* (1954) ruling by the U.S. Supreme Court that outlawed segregated schools, the EEO results were among the most influential factors leading to the desegregation of the American public school system.

The Coleman Report generated numerous follow-up analyses as well as new research on the differential effects of background and school factors on students' achievement, aspirations, and educational and occupational attainment. The direction of this research was influenced by public concern about racial and ethnic issues. A number of studies examined how school resources and school racial composition affected the achievement of black and white students (see reviews in Crain & Mahard, 1978; Spady, 1973). Because black students were shown to have higher achievement in majority white schools, the research was used to support efforts to desegregate public schools (Armor, 1972).

Coleman's (1966) landmark EEO study laid the foundation for the school effects research on between-school differences in educational opportunities. His later research contributed directly and indirectly to this growing body of work. At the same time, the research and debate on equality of educational opportunity influenced Coleman's thinking and played a role in his theoretical formulations about social systems. In particular, it influenced his last book, *The Foundations of Social Theory* (1990), arguably one of the foremost theoretical contributions to sociology of the 20th century.

The theoretical and empirical analysis of educational opportunity led Coleman to confront the dilemma posed by conflicting educational policies aimed at achieving equality of educational opportunity. The dilemma reflects the age-old tension between individual rights and the common good. On the one hand, if schools were to provide equal opportunities for all students, then the common good occasionally would have to take precedence over the goals of individual students. Schools would be forced to play a compensatory role, because students begin schooling with vast differences in background, ability, and skills. On the other hand, if schools were to be a meritocracy, then the needs and goals of individuals would be placed before those of the community in an effort to maximize individual talents and abilities.

Coleman's (1990) response to this dilemma was twofold. First, he rejected the goal of equality of educational opportunity for schools, regarding it as unrealistic and unattainable. Instead he suggested that the appropriate goal of education was to reduce, rather than to eliminate, inequality of educational opportunity. Coleman claimed that schools could decrease, but not eliminate, the vast differences among students created by variation in individual characteristics and social experiences. Second, and more important, his reflections on the tension between the individual and community goals led him to conceptualize social life as a contract, in which some rights are given over to the community and others are retained.

The fundamental insight and premise of *The Foundations of Social Theory* is that social life is about negotiating various rules to govern the actions of sets of persons. Coleman built his theory of purposive action on this premise, and he relied on the principle of maximization of utility to formalize it. In so doing, he linked the actions of individuals to those of the community. Combining the notion of rational choice with that of collective action, Coleman produced a theoretical structure to explain social life in all its various forms. This impressive sociological contribution to sociology benefited partly from his earlier work on equality of educational opportunity. Although *The Foundations of Social Theory* has not been available long enough for its impact to be felt, one might reasonably predict that it will provide a major theoretical framework for future studies in the sociology of education.

In considering whether the sociology of race and ethnicity influenced school effects studies, an interesting connection can be made. Both sociologists of race and ethnicity and sociologists of education became aware that the proximity of members of different racial and ethnic groups does not necessarily result in social integration. Responding to racial and ethnic tensions in society, sociologists of race and ethnicity moved beyond assimilation theory to posit different ways that minority groups could be incorporated into American society. At the same time, sociologists of education were learning, from the studies of school desegregation and from the experience of white flight, that only when certain conditions are present in a school and a community does desegregation lead to social integration. Discussions in the race and ethnicity literature of pluralism, interdependence, and conflict as possible alternate responses to racial and ethnic heterogeneity coincided with studies in the sociology of education that investigated the conditions under which school desegregation leads to racial and ethnic integration.

The similarity of these research issues suggests a possible influence of race and ethnicity research on school studies. However, an influence is difficult to detect. Research in the sociology of race and ethnicity is cited rarely by sociologists studying school desegregation; correspondingly, the theoretical ideas about alternate patterns of interracial and interethnic interaction are not found in sociology of education studies.

Another factor might lead one to predict an influence of race and ethnicity research on studies of equality of educational opportunity. Both areas focused on multiculturalism and its effects on individuals. Sociologists of race and ethnicity have examined ethnic identity and cultural boundaries in ethnically diverse settings. School effects researchers extended their studies of the racial composition of schools to include various ethnic groups and studied how the ethnic composition of a school affected students' achievement. Whether race and ethnicity research influenced school effects researchers to focus on ethnicity or whether this emphasis was simply due to the growing Chicano and Asian student population is unclear. Again, although the shared conceptual interest might suggest an influence, the sociology of education literature rarely refers to these ethnic studies.

Research on the Social Organization of Students and Within-School Processes

The school effects studies focused primarily on differences in educational opportunities across schools and paid little attention to differential opportunities for learning within schools. The research of the 1980s and 1990s corrected this oversight. Through systematic analysis of the ways schools channel educational opportunities to students within schools, the studies identified within-school and within-classroom processes that had the potential to distribute educational opportunities unequally across students.

Sociologists of education studying within-school processes examined how students are organized for instruction, how students gain access to the curriculum, and how school practices and policies affect students' learning. The studies identified mechanisms that created an unequal distribution of learning opportunities within a school and a classroom. They also demonstrated how non-white students could be particularly disadvantaged by these mechanisms.

One example of research on within-school processes is the study of grouping and tracking. Scholars examined whether the common practice of grouping students by ability for instruction created unequal opportunities for students to learn. Several studies found that ability grouping disadvantaged Black and other minority students by disproportionately assigning them to low-ability groups where instruction, pedagogy, and academic climate often were inferior to that found in higher ability groups (Alexander & McDill, 1976; Catsambis, 1994; Hallinan, 1991; Kubitschek & Hallinan, 1996; Oakes, Gamoran, & Page, 1992; Rist, 1970). They also determined that assignment to low-ability groups foreclosed certain course options later in a student's high school career (Hallinan, 1996). In addition, they showed that assignment to low-ability groups or tracks had a cumulative, negative effect on students' achievement, widening the distribution of achievement and increasing the disparity between the test scores and grades of White and minority students.

A second example of research on within-school processes is found in studies of the curriculum and instruction. Several studies reported that the quantity and quality of instruction affect the amount a student learns (Heyns, 1974, 1978; Oakes, 1985). Other research showed that the nature of classroom interactions, including students' participation, teachers' expectations, and peer tutoring, influences learning (e.g., Gamoran & Nystrand, 1991; Stodolsky, 1984). In general, school processes research demonstrated that students learn more when challenged by a demanding curriculum and by high expectations for performance and when provided with social support than in a less challenging and less supportive environment.

A third set of studies on within-school processes addressed issues related to students' disengagement from schooling and school failure. Researchers examined the determinants of students' deviant behavior and the school's response to these problems. They investigated the effects of grade retention and the causes of students' dropping out of school and identified student characteristics that increased the likelihood of low academic performance and failure (Alexander, Natriello, & Pallas, 1985; McNeal, 1997; Natriello, Pallas, & McDill, 1986; Roderick, 1994; Rumberger, 1995). Given the gap between the performance of White and non-White students, many sociologists focused on the school experiences of minority students (e.g., Jordan, Lara, & McPartland, 1996; Velez, 1989). They specified ways to improve the performance of low-achieving students through organizational, curricular, and instructional change.

Two connections can be made between the general concerns of race and ethnicity researchers and sociologists of education studying within-school processes. First, sociologists in both areas were concerned about equity issues. Sociologists of race and ethnicity examined political and social factors that created barriers to racial and ethnic interaction. Sociologists studying within-school processes identified inequitable instructional and organizational practices that disadvantaged minority students.

Second, sociologists of race and ethnicity have studied pluralism as a viable response to racial and ethnic diversity. Sociologists of education have demonstrated that pluralism is a workable model for interracial and interethnic relations in a school setting through studies showing the positive effects of student diversity and a multicultural curriculum on students' racial and ethnic attitudes and academic achievement. In addition, sociologists of education have examined the appropriateness of the curriculum and the methods of instruction found in majority white schools for non-white students and have demonstrated the benefits of a multicultural curriculum and school environment.

Despite the apparent overlap between interests of sociologists of race and ethnicity and sociologists studying within-school processes, it is difficult to point to an influence of race and ethnicity on within-school process studies. As in the case of the school effects research, sociologists examining school processes may have become interested in this area in response to wide societal concern about equity issues, rather than through an influence of sociological analyses of race and ethnicity. The empirical literature in both areas shows little exchange of ideas, and any commonality in the studies seems limited to the inclusion of race and ethnicity in the analyses.

Some sociologists have noted that recent research in the sociology of race and ethnicity has concentrated on racism as opposed to patterns of interracial and interethnic contact. One might ask whether this focus can be seen in the sociology of education. That is, can the recent study of school processes be described as a search for racism in school practices and policies? Examination of this work suggests that school process research focuses less on racism than on organizational practices and school policies that have unintended consequences for disadvantaged, minority students.

Sociologists of education currently are studying a number of issues, including school governance and financing, private versus public schools effects, school-to-work transitions, education from a life course perspective, and cross-cultural and cross-national determinants of achievement. Concerns about race and ethnicity may be seen in all these analyses. For example, studies of governance and school financing include comparisons of the effects of charter schools, magnet schools, and private schools on students from different racial and ethnic backgrounds. Research on long-term returns to schooling pays particular attention to differences in occupational attainment by race and ethnicity. Interpretations of research findings from cross-cultural and from cross-national studies of academic achievement explain the way cultural differences affect the learning process. Indeed, almost all recent research on schools has taken race and ethnicity into account in examining schooling processes and their outcomes. But again, if this research has been affected by theoretical perspectives and by empirical studies of race and ethnicity, this influence is difficult to detect.

Multiculturalism and Affirmative Action in Higher Education

Two major issues currently preoccupy sociologists who study institutions of higher education. These issues are multiculturalism and affirmative action. Multiculturalism includes the effort to incorporate the work of non-white, non-European, and female scholars into the curriculum. Affirmative action encompasses policies aimed at expanding the pool of applicants for admission to colleges and universities (and the job market) to insure consideration of all qualified applicants, regardless of race or ethnicity. Both of these issues tend to be seen through the lens of equality of educational opportunity.

Multiculturalism has been a subject of intense debate among scholars and activists. Racial and ethnic minorities and women have demanded that colleges and universities add their past and present scholarship to the traditional canon in the liberal arts curriculum. Sociologists of education have analyzed the multiculturalism debate from the perspective of both consensus and conflict theory. Glazer (1997) claimed that we have failed to incorporate blacks as equal members of American society. He argued that multiculturalism is a more viable approach to diversity than past efforts to assimilate minorities into a majority white society. However, he joins other sociologists in suggesting that multiculturalism may be a transitory state, which could eventually lead to assimilation or possibly to greater pluralism. Other social scientists (e.g., D'Sousa, 1995) have maintained that the demand for multiculturalism will weaken over time and that the traditional canon will be restored.

Affirmative action policies in education include a conscious effort to create and implement college admissions practices that provide equal opportunity for admission to all applicants. Francis (1993) pointed to three goals of affirmative action: compensation, to redress previous discrimination; correction, to alter present discrimination; and diversification, to create a multicultural society. Most recently, supporters of affirmative action have built their arguments on the benefits of creating racially and ethnically diverse institutions. Opponents of affirmation action argue that the practice discriminates against whites and conveys a negative judgment about the abilities of blacks.

Sociologists of education are studying the impact of affirmative action policies on college admissions. Building on their extensive research on equality of educational opportunity in elementary and in secondary schools, they are investigating equity issues related to criteria for college admission and for financial assistance. One such issue is the possible racial or ethnic bias created by the use of standardized test scores as an admissions criterion. A related issue is whether financial need should be a prerequisite for scholarships and for other forms of financial assistance.

Because the U.S. Supreme Court mandated that affirmative action policies may no longer be implemented to redress past discrimination or to counter current discrimination, the only remaining legal justification for affirmative action policies governing college admissions is to establish a multicultural or diverse student body. Sociologists of education have examined whether diversity has an impact on students' learning and on students' social attitudes and behaviors. Much of this research reports a positive effect of a racially and ethnically diverse college campus on student outcomes under conditions of institutional support for affirmative action programs (for a review of this literature, see Hallinan, 1998).

Because sociological research on multiculturalism is fairly recent, too few studies are available to trace an influence of sociology of race and ethnicity on this work. To date, most studies of multiculturalism are fairly descriptive, and they attempt to document the impact of efforts to adopt a multicultural curriculum on students' attitudes and behaviors. One might anticipate that sociologists of race and ethnicity will, in time, view multiculturalism as a critical factor in the evolution of patterns of racial and ethnic contact in American society. If this occurs, it could lead to cooperative work with sociologists of education on the effects of multiculturalism on race and ethnic relations among college and university students.

Neither sociologists of race and ethnicity nor sociologists of education have conducted a major survey of the consequences of affirmative action policies. Bowen and Bok's (1998) analysis of the performance of black and white students during matriculation at a sample of elite colleges and after graduation provides evidence of long-term benefits of affirmative action policies. At the same time, it raises concern about race differences in black and white academic achievement in college. Clearly, theoretical and empirical research on race and ethnicity and on educative processes would inform the debate about affirmative action policies and their consequences for student outcomes.

CONCLUSIONS

This chapter examines whether theory and research in the sociology of race and ethnicity has influenced theoretical and empirical research in the sociology of education. A comprehensive theory of race and ethnicity has yet to be formulated. For the most part, the sociology of race and ethnicity has relied on broad, societal theories of consensus and conflict and on more focused theories, such as assimilation, to describe social processes governing patterns of race and ethnic contact in America. In addition, sociologists of race and ethnicity have depended on the theoretical paradigms of subdisciplines, such as social stratification, demography, and social psychology, to explain the social dynamics of race and ethnicity.

Similarly, sociologists of education have failed to develop a broad theory of schooling in American society. Like the study of race and ethnicity, sociological research on schools has been built on theories of consensus and of conflict, as well as on subdisciplinary perspectives. Sociologists of education have relied on theoretically developed areas like social stratification, organizations, and social psychology for theoretical perspectives on schooling. Less theoretically elaborated areas, like the sociology of race and ethnicity, have not had a similar influence on sociological research on education.

Some of the conceptual perspectives in the study of race and ethnicity do appear, at least as assumptions, in research on schooling. Early studies of schools revealed a general acceptance of the assimilation hypothesis. Most studies focused on the educational trajectory of whites and assumed that blacks and other racial and ethnic groups followed the same trajectory. More recently, sociologists of education examined patterns of interracial and interethnic interactions in desegregated schools, mirroring some of the work on pluralism being conducted in the sociology of race and ethnicity. They also studied structural and contextual influences on interracial and interethnic attitudes and behavior, another interest of sociologists of race and ethnicity.

However, beyond a possible, modest influence of widely held general assumptions in the sociology of race and ethnicity, this area appears to have had little effect on the study of schooling in America. Given that racial and ethnic tension is one of the most persistent, contemporary social problems, greater collaborative effort is called for to understand the complex issues involved. Sociologists of race and ethnicity and sociologists of education would benefit from joint efforts to formulate a theory of race and ethnicity in an institutional setting. The two areas also would gain from collaborative empirical work aimed at explaining how societal institutions, like schools, provide opportunities and constraints that affect the race and ethnic relations of their members.

REFERENCES

Adorno, T. W., Frenkel-Brunswik, E., Levinson, D. J., & Nevitt, S. R. (1950). *The authoritarian personality*. New York: Wiley.

Alba, R. D., & Chamlin, M. B. (1983). Ethnic identification among whites. *American Sociological Review, 48,* 240–247.

Alexander, K., & McDill, E. (1976). Selection and allocation within schools: Some causes and consequences of curriculum placement. *American Sociological Review, 41,* 963–980.

Alexander, K. L., Natriello, G., & Pallas, A. M. (1985). For whom the school bell tolls: The impact of dropping out on cognitive performance. *American Sociological Review, 50,* 409–420.

Armor, D. J. (1972). The evidence on busing. *The Public Interest, 28,* 90–128.

Baldassare, M. (Ed., 1994). *The Los Angeles riots: Lessons for the urban future*. Boulder, CO: Westview Press.

Barth, E. A. T., & Noel, D. L. (1972). Conceptual frameworks for the analysis of race relations: An evaluation. *Social Forces, 50,* 333–348.

Bidwell, C. (1965). The school as a formal organization. In J. B. March (Ed.), *Handbook of organizations* (pp. 972–1022). Chicago: Rand McNally.

Blalock, H. M. (1967). *Toward a theory of minority-group relations*. New York: Wiley.

Bonacich, E. (1972). A theory of ethnic antagonism: The split labor market. *American Sociological Review, 37,* 547–559.

Bonacich, E. (1973). A theory of middleman minorities. *American Sociological Review, 38,* 583–594.

Bourdieu, P. P., & Passeron, J. C. (1990). *Reproduction in education, society and culture* (2nd ed.). London: Sage.

Bouvier, L. F. (1992). *Peaceful invasions: Immigration and changing America*. Lanham, MD: University Press of America.

Bowen, W. G., & Bok, D. C. (1998). *The shape of the river: Long-term consequences of considering race in college and university admissions*. Princeton, NJ: Princeton University Press.

Bowles, S., & Gintis, H. (1976). *Schooling in capitalist America: Educational reform and the contradictions of economic life* (paperback ed.). New York: Basic Books.

Campbell, R. T. (1983). Status attainment research: End of the beginning or beginning of the end? *Sociology of Education, 56,* 47–62.

Catsambis, S. (1994). The path to math: Gender and racial–ethnic differences in mathematics participation from middle to high school. *Sociology of Education, 67,* 199–215.

Coleman, J. S. (1968). The concept of equality of educational opportunity. *Harvard Educational Review, 38,* 7–22.

Coleman, J. S. (1988). Social capital in the creation of human capital. *American Journal of Sociology, 94,* S95–120.

Coleman, J. S. (1990). *Foundations of social theory*. Cambridge, MA: Belknap Press of Harvard University Press.

Coleman, J. S. (1994). A vision for sociology. *Society, 32,* 29–34.

Coleman, J. S., Campbell, E. Q., Hobson, C. J., McPartland, J., Mood, A., Weinfeld, F., & York, R. (1966). *Equality of educational opportunity*. Washington, DC: U.S. Department of Education.

Collins, R. (1979). *The credential society*. New York: Academic Press.

Cox, O. (1948). *Caste, class, and race: A study in social dynamics*. New York: Modern Reader Paperbacks.

Crain, R. L., & Mahard, R. E. (1978). School racial composition and black college attendance and achievement test performance. *Sociology of Education, 51,* 81–101.

Dahrendorf, R. (1959). *Class and class conflict in industrial society*. Stanford, CA: Stanford University Press.

D'Sousa, D. (1995). *The end of racism*. New York: The Free Press.

Farley, R., & Allen, W. A. (1987). *The color line and the quality of life in America*. New York: Russell Sage Foundation.

Francis, L. P. (1993). In defense of affirmative action. In S. M. Cahn (Ed.), *Affiirmative action and the university: A philosophical inquiry*. Philadelphia: Temple University Press.

Gamoran, A., & Nystrand, M. (1991). Background and instruction effects on achievement in eighth-grade English and social studies. *Journal of Research on Adolescence, 1,* 277–300.

Glazer, N. (1997). *We are all multiculturalists now*. Cambridge, MA: Harvard University Press.

Glazer, N., & Moynihan, D. P. (1970). *Beyond the melting pot: The Negroes, Puerto Ricans, Jews, Italians and Irish of New York City*. Cambridge, MA: MIT Press.

Gordon, M. (1964). *Assimilation in American life*. New York: Oxford University Press.

Greeley, A. (1971). *Why can't they be like us? America's white ethnic groups*. New York: Dutton.

Greeley, A. (1974). *Ethnicity in the U.S.: A preliminary reconnaissance*. New York: Wiley.

Hallinan, M. T. (1991). School differences in tracking structures and track assignments. *Journal of Research on Adolescents, 1*, 251–275.

Hallinan, M. T. (1996). Race effects on students' track mobility in high school. *Social Psychology of Education, 1*, 1–21.

Hallinan, M. T. (1998). Diversity effects on student outcomes: Social science evidence. *Ohio Law Journal, 59*(3), 733–754.

Hammond, P. E. (1966). Secularization, incorporation and social relations. *American Journal of Sociology, 72*, 188–194.

Heyns, B. (1974). Social selection and stratification within schools. *American Journal of Sociology, 79*, 1434–1451.

Heyns, B. (1978). *Summer learning and the effects of schooling*. New York: Academic Press.

Hout, M. (1984). Occupational mobility of black men: 1962 to 1973. *American Sociological Review, 49*, 308–322.

Jordan, W. J., Lara, J., & McPartland, J. M. (1996). Exploring the causes of early dropout among race–ethnic and gender groups. *Youth and Society, 28*, 62–94.

Katz, I., Hass, R. G., & Wackenhut, J. (1986). Racial ambivalence, value duality, and behavior. In J. F. Dovidio & S. L. Gaertner (Eds.), *Prejudice, discrimination, and racism*. New York: Academic Press.

Kim, I. (1981). *New urban immigrants, the Korean community in New York*. Princeton, NJ: Princeton University Press.

Kinloch, G. C. (1974). *The dynamics of race relations: A sociological analysis*. New York: McGraw-Hill.

Kubitschek, W. N., & Hallinan, M. T. (1996). Race, gender, and inequity in track assignments. In A. M. Pallas (Ed.), *Research in Sociology of Education and Socialization* (Vol. 11, pp. 121–146). Greenwich, CT: JAI Press.

Lieberson, S. (1980). *A piece of the pie: Blacks and white immigrants since 1880*. Berkeley, CA: University of California Press.

Lieberson, S., & Waters, M. C. (1988). *From many strands*. New York: Russell Sage Foundation.

Light, H. I. (1972). *Ethnic enterprise in America: Business and welfare among Chinese, Japanese, and Blacks*. Berkeley, CA: University of California Press.

Mann, H. (1832). *Common school education*. Rochester, NY.

Massey, D., & Denton, N. (1993). *American apartheid*. Cambridge, MA: Harvard University Press.

McNeal, R. B., Jr. (1997). High school dropouts: A closer examination of school effects. *Social Science Quarterly, 78*, 209–222.

Merton, R. K. (1968). *Social theory and social structure* (3rd ed.). New York: The Free Press.

Meyer, T. W. (1977). The effects of education as an institution. *American Journal of Sociology, 83*, 55–77.

Natriello, G., Palias, A. M., & McDill, E. L. (1986). Taking stock: Renewing our research agenda on the causes and consequences of dropping out. *Teachers College Record, 87*, 430–440.

Niemonen, J. (1997). The race relations problematic in American sociology: A case study and critique. *The American Sociologist, 28*, 15–54.

Oakes, J. (1985). *Keeping track: How schools structure inequality*. New Haven, CT: Yale University Press.

Oakes, J., Gamoran, A., & Page, R. N. (1992). Curriculum differentiation: Opportunities, outcomes, and meanings. In P. Jackson (Ed.), *Handbook of research on curriculum* (pp. 570–608). New York: Macmillan.

Parenti, M. (1967). Ethnic politics and the persistence of ethnic identification. *American Political Science Review, 61*, 717–726.

Park, R. E. (1950). *Race and culture*. Glencoe, IL: The Free Press.

Piore, M. J. (1979). *Birds of passage, migrant labor and industrial society*. New York: Cambridge University Press.

Portes, A., & Bach, R. L. (1985). *Latin journey, Cuban and Mexican immigrants in the United States*. Berkeley, CA: University of California Press.

Portes, A., & Manning, R. D. (1986). The immigrant enclave: Theory and empirical examples. In S. Olzak & J. Nagel (Eds.), *Competitive ethnic relations* (pp. 47–68). Orlando, FL: Academic Press.

Rist, R. (1970). Student social class and teacher expectations: The self-fulfilling prophecy in ghetto education. *Harvard Educational Review, 40*, 411–451.

Roderick, M. (1994). Grade retention and school dropout: Investigating the association. *American Educational Research Journal, 31,* 729–759.

Rosenberg, M., & Simmons, R. G. (1971). *Black and white self-esteem: The urban school child.* Washington, DC: American Sociological Association.

Rumberger, R. W. (1995). Dropping out of middle school: A multilevel analysis of students and schools. *American Educational Research Journal, 32,* 583–625.

Sassen-Koob, S. (1980). Immigrant and minority workers in the organization of the labor process. *Journal of Ethnic Studies, 1,* 1–34.

Schermerhorn, R. A. (1970). *Comparative ethnic relations: A framework for theory and research.* New York: Random House.

Sewell, W. H., Haller, A. O., & Portes, A. (1969). The educational and early occupational attainment process. *American Sociological Review, 34,* 82–92.

Sewell, W. H., & Hauser, R. M. (1975). *Education, occupation, and earnings: Achievement in the early career.* New York: Academic Press.

Solomos, J., & Back, L. (1994). Conceptualizing racisms: Social theory, politics and research. *Sociology, 28,* 143–161.

Spady, W. G. (1973). The impact of school resources on students. In F. N. Kerlinger (Ed.), *Review of research in education* (pp. 135–177). Itasca, IL: F. E. Peacock Publishers, Inc.

Stodolsky, S. (1984). Frameworks for studying instructional processes in peer work-groups. In P. Peterson, L. C. Wilkinson, & M. T. Hallinan (Eds.), The social context of instruction (pp. 107–124). San Diego, CA: Academic Press.

Turner, R. H. (1960). Sponsored and contest mobility and the school system. *American Sociological Review, 25,* 855–867.

Van den Berghe, P. (1967). *Race and racism: A comparative perspective.* New York: Wiley.

Van den Berghe, P. (1970). *Race and ethnicity.* New York: Basic Books.

Velez, W. (1989). High school attrition among Hispanic and non-Hispanic white youths. *Sociology of Education, 62,* 119–133.

Wilson, K. L. (1979). The effects of integration and class on black educational attainment. *Sociology of Education, 52,* 84–98.

Wilson, W. J. (1980). *The declining significance of race: Blacks and changing American institutions* (2nd ed.). Chicago: University of Chicago Press.

Yans-McLaughlin, V. (Ed., 1990). *Immigration reconsidered: History, sociology, and politics.* New York: Oxford University Press.

CHAPTER 4

Research and Theory on Equality and Education

Kathleen Lynch

INTRODUCTION

Sociologists have dominated the debate about equality in education over the last 25 years. They have challenged the psychological reductionism which so often overwhelms educational analysis in teacher education departments; they have identified the concept of truth itself as problematic in an education system where absolutism and certainty are all too frequently the dominant normative codes. There is a very real sense in which sociologists have been the most critical and reflective members of the academy of educationalists (Dale, 1992, p. 203; Wesselingh, 1996, p. 216). In a European context, the work of Bourdieu, Passeron and their colleagues in France (1977) has been especially influential in developing a critical class-based analysis of educational practice, while critical sociology of education has presented a challenge to the dominant educational paradigms in Canada (Livingstone, 1985), the United States (Apple, 1996), Australia (Connell, 1993) and Latin America (Torres & Rivera, 1994). Throughout the 1990s, feminist and postmodernist researchers have also challenged dominant discourses in education (Aronowitz & Giroux, 1991; Weiner, 1994)

There is, however, no one sociology of education. Major reviews of work in the field suggest that the sociological analysis of education is a disparate and eclectic sub-discipline of sociology (Arnot & Barton, 1992; Blackledge & Hunt, 1985; Hurn, 1978; Karabel & Halsey, 1977; Mehan, 1992; Torres & Rivera, 1994; Trent, Braddock, & Henderson, 1985). Given differences within the field, it is inevitable that there is great variability in the way in which

Kathleen Lynch • Department of Equality Studies, University College Dublin, Dublin, Ireland
Handbook of the Sociology of Education, edited by Maureen T. Hallinan. Kluwer Academic/Plenum Publishers, New York, 2000.

equality has been interpreted and defined. It is indeed because of its theoretical variability that sociology has had the capacity to be a critical and generative force for the development of an equality-related analysis in education.

The purpose of this chapter is to analyze research and theory in the sociology of education in the context of egalitarian theory generally, and critical and feminist theory in particular. While much mainstream sociology of education operates within an implicit normative paradigm, egalitarian theory challenges us to address ethical considerations about the purpose and value of research as core questions in theoretical and empirical analysis.

The chapter opens with an examination of the dominant methodological and conceptual frameworks within sociology of education over the last twenty years.[1] It briefly summarizes the contribution and limitations of different intellectual traditions in the analysis of equality, noting in particular the discrete and insulated character of much of the debate within the separate spheres. The normative orientation of sociology of education is the subject of the second section. It is suggested that political liberalism has been the dominant egalitarian paradigm among functionalists and interpretative researchers, although critical, feminist, post-structuralist, and postmodern theorists have presented a substantive radical challenge to this tradition in recent years.

The equality objectives informing sociological analysis are examined in the third section; some of the limitations of a Rawlsian-inspired model of social justice are also discussed. This is followed by an analysis of the epistemological foundations of sociological research on equality; the merits of both positivist and praxis-oriented approaches to knowledge for the realization of egalitarian change are assessed. The implications of failing to involve marginalized and oppressed groups in research design and production are then examined; new structures for research dialogue between researchers and marginalized groups and communities are proposed. The chapter closes with a brief summary and some concluding comments.

Research in sociology of education over the last 20 years has been dominated by liberalism. The focus has been on modification and adjustment, rather than on radical egalitarian reform. Although feminists and critical theorists have been highly critical of the education system, both as process and product, and identify the concept of education as an unmitigated good as problematic, they have not developed proposals which are sufficiently coherent and plausible to seriously challenge the powerful position of liberalism within educational theory and empirical research.

The same issue arises in relation to neo-Marxist critiques of the relationship between the politico-economic system and education. Critique is not substantiated with viable alternative proposals. In this chapter, it is suggested that theories of egalitarian change, that is, theories which are grounded in the institutional and political structures of educational reality, can only be successfully developed in a dialogical context. This dialogue should take place not only with a wide range of educationalists, policy-makers, and academics in cognate disciplines, but also with the marginalized and excluded groups who are the subjects of equality-based research in education. Those who are on the periphery need to be relocated at the center, negotiating and naming the purposes of research. Without a radical realignment of the power relations of research production, equality-related research will itself be contributing to the colonizing and oppressive process.

---

[1]This chapter does not purport to examine the vast literature on equality in education which is produced by the global community of sociologists working in the field. Such an undertaking would be a major study in its own right. What is examined primarily is a range of literature which is written or translated into English. The limitations of working out of a majoritarian linguistic and cultural perspective are acknowledged.

ANALYSING INEQUALITY:
CONCEPTUAL AND METHODOLOGICAL ISSUES

The Equality Empiricists

In their analysis of the work undertaken in the sociology of education in the preceding twenty years, Karabel and Halsey (1977) identified the research of the methodological empiricists as being a core part of the work of sociologists in the field of education. Working within both functionalist and neo-Weberian traditions, the methodological empiricists were primarily equality empiricists, in the sense that much of their research was centered on educational inequality. This tradition has continued to flourish since the late 1970s using large data bases to determine either the relationship between education and status attainment for different social groups, or the effects of schooling on the educational opportunities of particular social groups (Dronkers, 1983; Eckland & Alexander, 1980; Halsey, Heath, & Ridge, 1980; McPherson & Willms, 1987).

The work of the equality empiricists was paralleled by the work of stratification theorists who documented patterns of social mobility (among white men especially). While the focus of stratification research was not on the dynamics of education *per se*, it had implications for the work of egalitarian-focused sociologists of education as it documented the relative success or failure of different education strategies for the promotion of equality in society (Erikson & Jonsson, 1996; Shavit & Blossfeld, 1993). Numerous writers have noted how sociology of education was closely tied historically to stratification research (Apple, 1996; Mac an Ghaill, 1996).

Equality empiricism not only focuses on the mobility of various social groups between different sectors and fields of education, it also examines equality patterns within schools themselves. School-specific research examined the effects of schooling (especially tracking or streaming) on student outcomes, highlighting social class and racial and gender inequalities in access to learning. While this tradition was strongest in the United States (Alexander, Cook, & McDill, 1978; Gamoran, 1996; Hallinan, 1992; Oakes, Gamoran, & Page, 1992), there has been a burgeoning school effects research tradition in Europe also, although this work is not always equality-focused (Reynolds, Creemers, Nesselrodt, Schaffer, Stringfield, & Tessie, 1994).

The parameters within which the debate about equality in education takes place have been set by large scale empirical studies on the effects of schooling on life chances. Although these studies are not as dominant in the U.S. and Britain as they were in the 1970s (Weiss, 1995), they form the intellectual and political backdrop for much of contemporary research and thinking about equality in education, especially in the U.S. (Davies, 1995). These are the kinds of studies which tend to be funded by governments directly or indirectly, and they are often regarded in policy terms, if not in academic terms, as of central importance. The dominant intellectual paradigm which has been employed to interpret and explain these research findings has been structural-functionalism (Weiss, 1995).

Although a number of critiques and evaluations of the methodological and theoretical assumptions of the equality empiricists have been presented elsewhere (Apple, 1996; Apple & Weis, 1983; Bourdieu, 1973; Weiss, 1995; Wexler, 1987), it is worthwhile noting some of the limitations of the work here. Much of the research within this tradition framed social class inequality in education as a degendered and politically neutral issue thereby foreclosing intellectual debate about the complex and variable character of class-related inequalities. Bourdieu (1973) was especially critical of the atomistic representation of individuals divorced from structural relations within this type of sociological research. The work of the empiricists has also been critiqued by feminists and post-modernists for its objectivism and uncritical positivism. They claim that researchers represent themselves as detached and independent observers thereby concealing the paradigmatic and domain assumptions of their work. The fact that equality empiricists often work on research funded directly or indirectly by the State also means they are rarely in a position to subject the cultural politics of education or the role of the State to critical examination. Finally, status attainment research has been notable for its failure to explain educational outcomes for women and racial minorities (Kerchoff, 1984). Inequalities arising from disability or sexual orientation have also been generally ignored in the mainstream sociological tradition (Barton, 1996).

Yet there is an implied critique of social and political hierarchies within the work of the equality empiricists. It is assumed that people have a right to a more equitable redistribution of life chances, be that in terms of access to higher education, to high status jobs, or to advanced streams or tracks within a stratified system. However, when there are direct challenges to social hierarchies, as in the detracking research, it is the organizational manifestations of inequality which are critiqued, rather than the structural generators of racial, class, ethnic, and other inequalities. This perspective holds although it is clear that socioeconomic inequalities can and do seriously undermine the effects of internal egalitarian-oriented policies in schools and colleges (Blossfeld & Shavit, 1993).

Despite the aforesaid limitations, the work of equality empiricists has played an important role in the policy arena in certain European countries (including Sweden, the U.K., and, Ireland), in holding the State itself to public account. The use of national data in the analysis of poverty, and in the documentation of social class, religious, or gender differences in educational opportunities, has been very effective in countries such as Ireland in challenging the effectiveness of State policies for the promotion of equality in education and society generally (Callan, Nolan, B. Whelan, C. Whelan, & Williams, 1996; Cormack & Osborne, 1995). Brown, Halsey, Lauder, & Wells (1997: 37) suggest that this kind of political arithmetic is a vital tool of democracy in a world where inegalitarian ideologies are gaining hold. It helps inform the body politic, giving people access to knowledge which is detached from the powerful interests of government and media (Halsey, 1994).

Interpretive Research

Weberian-inspired interpretative sociology has a large following among educators in teacher education departments, which is where most sociological research on education is disseminated. Within this tradition there are a range of studies which are focused on the dynamics of interaction in schools and classrooms *per se* including the work of symbolic interactionists: Equality is not the central focus of much of this research however (Ball, 1987; Denscombe, 1985; Woods, 1983).

There is equality-focused work within the interpretative tradition which analyses systems of power, control, and influence, both in the micro-processes of school life and in the macroprocesses of educational systems. Unequal access to power at the corporate level is a central theme in the work of Archer (1984) and Collins (1979). Work by Bernstein (1973), DiMaggio (1982), Lareau (1989), and Mehan, Hetweck, & Lee Meihls (1985), illustrates how the operation of inequality in schools takes place in the micro-processes of school life; studies of the role of parents in education have been especially fruitful in explaining how privilege is perpetuated in schooling (Lareau, 1989; Wells & Serna, 1996). Interpretative approaches have also been adopted in the analysis of education policies (Arnot & Barton, 1992) and in deconstructing the dynamics of racial, sexual, and gender relations within classrooms and schools.

While it is generally assumed that work within the qualitative tradition tends to be interpretive in its approach, qualitative methods are employed by researchers from radically different intellectual traditions (Davies, 1995). Qualitative methods have been employed by neo-Marxists, feminists, and those who are eclectic in their theoretical approach to the research subject.

Ethnographic research within the interpretive tradition has deepened our understanding of inequality in education. It has highlighted the importance of cultural elements in the production and reproduction of inequality, refocused attention on the role of human agency in educational and social processes, and helped unravel the complex dialogical relationship between institutional practices and individual actions which contribute towards the perpetuation of inequality (Mehan, 1992).

However, as is true generally in the social sciences, ethnographic research is more effective at highlighting the failure of particular policies to promote egalitarian outcomes for particular groups than at specifying what lies beyond critique in terms of policy alternatives. Often what is lacking is a set of clearly defined alternatives or counterfactuals (Sayer, 1995) to present educational policies.

Critical Theory, Feminism, and Postmodernism

The lacunae presented by the distributive, generally macroscopic, focus of much of the equality-oriented studies of the 1960s and 1970s stimulated the development of the so-called new sociology of education in Britain in the early 1970s (Bernstein, 1973; Whitty, 1985; Young, 1971), and a closely associated neo-Marxist debate (Willis, 1977). A related critical tradition developed in the United States (Anyon 1980; Apple, 1979; Giroux, 1983; Wexler, 1987). These perspectives were paralleled by participatory action research which was broadly equality-oriented (Carr & Kemmis, 1986; Torres, 1990). Almost all of the early work within the critical tradition was focused on social-class related inequalities in education, moving from a focus on reproduction (Bowles & Gintis, 1976), to questions of resistance (Giroux, 1983; McRobbie, 1978), to postmodernist, feminist, and post-structuralist critiques (Aronowitz & Giroux, 1991; Lather, 1991; Wexler, 1987). Within France, Bourdieu and Passeron's work (1977) focused on cultural reproduction within a broadly structuralist and Marxist paradigm. A strong feminist tradition also developed at this time informed by both socialist and radical feminism (Acker, 1994; Arnot & Weiner, 1987; Spender 1980).

Working originally within a neo-Marxist framework, and subsequently with a strong feminist orientation in certain cases, writers within the critical tradition refocused the debate about equality in education from concerns about equal rates of consumption to questions about the nature of knowledge and patterns of power and control within education itself. Education was no longer defined as an unproblematic good; the more one got the better off one was. Critical theorists and researchers identified both the content of education, and the processes of influence and control within it, as problematic. This tradition has remained a minority one within the U.S. and a number of other countries (Apple, 1996; Wesselingh, 1996) although it was a powerful force in academic discourse in the U.K. for a number of years. Despite its pervasive impact on intellectual debate, Dale (1992, p. 214) claimed that this tradition did not exercise much influence on public policy in the U.K. He suggested that the relatively utopian character of much of the policy critique meant that change in the terms proposed was almost impossible to achieve. He suggested that even classroom-focused studies did not have an impact as they did not answer the questions which concerned educational practitioners.

The critical tradition which persisted within sociology of education into the 1990s was very different in its intellectual orientation to what was defined as critical thought in the 1970s and early 1980s. First, it began to challenge the simple correspondence models of reproduction exemplified in the work of Bowles and Gintis in the 1970s by incorporating notions of agency and resistance into debates. Second, it recognized the importance of non-class forms of social exclusion (gender, ethnicity, race, etc.) for understanding the patterning of domination and inequality in education (Morrow & Torres, 1995).

Increased research on issues of gender and ethnicity was paralleled by a gradual decline in the volume of empirical research being undertaken on social-class-related inequalities. Even the language of the debate changed from inequality to difference; the focus was on identity, culture, and recognition, rather than stratification, selection, and allocation. Postmodernist and poststructuralist analysis influenced both the language and the substance of educational thought (Mac an Ghaill, 1996). Issues of race, ethnicity, sexuality, and disability, so long neglected by sociologists in education, found a new and welcome prominence in educational and social analysis (Barton, 1996; Barton & Tomlinson, 1984; Hooks, 1981; Verma & Ashworth, 1986). It was not that issues of race, disability or ethnicity had been completely ignored in the past; they were not, especially in the U.S. where race was such a crucial issue. They had however, been defined as attributes of persons whose core was defined often in socio-economic (in functionalist analysis) or in social class terms (within the critical tradition). In the 1990s, however, race, ethnicity, gender, and/or disability were regarded as defining and essential identities, shaping the nature of all social experience. They were not defined as attributes, which people wore on the surface of some other more fundamental social class or socio-economic identity.

The emphasis on identity politics has inevitably focused greater attention on the process and curricula of schooling. The move from structuralism (be it of the functionalist or neo-Marxist kind) to post-structuralism has centered debate on process rather than outcome, on individual experience rather than on systems such as the state, or political operators and mediators within the education system. Although postmodernism and poststructuralism (including feminists within these traditions) have exerted a certain influence on contemporary writing in sociology of education there are many publications within the sociology of education which one could read without ever realizing that there were significant new developments in sociology in structuration theory and postmodernism (Shilling, 1993).

Discussion

The divisions between the broadly critical and positivist paradigms in education are visible, not only in the substantive differences in academic orientation between journals such as *Sociology of Education* and the *British Journal of Sociology of Education*, but also in the lack of communication between competing paradigms. The critical tradition is viewed by many of those within the positivist research tradition with theoretical and methodological distrust (Davies, 1995: Hammersley, 1995). Critical theorists view the claims to value neutrality of strong positivists with equal skepticism (Abraham, 1996).

That there are fundamental differences between perspectives is undeniable. However, these do not arise simply from the immanentist and teleological presumptions of critical theorists regarding the nature of social change as Davies (1995) has suggested. They arise also from the very real epistemological differences between broadly functionalist and interpretive, and critical modes of inquiry. Much of mainstream sociological research on education is essentially focused on reporting and analyzing inequalities rather than on changing them. The act of change is defined as a separate and discrete event from the act of analysis and inquiry. Critical theorists, on the other hand, regard knowledge production as praxis, an act of which documents the world, but which also works towards either domestication or freedom (Freire, 1972). Moreover, in so far as both traditions address policy concerns, they differ significantly in their policy audiences. For mainstream researchers, policy is as defined by educational administrators, teachers, government departments, and related power-brokers in education (see for example, the special edition of *Sociology of Education*, 1996, devoted to policy issues). Critical theorists generally take the policy perspective of those who are marginalized in society, as defined by the oppressed themselves (Lather, 1991). The research agenda as set by the managers and mediators of educational services is very different from the research concerns of those who are either marginal to the education system or who are minor beneficiaries within it.

Differences notwithstanding, the work of the equality empiricists, interpretative researchers, and critical theorists contribute in unique ways to our understanding of education and the realization of change within it. Empirical researchers, of all academic persuasions, provide essential documentation of patterns of inequality at both macrolevels and microlevels of social action. Without such documentation, challenges and resistance to particular policies and practices would take place in an informational void and would be all the more ineffective for that. For its part, critical analysis plays an important role in highlighting questions of value in research, and in introducing debates about the transformative potential of research in education. Such work is crucial for identifying the areas of education which can be used to challenge inequality, even if it suffers at times from a certain naiveté about the change-related potential of particular social actions. The feminist and postmodernist traditions, on the other hand, force educationalists and sociologists to engage in critical reflexivity about their own research thereby making the social relations of research production in education itself a subject of critique and investigation. Such reflexivity is vital for the development of new approaches to research and theory in the study of equality.

NORMATIVE CONSIDERATIONS

Baker (1998) has identified three basic conceptions of equality in contemporary egalitarian theory: basic equality, liberal equality, and radical equality. Basic equality is the principle which is fundamental to all egalitarian theory. It is the idea that all human beings are equal in dignity and worth, and are therefore equally worthy of concern and respect. It upholds the prohibition of inhuman or degrading treatment, and gives some recognition to the idea that all human beings have basic needs. It defines equality in fundamentally negative terms therefore, in terms of freedom from, rather than freedom to. Basic equality is therefore a rather minimalist view of equality.

While accepting the value of basic equality, liberal egalitarians move beyond this and espouse the protection of basic civil and political rights, including freedom of speech, freedom of movement, equality before the law, and freedom to own property. Liberalism is the fundamental philosophical premise underpinning the Universal Declaration of Human Rights and the European Convention on Human Rights. Liberal equality is most commonly associated in the policy field with the principle of equality of opportunity (Hall, 1986). It recognizes that society is stratified and proposes that equality policies should be directed towards equalizing opportunities for various types of mobility (educational, occupational, career, intergenerational, etc.) within a stratified system. The best known proponent of this tradition is Rawls (1971).

Radical egalitarians do not accept that major structural inequalities are inevitable in the way that liberal and basic egalitarians do. They argue for a radical change in the way that institutions and society are structured to promote equality. They focus especially on the importance of substantive economic and political equality, suggesting that liberals are merely concerned about ways in which to redistribute inequality across various groups, rather than how to eliminate major inequalities and hierarchies in the first place (Baker, 1987; Cohen, 1995; Nielsen, 1985; Young, 1990). Given that egalitarian theorists differ significantly therefore, in the way in which they define equality, it is important to locate sociological thinking within the wider egalitarian framework.

Education was and is an ethical enterprise. Even for those who do not subscribe to the modernist and enlightenment project of which education is such a central part, there is no denying that education is essentially about the realization of change in terms of some predefined sense of an educational good. It is almost inevitable therefore that what Shilling (1993) calls the "redemptive tradition" should be so strong in education. Even sociologists within the strong positivist tradition tend to regard education as a social good with definite redemptive effects, at least in this life!

What is not inevitable however, is the way in which inequality in education is widely interpreted, namely in liberal terms, as a problem of redistributing opportunities equally across social groups. Whether sociologists are measuring the effects of tracking, or examining patterns of mobility within different sectors of education, it is generally assumed that equality is being attained when marginalized or disadvantaged groups are increasing their entry rates to advanced or honors tracks, to prestigious universities or to high status jobs. The equality test is a proportionality one, proportionate representation in privileged positions. The structural inequalities endemic to hierarchies of knowledge, tracks, jobs, etc., are not the subject of investigation; they tend to be taken as given. There is also considerable evidence that most Western sociologists of education worked within a liberal political framework in the post-war era (Arnot, 1991; Lynch, 1995; Middleton, 1990). In addition, the need to redistribute opportunities was a core assumption underpinning status attainment theory, which remains the ascendant research tradition in American sociology of education (Davies, 1995, p. 1454).

There are a number of possible reasons why the liberal definitions of equality (be it in the weak sense of equal access, or the stronger senses of equal participation and outcome) came to dominate sociological research on education. One reason is undoubtedly the socio-political context within which it was created. Liberalism was the dominant political philosophy of the post-war years in most Western capitalist states. The goal was neither to re-order the structures of power and control, nor to reconstitute the ownership of industrial, agricultural, or service capital. The goal was to redistribute rather than restructure (Arnot, 1992, p. 43). Education was seen as a key instrument in this social design; it was a tool of social engineering. It offered an opportunity to combine the goals of personal fulfillment with the goal of economic development, without reordering hierarchies of capital, labor, culture, race, or gender. Expenditure on education met workers' demands for a greater equalization of opportunity and capital's demand for a skilled labor force. Education was also seen as the ideal tool in the realization of the modernist project of progressive development.

Given the applied nature of their research, and their need for major funding to undertake large-scale studies, sociologists of education were often more than willing to address questions about the effectiveness of education as a tool of social engineering. Major academic projects were often tied to State research objectives with academic shifts following political movements (Karabel & Halsey, 1977). As political philosophies shifted from liberal to conservative in the U.K. for example, educationalists also moved towards the right (Arnot & Barton, 1992). The ability of the State to redirect the sociological research agenda was especially evident in Britain during the eighteen years of Conservative government up to 1997. The equality project, even in a weak liberal form, was not the state project at that time. As sociologists were regarded as unduly critical of the State's agenda, sociological research on education was very poorly funded over the period. Sociologists worked under siege (Dale, 1992) being characterized by critics as irrelevant, politically biased, and demonstrating weak scholarship. By the 1990s, the conservative State project had succeeded in shifting the dominant sociological research agenda: concerns about accountability, choice, and effective schooling replaced inequality as core themes in the sociology of education (Arnot & Barton, 1992).

EQUALITY OBJECTIVES IN EDUCATION

Sociologists of education working within both quantitative and qualitative traditions tend to define equality objectives in terms of either access, participation, or outcome; they work out of a largely liberal and distributive view of social justice. Equality of access represents the minimalist conception whereby equality is defined in terms of access to different levels of education for relatively disadvantaged groups within a stratified society and educational system. Equal participation represents a stage beyond access, where equality is measured in terms of participation rates rather than just access rates, and/or in terms of the nature and quality of participation experienced by different groups within sectors and fields of education. Equality of outcome or success represents the third and most radical conception of equality which is found within liberal educational discourse. Within this tradition, equality is measured in terms of the educational attainments or success rates of marginalized groups within education. As participation in certain fields of education, notably university education, is often defined as the pinnacle of educational success, implicitly if not explicitly, there is a clear overlap between what is defined as equal participation and what is defined as equality of outcome or success at times.

Equality tends to be measured therefore in terms of how far any given disadvantaged group has progressed in accessing a hitherto inaccessible educational good. It establishes in particular, what proportion of the disadvantaged group have accessed a particular education position or privilege relative to their proportion in the general population and/or relative to some appropriate comparator group. Equality is deemed to be promoted if social class, gender, racial, or other inequalities/advantages in education are proportionately distributed across social groups; the closer the participation or success ratio is to one, the greater the equality achieved. As lengthy participation in second-level education has become almost universal in Western countries, proportionate access to different levels and types of higher education has become the commonest measure for assessing racial, religious, social-class, socio-economic, and occasionally, gender, inequality in education.

Measuring inequality in terms of the access/participation/success continuum makes an important contribution to sociological thought as it provides a clear map over time of how educationally stratified our society is in gender, social class, racial, or other terms. It lays down the empirical floor on which other analyses can build. Without such work, it would be very difficult to have a clear profile of what progress, if any, is taking place in educational opportunities for various groups vis-à-vis more advantaged groups.

However, liberal definitions of equality are but one possible set of definitions. A radical perspective suggests that while equality of access/participation/outcome are important, they tend to ignore fundamental problems of inequality of condition (Tawney, 1964). First, they do not address extant power and income differentials between social groups affecting their abilities to avail of opportunities in the first place. Second, they do not adequately address issues of equal status or respect which are fundamental to the realization of equality between groups differentially located in the cultural, ethnic, ability, religious, sexual, and other hierarchies in society. Third, they do not treat the content of education itself as fundamentally problematic. Working within a distributive view of social justice, it is generally assumed that more equals better, although both the process (pedagogy and organization) and product (curriculum) of education may be highly inegalitarin in their enactment, thereby reinforcing inequalities within the school/education system itself.

Liberal and Distributive Models of Social Justice

There are two dominant normative strands within sociological research on equality in education, namely the distributive and liberal traditions. The most fundamental underlying weakness of the distributive model of justice is its failure to question what kind of education is being provided; its indifference to the nature of education itself. A focus on distribution withdraws analytical attention from the role of curricular and pedagogical practice in the perpetuation of inequality. Yet as Connell (1993, p. 18) observes, "education is a social process in which the 'how much' cannot be separated from the 'what'. There is an inescapable link between distribution and content." The school or college curriculum is not neutral: its orientation includes class, gender, and race. It perpetuates particular cultural traditions at the expense of others, and in so doing reinforces images of what is or is not culturally valuable in a given society.

The failure to view the content of education as problematic is often associated with a reluctance to recognize cultural and other differences among those being educated. If one's cultural traditions and practices are not a valued part of the education one receives; if they are denigrated or omitted, then schooling itself becomes a place where one's identity is denied or one's voice is silenced. The process of schooling can create a sense of being inferior regardless of individual mobility outcomes. It can and does fail to provide equality of respect for all social groups, either by denying their identity in curricular selection or organization, or by adopting authoritarian forms of pedagogical relations which define learners as subordinate and passive recipients of knowledge.

Debates developing around identity politics, especially in feminist writing, have challenged traditional assumptions about the benefits of a simple distributive model of justice, especially when applied to a complex institution such as education (Fraser, 1995; Weiler, 1988; Young, 1990). Critical feminist and postmodernist analysis have identified not just the content of education as problematic, but also the organization of pedagogical relations. Drawing on the work of Freire (1972) especially, they have challenged the presumption that pedagogical practice can be divorced from outcome (Lather, 1991; Weiler, 1988).

Not only does the distributive model of justice not take sufficient account of differences, it also fails to provide a framework for analyzing equality of respect in pedagogical practice. Yet, the pedagogic act has a number of hidden or implicit messages about appropriate contexts and frameworks for learning which are quite distinct from the curriculum itself. These can be, and often are, anti-egalitarian (Bernstein, 1973; Bourdieu & Passeron, 1977). Learning within an hierarchical set of pedagogical relations in which the student is defined as a subordinate learner contradicts other egalitarian messages which may be given through the formal curriculum itself. This type of "banking education" (Freire, 1972) presents learning as a top-down process rather than a partnership process; it defines the learner as passive and subordinate, thereby reinforcing a power and status hierarchy between teachers and students which is anathema to the principle of equality itself. Such issues are not named as equality concerns within most of the empirical research literature on classrooms.

This is not to suggest that all mainstream education in schools is, to use Bourdieu's phrase, a system of "symbolic violence" for it is patently not; there are aspects of curricula which are owned by all groups (literacy, numeracy, critical analysis, scientific method, etc.). Moreover a certain amount of order and system organization is necessary in a group learning context. What is being suggested however, is that there is little debate in most countries about the ordering of pedagogical relations and the effects of hierarchical relations on equality-related attitudes and processes. In addition, equality of respect for minority and marginalized cultures and traditions is often only given token recognition within mainstream education.[2] What is necessary is a restructuring of the learning environment so that the hidden curriculum of pedagogical practice does not defeat other more fundamental egalitarian objectives which schools may be trying to promote, either through support programs or curricular reform.

Critical theorists and feminists have therefore been key players in moving the debate about equality beyond questions of distribution and beyond liberalism. They have argued for a concept of equality of condition which is premised on equality of respect in the organization of schooling itself - in terms of the structures of decision-making, the organization of curricular selection, and pedagogical relations.

Neo-Marxists have also addressed the problem of equality of condition, albeit from a more economistic and radical distributive perspective. They focus in particular on the importance of equality of economic condition outside of schooling for realizing all other equality objectives; they suggest that substantive equality in education, especially between social classes, is impossible in a highly class stratified society (Althusser, 1971; Bowles & Gintis, 1976). Unlike liberal educationalists, they do not believe that education (however it be equalized and re-structured internally) can be egalitarian without radical changes in the social relations of production, distribution, and exchange.

While few now subscribe to the strong economic determinism of the structural Marxists, there is validity to their more general argument regarding the importance of wider economic equality for the realization of equality within education. This has been borne out by a range of studies showing how educational reforms with a broadly egalitarian remit have not altered the nature of the relationship between social origins and educational attainment in a range of countries (Shavit & Blossfeld, 1993). The country which showed the weakest link between social origin and attainment was Sweden. This was a state which had the most consistent policy, over a 40 year period, of equalizing socio-economic conditions between social groups (Blossfeld & Shavit, 1993, p. 21). In effect, the equalization of life chances outside of schools had a direct effect on improving educational chances within schools (Erikson & Jonsson, 1996).

---

[2]At the very least we need the type of counter-hegemonic curricular developments which Connell (1993) proposes. Rather than create curricular ghettos for the disadvantaged, there is a need to *reconstruct the mainstream* to embody the interests of the least advantaged" (Connell, 1993, p. 44).

What this suggests is that inequality in education cannot be understood independently of other institutions and systems in society; in particular that it cannot be understood independently of the politico-economic subsystem. Without a radical redistribution of wealth and power outside of schools, substantive egalitarian change in the outcomes and processes of schooling is most unlikely. The reasons are simple: if education alone is made the principal site of change within the State, this allows powerful interests and classes, which may be disadvantaged by change, to use other politico-economic contexts of action to subvert the outcomes of egalitarian-oriented state policies. Research on the challenges to detracking in the U.S. shows how this can happen (Wells & Oakes, 1996). Moreover, education-specific groups who manage and mediate the education service are also able to resist change to the detriment of equality values (Lynch, 1989). While there is no neat synchrony between education mediators and the owners and controllers of power and wealth in society, the reality is that education decision-makers are more likely to be drawn from the same social groups as the economic and political elite than they are likely to be drawn from marginalized groups. Their own class and status position is frequently dependent on maintaining the existing order of cultural relations in education.

EMANCIPATORY PERSPECTIVES ON RESEARCH

Treating people equally is a fundamental premise of most ethical theories pertaining to the organization of society (Sen, 1992, p. 130). By implication therefore, inequality is construed in political theory and practice as both politically and morally undesirable. This has profound implications for the study of inequality: it supposes that inequality is not a morally neutral subject, not least because of the various forms of human misery experienced by those who are subjected to it. In studying inequality, we are investigating a social phenomenon which is itself in need of transformation. Given this, posing questions regarding the transformative dimensions of particular research approaches is not only justifiable, it is essential. Researchers need to ask if their work plays a role in either domesticating this inequality or in changing it. Failure to ask this question ignores a fundamental reality of the phenomenon under study itself, namely its ethical dimension.

The epistemological stance adopted within mainstream sociology of education has proved valuable in describing patterns of inequality in education. It has systematically documented the extent and nature of inequality in a wide range of different contexts; the empirical work undertaken in both the quantitative and qualitative traditions has kept the issue of equality in the public domain as an issue of ongoing concern for public policy-makers.

However, within the mainstream tradition, knowledge is not defined in the transformative sense as knowledge as praxis; it is presented as a set of facts about the world, be these interpretive or statistical facts. What is not overtly recognized is that knowledge has consequential as well as existential correlations. That is to say, little attention is given to identifying the change-related possibilities and limitations of particular frameworks or theories of inequality. The world is presented as a given with a past, but only occasionally as a place with a future which is open to change and intervention. Even when researchers focus on the policy implications of their findings, the issue of change is addressed as an addendum to the main study. The development of a theory of egalitarian-based change is not a core part of the theoretical agenda.

This is not to suggest that empirical research in the social sciences cannot and does not influence policy and promote equality of treatment in certain contexts . There is no doubt that it does, even thought the relationship between policy and research is by no means well defined (Epstein, 1996; Hallinan, 1996). However, most sociologists of education have not incorporated the analysis of the transformative potential of their work into the research design, and there is no necessary or inevitable change-specific outcome from much research on inequality (Chambers, 1983; Oliver 1992).

In addition, reflexivity is not encouraged within the mainstream tradition. It largely ignores the extent to which the defining and naming of particular perspectives on selected worlds, makes such worlds and perspectives more real. The way in which the worlds and stories are interpreted or defined creates particular emphases and poses certain policy options as more inevitable, feasible, and desirable than others. In addition, the naming of certain realities creates silences around those realities which are not named.

The silence problem is greatest in relation to those social realities which are difficult to document or even observe using the conventional methods of the social sciences; among these hidden realities are the relational systems of inequality. For inequality is fundamentally a relative phenomenon, and it is only through an understanding of relational systems of wealth, power, culture, control, definitions, etc. that we can understand how it is produced and reproduced. Yet, many relational systems are not overtly visible, not least because those living at different ends of the relational spectrum have no direct ties to each other which can be observed and easily documented. In addition, much of the powerful decision-making in both educational and financial life goes on in arenas to which social scientists are not and will not be given access. Without reflexivity most of these complex questions about the limitations of empiricism, the use of knowledge, the potential of knowledge to realize or forestall change, will not be addressed.

Both critical and feminist theorists have explored the transformative potential of their own writing. They have introduced reflexivity into social analysis, and attempted to identify routes for action, even though their efforts are, at times, construed as being naive, or even redundant (Dale, 1992; Hammersley, 1995). One of the more legitimate criticisms made about feminist and critical analysis perhaps is that they have been more effective on critique than they have been in identifying strategies for action and change. In recent years, for example, much emphasis has been placed on the notion of counter-hegemonic resistance through a radical pedagogy of transformation (Aronowitz & Giroux, 1991; Weiler, 1988). Based largely on a Freirean model of education as conscientisation, educationalists assume that teachers and educators can and will become agents of transformative action. As noted previously (Lynch, 1990), this thesis ignores the particular cultural and political configuration of relationships within which Freire's thesis emerged, and the complex interface between politics and policy which is required for change (Hallinan, 1996; Torres, 1990). It also oversimplifies the nature of power relations within education itself.

Critical theory also fails to address the wholeness of the education system. Transformative education could not occur without a simultaneous transformation of all the education subsystems including curriculum structures, management structures, organizational systems, teacher education, and State action. Yet, little serious attention is given to address the way in which changes in pedagogical practices might interface with other systems. The fact that a change in one sub-system may have little overall effect on other systems is not really recognized. Neither is the interface of interests between the politico-economic sites and the educational sites adequately understood in the context of realizing change.

Discussion

Attempts to isolate questions regarding the validity of scientific theories from moral or political values, generally in the name of value freedom (Abraham, 1996), leads to the analytical neglect of the transformative potential of research and theorizing. As inequality is a morally undesirable phenomenon, exclusive reliance on research methodologies to investigate it which are indifferent to the issue of emancipatory change can and do have a domesticating effect. At the very least, such research creates a new social reality about inequality, a sociological reality which generally exists outside and above those marginalized or disadvantaged groups about whom it is written. The research creates a community of academic owners of the documented inequality particular groups or persons experience. The experts name the world of others for their academic peers or for experts and/or policy-makers in the State or other organizations. This results, albeit inadvertently, in a process of colonization; sociologists and other experts can claim to know people in a way that they do not know themselves. This gives the experts information about people, and therefore power over them, which they are not in a position to challenge.

RESEARCH PARTNERSHIPS WITH MARGINALIZED GROUPS

As Bourdieu (1993, p. 37) has observed, intellectuals "tend to leave out of play their own game and their own stakes." Although academic writing creates virtual, textual, ethnographic and statistical realities about the nature of inequality in education, intellectuals are disinclined, for the most part, to subject their own analysis to reflexive critique. While there are exceptions to this especially in the critical, feminist, and post-modern traditions, such work is not typical of research undertaken in sociology of education. Yet, theoretical knowledge about equality in education has limitations imposed upon it by the conditions of its own performance.

One of these conditions is the cultural and political context of research. Much of the popular writing in sociology of education over the last 50 years has developed in Western capitalist states within a strong tradition of social reformism. In Europe and in the United States, educational sociology, as it was often known as in its early days, was tied closely to the analysis of education-related social reforms. Sociologists themselves were often central to the reform movement, and sociology of education was strongly focused on policy. In more recent times, sociology of education has become more diverse, and there is a large body of work which is not especially concerned with issues of equality. Much of the research on school effectiveness in particular reflects sociological flight to the agenda of the New Right with a focus on quality and accountability rather than equality.

The relations of research production within the academy are a further limiting condition on the work of researchers. The concept of the free-floating, disinterested intellectual may be part of the ideology of academia, it is not grounded in any sociological reality. Professional academics, no matter how radical their private political orientations, occupy a particular location within the class system (Bourdieu, 1993, pp. 36–48). In some respects, they occupy a contradictory class location, being part of the cultural elite while remaining socio-economically subordinate to powerful industrial and commercial interests (Davies, 1995). It is belonging to the cultural elite in society which provides them with the structural conditions to write; it gives them credibility over other voices and reinforces the perception of superiority which maintains the salary differentials between themselves and other workers.

Bourdieu (1993, p. 45) seems to suggest that there is no easy resolution to this dilemma for radical intellectuals. He proposes a radical, ongoing reflexivity wherein one prepares " the conditions for a critical knowledge of the limits of knowledge which is the precondition for true knowledge"; such practices, he suggests, would enable researchers to recognize the limits of their own understanding.

Even if academics do engage in ongoing reflexivity, this does not alter the structural conditions under which they work. Intellectuals work in institutions in which merit is measured, for the most part, is in terms of conformity to the dominant norms of intellectual and academic discourses. This includes not only writing within the dominant paradigm of one's discipline but also writing about what is currently intellectually fashionable. Without at least a nodding recognition of the important of the dominant discourses, then one's work is not likely to be published. And it is through their publications that intellectuals in universities are generally assessed.

The academy also penalizes those who attempt to redefine the purpose of the academy. Recognition is given generally only for work published or validated by one's academic peers. This acts as a very effective control on non-academic partnerships, limiting and containing interests within the safe confines of the university. It also works effectively to preclude intellectuals from involving themselves, and the university, in radicalizing initiatives due to the time commitments involved. Research involving genuine partnership and dialogue is time-consuming and unpredictable in its outcomes; it must also be accessible to those with whom it is conducted. Accessibility is not valued in most academic circles. Time spent in dialogue with marginalized groups does not produce career-rewarded publications unless it can be reconstituted for that purpose.

Thus, it is not surprising to find that marginalized groups have rarely been partners in research about themselves. Even teachers and pupils, who are so often the subjects of research, are rarely partners in research projects and virtually never in theoretical expositions (Van Galen & Eaker, 1995). Where sociologists have been involved in partnerships, it has mostly been, with the exception of a small number of activist writers, in a personal rather than a university capacity.

The question of partnership is especially problematic for marginalized groups or communities who are structurally excluded from the academy by virtue of their class position. Unlike debates about other equality issues in education, including gender, race, or disability, there has been no indigenous class-based analysis of educational inequalities (Lynch & O'Neill, 1994). Working class children, men, and women have all remained dependent on middle class sponsors—whether they are middle class by origin or by destination—to tell their story. In many respects, a form of intellectual and cultural colonization has continued in the social class field, which has been partially superseded in the race and gender areas by oppressed groups talking and researching for themselves about themselves.

If there is to be a move to create more egalitarian, emancipatory research methodologies involving genuine partnership, academic institutions will have to radically re-organize the relations of research production (Humphries, 1997). It would involve, at the very least, setting up research partnerships whereby those directly affected by inequality are given formal status to participate in the research process. This would challenge fundamentally the view of academic as expert witness on issues of equality/inequality. Such initiatives have implications for the operation of research programs and university life generally which extend far beyond issues of research methodology. They involve an equalization of perspectives on equality issues, rather than placing the academic voice as the leading expert one (Lynch, 1999).

While there has been a recent attempt to explore the relationship between research and policy in a special issue of *Sociology of Education* (1996), the specific focus here is on creating closer links between researchers, educators and policy-makers. With the exception of work by feminist educators, and philosophers (such as Humphries, 1997; Lather, 1991; Weiler, 1988), there has been little discussion of how to involve research subjects in defining the nature and purposes of research and theory in education . Neither have there been many attempts to identify the kinds of institutional and strategic practices required to implement a truly participatory methodology. Such elaboration is essential, however, if those who are prescribing dialogue are to be taken seriously. Otherwise, they will face the continued challenge posed by Sayer (1995) about the limits of radical theory, namely its failure to develop counterfactual proposals in the light of the critiques which it presents.

It is only through entering into partnership with those directly affected by injustice that workable counterfactual proposals can be systematically developed. Theories of egalitarian change need to be grounded in the lifeworld of the marginalized, not only for ethical reasons (Young, 1998), but also for practical reasons. Without ongoing dialogue academics are likely to prescribe utopian and partial solutions to inequality that will be duly disregarded, not only by those in power but by the very groups they claim to assist. There is a need to marry community perspective with normative prescription, scientific analysis, and policy appraisal.

Dialogical relationships are not only crucial for the understanding and promotion of equality within schools and classrooms (Freire, 1972), they are also crucial for the development of effective equality policies in education at the regional, national, or international level. The development of effective equality policies in education also means that professional educators and researchers must be working with rather than for marginalized groups. A dialogical relationship is essential because of the dangers inherent in any equality process that the marginalized group becomes either the object of charitable desire or a professional career/research interest. In either case, the danger is that the interest of the professional or the philanthropist will take precedence over the interest of the specific group. If this happens—and there is plenty of evidence of that it did in the disability area especially—the enactment of liberal reforms frequently become the central concern. These give legitimacy to the work of the professionals but have only marginal impact in terms of equality outcomes. Without real power sharing between the target equality group, policymakers, and professionals, colonization of the marginalized is often the unforeseen by-product of policy action. In other words, if the conditions of research production about inequality are exclusive, and do not involve the oppressed themselves as partners, then there is a very real sense in which the research process becomes part of the equality problem.

SUMMARY AND CONCLUSION

Sociology of education is a normatively-oriented discipline with a much greater focus on educational reform than radical change. While there is a radical tradition in sociology of education, this remains quite peripheral to much of its core analysis and research. What this has meant for the understanding and the realization of equality is that most intellectual attention is focused on amending present processes, systems, and structures, rather than analyzing the potential for radical transformation. The dominant models of explanation are those emanating from the functionalist tradition, although the development of both critical and feminist theory has moved the debate about equality from a simple concern with distribution to concerns about equality of respect and status within schools. This has made the processes and quality of schooling itself a central theme in the equality debate. The rise of identity politics within postmodernist analysis has also created new concerns in sociology of education. Difference is no longer defined in class, or even race or gender, terms; it also denotes differences in sexual orientation, ethnicity, religion, color, disability, age, etc. There has been a move therefore towards a concept of equality of condition, defined in terms of equality of respect or status, and power.

With the exception of those writing within a broadly neo-Marxist tradition, most sociologists of education have not focused on the issue of equality of economic condition as a core concern in their analysis. To the extent that sociologists have ignored economic inequalities and concentrated increasingly on status and power-related inequalities, they have peripheralized the debate about social-class-based inequality in education. While it may be entirely historically justified to move the debate about equality beyond issues of economic redistribution, the fact that those who are most economically marginalized remain the most oppressed within any given marginalized group, suggests strongly that addressing economic inequality remains fundamental to the realization of both distributive and non-distributive egalitarian objectives. It is difficult to imagine having substantive equality of respect between persons without an equalization of economic resources. Yet the liberal discourse which predominates in sociology of education systematically discourages the analysis of such issues.

Sociologists of education have been working within a liberal framework in much of their work. Although few articulate their liberal political premises, they form a deep structure of much intellectual thought in education. A fundamental assumption of much equality-based research is that effective equal opportunities policies can be implemented in and through education without radical equality of political and economic condition. There are strong grounds for believing that this position is untenable, not least because it chooses to ignore the dialectical relationship which exists between political power, material goods, and cultural property such as education. Economic capital is readily translatable into cultural capital. Without an equalization of income and wealth differentials, those with superior resources can always use these to improve their control over, and access to, credentialized cultural capital and thereby maintain their position of relative advantage. Equality is not only impeded in the simple distributive sense when significant income and wealth differentials exist however, it is also impeded in terms of equality of respect or status, as vulnerable groups struggle to define their own education and identity in the face of better endowed and/or more organized groups.

Status attainment theory is especially open to these criticisms. It endorses the notion of social mobility as a solution to the problem of inequality for marginalized peoples and groups. Working within a liberal political framework, it ignores the fact that even the most radical of the espoused objectives, equality of outcome, does not address the fundamental problem of hierarchies in power, wealth, and privilege. What it proposes is to replace or supplement the existing elite, within the economic, political, educational, and other hierarchies, with a new elite from hitherto disadvantaged groups. As the structural inequalities remain intact, then it is self evident that certain people must occupy highly disadvantaged positions. All that changes is the color, gender, etc., of those who are at the top or the bottom.

What liberals also often ignore is the fact that inequalities do not arise from the intrinsic nature or characteristics of marginalized or excluded groups; rather they arise from the way in which unique characteristics are addressed, be these differences of gender, disability, or ethnicity. Moreover, inequalities persist because positions are differentially rewarded or resourced in terms of wealth, power, and privilege, not because of the character of the people who occupy these positions. Yet much of the analysis centers on the marginalized or excluded group itself; this focuses attention on their difficulties and identities rather than the relational systems, structures, and institutions which generate their subordination in the first instance.

Liberal equality policies have come to predominate, not simply because these are the politics which are most politically palatable to the existing powerbrokers in education, but also because the marginalized peoples and groups at which these policies are supposedly directed are not an integral part of the decision-making process. Their voices, if represented at all, are mediated by professionals such as teachers, psychologists, doctors, social workers, health care workers, etc. and other service agencies outside their control. And mediated voices are not, by definition, organic voices. To move beyond the liberal agenda, it is essential that the oppressed groups, which have been marginalized in educational decision-making, are brought into the policy-making and research design process at all stages as equal partners. They need to be given full and adequate rights of self-representation guaranteed by adequate resourcing and education.

The second major theme of this paper therefore concerns the relationship between researchers, theorists, and the research subject. Despite the development of a more inclusive language within the research community in recent years, marginalized groups have not generally been involved in defining the terms and conditions under which research on themselves is undertaken. They have remained, with some notable exceptions, the subjects of sociological analysis, not the partners in its design and development. The fact that marginalized and oppressed groups have been witnesses rather than partners in the research process has meant that theories of inequality have been framed generally by those who are experientially removed from the immediate and direct experience of deep inequality.

If sociologists of education are to be more than chroniclers of injustice, they need to confront the ethical dilemma posed by researching the ethically loaded subject of inequality. We need to examine the transformative potential of our analysis on a systematic basis, rather than assume its effectiveness. Moreover, we also need to query the value and worth of our own work to determine whether it is, in Freire's words, a force for domestication or for freedom (1972). The only way in which this can be systematically determined is through direct dialogue and partnership with those about whom we research and write. Without such a partnership and joint ownership, it would be very difficult to develop any coherent theory of egalitarian change which would have genuine transformative potential.

Sociologists are not omniscient; the sociological window is but one window on the education world. If sociologists are to be effective in developing theories for equality-oriented practice, they also need to engage in collaborative research with academics outside their own discipline, and with educationalists and policy-makers. Both liberal and radical egalitarian theorists have much to contribute to the understanding of equality; both intellectual traditions have helped clarify the conceptual parameters of egalitarian policies and politics, while radical egalitarians have highlighted the interdependence of all forms of inequality, and the need for a structural, cross-institutional approach for the realization of change.

REFERENCES

Abraham, J. (1996). Positivism, prejudice and progress in the sociology of education: Who's afraid of values? *British Journal of Sociology of Education, 17,* 81–86.

Acker, S. (1994). *Gendered education; Sociological perspectives on women, teaching and feminism.* Milton Keynes, England: Open University Press.

Alexander, K. L., Cook, M., & McDill, L., (1978). Curriculum tracking and educational stratification: Some further evidence. *American Sociological Review, 43,* 47–66.

Althusser, L. (1971). Ideology and ideological state apparatuses. In L. Althusser (Ed.), *Lenin and philosophy and other essays.* New York: Monthly Review Press.

Anyon, J. (1980). Social class and the hidden curriculum of work. *Journal of Education, 162*(1): 67–92.

Apple, M. W. (1979). *Ideology and curriculum.* New York: Routledge and Kegan Paul.

Apple, M. W., (1996). Power, meaning and identity: Critical sociology of education in the United States. *British Journal of Sociology of Education, 17,* 125–144.

Apple, M. W., & Weis, L. (Eds., 1983). *Ideology and practice in schooling.* Philadelphia: Temple University Press.

Archer, M. (1984). *Social origins of educational systems.* London: Sage.

Arnot, M., (1991). Equality and democracy: A decade of struggle over education. *British Journal of Sociology of Education, 12,* 447–466.

Arnot, M. (1992). Feminism, education and the new right. In M. Arnot & L. Barton (Eds.), *Voicing concerns: Sociological perspectives on contemporary education reforms* (pp. 41–65). Wallingford, Oxfordshire, England: Triangle Books Ltd.

Arnot, M., & Barton, L. (Eds., 1992). *Voicing concerns: Sociological perspectives on contemporary education reforms.* Wallingford, Oxfordshire, England: Triangle Books Ltd.

Arnot, M., & Weiner, M. (Eds., 1987). *Gender and the politics of schooling.* London: Hutchinson.

Aronowitz, S., & Giroux, H. (1991) *Postmodern education.* Minneapolis, MN: University of Minnesota Press.

Baker, J. (1987). *Arguing for equality.* New York: Verso.

Baker, J. (1998). Equality. In S. Healy & B. Reynolds (Eds.), *Social policy in Ireland: Principles, practice and problems* (pp. 21–42). Dublin, Ireland: Oaktree Press.

Ball, S. J. (1987) *The micro-politics of the school: Toward a theory of school organisation.* London: Metheun.

Barton, L. (Ed., 1996). *Disability and society: Emerging issues and insights.* Harlow, Essex, England: Addison Wesley Longman

Barton, L., & Tomlinson, S. (Eds., 1984). *Special education and social interests.* Beckenham, UK: Croom Helm.

Bernstein, B. (1973) *Class codes and control Vol. 1: Theoretical studies towards a sociology of language.* London: Paladin.

Blackledge, D., & Hunt, B. (1985). *Sociological interpretations of education.* London: Croom Helm.

Blossfeld, H. P., & Shavit, Y. (1993). Persisting barriers: Changes in educational opportunities in thirteen countries. In S. Shavit & H. P. Blossfeld (Eds.), *Persistent inequality.* Oxford, England: Westview Press.

Bourdieu, P. (1973). Cultural reproduction and social reproduction, in R. Brown (Ed.), *Knowledge, education and cultural change.* London: Tavistock.

Bourdieu, P. (1993). *Sociology in question.* London: Sage.

Bourdieu, P., & Passeron, J. C. (1977). *Reproduction in education, society and culture.* Beverly Hills, CA: Sage.

Bowles, S., & Gintis, H. (1976) *Schooling in capitalist America.* New York: Basic Books.

Brown, P., Halsey, A. H., Lauder, H., & Wells, A. S. (1997). The transformation of education and society: An introduction. In A. H. Halsey et al. (Eds.), *Education: Culture, economy and society* (pp. 1–44). Oxford: Oxford University Press.

Callan, T., Nolan, B., Whelan, B., Whelan, C., & Williams, J. (1996). *Poverty in the 1990s: Evidence From the living in Ireland* Survey. Dublin: Oaktree Press.

Carr, W., & Kemmis, S. (Eds., 1986). *Becoming critical: Education, knowledge and action research.* Lewes, England: Falmer Press.

Chambers, R. (1983). *Rural development: Putting the last first.* Harlow, England: Longman.

Cohen, G. A. (1995). *Self-ownership, freedom and equality.* Cambridge: Cambridge University Press.

Collins, R. (1979). *The credential society. An historical sociology of education and stratification.* New York: Academic Press.

Connell, R. W. (1993). *Schools and social justice.* Philadelphia: Temple University Press.

Cormack, B., & Osborne, B. (1995). Education in Northern Ireland: The struggle for equality. In P. Clancy, S. Drudy, K. Lynch, & L. O'Dowd (Eds.), *Irish society: Sociological perspectives* (pp. 495–528). Dublin: Institute of Public Administration.

Dale, R. (1992). Recovering from a pyrrhic victory? Quality, relevance and impact in the sociology of education. In M. Arnot and L. Barton (Eds.), *Voicing concerns: Sociological perspectives on contemporary education reforms* (pp. 201–217). Wallingford, Oxfordshire: Triangle Books Ltd.

Davies, S. (1995) Leaps of faith: Shifting currents in critical sociology of education. *American Journal of Sociology, 100,* (6): 1448–1478.

Denscombe, M. (1985). *Classroom control: A sociological perspective.* London: Allen and Unwin.

DiMaggio, P. (1982). Cultural capital and school success. *American Sociological Review, 47,* 189–201.

Dronkers, J. (1983). Have inequalities in educational opportunities changed in the Netherlands? A review of empirical evidence. *Netherlands Journal of Sociology, 19,* 133–150.

Eckland, B. K. & Alexander, K. L. (1980). The national longitudinal study of the high school class of 1972. In A. Kerchoff (Ed.) *Research in Sociology of Education* (Vol. 1, pp. 189–222). Greenwich, CT: JAI Press.

Epstein, J. L. (1996). New contribution for sociology and education: contributing to school reform, *Sociology of Education, Special Issue on Sociology and Educational Policy,* 6–23.

Erikson, R., & Jonsson, J. O. (1996). *Can education be equalized: The Swedish case in comparative perspective.* Oxford, England: Westview Press.

Fraser, N. (1995). From redistribution to recognition? Dilemmas of justice in a "Post-Socialist" Age. *New Left Review, 212,* 68–91.

Freire, P. (1972). *Pedagogy of the oppressed.* New York: Penguin.

Gamoran, A. (1996). Curriculum standardization and equality of opportunity in Scottish secondary education: 1984–1990. *Sociology of Education, 69,* 1–21.

Giroux, H. (1983). *Theory and resistance in education: A pedagogy for the opposition.* Amhert: Bergin and Garvey.

Hall, S. (1986) Variants of Liberalism. In J. Donald & S. Hall (Eds.) *Politics and ideology.* Milton Keynes, England: Open University Press.

Hallinan, M. T. (1992). The organization of students for instruction in the middle school. *Sociology of Education, 65,* 114–127.

Hallinan, M. T. (1996). Bridging the gap between research and practice. *Sociology of Education, Special Issue on Sociology and Educational Policy,* 131–134.

Halsey, A. H. (1994). Sociology as political arithmetic. *British Journal of Sociology, 45,* 427–444.

Halsey, A. H., Heath, A., & Ridge, J. M. (1980). *Origins and destinations.* Oxford, England: Clarendon Press.

Hammersley, M. (1995). *The politics of social research.* London: Sage.

Hooks, B. (1981). *Ain't I a woman: Black women and feminism.* Boston: South End Press.

Humphries, B. (1997). From critical thought to emancipatory action: Contradictory research goals, *Sociological Research Online* [On-line], 2, (1). Available: www.socresonline.org.uk/socresonline/2/1/3.html.

Hurn, C. (1978). *The limits and possibilities of schooling.* Boston: Allyn and Bacon.

Karabel, J., & Halsey, A. H. (1977). Educational research: A review and interpretation. In J. Karabel & A. H. Halsey (Eds.), *Power and ideology in education* (pp. 1–85). New York: Oxford University Press.

Kerchoff, A. C. (1984). The current state of mobility research. *Sociological Quarterly, 25,* 139–153.

Lareau, A. (1989). *Home advantage: Social class and parental intervention in elementary education.* New York: Falmer Press.

Lather, P. (1991). *Getting smart: Feminist research and pedagogy with/in the postmodern.* New York: Routledge.

Livingstone, D. W. (1985). *A critical pedagogy and cultural power.* New York: Bergin and Garvey.

Lynch, K. (1989). *The hidden curriculum: Reproduction in education, a reappraisal.* Lewes, England: Falmer Press.

Lynch, K. (1995). The limits of liberalism for the promotion of equality in education. In E. Befring (Ed.) *Teacher education for equality: Papers from the 20th Annual Conference of the Association for Teacher Education in Europe,* Oslo College, Norway.

Lynch, K. (1999). Equality studies, the academy and the role of research in emancipatory social change. *Economic and Social Review, 30*(1), 41–69.

Lynch, K., & O'Neill, C. (1994). The colonisation of social class in education, *British Journal of Sociology of Education, 15,* 307–324.

Mac an Ghaill, M. (1996). Sociology of education: State schooling and social class: Beyond critiques of the New Right hegemony. *British Journal of Sociology of Education, 17,* 163–176.

McPherson, A., & Willms, J. D. (1987). Equalisation and improvement: Some effects of comprehensive reorganisation in Scotland. *Sociology, 21,* 509–539.

McRobbie, A. (1978). Working class girls and the culture of femininity. In Centre for Contemporary Cultural Studies Women's Studies Group, *Women Take Issue* (pp. 96–108). London: Hutchinson.

Mehan, H. (1992). Understanding inequality in schools: The contribution of interpretive studies. *Sociology of Education, 65,* 1–20.

Mehan, H., Hetweck, A., & Lee Meihls, J. (1985). *Handicapping the handicapped: Decision making in students' careers.* Stanford, CA: Stanford University Press.

Middleton, S. (1990). Women, equality and equity in liberal educational policies, 1945–1988. In S. Middleton, J. Codd, & A. Jones (Eds.), *New Zealand education policy today.* Wellington, New Zealand: Allen & Unwin.

Morrow, R. A., & Torres, C. A. (1995). *Social theory and education: A critique of theories of social and cultural reproduction.* New York: State University of New York Press.

Nielsen, K. (1985). *Equality and liberty: A defense of radical egalitarianism.* Totowa, NJ: Rowman and Allanheld.

Oakes, J., Gamoran, A., & Page, R. (1992). Curriculum differentiation: Opportunities, outcomes and meanings. In. P. W. Jackson (Ed.), *Handbook of research on curriculum,* (pp. 570–608). Washington, DC: American Educational Research Association.

Oliver, M. (1992). Changing the social relations of research production. *Disability, handicap and society,* 7, 101–114.

Rawls, J. (1971). *A theory of justice.* Oxford, England: Oxford University Press.

Reynolds, D., Creemers, B. P., Nesselrodt, A. Schaffer, E. C., Stringfield, S., & Teddlie, C. (Eds., 1994). *Advances in school effectiveness research and practice,* Oxford:, England: Pergamon Press.

Sayer, A. (1995). *Radical political economy: A critique.* Oxford, England: Basil Blackwell.

Sen, A. (1992). *Inequality reexamined.* Oxford, England: Clarendon Press.

Shavit, Y., & Blossfeld, H. P. (Eds., 1993). *Persistent inequality: Changing educational attainment in thirteen countries.* Boulder, CO: Westview Press.

Shilling, C. (1993). The demise of the sociology of education in Britain? Extended review. *British Journal of Sociology of Education, 14*(1), 105–112.

Sociology of Education (1996). Special Issue on Sociology and Educational Policy.

Spender, D. (1980). *Learning to lose: Sexism in education.* London: Women's Press.

Tawney, R. H. (1964 edition). *Equality.* London: Allen and Unwin.

Torres, C. (1990). *The politics of nonformal education in Latin America.* New York: Praeger.

Torres, C. A., & Rivera, G. G. (Eds., 1994) *Sociologia de la educacion: Corrientes contemporaneas,* (3rd. ed.), Buenos Aires: Mino y Davila Editores.

Trent, W., Braddock, J., & Henderson, R. (1985). Sociology of education: A focus on education as an institution. In E. Gordon (Ed.), *Review of research in education* (Vol. 12, pp. 295–335). Washington, DC: American Research Association.

Van Galen, J., & Eaker, D. J. (1995). Beyond settling for scholarship: On defining the beginning and ending points of postmodern research. In W. T. Pink & G. W. Noblit (Eds.), *Continuity and contradiction: The futures of the sociology of education* (pp. 113–132). Cresskill, NJ: Hampton Press.

Verma, G. K., & Ashworth, B. (1986). *Ethnicity and educational achievement in British schools.* London: Macmillan.

Weiler, K. (1988). *Women teaching for change: Gender, class and power.* Boston: Bergin and Garvey Press.

Weiner, G. (1994). *Feminisms in education.* Buckingham, England: Open University Press.

Weiss, L. (1995). Qualitative research in sociology of education: Reflections on the 1970s and beyond. In W. T. Pink & G. W. Noblit (Eds.), *Continuity and contradiction: The futures of the sociology of education.* Cresskill, NJ: Hampton Press.

Wells, A. S., & Oakes, J. (1996). Potential pitfalls of systematic reform: Early lessons from research on detracking. *Sociology of Education, Special Issue on Sociology of Education and Educational Policy,* 135–143.

Wells, A. S., & Serna, I. (1996). The politics of culture: Understanding local political resistance to detracking in racially mixed schools. *Harvard Educational Review, 66,* 93–118.

Wesselingh, A. (1996). The Dutch sociology of education: Its origins, significance and future. *British Journal of Sociology of Education, 17,* 212–226.

Wexler, P. (1987). *Social analysis of education: After the new sociology.* London: Routledge & Kegan Paul.

Whitty, G. (1985). *Sociology and school knowledge: Curriculum theory, research and politics.* London: Methuen.

Willis, P. (1977). *Learning to labour: How working class kids get working class jobs.* Westmead, UK: Saxon House.

Woods, P. (1983). *Sociology and the school: An interactionist viewpoint.* London: Routledge and Kegan Paul.

Young, I. M. (1990). *Justice and the politics of difference.* Princeton, NJ: Princeton University Press.

Young, I. M. (1998, January). Public address as a sign of political inclusion. [Public lecture given in Belfast, Northern Ireland].

Young, M. F. D. (Ed., 1971). *Knowledge and control.* Middlesex, England: Collier Macmillan.

CHAPTER 5

Structural Effects in Education

A History of an Idea

Robert Dreeben

There are strong reasons to believe that schools have an impact on the students who attend them. How large and what kind of impact and how to formulate and interpret it are questions that have drawn the attention of sociologists of education for several decades. This area of inquiry has roots in the general sociological question of how to understand the influence of social structure on individual conduct. The school effects example of this question has relied heavily on a particular kind of structural effects argument originating with Durkheim and has undergone conceptual elaboration since his time. In treating the problem of school effects, the position I adopt places strong emphasis on school organization because the impact of school-ing on students occurs in an organizational setting, and much of the research explicitly or implicitly takes that into account. This emphasis does not deny the importance of influences whose origins lie outside of organizations, but it does explain why I do not focus on them.

Structural effects arguments are explanatory. They deal with structural arrangements, their effects, and the mechanisms by which one influences the other; mechanisms are the heart of the explanation. Explanatory arguments require selection among substantive ideas and evidence about social phenomena, in the present case about what is organizationally important, and among methods—design, logic, and measurement. These two considerations, substance and method, although analytically distinct, are not wholly so in reality. There is tension between them because some substantive formulations overburden the available methods, and some methods limit the range of testable substantive ideas.

The problems that school organization, schooling, and their effects pose for explanatory arguments include the following: capturing the work activities of teachers, school officials,

ROBERT DREEBEN • Department of Education, University of Chicago, Chicago, Illinois 60637

Handbook of the Sociology of Education, edited by Maureen T. Hallinan. Kluwer Academic/Plenum Publishers, New York, 2000.

and students; the opportunities and constraints governed by time schedules, hierarchical and collegial arrangements, spatial settings, and curricular agendas; the relation of school and district organization to such lateral entities as the labor market for teachers and patterned parental interest organized in communities and in households; and patterns of action and interaction occurring in the context of these considerations. It has been easy to devise defensible indications of school outcomes in individual students, harder to identify appropriate structural properties of schools, and daunting to conceptualize and determine the mechanisms in play at points where structure and individuals come together in the ongoing work of schooling. Sociologists have approached school effects problems from a variety of perspectives using a variety of methodologies, but it is not my purpose to review them. This chapter is about the history of an idea—structural effects—that, I maintain, has held a pre-eminent position in efforts to understand schooling.

The burden of the argument is to show how this formulation, derived from Durkheim, flourished in the intellectual environment of the Columbia Department of Sociology from the late 1930s to the late 1950s, became transformed over the next 10 years in Coleman's work, and subsequently achieved long-term durability despite evidence of its limitations. The structural effects formulation, although not unknown in other areas of sociology (e.g., Berelson, Lazarsfeld, & McPhee, 1954; Bulmer, 1984; Davis, 1961, 1966; Kerr & Siegel, 1954; Key, 1950; Kobrin, 1951; Lieberson, 1958; Schwartz, 1975; Shaw, 1924; Shaw & McKay, 1942; Stinchcombe, 1959; Stolzenberg, 1978), does not appear to be as dominant elsewhere as in studies of schools.

Two studies stand out for having made the structural effects formulation explicit. In 1959, Wilson published "Residential Segregation of Social Classes and Aspirations of High School Boys." His analytic scheme, which treated social class at the individual and school levels, became paradigmatic in the treatment of how schools influence aspirations, attainment, and other life chances. Blau published "Structural Effects" (1960) in the same journal a few months later. Both articles employed the same structural effects formulation but extracted it from strikingly different origins. Blau's (1955, 1960) study derived from a Columbia sociology tradition concerned with structural analysis; Wilson's came from work on stratification and the social psychology of group influences on individuals. Blau expressed his formulation generally, to apply beyond his study of public service agencies (1955); Wilson's dealt just with schools. The principle underlying both was that net of the effect of an individual characteristic believed to shape a pattern of conduct, a group property based on the aggregation of that characteristic influences that conduct.

Wilson (1959) opened with three propositions. First, social classes differ according to their value systems, a claim based on Hyman's study, "The Value Systems of Different Classes" (1953), which argued that individuals tend to have value preferences related to their social class membership, and that classes can be characterized according to their values. This position held currency at the time, informing studies of class-based and ethnic-based patterns of child rearing (e.g., Bronfenbrenner, 1958; Miller & Swanson, 1958; Strodtbeck, 1958). Wilson saw individual values originating in the value climate of school society (p. 836), based on the class composition of residential neighborhoods, providing "a significant *normative reference* influencing the educational aspirations of boys from varying strata . . . " (p. 837; my italics). Second, according to early studies of status attainment (Kahl, 1953; Sewell, Haller, & Straus, 1957), the educational aspirations of students are related to their social origins. Third, consistent with evidence adduced by Asch (1952), Katz and Lazarsfeld (1955), and Newcomb (1958), individual conduct and judgment are shaped by hierarchic pressures from superordinates and by lateral ones from peers. Together these propositions identify Wilson's position on how schools exert normative influence on individual aspirations.

Blau's (1955, 1960) view of structure was more complex and nuanced than Wilson's, and was not limited to normative force. The logic of structural effects reasoning in both works was identical, but the conceptual development differed. Blau drew attention to Durkheimian social facts. He distinguished social facts based on "common values and norms embodied in a culture or subculture" from those based on "networks of social relations" (1960, p. 78) expressed in social interactions organized around individuals' social positions and subgroup memberships. Wilson (1959) expressed structure narrowly as normative climate, with his infusion of school structure with normative meaning being entirely speculative. Blau extended the meaning to include social cohesiveness and networks of worker interaction, within and across levels of hierarchy and between workers and clients, and identified through empirical observation.

THE DURKHEIMIAN TRADITION

Juxtaposing collective and individual considerations to explain conduct is central to Durkheim's analysis of social facts: "ways of acting, thinking, and feeling, external to the individual, and endowed with a power of coercion, by reason of which they control him" (Durkheim, 1895/ 1938, p. 3). Social facts can include, for example, systems of currency, professional practices (p. 2), technical methods of production (p. 3), "legal and moral regulations, religious faiths, financial systems, etc." (p. 4), and forces external to individuals that constrain their conduct. Social facts vary from the most to the least articulated and structured (pp. 8–12). He stressed that even though individuals act freely according to their own dispositions, their conduct in the context of social facts showed "astonishing regularity" (p. 94).

Durkheim, (1897/1951) employed the concept of social facts in *Suicide*, which contains apposite examples of structural effects reasoning; namely, a state of society, a rate of individual conduct, and a linking mechanism. For example, he examined the impact of family circumstances on suicide rates, taking into account sex, marital condition, the presence of children, and age (p. 197–198). To demonstrate the causative impact of social states, he showed, against a baseline rate among the unmarried, in the relevant age categories, how the presence of children reduced the suicide rate among husbands and widowers with children, compared to those without children; the same pattern held among wives and widows, with rates differing in magnitude by sex. His explanation for the prevention of (egoistic) suicide emphasized the integrative state of domestic society (p. 201) and "the intensity of the collective life circulating in it" (p. 202); it discounted one based on the affectionate feelings of parents for their children.

Durkheim (1897/1951) did not observe social integration or the events of family life indicative of it; he conjectured about them to identify a social mechanism that linked structural properties of families with conduct (rates of spousal and parental suicide). He applied a similar explanatory logic to analyze varying suicide rates in geographical regions that differed in the proportion of Catholics and Protestants and to suicide rates in the military (as well as to other topics), demonstrating the importance of both deviance from and conformity to social norms (e.g., the proscription against suicide in both confessions). Later work on school effects grew from his conception of social facts and structural effects, cultivated by sociologists at Columbia, in an oddly inconspicuous way.

Blau's early studies of organizational work groups fell squarely in the Durkheimian tradition, with debts also to Weber and to Simmel. His studies of public agencies distinguished two kinds of work groups characterized by prevailing value orientation toward clients, classified case workers according to this orientation, and ascertained their conduct in serving clients. Findings showed that group values influenced conduct in the same direction among individuals who both resembled each other and differed in their orientations (1960, p. 181), hence the structural effect. The mechanism entailed sanctioning through social interaction in work groups: perfunctory service to clients received social disapprobation, dedicated service brought approval and respect.

In "Structural Effects," Blau (1955, 1960; Blau & Scott, 1962, pp. 87–115) described how the normative and interactive elements of climate jointly affected conduct. His formulation involved detailed observations of sanctioning, consulting, helping, supervising, and other activities transpiring over time through the interactions of daily work, not just the identification of group properties and of individual characteristics. As his treatment of patterns of consultation and rule enforcement and of collegiality and authority in public agencies showed (1955), he saw both conformity to and violation of norms in the framework of how authority is exercised and in workers' relations to their superiors and their clients. The conceptual strategy for treating structural effects differed from Wilson's (1959) which privileged normative influences as the mechanism by which structure influenced aspirations.

THE COLUMBIA TRADITION

Substance

Relations between social structure and patterns of individual conduct received extensive attention from the 1930s through the 1950s in the Department of Sociology at Columbia, especially from Merton and Lazarsfeld. The connection between their contributions (and of their students Blau and Coleman, among others) and Durkheim is unmistakable. Hauser (1971, pp. 13–14) was the first to point out the influence of Columbia sociology on the later use of contextual analysis (structural effects) in education.

One of Merton's elaborations of Durkheim appeared in his essay on deviance, "Social Structure and Anomie" (1938), whose "primary aim is to discover how *some social structures exert a definite pressure upon certain persons in the society to engage in non-conformist rather than conformist conduct*" (p. 672; Merton's italics). The argument linked rates of behavior to elements of social structure. The latter referred to conjunctions of "cultural goals" (cultural structure, or values), and "institutional norms" (prescription, preference, permission, proscription) as they applied to the means of pursuing legitimate objectives (p. 673). As to conduct, where Durkheim stressed the external constraint of social facts, Merton recognized normative constraint on the use of means and viewed conduct as "types of [role] adaptation" (p. 676) to circumstances defined by culturally valued goals and institutionalized means. The acceptance and/or rejection of such goals and means defined the five "modes of individual adaptation" (conformity, innovation, ritualism, retreatism, and rebellion p. 676) of his familiar typology. Individuals behave more like actors in Merton's scheme than in Durkheim's; they cope in patterned ways with conjunctions and disjunctions between goals and means. Merton dispensed with the idea of social current; variants of it (e.g., value community, ethos), however, reappeared later in research on school effects.

About two decades after "Social Structure and Anomie" appeared, Merton (1957a) elaborated on it in "Continuities in the Theory of Social Structure and Anomie" and modified the definition of social structure. The 1938 definition of "cultural structure" remained the same, but by 1957 social structure referred to "that *organized set of social relationships* in which members of the society or group are variously implicated" (p. 162; my italics). This revision did not displace the earlier definition of social structure as legitimized means, but rather took account of individuals' situations as they acted. Social structure consisted of positions and statuses that limited or enabled the culturally prescribed actions of the individuals occupying them (p. 162). This formulation identified situations—structural circumstances (later elaborated as "opportunity structure"; Merton, 1959, 1995; Stinchcombe, 1990)—based, for example, on status or on class (though not limited to them), affecting the likelihood that individual conduct will utilize institutionalized means.

Merton advocated the detailed description of social conduct. Discussing Cohen's *Delinquent Boys* (1955), for example, he noticed the careful portrayal of the nonutilitarian character of delinquent behavior ignored by previous writers on the topic and not adequately addressed by the theory of anomie. To explain delinquent behavior,

> one must presumably look to the social interaction among these like-minded deviants who mutually reinforce their deviant attitudes and behavior which, in the theory, result from the more or less common situation [of disjointed ends and means] in which they find themselves. (Merton, 1957a, pp. 178–9)

He maintained that not all individuals exposed to the same conditions deal with them the same way. That not all aspects of conduct are explained by the theory of anomie, and that rates of conduct vary under the same circumstances suggest that attention must be paid to the mechanisms (Merton, 1949) by which social conditions influence conduct. This is to explain why, given common circumstances, some engage in certain patterns of action whereas others do not. These mechanisms, he believed, can be found in patterns of interaction (though not only there) revealed in appropriate descriptions of social phenomena. He followed a similar line of analysis in "Bureaucratic Structure and Personality" (1940) to explain the structural origins of bureaucratic overconformity, a type of deviance.

Merton's essays of the 1930s and 1940s developed a theoretical position that drew on and elaborated on Durkheim's treatment of how social structure and individual conduct were connected. The arguments built theoretical principles from illustrations and from the clarification of concepts. In later work, inspired by the depiction of World War II military life found in *The American Soldier* (Stouffer, Lunsdaine, et al., 1949a; Stouffer, Suchman, deVinney, Star, & Williams, 1949b), he pursued this problem area with greater reliance on quantitative analysis than in the past. The landmark publication illustrating this was the essay, "Contributions to the Theory of Reference Group Behavior" (Merton & Kitt, 1950). One of its tasks was to develop propositions that subsumed ostensibly disparate findings in *The American Soldier*, a treasury of survey evidence on soldiers' beliefs, attitudes, assessments of circumstances, definition of situations, complaints, and satisfactions related to their structural locations in both civilian and in military life. These locations were defined by opportunities and by constraints influencing how soldiers tried to achieve culturally emphasized goals using institutionalized means (Merton, 1959; 1964 p. 216; Stinchcombe, 1990).

Although Merton and Kitt (1950) devoted much of the text to this task, they also dwelt on how to characterize such elements of social structure as opportunities for promotion in different branches of the Army (p. 53), group contexts defined by aggregating individual characteristics (p. 71), the "open or closed character of the social structure" (p. 89), and social aggregates defined as actual groups or as categories.

> Once ... indices [of social structure] are established, it becomes possible to have systematic. . .comparisons of the behaviors of people of similar class status living within differently proportioned class structures ... [O]ther types of social differentiation can be indexed by the frequency distributions of various statuses (education, race, age, *etc.*) and combined with the systematic study of individuals similarly situated within these varying structures. (p. 83)

This statement expresses the logic of structural (contextual) effects. The Merton–Kitt essay was primarily a work of social psychology. Identifying group characteristics was subsidiary and was treated primarily to identify definitions of situations that influenced attitudes, self-assessments, mobility, and individual action. Merton (1957b) later reanalyzed and elaborated the 1950 essay in "Continuities in the Theory of Reference Groups and Social Structure", which devoted more attention to social organization and group properties than its predecessor.

In part of "Continuities' ... " Merton (1957b) reworked the 1950 essay to expand his views on the properties of groups. Among them were the concepts of collectivity (a group whose members interact, share, and abide by norms) and category (aggregates of persons with similar characteristics [e.g., age, sex, race], but who do not necessarily interact or share norms). Social categories can become transformed into cohesive collectivities, but the distinction between collectivities and categories suggests that aggregating individual characteristics into social categories does not necessarily indicate a normative climate. Identifying climates requires demonstrating that a category is also a collectivity exerting normative influence. He devoted part of this essay to an inventory of structural properties: among them clarity of definition of membership, completeness of membership, differentiation, visibility of conduct, group autonomy or independence, and toleration of deviant or variant behavior (pp. 308–326), thereby expanding the idea of structure beyond Durkheim's concept of social facts and his treatment of how social facts influence conduct through "Attachment to Groups" in *Moral Education* (Durkheim, 1902–1903, 1961).

These essays, and others not cited here, were emblematic of a Columbia tradition of dealing with the connection between individuals and social structure. Another characteristic of that tradition was the priority given to single and to comparative organizational case studies relying on observational, survey, documentary, and intensive interview methodologies, among them Blau's *Dynamics of Bureaucracy* (1955), Gouldner's *Patterns of Industrial Bureaucracy* (1954), and Lipset, Trow, and Coleman's *Union Democracy* (1956). These studies examined variations in the division of labor, authority relations, cohesion, rules and norms, personnel policies, methods of production, work and nonwork activities, controls, sanctions, and patterns of interaction among workers and officials and between them and others situated outside the work setting. They demonstrated connections between social structure and individual conduct through descriptions of ongoing social events, portraying social life in organizations with greater richness and variety than Durkheim could express by demonstrating empirical relations between rates of social conduct and aggregate group characteristics. What distinguished this work was not so much its fieldwork methodology (although that was important), but that it conceptualized ongoing social processes and their relation to organizational structure.

Method

Kendall and Lazarsfeld (1950), in "Problems of Survey Analysis," also employed evidence from *The American Soldier* (Stouffer, Suchman, et al., 1949b; Stouffer, A. A. Lumsdaine, et al., 1949a), but to develop a general logic of survey analysis. They examined, for example, the case of soldiers with higher levels of education being more likely than those with lower levels to say that they had volunteered or should not have been deferred. Kendall and Lazarsfeld interpreted the finding by arguing that better educated soldiers accepted induction because they came from civilian environments in which few men were deferred, and thus had no legitimate expectation of deferment because of their education (p. 149). This interpretation was based on soldiers' membership in a social category (i.e., an environment with infrequent deferments) affecting their self-assessments and beliefs about the appropriateness of being in the Army; based primarily on soldiers' thought processes, it may or may not have been correct. Whatever the case, the purpose of the exercise was more to develop a logic of analysis than to pursue the substantive details empirically.

To explore structural effects, Kendall and Lazarsfeld (1950) developed a formalization of connections between descriptions of individuals (personal data) and of aggregates, interactions, categories, and groups (unit data), creating a typology to represent how personal data and unit data are layered to express relations among levels of aggregation. This effort concluded with a discussion of whether personal data and unit data can be used interchangeably, a question that comes down to us as ecological correlation (Robinson, 1950) and as the ecological fallacy (Selvin, 1958, 1960). "Our main interest here is directed toward the *logical relationship* between personal data and unit data" (Kendall & Lazarsfeld, p. 188; my italics), toward developing general principles of data analysis applicable to surveys regardless of content. This enterprise differed from Merton's.

Lazarsfeld and Menzel (1961), paralleling Merton's (1957b) classification of group characteristics, developed "A Typology of Properties Describing 'Collectives' and 'Members'" (p. 526). Selvin and Hagstrom (1963) later proposed a more systematic version of the Kendall–Lazarsfeld–Menzel scheme. The former referred to properties intrinsic to any level of group—individual, pair, primary and secondary group, total society—each of which could be aggregated upward, so that an "integral characteristic becomes the basis for aggregative characteristics of successively higher-level groups" (p. 404); moving toward smaller units, "an individual or a group below the total society can be described 'contextually' by the characteristics of successively larger groups to which it belongs (p. 404). Selvin (1960) also identified subtle and insidious forms of the ecological fallacy. This interest in group properties, in levels of aggregation, and in the connection between social structure and individual conduct characterized Columbia sociology for more than two decades, but scholars located elsewhere also contributed: Robinson (1950) on ecological correlation; Inkeles (1963) on the relation between psychological and sociological levels of analysis; Davis (1966) and his colleagues on statistical problems in analyzing individual and collective evidence (Davis, Spaeth, & Huson, 1961; Tannenbaum & Bachman, 1964).

There are palpable differences between styles of work emphasizing general analytic methods and those focused on descriptive analysis, though they should not be exaggerated. Related to this distinction is a preference for the generalizing efforts of surveys and the particularizing character of case studies, though neither one precludes the other. An early attempt to reconcile the two can be found in Coleman's essay, "Relational Analysis: The Study of Social Organizations with Survey Methods" (1958-59), a discussion of how to develop indices of social structure using surveys. He drew his examples from Columbia studies exemplifying structural effects and the use of sociometric methods to characterize networks. (*The Adolescent Society* [Coleman, 1961] employed this strategy.) A major theme of his article, however, was to show how advancements in computer technology could contribute to new survey methods designed to investigate social organization (1958–59, p. 28) by adapting them to deal with relationships as units of analysis and by avoiding the atomism of past survey methodology.

It would be misleading to suggest that Columbia sociology at the time bifurcated into methodological and substantive camps. Yet the affinities between Merton and Blau, on the one hand, and between Lazarsfeld and Coleman, on the other, are unmistakable. Blau's agenda was to explore the nature of work and authority in organizations. He employed a Durkheim-inspired methodology to examine substantive propositions about organizations derived largely from Weber (via Merton, 1940; Merton, Gray, Hockey, & Selvin, 1952). Coleman contributed to the organizational analysis of the International Typographical Union (Lipset et al., 1956) but later moved away from questions about organizational structure and toward the application of survey methods to studying school organization and its effects. The subsequent history of the sociology of education was powerfully influenced by this development in his thinking, particularly by *Equality of Educational Opportunity* (Coleman et al., 1966), a study whose reliance on survey methods minimized the attention it could pay to the particulars of school organization. That history was also influenced by the fact that those who participated in Columbia's tradition of organizational analysis (e.g., Blau, 1955; Chinoy, 1955; Gouldner, 1954; Lipset, 1950; Lipset et al., 1956; Selznick, 1949; Sills, 1957) had little if any interest in research on educational organization (save for Blau's [1973] and Lazarsfeld and Thielens's [1958] studies of academia).

Lazarsfeld and Merton (1954) addressed the difference between the two styles of social science in their essay "Friendship as A Social Process" on the formation of and change in friendship patterns among residents of housing projects to demonstrate both the complementarity and distinctiveness of the two perspectives (p. 19). Merton's section of the essay dealt with how friendships form, continue, and dissolve (p. 24); it conceptualized interaction and social process and the structures emerging from them over time. Lazarsfeld's section formalized the argument. The implication of this joint effort was that methodology should be directed as much to understand the structure, the interaction patterns, and the mechanisms of social process as to codify the analysis of empirical associations. The larger point was that the two perspectives were applied together, guided by the formulation and analysis of a substantive question. Lazarsfeld's section brought little to the essay that was not already available in Kendall and Lazarsfeld (1950), except as it applied to friendship. It is hard to imagine Lazarsfeld's section preceding Merton's, which is not to gainsay the former's contribution to identifying gaps in the substantive argument and in generalizing it. The Lazarsfeld–Merton essay brought together two strands of the Columbia tradition, one based on the logic of survey analysis, the other on organizational studies and their concern with social form and process. It is difficult to detect any residue it may have left in later studies of school effects.

COLEMAN'S CONTRIBUTION

Equality of Educational Opportunity (EEO; Coleman et al., 1966) manifested an implicit connection between the idea of school climate and its intellectual antecedents in Durkheim, mediated through Columbia sociology. A curiosity of this work is the inexplicitness of its conceptual scheme and origins. That EEO does not treat its own origins, however, does not mean it lacks them. The conventional view is that EEO employed the economic formulation of the production function, a form of input–output analysis (Averch, Carroll, Donaldson, Kiesling & Pincus, 1972; Hanushek, 1986; Lau, 1979), and in a partial sense this is so. It was also propelled by an unexpressed argument originating in the same traditions that generated the formulations of Wilson and Blau. The structure–conduct linkage in that argument, moreover, is highly compatible with the input–output logic of production functions.

EEO's (Coleman et al., 1966) conception of school organization can be read from Section 3.2, "Relation of School Factors to Achievement" (pp. 290–325). That analysis included aggregated school characteristics (e.g., average teacher educational level, racial composition), individual characteristics statistically controlled (e.g., social background, race/ethnicity), and school properties (e.g., facilities and curriculum) to assess their impact on individual achievement. It led to such conclusions as the following: "The higher achievement of all racial and ethnic groups in schools with greater proportions of white students is largely, perhaps wholly, related to effects associated with the student body's educational background and aspirations" (p. 307); this is a standard structural effects proposition. EEO also contained analyses that related school facilities and curriculum (e.g., labs, accelerated curriculum, guidance facilities, teacher characteristics, grouping and tracking; and school size—aggregated or global school properties) to individual achievement. What happens in schools and what mechanisms operate so that such properties influence individual achievement? We don't know.

Although the logic of EEO's (Coleman et al, 1966) analysis is clear, it contained no conceptualization and description of school organization and the schooling process beyond the summation of plausible but ad hoc school characteristics. The contrast with *Union Democracy* is striking. In his studies of schools Coleman over time de-emphasized the substantive treatment of work and its settings, of occupation, and of organizational structure that characterized *Union Democracy* (and other organizational studies). This was anomalous in light of his report on the major intellectual influences on him during his years at Columbia (Coleman, 1990a). In that account, he described how Lipset approached the difficulties of combining "macrosocial problems and sample survey techniques" (p. 95).

> Although quantitative analyses of the survey data can be found throughout the book and indeed are central to the study, it was the *framework of ideas from social theory* that generated the analyses . . . [T]he initial ideas were richly developed, elaborated, and modified by the data (p. 95; Coleman's italics),

gathered by observation and by interview, and gathered from historical materials and from union publications. Despite the positive sentiments he expressed in his retrospective essay, he proceeded to follow an approach to educational research that drew far more from Lazarsfeld than from Lipset and others in the Columbia organizational tradition, as evidenced by his first book, *The Adolescent Society* (Coleman, 1961), later by EEO and subsequently by his studies of the public and private educational sectors. The latter relied on evidence from large-scale cross-sectional and later longitudinal surveys whose formulation and design bore Lazarsfeld's stamp; through them he became a major force in shaping how we look at schools and their effects.

The Adolescent Society (Coleman, 1961) employed survey methods to investigate 10 secondary schools. The formulation of both adolescent society and of school was built on the concept of "value climate" to explain patterns of individual behavior, with climate referring both to a societal phenomenon, similar to Durkheim's notion of "current," and to its manifestations in different schools. The book employed a conception of adolescence as a life-cycle stage where "the child of high-school age. . .is 'cut off' from the rest of society, forced inward toward his own age group, made to carry out his whole social life with others his own age . . . [and] maintains only a few threads of connection with the outside adult society" (p. 3).

The value climate of schools was the main organizing principle, but whether it was the main force at work is an open question (Coleman, 1961). The chapter "Scholastic Effects of the Social System," for example, presented a familiar kind of contextual analysis: within schools, Coleman showed relations between the education of students' parents and academic outcomes (e.g., hours per day studying, intention to go to college). Identifying the source of variation in outcomes is difficult, however; although the text attributed it sometimes to the value (or so-cial) climate of the schools, one cannot distinguish this influence from the variety of other school characteristics identified (but not treated systematically) or from the societal notion of adolescent culture. Though he gathered information about the schools, he treated them as internally undifferentiated and thereby put mechanisms linking adolescent culture to outcomes out of reach. (Note that although he presented sociograms that differed by school, these fig-ured in identifying different kinds of adolescent subgroupings, not in explaining scholastic effects.) This study, along with Wilson's (1959) article, solidified the concept of the school value climate as a conventional assumption in subsequent work on school effects.

EEO (Coleman et al., 1966) took an additional step away from organizational analysis, bolstered by the advent of high-speed computers that handled multivariate regression with huge samples of participants and many variables. This capacity allowed the use of large-scale surveys for their obvious advantages, while reducing the likelihood of considering aspects of school organization and functioning not readily revealed by such methods. It would be wrong to argue, however, that EEO took no substantive position on school organization. That posi-tion, however, could only be inferred from the actual variables employed to describe school characteristics because EEO lacked explicit substantive arguments about social structure, the schooling process, and how work is organized and carried out. Yet, no one else at that time had developed persuasive formulations of these matters with respect to schools and to schooling even though this sort of conceptualizing had occurred in other fields, most notably in studies of industry, of government, of hospitals, of voluntary associations (political parties and unions), and of the military.

EEO's (Coleman et al., 1966) influence on the subsequent agenda of the sociology of education has been colossal. It became a prototype (with variations) for later investigations rooted more in the Lazarsfeld than in the Merton style, exploiting the advantages of survey design and analysis more than the substantive investigation of school organization and of schooling. It stimulated the employment of large surveys to study educational effects, solidi-fied the use of structural (contextual) effects designs, and introduced school properties other than normative climate into the analysis of school effects. Yet it provided little direct stimula-tion to the analysis of school structure, educational work, and the schooling process—to the issues that the substantive tradition at Columbia might have inspired in studies of education, but did not.

FURTHER DEVELOPMENTS: PRO AND CON

EEO (Coleman et al., 1966) was not the sole influence on future approaches to educational effects; other investigations pursued parallel interests employing similar formulations. Michael (1961), analyzing evidence from a national study, aimed to discover whether family status or ability was a better predictor of college attendance depending on the social-class climate of the school, with individual family status held constant. This work recast earlier studies by Kahl (1953) and by Sewell and colleagues (1957) into a structural effects framework, but it did so by conflating a variety of other school characteristics (e.g., percent seniors enrolled in college curriculum, size of community library, seniors whose best friend plans college, etc.) with class-based school climate. Michael (1961) expressed his argument in a predictive frame-work and demonstrated conditional relations among ability, family status, school climate, and college plans—as anticipated. Even though this study was not designed to explore the mean-ing of climate or to discover how it fit into some causal process, it inadvertently anticipated difficulties that would subsequently emerge: when a variety of school properties are treated simultaneously with aggregate status under the rubric of climate, it is impossible to tell whether school climate or other conditions correlated with it influence the outcome.

In contrast, Rogoff's [Ramsøy] (1961) analysis of the same data was an attempt to identify the "social process," sequence of events, and "social mechanisms" (p. 241) by which amount of education is directly related to adult social status. She considered three explanations: family influences on academic motivation, the positive scholastic impact of schools on able students whatever their class origins, and community compositional influences both in support of schools as cultural institutions and manifest in school normative climate (pp. 242–243). With respect to structural effects, she noted the importance of the classroom, through the mechanism of its rewards and punishments, as an influence on ability and motivations and as resulting in differing levels of achievement; that is, interaction effects between talent and the school's system of rewards. She also considered the contextual effects of town, suburban, and city school location, presumably operating through normative climates. However, why climates should vary by type of community is not clear. Rogoff was clearly interested in the problem of mechanisms and saw them residing in the "educational experience" (p. 250) that schools provide. However, in the absence of direct evidence about the classroom and its "reward–punishment system," and of the normative impact of communities and schools, mechanisms remained conjectural.

Boyle (1966a), reviewing earlier studies of socioeconomic composition effects, asked why there should be contextual effects and by what mechanisms they occurred: peer group culture, the pedagogical characteristics of schools, values and attitudes, or scholastic abilities (p. 628). He devised two explanatory arguments: first, schools differ in their success at developing knowledge and skills; second, they influence attitudes, values, and motivation to attend college. Concerning the first, Boyle drew upon Rogoff's (1961) idea that the structure of national educational systems (p. 631) should be taken into account (e.g., the decentralized character of the American system, allowing variation in educational quality school-by-school, in contrast to the more provincially centralized Canadian system). Second, he alluded to the normative pressure generated among students related to the social-class composition of schools. Limitations of his data prevented Boyle from employing satisfactory measures of instructional adequacy. He ended up interpreting his evidence as Wilson would have ("students in generally middle-class schools who lack . . . [a strong academic background] appear to be carried along by the majority" [p. 634]; note the similarity to Berelson and associates' concept of the "breakage effect" [1954, pp. 98–101]). In so doing he presented a structural effects argument that spanned several levels of educational systems including the knowledge-imparting curricular function of schools in addition to normative climate transmitted through interaction.

By the late 1960s, the drift of investigations revealed the widespread currency of structural effects arguments, but Sewell and Armer (1966a) expressed doubt about them. Their position resembled Wilson's: neighborhood contexts represent subcommunities reflected in the composition of student populations within which normative climates form that influence the aspirations of all youth, irrespective of individual social status and ability (pp. 161–162). Sewell and Armer maintained, however, that neighborhood context made little contribution to explaining college plans independent of "traditional variables" (p. 167), an assessment affirmed by Brown and House (1967) and by Hauser (1970, 1971). Their conclusion also took a poke at recent claims about neighborhood effects, which "may be traced to popular assessments of American education by various educational authorities" (p. 160), a snide reference to Conant (1961) and his book, *Slums and Suburbs*.

Proponents of contextual analysis (Boyle, 1966a; Michael, 1966; Turner, 1966) leapt to their own defense; Sewell and Armer (1966b) rejoined. Most of this debate addressed technicalities of definition, of method, of design, of inference, and of causal order. Little of it addressed the substantive meaning of context and what happens in neighborhoods and schools, which, according to Sewell and Armer, "need to be measured directly and appropriately *rather than inferred from the social-class composition* of the school or the neighborhood" (p. 711; my italics). Michael (1966), taking umbrage at Sewell and Armer's (1966b) dig at educational authorities, thought that sociological paternity should prevail because Durkheim's *Suicide* was published sufficiently long ago "to elevate contextual analysis from the status of fad to tradition" (1966, p. 706). Aside from the parties to this debate airing technical matters, Sewell and Armer (1966b) raised an important point about structural effects arguments (but without supplying substantive remedies): the need for more direct measurement of what context means and less reliance on conjectural inference from compositional measures.

The period from the late 1960s through the 1980s witnessed further developments in the area of structural effects, some extending and elaborating it, others questioning its conceptual and methodological soundness. Earlier, Robinson (1950) aimed a salvo at its underpinnings. He doubted "whether ecological correlations can validly be used as substitutes for individual correlations" (p. 357), except under unlikely conditions, because a correlation between two characteristics of individuals in a population will not necessarily be the same when calculated in subgroups. Hauser (1970) extended this line of criticism with a broader methodological critique in "Context and Consex: A Cautionary Tale" and in a more complete and detailed statement in *Socioeconomic Background and Educational Performance* (1971). The logic of his argument was similar, the intent different. He was more concerned with how to establish structural conditions as causes of individual conduct than with whether ecological correlation will serve as a defensible expedient when individual-level data are unavailable.

> The contextual fallacy occurs when residual differences among a set of social groups, which remain after the effects of one or more individual attributes have been partialed out, are interpreted in terms of *social or psychological mechanisms* correlated with group levels of one of the individual attributes. (1970, p. 659; my italics)

Criticizing Blau, Hauser (1970) noted that equating group differences with "the social" and individual differences with "the psychological" represented "a misunderstanding of statistical aggregation and of social process" (p. 13). He was mainly concerned with properly modeling social process, jointly implicating both individual and structural considerations, though he did not construct a substantive argument about school organization and schooling. (Blau's analysis, however, did not really depend on a sharp distinction between the "social" and the "psychological.") Hauser questioned the defensibility of contextual arguments: they can be arbitrary, because selecting one contextual variable does not rule out the appropriateness of others or of individual explanations. They fail to identify internal mechanisms because they assign school-level properties to all students and do not distinguish selection based on the dependent variable from a contextual effect (Hauser, 1971, p. 32, 1974). A key issue was whether mechanisms can be identified, a point where Hauser joined Sewell and Armer.

Campbell and Alexander (1965) also found difficulty with structural effects arguments over the issue of mechanisms. They drew on earlier research that emphasized the significance of personal interaction with school peers. " . . . [A]nalyses of 'structural effects,'" they maintained, must move "from the characteristics of the total system to the situation faced by the individual due to the effects of these characteristics and then from the social situation confronting the individual to his responses to it" (pp. 284–285). Context represented opportunities for interaction with friends planning to attend college. The larger the pool of high socioeconomic status peers in the school, the greater the chance of finding such friends (an argument reminiscent of *Union Democracy's* discussion of the relation between chapel size and political participation). They found that the correlation between school status and college plans was reduced with friends' status (a proxy for peer group relations) held constant, but that between friends' status and plans was not reduced with school status held constant. This suggested that interaction among friends was the mediating mechanism, constrained by opportunities for interaction, rather than by school climate. Campbell and Alexander brought a familiar line of reasoning into play: individuals' values and attitudes develop through sustained interaction in social situations with others who are important to them. The mechanism is reciprocal interaction among friends, rather than the direct normative influence of school climate on conduct (Alexander & Campbell, 1964).

STRUCTURAL EFFECTS POST-EEO

The body of work just discussed was less about the nature of schools and schooling than about contextual analysis based primarily on neighborhoods and on schools as climates and on interaction among peers. EEO (Coleman et al., 1966) brought school characteristics into prominence because its commission (by the Civil Rights Act of 1964) mandated the examination of the degree to which White and Black students, as well as other minority group students, attended schools of comparable quality. It thus entered the realm of public policy controversy over civil rights, social equality, school desegregation, and educational excellence. This policy preoccupation would turn out to have a long life and influence how structural effects arguments colored school reform thinking in the 1980s and 1990s.

Publications appeared in the early 1970s reacting to EEO (Coleman et al., 1966), Mosteller and Moynihan's *On Equality of Educational Opportunity* (1972) prominent among them. Several of its constituent essays employed structural effects arguments; Armor's, for example, (1972, p. 176) noted problems of interpretation attributable to the ecological fallacy. McDill and Rigsby's *Structure and Process in Secondary Schools* (1973) questioned the overreliance on aggregate socioeconomic status to define school climate, an indirect measure from which normative influence was inferred (p. 20). Acknowledging that curriculum, teacher quality, physical facilities, structural features, and socioeconomic composition were proper subjects of investigation, they "concentrate[d] primarily on differences in what has been called educational and social climates among schools" (p. 2), measured directly rather than inferred. (For example, an emphasis [i.e., climate] on "Academic Emulation," based on questions tapping the academic side of school life, referred to a "general academic and intellectual tone" [p. 38]; similar concepts applied to five other dimensions of climate.) This conception was based on their belief that structural characteristics "are simply too gross" (p. 118) to explain academic performance, and on their earlier findings showing that the effects of nonclimate (structural) school characteristics were small (McDill, Rigsby, & Myers, 1969). They tested their conception of climate against the indirect form (inferred from aggregate school characteristics) and assessed the results of earlier studies of whether peer-group processes represented mechanisms by which climate influenced achievement and college plans. McDill and Rigsby reinforced the normative meaning of school climate.

Others (Brookover, Beady, Flood, Schweitzer, & Wisenbaker, 1979; Rutter, Maughan, Mortimore, & Ouston, 1979) expressed disbelief that the effects of school differences on achievement were as small as EEO (Coleman et al., 1966) reported. Brookover's methodology (like McDill and Rigsby's) used teachers, students, and principals as informants, summarizing their perceptions of norms and structure at the school level, and summed multiple indices of climate and structure into global measures. The result was to obscure how the components of school organization fit together and which components of the summary singly or in combination affected the outcomes (as in Michael, 1961). The mechanisms by which school organization and climate influenced outcomes (themselves aggregated) were indeterminate because there was no way to ascertain which students, whose achievement was expressed as a school rate, were subject to climate effects.

A study of 12 London secondary schools (Rutter et al., 1979) argued that EEO (Coleman, et al., 1966) was

> quite unable to consider whether children were influenced by differences in things such as the style or quality of teaching, the types of teacher–child interaction in the classroom, the overall social climate of the school, or its characteristics and qualities as a social organisation. (pp. 5, 31)

Rutter accordingly examined whether children's school experiences made a difference in outcomes. Acknowledging the importance of classroom instruction, he considered not the "details of curriculum," but "the broader curriculum of the social environment within which lesson teaching takes place" (p. 54). He gathered observations of classrooms, of school entry patterns, and of student placements in different kinds of courses and aggregated them at the school level to derive an abstract, global notion of school structure. This meant conceptually subordinating the direct influences of classroom organization, teaching practices, and social interaction (pp. 62–64) on students' experience. He maintained that the importance of school events and behavior was their contribution to "the *establishment of an ethos* which would enable *all* those in the school to function well" (p. 56; my italics).

This analysis distinguished several kinds of school process (e.g., academic emphasis, teacher action, rewards and punishments, etc.), each represented by a set of items and correlated with four school-level measures of outcome: attendance, student misbehavior, academic attainment, and delinquency. The numerous correlations differed widely in magnitude, which led to speculation about whether "process" should be construed as a multitude of unstable, substitutable effects or as a coherent phenomenon, identified by combining those items into a single index, strongly related to the outcomes. Rutter (1979) concluded:

> [T]he association between *combined* measure of overall school process and each of the measures of outcome was much stronger than any of the associations with individual process variables" [i.e., taken one at a time] . . . The implication is that the individual actions or measures may combine to create a particular *ethos*, or set of values, attitudes and behaviours which will become characteristic of the school as a whole. (p. 179; Rutter et al.'s italics)

The correlation of the global scale with the outcomes was strong. However, difficulties of interpretation arise, attributable to the combining of variables and to the familiar uncertainties of ecological correlation. Despite its critical posture toward EEO, the study employed the same form of analysis: it summed elements of school structure and operation and related them to outcomes, thereby sacrificing the portrayal of internal school life and the mechanisms by which ethos might affect outcomes.

The prevailing school effects formulation had by the late 1970s thoroughly absorbed Wilson's version of Durkheim's perspective. Though Blau and Wilson employed the same analysis, Wilson's conception, not Blau's, gained currency in its own right and also indirectly through Coleman's. It is also interesting that Durkheim's, Merton's, and Blau's concerns with deviance dropped from sight, as if conventionally salutary academic values could not have unanticipated consequences of a negative sort (Stinchcombe, 1964). Sociologists of education could have drawn from Blau as well as from other contributors to the field of organizations, such as Etzioni (1975), Homans (1950, 1974), Perrow (1970, 1972), and Stinchcombe (1959, 1965). The field might then have developed in quite different directions.

Since the late 1970s, studies employing structural effects arguments continued to appear (e.g., Alexander & Pallas, 1985; Kerckhoff, 1993; Lee & Bryk, 1988; McPartland & McDill, 1982; Willms, 1985) along with others showing the limits of their explanatory capability. Alwin and Otto (1977), for example, assessed the strength of aggregate school properties on aspirations and whether within-school variation in student characteristics accounted for those effects. It didn't and the context (climate) effects were small. Bidwell and Kasarda (1980) showed how reliance on aggregate measures reduced explanatory power and also drew attention to the importance of internal school processes—schooling—as mechanisms accounting for achievement differences. Gamoran (1987), analyzing the stratification of high school learning opportunities, showed that in six curricular areas, measures of school composition and course offerings added virtually nothing to the amount of variation in learning explained, and with few exceptions changed by trivial amounts, the values of coefficients representing student characteristics entered earlier into regression equations.

SCHOOL COMMUNITY

From the 1960s onward, public policy agendas shaped research on the effects of schools, first centered thematically on equality, and later on the alleged failures of schools and the proposed remedies of choice, vouchers, tax credits, charter and private schools, site-based management, decentralization, and community governance. Coleman, Hoffer, and Kilgore's *High School Achievement* (1982), Coleman and Hoffer's *Public and Private High Schools* (1987), and Bryk, Lee, and Holland's *Catholic Schools and the Common Good* (1993) represent works written in a genre of policy reform. All employed structural effects reasoning.

This interest in policy represented a thematic shift from research written to explore sociological themes without a policy subtext. There is an affinity between the stress on normative school climate in this work and its intent to reform schools, because attempts to effect change tend to be guided by value-laden definitions of desirable conditions and by the means to reach them. These three studies concerned themselves with applying the alleged benefits of private schools to the betterment of public schools. They also shared a premise that such different educational outcomes as achievement in school subjects, rates of dropping out, and student indiscipline, among others, can be explained by global properties of schools. The evidence they adduced shows that these outcomes vary according to their location in *sectors* of the educational system: public, Catholic, and private non-Catholic. Sectoral analyses compare individuals identified by their school attendance in one of the sectors and treat schools as possessing the characteristics of their respective sectors. School differences within sectors receive some attention; differences in educational experience within schools do not.

High School Achievement (Coleman et al., 1982) began with a discussion of policy considerations bearing on academic performance, post-high school educational plans, character development, and school safety and discipline, along with such undesirable outcomes as segregating talented students, fostering religious and racial divisiveness, and exaggerating competitiveness. It described the terms of public debate about whether private schools foster positive or negative outcomes more than public schools (pp. 4–5). Underlying the public–private distinction was the idea that public sector schools were organized around residence and that Catholic schools were organized around religious identity (p. xxix). These two principles of organization applied both to schools and to sectors, making them in effect conceptually isomorphic. The policy framework governing the comparison of public and private sectors (and schools) subordinated internal differences in school structure and schooling to commonalities across schools within sectors, thereby emphasizing differences between sectors. Yet precedent existed for treating the internal structure and operation of schools (e.g., Barr & Dreeben, 1977; Bidwell, 1965; Bidwell & Kasarda, 1980; Bossert, 1979; Fichter, 1958; McPherson, 1972; Metz, 1978; Rosenbaum, 1976; Sørensen, 1970; Sørensen & Hallinan, 1977; Stinchcombe, 1964; Swidler, 1979; Waller, 1961).

Coleman and associates (1982) showed that patterns of academic course taking, indiscipline, future academic plans, self-esteem, academic performance by subject (reading, vocabulary, and mathematics), and other considerations favored the Catholic sector (and other private sectors) over the public sector and for different student subpopulations. The mechanisms accounting for sectoral differences in outcome were coursework, homework, attendance, positive disciplinary climate, and good student behavior (p. 171). Accepting these conclusions at face value, however, requires hesitation because the characteristics of student populations and schools were measured by sector as if there were no structural variation within schools and among schools within sectors. This is because the initial residential versus religious community distinction provides no conceptual basis for considering within-sector and within-school variation. Sectoral differences can appear even when relations between school characteristics and outcomes deviate from the sectoral pattern or even contradict it (Hauser, 1971; Kendall & Wolf, 1949). However, if school deviations from a sectoral pattern occur, explaining school variation within sectors remains an issue that draws attention to events and to structures internal to schools.

Another analysis (Coleman and associates, 1982) demonstrated the relation of parental education and race/ethnicity, respectively, to achievement in each sector; it showed parental education to be less strongly related to student achievement in the Catholic sector than in the public sector (pp. 144). Parallel findings held for race/ethnicity. This pattern, called the "common school effect," was said to indicate that achievement differences in Catholic schools were less responsive to student class, race, and ethnic distinctions than in public schools. (Lee and Bryk, 1988, for example, adopted as a "premise that there is a more equitable distribution of achievement in Catholic schools than in public schools" [p. 79].)

Generalizations about the Catholic school advantage, the common school effect, and the relation between school and sector are germane to structural effects analysis. Coleman and Hoffer (1987) introduced the concepts of "functional" and "value" community to elaborate the meaning of sector and school. They based this distinction on the following historical narrative. In the 19th century there was coincidence between two school tasks: extending children's perspectives beyond the family to the wider culture (the public school perspective) and expressing families' values (the private school perspective). In time, because of immigration and the ensuing increase in ethnic and religious diversity, technological change, urbanization, and the growth of mass media, the historical coincidence disintegrated and yielded three separate and at times conflicting "orientations" to school organization: schools as agents "of the larger society" freeing children from parental constraints (pp. 24–25), of the religious community," and "of the individual family" (p. 24). (Historical scholarship [e.g., Axtell, 1974; Bridenbaugh, 1964; Brown, 1996; Demos, 1970; Kaestle, 1973, 1983; Morgan, 1966; Vinovskis, 1985) identifies aims of public schooling as combating parental neglect of children's educational needs, as creating an informed republican citizenry, and also as reflecting social cleavages within communities. These considerations cast some doubt on the primary significance of the three orientations.)

"Functional community" referred to

'closure' between the adult communities and the communities of youth in high school: Parents knew who their children's friends were and knew their parents. The norms that pervaded the school were in part those dictated by the needs of youth themselves, . . . but in part those established by the adult community and enforced by the intergenerational contact that this closure brought about" (Coleman & Hoffer, 1987, p. 7; Coleman elaborated these ideas in his later work on social capital [1988, 1990b, pp. 300–321]).

"Value community" referred to consensual commitment to a set of values; solidarity across (or within) generations is not necessarily entailed. Functional communities can exhibit value consensus or cleavage, but value communities, exemplified by magnet and nonreligious private schools that attract students from different residential locations, are not necessarily functional ones. Religious schools are both functional and value communities because they engage families who attend the same religious observances. Religious attendance expresses value consensus, the social cement that ties generations together by virtue of residential propinquity, the social visibility derived from it, and a presumed tendency of parents to sanction the conduct of neighbors' children. There is an affinity between these concepts and notions of school climate: a normative component and an interactional sanctioning one. Coleman and Hoffer, employing the concept of social capital, construed the religious school as embedded in a unified residential–church–school community. This treatment of community mechanisms, however, intended to link school (sector) to individual outcomes, is as conjectural as Durkheim's and others' speculations—however plausible—about mechanisms intervening between social structure and individual conduct.

Coleman and Hoffer (1987) reported achievement gains from grades 10 to 12 (pp. 63–83), consistent with Coleman and associates (1982; a cross-sectional study), indicating Catholic sector advantages in gains over public ones, with the following interpretation: "the differences in economic resources of the schools are less important [Catholic schools being least well endowed economically] than the differences in social resources—the functional or value communities that reinforce the demands made by the schools" (Coleman & Hoffer, 1987, p. 68). This argument stressed that functional communities value academic achievement (p. 61); but, as Peshkin's (1986, pp. 56–58) observations of a fundamentalist Christian school (also a functional community) that subordinated academic to spiritual values demonstrated, they need not.

Although Coleman and Hoffer (1987) continued to treat (following Coleman et al., 1982) the academic emphasis of the Catholic school curriculum, the community perspective dominated. Coleman and Hoffer extended it to examine sector dropout differences in student subpopulations distinguished by grades, absences, probation, and disciplinary problems. They found a Catholic school advantage over schools organized by value community (private) and by residence (public), and obtained similar results (higher achievement, lower dropout rates) among students from economically, racially, and ethnically disadvantaged households, and among those experiencing family "deficiencies" (i.e., single parents, working mothers [p. 118]. Achievement in Catholic schools was higher and dropping out was lower among Catholic students compared to non-Catholic ones and among church attenders over nonattenders. Catholic schools showed higher levels of achievement than public schools among minority students compared with non-Hispanic Whites. What accounted for these differences were students enrolling in academic programs, doing homework, and taking academic courses; school discipline; and a school population of higher social and academic standing. Yet, interpretation requires caution. The analysis was based on sector, not on school differences; what holds for sectors might not hold for schools.

Coleman and Hoffer's (1987) functional community explanation applied to dropping out of school invoked the egoism argument from Durkheim's (1897/1951) *Suicide*. Catholic schools are integrated religious communities defined by a single curriculum, discipline, and homogeneous social composition and by the religiosity of students, not just as individuals, but as indicative of school climate, because both church attenders and nonattenders at Catholic schools outperform their public school counterparts. Non-Catholic private schools, paralleling the normative strictures of Protestantism, suffer an excess of individualism; public schools experience anomie. Regarding dropouts:

> As in Durkheim's examination of suicide rates in social environments that are integrating and those that are isolating, this examination of dropout rates shows the powerful effects of a socially integrated community in reducing the likelihood of leaving the system . . . In contrast the individualistic settings of the other private schools increase the likelihood of middle-class dropout . . . (Coleman & Hoffer, 1987, p. 148)

The interpretation, then, was based on the relation between context and individual conduct but not on the mechanism. From Durkheim, we cannot tell whether Protestant and Catholic *individuals* committed suicide at higher rates in Protestant or Catholic *areas*. With Coleman and Hoffer (1987), because the Catholic *sector* shows lower rates of dropping out, presumably because of functional communitarianism, we cannot tell whether that characteristic of *schools* accounts for lower school dropout rates, and if so whether communitarianism is the mechanism, in either Catholic or public schools.

Bryk and associates (1993) also addressed the problem of mechanisms. The difficulty in Coleman's work, in their view, was that it "provides only limited information about *how* these Catholic school effects might accrue . . . " and "about the internal organization of Catholic secondary schools" (p. 59; Bryk et al's italics). They stressed the importance in Catholic schools of an academic orientation, based on belief and normative preference—"an institutional pull" (p. 118)—reflecting "a widely held belief among Catholic school educators that a traditional academic curriculum is appropriate for most adolescents" (p. 105). This belief is expressed in the emphasis on college preparatory courses and in assigning students to programs rather than letting them choose, the latter partly explained by many Catholic schools not offering nonacademic programs. Public sector high schools, in contrast, tend to be tracked. This reaction to Coleman's lack of attention to internal school organization led to revisiting the Catholic school advantage and the common school effect.

Bryk and associates (1993) also developed a communitarian argument. Employing qualitative and quantitative methods, they discussed the development of Catholic schools during the post-Vatican II period as caring, personalistic, and solidary communities (p. 142). The qualitative analysis consisted of field work in seven Catholic high schools, which included observations of classrooms and of school events, interviews with students and with staff, and analysis of statements of purpose and of value commitment. They organized this material into a general portrait of Catholic schools by combining descriptive elements from the cases, a summary procedure that yielded a composite description of commonalities, but without a systematic treatment of school differences. The result was a profile representation of schools in the Catholic sector. However, as Selvin (1960) pointed out, profiles have vulnerabilities, because global aggregates (like sectors comprising schools or schools comprising internal structures) might not characterize their constituent units.

Examining the impact of public, of religious, and of other private schools raises questions about how to express the connection between sectors and schools, the properties of school organization, and the mechanisms through which educational outcomes are produced. The common school effect touches all three questions. The relation between race and achievement calculated on individuals in each *sector*, for example, cannot be ascertained in single-race schools, which are numerous in the Catholic sector (5.8% Black, 7.5% Hispanic enrollments [Coleman et al., 1982, p. 31; almost identical proportions in Bryk et al., p. 70) and in the public sector with many all minority schools. Here is a case where it is unlikely that the proportion of minority students in the sector will resemble that in the schools. The case also opens the issue of whether schools with minority student proportions of different sizes make the same social, programmatic, instructional, and curricular provisions and achieve a common school effect to the same degree. Although a communitarian climate combined with a unified academic curriculum may be associated with a weak relation between social background and achievement (the common school effect) calculated on a sectoral population of students, it is equally plausible that such an association can vary or not appear school-by-school and can be attributed to the varied ways schools deal with their student populations. A test of this effect needs to rely on within-school variations—a persuasive one on school populations with substantial representations of racial/ethnic groups. It should also attend to the identification of mechanisms and whether they differ by school composition.

The findings (Bryk, et al., 1993; Lee & Bryk, 1989) showed that sector differences in achievement diminish in size when the academic organization of schools is taken into account, and that sector differences favoring Catholic schools in teacher commitment and in student engagement are diminished when communitarian aspects of schools are introduced. How to interpret this evidence depends on how one understands academic and communitarian organization and their measurement (Bryk and associates, 1993, p. 286). Again questions about mechanisms arise, two in particular: one pertains to how school organization is formulated; the other to whether student selection can account for both the Catholic school advantage and the common school effect.

The treatment of academic and communitarian school organization rests on global characterizations of schools (principals' reports about schools, school averages, and such characterizes as size and sector [Bryk and associates, 1993, p. 189], but not on within-school variation in structure and operation). The examination of how communitarian organization (Bryk and associates, 1993, pp. 279–282) relates to teacher commitment and to student engagement by school is based on a combination of 23 measures into a "community index," a procedure that does not reveal the patterning of these measures *within* schools, how they function to influence achievement, or how they function to produce a common school effect. The procedures employed in the chapter "Variations in Internal Operations" were based on school-level summaries of internal operations, not on within-school variations, the same logic of contextual analysis found in earlier studies (Brookover et al., 1979; McDill & Rigsby, 1973; Rutter et al., 1979).

With respect to mechanisms, the question is whether school influences can be demonstrated without also taking into account the constituent units of school organization, the activities of teachers and school officials, and the contingencies they face. Although the observations of school personnel can be summarized to provide a global indication of community and solidarity, and schools can be compared on that basis, one does not know whether, for example, all departments, teachers of the same subject or grade, or subgroups organized on some other basis share this quality or whether community and solidarity of units can create cleavages in the whole, as Loveless (1994) has shown in connection with the untracking issue. Teachers and administrators may agree on school goals and values when framed abstractly but not necessarily on specific goals and the means to accomplish them, and they might not employ those means in their activities. As Pallas (1988) observed, climate differences between schools are modest in size, substantial variation and disagreement exist within schools as expressed in teachers' reports about what the climate is, and climate can be viewed as an outcome as well as a cause. The use of global organizational indices tends to obscure these differences, the patterns of action and interaction in the work of schools, the directionality of causation, and the conceptual basis on which an argument about mechanisms can be constructed.

The selectivity controversy pertains to whether the advantage of Catholic schools over public schools is attributable to academic and communitarian organization or to advantaged students selecting Catholic schools. It has been treated largely as a problem in assessing self-selection bias (Murnane, Newstead, & Olsen, 1985; Neal, 1997) in forming the composition of school populations. This perspective ignores selectivity from the supply side as a component of internal school structure and operation, while fastening on the demand (household choice) side of enrollment. What's more, it neglects selectivity as an aspect of school operation.

Bryk and associates (1993) observed that Catholic sector secondary schools express their academic and communitarian values in curricular and social organization. Making these values known (see the example of one school's statement of its philosophy [pp. 146–147]) is part of the student selection process, of establishing self-definitions, or of establishing charters (Meyer, 1970, 1977), a practice also familiar to private to magnet, and to vocational schools. Parents selecting a kind of school and schooling is partly a response to what schools publicize about themselves. If schools claim to be academic and possess certain social and spiritual qualities, students and their parents interested in this kind of schooling (Greeley, 1982, p. 22), irrespective of background, will be more likely to seek admission than those looking for something different. From the pool of admission seekers, schools select students they believe will prosper under their academic regimen and form of social life. Selection occurs on both the supply and the demand sides. On the former, schools that can do so select students; those that cannot select them use other means to adapt the school's offerings, academic and social, to the population. Controversies about selection bias have concentrated on the wealth and status advantages of the Catholic school population, as if such advantages were proxies for academic proclivities and talents. Bryk and associates' (1993, p. 252) evidence showed academic background correlating 0.21 and 0.30 with social class and –0.04 and –0.11 with minority status among Catholic students and public school students, respectively. These weak relationships indicate the leeway that academic schools have in selecting academically interested students whatever their class and minority origins. Given the claims for Catholic school advantage and a common school effect, selection on both the supply and the demand sides needs to be examined as a matter of internal school organization and functioning. It cannot be addressed convincingly through structural effects reasoning that relies on such broad categorical measures as sector and averaged school properties.

The nonselectivity of most public schools raises similar issues. The availability of Catholic, private, and public charter and magnet schools alters the attendance distribution of the school-going population, at least in metropolitan areas. When students attending these schools leave the larger pool, nonselective public schools become the only option for those who remain. The schools must accordingly organize themselves to serve populations diverse in the languages spoken, the variety of vocational and academic interests, degrees of student indifference and inconsistency of attendance, the mix of special education constituencies, and the presence of students with disrupted family lives. For characterizing the variety of organizational and programmatic alternatives present in the public school domain (see Page, 1999), for a relevant discussion), the available evidence from large surveys has been insufficiently informative to indicate how they operate under prevailing conditions; the opprobrious metaphors of "bureaucracy" (Bryk et al., 1993, p. 294) and "shopping mall" (Powell, Farrar, & Cohen, 1985), frequently used to characterize public schools, are conceptually not up to the task.

CLOSING OBSERVATIONS: THE STATICS OF STRUCTURAL EFFECTS

The structural effects argument developed out of Durkheim's claims for the significance of social facts in accounting for stable rates of individual conduct. The connection between Durkheim and recent investigations of school effects, mediated through Columbia contributions to general sociology, looks linear from a distance but convoluted up close. Durkheim's (and others') ideas about the relation between social structure and individual conduct underwent elaboration at Columbia in distinct yet related directions: first, in studies focused on organizational structure and events, interactions among people at work, and short-term historical change; second, in methodological investigations designed to formulate general principles of survey analysis.

The significance of Columbia sociology for how the subsequent study of school effects took shape rested in both the presence and the absence of its influence. The first direction stressed *organizational* case studies rather than organizational *case studies*. Their contribution regarding structure and conduct came more from the substantive analysis of organizations than from case study methodology. As to structural effects, Blau was a key figure in elaborating on that idea as an outgrowth of his substantive agenda (as shown by his extraction of structural effects reasoning from *The Dynamics of Bureaucracy* [1955]), not mainly as a mode of data analysis. *Dynamics* was emblematic of the organizational side of the Columbia tradition. Although instrumental in developing structural effects argumentation in general, his work (and that of others from Columbia) exerted little if any direct substantive impact on later developments in school effects research. No one working in the sociology of education in the middle to late 1950s, moreover, showed much interest in school organization. Not until 1965 did an important contribution to that area of study appear (Bidwell, 1965), and a long time subsequently passed before others gained interest.

A different picture emerges from the second direction. Structural effects was one of several themes developing out of Lazarsfeld's and his students' contributions to principles of survey analysis. Their later application to education in general and to school effects in particular can be attributed primarily to Coleman. Of the participants in the Columbia milieu of the 1950s, he was almost alone in later devoting a substantial proportion of his intellectual efforts to educational topics. (An exception is Trow, who, however, wrote largely about higher education.) Most noteworthy were *The Adolescent Society* (1967) and EEO (1966), as well as his influence on the design of large, nationwide surveys of education from the mid-1960s onward. Those contributions were as important for what they did not take from Columbia as for what they did. Coleman did not apply the substantive agenda of the Columbia organizational studies to the analysis of schools, nor did he continue the research style of the case studies. There was certainly an organizational side to his approach to school effects, but it was conceptually implicit and fashioned out of the empirical materials that large surveys could yield; namely, global variables and aggregations of individual-level data resembling the nonsubstantive schemes of aggregation developed by Lazarsfeld, Kendall, Menzel, Selvin, and Hagstrom. The later acronymic surveys were not substantively designed around conceptions of school organization and how it operated. My speculation is that his views about policy analysis assigned greater persuasiveness to evidence gathered from nationwide surveys than from intensive organizational analyses.

Studies of school effects followed Wilson's formulation, schematically similar to Blau's but substantively unconnected to organizational analysis. His position contained a rather narrow (in hindsight) view of structure as the aggregation of individual characteristics and of normative climate as the dominant mechanism influencing individual outcomes. The normative climate perspective endured as a thread running through structural effects studies for decades to come. Although prominent, it was and is not the only mechanism employed in investigations based on structural effects arguments. The alleged influences of school composition based on race, on sex, or on teacher qualifications, for example, did not necessarily represent normative versions of such arguments but are nevertheless examples of the general scheme.

Traditions other than Columbia's could have led to the emergence of a sociology of education that paid significant attention to the substance of school organization, its inner workings, and its effects. Abbott's (1997) analysis of the Chicago School, developing around Thomas, Park, and Burgess (like Merton's [1995] of Columbia), for example, maintained that

> ... [T]he Chicago School thought—and thinks—that one cannot understand social life without understanding the arrangements of particular social actors in particular social times and places ... [N]o social fact makes any sense abstracted from its context in social (and often geographic) space and social time. (Abbott, 1997, p. 1152)

His portrayal of the Chicago School fastened on the "interactional fields" (p. 1156) of ethnic groups, of neighborhoods and other segments of cities, of occupational groups, and the like. The common ground between this conception of what is sociologically important and that prevailing earlier at Columbia is plain. Despite that similarity, neither a sociology of education nor a concern with school effects developed in Chicago (at least not until after the mid-1960s, and then not based on the patron saints of the Chicago School). Chicago sociology showed little concern with organizational structure or with education and schooling (Becker, 1952, 1953, was an exception), focusing more on other units of society: neighborhoods, occupations, urban areas, and racial ethnic groups. The Chicago version of Durkheim focused on area rates of crime, delinquency, and forms of social disorganization, excluding analogous patterns of educational phenomena.

Hindsight reveals the legacy that Durkheim's (1897/1951) *Suicide* left for the study of school effects. Along with the *Rules* (1895/1938), it laid the groundwork for a sociology based on social facts. It also employed methods that relied on evidence drawn from public records, an analogue of survey evidence collected for later secondary analysis prompted by questions different from those generating the original surveys. Although we remember social facts as external and constraining (and Durkheim's political reasons for a superindividual definition of them), they also represent static indices of social conditions: the proportion of Catholics and Protestants in given geographic areas defined religious society; the configuration of sex, marital status, and parenthood defined domestic society; and so forth. The substantive core of his enterprise was to identify a mechanism—social integration—to explain why certain social facts account for stable rates of suicide. That effort was hampered by limitations of the evidence, which provided no direct information on how church polities operated and family life transpired or of social integration. We continue to admire the ingenious research design of his secondary analyses and his digging into public records to find intervening and contingent conditions to argue the explanatory case for the mechanism of integration. He looked a lot like a late 20th century student of school effects rummaging through a body of available survey data short on evidence about the mechanisms of schooling. His interpretations were plausible but speculative. Halbwachs (1978), Henry and Short (1954), Hyman (1955), and Inkeles (1963), for example, identified different mechanisms from Durkheim in linking social states and rates of suicide.

In my view, the conceptual vulnerability of structural effects argumentation, as it has been applied to explaining school effects, is that it rigidifies social structure and social process. This is primarily a substantive problem; secondarily a methodological one occasioned by a shortage of appropriate evidence that encourages ransacking the code sheets of large surveys to construct measures of convenience. When this occurs, evidence and method constrain substance. The rigidity occurs because of an implicit belief that school organization and process can be appropriately represented by time-frozen, global, aggregate, and averaged measures of school characteristics made to stand for the situational, contingent, and temporal events and activities of schooling. What is substantively important about school organization and schooling, moreover, needs to be argued in its own terms rather than selected from the cafeteria of survey offerings.

A second source of rigidity derives from Durkheim's conception of social facts, where the order of causality runs from structure to individual conduct. The prevailing policy environment continues to be hospitable to studies that investigate the impact of schools on achievement, but that does not justify conceptually the causal priority of school structure. Elements of schooling and of school structure can be understood, for example, as results rather than as causes of social action and interaction as participants in schools over time follow the routines and confront the contingencies arising in their work. Although certain structural aspects of school organization have remained remarkably stable since the 19th century (e.g., age grading, classrooms as sites for teaching, textbook-driven instruction), other aspects can be seen both to shape and to respond to alterations in the course of events, to shocks to the system, to the evaluation and rethinking of customary ways of doing things, and the like. Schools, like other organizations, deal with the continuity, change, and disruption of circumstances; for this reason, adopting the structure–conduct sequence of causality does injustice to our understanding of schools and of schooling, even in longitudinal surveys. Though such surveys take the passage of time into account, they usually observe changes in outcomes (e.g., gain scores) while treating school characteristics as unchanging. The impact on individuals and on the structure of school organization itself, caused by changes in the events and practices of schooling, thereby escapes attention.

Following a substantive agenda different from what is usually found in conventional treatments of structural effects, a number of studies have treated the events and processes of schooling. Consider some apposite examples. Metz (1986) showed how teachers and school district officials created varied curricular, instructional, and evaluational arrangements (i.e., structures and practices based on newly formulated instructional philosophies) in three magnet schools, following shifts in their racial/ethnic composition, responding to opportunities and problems arising from court-ordered desegregation. Barr and Dreeben (1983) described how teachers established and modified classroom reading group arrangements (i.e., creating new structures) to deal with both the initial ability distribution of classes and variations in students' learning trajectories over the school year. DeLany (1991) demonstrated how a school administrator charged with responsibilities for time scheduling and for course scheduling coped with unanticipated changes in the size of enrollment and in the composition of the teaching staff, thereby shifting past patterns of both curricular offerings and student course-taking. Bidwell and Quiroz (1991) showed how different types of workplace control (domination, rules, consultation, and markets) emerged out of attempts by school personnel to deal with contingencies arising from differences in school size and in client power and how these intervening modes of control then influenced teachers' orientations to and conduct of instruction (Bidwell, Frank, & Quiroz, 1997).

These examples portray teachers and school officials dealing with the properties of school populations and other circumstances, not by construing them as indices of climate, but as organizational arrangements and modes of conducting work that in turn influence schools' internal operation and student outcomes. They evoke a sense of schools as active organizations, reminiscent of older organizational studies, using evidence collected specifically for the purposes of the investigation (e.g., strategic comparisons of cases) without relying mainly on the available large surveys. Yet not all conceptions of school organization concentrate on the internal workings of schools or on mechanisms construed in such terms. With reference to the most stable aspects of schools and schooling, for example, the institutional perspective has drawn attention to how schools are linked structurally to the impersonal systems of the modern economy and the nation–state (Meyer & Rowan, 1978; Weber, 1978). Those linkages can be identified more readily from analyses of historical developments in the larger society and in organizations (e.g., demographic patterns, technological developments, social movements, governmental actions, shifts in educational demand, migration; [Craig. 1981; Stinchcombe, 1965]) than from the locked-in-time indices usually employed in structural effects arguments.

Abbott's (1997) assessment of general sociology seems appropriate to the area of school effects: "Most of our current empirical work concerns decontextualized facts with only a tenuous connection to process, relationship, and action" (p. 1158). That area of investigation has been dominated by, though not limited to, a kind of structural effects reasoning in which the "decontextualized facts" of global and aggregate indices have stood for both structure and process, the latter frequently identified more by conjecture than by examination, and in which causality has been considered to be unidirectional. These are substantive difficulties that cannot be addressed simply by employing alternate methods of studying school organization. Their resolution requires devoting attention to substantive conceptual agendas of school organization and schooling.

ACKNOWLEDGMENTS. I am grateful to Rebecca Barr, Charles E. Bidwell, and John W. Meyer for their valuable readings and comments on an earlier draft of this chapter.

REFERENCES

Abbott, A. (1997). Of time and space: The contemporary relevance of the Chicago School. *Social Forces, 75,* 1149–1182.

Alexander, C. N., & Campbell, E. Q. (1964). Peer influences on adolescent aspirations and attainments. *American Sociological Review, 29,* 568–575.

Alexander, K. L., & Pallas, A. M. (1985). School sector and cognitive performance: When is a little a little? *Sociology of Education, 58,* 115–127.

Alwin, D., & Otto, L. B. (1977). High school context effects on aspirations. *Sociology of Education, 50,* 259–273.

Armor, D. J. (1972). School and family effects on black and white achievement: A reexamination of the USOE data. In F. Mosteller & D. P. Moynihan (Eds.), *On equality of educational opportunity* (pp. 168–229). New York: Vantage Books.

Asch, S. E. (1952). *Social psychology.* New York: Prentice-Hall.

Averch, H. A., Carroll, S. J., Donaldson, T. S., Kiesling, H. J., & Pincus, J. (1972). *How effective is schooling? A critical review and synthesis of research findings.* Santa Monica, CA: Rand.

Axtell, J. (1974). *The school upon a hill: Education and society in Colonial New England.* New Haven, CT: Yale University Press.

Barr, R., & Dreeben, R. (1977). Instruction in classrooms. In L. S. Shulman (Ed.), *Review of research in education 5* (pp. 89–162). Itasca, IL: F.E. Peacock.

Barr, R., & Dreeben, R. (1983). *How schools work.* Chicago: University of Chicago Press.

Becker, H. S. (1952). Social-class variations in the teacher–pupil relationship. *Journal of Educational Sociology, 25,* 451–465.

Becker, H. S. (1953). The teacher in the authority system of the public schools. *Journal of Educational Sociology, 27,* 128–141.

Berelson, B. R., Lazarsfeld, P. F., & McPhee, W. N. (1954). *Voting: A study of opinion formation in a presidential campaign.* Chicago: University of Chicago Press.

Bidwell, C. E. (1965). The school as a formal organization. In J. G. March (Ed.), *Handbook of organizations* (pp. 972–1022). Chicago: Rand-McNally.

Bidwell, C. E., Frank, K. A., & Quiroz, P. A. (1997). Teacher types, workplace controls, and the organization of schools. *Sociology of Education, 70,* 285–307.

Bidwell, C. E. & Kasarda, J. D. (1980). Conceptualizing and measuring the effects of school and schooling. *American Journal of Education, 8,* 401–430.

Bidwell, C. E. & Quiroz, P. A. (1991). Organizational control in the high school workplace: A theoretical argument. *Journal of Research on Adolescence, 1,* 211–229.

Blau, P. M. (1955). *The dynamics of bureaucracy: A study of interpersonal relations in two government agencies.* Chicago: University of Chicago Press.

Blau, P. M. (1960). Structural effects. *American Sociological Review, 25,* 178–193.

Blau, P. M. (1973). *The organization of academic work.* New York: Wiley.

Blau, P. M., & Scott, W. R. (1962). *Formal organizations: A comparative approach.* San Francisco, CA: Chandler.

Bossert, S. T. (1979). *Tasks and social relationships in classrooms: A study of instructional organization and its consequences.* Cambridge, England: Cambridge University Press.

Boyle, R. P. (1966a). The effects of the high school on students' aspirations. *American Journal of Sociology, 71,* 628–639.

Boyle, R. P. (1966b). On neighborhood context and college plans (III). *American Sociological Review, 31,* 706–707.

Bridenbaugh, C. (1964). *Cities in the wilderness: The first century of urban life in America, 1625–1742.* New York: Knopf.

Bronfenbrenner, U. (1958). Socialization and social class through time and space. In E. E. Maccoby, T. M. Newcomb, & E. L. Hartley (Eds.), *Readings in social psychology* (pp. 400–425). New York: Henry Holt.

Brookover, W., Beady, C., Flood, P., Schweitzer, J., & Wisenbaker, J. (1979). *School social systems and student achievement: Schools can make a difference.* New York: Praeger.

Brown, A. F., & House, J. H. (1967). The organizational component in education. *Review of Educational Research, 37,* 399–416.

Brown, R. D. (1996). *The strength of a people: The idea of an informed citizenry in America, 1650–1870.* Chapel Hill, NC: University of North Carolina Press.

Bryk, A. S., Lee, V. E., & Holland, P. B. (1993). *Catholic schools and the common good.* Cambridge, MA: Harvard University Press.

Bulmer, M. (1984). *The Chicago school of sociology: Institutionalization, diversity, and the rise of sociological research.* Chicago: University of Chicago Press.

Campbell, E. Q., & Alexander, C. N. (1965). Structural effects and interpersonal relationships. *American Journal of Sociology, 71,* 284–289.

Chinoy, E. (1955). *Automobile workers and the American dream.* New York: Doubleday.

Cohen, A. K. (1955). *Delinquent boys: The culture of the gang.* Glencoe, IL: The Free Press.

Coleman, J. S. (1958–59). Relational analysis: The study of social organization with survey methods. *Human Organization, 17,* 28–36.

Coleman, J. S. (1961). *The adolescent society.* Glencoe, IL: The Free Press.

Coleman, J. S. (1990a). Columbia in the 1950s. In B. M. Berger (Ed.), *Authors of their own lives: Intellectual autobiographies by twenty American sociologists* (pp. 75–103). Berkeley, CA: University of California Press.

Coleman, J. S. (1990b). *Foundations of social theory.* Cambridge, MA: Harvard University Press.

Coleman, J. S., Campbell, E. Q., Hobson, C. J., McPartland, J., Mood, A., Weinfeld, F. D., & York, R. L. (1966). *Equality of educational opportunity.* Washington, DC: U.S. Government Printing Office.

Coleman, J. S., & Hoffer, T. B. (1987). *Public and private high schools: The impact of communities.* New York: Basic Books.

Coleman, J. S., Hoffer, T. B., & Kilgore, S. B. (1982). *High school achievement: Public, Catholic, and private schools compared.* New York: Basic Books.

Conant, J. B. (1961). *Slums and suburbs: A commentary on schools in metropolitan areas.* New York: McGraw-Hill.

Craig, J. E. (1981). The expansion of education. In D. C. Berliner (Ed.), *Review of research in education 9* (pp. 151–213). Washington, DC: American Educational Research Association.

Davis, J. A. (1961). *Great books and small groups.* New York: The Free Press.

Davis, J. A. (1966). The campus as a frog pond: An application of the theory of relative deprivation to career decisions of college men. *American Journal of Sociology, 72,* 17–31.

Davis, J. A., Spaeth, J. L., & Huson, C. (1961). A technique for analyzing the effects of group composition. *American Sociological Review, 26,* 215–226.

DeLany, B. (1991). Allocation, choice, and stratification within high schools: How the sorting machine copes. *American Journal of Education, 99,* 181–207.

Demos, J. (1970). *A little commonwealth: Family life in Plymouth Colony.* New York: Oxford University Press.

Durkheim, É. (1938). *The rules of the sociological method* (S. A. Solovay & J. H. Mueller, Trans.). Glencoe, IL: The Free Press. (Original work published 1895)

Durkheim, É. (1951). *Suicide: A study in sociology* (J. A. Spaulding & G. Simpson, Trans.). Glencoe, IL: The Free Press. (Original work published 1897)

Durkheim, É. (1961). *Moral education: A study in the theory and application of the sociology of education* (E. K. Wilson & H. Schnurer, Trans.). New York: The Free Press. (Original work published 1902–1903)

Etzioni, A. (1975). *A comparative analysis of complex organizations: On power, involvement, and their correlates.* New York: The Free Press.

Fichter, J. H. (1958). *Parochial school: A sociological study.* Notre Dame, IN: University of Notre Dame Press.

Gamoran, A. (1987). The stratification of high school learning opportunities. *Sociology of Education, 60,* 135–155.

Gouldner, A. W. (1954). *Patterns of industrial bureaucracy.* Glencoe, IL: The Free Press.

Greeley, A. M. (1982). *Catholic high schools and minority students.* New Brunswick, NJ: Transaction.

Halbwachs, M. (1978). *The causes of suicide.* (H. Goldblatt, Trans.). New York: The Free Press. (Original work published 1930)

Hanushek, E. A. (1986). The economics of schooling: Production and efficiency in the public schools. *Journal of Economic Literature, 24,* 1141–1177.

Hauser, R. M. (1970). Context and consex: A cautionary tale. *American Journal of Sociology, 75,* 645–664.

Hauser, R. M. (1971). *Socioeconomic background and educational performance.* Washington, DC: American Sociological Association.

Hauser, R. M. (1974). Contextual analysis revisited. *Sociological Methods and Research, 2,* 365–375.

Henry, A. F., & Short, J. F. (1954). *Suicide and homicide.* Glencoe, IL: The Free Press.

Homans, G. C. (1950). *The human group.* New York: Harcourt, Brace.

Homans, G. C. (1974). *Social behavior: Its elementary forms.* New York: Harcourt, Brace, Jovanovich.

Hyman, H. H. (1953). The value systems of different classes: A psychological contribution to the analysis of stratification. In S. M. Lipset & R. Bendix (Eds.), *Class, status and power: A reader in social stratification* (pp. 426–442). Glencoe, IL: The Free Press.

Hyman, H. H. (1955). *Survey design and data analysis: Principles, cases and procedures.* New York: The Free Press.

Inkeles, A. (1963). Sociology and psychology. In S. Koch (Ed.), *Psychology: A study of a science* (Vol. 6, pp. 317–387). New York: McGraw-Hill.

Kaestle, C. F. (1973). *The evolution of an urban school system: New York City, 1750–1850.* Cambridge, MA: Harvard University Press.

Kaestle, C. F. (1983). *Pillars of the republic Common schools and American society, 1780–1860.* New York: Hill & Wang.

Kahl, J. A. (1953). Educational and occupational aspirations of 'common man' boys. *Harvard Educational Review, 23,* 186–203.

Katz, E., & Lazarsfeld, P. F; (1955). *Personal influence.* Glencoe, IL: The Free Press.

Kendall, P. L., & Lazarsfeld, P. F. (1950). Problems of survey analysis. In R. K. Merton & P. F. Lazarsfeld (Eds.), *Continuities in social research: Studies in the scope and method of* "The American Soldier" (pp. 133–196). Glencoe, IL: The Free Press.

Kendall, P. L., & Wolf, K. M. (1949). The analysis of deviant cases in communications research. In P. F. Lazarsfeld & F. Stanton (Eds.), *Communications research, 1948–49* (pp. 152–157). New York: Harper.

Kerckhoff, A. C. (1993). *Diverging pathways: Social structure and career deflections.* Cambridge, England: Cambridge University Press.

Kerr, C., & Siegel, A. (1954). The interindustry propensity to strike—An international comparison. In A. Kornhauser, R. Dubin, & A. Ross (Eds.), *Industrial conflict* (pp. 189–212). New York: McGraw-Hill.

Key, V. O. (1950). *Southern politics in state and nation.* New York: Knopf.

Kobrin, S. (1951). The conflict of values in delinquency areas. *American Sociological Review, 16,* 653–661.

Lau, L. J. (1979). Educational production functions. In D. M. Windham (Ed.), *Economic dimensions of education* (pp. 33–69). Washington, DC: National Academy of Education.

Lazarsfeld, P. F., & Menzel, H. (1961). On the relation between individual and collective properties. In A. Etzioni (Ed.), *Complex organizations: A sociological reader* (pp. 422–440). New York: Holt, Rinehart and Winston.

Lazarsfeld, P. F., & Merton, R. K. (1954). Friendship as social process: A substantive and methodological analysis. In T. Abel & C. H. Page (Eds.), *Freedom and control in modern society* (pp. 18–66). New York: Van Nostrand.

Lazarsfeld, P. F., & Thielens, W. (1958). The academic mind. Glencoe, IL: The Free Press.

Lee, V. E., & Bryk, A. S. (1988). Curriculum tracking as mediating the social distribution of high school achievement. *Sociology of Education, 61,* 78–94.

Lee, V. E., & Bryk, A. S. (1989). A multilevel model of the social distribution of high school achievement. *Sociology of Education, 62,* 172–92.

Lieberson, S. (1958). Ethnic groups and the practice of medicine. *American Sociological Review, 23,* 542–549.

Lipset, S. M. (1950). *Agrarian socialism: The Cooperative Commonwealth Federation in Saskatchewan.* Berkeley, CA: University of California Press.

Lipset, S. M., Trow, M. A., & Coleman, J. S. (1956). *Union democracy. The internal politics of the International Typographical Union.* Glencoe, IL: The Free Press.

Loveless, T. (1994). The influence of subject areas on middle school tracking policies. In A. M. Pallas (Ed.), *Research in sociology of education and socialization* (Vol. 10, pp. 147–175). Greenwich, CT: JAI Press.

McDill, E. L., & Rigsby, L. C. (1973). *Structure and process in secondary schools: The academic impact of educational climates.* Baltimore: Johns Hopkins University Press.

McDill, E. L., Rigsby, L. C., & Meyers, E. D. (1969). Educational climates of high schools: Their effects and sources. *American Journal of Sociology, 74,* 567–586.

McPartland, J. M., & McDill, E. L. (1982). Control and differentiation in the structure of American education. *Sociology of Education, 55,* 77–88.

McPherson, G. (1972). *Small town teacher.* Cambridge, MA: Harvard University Press.

Merton, R. K. (1938). Social structure and anomie. *American Sociological Review, 3,* 672–682.

Merton, R. K. (1940). Bureaucratic structure and personality. *Social Forces, 18,* 560–568.

Merton, R. K. (1949). Manifest and latent functions. In R. K. Merton, *Social theory and social structure* (pp. 73–138). Glencoe, IL: The Free Press.

Merton, R. K. (1957a). Continuities in the theory of social structure and anomie. In R. K. Merton, *Social theory and social structure* (revised and enlarged edition, 161-194). Glencoe, IL: The Free Press.

Merton, R. K. (1957b). Continuities in the theory of reference groups and social structure. In R. K. Merton, *Social theory and social structure* (revised and enlarged edition, pp. 281–386). Glencoe, IL: The Free Press.

Merton, R. K. (1959). Social conformity, deviation, and opportunity-structure. *American Sociological Review, 24,* 177–189.

Merton, R. K. (1964). Anomie, anomia, and social interaction: Contexts of deviant behavior. In M. B. Clinard (Ed.), *Anomie and deviant behavior: A discussion and critique* (pp. 213–242). New York: The Free Press.

Merton, R. K. (1995). Opportunity structure: The emergence, diffusion, and differentiation of a sociological concept. In F. Adler & W. S. Laufer (Eds.), *The legacy of anomie theory: Advances in criminological theory* (pp. 3–78). New Brunswick, NJ: Transaction.

Merton, R. K., Gray, A. P., Hockey, B., & Selvin, H. C. (Eds., 1952); *Reader in bureaucracy.* Glencoe, IL: The Free Press.

Merton, R. K., & Kitt, A. S. (1950). Contributions to the theory of reference group behavior. In R. K. Merton & P. F. Lazarsfeld (Eds.), *Continuities in social research: Studies in the scope and method of "The American Soldier"* (pp. 40–105). Glencoe, IL: The Free Press.

Metz, M. H. (1978). Classrooms and corridors: The crisis of authority in desegregated secondary schools. Berkeley, CA: University of California Press.

Metz, M. H. (1986). *Different by design: The context and character of three magnet schools.* New York: Routledge & Kegan Paul.

Meyer, J. W. (1970). The charter: Conditions of diffuse socialization in schools. In W. R. Scott (Ed.), *Social processes and social structures* (pp. 564–578). New York: Holt, Rinehart, and Winston.

Meyer, J. W. (1977). The effects of education as an institution. *American Journal of Sociology, 83,* 55–77.

Meyer, J. W., & Rowan, B. (1978). The structure of educational organizations. In M. W. Meyer (Ed.), *Environments and organizations* (pp. 78–109). San Francisco, CA: Jossey-Bass.

Michael, J. A. (1961). High school climates and plans for entering college. *Public Opinion Quarterly, 25,* 585–595.

Michael, J. A. (1966). On neighborhood context and college plans (II). *American Sociological Review, 31,* 702–706.

Miller, D. R. & Swanson, G. E. (1958). *The changing American parent: A study in the Detroit area.* New York: Wiley.

Morgan, E. S. (1966). *The puritan family: Religion domestic relations in seventeenth-century New England.* New York: Harper and Row.

Mosteller, F., & Moynihan, D. P. (Eds., 1972). *On equality of educational opportunity.* New York: Vantage Books.

Murnane, R. J., Newstead, S., & Olsen, R. J. (1985). Comparing public and private schools: The puzzling role of selectivity bias. *Journal of Business and Economic Statistics, 3,* 23–35.

Neal, D. (1997). The effects of Catholic secondary schooling on educational achievement. *Journal of Labor Economics, 15*(pt. 1), 98–123.

Newcomb, T. M. (1958). Attitude development as a function of reference groups: The Bennington study. In E. E. Maccoby, T. M. Newcomb, & E. L. Hartley (Eds.), *Readings in social psychology.* New York: Henry Holt.

Page, R. N. (1991). *Lower-track classrooms: A curricular and cultural perspective.* New York: Teachers College Press.

Pallas, A. M. (1988). School climate in American high schools. *Teachers College Record, 89,* 541–554.

Perrow, C. (1970). *Organizational analysis: A sociological view.* Belmont, CA: Wadsworth.

Perrow, C. (1972). *Complex organizations: A critical essay.* Glenview, IL: Scott Foresman.

Peshkin, A. (1986). *God's choice: The total world of a fundamentalist Christian school.* Chicago: University of Chicago Press.

Powell, A. G., Farrar, E., & Cohen, D. K. (1985). *The shopping mall high school.* Boston: Houghton Mifflin.

Robinson, W. S. (1950). Ecological correlations and the behavior of individuals. *American Sociological Review, 15,* 351–357.

Rogoff [Ramsøy], N. (1961). Local social structure and educational selection. In A. H. Halsey, J. Floud, & C. A. Anderson (Eds.), *Education, economy, and society* (pp. 241–251). New York: The Free Press.

Rosenbaum, J. E. (1976). *Making inequality: The hidden curriculum of high school tracking.* New York: Wiley.

Rutter, M. S., Maughan, B., Mortimore, P., & Ouston, J. (1979). *Fifteen thousand hours.* Cambridge, MA: Harvard University Press.

Schwartz, B. (1975). *Queuing and waiting: Studies in the social organization of access and delay.* Chicago: University of Chicago Press.

Selvin, H. C. (1958). Durkheim's Suicide and problems of empirical research. *American Journal of Sociology, 63,* 607–619.

Selvin, H. C. (1960). *Problems in the use of individual and group data.* Unpublished manuscript, University of California at Berkeley.

Selvin, H. C., & Hagstrom, W. O. (1963). The empirical classification of formal groups. *American Sociological Review, 28,* 399–411.

Selznick, P. (1949). *TVA and the grass roots: A study in the sociology of formal organization.* Berkeley, CA: University of California Press.

Sewell, W. H., & Armer, J. M. (1966a). Neighborhood context and college plans. *American Sociological Review, 31,* 159–168.

Sewell, W. H., & Armer, J. M. (1966b). Reply to Turner, Michael, and Boyle. *American Sociological Review, 31,* 707–712.

Sewell, W. H., Haller, A. O., & Straus, M. (1957). Social status and educational and occupational aspiration. *American Sociological Review, 22,* 67–73.

Shaw, C. R. (1924). *Delinquency areas.* Chicago: University of Chicago Press.

Shaw, C. R., & McKay, H. D. (1942). *Juvenile delinquency and urban areas: A study of rates of delinquency in relation of differential characteristics of local communities in American cities.* Chicago: University of Chicago Press.

Sills, D. L. (1957). *The volunteers: Means and ends in a national organization.* Glencoe, IL: The Free Press.

Sørensen, A. B. (1970). Organizational differentiation of students and educational opportunity. *Sociology of Education, 43,* 355–376.

Sørensen, A. B., & Hallinan, M. T. (1977). A reconceptualization of school effects. *Sociology of Education, 50,* 273–289.

Stinchcombe, A. L. (1959). Bureaucratic and craft administration of production: A comparative study. *Administrative Science Quarterly, 4,* 168–187.

Stinchcombe, A. L. (1964). *Rebellion in a high school.* Chicago: Quadrangle Books.

Stinchcombe, A. L. (1965). Social structure and organizations. In J. G. March (Ed.), *Handbook of organizations* (pp. 142–193). Chicago: Rand McNally.

Stinchcombe, A. L. (1990). Social structure and the work of Robert Merton. In J. Clark, C. Modgil, & S. Modgil (Eds.), *Robert K. Merton: Consensus and controversy* (pp. 81–95). London: Falmer.

Stolzenberg, R. M. (1978). Bringing the boss back in: Employer size, employee schooling, and socioeconomic achievement. *American Sociological Review, 78,* 813–828.

Stouffer, S. A., Lumsdaine, A. A., Lumsdaine, M. H., Williams, R. M., Smith, M. B., Janis, I. L., Star, S. A., &

Cottrell, L. S. (1949a). *The American soldier II: Combat and its aftermath*. Princeton, NJ: Princeton University Press.

Stouffer, S. A., Suchman, E. A., deVinney, L. C., Star, S. A., & Williams, R. M. (1949b). *The American soldier I: Adjustment during army life*. Princeton, NJ: Princeton University Press.

Strodtbeck, F. L. (1958). Family integration, values, and achievement. In D.C. McClelland, A. L. Baldwin, U. Bronfenbrenner, & F. L. Strodtbeck (Eds.), *Talent and society: New perspectives in the identification of talent* (pp. 135–194). Princeton, NJ: Van Nostrand.

Swidler, A. (1979). *Organization without authority: Dilemmas of social control in free schools*. Berkeley, CA: University of California Press.

Tannenbaum, A. S., & Bachman, G. G. (1964). Structural versus individual effects. *American Journal of Sociology, 59*, 585–595.

Turner, R. H. (1966). On neighborhood context and college plans (I). *American Sociological Review, 31*, 698–702.

Vinovskis, M. A. (1985). *The origins of public high schools: A reexamination of the Beverly high school controversy*. Madison, WI: Wisconsin.

Waller, W. (1961). *The sociology of teaching*. New York: Russell and Russell.

Weber, M. (1978). *Economy and society* (Vol. 2, G. Roth & C. Wittich, Trans.). Berkeley, CA: University of California Press. (Original work published 1968)

Willms, J. D. (1985). Catholic-school effects on academic achievement: New evidence from the high school and beyond follow-up study. *Sociology of Education, 58*, 98–114.

Wilson, A. B. (1959). Residential segregation of social classes and aspirations of high school boys. *American Sociological Review, 21*, 836–845.

CHAPTER 6

School Effects

Theoretical and Methodological Issues

AAGE B. SØRENSEN
STEPHEN L. MORGAN

INTRODUCTION

Schools are charged with many tasks: the preservation of order through the socialization of children, the maintenance of a productive labor force, the promotion of tolerance, the cultivation of talent, and the prevention of crime and loitering. The satisfactory accomplishment of these objectives, except perhaps the last, is dependent on the capacity of schools to increase individual knowledge, skills, and maturity. Social scientists have many theories about the influence of schools but often little evidence supporting these theories.

The gap between theory and evidence persists for at least three reasons. First, in order to evaluate theories about the influence of schools we need measures of the many possible outcomes of schooling. Unfortunately, we have reasonably good measures for only a few outcomes: cognitive skills and knowledge, economic growth, and labor market success. Second, schools contribute to individual change in interaction with other institutions, most notably the family. The disentanglement of the interacting contributions of schools and these associated institutions is a daunting methodological challenge. Schools have a near monopoly on instruction in some areas, such as trigonometry, and in these areas school effects can be identified.

AAGE B. SØRENSEN AND STEPHEN L. MORGAN • Department of Sociology, Harvard University, Cambridge, Massachusetts 02138

Handbook of the Sociology of Education, edited by Maureen T. Hallinan. Kluwer Academic/Plenum Publishers, New York, 2000.

However, the contribution of schools to psycho-social maturity is clearly very difficult to disentangle from influences of other agents of socialization. Finally, the confounding effects of unobservable individual heterogeneity, especially in genetic endowments, further compli-cate efforts to isolate the effects of schools.

In this chapter, we discuss theory and evidence on school effects. We address the topic, as it has been addressed by almost all past research in the sociology of education, as a question of how much difference characteristics of schools make for student learning in areas where we have measures of learning outcomes, usually based on performance on standardized tests of achieve-ment. As a result, this chapter, like the sub-discipline of sociology of education, focuses analysis on a subset of the effects of schools noted above. This narrow focus is justified to some extent by the attentions of policymakers and parents, whose decisions—the allocation of funding and residential/school choice, respectively—are influenced by beliefs about the causes of varia-tion among schools in learning outcomes such as mathematics skills and verbal competence.

Research in this tradition is based upon measurement of the impact of differences among schools on learning outcomes. If stable associations of outcomes with differences across schools are established, the conclusion that school effects are strong—a position already held by many policymakers and parents—is supported. However, it is important to recognize that the ab-sence of associations between school differences and learning does not support the conclusion that schools are unimportant. For example, if all schools successfully produce the same level of achievement among students on some outcome, no impact will be inferred from an exami-nation of variation across schools with different characteristics. Nonetheless, the effect of schooling may still be powerful, especially if uniform achievement across schools compen-sates for inequality in outcomes that would otherwise arise from individual differences in family background and genetic endowments. The possible existence of such a research find-ing justifies a distinction between the effects of schools (i.e., the effect of variation among schools on outcomes) and the effect of schooling (i.e., the overall effect of the schooling process). When studied at the individual level, the effect of schooling is the major focus of research on the effects of educational attainment. The preoccupation of this strand of research is the disentanglement of the individual effects of family background and genetic ability, not the identification of the influence of different school practices on learning. Interest in the macro-social effect of variation in schooling processes has generated little empirical research, with the exception of research in economics on the effect of education on economic growth that was the inspiration for the early development of human capital theory (e.g., Schultz, 1961). A more recent example of macro-social research on the measurement of the economic effect of schooling has been provided by Angrist and Krueger (1991).

The narrow specification of the research question, however, has the virtue of suggesting research designs which allow for straightforward identification and estimation of the effects of schools. If we could take a sample of schools that differ in organization and/or resources and then either allocate identical students or randomly assign a sample of nonidentical stu-dents to various schools, observed variation in learning across these schools would then rep-resent the differential effectiveness of schools. Unfortunately, neither version of this research design is feasible. The identification of identical individuals, even if they existed, is impos-sible. Furthermore, although experiments abound in educational research, random assignment of students to treatments is rare, perhaps because the design is considered unethical, even if, as is unlikely, parents would allow their children to participate in any such study. There are notable exceptions: the so-called Perry Preschool Project (e.g. Barnett, 1995) on the effect of intensive preschool programs—a large-scale randomized experiment in Tennessee to estab-lish the effect of class size on student performance (discussed in Mosteller, 1995), and the experiments on the expectancy effect by Rosenthal and Jacobson (1968).

The approximation in common use to the ideal experimental design is the statistical estimation of linear models that control for variation, among students, that confounds the estimation of school effects. The use of statistical methods, in particular regression analysis, to control for variation in individual endowments that are relevant for learning has become the standard methodology. Control variables—measured attributes of students and, more recently, assumed functions of unmeasured variables that produce non-random selection of students into schools—are entered alongside the school characteristics of interest in linear-additive models with measures of level of achievement, or gains in achievement, as dependent variables. The only commonly acknowledged weakness of this approach, much emphasized in debates about the magnitude of school effects, is the indeterminate nature of guidelines on which control variables should be included in any model. As a result, the mantra "Many controls are better than few controls" guides most research practice. The avowed purpose of including a maximal set of control variables is to eliminate all possible sources of individual variation that could confound the estimation of a school effect.

Many results have been obtained from research conducted in this manner. However, no consensus exists on the magnitude or source of school effects on learning, especially in relation to the effects of individual endowments. Debates about the relative merits of findings typically focus on methodological issues. While we discuss methodological issues in this chapter, we first examine more fundamental theoretical issues. Theory precedes estimation, for it is theory that determines the type of model that needs to be estimated. Only with a perfectly tailored randomized experiment can estimation proceed without explicit reference to theory, though theory, of course, must guide the experimental design.

The choice of models in regression analysis is usually not seen as a matter of theory by sociologists and educational researchers. Theory, at most, is considered relevant for the choice of control variables to include in a model. Nevertheless, an additive model does represent a theory about how school effects, or effects of any kind, are produced. If a researcher includes a set of school characteristics alongside a set of individual variables, then an implicit assumption is maintained: the effects of school characteristics add to the effects of individual characteristics on learning. In other words, students are provided with additional resources relevant for learning when they enter a school. Students may, for example, be motivated to try harder in schools with certain characteristics. The increased motivation of students may then increase academic achievement, regardless of students' abilities and the opportunities to learn that are provided the students by schools. This may be a reasonable theory about how schools affect learning, but it is not the only mechanism by which learning is achieved. If, instead, learning is jointly dependent on the student's efforts, abilities, and opportunities to learn, then the effect of effort on achievement will depend on the student's opportunities for learning, or how much is taught in a school. This alternative theory suggests that effort and ability will have no effect on learning in schools that teach nothing. The mechanism at the heart of this theory requires a nonlinear specification of the learning process that we later detail. An innocuous sounding assertion, this simple stipulation has strong implications for inferences about school effects in empirical research.

PAST SCHOOL EFFECTS RESEARCH

The school effects literature is large. Any proposal for improving the performance of schools can be considered a theory about school effects, and any study that claims that a school characteristic makes a difference for learning could be said to constitute a contribution to school effects research. In this chapter, we mostly consider large-scale quantitative studies of the effect of school organization and resources on learning outcomes, and because James S. Coleman's contributions dominate the field, we first survey his seminal research in the sociology of education.

Coleman's Research on School Effects

Coleman began his first study of schools in 1957 when he became an assistant professor at the University of Chicago. A study of adolescent subcultures based on surveys of students in ten high schools in northern Illinois, his first research was published as *The Adolescent Society* (Coleman, 1961). In the preface, Coleman noted two reasons for undertaking the study. Interested in how schools might be made more effective, Coleman (1961) conducted the research because of ". . . a deep concern I have had, since my own high school days, with high schools and with . . . ways to make an adolescent's experience with learning more profitable. . . . " (p. vii). Coleman was also motivated by an interest in different types of status systems and the value systems that they reflect. Coleman's interest in documenting the effects of high schools on learning did not receive much attention in *The Adolescent Society,* possibly because the empirical evidence he gathered about these effects proved more difficult to interpret than he anticipated. Instead, *The Adolescent Society* focuses on social rather than educational processes, cataloguing the social systems created in the ten high schools and in the adolescent subcultures associated with them. Nevertheless, the policy prescriptions Coleman (1961) drew from his analysis were about how to change these subcultures in order to encourage learning and academic achievement.

Coleman's interest in the effects of schools on individual learning became his main preoccupation in educational research for almost four decades. The link between the two concerns motivating *The Adolescent Society* (Coleman,1961)—school effectiveness and schools as social systems—was always clear to Coleman, and his interest in the social systems created in schools reemerges in his last substantial research project in the sociology of education.

Coleman completed three major reports after *The Adolescent Society.* The first Coleman Report (for a while known as the Coleman–Campbell Report) was the massive *Equality of Educational Opportunity*, probably still the largest social science research project ever completed (Coleman et al., 1966). The report's finding of small effects, relative to those of family background, of school resources and facilities on students' achievement created considerable controversy in both academic and policy circles. The second Coleman Report (Coleman, Kelly, & Moon, 1975) was a study of trends in desegregation in American schools. This report did not focus directly on school effects or educational processes but instead focused on the most important policy consequence of the *Equality of Educational Opportunity* report for policy— the use of busing to integrate schools in order to increase the academic achievement of minorities. This second report was widely interpreted to deny the benefits of desegregation documented in the first report and was strongly attacked by many, including many of Coleman's fellow sociologists. The interpretation was incorrect. Coleman did not doubt the relevance of student body composition for schools' educational climates. Rather, he doubted the long-term benefits of busing as a remedy for segregation

The third major piece of educational research Coleman directed, the *High School and Beyond* study, again defined the research agenda by reporting on differential school effectiveness. For this report, however, Coleman and his colleagues focused on differences between public and private schools (published as Coleman, Hoffer, & Kilgore, 1982, and later updated in Coleman & Hoffer, 1987, with additional evidence). The effects of schools, which were said to have been denied by Coleman in the *Equality of Educational Opportunity* report, were now emphasized. Roles reversed, and Coleman's critics now denied the existence of school effects, at least across the private and public sectors.

The overall impact of Coleman's research in the sociology of education is extraordinary, influencing policy and research as no other sociological enterprise. *Equality of Educational Opportunity* (Coleman et al., 1966) was never replicated, though the data were re-analyzed (see Mosteller & Moynihan, 1972). The public versus private school research inspired other research on school effectiveness, not only in an attempt to reassess Coleman's conclusions, but also to more broadly assess how school resources and organization can affect educational performance and how incentives for improving the performance of schools, such as voucher systems, might promote better school organization and practices. This follow-up research has been primarily conducted by economists and political scientists (Chubb & Moe, 1990; and Hanushek, 1986, 1996). The controversy about the magnitude and source of the effects remains vibrant (Berliner & Biddle, 1997), especially about the incentive systems that are suggested by research. The controversy to date has been dominated by political issues, focusing on the distributional consequences of voucher systems and the ability of traditional interest groups, such as teacher unions and public bureaucracies, to maintain control over the organization and funding of schools.

Most of the controversies surrounding Coleman's school effects research have been based on methodological disputes. As noted above, we emphasize theoretical issues rarely discussed in the relevant literature. Our first task in this chapter is to identify Coleman's implicit theory of school effects.

Coleman's Theory of School Effects

Over the stretch of time in which he was engaged in research on schools, Coleman changed in his ideas about school effectiveness and the link between school effectiveness and social systems. However, there is more continuity in his ideas than is generally recognized. Coleman pursued the same questions, and his alleged reversals of conclusions are much less dramatic than the controversies around these conclusions suggest. The continuity of the questions that guided Coleman's research allows us to identify a theory of school effects on learning.

Coleman may well have been the leader of the discipline of sociology who was most committed to the creation of a science of sociology based on Durkheim's contention that social systems shape and perhaps determine individual action. Coleman's work is not usually identified as Durkheimian, for he also devoted much effort to the development of rational choice theory and methodological individualism where his major concern was the analytic movement from the individual actor level to the macrostructural level (or, conceptually, from microeconomic ideas to Durkheimian perspectives on social structures). However, although building grand theory, his empirical research, including his educational research, made little use of rational choice theory and remained straightforwardly Durkheimian. Although perhaps least apparent in *Equality of Educational Opportunity*[1] (Coleman et al., 1966), Coleman's fascination with the connection between social systems and educational outcomes is most pronounced in *The Adolescent Society* (Coleman, 1961) and in *Public and Private High Schools: The Impact of Communities* (Coleman & Hoffer, 1987).

---

[1] Coleman deplored this later, characterizing the *Equality of Educational Opportunity* research as not really sociological research (personal communication).

By Durkheimian perspective we mean that Coleman saw social systems as the fundamental determinant of action. Social systems create the outcomes of educational processes by determining individuals' values and motivation. In *The Adolescent Society*, Coleman (1961) argues that the status systems established in peer groups shape students' attention and effort in school. Learning is an individual enterprise with individual level successes measured in grades that indicate relative standing. Success for some students constitutes failure for others. For Coleman, the predominant influence of an adolescent subculture on individual scholastic achievement is negative. Coleman proposed how this might be changed by making scholastic achievement more of a source of collective effort and pride, similar to interscholastic sports. He also, presumably in continuation of these ideas, initiated a research and development effort to create educational games that make social processes support efforts at learning and achievement. However, the evidence is weak for the linkage between social systems and educational outcomes in *The Adolescent Society* (Coleman, 1961). Coleman devotes a chapter to the topic and finds no relationship between the value systems of schools and the performance of students measured as grades obtained relative to the measured I.Q. of students. He presumably took I.Q. to be a measure of a student's intellectual endowment, and then assessed the impact of adolescent culture on performance relative to the potential given by this endowment. Coleman never again used this dependent variable or made a distinction between achievement and ability.

The *Equality of Educational Opportunity* (Coleman et al., 1966) report addressed the problem of schools and their relevance for learning in a very different fashion. As a research report prepared for policymakers, almost nothing is written about the conceptual framework for the analysis. However, on page 36, Coleman writes:

> the question of this report becomes a simple one: How well do the schools of our nation provide such opportunity for minority group children who would otherwise begin adult life with a distinct disadvantage? . . . To answer such a question . . . requires a variety of approaches. Most fundamental, of course, is the question of how well schools reduce the inequity of birth . . . ; that is, what results do schools produce? (Coleman et al., 1966, p. 36).

This is the main statement of the guiding research question, and it also provides an implicit theory of the educational process. The theory is that schools can somehow modify the inequality in educational outcomes created by birth (i.e., created by the family of origin and observable across characteristics such as race, ethnicity, and socioeconomic status). In Coleman's language from *The Adolescent Society* (1961), the question can be formulated as how the social system of the school can modify the social system created by families of origin.

The relationship between family and school was of little concern in *The Adolescent Society* (Coleman, 1961). This relationship was the source of the major finding of *Equality of Educational Opportunity* (Coleman et al., 1966). Another important difference between the two studies was the measure of academic achievement used. While *The Adolescent Society* (1961) saw the impact of the social system of the school on grades relative to a student's I.Q., the outcome in the *Equality of Educational Opportunity* report is academic achievement measured by a standardized test. No independent measure of mental ability was obtained, increasing the burden on the explanatory power of the theory of educational processes being proposed.

As noted, Coleman and colleagues used a largely implicit theory in the *Equality of Educational Opportunity* (1966). Two social systems were compared—one characterizing the family of origin and one created by the school. In practice, the research focus was the measurement of which of these two systems explained the most inequality (or variance) in educational achievement. This question does not have a straightforward answer because variables characterizing schools are highly correlated with variables characterizing families. Therefore, the result of the decomposition of variance depends on the causal assumptions maintained. The validity of the assumptions became an important controversy surrounding the *Equality of Educational Opportunity* report, as we later discuss. However, the main conclusion is now accepted wisdom: family is much more important for inequality of achievement than the school characteristics that can be purchased with economic resources.

Equality of Educational Opportunity finds that a few school characteristics that reflect the social systems created in schools have some importance for achievement. Consistent with a conjecture of *The Adolescent Society*[2], this finding suggests that those things that can be purchased with money are unimportant, while those reflecting social processes are important. However, the measures of the social system in *Equality of Educational Opportunity*—the average socioeconomic characteristics and racial composition of the student body—are much less sophisticated than those of *The Adolescent Society* (Coleman, 1961). *Equality of Educational Opportunity* presents very elaborate analyses showing that minority students' performance is affected by the composition of the student body—a finding that was to become important for policy and for practice because it was used to justify busing of children to achieve racial balance. In light of the importance of the busing controversies, it is ironic that there was a coding error in the construction of the student body composition variable that may have led Coleman et al. to misinterpret the effect of student body composition (see Smith, 1972).

The main conclusion of *Equality of Educational Opportunity* (Coleman et al., 1966) was based on the decomposition of variance in additive models for the level of academic achievement. This is a particular way to summarize effects in regression analysis. These models are an implicit acceptance of the theory of education that suggests that the influence of families and schools on educational outcomes can be added together. In *The Adolescent Society*, Coleman (1961) saw learning as an outcome that is created by students with different abilities who apply themselves in different degrees to learning. The theory of *Equality of Educational Opportunity* suggests that schools and families create both the abilities and the effort to apply these abilities.

The theory in *Equality of Educational Opportunity* (Coleman et al, 1966) is made even more demanding by the dependent variable adopted. To assess school effects, an outcome measure is needed that can be compared across schools. American schools teach a number of different things to the same age students. In a study as large as *Equality of Educational Opportunity*, the only possible comparable measure is one that is much closer to a measure of student aptitude than to what students have actually learned. Thus, very little of the variation in the achievement measure that is the dependent variable will reflect what students have been taught and thus the outcome of what actually is the main activity in schools. Only to the extent that schools influence student ability and effort, over and above the influence of early socialization and of genes, will schools cause variation in student outcomes measured with these achievement tests.

In the first publication from the *High School and Beyond* study (Coleman et al., 1982), level of achievement was again the main dependent variable. However, gains in achievement were also analyzed, using synthetic gain scores constructed from cross-sectional data. In the second main publication from the study (Coleman & Hoffer 1987), gain scores were analyzed directly. By using gain scores, the demands of the additive theory were reduced. Gains in

---

[2]In *The Adolescent Society*, Coleman noted with approval an unpublished study from Connecticut showing that per-pupil school expenditure had no relationship to the achievement of students relative to their I.Q.

achievement are outcomes schools presumably can influence, assuming achievement is measured so it reflects what can be learned in schools. A measure comparable across all schools is still needed, and the tests used in *High School and Beyond* (Coleman et al., 1982) seem to measure aptitude, reducing the direct connection to what may be taught in schools. However, Heyns and Hilton (1982) argued that the tests do measure something schools can influence.

The mechanisms that produced the dependent variable again did not receive much attention in the *High School and Beyond* (Coleman et al., 1982) research. Coleman and Hoffer (1987) showed that private and public schools differ in many ways: in course offerings, in organizational differentiation, in parental involvement, in discipline, in homework, size, and so on. However, these characteristics were never directly related to achievement outcomes in a manner that suggests how they affect achievement. Instead, theoretical attention was devoted to the specification of how the social systems created in schools can become effective agents for creating student behavior that is conducive to learning. Thus, the main focus is the same as in *The Adolescent Society* (Coleman, 1961). In *Private and Public High Schools* (Coleman & Hoffer, 1987), Coleman changed the emphasis of what was important about school social systems. The direct emphasis on peer-group cultures (in *The Adolescent Society*) and on student body composition (in *Equality of Educational Opportunity*) was replaced by attention to the attributes of the school social systems that could make them extensions of the family, in order to create a mutually reinforcing community.

Coleman and Hoffer (1987) noted that some schools simply extend the values of the family; nonreligious private schools and some public schools of choice attract students on the basis of their own and their parents' values. In contrast, some religious private schools, Catholic schools in particular, not only share values, but are a part of a functional community that reinforces these values. Religious schools are high in social capital, a concept that became important for Coleman and for others. These schools are easy to manage and their pupils are easy to teach. The social structures that envelop students generate beneficial effects on students' learning.

The basic form of the new theory is the same. The network structures that create social capital add together family and school effects to create powerful social influences that promote educational outcomes. Students immersed in social systems rich in social capital gain in academic achievement presumably because they work harder and with greater aptitude in schools rich in social capital. The theory is perhaps a bit less ambitious than the theory implicit in *Equality of Educational Opportunity* (Coleman et al., 1966). However, it is much more ambitious than the theory of *The Adolescent Society* (Coleman, 1961), for there schools are only asked to affect the grades that students obtain relative to their ability.

In *Public and Private Schools* (Coleman & Hoffer, 1987), the criteria for testing the theory also changed. Coleman no longer gauged the relative explanatory power of family and school. Instead, he assessed the significance of the effect of social capital. Unfortunately, the used data had no direct measure of social capital. As a result, Coleman and his associates could not directly test their social capital hypothesis and instead relied on an interpretation of the association between school sector and achievement gains. When the assertion that Catholic schools have the highest social capital is coupled with the empirical finding that Catholic school students score slightly higher on standardized tests of achievement, the theory of social capital seems to have some support. Methodological attention therefore focused on establishing the significance of sector effects, net of the selection of students with different abilities into different school sectors. Because no direct measure of ability is available in the *High School and Beyond* data, Coleman and his associates use measures of family background as proxy variables for ability (and perhaps other confounding variables).

   In Coleman & Hoffer (1987), the family background variables are used in an additive model with gains in achievement as the dependent variable. The model is then estimated separately for each school type. This implies an interaction between school type and the influence of family background (and achievement at the sophomore level) on gains between sophomore and senior year. The conjecture that high social capital supports family and school structures might suggest to some that the interaction should be such that the family background variables are more important in schools with strong ties between the family and the school system. However, Coleman & Hoffer (1987) evidently conceived of the matter in just the opposite manner. Schools with high social capital, such as Catholic schools, should reduce the influence of family background variables, he argued. In the language of *Equality of Educational Opportunity* (Coleman et al., 1966), the variance explained by family variables should be lower in Catholic schools. A smaller effect of family socioeconomic status on achievement gains is indeed found for Catholic schools than is found for public schools, supporting the conclusion that parochial schools are common schools that reduce the impact of social origin.

   The theory of schooling implicit in Coleman & Hoffer (1987) project is more complex than in the *Equality of Educational Opportunity* report. The earlier theory suggested that academic achievement was produced by two sets of forces—one set formed by the family and another by the school—and the salient question is the relative importance of the two. The new theory suggests that the degree of integration of the community social system, formed by school and family structures, determines the degree to which the comprehensive community social system produces learning and reduces the deficits some children bring to schools. The implicit model is one in which high social capital adds to the academic achievement of everyone and reduces the importance of family background. In other words, some school and community characteristics interact with family background.

   The argument for the importance of an interaction effect between school characteristics and family background seems indeed the proper specification of the statement of the *Equality of Educational Opportunity* report: "Most fundamental, of course, is the question of how well schools reduce the inequity of birth. . . . " (Coleman et al., 1966, p. 36). This question could not be answered in *Equality of Educational Opportunity* because Coleman never interacted school characteristics with family background characteristics.

   The specific interaction between school characteristics and family background, implicitly proposed by Coleman, is compensatory in nature. Good schools reduce the inequity of birth because the social systems created by good schools reduce the importance of family background. However, this is not the only possible direction of the effect of the interaction between school characteristics and family background characteristics, as we will demonstrate below.

   The Adolescent Society (Coleman, 1961) research considered school effectiveness as a question of how schools might affect the relationship between I.Q. and achievement. If we consider I.Q. a measure of family background, then the question is exactly the same as the one addressed by *Public and Private Schools* (Coleman & Hoffer, 1987) and formulated, but not addressed, in *Equality of Educational Opportunity* (Coleman et al., 1966). There is indeed consistency in Coleman's theory of how schools affect educational processes.

Conceptions of School Effects in Other Research

Coleman's school effects research defined the basic questions addressed by most other school effects research. Hanushek (1986) reviewed 147 studies of the effect of school characteristics on learning and found no systematic pattern of the effect of class size, teacher/pupil ratio, teacher education and experience, teacher salary, and per pupil expenditure on achievement. Most of these studies used administratively collected data from schools and school districts. The data showed a positive correlation between school expenditures and achievement, but revealed that the strength of the relationship disappears when family background is controlled.

Hanushek (1986) also reviewed several classroom-level studies that showed clear differences in teacher effectiveness (e.g., Hanushek, 1971; Murnane & Phillips, 1981). Some teachers do significantly better than other teachers in improving students' achievement test scores, controlling for background characteristics of these students. However, these total effects of teachers are not related to easily observable characteristics of teachers, such as their education and experience. Teacher effort and ability at teaching does appear to matter, but the relevant characteristics are not identified in the measures used in large scale research.

Other varieties of research have been pursued over the last few decades. A number of studies that investigated learning outcomes in one or a few schools claimed to provide evidence of what makes a school effective (e.g., Goodlad, 1984; Lightfoot, 1983; Powell, Farrar and Cohen, 1985, Sizer, 1984). These studies tended to be cross-sectional, based on small samples, and qualitative. They therefore fell outside of the review we are undertaking. Bryk, Lee & Holland (1993) focused on the common-school conception of Catholic schools, providing both qualitative and illustrative quantitative evidence.

Much attention has been focused on the average performance of U.S. schools, both over time and in comparison with the schools of other nations (for an overview of this evidence see Hanushek, 1994a). The former is investigated by comparing SAT scores and other average achievement test scores over time for the nation as a whole. The trend is a marked decline in SAT scores, but this partly reflects changes in the composition of test takers. Comparisons of achievement test scores given to representative samples show very little change. Nonetheless, the gap between Whites and minority groups has narrowed over the last three decades (Jenck & Phillips, 1998). Comparisons with the schools of other nations show that US students perform worse than students from many other nations. An important characteristic of U.S. schools revealed in these comparisons is that there is a great deal of variation in performance and in student body composition among states (see National Center for Educational Statistics, 1993). There is also a great deal of variation among U.S. schools in what schools teach and require in mathematics of their students. This variation presumably accounts for a major part of the difference between the United States and nations with more uniform standards and curricula. When course taking is taken into account, U.S. students taking advanced courses do as well, if not better than the average Japanese student (Westbury, 1992). If all students learned from the same textbooks, the U.S. deficit might also decrease. Schools decide what textbooks to use and can require students to take certain courses. Thus, the practices of American schools do matter and can be altered.

Throughout the long period of stagnation in performance, spending on schools has increased dramatically. Thus, schools deliver less per dollar than they did previously. Much of the debate about this lamentable state of affairs has focused on providing incentives for schools to do better. A large number of innovations—charter schools, magnet schools, school choice, performance contracting, and voucher systems—have been proposed, but research evaluating these innovations is (so far) inconclusive. Whatever insight this research provides about the effectiveness of the incentive systems and innovations, it provides very little insight into what specifically schools can do to improve their own incentives to educate students. A notable exception is the research conducted by Chubb and Moe (1990).

Chubb and Moe (1990) suggested an elaborate theory of how variation in school effectiveness reflects the institutional context of schools, especially the institutions of direct democratic control by which schools have traditionally been governed. This system, and the bureaucracies it creates, constrains the shape of school organization that is important for learning outcomes. In contrast to the effective schools literature, which makes similar claims with qualitative evidence, Chubb and Moe (1990) offered quantitative evidence using the same *High School and Beyond* data analyzed by Coleman (1961). In contrast to the private versus public school research conducted by Coleman and associates, which hypothesized that school organization (shaped by social capital) accounts for the difference between private and public schools, Chubb and Moe introduced measures of what they consider to be the relevant aspects of school organization, believed to be related to gains in achievement. They used the same basic model as Coleman and Hoffer (1987)—a linear model for gains in achievement where measures of school characteristics are introduced alongside measures of family background variables and initial level of achievement.

Chubb and Moe delineated four sets of organizational characteristics of schools: personnel, goals, leadership, and practice. They constructed measures of each set of characteristics by comparing high achieving and low achieving schools and then build a composite index of effective school organization. Finally, they showed that this effective school measure is a strong predictor of gains in achievement. According to their results, the predicted achievement gain, resulting from moving from the lowest to the highest quartile on effective school organization, is about equal to the gain that would be achieved by moving from the lowest to highest quartile of family background. As a result, they concluded that the effect of good school organization is comparable in size to the influence of each student's family background. They also found no effect of racial composition. The findings of Chubb and Moe, if true, are a substantial revision of the main conclusions of the *Equality of Educational Opportunity* (Coleman et al., 1966) report. However, it is important to note that these results on 10th-grade to 12th-grade achievement gain are obtained net of academic achievement in Grade 10, which Chubb and Moe (1990) interpreted as a measure of ability. A substantial effect of family background presumably is mediated by 10th-grade scores. Also, Coleman and associates (1966) used variance explained, rather than estimates of regression coefficients, as the basis for their conclusions.

Chubb and Moe (1990) proceeded to show how effective school organization depends on the institutional setting, as this was their main argument. However, with only one exception, they were unable to cast much light on what schools with effective organizations actually do to produce more learning. They found no effect of the amount of homework required, graduation requirements, administrative routines in the classroom, or discipline. They did find a substantial effect of the percentage of students in a school who are educated in the academic track. Schools in which students take more demanding courses produce more learning. A similar difference in track organization also accounts for most, if not all, of the difference between public and private schools (Alexander & Pallas, 1983; Coleman & Hoffer, 1987). Thus, the only direct effect established between effective school organization and learning is that effective schools have more demanding academic programs. Something other than the instructional program may explain why schools with high goals, functional communities, strong leaders, dedicated teachers, involved parents, and professional teachers produce more learning. However, neither Coleman and Hoffer (1987), nor Chubb and Moe (1990), demonstrated the direct relevance of these organizational variables for learning. The importance of teachers, academic programs, and curricula suggest a simple theory about how important school effects come about. Schools that teach more material produce more learning. In the next section, we further develop this theory.

TOWARD A THEORY OF SCHOOL EFFECTS

Conclusions from school effects research have shifted from the claim that schools make little difference for learning to the alternative claim that organizational features of schools make a lot of difference. Underneath the most recent claims is the relatively uncontroversial finding that the main effects of schools are effects of their academic programs. Differences in teaching programs are also what appears to account for the results of the international comparisons of the performance of U.S. schools with the schools of other nations. In short, schools make a difference by teaching students.

This simple conclusion suggests that research on school effects should pay more attention to variables measuring teaching effort and curricula—variables that measure the opportunities for learning provided by schools. When these variables are added to the regression equations typically estimated in school effects research, opportunities for learning should further explain achievement. However, simply adding variables providing measures of opportunities for learning to the standard additive models is not necessarily the correct specification. The effects of opportunities for learning may not simply add to the effects of student endowments. Rather, it is more likely that the effects of opportunities for learning interact with the effects of student endowments.

Suppose, to take an extreme example, that we have a school in which no English is taught. All instruction is in Hungarian and about Hungarian topics. Furthermore, parents who send their children to this school speak Hungarian and nothing but Hungarian. If given the standard English verbal ability test analyzed in educational research, students from this school would all achieve the same score. Students would not have been taught anything relevant for performance on the English test. No effect of family background on learning outcomes in this school would be observed, for no learning relevant for the test has taken place.

Suppose, in contrast, that there is a school with an extremely rich curriculum in mathematics. Students can progress from very simple algebra to very advanced mathematical topics. Every progression in this curriculum depends on how well a student has learned the previous step, and the speed of learning of each step depends to some degree on the student's background (because his mental ability is correlated with his family's socioeconomic status). The cumulative nature of the material, coupled with the relevance of ability for the completion of each stage in the curriculum, implies both that learning increases with the number of stages in the curriculum and that the correlation between mental ability and the amount learned increases with the number of stages in the curriculum. The assumption of a correlation between family background and mental ability ensures that, other things equal, the more instructional material that is covered in a period of instruction, the higher the observed effect of family background on academic achievement.

These simple ideas suggest that there are two components to the educational process in schools: what students are taught and how much they learn of what they are taught. Schools, classrooms, and other instructional groups differ in what and how much is taught. Students will differ, by ability and effort, in how much they learn. Student ability and effort can change over time as a result of learning and as a result of motivational processes associated with the social systems to which they belong. Schools can influence how much a student will learn by how much they try to teach and by changing student effort.

A simple formal representation, originally proposed in Sørensen and Hallinan (1977), expresses these ideas. Denote by $y_i(t)$ the amount a student, i, has learned by time t of material in an instructional period, or a course, where instruction began at Time 0. Let $v_c(t)$ be a measure of how much material has been presented by time t in classroom c. The amount, $y_i(t)$, students will have learned of this material in the period from Time 0 to Time t depends on students' ability and effort. Denote jointly ability and effort expended by s_i, and assume, for now, that s_i remains constant throughout the learning process. Ability and effort of course vary across individuals.

Learning is related to teaching by the simple differential equation:

$$\frac{dy_i(t)}{dt} = s_i dv_c(t) \tag{1}$$

The increase in achievement, $dy_i(t)$, for each increment of time, dt, is a function of how much has been taught, or $dv_c(t)$, and on the students's ability and effort, s_i. Using simple methods of integration, the solution is

$$y_i(t) - y_i(0) = s_i[v_c(t) - v_c(0)], \tag{2}$$

which gives the amount learned by time t as a function of how much has been taught in the period and of the student's ability and effort. The simple formulation of Equations (1) and (2) provides one elementary but fundamental insight. Opportunities for learning interact with the effort and ability of students in producing learning. If nothing is taught, nothing is learned. Individuals have to learn from something, perhaps their own experiences, perhaps their text-books, perhaps their teachers. If they have nothing to learn from, they will learn nothing. Moreover, ability and effort determine how much will be learned in a period of time. If two students are exposed to the same material, the student with the highest ability and/or effort will learn the most. Ability and effort are here conceived of as individual characteristics, varying among students, but treated as constant over the period of time studied. Because there should be no ambiguity about the usage, the subscript i is dropped in the sequel. The amount of material taught by time t varies across classrooms because of differences in curricula and in teacher effort. In most of the discussion that follows, $v_c(t)$, is treated as a school characteristic and within-school differences between classrooms are ignored. In empirical work, it may be possible to estimate the variation in v(t) across both schools and classrooms depending on data availability. However, the presentation here is theoretical and we therefore also drop the subscript c in the remainder of this chapter.

The implications of the interaction between ability and effort, on the one hand, and op-portunities for learning, on the other, may be seen by introducing variables that are correlated with the ability and effort of students. Assume that we have measures of a student's endow-ments, such as family background variables and other variables (perhaps school characteris-tics) that influence the efforts of students. Assume further that we are uninterested in how these variables actually produce ability and effort, so that a linear formulation is adequate. Thus, we specify s as $s = c_0 + c_1 x_1 + c_2 x_2 \ldots c_n x_n$, and thus re-express Equation (2) as

$$y(t) - y(0) = [v(t) - v(0)](c_0 + c_1 x_1 + c_2 x_2 \ldots c_n x_n) \tag{3}$$

The regression of y(t)–y(0), or gains in achievement over a period, on variables that measure not only ability and effort but also school characteristics is the common practice in school effects research. Equation (3) shows that if the simple mechanism for learning pro-posed here is correct, then the coefficients of the x variables will depend on v(t)–v(0), the amount of instructional material presented in the period over which the gain in achievement is measured. The larger v(t)–v(0) is, the larger the estimates of these coefficients will be. Schools that cover extensive material in their instruction provide many opportunities for learning and will create more growth in achievement. If opportunities for learning are not measured and included in the model, the estimated coefficients of the x variables will reflect these unmeasured and omitted variables. More opportunities for learning will create larger observed effects of the variables that measure the individual endowments that determine ability and effort.

There are several objections that may be raised against the formulation proposed by Equation (3). First, it assumes that effort and ability are constant over the period studied. This is not a reasonable assumption if a student's ability to learn new material depends on what is already known and a student's effort depends on past success. These are both reasonable mechanisms. However, for short periods of time, such as the 2-year period covered by the panel data commonly analyzed in school effects research, the assumptions of stable effort and ability may be reasonable.

A much more serious problem is that direct measures of opportunities for learning are usually not available. Data available for research on school effects usually do not measure what and how much schools teach, though an instructive exception is provided by Barr and Dreeben (1983). This makes it impossible to estimate Equation (3) directly. The solution to this problem adopted in Sørensen and Hallinan (1977) is to assume a particular dependency of $v(t)$ on time. Assume that the amount of new material presented, $dv(t)$, declines over time in proportion to what has already been taught, or $dv(t)/dt = b\,v(t)$, with the constraint that $b < 0$. This expression is again a simple differential equation. When solved, see Sørensen and Hallinan (1977) for details, one obtains the function

$$v(t) = \frac{1}{b}\,(e^{bt} - 1).$$

(4)

By letting $t \rightarrow \infty$ as less and less new material is presented, we can show that the total amount of material presented is $-1/b$, so that b directly determines the opportunities for learning. The smaller b is in absolute magnitude, the more opportunities there are. The formulation (4) assumes that $v(0) = 0$, but the specification implies a simple linear differential equation for learning, $dy(t)/dt = s + by(t)$, that can be solved for any period of time. The solution is

$$y(t_2) = c_0{}^* + b^* y(t_1) + c_1{}^* x_1 + c_2{}^* x_2 \ldots . c_n{}^* x$$

(5)

where $b^* = e^{b\Delta t}$, and each of the c^* coefficients have the form, $c^* = c/b(e^{b\Delta t}\,\Delta 1)$. Here $\Delta t = t_2 - t_1$, the period of observation (e.g., 10th to 12th grade). From estimates of b^*, one can obtain b as in $b^*/\Delta t$, and using this estimate, one can also generate the parameters c from the c^*s. Note that b^* is a function of b and time. Estimates of b^* are between zero and 1, since b is assumed to be less than zero, For given time periods, a larger b^* suggests more opportunities.

Equation (5) is the lagged regression model estimated by Coleman and Hoffer (1987), Chubb and Moe (1990), and many others. However, the proposed derivation, and the resulting parametrization, allows for the estimation of the fundamental forces governing learning: the opportunities for learning characterizing schools and the individual endowments of students, perhaps augmented by their schools. Such estimates were presented for various school characteristics in Sørensen and Hallinan (1977), for ability groups in Sørensen and Hallinan (1986), for academic tracks in Sørensen (1987), and for public versus Catholic schools in Sørensen (1996). All of these applications provided results consistent with the ideas suggested above. The models were estimated individual level models. Multilevel models would have been more appropriate because the b^*s are school (track or ability) characteristics. This would have provided better estimates, but the use of multilevel analysis would not change the conceptual points emphasized. In the analysis of the Catholic versus public school differences, estimates for b in different subject areas suggest that Catholic Schools do indeed provide more opportunities for learning, in addition to whatever effects the functional communities have on the efforts of students (Sørensen, 1996). This appears to be mainly a result of more students being allocated to academic tracks in Catholic schools, as noted above.

The conception of how school effects are produced proposed here is very different from what Coleman proposed in the additive models used in *Equality of Educational Opportunity* (Coleman et al, 1966) and subsequent school effects research. The additive models used assumed that schools can shape the minds and motivations of students in order to overcome the influence of family background. Additive models pay no attention to the interaction between student endowments and opportunities for learning, or the process of education.

In response to an early version of the model proposed, Hauser (1978) argued that it is unreasonable to assume that school effects are produced primarily by opportunities for learning. He suggested that there may be considerably more learning going on in a boot camp where relative achievement levels are in flux than in a perfunctorily led high school class where relative learning differences persist. Evidently, Hauser conceived of learning as change in students' ability and effort only. Furthermore, Hauser seemed only to allow school effects that change students relative to each other. This is an unreasonably restrictive definition of school effects: schools only matter if they make the bright dull and the dull brighter, as can be detected by the variance partitioning produced by simple cross-sectional models.[3]

Hauser (1978), Coleman and associates (1966), Chubb and Moe (1990), and others conceived of schooling as a process whereby schools somehow add to, or subtract from, the intellectual resources of students. This is an attractive scenario, for it implies that schools should be able to produce gifted students and more equal educational outcomes. At least all students attending the same schools should come out pretty much alike, and all students in America should become equal if schools are equally equipped with the things that mold young minds. This, in turn, would mean that schools can achieve equality of results, as well as equality of educational opportunity, if those who are in charge of schools think that this is an important goal.

This conception of the educational process and of the role of schools is an important one in American culture. The comprehensive system of secondary education, or the "common school" (Cremin, 1951), is a unique American institution designed to achieve a basic equality of educational outcomes. The institution has been imitated in a number of European countries, as a replacement for, or an alternative to, the very selective and highly differentiated European school systems, designed originally to achieve the opposite of the American schools: maximum feasible inequality of educational outcomes (see, for example, Kerckhoff (1993), who presented an exemplary illustration of the contrast in an empirical analysis of schooling processes in the U.K., emphasizing the long-term consequences of processes creating inequality).

The American goal of the common school is not an easy one to achieve, at least not if it is taken literally. Presumably, schools would add to the ability and effort of children primarily by teaching and thus by creating opportunities for learning. If equal outcomes are desired, these opportunities should be allocated so that the least able receive the most opportunities and the most able the fewest. This is not usually what occurs in schools. One main reason may

---

[3]A number of implications for policy of the debate between Hauser and Sørensen about the nature of school effects are developed by Hoaglin et al. (1982).

be that such an allocation of opportunities is in direct contradiction to another popularly accepted educational goal; the goal of providing each student with the opportunity to achieve to the maximum of his or her potential.

Providing students with more opportunities for learning produces more inequality in academic achievement. This is easily seen from the conception of learning and teaching proposed here. Opportunities for learning determine the parameters of Equation (5) in such a manner that the variance of y(t) in the long run will become $s^2_{y(max)} = (-1/b)^2 \sigma^2_s$. In this case, y(max) is the eventual academic achievement, and σ^2_s is the variance in student intellectual resources. Clearly, as more opportunities are provided, more variance or inequality in academic achievement will be created, for given inputs. From Equation (5), it can also easily be seen that the variance in achievement will increase over time until it reaches the value $\sigma^2_{y(max)}$. There is empirical support for this prediction about the increase in inequality in achievement in the form of a phenomenon called fan spread. For example, Willms and Jacobsen (1990) reported that while students tend to maintain their initial position in the distribution of mathematics achievement from grades 3 to 7, there is an increase in the variance in the scores in later grades that is consistent with the suggsted predictions suggested.

In fact, the goal of providing each student with the opportunities to achieve the maximum of his or her potential has stronger implications. Such a goal implies that those with the greatest intellectual resources should have the most favorable opportunities for learning. For this reason, ability grouping and similar arrangements are often adopted in the lower grades in tandem with elaborate curriculum differentiation in the higher grades. Schools that provide the most opportunities to the most able students are also schools that maximize differences among students in academic achievement. The goal of maximizing each student's academic achievement, therefore, implies the maximization of inequality of educational outcomes given individual endowments.

If we consider good schools to be schools that try to teach a lot, and if the model proposed previously is true, then good schools increase the effect of family background. This is, of course, the exact opposite of Coleman's prediction (Coleman et al., 1966). His conception of a good school does not emphasize the amount of teaching taking place, but the strength of functional communities that may be created in schools. These characteristics of good schools reduce the effect of family background, he argued. In Catholic schools the effect of family background on learning should be lower than in public schools. Coleman, Hoffer, and Kilgore (1982) and Coleman and Hoffer (1987) showed that there seems to be an advantage for minority students and to students with disadvantaged family backgrounds who attend Catholic schools. There are two explanations for this result. Coleman's would be that it reflects the higher effort by all students produced by functional communities. However, the pattern could also result from selection into Catholic schools by highly motivated parents of disadvantaged youth, as argued by Goldberger and Cain (1982), so that the allegedly disadvantaged students are, in fact, nontypical as shown by their parents' school choices. Coleman did not address these selection issues related to his common school idea (see Heckman & Neal, 1996, for a discussion).

If the smaller effect of family background in Catholic schools is not due to selection, then the result suggests that the theory about the effect of opportunities is wrong, or that Catholic schools provide fewer opportunities for learning, or that the functional communities overcome the increased differentiation caused by better opportunities for learning in Catholic schools. It can be shown, using inclusion in the academic track as an indicator of opportunities for learning, that there indeed is a stronger effect of family background on achievement for students in the academic tracks compared to other students (Sørensen, 1987), suggesting that the interaction effect between background and opportunities for learning does indeed exist. It is also possible to show that Catholic schools provide more opportunities for learning than public schools (Sørensen, 1996). Thus, it would seem that selection bias is indeed important, or that functional communities change students substantially, as suggested by Coleman's Durkheimian educational theory. In other words, if there is no selection bias, then Coleman & Hoffer's (1987) common school scenario implies that functional communities make students so much alike that the increased opportunities for differentiation provided by the richer teaching in Catholic schools do not result in more inequality in these schools, but in less.

METHODOLOGICAL ISSUES

No other sociological research has attracted as much attention and controversy as the school effects research conducted by Coleman and his associates. Almost all of the debate surrounding these studies focused on methodological issues of study design, measurement, sampling, and statistical analysis techniques. The magnitude of reported effects was disputed. In the first Coleman report, these effects were minimal. In the public/private school research, they were substantial. Much of the debate over these effects focused on whether regression analysis adequately controls for the individual endowments that influence learning outcomes. This section briefly surveys these issues, as well as an unresolved statistical problem of the lagged regression model that has become the common model for the estimation of school effects.

The Magnitude of School Effects

The well-known conclusion of *Equality of Educational Opportunity* (Coleman et al., 1966) is that school resources—instructional and economic—make very little difference for the academic achievement of students. This conclusion was drawn from a comparison of the amount of variance explained by the set of variables measuring school characteristics and the amount of variance explained by individual endowments. The choice of this methodology clearly reflects the statistical and computational capacities that were available at the time of the study. The use of regression analysis by social scientists on large datasets was still in its infancy in the early 1960s. Coleman needed a way to express the effect of a large group of variables simultaneously, and the partitioning of explained variance seemed a straightforward and feasible approach given the computational resources that were available. Using this measure of effect, *Equality of Educational Opportunity* (Table 3.24.1) reported that district per pupil expenditure accounts for a mere .09% of the variance in academic achievement for Black students in the North and .29% for White students in the North.

There are two problems with this approach. One received much attention in the debate about the *Equality of Educational Opportunity* report—the causal ordering of the various groups of variables. Because schools with good resources tend to have students with high family background, groups of variables summarizing each are therefore highly correlated and share substantial amounts of variance. The total amount of variance explained by a group of variables is therefore a poor measure of the importance of the group of variables. The order in which the variables are entered becomes important. Hanushek and Kain (1972, p. 127) showed that school characteristics account for 8.08% of the variance in achievement, if this group of variables is entered first. In contrast, the family background variables account for 7.77% of the variance when they are entered first. When entered last, school resources and instructional facilities account for an additional 2.12 % of the variance.

Coleman and his collaborators on *Equality of Educational Opportunity* (1966) defended their assumptions of causal order by pointing out that family background is causally prior to school characteristics. However, the opposite may be true if students choose schools freely and their choices depend on the facilities of the schools, as noted by Hanushek and Kain (1972). The assumption of Coleman and his colleagues was embedded in the standard interpretation of the results of the study, and for a group of neighborhood schools, the assumption may be reasonable.

However, the interpretation remains ambiguous. The amount of variance explained by schools would be 100% if schools caused all the variation in educational outcomes so that schools produce equal educational outcomes for all their students, regardless of student body composition. However, the outcome of explaining 100% of the variance could also result from schools having no effect at all. This would occur if schools were completely homogeneous in terms of student bodies so that students are all alike within schools and different between schools. In the latter case, even if schools have no effect on academic achievement, school characteristics would perfectly predict the achievement differences caused by individual endowments. If there was no variation within schools in individual endowments, all of the effects of these endowments on achievement would mistakenly be attributed to schools in the standard regression analysis.

There is no way to differentiate these two interpretations without recourse to theory, a randomized experiment, or an unverifiable assumption that we have measured all determinants of achievements and the standard linear additive specification is the true model. Standard school effects research offers none of these alternative guaranties.

The use of amount of variance explained as an effect measure has other problems. Variance explained depends on the variances of the variables. Anyone browsing through the *Equality of Educational Opportunity* report (1966) will find a bewildering variation in the R^2s and contributions to R^2s among the various regional, grade, and racial groups that are largely uninterpretable. These variations clearly reflect variation across groups in population variances, errors of measurement, and the like. None of this variation says anything about the effectiveness of schools. Cain and Watts (1970) pointed this out and argued for converting the variables into some dollar metric and the use of (metric) regression coefficients when evaluating their policy implications. Coleman (1972) converted the variance-explained measures to standardized regression coefficients, for a long time popular measures of relative importance. These measures suffered from the same dependence on population variances as the variance measures.

More recently, school effects research has relied on regression coefficients to assess the magnitude of effects. In the private/public schools research, almost all attention has been focused on the statistical significance of coefficients, in particular those for school sector. Statistical significance is important for our willingness to believe in a result. It is not a guide to the magnitude of the effect because statistical significance also depends on population variances, on sample variances, and on sample size. There nevertheless has been a tendency to confound statistical significance with substantive importance.

Coleman and Hoffer (1987) converted the regression coefficient estimates into grade equivalents and claimed that average public school students would gain from 1 (in reading, writing, and mathematics) to .02 (in science) grade equivalents if they were instead enrolled in Catholic schools. This seems to mean that in important subjects, Catholic school students gain an extra year of schooling over public school students. Over the 2-year period covered by these data, this is a large effect of Catholic schooling, perhaps too large to be believable.

The private/public school research by Coleman and his associates makes no attempt to compare school effects to family background effects, the issue that so much occupied them in the *Equality of Educational Opportunity* report (1966). School effects are in a different metric than the family background variables, and direct comparison is impossible based on raw regression coefficients. Chubb and Moe (1990), nevertheless, argued that their school organization variable is important because if one moves from the bottom to the top quartile in school organization the gain is even greater than when moving from the bottom to the top quartile in family background. This is a comparison no different from the comparison of variance explained. Unless one believes that effort expended by moving around quartiles is a proper metric, the effects remain incomparable.

Effects of dollars invested in a school might be an appropriate metric because its effect can be compared to investments in other activities. Hanushek (1986), as noted previously, found no systematic effect of school expenditures on learning. His meta-analysis was of patterns of significance and not of the magnitude of effects. Hedges, Laine, and Greenwald (1994) reanalyzed the same set of studies with a different methodology and found a different pattern of effects in terms of statistical significance, suggesting more support for an effect of school expenditures. They also attempted to estimate the magnitude of the effect of dollars invested in schools and found that a 10% increase in real resources produced a 70% increase in a standard deviation of achievement. Hanushek (1994b), in his response, pointed out that the expenditure on schools increased by 100% over 25 years, thus suggesting an increase of seven standard deviations in achievement! In fact, performance has at best remained constant over this 25-year period.

Parents believe that schools make an important difference, important enough to justify additional expenses for private schooling and housing choices to allow their children to go to what they consider to be good public schools. The result is a confounding of school characteristics and individual endowments that has occupied school effects research ever since the publication of *Equality of Educational Opportunity* (Coleman et al., 1966). It is probably meaningless to say which is more important. It is not meaningless to compare expenditures on schools to expenditures on social programs providing a higher standard of living for the poor and more income security for them. These comparisons remain to be done.

Selection Issues

The ideal design for the establishment of school effects would seem to be the randomized experiment noted in the introduction. Short of the ideal design, researchers rely on the use of control variables in regression analysis, usually measures of individual endowments. If these controls are inadequate or are improperly specified, estimates of school effects are biased. This issue has occupied much of the methodological criticism of school effects research and started with the debate over the *Equality of Educational Opportunity* report (Coleman et al., 1966) and its assumption about the causal order of family background variables and school characteristics. Again, the issue dominated the attention of the debate about the research on public and private schools, but by then a new language had been developed by statisticians and by econometricians to explain the sources of bias. The main criticism of the research was that the controls used by Coleman were inadequate, resulting in sample selection bias (see, for example, Goldberger & Cain, 1982; Murnane, Newstead, & Olsen,1985).

Coleman, Hoffer, and Kilgore (1982) used 17 family background variables as controls. However, this did not seem adequate to the critics who pointed out that unmeasured endowment variables might still bias upward the effect of private schools. A set of sophisticated statistical techniques to handle sample selection bias was being developed at the time Coleman's critics attacked the public and private school research (see Winship & Mare, 1992, for a review of these techniques). There are two issues involved—model misspecification and unobservable causes of self-selection. If the nonrandom allocation of students to public schools and to private schools is not adequately controlled by entering the correct specification of all relevant family background variables and other observable characteristics of students (i.e., parents' education is included as a linear additive effect when a nonlinear specification is more appropriate), then bias in the school effects coefficients can result. The second source of bias in the estimates of school effects can arise from the nonrandom allocation of students to school sectors on the basis of an unobserved determinant (i.e., parents are more likely to pay for what they consider a high-quality private education if they rightly judge their children to have an unusually strong genetic endowment of cognitive ability). The first source of bias can be handled with a technique developed by Rosenbaum and Rubin (1983) to estimate the sector effects separately for groups of students having the same propensity to attend private schools, although constructing (and defending the chosen construction of) the propensity score can be quite difficult. Coleman and Hoffer (1987) attempted this sort of correction and reported that it did not change their conclusions. The second source of bias can be tackled by a two-stage estimation procedure, associated with the labor economics research of Heckman (1979), that supplies an estimate of the error term with which the school effects variables are purportedly correlated. Applied by Noell (1982) to the private/public sector effects estimate, no significant impact of unmeasured variables on the sector effect was detected.

Finally, control variables can also magnify selection bias, as often happens when researchers do not use an explicit theory to model the mechanisms that produce school effects. We proposed previously that schools may affect learning in two ways—by providing opportunities for learning and by changing the ability and effort of students. These latter atmospheric effects of schools presumably also affect parents. With the desire to control for all relevant characteristics of family background, researchers often include family-level variables that might be partly determined by schools. Such variables include items in the home—number of books, dictionaries, pocket calculators—all items used in the research on private and public schools. Similarly, parents presumably react to the ability and effort of students by adjusting their aspirations and expectations to the school performance of their children. These variables are commonly used to measure family background. Finally, even the standard family background variables, parents' education and socioeconomic status, may change meaning as a result of the operation of schools. These variables are indicators of cultural aspects of the home background, and if schools change students, schools also change what these variables measure.

Statistical Issues

The estimation, in early schools effects research, of linear models for the level of academic achievement using ordinary least squares presents no special statistical problems. However, in almost all recent school effects research, the dependent variable has been the gain in achievement, say between 10th and 12th grade, and this may cause problems. The commonly used model is

$$y(t_2) - y(t_1) = c_0^* + b^* y(t_1) + c_1^* x_1 + c_2^* x_2 \ldots \ldots c_n^* x_n \tag{6}$$

If the left-hand side is replaced by $y(t_2)$ alone, as in Equation (5), the estimates of the c_i coefficients are the same, but the coefficient for $y(t_1)$ becomes $b^* + 1$. Equation (6) is referred to as the regressor variable model in the psychometric literature, and the variant with only $y(t_2)$ as the dependent variable is known as the lagged model in the econometrics literature. These formulations, with $y(t_1)$ on the right-hand side, are usually seen as preferable to other models because they avoid the problems caused by the well-known unreliability of the change score, $y(t_2) - y(t_1)$, and they capture the regression toward the mean that otherwise may seriously bias other coefficients correlated with $y(t_1)$. Interpretations of the model vary. Chubb and Moe (1990) saw $y(t_1)$ as a measure of ability affecting level of achievement at Time 2. Coleman and Hoffer (1987) took the model as one for gains in achievement. Equation (6) is identical to Equation (5) and therefore also represents the estimation equation for the model of learning we have described previously with the model for change in $v(t)$ over time given in Equation (4).

The regressor variable method (or the lagged model) is not free of problems. If it is used to estimate the difference in achievement gain for two groups with different initial levels of achievement, such as Catholic and public schools, measurement error in y will produce under adjustment for the initial difference between the two groups (see Judd & Kenny 1981, Chapter 6; and Willett 1988 for further explanation). Allison (1990) proposed the estimation of models of the change score without $y(t_1)$ as a right-hand-side variable in order to avoid the bias caused by measurement error in $y(t_1)$. When the effect of the x_i variables occurs after $y(t_1)$ is obtained, Allison showed that the measurement error problem disappears.

Allison's (1990) argument amounts to estimating the fixed-effect (or first difference) model from the econometrics literature. This model is obtained by assuming a model for the levels of achievement at Time 1 and Time 2 and then subtracting the two models. This results in the equation

$$y(t_2) - y(t_1) = b_0 + b_1 \Delta x_1 + b_2 \Delta x_2 \ldots b_n \Delta x_n \tag{7}$$

where b_i are the coefficients to the x variables that change between Time 1 and Time 2. Constant variables, including unmeasured variables that remain constant over the period, disappear and are eliminated as sources of bias. Such fixed-effects models have become very popular for the treatment of panel data. Following Allison, they may also seem appropriate for the estimation of models for achievement gains, removing the problem caused by measurement error in $y(t_1)$ or by unmeasured variables correlated with $y(t_1)$.

It is important to note that the fixed-effect or the change score model assumes that changes in y_t are produced by changes in independent variables. In other words, the fixed-effect model assumes that academic achievement only increases with an increase in some determinant of learning. This is not a reasonable assumption for the type of variables and processes usually investigated in school effects research. Measured family background variables usually do not change markedly over time. In any event, to the extent that the background variables are measures of stable ability differences, the mechanism by which they affect learning is one where the level of ability, or cultural resources in the home, affects gains in achievement. This is also what the learning model, suggested previously, assumes. Furthermore, the opportunities for learning provided by a school may be considered stable characteristics of schools.

The statistical advantage of the change score or fixed-effect model holds when ordinary least squares are used. The lagged models, of which Equation (6) is an example, have generated a rich literature in econometrics (e.g., Greene, 1993) in the context of time series models. Here the proposed solution to the biases caused by $y(t_1)$ is to use instrumental variables. The lagged models do seem more appropriate for studying learning outcomes of schools than the fixed effect model. However, an instrumental variables approach to overcome the statistical problems with measurement error in the lagged variable has not yet made an appearance in the school effects literature.

CONCLUSION

No body of sociological research has generated as much controversy as the school effects research conducted by James S. Coleman. The policy implications have been unpopular with many of the interest groups associated with schools. Because the conclusions were based on some of the largest quantitative research enterprises conducted, much effort has been invested in finding methodological faults and problems with the research. We have reviewed some of these methodological problems, and clearly some conclusions are dubious and are based on procedures and methods that now seem inadequate. Nevertheless, we find that the most serious problems are conceptual. School effects research has paid very little attention to the issue of how school effects are brought about, and when the research has proposed such mechanisms, as in the research on Catholic and on public schools, they have not been empirically established.

We propose the use of a nonlinear specification of how the learning process depends on student endowments and the main activity of schools, teaching. The model is based on a simple theory of how learning outcomes are produced, a theory that has important implications for how one should go about conducting school effects research. However, we are doubtful that such an approach will gain wide acceptance in future school effects research.

There is a serious dilemma for policy oriented sociological research here. Sociologists have few well-specified theories that result in acceptable mathematical models for processes, and those theories that do exist, such as the one we outlined above, are unlikely to be agreed upon. This means that sociologists are unlikely to propose that a policy recommendation be based on models that deviate from the standard linear statistical models we are taught to use by statisticians. Statisticians do not have sociological theories. They, therefore, propose models that are parsimonious. This is a virtue, but the result may be an incorrect representation of the processes under study. The simple additive model for academic achievement from our perspective is a poor theory. However, it is the only theory likely to be believed by the research community at large and the policymakers informed by this community. Sociologists therefore must choose between believing their own theories while accepting the difficulty of getting the models they imply accepted, or instead ignoring the implications of their own theories in order to provide standard statistical descriptions.

ACKNOWLEDGMENT: The research was supported by a grant from the American Educational Research Association which receives funds for its AERA Grants Program from the National Science Foundation and the National Center for Education Statistics (U.S. Department of Education) under NSF Grant #RED-9452861. Opinions reflect those of the authors and do not necessarily reflect those of the granting agencies. We are indebted to Susan Dumais, Deborah Hordon, Gabriella Gonzalez, and Shannon Hodge for research assistance.

REFERENCES

Alexander, K. L., & Pallas, A. M. (1983). Private schools and public policy: New evidence on cognitive achievement in public and private schools. *Sociology of Education, 56,* 170–182.

Allison, P. D. (1990). Change scores as dependent variables in regression analysis. *Sociological Methodology, 20*, 93–114.

Angrist, J. B., & Krueger, A. B. (1991, November). Does compulsory school attendance affect schooling and earnings? *The Quarterly Journal of Economics, CVI*(4), 980–1014.

Barr, R., & Dreeben, R. (1983). *How schools work*. Chicago, IL: Chicago University Press.

Barnett, W. S. (1995). Long-term effects of early childhood programs on cognitive and school outcomes. *The Future of Children*, 5, 25–50.

Berliner, D. C., & Biddle, B. J. (1997). *The manufactured crisis*. White Plains, NY: Longman.

Bryk, A. S., Lee, V., & Holland, P. (1993). *Catholic schools and the common good*. Cambridge, MA: Harvard University Press.

Cain, G. G., & Watts, H. W. (1970). Problems in making policy inferences from the Coleman Report. *American Sociological Review, 35*, 228–242.

Chubb, J. E., & Moe, T. M. (1990). *Politics, markets, and America's schools*. Washington, DC: Brookings.

Coleman, J. S. (1961). *The adolescent society*. New York, NY: The Free Press.

Coleman, J. S. (1972). The evaluation of "equality of educational opportunity." In F. Mosteller & D. P. Moynihan (Eds.), *On equality of educational opportunity* (pp. 146–167). New York, NY: Random House.

Coleman, J. S., Campbell, E. Q., Hobson, C. J., McPartland, J., Mood, A., Weinfeld, F. D., & York, R. L. (1966). *Equality of educational opportunity*. Washington, DC: U.S. Government Printing Office.

Coleman, J. S., Kelly, S., & Moore, J. (1975). *Trends in School Segregation, 1968–1973*. Washington, DC: The Urban Institute.

Coleman, J. S., & Hoffer, T. (1987). *Public and private schools: The impact of communities*. New York: Basic Books.

Coleman, J. S., Hoffer, T., & Kilgore, S. (1982). *High school achievement*. New York: Basic Books.

Cremin, L. A. (1951). *The American common school*. New York: Knopf.

Goldberger, A. S., & Cain, G. G. (1982, April/July). The causal analysis of cognitive outcomes in the Coleman, Hoffer and Kilgore Report. *Sociology of Education, 55*, 103–122.

Goodlad, J. I. (1983). *A place called school: Prospects for the future*. New York: McGraw-Hill.

Greene, W. (1993). *Econometric analysis. 2nd Edition*. Englewod Cliffs, NJ: Prentice-Hall.

Hanushek, E. A. (1971, May). Teacher characteristics and gains in academic achievement. *American Economic Review, 60*, 280–288.

Hanushek, E. A. (1986, September). The economics of schooling: Production and efficiency in public schools. *Journal of Economic Literature, 24*, 1141–1177.

Hanushek, E. A. (1994a). *Making schools work*. Washington, DC: The Brookings Institution.

Hanushek, E. A. (1994b). Money may matter somewhere: A response to Hedges, Laine, and Greenwald. *Educational Researcher, 23*, 5–-8.

Hanushek, E. A. (1996). A more complete picture of school resource policies. *Review of Educational Research, 66*, 397–409.

Hanushek, E. A., & Kain, J. F. (1972). On theVValue of "Equality of Educational Opportunity" as a guide to public policy. In F. Mosteller & D. P. Moynihan (Eds.), *On Equality of Educational Opportunity* (pp. 69–115). New York: Random House.

Hauser, R. M. (1978). On "A reconceptualization of school effects." *Sociology of Education, 51*(1), 86–73.

Heckman, J. J. (1979). Sample bias as a specification error. *Econometrica, 47*, 153–162.

Heckman, J. J., & Neal, D. (1996). Coleman's contribution to education: Theory, research styles and empirical research. In J. Clark (Ed.), *James S. Coleman* (pp. 81–102). London: Falmer Press.

Hedges, L. V., Laine, R. D., & Greenwald, R. (1994, April). Does money matter? A meta-analysis of studies of the effects of differential school inputs on student outcomes. *Educational Researcher, 23*, 5–14.

Heyns, B., & Hilton, T. L. (1982, April/July). The cognitive tests for high school and beyond: An assessment. *Sociology of Education*, 55, 89–102.

Hoaglin, D. C., Light, R. J., McPeek, B., Mosteller, F., & Stoto, M. A. (1982). *Data for decisions*. Cambridge, MA: Abt Books.

Jencks, C. S., & Phillips, M. (1998). *The Black-White Test Score Gap*. Washington, DC: Brookings Institution Press.

Judd, C. M., & Kenny, D. A. (1981). *Estimating the effects of social interventions*. New York: Cambridge University Press.

Kerckhoff, A. C. (1993). *Diverging pathways: Social structure and career decisions*. New York: Cambridge University Press.

Lightfoot, S. L. (1983). *The good high school: Portraits of character and culture*. New York: Basic Books.

Mosteller, F. (1995). The Tennessee study of classs size in the early school grades. *The Future of Children*, 5, 113–127.

Mosteller, F., & Moynihan, D. P., (Eds.). (1972). *On equality of educational opportunity.* New York: Random House.

Murnane, R., Newstead, S., & Olsen, R. J. (1985). Comparing public and private schools: The puzzling role of selectivity bias. *Journal of Business and Economic Statistics, 3,* 23–35.

Murnane, R. J., & Phillips, B. (1981, March). What do effective teachers of inner-city children have in common. *Social Science Research, 10,* 83–100.

National Center for Educational Statistics. (1993). *Education in the states and nations: Indicators comparing U.S. states.* Washington, DC: U.S. Department of Education, Office of Educational Research and Improvement.

Noell, J. (1982, April/July). Public and Catholic schools: A Reanalysis of "Public and Private Schools." *Sociology of Education, 55,* 123–132.

Powell, A. G., Farrar, E., & Cohen, D. K. (1985). *The shopping mall high school: Winners and losers in the educational marketplace.* Boston: Houghton Mifflin.

Rosenbaum, P. R., & Rubin, D. B. (1983). The central role of the propensity score in observational studies for causal effects. *Biometrika, 70,* 41–55.

Rosenthal, R. & Jacobson, L. (1968). *Pygmalion in the classroom: Teacher expectation and pupils' intellectual development.* New York: Holt, Rinehart and Winston.

Schultz, T. (1961, March). Investment in human capital. *American Economic Review, 51,* 1–17.

Sizer, T. R. (1984). *Horace's compromise: The dilemma of the American high school.* Boston: Houghton Mifflin.

Smith, M .S. (1992). Equality of educational opportunity: The basic findings reconsidered. In F. Mosteller & D. P. Moynihan (Eds.), *On equality of educational opportunity* (pp. 230–342). New York: Random House.

Sørensen, A. B. (1987). The organizational differentiation of students in schools as an opportunity structure. In M. T. Hallinan (Ed.), *The social organization of schools: New conceptualizations of the learning process* (pp. 103–130). New York: Plenum.

Sørensen, A. B. (1996). Educational opportunities and school effects. In J. Clark (Ed.), *James S. Coleman* (pp. 207–225). London: Falmer Press.

Sørensen, A. B., & Hallinan, M. T. (1977). A reconceptualization of school effects. *Sociology of Education, 50,* 522–535.

Sørensen, A. B., & Hallinan, M. T. (1986, Winter). Effects of ability grouping on growth in academic achievement. *American Educational Research Journal, 23*(4), 519–542.

Westbury, I. (1992). Comparing American and Japanese achievement: Is the United States really a low achiever? *Educational Researcher, 21*(5), 18–24.

Willett, J. B. (1988). Questions and answers in the measurement of change. *Review of Research in Education, 1988–89,* 345–422.

Willms, J. D., & Jacobsen, S. (1990). Growth in mathematics skills during the intermediate years: Sex differences and school effects. *International Journal of Educational Research, 14,* 157–174.

Winship, C. & Mare, R. D. (1992). Models for Sample Selection Bias. *Annual Review of Sociology, 18,* 327–350.

PART II

DEVELOPMENT AND EXPANSION OF EDUCATION

CHAPTER 7

Development and Education

COLETTE CHABBOTT

FRANCISCO O. RAMIREZ

INTRODUCTION

A positive relationship between education and economic, political, and cultural development is widely assumed throughout much of the modern and modernizing world, yet research suggests that this relationship is problematic. The problem has two aspects. First, although many empirical studies show a positive relationship between many forms of education and individual economic, political, and cultural development, the effects of education on development at the collective level are ambiguous. Second, at the same time evidence of this for ambiguity has been mounting, faith in education as the fulcrum for individual and for collective development has been growing in the form of international education conferences and declarations and national-level education policies.

This chapter explores two aspects of the problem in distinct ways. First, in the sections on the effects of education on development and the effects of development on education, we review the empirical relationship between education and development, drawing on several decades of cross-national studies. Second, in Section 4, we examine the way education as an instrument to attain national progress and justice has been produced and diffused via development discourse, development organizations, and development professionals. Although the types of education prescribed varied from one decade to another, throughout the post-World War II period, education for all became an increasingly important component in the global blueprint for development.

How did this blueprint come to be so widely disseminated? We suggest that two ration-

COLETTE CHABBOTT • School of Education, Stanford University, Stanford, California 94305-3096. *Present address:* Board on International Comparative Studies in Education, National Academies of Science, Washington, DC 20007
FRANCISCO O. RAMIREZ • School of Education, Stanford University, Stanford, California 94305-3096.
Handbook of the Sociology of Education, edited by Maureen T. Hallinan. Kluwer Academic/Plenum Publishers, New York, 2000.

ales played a major role in buttressing confidence in the relationship between education and national development. The first constructs education as an investment in human capital, which will increase the productivity of labor and contribute to economic growth and development at the societal level. This rationale is closely tied to global norms about science, progress, material well-being, and economic development. The second general rationale constructs education as a human right, imagining education as the prime mechanism for human beings to better themselves and to participate fully in the economy, politics, and culture of their societies. This rationale is tied to notions of justice, equality, and individual human rights.

Our assessment of the literature on education and development leads us to two general conclusions. First, there are many gray areas regarding the evidence on the links between development and education. Sweeping assertions regarding the positive or negative effects of one on the other miss the mark. This is slowly but steadily recognized in calls to move beyond the earlier either/or formulations and attempts to delineate the conditions under which links between development and education are most likely to occur (Fuller & Rubinson, 1992; Rubinson & Brown, 1994). Moreover, many current studies go beyond examining the reciprocal ties between educational expansion and increased wealth; all sorts of research issues regarding the quality of education and the quality of life itself are on the rise. The scope of the development and education literature has expanded.

However, the second general conclusion is that much confidence in the positive ties between education and development persists in the development practitioner literature and in public discourse about education and development. Sociological attention needs to be directed to the power of the taken-for-granted, that is, to the institutionalization of diffuse beliefs, practices, and routines regarding the links between development and education (Meyer, 1977). Attention also needs to be directed to the social effects of widely diffused, taken-for-granted notions about education and development. These effects include the proliferation and spread of development discourse, development organizations, and development professionals, all of which celebrate and promote expanded visions of education as human capital and as a human right (Chabbott, 1996). These visions have a significant impact on what educational statistics are collected, how development progress is measured, and what education policies nation–states are encouraged to adopt.

To reiterate, these two general conclusions constitute an interesting paradox: despite growing scholarly acknowledgment that our understanding of the link between education and development contains many gray areas, public confidence in these links, manifest in national policies and in international declarations, continues to mount. It is this paradox that motivates our review of the literature and our delineation of new research directions in the study of development and education.

EFFECTS OF EDUCATION ON DEVELOPMENT

This section examines the effects of education on economic, political, and cultural development. We assess evidence of both individual and societal level effects.

Economic Development

The impact of education on the economy is often studied by considering the effect of education on individual productivity or its influence on national economic growth. The idea that increased exposure to school would increase productivity is at the heart of human capital theory. The pioneering work of Schultz (1963) suggested that the acquisition of more schooling involved more than mere enhanced consumption. Humans were increasingly investing in the development of their cognitive capacities and skills, and these investments, in the form of additional schooling attained, had payoffs both for them and for their societies. These investments were conceptualized as investments in human capital formation; today human capital is a pervasive feature of development discourse, a point to which we return in the third section. Much economic research focuses on the relationship between schooling and productivity at the individual level of analysis. It is to these studies that we now turn, before reviewing analyses at the societal level.

Almost from the outset of this research program, wages were used as a proxy for productivity (Denison, 1962). Given core economic assumptions about labor markets and the efficiency of resource allocation, the premise that more productive workers would be compensated with greater wages seemed plausible. These assumptions are consistent with the premises underlying the functionalist theory of social stratification. There are indeed many empirical studies showing the expected positive associations between schooling and wages in many different countries (Psacharopoulos & Woodhall, 1985; but see Lundgreen, 1976, for contrary evidence). Rate-of-return studies have become a staple of the economics of education, and more recently, of its application to research in less developed countries. Much of this research effort seeks to distinguish between the private and the social returns of different levels of schooling (primary v. higher education). Since the 1970s, Psacharopoulos (1973, 1989) has argued that the private and social returns are greater for primary education rather than for higher education and that this difference is greater in the less developed countries. More recent research, however, suggests that rates of return to tertiary education may be higher than rates for lower levels of education, particularly during sustained periods of industrialization (Carnoy, 1998; Ryoo, Nan, & Carnoy, 1993).

These generalizations have often lead to policy recommendations for less developed countries as to where investments in education would be most fruitful. As further studies called for more qualified generalizations, policy recommendations were altered or reversed (see discussion of discourse in "On Mechanisms for Diffusion"). For example, vocational schooling was recommended by donor organizations in the 1950s and 1960s and then the recommendation was scrapped, resulting in some serious costs to the client countries (Samoff, 1995).

Within this research tradition several studies have examined the effects of schooling on the productivity of women, comparing their wages with those of less educated women as well as with men with varying degrees of schooling. As is the case with the earlier studies of education and productivity among men, these relatively newer inquiries do not report identical results across countries. But here too some generalizations are warranted: as was the case with respect to men, there are private and social rates of return to women's schooling (Schultz, 1993). This is true in both the more developed and the less developed countries (Stromquist, 1989). In some countries the rate of social and/or private return to girls' schooling is actually greater than for boys' schooling. These findings have been emphasized in many government reports justifying investments in women's schooling, leading to a major push in the 1990s for girls' education projects in developing countries.

The dominant conceptualization and measurement of productivity in these studies has not gone unchallenged. Labor market economists have noted the degree to which schooling credentials may distort the market, thereby weakening the tie between productivity and wages (Carnoy, 1995; Knight & Sabot, 1987). To the extent that this is true, increased worldwide emphasis on formal schooling may increase the tendency to use formal degrees as certification for those seeking jobs, thereby increasing individual returns to schooling without neces-sarily increasing individual productivity (Collins, 1971). Some empirical studies question any direct evidence of a positive schooling effect on productivity (Berg, 1970), but more recent research on farmer education and on farmer productivity yields positive results (Lockheed, Jamison, & Lau, 1988; see also Honig's [1996] study of education and profitability among Jamaican microentrepreneurs). The broader sociological critique is that simply expanding the number of individuals with more schooling does not necessarily result in an increase in more productive jobs (Collins, 1979). From this perspective schooling is primarily a sorting and allocating machine; schools are organizations of stratification, with the more credentialed outcompeting the less credentialed for the better paying jobs (Spring, 1972).

None of this implies that the more credentialed are necessarily more productive. When the society is conceptualized as a more closed system, the process is imagined as a simple repro-duction of the hierarchical order, as social elites are more able to secure educational advantages for their children (Bowles & Gintis, 1976; but see Olneck & Bills, 1980). When a more open society is imagined, much intense competition and conflict ensues between social classes, between ethnic and religious groups, and more recently between women and men. None of this, however, was hypothesized to lead to increased productivity. The credential society was not to be confused with a more productive one (Collins, 1979). Thus, the optimism of an earlier era gave way to more skeptical and more critical outlooks in the sociology of development and educa-tion. This change in tone was even more pronounced when examining the effects of education on political and cultural development, a point emphasized later in this chapter.

A more recent appraisal of the literature makes explicit a methodological point implied in some of the earlier critiques and offers a fresh reformulation of the central question. The methodological point is a straightforward levels-of-analysis point: even if it were established that more schooling resulted in greater individual productivity, effects of schooling on pro-ductivity at the individual level do not necessarily lead to economic growth at the societal level. To arrive at the latter inference, one needs to compare societies, not individuals (see the papers in Meyer & Hannan, 1979). The brain drain literature partially suggests what happens to societies that have not been able to create more productive jobs for their more productive workers. The substantive reformulations call for the identification of the conditions under which educational expansion leads to economic growth (Fuller & Rubinson, 1992; Hanushek & Kim, 1996). In what follows we first examine cross-national studies of the influence of educational expansion on economic growth and then we turn to studies that specify the effects of some forms of schooling.

The study of Harbison and Meyers (1964) was among the first to undertake cross-na-tional efforts in this domain. This study reported a positive association between a country's level of educational enrollments and economic wealth and emphasized the stronger economic effect of secondary education. Because the study relied on a cross-sectional design it could not ascertain the direction of causality, thereby raising the chicken and egg question: does economic development lead to educational expansion, or vice versa (Anderson & Bowman, 1976)? Moreover, earlier research was often bivariate in character or did not include a suffi-cient number of reasonable control variables in the analyses. In the 1980s and the 1990s, however, cross-national researchers have attacked this issue utilizing multivariate analyses of panel data. These studies show that primary and secondary schooling have stronger effects on economic development than higher education (Benavot, 1992b; Meyer & Hannan, 1979). Moreover, the economic effects of expanded schooling seemed stronger for poorer countries. Interestingly enough this generalization is consistent with the main inference in Harbison and Meyers emphasizing the weaker economic effect of higher education. A similar conclusion is drawn by researchers undertaking a time series analysis of the economic consequences of the expansion of higher education in the United States (Walters & Rubinson, 1983).

In these analyses the independent variables of interest do not distinguish between types of schooling or curricula or between the different populations undergoing greater schooling. If some types of schooling more directly contribute to economic growth than other types, isolating their effects requires more refined measures than simple statistics estimating secondary or tertiary enrollments as a percent of the typical age cohort for this level of schooling. Working with different research designs and methods of analysis, several studies suggest a common and positive economic outcome of more scientific and technical forms of schooling. Focusing on lower levels of schooling in both France and Germany, some studies indicate that the expansion of more technical tracks had distinctive positive effects not found in the growth of the more classical tracks (Garnier & Hage, 1990; Garnier, Hage, & Fuller, 1989; Hage & Garnier, 1990; 1992). The researchers reasoned that the skills learned in these tracks were more relevant to the needs of the economy than the greater emphasis on high culture in the classical tracks. Another study examined the effects of varying curricular emphases in primary education on economic development. This analysis shows that, net of other influences, a stronger emphasis on science in the curriculum positively influences economic development (Benavot, 1992a). Shifting from lower levels of schooling to higher education, other cross-national investigations focused on the influence of different fields of study in higher education on the economy. The key cross-national finding is that greater enrollments in science and engineering positively influence economic development (Ramirez & Lee, 1995; Schofer, Ramirez, & Meyer, 1997).

Taken as a whole these findings suggest the plausibility of knowledge claims linking scientization in education and the growth of the economy. However, much more research is needed to test the implications of the general claim. Note, for example, that a time series analysis of the economic effect of science and engineering graduates in the United States failed to find a significant impact (Walters & O'Donnell, 1990). Furthermore, Schofer and associates (1997) found that some aspects of prestigious science activities, such as research and patents, have a negative economic effect. Finally, although many of these studies did not include a significant number of developing countries, they are sometimes used to justify fairly explicit policy recommendations for developing countries from international development organizations (described in "On Translating International Development into Educational Discourse").

A second direction in this domain disaggregates the educational effects by gender. Benavot (1989), for example, shows that women's share of secondary education positively influences the economy whereas the female tertiary enrollment variable fails to do so. Further studies may estimate the effects of female and male enrollments in different fields in higher education. This research direction would integrate the growing interest in isolating science effects with the expanding focus on gender-related outcomes. A recent cross-national study of science education at the secondary level concluded that girls do not necessarily have a predisposition against science. The participation and achievement of girls in secondary science varies widely between countries (Caillods, Gottelmann-Duret, & Lewin, 1996; a similar finding for math achievement is reported in Baker & Jones, 1993).

Political Development

The same optimism regarding the economic benefits of expanded schooling also led to an emphasis on political gains. One major line of inquiry focused on the effects of schooling on the political knowledge, values, and attitudes of individuals. Studies of the political socialization effects of education reflect this research tradition. A more macrosociological approach directly examined the effects of education on political democracy and on national integration. At both the individual and societal levels of analysis, the initial work seemed to be grounded in a much greater confidence in the transformative powers of schooling than later studies.

A major generalization from the political socialization literature is that individuals with more schooling were more likely to know more about their political systems and to have more positive political values and attitudes. The latter were often defined as participatory, democratic, and tolerant values and attitudes. Comparative studies of political socialization include the pioneering work of Almond and Verba (1963) as well as that of Torney and Hess (1969). Some studies compared adults with varying levels of schooling whereas others compared children in different national contexts exposed to different curricula (see, for example, Torney's (1976) cross-national study of civics education). The underlying assumption was that in democratic societies schools were instruments of democracy and more schooling thus led to more democratic outlooks and practices. Just exactly how schools accomplished this goal was unclear, with some arguments emphasizing curriculum and teachers as organizational resources, whereas broader sociological accounts stressed the citizenship-conferring character of the school as an institution (Dreeben, 1968; Meyer, 1977).

This political socialization research direction continues in the form of the current and ongoing second international study of civic education and also in comparative case studies of education, democracy, and human rights, such as Starkey (1991). Many of the new democracies seem especially interested in understanding how schools can shape democratic orientations. However, more recent studies raise questions about earlier generalizations. Weil (1985), for example, showed that the link between schooling attained and political tolerance varies across countries. In countries with a more authoritarian legacy or regime, better educated people are not more politically tolerant. This kind of finding suggests that in this domain of inquiry, one should also eschew unqualified generalizations. The political context within which schools operate may be an important contingency in ascertaining the relationship between education and politically democratic beliefs and values.

These studies raise some of the same issues of conceptualization and measurement as those earlier mentioned with respect to schooling and productivity. The reliance on paper-and-pencil tests as assessments of democratic orientations can be challenged; perhaps more educated actors are better prepared to figure out the correct responses and therefore inflate their scores. This criticism, however, begs the question as to why the more educated are better able to ascertain the more normatively acceptable political response.

Even if we did accept the face validity of the earlier findings, the levels-of-analysis argument made earlier with respect to schooling and economic development applies here, too. That is, one cannot infer the positive effects of expanded education on political democracy on the basis of individual data on schooling and values. The impact of education on the systemic rules of the game that constitute political democracy need to be directly studied, not inferred from individual-level data.

Much comparative theorizing argued or presupposed that an educated citizenry was essential for the establishment and maintenance of a political democracy. In this context the United States was often invoked as a country that both expanded schooling and political democracy relatively early in its history (Lipset, 1963). Comparative evidence supporting this generalization was found for both more developed (Cutright, 1969) and less developed countries (Adelman & Morris, 1973). These and other studies typically employed cross-sectional research designs, raising the same set of issues generated in response to the early work on education and economic development. Using the same indicators of political democracy earlier analyzed but extending these measures over time, one study showed that participation in lower levels of schooling (but not in higher education) positively affected political democracy (Ramirez, Rubinson, & Meyer, 1973). However, a more recent study with more and better measures of political democracy found significant effects of higher education (Benavot, 1992b). This study also shows that the effects of education vary across time periods, further suggesting the more conditional character of the relationship between educational expansion and political democracy.

Other studies have focused on political order and national integration. Some scholars feared that a bloated system of higher education would result in political instability; cross-national analyses showed no such effects (Gurr, 1971). There is also no evidence that educational expansion influences the type of political regime in a country (Thomas, Ramirez, Meyer, & Gobbalet, 1979). A more qualitative assessment of the role of education in promoting national integration in Malaysia concluded that education has failed to bolster national integration (Singh & Mukherjee, 1993), in stark contrast with the enormous faith placed in the nation-building potential of education in the 1950s and 1960s (see the papers in Coleman, 1965).

Cultural Development

Though closely related to studies of both economic and political development, modernization theory and research also focused on forms of personal development that were related to cultural development. Modernization theorists drew on Parson's (1957) theories of structural differentiation to explain how institutions multiply and the simple structures of traditional society become more complex in response to changes in technology and/or values. For most of these theorists, modernization was roughly equivalent to Westernization.

McClelland (1961), for example, argued that child-rearing practices tied to Western notions of individualism and progress give rise to a greater number of individuals with high levels of need achievement, which in turn produce an achieving society, driven by the need to achieve ever higher levels of output and productivity. These child-rearing practices and similar efforts in school lead to the formation of personal modernity, a condition characterized by a high sense of optimism, efficacy, and self-direction (Inkeles & Sirowy, 1983; Inkeles & Smith, 1974). Several case studies sought to document the passing of traditional society in part as a function of expanded schooling. More recent work examining the effect of varying types of educational experiences on personal modernity among Algerian students shows that more modern orientations are positively influenced both by instruction in French and by field of study, with science students exhibiting more modern outlooks than those in the humanities (Coffman, 1992). This study suggests that not all educational experiences may have the same modernization consequences. Whereas literacy may be in some generic sense modernizing, it may also be compatible with personal orientations quite different from those depicted by the theory.

Whether modernization could be distinguished from Westernization was a recurring issue in this literature. Just as there were those who argued that there were multiple paths to economic development, some researchers contended that there were diverse personal orientations and institutional arrangements compatible with undertaking modernization. Additionally, just as a causal link between more schooling and both more productive and more democratic individuals did not necessarily add up to economic growth and political democracy, respectively, so too a tie between expanded education and more modern persons would not suffice to justify causal inferences at the societal level. Cross-national comparisons at the societal level were needed. The literature contains early efforts to conceptualize societal modernization and the contribution of schooling to societal modernization (Black, 1967; Eisenstadt, 1963). However, the concept proved to be more complex than either economic development or political democracy. Few studies more attempted directly assess the impact of education on societal modernity.

One obvious avenue of research involves the influence of education on inequality, because part of what it means to be a modern society is to be a more open and, thus presumably, a more egalitarian society. Despite a plethora of cross-national studies on income inequality, little work has examined whether there is less income inequality in countries with more expanded education. One unpublished study suggests no effects (Shanahan, 1994); this finding is consistent with more structural theories of social inequality (Boudon, 1974). Little work has directly examined the influence of education on other forms of inequality; for example, between women and men. At the individual level of analysis, one study shows that more educated people are not necessarily more supportive of government efforts to reduce inequality between men and women (Davis & Robinson, 1991). More societal-level analyses indicate that the expansion of women's share of higher education positively influences their share of the paid labor force (Weiss, Ramirez, & Tracy, 1976). It is often assumed that women's expanded access to education will have broad, positive development effects, but much more research in this area is needed.

Summary

At the individual level of analysis, we find evidence that schooling positively influences wages but debate continues on whether wages are an adequate measure of productivity. There is also support for the hypothesis that more educated individuals are more politically active, though the effects of schooling on political tolerance are more variable. Lastly, more schooled individuals exhibit some values in line with modernization theory, but whether this is simply evidence of greater Westernization in general remains unsettled.

None of these findings, however, warrant societal-level inferences. Direct cross-national comparisons have increasingly been undertaken. Whereas earlier work emphasized global educational effects, more recent studies distinguish between the effects of different types of schooling and those brought about by different kinds of populations undertaking education. There is partial support for arguments emphasizing the economic benefits of expanded schooling, especially more technical forms. In contrast, the political or cultural consequences of educational expansion and the educational source of political or cultural development remain to be explored.

EFFECTS OF DEVELOPMENT ON EDUCATION

The chicken and egg question regarding the relationship between education and economic development also applies to the ways in which education affects political and cultural development. Perhaps education is more a consequence of economic, political, and cultural development rather than its cause, or perhaps causation is reciprocal. Much of this literature directly operates at the societal level, with the expansion of the educational system as a main dependent variable. More recent studies focus on specific aspects of the educational system, such as curricular emphases or specific fields of study, or on the access and attainment of specific populations, such as women. In what follows we focus primarily on these cross-national studies.

Some of the literature focuses on the rise and expansion of mass schooling whereas other studies deal with the formation and growth of higher education. Links between schooling and market forces and between schooling and the state have also been analyzed in this research tradition. This review first considers studies of mass schooling, then turns to research on higher education. We cover only studies in which educational outcomes are examined as a function of development variables.

Mass Schooling

Historians and sociologists increasingly recognize that the rise of mass schooling cannot be adequately accounted for as an outcome of industrialization (Maynes, 1985; Ramirez, 1997). This general observation is well illustrated in a case study of the rise of mass schooling in Sweden, a study that reveals the compatibility of mass schooling with a preindustrial economic base (Boli, 1989). Despite the popularity of both more conservative and more radical variants of logic of industrialization arguments, historical evidence fails to support the favored causal claim that mass schooling arose as a function of economic development. Nor is it the case that the expansion of primary school enrollments is mainly driven by economic development. Cross-national multivariate analysis of panel data shows that much primary enrollment growth is unrelated to various measures of economic development (Meyer, Ramirez, Rubinson, & Boli-Bennett, 1977; Meyer, Ramirez, & Soysal, 1992). Throughout the 20th century mass schooling has expanded in more developed and in less developed countries.

An alternate set of claims revolves around political factors. Historians and sociologists have linked the rise of mass schooling to the rise of the nation–state (Bendix, 1964; Reisner, 1927). Mass schooling for the production of loyal citizens is indeed a theme in the rise of mass schooling. However, there is no evidence that the more integrated nation–states were the ones that early on launched mass schooling (and as noted in the prior section, the success of mass schooling in promoting national integration has been challenged). Nor is a simple democratic story plausible, as mass schooling emerged in both more democratic and more authoritarian regimes in North America and in Western Europe in comparable time periods (Ramirez & Boli, 1987). The aforementioned cross-national analyses of primary educational expansion also failed to show convincing political and societal modernization effects.

In the post-World War II era the commitment to expand mass schooling cuts across all sorts of national boundaries and socioeconomic formations. The mixed evidence notwithstanding, there is much official and popular confidence in the transformative powers of schooling. There is also much worldwide consensus on the right of all to schooling. The erosion of primary enrollments in this country or in that region can thus be discussed as both an economic and a moral crisis (Fuller & Heyneman, 1989), a crisis that increasingly commands the attention of both national authorities and transnational organizations. This point is re-examined in the section on translating international development into educational discourse.

These findings may be interpreted along more historicist accounts of the rise of mass schooling (see, for example, many of the chapters in Mangan, 1994) or, alternately, from more generalizing sociological perspectives that emphasize the role of transnational forces. The historical approach suggests that, via multiple paths, different economies, polities, and civil societies converged on the value of expanding mass schooling. In contrast, macrosociologists have postulated that a single model of progress and justice formulated at the world level contributes to commonalities in mass schooling outcomes in otherwise diverse societies. The influence of these models triggered education as a nation-building project, quite apart from its actual impact on nation building and on related development activities. In some societies, though, the nation was more directly managed by the state whereas in others nation building involved social movements loosely coupled to the state bureaucracy.

In the 18th and 19th centuries the role of education within these emerging models was much more modest than its present status. Schooling for the masses literally started as schooling for differentiated and subordinated strata, but increasingly schools were imagined as beacons of progress and as pillars of the republic. This elevated view of schooling emerged even as nation–states themselves emerged as imagined, progress-seeking communities of solidarity (Anderson, 1991). By the late 19th century one could assert that the Franco–Prussian War had been won by the Prussian schoolmaster. Throughout the 20th century the putative links between schooling and development grew, less as a function of varying levels of societal development and more as an outcome of the common articulation of world development blueprints (Ramirez, 1997). Later we address the mechanisms through which world development blueprints are established and disseminated.

More recent studies have examined the impact of varying levels of development on curricular content and emphases (Kamens, Meyer, & Benavot, 1996). These studies show surprisingly similar trends in curricular development, trends that seem unrelated to the requirements of local economic or political structures or to the interests of local masses or elites (see the chapter by McEneaney and Meyer in this volume for a review of this literature.) Other cross-national research has focused on the changing trends in curricular requirements for girls and for boys in primary and secondary schooling, trends that suggest gender de-differentiation (Ramirez & Cha, 1990). This study also suggests that the growth of mass schooling involved expanding schooling for both boys and girls.

Higher Education

Earlier case studies of the development of higher education focused on cross-national organizational and institutional differences and sought to explain these differences (Clark, 1977a, 1977b). In these and in related cross-national studies, variations in levels of political centralization account for variations in the degree to which higher education is regulated by state authorities (Ramirez & Rubinson, 1979). Variations in academic governance structures have also been examined as a function of both market forces and state legacies. In this tradition a recent comparative study concluded that systems that strongly differentiate at the secondary level are more likely to have lower degrees of differentiation at the higher level (e.g., Germany) than those with relatively low levels of secondary school differentiation (e.g., the United States, Windolf, 1997). This analysis also suggests that the response of higher education expansion to market forces (business cycles) will be greater in societies where markets are more influential than state bureaucracies, moreso in the United States than in Germany.

The expansion of higher education has not always been regarded as evidence of progress. Not only was there greater skepticism regarding its positive effects, the elite character of higher education was taken for granted until well after World War II. Increasingly, higher education has become nearly a mass institution in some countries, whereas in others the aspiration to turn higher education into a more mass-friendly setting is evident. There is little evidence that the expansion of higher education is mainly a function of the level of economic growth; there is much evidence that the expansion of women's share of higher education is a worldwide trend (Kelly, 1991). In less developed countries the newness of the system of higher education positively influences the growth of women's share, a process that suggests that the age of a country influences its receptivity to changing world emphases on who should enter into higher education (Bradley & Ramirez, 1996).

There is also evidence that the content of higher education is becoming more diversified and more present-oriented in its coverage. Despite their distinctive historical legacies and thick cultural milieus, more universities and especially the many newer ones seem more connected to both mass schooling institutions and to broad development concerns than in prior eras (Frank, Wong, Meyer, & Duncan, 1996). Perhaps it is true that more peoples and more societies are organizing themselves as if there were "no salvation outside higher education" (Shils, 1971). This may explain some of the internal opposition to external pressures to curb the growth of costly higher education or to defray some of the costs with user fees and tuition. These pressures are often applied by the World Bank as part of programs to rationalize resource allocations in the education sector.

Summary

The emergence and expansion of mass schooling is difficult to account for as a function of national or societal properties, such as the level of development. The extent to which schooling is more directly linked to state bureaucracies or more open to market forces varies in large part as a consequence of how much society itself is market- or state-driven. However, the worldwide character of the expansion and the universalistic nature of the rationale for expansion suggests that external factors play a significant role.

We find more cross-national variation in the internal organization of higher education, but here too the historical trend is in the direction of greater massification. Thus, massification of both basic schooling and higher education in the 20th century appear to be attuned to transnational blueprints for promoting development through education. Individual-level demands for more schooling are on the rise, with issues of gender commanding greater attention than in past decades. Increasingly the core debates hinge on what constitutes quality education, which is increasingly construed as the key to development.

We are left with our paradox: to date, empirical research has been unable to establish universal causal links between education writ large and development, especially at the societal level of analysis. Nevertheless, by the end of the 20th century, common blueprints of education for development appear in many international education declarations and covenants, as well as in national strategies and policies. The next section focuses on the mechanisms through which these blueprints have been produced and diffused throughout the world.

MECHANISMS FOR DIFFUSION

In the post-World War II era, common blueprints emphasizing education for development have emerged and have been rapidly disseminated. The result has been an increase in common educational principles, policies, and even practices among countries with varying national characteristics. Attempts to explain the growth of educational isomorphism* have empha-

---

*The term isomorphism means the tendency for collectivities engaged in similar enrterprises to adopt similar social structures (DiMaggio & Powell, 1983).

sized coercion, imitation, and conformity to norms (Berman, 1983, 1997; Meyer, Nagel, & Snyder, 1993). Missing from most of this literature is an analysis of the mechanisms that generate this isomorphism. This section addresses this gap in the following four subsections. First, we trace the translation of abstract, rarified ideas about progress and justice into rational discourse about education and development at the global level. Second, we describe the formalization of that discourse into international development organizations. Finally, we look at the role of international development professionals in institutionalizing and modifying that discourse about education and development.

Figure 7.1 outlines our argument, starting from the premise that world ideas about progress and justice translate into discourse about development and, more specifically, about education and development. This rationalizing discourse facilitates the rise of both networks of development professionals and international development organizations. These professionals and or-

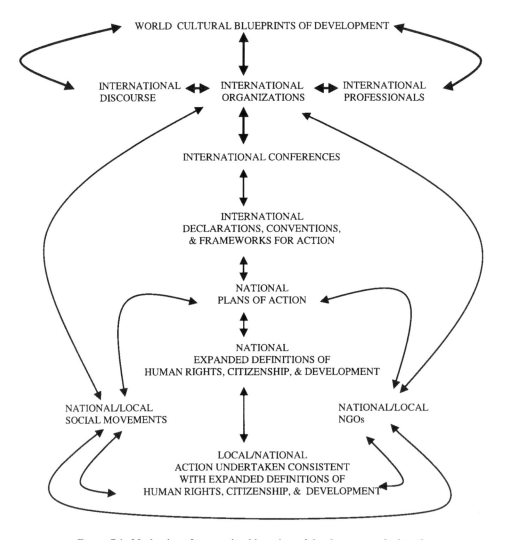

FIGURE 7.1. Mechanisms for carrying blueprints of development and education.

ganizations, in turn, sharpen and standardize the discourse by coordinating activities that showcase discourse. International conferences are one example of these types of activities; between 1944 and 1990, various United Nations organizations sponsored more than 16 global conferences on specific areas of development, such as family planning, water and sanitation, and food. Each of these conferences brought together not just national delegations but also scores of international development organizations.

By the time of the first Education for All Conference in 1990, standard products of these conferences included nonbinding declarations and frameworks for action. These declarations and their associated frameworks typically invoke the highest ideals of progress and justice, thereby making it practically mandatory for national delegations to endorse them. Given the prominent role played by ideals in both the declaration and framework for action, the national plans developed subsequent to the conference often incorporate expanded definitions of human rights, citizenship, and development.

For most of the postwar period this conference–declaration–national plan cycle contributed to a significant amount of loose coupling (Meyer et al., 1993; Nagel & Snyder, 1989) between on the one hand, national education policies produced in response to international norms and, on the other hand, the implementation of these policies at the subnational level. In recent years, however, the governmental international development organizations have increasingly recruited and supported the participation of international, national, and local nongovernmental organizations (NGOs) in international conferences. They also support NGO efforts to monitor the implementation of declarations and national plans of action at the national and the local levels. With the advent of new, inexpensive electronic communications, local NGOs can publicize national plans at the national and the local level and can draw international attention when national governments fail to implement those plans (see, for example, Social Watch, 1996). Fisher (1998) suggested that this may lead to tighter coupling between international norms and action at the subnational level.

The following subsections describe the process shown in Figure 7.1 in greater detail as it relates to education and development. Note that most arrows in Figure 7.1 are two way, indicating that these nodes are reciprocal and iterative. In general, over time, links between education and development grow tighter and more institutionalized; the meaning of development and, by extension, of education broadens; and emphasis shifts from an exclusive concern with collective economic growth to incorporate individual rights and justice.

Expanding Discourse and Organizations

Since the end of World War II, a world culture emphasizing progress and justice (Fagerlind & Saha, 1983; Meyer, Poll, Thomas, & Ramirez, 1997; Robertson, 1992) produced a rationalizing discourse about development, and, over time, constructed a central role for education in the development process. The most legitimate actors became nation–states with broad national and individual development goals and with individual citizens whose education was linked to their development and the development of their nation–state.

An expanded definition of development derives from the United Nations' (UN) 1948 Universal Declaration of Human Rights (United Nations, 1948). The Declaration makes explicit each individual's rights to a minimum standard of living but does not specify how that standard will be ensured: "Article 25, Para 1. Everyone has the right to a standard of living adequate for the health and well being of himself (sic) and of his family, including food, clothing, housing, and medical care and necessary social services. . . . "

Later efforts, however, to translate the nonbinding 1948 Declaration into binding international covenants led to further elaboration of the imperative for states to provide for individual development and of the wealthier states to provide assistance to poorer states to help them fulfill this responsibility.

Article 11, Para 1. The States Parties to the present Covenant recognize the right of everyone to an adequate standard of living . . . and to the continuous improvement of living conditions. The States Parties will take appropriate steps to ensure the realization of this right, recognizing to this effect the essential importance of international co-operation based on free consent. (United Nations, 1966)

These documents helped to create a world of developed and developing countries, with the former encouraged to provide the latter with foreign aid or development assistance. Originally, multilateral organizations, such as the UN, expected to be the main conduits of this development assistance. The advent of the Cold War, however, circumvented the UN's coordinating mandate (Black, 1986); by the 1950s, many Western countries began channeling development assistance through primarily religious organizations and through NGOs already established in former colonies, a practice that has grown over time (Organization for Economic Cooperation and Development, 1988). In addition, in the 1960s and 1970s, most high-income countries also formed bilateral governmental development organizations. As a result, by the early 1990s, there were about 250 multilateral, 40 bilateral, and 5,000 international nongovernmental development organizations (Chabbott, 1996). Over time, as their density increased, these organizations became increasingly bureaucratized and professionalized. Although initially focused on sectors immediately associated with economic production (such as agriculture or infrastructure), international development organizations eventually broadened into all social and economic sectors, including education.

In addition, both of the documents excerpted previously emphasize that the target of development is not the national economy—the traditional "wealth of nations"—but everyone. Individual development became the means to national development and individual development was equated with individual education in many UN documents. The best known of these include Article 26 of the Universal Declaration of Human Rights (United Nations, 1948), which defines education as a human right, and Articles 13 and 14 of the International Covenant on Economic, Social, and Cultural Rights (United Nations, 1966), which expands on this theme. In 1990 more than 150 nations accepted by acclamation the Declaration of Education for All, reiterating these rights and consequences and reaffirming their belief in the relationship between development and education at the global, national, and individual levels:

1. Recalling that education is a fundamental right . . . ;
2. Understanding that education can help ensure a safer, healthier, more prosperous and environmentally sound world, while simultaneously contributing to social, economic, and cultural progress, tolerance, and international cooperation;
3. Knowing that education is an indispensable key to, though not a sufficient condition for, personal and social improvement . . . UNESCO 1993)

Note that this passage sets out both normative (education as a right) and instrumental (education as an essential input to development) arguments to promote education. For most of the postwar period, instrumental arguments, often drawing on human capital constructs (Schultz, 1963), dominated liberal organizations (i.e., the World Bank, USAID). In contrast, normative arguments tended to prevail among more progressive funders (i.e., the UN agencies, the Nordic bilateral organizations; Buchert, 1994)

Finally, the universalistic focus in the development discourse, that is, everyone, increased emphasis within international development agencies on individual welfare and on broad participation in the development process. By the late 1980s, this translated into an increasing focus on previously marginalized groups, such as ethnic minorities and women. Education became a central theme in efforts to raise these groups to a higher status.

In summary, we have described the mechanism by which discourse at the global level about the nature of development simultaneously prompted the expansion of discourse about education and development, the formation of international development organizations, and the proliferation of activities to promote it, such as international conferences. The next section examines the evolution of the content of discourse about education in the context of shifting discourse about development. Whereas in this section, development discourse facilitated the creation of a field of international development organizations, in the next we show how, once created, these organizations generate secondary discourse that results in an emphasis on different levels and types of education in different decades.

Translating International Development into Educational Discourse

Since the end of World War II, institutionalized discourse on development within the UN justified the formation of dozens of formal UN-affiliated organizations with the express purpose of operationalizing the UN's Charter, Declaration, and Covenants. The UN's commitment to promoting education as a human right was manifest in the relatively early creation of the United Nations Educational, Scientific, and Cultural Organization (UNESCO, f. 1946). Jones (1990) emphasized the importance of the objective, material needs of the Allies to rebuild education systems shattered by World War II in establishing UNESCO as an action-oriented organization. An emphasis on psychology and on international peace was deeply embedded in UNESCO, which popularized Clement Atlee's notion that "wars begin in the minds of men." Illiteracy—or the lack of exposure to the socializing influence of schooling—was therefore constructed as a threat to peace (Jones, 1990). In addition, UNESCO's early education approaches, such as fundamental education, assumed a causal link between education and development. Margaret Mead, one of a series of social scientists and humanitarians called upon to help UNESCO define its mission, declared:

> The task of Fundamental Education is to cover the whole of living. In addition, it is to teach, not only new ways, but the need and the incentive for new ways . . . if the new education is to fill the place of the old, it has to cover all areas of living . . . In many countries new fundamental education is carried on by teams including social workers, graduate nurses, agricultural assistants, home economists, hygiene experts. (quoted in Jones, 1990)

UNESCO's mandate envisions the organization as the main conduit for much development assistance. Like other UN organizations, UNESCO suffered a major setback with the advent of the Cold War. Since then, many bilateral organizations, and even some other UN organizations, created education sections. In addition, several other intergovernmental organizations specializing in educational development emerged, such as the International Institute for Educational Planning (IIEP, f. 1963; see King, 1991 for a more complete catalog of international educational development organizations). Although UNESCO tried from time to time to mount ambitious global level programs, such as the World Literacy Program, its main contribution to educational development became reports, pilot projects, and conferences (Jones, 1990).

Many factors contributed to the rise of what Cox (1968) called the ideology of educational development. UNESCO's regional conferences helped to create common vocabulary and goals. A group of American economists (Becker, 1964; Schultz, 1963) provided the rational link between education and development in the form of human capital theory. U.S. foundations supported both economic research and expanded support for the study of education and development in other countries (Berman, 1992). Finally, international development organizations expanded their education departments, promoted specific education policies and projects, and funded new educational and research networks in developing countries (McGinn, 1996).

The education policies promoted by the international development organizations, however, do not necessarily derive from the educational research described in earlier sections, rather they tend to mirror the shifting ideas about national development (Berman, 1997; Coombs, 1985; Watson, 1988). Table 7.1 is a simplified mapping of the major approaches to national development in the decades since World War II, as articulated in the mainstream practitioner literature (Arndt, 1987; J. Lewis & Kallab, 1986; J. P. Lewis, 1988; Meier, 1995). Alongside these development approaches, we show the corresponding discourse about educational development and the educational priorities associated with this discourse (P. Jones, 1997; P. W. Jones, 1990, 1992). To emphasize the overlapping quality of many of these ideas, the lines demarcating decades are dashed, not solid.

Although there is much overlap in these decades, trends are evident. First, the concept of development shifts from national control and orientation to international funding and global orientation. Second, we see increasing complexity in the way the process of development is imagined, with newer approaches subordinating but not entirely replacing older ones. But, most important, we see national development increasingly defined in terms of individual welfare, rather than simply in terms of national economic growth and, concurrently, a push to use

TABLE 7.1. **Themes in National Development and Educational Development Discourse, 1950–1995**

Decade	Development discourse	Educational development discourse	Educational priorities
1950s	Community development Technology transfer	Fundamental education (1949–1955) Functional education	Rural extension training Adult literacy for health & agriculture
	Comprehensive national planning Industrialization	Manpower planning	Universal primary education
1960s	Modernization	Human capital theory	Formal secondary and higher schooling
	Economic growth Dependency	Manpower planning Functional education	Technical and vocational training Vocationally oriented literacy
1970s	Basic human needs Growth with equity	Basic education Equalizing educational opportunity	Formal primary schools Nonformal education for youth and adults
	Integrated rural development New International Economic Order	Teaching "neglected groups" Pedagogy of the oppressed	Literacy education Adult/lifelong learning
1980s	Poverty reduction	Human resources development	Formal primary and secondary schools
	Structural adjustment	Educational efficiency and effectiveness Quality learning	Education administration and finance
1990s	Sustainable human development	Meeting basic learning needs	Universal formal primary and secondary schools
	Poverty alleviation Social dimensions of adjustment	Quality learning Girls' education	Quality of classroom teaching and curriculum

universal access to primary education as a key measure of both individual welfare and national development. This rationalization—that individual welfare, particularly individual access to quality education is at the very center of development—creates the foundation on which to build broader, normative arguments for education and for development.

Beginning in the second row of Table 7.1, the comprehensive economic development planning approach promoted in the 1950s by a variety of governments and international donor organizations assumed that each nation–state was a relatively autonomous, self-contained unit. Prudent management of domestic resources was the supposed determinant of national development, and it might be achieved with little help from the outside world. During this decade, UNESCO implemented fundamental and later functional education programs, introducing literacy as a part of a broad approach to community development. Universal primary education was assumed to be a low-cost activity that required locally trained teachers and no scarce foreign exchange.

In the 1960s, rapid economic growth became prerequisite to development, still promoted by central planning. Educational planners urged developing countries to focus their limited budgets on formal secondary and higher schooling in subjects related to industrialization. Technical and vocational training also received support, as well as vocationally oriented literacy. Education was rarely mentioned as a right, but rather as instrumental to industrial development.

In the 1970s, as some speculated that economic growth was increasing, rather than decreasing the ranks of the impoverished in many countries, the concept of development was expanded to include social as well as economic aspects. During this decade, basic human needs emerged, along with the idea that the international community had a responsibility to meet these needs in nation–states where weak economies and administrative infrastructure rendered it impossible for national governments to do so. Some more radical analyses extended the responsibilities of the international community even further, suggesting that a New International Economic Order might be necessary to address chronic social and economic imbalances at the world level that favored the rich countries and maintained the economic disadvantages of the poorer ones.

In this context, a basic education, capable of equipping both adults and children to participate more fully in their societies, became the focus of development agency attention. Education was the way to equalize economic opportunity and to incorporate previously neglected groups. Along with formal primary schools, UNESCO in the 1970s emphasized adult literacy and lifelong education, and various international development organizations explored the potential of nonformal, that is, out-of-school, education.

In the 1980s, structural adjustment brought home the message that no nation is an island; all are part of the world financial system. This implied that nation–states—both developed and developing—should adjust their domestic economic policies and structures to conform to the international system, not vice versa, and that those nation–states that do not keep their financial house in order will forfeit some degree of their financial sovereignty.

Although manpower planning of the 1950s failed to prepare most countries to handle the educational crises in the 1960s and 1970s, a variation on it—human resources development—became very popular in the 1980s. With education defined as a basic human need, human resources development became a prerequisite to social or human development and momentum built toward establishing minimum standards of basic education for all individuals, particularly previously disadvantaged groups (Allen & Anzalone, 1981). More emphasis was placed on formal primary and secondary schools, particularly on improving efficiency and their ability to serve all citizens.

Western nation–states reacted to global recession in the early 1990s with cutbacks in development assistance to both multilateral and bilateral organizations. This reinforced the influence of the World Bank in education in developing countries. The Bank maintained its large structural adjustment loans and continued to employ more social science researchers than any other international development organization (Jones, 1997). By the early 1990s, however, the World Bank was coupling its structural adjustment loans with social dimensions of adjustment packages. In general, these packages were designed to strengthen the borrower country's capacity to monitor the effects of structural adjustment on the poor and to channel compensatory program funds through grassroots NGOs. By the mid-1990s, World Bank literature was speaking of development with a human face and about sustainable human development rather than aggregate economic growth.

The World Bank joined with UNESCO, UNICEF, and the United Nations Development Programme (UNDP) to sponsor the World Conference on Education for All (1990, Jomtien, Thailand). Whereas instrumental arguments lingered just below the surface in much of the focus on girls' education, normative arguments showed up in the claim of universality in the title of the conference, of human beings having inalienable learning needs (Inter-Agency Commission. World Conference on Education for All, 1990), and of underlying equity concerns embedded in calls for quality education for all (King & Singh, 1991).

The World Bank, convinced that the social returns to primary schooling were higher than for any other type of schooling, promoted formal primary and secondary schools. In the interest of equity, both the Bank and other international development organizations devoted more attention in the 1990s to school quality, both in terms of classroom teaching and curriculum. Most countries now have a national policy mandating universal primary education and the decade has been marked by interest in alternate ways to get children, particularly girls, in remote and/or conservative areas into modern schools (Ahmed, Chabbott, Joshi, & Pande, 1993).

In summary, the measures of development as an international and a national concern have changed since the 1950s from a narrow focus on national economic growth to incorporate measures of individual welfare and human rights. At the same time, the locus of responsibility for the development imperative has shifted from the national to the global level. Finally, education became inextricably linked with notions of development, and the levels and types of education emphasized in different decades mirror trends in broader development discourse, not necessarily empirical research on education and development.

None of the education approaches described previously (fundamental education, functional education, quality learning for all, etc.) was fully implemented and therefore the postulated contribution of education to development that each claimed has never been empirically established. However, these theories about the relationship between education and development were asserted and reiterated at hundreds of international conferences in the postwar period, many of them aimed particularly at officials in low-income countries and in international development agencies. The role of professionals in promoting these conferences that, in turn, promoted different levels and types of education because of their putative links to development, is the subject of the next section.

Professionalizing Educational Development

Between the end of World War II and the beginning of the 1980s, the background and composition of the staff of international development organizations changed significantly. Originally recruited from former colonial officers, from children of missionaries, and from war relief workers, newer staff includes former volunteers with organizations like the Peace Corps and International Voluntary Service and highly educated, expatriate officials from developing countries, fleeing political upheaval or in search of a larger professional milieu (Chabbott, 1996).

The work of the staff in governmental and nongovemmental development organizations has grown more bureaucratic and professionalized over time. Development professionals have created and are now sustained by a network of support organizations and publications. For example, membership in the Society for International Development (f. 1957) now includes close to 10,000 individuals and over 120 organizations or agencies in 60 countries. The bimonthly International Development Abstracts (f. 1982) covers more than 500 journals and other serial publications and the Development Periodicals Index (f. 1991) lists about 600. With respect to the education sector, the study of developing countries has occupied considerable space in major comparative and international educational journals and conferences since the 1950s. By the late 1970s, specialization in educational development led to the establishment of at least one journal (the International Journal of Educational Development, f 1981); a dozen postbaccalaureate degree programs, such as the Stanford International Development Education Committee (f. 1965); and associations, such as the Nordic Association for the Study of Education in Developing Countries (f. 1981).

In spite of their efforts to professionalize, the routine barriers created by lengthy tours overseas and by preoccupation with the politics of securing government funding tend to isolate development professionals from the Western academic community. Like professionals in all fields, many intend but few are able to remain up-to-date with new developments in their fields, such as debates in recent decades about the gray nature of the relationship between education and development.

Nonetheless, these professionals play a role in the rise in interest in education and overseas development in Western schools of education. For example, volunteer teachers returning from service with relief agencies and with later development agencies (i.e., pre-professionals in our terms), such as the American Friends Service Committee and the Peace Corps, brought new interest in developing countries to international education departments in graduate schools of education. In addition, development agencies funded short-term and long-term training for officials and academics from developing countries, creating an important source of revenue for some schools of education. The Ford Foundation funded the creation or expansion of development departments in many schools of education in the United States. Most directly, development agencies generated a demand for experts in education who could provide advice to ministries of education in developing countries. Within academia, the study of education in developing countries usually resided in a broader department of comparative and/or international education in a school of education.

Despite their symbiosis, the challenge to human capital theory mounted in academic circles rarely surfaced in professional educational development circles. Instead, professional debates have focused more on the relative strength of instrumental (education as an input to economic growth) versus human rights justifications for education and for the value of different levels of education in different contexts. Faith in the power of education to address core development concerns has grown over time, as described in the preceding section. This faith culminated in the 1990 World Conference on Education for All (EFA).

As noted previously, since the late 1950s, international development conferences have proved a popular way for chronically underfunded international development organizations to move the development agenda forward, to raise global awareness about a particular problem, and to call on nation–states to bring resources to bear on that problem. By 1990, various UN and other donor organizations had sponsored hundreds of world and regional educational conferences and had produced more than 77 recommendations to education ministers and about a dozen general declarations on the subject of education.

By 1990 all of the components of the blueprint described earlier in Figure 7.1, which allowed international development professionals to legitimately initiate, sponsor, and follow up world development conferences, were in place. The blueprint includes creating a sense of crisis about some sector at the global level (Coombs, 1968, 1985); mobilizing governmental consensus around a non-binding declaration and a framework for action; generating national plans of action; generating additional national and international funding for those plans; establishing international means to monitor compliance with national plans; and, wherever possible, translating the subject of the conference into a binding international covenant or defining it more forcefully as a human right (UNESCO, Education for All Forum Secretariat, 1993).

In addition, the Education for All conference was one of the first global conferences to invite development NGOs, both international ones and those formed in developing countries, as full participants. These NGOs later helped to monitor national governments' compliance with agreements made at the conference. Equipped with inexpensive facsimile machines and electronic mail connections to other groups and organizations around the world, local NGOs are able to report lags in government efforts to turn international commitments into action (Social Watch, 1996).

The impact of EFA on literacy and on primary school enrollments, or even on international development assistance levels to education, has yet to be assessed (Bennell & Furlong, 1998; Hallak, 1991). Meanwhile, the effects of the EFA Conference and other international development projects on the way education is defined, organized, and appears at the global, national, and classroom levels, particularly in low-income countries, remains to be explored.

Summary

International development professionals have invoked taken-for-granted ideals to mobilize both nation–states and NGOs around a menu of technical–functional education needs. These ideals, the professionals' claims of technical–functional expertise, and the degree to which the professionals have gained global acceptance of certain activities, such as international conferences, increase the influence of these professionals beyond their individual or collective social, economic, or political status.

In this sense development professionals should not be mainly construed as powerful agents pursuing their own interests or those of their nation–states of origin. These professionals have, along with other mechanisms, played an important role in recent decades in diffusing blueprints of education and in the development and the expansion of different levels and types of education in different decades. They have mainly accomplished this by enacting the role of objective experts and of rational managers, engaged in highly legitimate activities, associated with some of the most taken-for-granted notions of progress and justice at the global level.

CONCLUSIONS

The relationship between education and development is a problematic one. Individual schooling tends to raise individual wages, make individuals more politically active (though not necessarily more tolerant), and promote modern attitudes. Whether these effects can be largely attributed to education or whether, instead, they are evidence of more general processes of Westernization remains to be explored.

The effects of different types of education at the societal level, on national economic, political, and/or cultural development, are ambiguous. Mass education has had a positive and relatively robust effect on national development. The effects of higher education on societal development, in contrast, have not been significant and/or consistent.

The effects of development on education are no less problematic. Mass schooling is not, as was previously asserted, a rational response to increasing demand for literate workers in the course of modernization; in both developed and developing countries, mass education was instituted far in advance of any functional need for it. Instead, since the end of World War II, the expansion of education appears to be attuned to the transnational blueprints for promoting development through education.

These blueprints are reflected in international development discourse articulated by development professionals in international organizations and diffused through the various activities of those organizations, including international conferences. The blueprints are informed by broad and pervasive world models of progress and justice, in which education is valued both as a human capital investment and as an inalienable human right. Nation–states are expected to commit themselves to education for development goals and strategies and they frequently do so, independent of local economic, political, or social conditions. The results are familiar ones: loose coupling between policies and practices and practices out of sync with local realities.

The institutionalization of these blueprints tends to lower the effects of national development on educational expansion, because all countries now engage in such expansion; increase the effects of national development on educational quality, as more national resources are channeled to education; increase individual returns to education by increasing credentialism; and decrease collective returns because all countries are expanding education at the same time. Further studies are needed to measure the magnitude of these and other effects.

More broadly, further studies are needed to focus on the conditions that produce stronger ties between education and development. Many prior reviews of the education and development literature have made this point, emphasizing the influence of varying societal and educational conditions on, for example, schooling and productivity (Rubinson & Brown, 1994). This review suggests that a new generation of studies should examine the institutionalization of world blueprints and their transnational carriers. The scope, coherence, specificity, and status of these blueprints varies over time. The degree to which transnational carriers cooperate or compete, specialize or overlap in area or content focus, are viewed as merely reflecting national interest, or are celebrated as autonomous beacons of professionalized expertise, also varies. Much research is needed to ascertain whether and in what ways this variation in world blueprints and their transnational carriers conditions ties between education and development at both the societal and individual level of analysis.

REFERENCES

Adelman. I., & Morris, C. T. (1973). *Economic growth and social equity in developing countries.* Stanford, CA: Stanford University.

Ahmed, M., Chabbott, C., Joshi, A., & Pande, R. (1993). *Primary education for all: Learning from the BRAC experience.* Washington, DC: Academy for Educational Development.

Allen, D. W., & Anzalone, S. (1981). Basic needs: New approach to development—But new approach to education? *International Review of Education, 27*(3), 209–226.

Almond, G., & Verba, S. (1963). *The civic culture*. Princeton, NJ: Princeton University Press.

Anderson, B. (1991). *Imagined communities* (2nd ed.). London: Verso.

Anderson, C. A., & Bowman, M. J. (1976). Education and economic modernization in historical perspective. In L. Stone (Ed.), *Schooling and society* (pp. 3–19). Baltimore, MD: Johns Hopkins University Press.

Arndt, H. W. (1987). *Economic development: The history of an idea*. Chicago: University of Chicago.

Baker, D. P., & Jones, D. P. (1993). Creating gender equality: Cross-national gender stratification and mathematical performance. *Sociology of Education, 66*(2, April), 91–103.

Becker, G. (1964). *Human capital: A theoretical and empirical analysis, with special reference to education*. New York: National Bureau of Economic Research (Columbia University Press).

Benavot, A. (1989). Education, gender, and economic development: A cross-national study. *Sociology of Education, 62*, 14–32,

Benavot, A. (1992a). Curricular content, educational and expansion, and economic growth. *Comparative Education Review, 36*, 150–174,

Benavot, A. (1992b). Educational expansion and economic growth in the modern world, 1913–1985. In B. Fuller & R. Rubinson (Eds.), *The political construction of education* (pp. 117–134). New York: Praeger.

Bendix. R. (1964). *Nation-building and citizenship*. Berkeley, CA: University of California Press.

Bennell, P., & Furlong, D, (1998). Has Jomtien made any difference? Trends in donor funding for education and basic education since the late 1980s. *World Development, 26*(1), 45–59,

Berg, L. (1970). *Education and jobs: The great training robbery*. Boston: Beacon.

Berman, E. H. (1983). *The influence of the Carnegie, Ford, and Rockefeller Foundations on American foreign policy: The ideology of philanthropy*. Albany, NY: State University of New York Press.

Berman, E. H. (1992). Donor agencies and third world educational development, 1945–85. In R. F. Arnove, P. G. Altbach, & G. P. Kelly (Eds.), *Emergent issues in education: Comparative perspectives* (pp. 57–74). Albany, NY: State University of New York Press.

Berman, E. H. (1997). The role of foundations, bilateral, and international organization in the diffusion of the modern school. In W. K. Cummings & N. F. McGinn (Eds.), *International handbook of education and development: Preparing schools, students and nations for the twenty-first century* (pp. 137–152). New York: Pergamon.

Black, C. E. (1967). *The dynanics of modernization*. New York: Harper and Row.

Black, M. (1986). *The children and the nations: The story of UNICEF*. Potts Point, Sydney, Australia: P.I.C. Pty Ltd.

Boli, J. (1989). *New citizenship for a new society: The institutional origins of mass schooling in Sweden*. New York: Doubleday.

Boudon, R. (1974). *Education, opportunity, and social inequality: Changing prospects in western society*. New York: Wiley.

Bowles, S., & Gintis, H. (1976). *Schooling in capitalist America*. New York: Basic Books.

Bradley, K., & Ramirez, F. (1996). World polity and gender parity: Women's share of higher education, 1965–985. *Research in Sociology of Education and Socialization, 11*, 63–92.

Buchert, L. (1994). Education and development: A study of donor agency policies on education in Sweden, Holland, and Denmark. *International Journal of Education Research, 14*(2), 143–157.

Caillods, F., Gottelmann-Duret, G., & Lewin, K. (1996). *Science education and development: Planning and policy issues at secondary level*. Paris: Unesco, International Institute for Educational Planning.

Carnoy, M. (1995). The economics of education, then and now. In M. Carnoy (Ed.), *International Encyclopedia of Economics of Education* (2nd ed., pp, 1–7). Oxford, England: Pergamon,

Carnoy, M. (1998). *Notes on the production and use of knowledge in the education sector*. Stanford, CA: Stanford University School of Education.

Chabbott, C. (1996). *Constructing educational development: International development oganizations and the World Conference on Education for All*. Unpublished doctoral dissertation, Stanford University, School of Education, Stanford, California.

Clark, B. (1977a). Structure of post-secondary education. In A. Knowles (Ed.). *International encyclopedia of higher education* (Vol. 8). San Francisco, CA: Jossey-Bass.

Clark, B. (1977b). *The Changing Relations between Higher Education and Government: Some Perspectives from Abroad*. New Haven, CT: Institute for Social Policy Studies.

Coffman, J. M. (1992). *Arabization and Islamization in the Algerian university*. Unpublished doctoral dissertation, Stanford University, Stanford, California.

Coleman, J. S. (Ed., 1965). *Education and political development*. Princeton, NJ: Princeton University Press.

Collins, R. (1971). Functional and conflict theories of educational stratification. *American Sociological Review, 36*, 1002–1019.

Collins, R. (1979). *The credential society: A historical sociology of education and stratification.* New York: Academic Press.

Coombs, P. H. (1968). *The world educational crisis: A systems/analysis.* New York: Oxford University Press.

Coombs, P. H. (1985). *The world crisis in education: The view from the eighties.* New York: Oxford University Press.

Cox, R. W. (1968). Education for development. In R. N. Gardner & M. F. Millikan (Eds.), *The global partnership: International agencies & economic development* (pp. 310–331). New York: Frederick A. Praeger,

Cutright, P. (1969). National political development: Measurement and analysis, In M. Eckstein & H. Noah (Eds.), *Scientific investigations in comparative education* (pp. 367–383). New York: Macmillan.

Davis, N. J., & Robinson, R. V. (1991). Men's and women's consciousness of gender inequality: Austria, West Germany, Great Britain, and the United States. *American Sociological Review, 56,* 72–84.

Denison, E. (1962). *The sources of economic growth in the United States and the alternatives before us.* New York: Committee for Economic Development.

DiMaggio, P. J., & Powell, W. W. (1983). The iron cage revisited: Institutional isomorphism and collective rationality in organizational fields. *American Sociological Review, 48*(April), 147–160.

Dreeben, R. (1968). *On what is learned in school.* Reading, MA: Addison Wesley.

Eisenstadt, S. N. (1963). *The political systems of empires.* New York: The Free Press.

Fagerlind, I., & Saha, L. (1983). *Education and national development: A comparative perspective.* Elmsford, NY: Pergamon.

Fisher, J. (1998). *Non-governments: NGOs and the political development of the third world.* West Hartford, CT: Kumarian.

Frank, D., Wong, S.-Y., Meyer, J., & Duncan, S. (1996). *Embedding national society: History as a map of the world: 1895–1994.* Paper presented at the Annual Meeting of the American Sociological Association, New York.

Fuller, B., & Heyneman, S. P. (1989). Third world school quality: Current collapse, future potential. *Educational Researcher, 18*(2, March), 12–19.

Fuller, B., & Rubinson, R. (Eds., 1992). *The political construction of education: The state, school expansion, and economic change.* New York: Praeger.

Garnier, M., & Hage, J. (1990). Education and economic growth in Germany. *Research in Sociology of Education and Socialization, 9,* 25–53,

Garnier, M., Hage, J., & Fuller, B. (1989). The strong state, social class, and controlled school expansion in France, 1881–1975. *American Journal of Sociology, 95,* 279–306.

Gurr, T. (1971). A causal model of civil strife: A comparative analysis using new indices. In J. V. Gillespi & B. A. Newvold (Eds,), *Macro-quantitative analysis: Conflict, development, and democratization.* Beverly Hills, CA: Sage.

Hage, J., & Garnier, M. (1990). Social class, the hesitant state, and the expansion of secondary schools in Britain, 1870–1975. *Research in Sociology of Education and Socialization, 9,* 55–80.

Hage, J., & Garnier, M. (1992). Strong sates and educational expansion: France versus Italy. In B. Fuller & R. Rubinson (Eds.), *The political construction of education* (pp. 155–171). New York: Praeger,

Hallak, J. (1991). *Education for all: High expectations or false hopes.* Paris: UNESCO. Institute for International Educational Planning.

Hanushek, E., & Kim, D. (1996). *Schooling, labor force quality, and the growth of nations.* Unpublished manuscript, University of Rochester, Department of Economics, Rochester, New York.

Harbison, F., & Myers, C. (1964). *Education, manpower, and economic growth.* New York: McGraw-Hill.

Honig, B. (1996). Education and self-employment in Jamaica. *Comparative Education Review, 40*(2), 177–193.

Inkeles, A., & Sirowy, L. (1983). Convergent and divergent trends in national educational systems. *Social Forces, 62*(2, December), 303–333.

Inkeles, A., & Smith, D. H. (1974). *Becoming modern: Individual change in six developing countries.* Cambridge, MA: Harvard University Press.

Inter-Agency Commission. World Conference on Education for All. (1990). *Meeting basic learning needs: A vision for the 1990s.* Paris: World Conference on Education for All.

Jones, P. (1997). On world bank education financing. Review article. *Comparative Education, 33*(1, March), 117–129.

Jones, P. W. (1990). UNESCO and the politics of global literacy. *Comparative Education Review, 34*(1), 41–60.

Jones, P. W. (1992). *World bank financing of education: Lending, learning and development.* New York: Routledge.

Kamens, D. H., Meyer, J. W., & Benavot, A. (1996). Worldwide patterns in academic secondary education curricula. *Comparative Education Review, 40*(2), 116–138.

Kelly, G. (1991). Women and higher education. In P. G. Altbach (Ed.), *International Higher Education: An encyclopedia* (pp. 297–323). New York: Garland Publishing Company.

King, K. (199 1). *Aid and education in the developing world: The role of the donor agencies in educational analysis*. Essex, UK: Longman.

King, K., & Singh, J. S. (1991). *Improving the quality of basic education*. Paper presented at the Conference of Commonwealth Education Ministers, Barbados.

Knight, J. B., & Sabot, R. H. (1987). The rate of return on educational expansion. *Economics of Education Review, 6*(3), 255–262.

Lewis, J., & Kallab, V. (Eds., 1986). *Development stages reconsidered* (Vol. 5). New Brunswick, NJ: Transaction.

Lewis, J. P. (Ed., 1988). *Strengthening the poor: What have we learned* (Vol. 10). New Brunswick, NJ: Transaction.

Lipset, S. M. (1963). *The first review nation*. Garden City, NY: Doubleday.

Lockheed, M., Jamison, D., & Lau, L. (1988). Farmer education and farmer efficiency: A survey. In T. King (Ed.), *Education and income* (pp. 111–152). Washington, DC: World Bank.

Lundgreen, P. (1976), Educational expansion and economic growth in the nineteenth century Germany: A quantitative study. In L. Stone (Ed). *Schooling and society* (pp. 20–76). Baltimore: Johns Hopkins,

Mangan, J. A. (Ed., 1994). *A significant social revolution: Cross-cultural aspects of the evolution of compulsory education*. London: Woburn Press.

Maynes, M. J. (1985). *Schooling in western Europe: A social history*. Albany, NY: State University of New York Press.

McClelland, D. (1961). *The achieving society*. New York: The Free Press.

McGinn, N. (Ed., 1996), *Crossing lines: Research & policy networks for developing country education*. Westport, CT: Praeger.

Meier, G. (1995). *Leading issues in international development* (6th ed.), New York: Oxford University Press.

Meyer, J., Boli, J., Thomas, G. M., & Ramirez, F. O. (1997). World society and the nation state. *American Journal of Sociology, 103*(1), 144–181.

Meyer, J. W. (1977). The effects of education as an institution. *American Journal of Sociology, 63,* 55–77.

Meyer, J. W., & Hannan, M. T. (Eds., 1979). *National development and the world system: Educational, economic, and political change, 1950–1970*. Chicago: University of Chicago.

Meyer, J. W., Nagel, J., & Snyder, C. W., Jr. (1993). The expansion of mass education in Botswana: Local and world society perspectives. *Comparative Education Review, 37*(4, November), 454–475.

Meyer, J. W., Ramirez, F. O., Rubinson, R., & Boli-Bennett, J. (1977). The world educational revolution, 1950–1970. *Sociology of Education, 50*(0ctober), 242–258.

Meyer, J. W., Ramirez, F. O., & Soysal, Y. (1992). World expansion of mass education, 1980. *Sociology of Education, 65*(2), 128–149.

Nagel, J., & Snyder, C. W. (1989). International funding of educational development: External agendas and internal adaptations—the case of Liberia. *Comparative Education Review, 33*(1), 3–20.

Olneck, M. R., & Bills, D. B. (1980). What makes Sammy run? An empirical assessment of the Bowles–Gintis correspondence theory. *American Journal of Education, 89*(1), 27–61.

Organization for Economic Cooperation and Development. (1988). *Voluntary aid for development: The role of non-governmental organisations*. Paris: OECD.

Parsons, T. (1957). The school class as a social system. *Harvard Education Review, XXIX*(4) 297–318.

Psacharopoulos, G. (1973). *Returns to education*. San Francisco, CA: Jossey Bass.

Psacharopoulos, G. (1989). Time trends of the returns to education: Cross-national evidence. *Economics of Education Review, 8,* 225–231.

Psacharopoulos, G., & Woodhall, M. (1985). *Education for development: An Analysis of investment choices*. New York: Oxford University Press.

Ramirez, F., & Boli, J. (1987). The political construction of mass schooling: European origins and worldwide institutionalization. *Sociology of Education, 60,* 2–17.

Ramirez, F., & Lee, M. (1995). Education, science, and development. In G. A. Postiglione & L. W. On (Eds.), *Social change and educational development* (pp. 15–39). Hong Kong: University of Hong Kong,

Ramirez, F., & Rubinson, R. (1979). Creating members: The political incorporation and expansion of public education. In J. Meyer & M. Hannan (Eds.), *National development and world system* (pp. 72–84). Chicago: University of Chicago Press.

Ramirez, F., Rubinson, R., & Meyer, J. (1973, September). *National educational expansion and political development: Causal interrelationships, 1950–1970*. Paper presented at the SEADAG Seminar on Education and National Development, Singapore.

Ramirez, F. O. (1997). The nation–state, citizenship, and educational change: Institutionalization and globalization. In W. K. Cummings & N. F. McGinn (Eds.), *International Handbook of Education and development: Preparing schools, students and nations for the twenty-first century* (first ed., pp. 47–62). New York: Pergamon.

Ramirez, F. O., & Cha, Y.-K. (1990). Citizenship and gender: Western educational development in comparative perspective. *Research in Sociology of Education and Socialization, 9,* 153–173.

Reisner, E. H. (1927). *Nationalism and education since 1789.* New York: MacMillan.

Robertson, R. (1992). *Globalization: Social theory and global culture.* London: Sage.

Rubinson, R., & Brown, I. (1994). Education and the economy. In N. J. Smelser & R. Swedborg (Eds.), *The handbook of economic sociology* (pp. 583–599). Princeton, NJ: Princeton University Press.

Ryoo, J.-K., Nam, Y.-S., & Carnoy, M. (1993), Changing rates of return to education over time: A Korean case study. *Economics of Education Review, 12*(1), 71–80.

Samoff, J. (1995). *Analyses, agendas, and priorities in African education: A review of externally initiated, commissioned supported studies in Africa, 1990–94 (Inventory and analytic overview of African education sector study).* Paris: UNESCO: Working Group on Education Sector Analysis Lead Agency, Association for the Development of African Education.

Schofer, E., Ramirez, F., & Meyer, J. (1997). *The effects of science on national economic development 1970–1990.* Toronto, Ontario. Paper presented at the American Sociological Association.

Schultz, T. P. (1993). Returns to women's education. In E. M. King & M. A. Hill (Eds.) *Women's education in developing countries* (pp. 5–93). Washington, DC: The World Bank.

Schultz, T. W. (1963). *The economic value of education.* New York: Columbia University Press.

Shanahan, S. (1994). *Education and inequality: A cross-national analysis.* San Diego, CA: Paper presented at the annual meeting of the Pacific Sociological Association, March.

Shils, E. (1971). No salvation outside higher education. *Minerva, 6,* 313–321.

Singh, J. S., & Mukherjee, H. (1993). Education and national integration in Malaysia: Stocktaking after thirty years of independence. *International Journal of Educational Development, 13*(2), 89–102.

Social watch. (1996). *Social watch: The starting point.* Montevideo, Uruguay: Instituto del Tercer Mundo.

Spring, J. (1972). *Education and rise of the corporate state.* Boston: Beacon Press.

Starkey, H. (Ed., 1991). *Socialisation of school children and their education for democratic values and human rights.* Amsterdam: Council of Europe/Swets and Zeitlinger.

Stromquist, N. (1989). Determinants of educational participation and achievement of women in the Third World: A review of the evidence and a theoretical critique. *Review of Educational Research, 59*(2), 143–183,

Thomas, G., Ramirez, F., Meyer, J. W., & Gobbalet, J. (1979). Maintaining national boundaries in the world system: The rise of centralist regimes. In J. W. Meyer & M. Hannan (Eds.), *National development and the world system.* Chicago: University of Chicago Press.

Torney, J., Oppenheim, A. N., & Farnen, R. F. (1976). *Civic education in ten countries: An empirical study* (ERIC). New York: Wiley.

Torney, J. V., & Hess, R. D. (1969). Teachers, students, and political attitude development. In G. Lesser (Ed.) *Psychology and the Educational Process.* Glenview, IL: Scott Foresman.

UNESCO. Education for All Forum Secretariat. (1993). *Education for all: Status and trends.* Paris: UNESCO.

United Nations. (1948). Universal declaration of human rights. San Francisco, CA: United Nations.

United Nations, (1966). International covenant on economic, social, and cultural rights. New York: United Nations.

Walters, P. B., & O'Donnell, P. J. (1990). Post-World War II higher educational expansion, the organization of work, and changes in labor productivity in the United States. *Research in Sociology of Education and Socialization, 9,* 1–23.

Walters, P. B., & Rubinson, R. (1983). Educational expansion and economic output in the United States, 1890–1969: A production function analysis. *American Sociological Review, 48*(4, August), 480–493.

Watson, K. (1988). Forty years of education and development: From optimism to uncertainty. *Educational Review, 40*(2), 137–174.

Weil, F. (1985). The variable effect of education on attitudes: A comparative historical analysis of anti-semitism using public opinion survey data. *American Sociological Review, 50,* 458–475.

Weiss, J. A., Ramirez, F. O., & Tracy, T. (1976). Female participation in the occupational system: A comparative institutional analysis. *Social Problems, 23,* 593–608.

Windolf, P. (1997). *Expansion and structural change: Higher education in Germany, the United States, and Japan, 1870–1990.* Boulder, CO: Westview Press.

CHAPTER 8

The Content of the Curriculum

An Institutionalist Perspective

ELIZABETH H. MCENEANEY
JOHN W. MEYER

INTRODUCTION

The educational system is foundational in contemporary society, providing the basic substantive content thought to be necessary for society as it is, and for society as it is to become in a future imagined community (Anderson, 1991). Schooled education is supposed to provide the cultural content required for a very wide and increasing variety of modern roles. And it provides the most legitimated substantive basis for allocation of people into roles running from the occupational and economic, the political and organizational, and even personal and familial relationships. For all of these types of roles, socialization and training through education are understood to provide the underlying cultural content. This chapter reviews the nature of the content involved, and its changes over time as the modern system expands.

Two broad aspects of education are involved. The one that has received predominant attention in the research literature highlights the allocational function of education, with subsequent implications for inequalities in curricular content. The other aspect stresses how mass educational systems are involved in a very different type of fundamental social change—the construction of participatory and equal individual persons as the primary social unit in society. Far from educational sorting and stratifying, this second function is built on the principle of an

ELIZABETH H. MCENEANEY • Department of Sociology, University of Nevada-Las Vegas, Las Vegas, Nevada 89154-5033   JOHN W. MEYER • Department of Sociology, Stanford University, Stanford, California 94305

Handbook of the Sociology of Education, edited by Maureen T. Hallinan. Kluwer Academic/Plenum Publishers, New York, 2000.

expanded universal citizenry, regardless of a student's social status. This function of education has many implications for curricular content; these are, to some degree, in tension with the demands on the curriculum to respond to schooling's allocational role. We discuss these two perspectives in turn: their general vision of education, their implicit theories about the curriculum, and associated lines of empirical research.

ALLOCATION IN A DIFFERENTIATED
SOCIAL WORLD

Current work in the sociology of education gives surprisingly little attention to the substantive content of the curriculum. In this section, and in the following one, we explain why this follows from the dominant intellectual perspectives. Then we turn to alternate perspectives that suggest a refocusing of research efforts on the analysis of the curriculum.

The view exerting the most leverage on sociological research on the curriculum is that as modern society becomes increasingly differentiated, education plays the central part in allocating individuals into the differentiated social roles involved. Attention has gone to the stratificational side and to the awareness that education is the crucial factor in producing stratified outcomes (e.g., Blau & Duncan, 1967; Arum & Shavit, 1995; Shanahan, Elder, & Miech, 1997; Caspi, Wright, Moffett, & Silva, 1998). The focus has not been on the actual cultural content built into education but on the way variations in schooled content are mechanisms in social allocation. Thus Bourdieu (1984; Bourdieu & Passeron, 1977) saw French education as producing and selecting people in terms of quite arbitrary cultural capital; Collins (1979 and elsewhere) supposed that the content and values involved were (perhaps somewhat less arbitrarily) those of dominant groups; Apple (1990) saw the culture involved as reinforcing a system of economic dominance.

Thus curriculum, in the contemporary sociology of education, refers to two phenomena little related to substantive content. First, to those concerned with inequalities in achievement and attainment, it refers to educational tracking. The idea is that curricular tracks are variably and unequally available to students of different social status, gender, or ethnicity, and that participation in these different tracks affects a variety of desired outcomes. Studies focusing on tracking take an interest in the substantive curriculum mainly when variations in it seem clearly related to prior or subsequent social stratification. They do not, for instance, attend to what is studied in mathematics courses: they attend to whether variation in gender is related to variation in the number or to hierarchical levels of the courses that are taken.

Second, curriculum means a hidden curriculum. The social arrangements of school and classroom are thought to communicate cultural content. Some ideas here stress the universalized participation involved in the expectations communicated (Dreeben, 1968; Parsons, 1962). More often, attention goes again to the stratification system: variations in students' status produce variation in the implicit knowledge built into their instruction, or they produce exclusion from higher expectations and opportunities. Another focus of attention is that the implicit knowledge carried in the system is consistent only with the arbitrary culture of higher status groups, so that lower status students are disadvantaged. It turns out then, that students acquire a kind of membership in society—a membership that may sharply differ for those being trained to command and those being trained to obey. The substantive content of the knowledge involved is less important than the roles being acquired—and the research tradition stresses status variation in these roles.

BEYOND THE CONCERN WITH STRATIFICATION

The research inattention to curricular content arises, not because sociologists think the matter unimportant, but because they tend to see it as obvious. In this, they share in a common modern culture in which the importance of education—and the main lines of the curriculum—are highly institutionalized social and individual goods. Both mass and elite education have expanded enormously in the modern period, with increasingly taken-for-granted assumptions that these structures are central ingredients of both individual and societal development. The social scientific baseline theory involved is functional: education is necessary for appropriate socioeconomic and technological development (while perhaps preserving existing class, gender and ethnic/racial hierarchies), and its content is driven by the functional exigencies of that project. Mass education produces a population suited for participation in this industrial, capitalist order: elite education produces the leading and specialist components. From this point of view, the details of an educational system's curricular content follow straightforwardly from social structures or characteristics in the real and particular society at hand. Curricular timetables, textbooks, and other materials are the end products of power struggles of varying intensity to define the "one best way" of meeting national (or in some cases sub-national) needs. Case studies focus on the more spectacular conflicts (Carnochan, 1993; Larson, 1989), far less on the end products of these conflicts. In an earlier period in which the institutionalized dominance of education was less well established, social theorists like Durkheim (1922 [1956]) felt it necessary to argue the matter, spelling out a story of the necessary content of modern education. Now it is mostly established.

This means that in both the common culture and in sociological discourse, attention goes, not to the main and now obvious aspects of the curriculum, but to the margins where social uncertainty and conflict appear. So both the public and the sociologists attend to more peripheral issues, that are paradoxically associated with more intense conflict than core aspects of the curriculum. Are women and minorities adequately represented in history and literature? What is the place of detailed sex education? Which strategies for reading instruction are best? Is prayer appropriate, or instruction in the Bible? How much effort, and what kind, should go into writing training? Should parents be required to pay in order for their child to participate in so-called extracurricular activities? The main outlines—the investments of time and instruction in national language, mathematics, science, social science, the arts, and physical education—are little analyzed.

The lack of attention to curricular content in these areas is surprising given that student outcomes and achievement are increasingly subject to intensive international comparison (most recently, for example, in the Third International Mathematics and Science Study [Beatty, 1997]). The actual content of these tests receives virtually no attention,* just as the content of classroom instructional materials and practice and curricular benchmarks and standards escape

---

*Two recent controversies over the content of standardized tests in the U.S. provide support for our contention that attention is drawn to marginal content and stratification effects. Passages from award-winning writers Alice Walker and Annie Dillard in California's never-implemented CLAS test were charged with being "anti-religious" and "anti-meat-eating" respectively (Chavez & Matthews, 1995), while the content of the Educational Testing Service's PSAT was criticized because boys have consistently won more National Merit Scholarships based on the tests than girls. The test has been revised to include open-ended writing tasks, in which girls tend to outperform boys, as a means of mitigating this stratified outcome. The point that an open-ended writing requirement might be an appropriate measure of achievement in its own right did not appear to be central to the debate about whether to change the test.

analysis in themselves. In such matters, if a modern sociologist has some information, it is because the sociologist has children in school—the research literature has little to say.

The taken-for-granted quality of the curriculum accounts for the peculiarly deflected modern sociological critique of it noted previously. The sociologists imagine that the functionally natural curriculum may be distorted by forces of power and interest, and/or by inertial tradition. Theories are about these possible distortions, not the main structure itself.

One set of conflict theories suggests that the curriculum may be used to reproduce arbitrary stratificational hierarchies. Thus functionally useless knowledge—linked to the tastes of higher status groups—is used to perpetuate class distinctions (Bourdieu, 1984; Bourdieu & Passeron, 1977). Alternately, dominant ethnic, cultural, or gender forces may use the educational system to reinforce their dominance (Collins, 1979; Frazier & Sadker, 1973) and gain advantages in educational selection.

In a second set of critical (but more functional) theories, such processes may be reinforced by tracking systems differentially training children from different classes (e.g., Bowles & Gintis, 1976; Giroux, 1981), or by giving differential access to the important knowledge. The knowledge is seen as functional, but tracks and variations in hidden curricula may transmit it in differential and unfair ways, reproducing class structures. This line of argument is highly developed in British curricular research (Bernstein, 1990; Goodson, 1987; 1992) and other countries where track differences have been extreme (e.g., Broaded, 1997, on Taiwan). But many studies also examine carefully the somewhat more muted versions in the United States (e.g., Gamoran, 1992; Hallinan, 1987; Oakes, 1985). A variation on the theme of tracking is the considerable attention given to differential access to opportunities to learn (e.g., Stevenson, Schiller, & Schneider, 1994). Scholarly attention to the stratificational effects of the hidden curriculum is also widespread (Anyon, 1980; Bourdieu & Passeron, 1977; Bowles & Gintis, 1976; Gillborn, 1992; Weisz & Kanpol, 1990; Willis, 1981).

Third, in more extreme critical theories, the whole curricular structure may be distorted in hegemonic reinforcement of a whole social structure that is itself dominated by class interest and power. The curriculum may reinforce, not modernity but tradition or dominance, lending the weight of legitimacy to what should be seen as illicit past or present hegemony (Apple, 1990; Bacchus, 1996; Freire, 1970). The view here is that education should be functional for a more progressive society, but is in fact a celebration of the asymmetrical power built into the present society as a whole, and turns this power into legitimated authority. These studies, as well as those highlighting the hidden curriculum, have been critiqued primarily on a methodological basis by Ladwig (1996).

AN INSTITUTIONALIST PERSPECTIVE ON THE CURRICULUM

We turn now to a conception of education, and the curriculum, as an institutionalized system building a broad cultural base or model of modern society that emphasizes expanded and universal participation. As opposed to approaches aiming to explain variation, institutionalist theories seek to explain isomorphism or standardization of social phenomena, often as it occurs at the global level. Recent institutionalist perspectives on education question a fundamental, yet taken-for-granted, theory that societal development is generated solely and in an aggregated fashion through the development of individuals who have appropriate training, attitudes, and levels of productivity. Based on such an understanding, reformers routinely point to the inadequate level of some aspect of societal development and propose changes in state-sponsored development of individual persons (e.g., formal mass education). Yet, the presumed links in the long causal chain theoretically leading to societal development have not been established empirically (Meyer, Ramirez, & Soysal, 1992). Institutionalist views of education emphasize the normative, ideological basis for this theorized prescription for development, and therefore, turn their attention to the proliferation of organizational forms and cultural models that conform to the values implicit in this taken-for-granted theory of societal development. Resonance with these values may be enough to sustain change, aside from actual effects on children, workers, or societies. Such a perspective has been used to account for dramatic increases in mass educational enrollments that appear to be decoupled from material conditions within nation-states (Meyer, Ramirez, et al., 1992), and can be usefully applied to analysis of the change and diffusion of curricular forms as well.

Two shifts in perspective, from those discussed in the previous section, are involved. First, attention is given to the obvious fact that expanded modern educational systems try to organize many years of the lives of all persons in society around the learning of a common standardized broad culture. Educational systems allocate status, to be sure, but first they create a huge common base of knowledge and culture, the analysis of which is certainly important. Second, they do this in terms, not of the functional particulars of local or even national actual social and power systems, but of sweeping and surprisingly universal models of society. The models involved tend to conform to visions of society more than to current realities, and to visions that are now worldwide in character (Meyer, Kamens et al., 1992). They deserve closer study.

From an institutional view, the content of the curriculum is ripe for careful analysis. This vision of the role of education supposes that the modern system and its goals of imagined communities rest on a broad culture creating and emphasizing shared knowledge and values. Education provides the locus for these. Beyond the role of schooling in stratification, the focus is on the construction of shared cultural understandings—the building of the assumptions taken for granted in modern theory and policy. This line of thought parallels some critical theorists' interests in hegemony, as opposed to more naked exertions of power and influence.

A most central social status in the modern system and in its imagination is one on which all are to be equal, and all are to be participants: citizenship, personhood, human being. The great modern culture is to be built into all persons through universalized mass education (including, increasingly, secondary education and modern mass university instruction). All are to be citizen-persons, and all are to be expanded participants in a great modern order. Thus, from this second view, modern mass educational systems are fundamentally engaged in a project of constructing *individuals* who understand themselves and others as having interests and the capacity to act rationally on them.

One clear manifestation of this role is that the curriculum is increasingly organized around choice. Electives are built into the primary level curriculum, while university-level programs are organized around distribution requirements insuring adequate breadth of knowledge while preserving student choice. The differentiation and elaboration of the modern curriculum is therefore not always tightly related to the vertical stratification system. Instead, institutional critiques suggest a lateral differentiation of the curriculum to accommodate the participation of newly-constituted individuals on a massive scale. Mainstream sociological critiques of the curriculum are correct in their concern that schooling fails to empower students from all social groups. What the institutional critique emphasizes, however, is the degree to which modern curricular content already takes a participatory form and style, perhaps decoupled from structural changes that widen actual opportunities for students upon completion of their formal schooling. The educational system has been under sustained and highly legitimated pressures for reform from progressive and democratic critics for several centuries, and to a considerable extent the curriculum incorporates their vision.

Institutionalist studies of the curriculum also refocus attention on the main outlines of the curriculum, with a new perspective on the functionalist assumptions taken for granted in both the common culture and the sociological criticisms of the curriculum as deflected by power, interest, and forces of inequalitarian traditions. They start from the obviously highly cultural and highly institutionalized character of the modern society, which is in fact as much a cultural model as any social praxis (Thomas, Meyer, Ramirez, & Boli, 1987). And they start from the fact that education itself is also an abstracted cultural model, and part of the model of modernity. Useful implications follow, many of which have been followed up in empirical research:

First, education and the curriculum are constructed out of models of modernity and its educational requirements, rather than solely out of socioeconomic modernity itself. Immediate interests or functional requirements are often poor predictors of education and curricula, which are greatly affected by the political-cultural dominance of ideological or cultural models. Both educational expansion (Meyer, Ramirez, et al., 1992) and curricular structures (Benavot, Cha, Kamens, Meyer, & Wong, 1991) are little predicted by economic development or complexity, or by variations in local structures of power and interest. They have cultural roots in institutional ideologies (themselves functional theories). General models of modernity are highly developed, rationalized, and professionalized in the modern system; specific models of education and curricula are also highly articulated as pictures of human and social development, and are carried by rationalized and professionalized structures.

Second, the cultural models involved tend to be very widespread around the world, so that educational forms and curricular structures evolve and change in rather isomorphic ways worldwide. Thus, educational expansion, in terms of entitlements and enrollments, has been a worldwide process (Meyer, Ramirez, et al., 1992), as have curricular development and change (Benavot et al., 1991). Nations around the world are aligning themselves in terms of the inclusion of, and time commitments to, various school subjects.

Third, curricular change is often better predicted by an educational system's linkages to evolving models in world society than by any local pressures of function and interest. Expansion goes on in extremely poor countries at least as rapidly as in the core; curricular modernization may also flow rapidly to the Third World—perhaps even more rapidly given the weak standing of local interests and traditions. For example, innovations in science education, such as those in the spirit of Science, Technology, and Society (STS) reforms find expression in primary textbooks earlier in many developing countries than in such core countries as the United States, Germany, and France. In both science and mathematics, developing countries pay particular and early attention to establishing the personal relevance of the curricular content (McEneaney, 1998).

ALLOCATION VERSUS UNIVERSAL PARTICIPATION

The world is now organized as a set of nation-state societies. Each more or less controls its own educational system, but almost all are organized around standardized and sweeping wider models of what imagined society is. We thus turn to an analysis of the dominant model of society, and how this model leads to the contemporary curriculum.

The two forces outlined above push modern education in directions that are not quite consistent. The first force, for legitimated selection and differentiation, is partly inconsistent with the second force for universalized expansion. However, the inconsistency is by no means complete; much of the modern resolution lies in the expansion of the mass educational base on which differentiated selection can occur. Selection processes are perhaps even more thoroughly legitimated in this context, which emphasizes participation. Specifically, modern educational systems celebrate participation, both in terms of enrollments and in the cultural content imparted. This stands in opposition to Young's (1961) more narrow vision of meritocracy. In addition, much differentiation can take the form of lateral differentiation, rather than strictly vertical selectivity. This lateral differentiation emerges as a kind of cultural map, covering an ever increasing range of the social and natural world. By invoking the metaphor of a map, we wish to emphasize that the laterally-differentiated curriculum involves far more openness and choice than suggested by accounts highlighting vertical differentiation. Consequently, the modern curriculum underscores proper attitudes and orientations as it edges toward becoming free of technical content. We highlight this type of differentiation at the end of this paper. Attention to the second force—the pressure for expanded and universalized participation—leads naturally to direct attention to the actual substantive content of educational curricula. Thus, this chapter gives emphasis to this issue.

CURRICULUM AND THE NATION-STATE

If educational curricula are constructed as part of models of modern society, how is this society conceived? One might suppose it to be autonomous local communities or groups, or primordial racial and ethnic groups. But these entities, in the modern system, are not highly rationalized, and on their own generate little by way of formal education. Society in the modern system generally means the nation-state, or local units conceived as components of this wider nation-state (as in federalist countries).

This nation-state society, in the contemporary system, has a great deal of standardized commonality to it (Meyer, Boli, Thomas, & Ramirez, 1997). Thus, curriculum emerges in an imagined community of a more abstractly defined nation (Anderson, 1991), and its development is to reflect the ideal norms of an imagined social enterprise. Thus we may find rather similar educational and curricular forms and content in societies that differ by factors of fifty to one in economic development; or by unquantifiable dimensions in traditional cultural roots (Meyer, Kamens & Benavot with Cha & Wong, 1992). Practical functional and power realities also differ greatly among countries. The societies differ, but the idealized models of society, around which education and curricula are built, vary much less. Society occurs in a rationalized natural and social environment, universalistic and analyzable; it does not, principally, occur in a mystified or particularistic cosmos, with distinct gods and spirits and with special natural laws and forces. It is thus important for educational curricula to carry much information about this wider environment in natural and social sciences.

Society is made up of individual persons whose knowledge and commitments matter; it is built on individual citizenship. Even in the most centralized or authoritarian forms, society is not simply an authoritative structure that controls, as peasants, conforming people at the bottom: modern mass education arises because society is conceived to depend on people, not simply mechanically control them. Education must, therefore, integrate the people in a common national culture, and knowledge about the environment and social structure must be instilled in these people. It is also important that the people understand their own rights and responsibilities, and carry the capacity for effective and responsible voluntary action.

Society is itself a rationalized and differentiated structure, oriented toward progress. It is important for education to prepare and select people for positions in this differentiated system. Specialized instruction is necessary, especially as points of occupational allocation are reached. It is also necessary for everyone to understand the overall structure and share in its professive goals. Thus, mass education must provide instruction in history and civics, and religious or moral education of some sort.

Finally, each sovereign nation-state, especially in the high period of nationalism, has its own claimed primordial base in history and culture (and sometimes in ethnicity and religion). In a historically very competitive environment, its autonomous authority, against the powers around it, rests on such claims. It is important to transmit this cultural material in education, through art, through literature, through distinctive national language and culture, and through special national history.

These themes take on more meaning if we stress what the modern educational curriculum does not do. First, with rare exceptions (Kamens, 1992), it does not stress the importance and authority of a transcending tradition. In both mass and elite education, classical languages play a minor role (Cha, 1991), as do very traditional and ritualized forms of linear national or classical history (at the secondary level: S.-Y. Wong, 1991; at the tertiary level: Frank, Wong, Meyer, & Ramirez, 2000; Frank, Schofer, & Torres, 1994), and as do traditional literary canons: few curricular systems emphasize the learning of classic national poetry and literature, let alone generate traditional forms of memorization of such material. In many countries, some religious instruction remains (Cha, Wong & Meyer, 1992), but this rarely takes older forms involving instruction in doctrine and in sacred tests. In some cases, religious instruction enjoys a renaissance as a means to counter encroaching Western values, but Tan (1997) documented the failure of this strategy (and subsequent repeal of required religious instruction) in Singapore in the 1980s. The curriculum is focused on the myth of a modern rationalized society and culture, not on myths of tradition.

Second, the curriculum has a national or universal orientation and rarely stresses knowledge of local society and culture, although massive numbers of students will in fact live under the controls of such local structures. Local languages disappear at a great rate (Cha, 1991; de Swaan, 1993). Local history and culture are rarely emphasized.

Third, especially in long cycles of mass education, the curriculum stresses universalized models of knowledge and action and is little adapted to actual roles young people will play. Students of differing class, gender, urbanization, and ethnicity are likely to be allocated into occupational and other roles that differ greatly in functional requirements; despite this, modern mass educational curricula attempt universalized instruction. They do not plan dramatically different curricula for males and females (Ramirez & Cha, 1990), or for children of differing social class, or for rural and urban students. Further, while most aspects of the modern curriculum are legitimated as generally useful (e.g., language, mathematics), astonishingly little effort is made to immediately instrumentalize the curriculum. The point is to instill generalized knowledge and perspective—not to train young people for very specific needed skills—despite continuing traditionalist criticisms that important sacred, technical, or functional knowledge is being lost (Bennett, 1992; Bloom, 1987; Hirsch, 1988).

DIMENSIONS OF CURRICULAR CHANGE

The ideas above suggest that if we want to explain curricular change over time, we should look at world-level change, since models (more than local social and economic structures) of education and of modern society evolve at the world level (Meyer et al., 1997). We should also consider how general models of modern society and of education are changing, over and above immediate local constellations of power, interest, and function. In general, curricular content develops in a way that de-emphasizes the sacred qualities of school knowledge. Instead, the curriculum highlights a picture of society as thoroughly manageable and rational-ized, composed of agentic individuals, a society which is global in scope. The natural environ-ment is also constructed in the modern curriculum as lawful and controllable. Understandings about expertise change. Experts and expert knowledge are still prized (indeed, often thought to be central to national development), but increasingly, curricular materials portray all stu-dents as being potential experts. Some general themes follow:

1. Expanded Rationalization of Society

Throughout the twentieth century, and especially in the last fifty years, models of society and social development have been greatly elaborated. Many more domains are thinkable and dis-cussable in modern terms, and are understood to require social management. Economies are rationalized and conceptualized, and such issues as unemployment, capital investment rates, scientific and technical development, and labor quality are routine public responsibilities. Political life is similarly elaborated and analyzed, as are many dimensions of social life. So matters of family life (spousal and child abuse, child reading, family poverty and breakup, and reproduction control) come under public scrutiny as do all sorts of issues about social inequal-ity. Recent proposals, for example, would mandate instruction regarding the issue of domestic violence (Melear, 1995; Reuben, 1996). Specialized curricula in higher education routinely reflect such issues. Two examples are the rise in the Social Problems course as a typical introduction to sociology and the proliferation and breadth of Public Policy programs in American universities. Topics of these kinds also show up in mass education; in history that incorporates social elements more than political ones, in literatures that touch on many issues previously private (e.g., mental health, sexuality), in scientific and social scientific analyses. In this sense, for example, the more systemic orientation of contemporary German secondary school history textbooks—with their focus on *conditions* producing industrialization, capital-ism, and welfare states as opposed to the "great man approach"—epitomizes modernity (Berghahn & Schissler, 1987).*

2. Expanded Construction of the Individual

Contemporary models of society, especially in the post-War period of dominant liberalism, put increasingly elaborated models of the individual citizen, human, and person at the center of society. This person is now a rich and complex entity, whose economic, political, and social choices and capacities are conceived to be the motor of social development, and whose human rights are foundational. This produces three broad effects on curricula.

First, the content of the curriculum increasingly focuses on the rights and capacities of the individual. History of the polity and state give way to social studies of individuals in society (S.-Y. Wong, 1991); scientific instruction and literary tastes emphasize individual choices, rights, and standing (see Frank, Meyer, & Miyahara, 1995 on psychology); art and

---

*Rohe (1987) argues that, in contrast to Great Britain's tendency to highlight protagonists, Germany's emphasis on the broadly systemic is an inevitable result of its lack of heroes (and too easily identified villains) in twentieth century history. Though Germany's particular historical trajectory may have led it to this curricular orientation relatively early, the trend toward more systemic treatments in history and other subjects is more accurately seen as global in scope.

music emphasize individual expression more than collective traditions; and so on. These changes appear in mass education, but also in more specialized elite training systems.

Second, there is an attempt to universalize participation in the expanded curriculum. For instance, worldwide movements stress the expansion of mass education—as in the Education for All Movement (Chabbott, 1996)—and the more complete incorporation of females, racial and ethnic and regional minorities, and lower status groups (United Nations Children's Fund, 1992). Ideas that lower status groups should only be trained for limited roles in society are in ill repute: the effort is to bring the expanded curriculum to each and every child. Hence, educational systems around the world embrace literacy in a widening range of subject areas— more fundamentally as a metaphor than as a specified set of skills (McEneaney and Wong, 1997). Challenges to this model are viewed as heresy.*

This trend is apparent not only in discourse at the policy level. Curricular materials themselves become vastly more participatory in character. Elementary science and mathematics textbooks from around the world greatly expand depiction of people over time, including females and racial/ethnic minorities. The participation exhibits a universality in that this increasing frequency of depictions of ordinary people far outstrips depictions of famous scientists and mathematicians (McEneaney, 1998). Similar shifts in emphasis are found in social studies curricular outlines. Topics highlighting the centrality of the abstracted individual increase (e.g., Individual and his/her environment) as do requirements involving field trips or experiments (McEneaney & Wong, 1997).

Third, there are sustained efforts to recognize the interests and developmental needs of the child—now conceived as a person—in the educational process. It is an important consideration—over and above social functional needs—to find ways to interest and involve the student, and to organize curricula to be relevant to the student as a developing person. In art and literature, canons are weakened, and efforts are made to find materials that appeal to the students (Bryson, 1998). Science, mathematics, and social science curricula are redesigned to make sense to the student more than to the traditional authority structure. Owl excrement thus becomes a worthy object of scientific investigation in one primary science textbook recently approved for California public schools. By the middle of the twentieth century, arithmetic textbooks from many countries had become adorned with characters sporting smiles and engaging in slapstick in ways that appear to have precious little relation to the mathematical ideas presented. Later, these interest-enhancement devices become more integrated in the overall structure of the textbooks, but the aim remains constant (McEneaney, 1998).* Language itself changes from more high cultural forms to democratized ones, and great efforts are made to edit the language to be appropriate to the development of the target students. An extreme example is the proposal to recognize Ebonics in the Oakland, California public schools, but so are the elaborate attempts to fill basal readers with age-appropriate vocabulary. Grammar, of course, is de-emphasized and instruction in Latin, primarily viewed as a means to

*When physicist Morris Shamos (1995), for example, questioned the instructional objective of universal scientific literacy, his views received a distinctly chilly reception by educationalists (Evans, 1997).

*This pedagogical orientation highlighting the aesthetic and developmental needs of children is not limited to official curricular frameworks or textbooks and curricular materials intended for formal systems of education. U.S. marketing for a briskly-selling CD-ROM game, "Grossology," earnestly asserts its effectiveness in imparting appropriate scientific knowledge and attitudes. Similarly, "Beakman's World," an award-winning Saturday morning television show on CBS, claims to offer "whacked-out" science, clearly intended to stimulate the child's interest (CBS Kidszone - Beakman's World, 1998). German television offers "Lach und Sach" [*trans.:* "Smiles and School Science"]. These examples remind us that curricula are usefully viewed as cultural products not entirely discontinuous with popular culture.

impart the structure of language, has virtually disappeared because it is ill-suited to the expressive requirements of the modern curriculum. All these changes attempt to emphasize the active participation and interest of the student.

Thus, great drifting changes appear in the curriculum. At the secondary level, classical curricula tend to disappear, replaced by comprehensive ones (Kamens & Cha, 1992). In primary education, progressive traditions tend to dominate in many areas (S. Wong, 1991; S. Y. Wong, 1991; McEneaney, 1998). Although the change may have originated at lower levels, it is apparent now at higher levels. At the university level, enormous curricular expansion occurs. Worldwide, the mean number of academic departments and faculties in universities has increased dramatically since the 1960s (World List, 1969; World List, 1995). Gender studies becomes requisite in a growing number of American universities, though the particular conceptualization of gender varies dramatically across instructors and across departments within any particular institution (Christopher, 1995). Formal internship programs, intended to be hands-on, proliferate, as do leadership development programs (Golde & McEneaney, 1998). Such programs often offer college credit. Even modern management training programs have this flavor—de-emphasizing specific technical knowledge in favor of rationalizing broader areas of work life in a non-technical way (e.g., managing stress, morale, communication). Hence, although shifts in the curriculum reflecting an expanded construction of the individual originated at the primary school level, the changes are now apparent at the tertiary level and beyond.

3. Expanded Rationalization of the Natural Environment

The model of the modern society locates this society in increasingly complex relations with an increasingly rationalized natural environment. The physical, social, psychological, and moral context of society is scientized, and science becomes a generalized umbrella of understanding—a mentality appropriate and necessary for every member of society. The long-term expansion of science instruction continues (Benavot et al., 1991), and the topics included in science expand, now including all sorts of social and psychological material (McEneaney, 1998). The Sachunterricht (literally "object instruction") style of primary school science in German-speaking countries is a good example; making no firm distinction between theorizing about the natural and social environment, the portrayal is of an analyzable, but highly interrelated world. In one fourth grade textbook, for example, the physics of bicycles is followed rather seamlessly by a discussion of transportation as a human need and traffic congestion as a social problem (Herbert et al., 1993). It is not simply a case of science curricula appropriating social arenas—civics instruction, too, broadens to include consideration of citizenship in relation to environmental issues and the natural world (Rauner, 1998). The student must learn that everything in the wider environment can and should be analyzed scientifically, and that individual and social relations with this environment extend to all sorts of domains of activity (from garbage to natural resources to human sexuality).

4. Globalization: Transcending the National State

The model of the modern society increasingly locates this society in a global context, economically, politically, socially, and culturally. Emphasis on national autonomy, autarky, and primordial tradition is weakened. Thus, the curriculum must be globalized, to create a broader understanding. History and social studies emphasize transnational elements (Frank et al., 2000), and civics instruction dramatically shifted in the 1980s and 1990s to a model of the "postnational citizen" of the world (Rauner, 1998). Science is applicable everywhere (now less overtly linked to the notion of progress in textbooks, its utility is merely assumed); art and literature incorporate more global and eclectic materials. Albarea (1997), for example, argued in support of music instruction as an "intercultural" dimension of lifelong education, suggesting that educating "multimusical" individuals might be a basis on which to develop a "pluralist European identity." Foreign languages and cultures must be incorporated (on language, see Cha, 1991).

5. Glocalization (Robertson, 1992): Transcending the National State

Modern society models increasingly step back from the picture of national unity around the state as the core entity. Society now includes legitimated diversity, all to be seen in a universalistic context. As a result, local and regional cultures and histories have become more relevant, and society is seen as composed of many different groups (women, ethnic minorities, religious groups, age groups), whose conditions and interests and cultures have standing. History, literature, art, and language all broaden, and the curriculum should include materials relevant to a society now seen as more diverse. Thus, the French state, having devoted itself for centuries to the unification of national culture and the extirpation of local ones, now provides instruction in eight different regional language/cultural groups. Although this might seem to contradict Cha's (1991) study that documents the worldwide decline of curricular emphasis on local languages, admitting a degree of localism is understood, in the modern curriculum, as insuring personal relevance through individual expressiveness.

Broadening, then, walks a fine line between emphasis on the transnational/universal and homage to the particular/local. Across subject areas, the incorporation of local elements has a programmatic and formulaic feel: enough to satisfy "relevance" criteria, yet not so much as to undercut the notion that the knowledge has universal standing. As such, arithmetic textbooks of the 1980s and 1990s from a diverse range of countries include a few pages celebrating the symmetry and geometry of locally-produced art, often folk art. This nearly obligatory bow to the local does not, however, disrupt the overall flow of instruction, since it is typically sprinkled throughout the book, rather than organized into a chapter, and quite frequently serving as decoration, lacking direct links to classroom activities or exercises.

In a similar vein, multiculturalism has nearly hegemonic standing in American classrooms, though the treatment is usually highly eclectic. Drew (1997, p. 298) criticizes this "cultural tourism" noting that "students are free to travel, to observe, [but also] to remain removed from and unaffected by the material conditions . . . represented" in multicultural readers. More generally, then, it is clearly true that this lateral expansion of the curriculum need not include a deepening political or even emotional commitment to the issues at hand. What the curriculum requires is far more subtle: a commitment to a particular view of self in environment, of individuals imbued with choices and capacities in a rationalized, lawful world.

CURRICULAR CHANGE AND MODERN FORMS OF CULTURAL TASTE

There are striking parallels between contemporary curricula and the evolution of patterns of cultural taste. The laterally expanded, eclectic, and differentiated curriculum develops in clear association with much discussed trends in cultural standards in general, which tend to move away from highly stratified forms toward models celebrating diversity. In one sense, whether derived from political conflict or a less overtly conflictual alignment to cultural models, curricula can be viewed as a national expression of taste. Curricula are detailed statements about national preferences: a preferred natural and social world, a preferred history, a preferred understanding of children as learners. Importantly, while curricula once outlined knowledge appropriate for elites, they now specify what is appropriate for everyone. There is perhaps greater and more consistent pressure on nation-states to cultivate high-status tastes than there is on individuals. Nevertheless, the literature on the historical trends in the relationship between the social status and the cultural tastes of individuals is pertinent. Hence, we now ask the reader to make a conceptual leap to apply theories about the tastes of individual persons to another social unit: national educational systems.

Bourdieu's (1984) groundbreaking empirical analysis in France suggests that higher social status is associated with greater cultural "distinction," that is, a narrower range of cultural preferences. His most impressive analysis of the special case of France may have misled analysts of the general phenomenon of cultural capital. He sees it as tightly linked to the stratification of a class and status structure; it is probably more generally true in the modern world that the really valued forms of cultural capital stress comprehensive and eclectic knowledge and capacity more than a few specialized elite forms. Thus, in contrast, there is growing empirical evidence of a historical shift toward "omnivorousness" among high-status individuals (Peterson & Kern, 1996; Peterson & Simkus, 1992). Peterson and Kern note that cultural omnivorousness is not the same as being indiscriminant in one's cultural preferences, but an "openness to appreciate everything" (1996, p. 904). Bryson (1996) operationalizes this cultural openness or tolerance as *not disliking* various styles of music, and demonstrates that more highly educated people have a broad familiarity with a diversity of musical genres, excluding only those genres (e.g., heavy metal) more specifically associated with low-status people.

So it is with the modern curriculum. Originally, it emphasized narrow, technically specialized content. Over time, it has become omnivorous in its lateral expansion, and eclectic in its juxtaposition of topics. In this context, the fact that American high schools have settled into teaching sexual abstinence while handing out condoms is not so surprising. In addition, it becomes conceivable to teach creationism one day and Darwin's theory of evolution the next. Cultivating an entitlement to choose is central, however, so that students may be asked to select one novel to read from a breathtakingly diverse list of authors, or to make up and solve their own algebra problem in math class. Above all, the modern curriculum is tolerant in the sense that all arenas of the social and natural world are portrayed as equally worthy of rational analysis. Popular culture and leisure studies thus become worthy of academic attention at the college level. It would be wrong to view this change as empowering or spearheading fundamental social change. We can apply Drew's critique of multicultural readers much more broadly to the whole of the modern curriculum—as cultural tourism designed to eliminate disliking, rather than instilling particular commitments or technical expertise.

REFORM AND RESISTANCE

The long-term curricular changes we have discussed receive relatively little attention. Most policy discussions, overwhelmed by the urgency of change, tend to be insensitive to how much change is routine. This arises because much change effort takes the form of dramatic reform movements, and organizational reforms tend ultimately to be seen as relative failures. It seems to the intellectual observers that needed reforms fail, and that reactionary resistance is dominant. This is, as we discuss in this chapter, unrealistic; in fact, long-term trends systematically parallel the goals of reformers, and surprisingly little evidence of effective reaction can be found.

Much of the change we have described occurs in routinized ways, as teachers and policymakers adapt to changing wider cultural models and contexts. In decentralized educational systems such as the American system, no single policy center manages all the adaptation, and in rather decoupled ways shifts occur in national, state, district, school, and classroom instructional patterns (Meyer & Rowan, 1978). There is little organizational coherence to it, and those who attempt organizationally-controlled change often experience the decoupling involved as failure. This misses the point that all policy levels from national state to the classroom teacher tend to adapt to widespread institutional changes. There would, for instance, be no good way to discover the impact of the modern environmental movement on American education. Special district, state, or national programs may or may not have much direct effect, but clearly American teachers are much more likely to include environmental projects and materials than in the past.

In more centralized, and typical, educational systems, curriculum is tied more closely to a single national control system, and classroom teachers are more likely to follow along (Stevenson & Baker, 1991). Change, on the dimensions discussed above, may be routine and bureaucratic, but is more concretely situated. In either case, much curricular change is routine, and socially of little visibility. This arises because curricular change tends to be rooted in general cultural changes in models of the modern society: it is taken for granted that the curriculum reflects these models, and is naturally functional for them. With the rise of widespread modern environmentalism, for instance, it would seem natural to practically all participants that children should receive instruction in recycling—and such instruction may be relatively routine even in developing countries in which actual recycling plays little part. Similarly, with the rise of modern principles of gender equality, it seems obvious that the curriculum will reflect this, even in societies in which gender equality plays little actual role (Ramirez & Cha, 1990).

However, with the expansion and penetration of modern models of society, gaps are often perceived between changing social reality or mythology and the curriculum: the modern system is fertile ground for educational and curricular reform movements. With current perceptions of gaps between the imagined modern economy and actual science and mathematics curricula, for instance, there have been worldwide movements for reform in these curricula (American Association for the Advancement of Science, 1992; National Education Goals Panel, 1997; United Nations Educational, Scientific, and Cultural Organization, 1991). These occur in countries with developed economies, but also in countries in which development is only an imagined model.

Even in cases where reforms are pursued in conservative styles (e.g., with reference to needed higher standards of achievement), the actual agendas involved tend to follow directions noted in our previous discussion: expanded rationalization, greater participation (including student centrism), more globalization, and less traditionalism. The conservative American pressures for improved test scores in science and in mathematics, for instance, when turned into concrete curricular change, in fact take quite a progressive direction on exactly the dimensions we have discussed.

When reform movements occur, they receive much public and social scientific attention, and substantial literatures arise. Overstated proposals and policies for reform are routine, and criticisms of their failures are also routine. Much of it is shadow boxing, in the sense of back-and-forth discussions of unimplemented and unimplementable ideologies; in order for a proposal to be perceived as a reform, it is most likely to be quite unrealistic and unrealizable (Meyer, 1992). Commentators have described the waves of educational and curricular fads and fashions (often encapsulated as buzzwords) as "change without reform" (Cuban, 1997; see also Tyack & Cuban, 1995). The entire pattern of discussion, however, focuses on the reform tip of the iceberg of educational change, and tends to ignore the long-term and very striking drifts characterizing curricular change.

Resistances exist as well. Change, and especially reform movements, generate reactive oppositional discourse. In addition, throughout the history of modern education, much traditionalist discourse is routine; programs are suggested that go back to various basics of history, language, science, mathematics, and culture. Overall, it is striking how little impact most of this has, in developed countries or in world education as a whole. Following is a discussion of several factors involved.

First, dramatic reforms may be more difficult to implement in dominant or hegemonic educational systems in which previous forms are well institutionalized. The literature on British curriculum suggests the entrenched resistance power of the established academic and class forces; something of the same resistance may be found in hegemonic America (despite its progressive history). Resistance may be more effective in higher levels of mass education, in which it can be accompanied by the conservative power of the university academics (e.g., Slaughter, 1997) and their selection tests.

Second, reform may be easier to adopt but more difficult to implement under Third World conditions, in which limitations of teacher training and resources slow rates of effective change. Some studies have documented general shifts in textbooks and curricular outline content and emphasis (McEneaney, 1998; Rauner, 1998; Meyer et al., 1992) as well as more specific changes in, for example, constructions of gender in materials from developing and former Eastern bloc countries (Walford, 1983). Yet, Altbach (1988) warns that the lack of material infrastructure often prevents these curricular materials from being used as intended in classrooms Some systems simply cannot afford textbooks for children; others, for example, cannot manage to deliver printed and purchased textbooks to rural schools in a timely manner due to inadequate roads.

Third, expansive reforms may proceed more slowly in educational systems constrained by traditional testing forms; the greater the selectivity of a system, the more powerful these institutions may be. Curricular materials in current and former British colonies, for instance, seem highly attuned to meeting the requirements of the traditional British or British-inspired "O" and "A" level examinations (Eisemon, 1990). In primary science, this is associated with a persistent espousal of academic and disciplinary emphasis rather than with more applied portrayals of science (McEneaney, 1998). One factor facilitating long-term expansive curricular change in the United States has been the weak power of both selectivity and traditional standardized achievement testing in the educational system.

Overall, however, the surprising characteristics of modern curricular change lie in the routine and taken for granted ways in which so much of it happens. In the United States, there are isolated elements of the curriculum that appear to act as lightning rods, occasionally drawing the attention and ire of parents and community members, but as noted previously, these topics tend to be relatively marginal, and conflicts tend to be resolved through inclusion rather than through hard-line exclusion. Furthermore, the United States, granting parents the status to participate in this way, is an anomaly—the vast majority of curricular change in most countries is funneled through professionalized channels and cultures, generating little overt conflict in the broader society. This arises because the curriculum is embedded in changing wider models of society, and in these models the curriculum takes on an obvious quality.

With rapid curricular evolution, through this century and especially through recent decades, naturally traditionalist complaints arise and receive much attention (Bennett, 1992; Bloom, 1987; Finn, 1991; Hirsch, 1988). The broad and driven commitment to progressive forms that we have described makes these complaints seem very threatening, and proponents of modernization often see their curricular world as being destroyed. Complaints consequently arise that students no longer learn real history and geography, or real disciplined science, or literature and language, or artistic and cultural traditions. Scandals are promulgated—American children cannot find Atlanta on a map, cannot properly parse sentences or the atom, cannot correctly do calculations, do not know when or what the Civil War was or was about, and so on. Efforts are made to emphasize various basics on such matters. Our point is that the main evolution goes quite the other way, toward more expansive, participatory, and broadened conceptions of knowledge, involving the development and interests of the student rather than the authority of received knowledge. It is very difficult to find, in any country, real movements in the opposite direction, apart from decorative adaptations, such as dramatic emphases on nationalist history and the authority of religious/ethnic traditions, formalized elite and disciplinary science with long sequences of rigidly required topics, or emphases on the learning of sacred canons of art and literature.

DIFFERENTIATION

We have discussed the way the modern curriculum—particularly in mass education—evolves as an expanded and universalized cultural map. Wider and wider arenas of rationalization are incorporated, and made relevant to universal student populations. This broad trend runs in opposition to those more instrumentalist theories of modern society and education that stress the impact of social differentiation—perhaps functional differentiation, but more often in sociological thinking differentiation in power, resources and status. These lines of thought would predict more, not fewer, barriers; more and earlier specialization and differentiation, not less and later specialization. Nevertheless, as we have stressed, educational reality has involved extended and expanded mass educational curricula, with differentiation coming in later and less dramatically. The rise of comprehensive and expanded secondary education has been an exemplification of this. Still, the actual structure of modern society has indeed seen rapid occupational differentiation, and the expansion and differentiation of knowledge specialties. It is important to note how this has occurred.

Older systems of highly stratified education have certainly been undercut. Around the world, educational expansion nudges secondary education toward universality, as enrollments in higher education multiply. Formal highly stratified tracking (e.g., at the senior secondary level) has been weakened. Already in decline as an elite institution before reunification, the German gymnasium is rapidly embracing a more comprehensive orientation, as a dramatically lower proportion of secondary level students choose lower track programs in the Realschule and Hauptschule. This development is paralleled in the breakdown of distinction in the training of teachers at different levels. In developing countries, upper secondary teachers once received considerably more academic and professional training than teachers at lower levels. As more resources are invested in teacher training, the trend is toward more equitable levels of training, with required years of training for primary and junior secondary teachers approaching that for upper secondary teachers. (UNESCO, 1976, UNESCO, 1996). Hence, the older form of storing elite knowledge in elite curricula is clearly not the dominant trend in any national educational system.

Instead, the modern mode for dealing with occupational and knowledge differentiation has been to diversify curricula within a broadly comprehensive mode. The key notion is choice: wider varieties of special instruction in secondary education and the universities are to be found—one can major in anything from classics to cows and wine in an American university, and secondary schools have a dramatically expanded cafeteria of programs (Powell, Farrar, & Cohen, 1985). Increasingly, however, allocation into these various programs is managed, not by elite selection and testing rules, but by choices made by individual students and their families. This maintains myths of democratic and participatory universalism, while enabling the curriculum to contain the most astonishing variety of specialties. Sociologists looking at this system can naturally find much hidden stratification in it: they miss the larger point that the whole system increasingly rests on expanded choice and participation rights. School counselors in America, for instance, function little as the old-style gatekeepers—increasingly they presume high aspirations, and play roles as guiding student choice (Rosenbaum, Miller & Krei, 1996; Schneider & Stevenson, 1999). Flows of information to low-income families about these choices may be disrupted (through neglectful or absent counseling and other means) but our point is that the system relies rather unquestioningly on the premise of choice.

DEVELOPING PROPERTIES OF THE MODERN CURRICULUM

We now summarize our observations and arguments on contemporary school curricula and implications for the direction of change in the future. At many points, there is evidence supporting these arguments; at others, they function as hypotheses for future work.

Social Studies

Traditional national and civilizational history and geography, built around linear sequences; around the political and military development of the state and its elites; and around the geography of the sacred national territory; are weakened and receive less emphasis (Frank et al., 2000). At the elementary level, they are replaced by more eclectic social studies, linking the putative interests and the child as a person to a broad society in which this person is to participate. History itself is more social, and social studies replaces much of it (S.-Y. Wong, 1991). The substance covers both local and international matters in part removed from the tight boundaries of time and space; there is a chapter on the Dakota, then on an African family and community, then on the local community. At senior secondary and university levels, the same changes appear, with emphases on the social sciences, on international society, on human diversity, and on the individual.

Science

Science as external elite knowledge is weakened, and students are less exposed to traditional categories; they learn the general importance for everybody of the scientific attitude and perspective, learn to think about science as related to their own identities, activities and interests, and are less obligated to know tight bundles of official knowledge. Instruction no longer emphasizes the parts of the leaf, the length of rivers, the types of clouds, or long lists of beneficial and harmful plants and chemicals; it focuses on the more diffuse understanding of processes, such as the interdependencies involving the rain forest, drought and desertification, recycling, and so on. At higher levels, great diversity appears, with greatly enlarged choices about what to be scientific about and how to do it. Time commitments in mass curricular outlines to science increase dramatically over the course of the century (Kamens & Benavot, 1991).

Language and Literature

The emphasis goes toward the student's capacity for expression and understanding, and away from a focus on students' subordinating themselves to correct use of elite forms (e.g., grammar, spelling, elaborate formal constructions). The literature emphasized is no longer the sacred canon of national or civilizational texts: any text that engages the student can be used to promulgate participative comprehension and broadened understanding. At higher levels, great diversity appears, and it is reasonable to let students choose among literatures of all sorts: science fiction, romance novels, authors reflecting feminist or ethnic perspectives, and literature from anywhere in the world.

Mathematics

Here, logical traditions retain more force. Time commitments to mathematics in national curricula remain fairly stable historically (Kamens & Benavot, 1991). But still there is a notable shift from the most traditional and deductive structures, like geometry and trigonometry, toward an understanding and collecting of data, applications of statistics and various computer analyses, and the like. Instructionally, calculative correctness is subordinated to proper understanding. At higher levels, diversity and choice appear.

Art and Culture

Emphasis on canonical sacred traditions declines, and cultural emphases become eclectic and organized around the interests and participation of the student. The student is to understand a broad range of national and cultural forms, and is to do so in ways that emphasize participation and interest. Paralleling curricular treatments of literature, the expressive possibilities of art and culture are themselves worthy of consideration.

Civics

Emphases on the detailed rules and structures of government decline. The student is to learn broader principles of human rights and responsibility, of democratic political structure, and of the wider international and ecological environment. Involvement and participation are more important than technical knowledge, and the student is to learn to do these things from a validated individual point of view (Rauner, 1998). At higher levels, an eclectic understanding of the political system is more important than detailed knowledge of government.

Overall

Schooled knowledge moves from authoritative structures of fact and skill and discipline to dramatic emphases on (a) broadened individual participation in (b) a rationalized knowledge system that functions as an umbrella of understanding and comprehension. The student does not need to know where Egypt is, or much about its history, but needs to understand that the same general principles apply there as everywhere else: tolerance, universalism, the capacity to understand and at least hypothetically communicate, are the targets. The student is scripted to be an empowered member and participant in a very broad society and nature, not to be subordinated to an exogenously authoritative elite culture.

DISCUSSION AND CONCLUSION

We began our discussion with a consideration of two different, but not entirely oppositional pressures on mass educational curricula. In the first, a view of modern society as increasingly complex and differentiated suggests that the curriculum itself should become more hierarchical, doling out elite knowledge only selectively, with heightened stratification and hierarchy the inevitable result. In the second, the focus is on society as resting on a broad, shared culture in which the increasingly elaborated notion of modernity is a powerful model. We have explicated the nature of curricular change which follows from this modernist project of constructing individuals. Theories stemming from the first view implicate local conditions and structures, suggesting that curricula mirror (or are direct products of) actual material conditions. We highlight how curricula evolve in concert with cultural models of modernity (of which education is a part), which are fundamentally global in scope. These models undoubtedly have hegemonic influence, but they shape curricula that are less oriented toward overt control and regulation of students than is commonly assumed. Power and influence undoubtedly operate in this process, but much more through the thorough rationalization and professionalization of the field than open conflict.

In each case, curricula are seen as embedded in a social context, practically as a matter of course, but we argue that the former fails to account for the vast majority of curricular change. In short, we advocate a dramatically wider consideration of social context in recognition of the highly institutionalized character of mass schooling, a social context that goes beyond local interests and power plays to include cultural models, global in scope, which are elaborated in imagined communities.

We are not alone in this critique, though little of it appears in the mainstream American sociological literature. Hlebowitsh (1997, p. 509) decries the tendency to choose a chronology of social control to account for curricular change, and suggests that the conceptualization of curriculum as an object of social inquiry is too narrow, "and gone mad with overtly ideological constructions." Englund remarks that the literature neglects the "meaning-creating content of socialization," relegating it to a taken-for-granted (1997, p. 267). Claiming the sociology of curriculum knowledge as a central problem in the study of schooling, Popkewitz offers a notion of how power operates in a view of the curriculum as culturally constructed. Drawing on Foucault's notions of governmentality and regulation, he writes: "curriculum inscribes rules and standards by which reason and individuality are constructed . . . The regulation [curriculum produces] is not only what is cognitively understood; it produces sensitivities, dispositions, and awarenesses" (1997, p. 145).

Clearly, sociological analysis of the curriculum and its relationship to enduring patterns of inequality are important and have obvious policy relevance. However, much curricular change occurs at the level Popkewitz highlights, and the inculcation of modern sensitivities tends not to draw public or scholarly scrutiny.

ACKNOWLEDGMENTS: The authors share equal responsibility for this chapter. We wish to thank David J. Frank, Gero Lenhardt, Francisco O. Ramirez, and the members of the Stanford Workshop on Comparative Political and Educational Systems for their valuable comments.

REFERENCES

Albarea, R. (1997). L'Éducation musicale pour la formation d'une identité europeénne pluraliste. *International Review of Education, 43,* 61–72.

Altbach, P. (1988). Textbooks and the Third World: An overview. In P. Altbach and G. Kelly (Eds.), *Textbooks in the Third World: Policy, content and context* (pp. 3–18). New York: Garland.

American Association for the Advancement of Science (AAAS). (1992). *Benchmarks for science literacy.* New York: Oxford University Press.

Anderson. B. (1991). *Imagined communities: Reflections on the origin and spread of nationalism* (revised ed.) New York: Verso.

Anyon, J. (1980). Social class and the hidden curriculum of work. *Journal of Education, 162,* 67–92

Apple, M. W. (1990). *Ideology and curriculum* (2nd ed.). New York: Routledge.

Arum, R., & Shavit, Y. (1995). Secondary vocational education and the transition from school to work. *Sociology of Education, 68,* 187–204.

Bacchus, K. (1996). Curriculum development in a colonial society. *Education and Society, 14,* 3–21.

Beatty, A. (Ed., 1997). *Learning from TIMSS: Results of the Third International Mathematics and Science Study.* Washington, DC: Narional Academy of Sciences, National Research Council.

Benavot, A., Cha, Y.-K., Kamens, D., Meyer, J. W., & Wong, S.-Y. (1991). Knowledge for the masses: World models and national curricula, 1920–1986. *American Sociological Review 56,* 85–101.

Bennett, W. (1992). *The de-valuing of America: The fight for our culture and our children.* New York: Summit Books.

Berghahn, V., & Schissler, H. (Eds., 1987). *Perceptions of history: International textbook research on Britain, Germany and the United States.* New York: St. Martin's Press.

Bernstein, B. (1990). *The structuring of pedagogic discourse: Class, codes and control* (Vol. 4). New York: Routledge.

Blau, P., & Duncan, O. D. (1967). *The American occupational structure.* New York: Wiley.

Bloom, A. (1987). *The closing of the American mind: How higher education has failed democracy and impoverished the souls of today's students.* New York: Simon and Schuster.

Bourdieu, P. (1984). *Distinction: A social critique of the stratification of taste.* Cambridge, MA: Harvard University Press.

Bourdieu, P., & Passeron, J.-C. (1977). *Reproduction in education, society and culture.* Beverly Hills, CA: Sage.

Bowles, S., & Gintis, H. (1976). *Schooling in capitalist America: Education reform and the contradictions of economic life.* New York: Basic Books.

Broaded, C. M. (1997). The limits and possibilities of tracking: Some evidence from Taiwan. *Sociology of Education, 70,* 36 –53.

Bryson, B. (1996). 'Anything but heavy metal': Symbolic exclusion and musical dislikes. *American Sociological Review, 61,* 884–899.

Bryson, B. (1998). *Institutionalizing multiculturalism: Symbolic and organizational boundaries in American universities.* Unpublished doctoral dissertation, Department of Sociology, Princeton University, Princeton, New Jersey.

Carnochan, W.B. (1993). *The battleground of the curriculum.* Stanford, CA: Stanford University Press.

Caspi, A., Wright, B., Moffitt, T., & Silva, P. (1998). Childhood predictors of unemplpyment in early adulthood. *American Sociological Review, 63,* 424–451.

CBS Kidszone–Beakman's World (1998). Http://marketing.cbs.com/kidszone/shows/beakman.html.

Cha, Y.-K. (1991). The effect of the global system on language instruction, 1850–1986. *Sociology of Education, 64,* 19–32.

Cha, Y.-K., Wong, S.-Y., & Meyer, J. M. (1992). Values education in the curriculum: Some comparative empirical data. In J. W. Meyer, D. Kamens, & A. Benavot, with Y.-K. Cha, & S.-Y. Wong. *School knowledge for the masses: World models and national primary curricular categories in the twentieth century*. London: Falmer Press.

Chabbott, C. (1996). *Constructing educational development: International development organizations and the World Conference on Education For All*. Unpublished doctoral dissertation, School of Education, Stanford University, Stanford, California.

Chavez, K., & Matthews, J. (1995, October 17). Wilson approves test gauging student skills. *San Francisco Examiner*, p. A-5.

Christopher, S. (1995). *Required knowledge*. Unpublished Ph.D. Dissertation, School of Education, Stanford University.

Collins, R. (1979). *The credential society*. New York: Academic Press.

Cuban, L. (1997). Change without reform: The case of Stanford University School of Medicine, 1908-1990. *American Educational Research Journal, 34*, 83–122.

de Swaan, A. (Ed., 1993). The emergent world language system. *International Political Science Review*. 14 (Special Issue).

Drew, J. (1997). Cultural tourism and the commodified other: Reclaiming difference in the multicultural classroom. *The Review of Education/Pedagogy/Cultural Studies, 19*, 297–309.

Durkheim, E. (1922 [1956]). *Education and sociology*. Glencoe, IL: The Free Press.

Eisemon, T. (1990). Examinations policies to strengthen primary schooling in African countries. *International Journal of Educational Development, 10*, 69–82.

Englund, T. (1997). Toward a dynamic analysis of the content of schooling: Narrow and broad didactics in Sweden. *Journal of Curriculum Studies, 29*, 267–287.

Evans, R. (1997). A challenge to the science education community: Morris H. Shamos' "The myth of scientific literacy." In W. Gräber & C. Bolte (Eds.) *Scientific Literacy* (pp. 103–120). Kiel, Germany: Institüt für die Pädagogik der Naturwissenschaften.

Finn, C. (1991). *We must take charge: Our schools and our future*. New York: The Free Press.

Frank, D. J., Schofer, E. & Torres, J. C. (1994). Rethinking history: Change in the university curriculum: 1910–90. *Sociology of Education, 67*, 231–242.

Frank, D. J., Meyer, J. W. & Miyahara, D. (1995). The individualist polity and the centrality of professionalized psychology. *American Sociological Review, 60*, 360–377.

Frank, D. J., Wong, S. Y., Meyer, J. W., & Ramirez, F. O. (2000). Embedding national societies: Worldwide changes in university history curricula, 1985–1994. *Comparative Education Review, 44*, 29–53.

Frazier, N., & Sadker, M. (1973). *Sexism in school and society*. New York: Harper and Row.

Freire, P. (1970). *Pedagogy of the oppressed*. New York: Seabury.

Gamoran, A. (1992). The variable effects of high school tracking. *American Sociological Review, 57*, 812–828.

Gillborn, D. (1992). Citizenship, 'race' and the hidden curriculum. *International Studies in Sociology of Education, 2*, 57–75.

Giroux, H. (1981). *Ideology, culture and the process of schooling*. Philadelphia: Temple University Press.

Golde, C., & McEneaney, E. (1998). The student affairs profession and the chartering of student activism. Unpublished manuscript, Department of Sociology, University of Nevada Las Vegas.

Goodson, I. (1987). *School subjects and curriculum change*. London: Falmer Press.

Goodson, I. (1992). On curriculum form: Notes toward a theory of curriculum. *Sociology of Education. 65*, 66–75.

Hallinan, M. (1987). *The social organization of schools: New conceptualizations of the learning process*. New York: Plenum.

Herbert, M., Bunk, H.-D., Klotz, B., Knauf, A., Knauf, T., & Sannwaldt-Hanke, K. (1993). *Mein Entdeckerbuch 4*. Stuttgart: Ernst Klett Schulbuchverlag.

Hirsch, E. D. (1988). *Cultural literacy: What every American needs to know*. New York: Vintage Books.

Hlebowitsh, P. (1997). The search for the curriculum field. *Journal of Curriculum Studies, 29*, 507–511.

Kamens, D. (1992). Variant forms: Cases of countries with distinct curricula. In J. W. Meyer, D. Kamens, & A. Benavot with Y. K. Cha & S. Y. Wong. *School Knowledge for the Masses* (pp. 74–82). Washington, DC: Falmer Press.

Kamens, D. & Benavot, A. (1991). Elite knowledge for the masses: The origins and spread of mathematics and science education in national curricula. *American Journal of Education, 99*, 137–180.

Kamens, D., & Cha, Y.-K. (1992). The formation of new subjects in mass schooling: Nineteenth century origins and twentieth century diffusion of art and physical education. In J. W. Meyer, D. Kamens, & A. Benavot, with Y.-K. Cha & S.-Y. Wong, *School knowledge for the masses: World models and national primary curricular categories in the twentieth century* (pp. 152–164). London: Falmer Press.

Ladwig, J. (1996). *Academic distinctions: Theory and methodology in the sociology of school knowledge*. New York: Routledge.

Larson, E. (1989). *Trial and error: The American controversy over creation and evolution*. New York: Oxford University Press.

McEneaney, E. (1998). *The transformation of primary school science and mathematics: A cross-national analysis, 1900-1995*. Unpublished doctoral dissertation, Department of Sociology, Stanford University, Stanford, California..

McEneaney, E., & Wong, S.-Y. (1997, August). *Toward a theory of global curricular change: The cases of social studies, science and mathematics*. Annual meeting of the American Sociological Association, Toronto, Ontario.

Melear, C. (1995). Multiculturalism in science education. *The American Biology Teacher, 57*, 21–27.

Meyer, J. W. (1992). Innovation and knowledge use in American public education. In J. W. Meyer & W. R. Scott (Eds.) *Organizational environments: Ritual and rationality* (pp. 233–260). Newbury Park, CA: Sage.

Meyer, J. W. & Rowan, B. (1978). Institutionalized organizations: Formal structure as myth and ceremony. *American Journal of Sociology, 83*, 340–363.

Meyer, J. W., Boli, J., Thomas, G. M., & Ramirez, F. O. (1997). World society and the nation-state. *American Journal of Sociology, 103*, 144–181.

Meyer, J. W., Kamens, D., & Benavot, A., with Cha, Y.-K. & Wong, S-Y. (1992). *School knowledge for the masses: World models and national primary curricular categories in the twentieth century*. London: Falmer Press.

Meyer, J. W., Ramirez, F. O., & Soysal, Y. N. (1992). World expansion of mass education, 1870–1980. *Sociology of Education, 65*, 128–149.

National Education Goals Panel. (1997). *The National Education Goals Report: Building a nation of learners, 1997*. Washington, DC: U.S. Government Printing Office.

Oakes, J. (1985). *Keeping track*. New Haven, CT: Yale University Press.

Parsons, T. (1962). *Toward a general theory of action*. Cambridge, MA: Harvard University Press.

Peterson, R., & Kern, R. (1996). Changing highbrow taste: From snob to omnivore. *American Sociological Review, 61*, 900–907.

Peterson, R., & Simkus, A. (1992). How musical tastes mark occupational status groups. In M. Lamont & M. Fournier (Eds.), *Cultivating differences: Symbolic boundaries and the making of inequality* (pp. 152–186). Chicago: University of Chicago Press.

Popkewitz, T. (1997). The production of reason and power: Curriculum history and intellectual traditions. *Journal of Curriculum Studies, 29*, 131–164.

Powell, A., Farrar, E., & Cohen, D. (1985). *The shopping mall high school: Winners and losers in the educational marketplace*. Boston: Houghton Mifflin.

Ramirez, F. O., & Cha, Y.-K.(1990). Citizenship and gender: Western educational developments in comparative perspective. *Research in Sociology of Education and Socialization, 9*, 153–174.

Rauner, M. (1998). *The worldwide globalization of civics education topics from 1955–1995*. Unpublished doctoral dissertation, School of Education, Stanford University, Stanford, California..

Reuben, R. (1996). The forgotten victims: New ABA domestic violence program reaches out to children. *ABA Journal, 82*, 104–105.

Robertson, R. (1992). *Globalization: Social theory and global culture*. London: Sage.

Rohe, G. (1987). The constitutional development of Germany and Great Britain in the nineteenth and twentieth centuries in German and English history textbooks: A study of comparative political culture. In V. Berghahn & H. Schissler, H. (Eds.), *Perceptions of history: International textbook research on Britain, Germany and the United States* (pp. 51–70). New York: St. Martin's Press.

Rosenbaum, J., Miller, S., & Krei, M. (1996). Gatekeeping in an era of more open gates: High school counselors' views of their influence on students' college plans. *American Journal of Education, 104*, 257–279.

Shanahan, M., Elder, G., & Miech, R. (1997). History and agency in men's lives: Pathways to achievement in cohort perspective. *Sociology of Education, 70*, 54–67.

Shamos, M. (1995). *The myth of scientific literacy*. New Brunswick, NJ: Rutgers University Press.

Slaughter, S. (1997). Class, race, and gender and the construction of post-secondary curricula in the U.S.: Social movement, professionalization and political economic theories of curricular change. *Journal of Curriculum Studies, 29*, 1–30.

Stevenson, D., & Baker, D. (1991). State control of the curriculum and classroom instruction." *Sociology of Education 64*, 1–10.

Stevenson, D., Schiller, K. & Schneider, B. (1994). Sequences of opportunities for learning. *Sociology of Education, 67*, 184–198.

Schneider, B., & Stevenson, D. (1999). *The ambitious generation: America's teenagers, motivated but directionless.* New Haven, CT: Yale University Press.

Tan, J. (1997). "The rise and fall of religious knowledge in Singapore secondary schools." *Journal of Curriculum Studies, 29,* 5, 603–624.

Thomas, G. M., Meyer, J. W., Ramirez, F. O., & Boli, J. (1987). *Institutional structure: Constituting state, society, and the individual.* Newbury Park, CA: Sage.

Tyack, D., & Cuban, L. (1995). *Tinkering toward utopia: A century of public school reform.* Cambridge: Harvard University Press.

UNESCO. (1976). *World guide to higher education: A comparative survey of systems, degrees and qualifications.* New York: Unipub.

UNESCO. (1996). *World guide to higher education: A comprehensive survey of systems, degrees and qualifications* (3rd ed.). Paris: UNESCO Publishing.

UNESCO. (1991). *Science for all and the quality of life.* Bangkok: UNESCO Principal Regional Office for Asia and the Pacific.

United Nations Children's Fund. (1992). *Educating girls and women: A moral imperative.* New York: United Nations.

Walford, G. (1983). Science education and sexism in the Soviet Union. *School Science Review, 18,* 18–19.

Weisz, E., & Kanpol, B. (1990). Classrooms as socializing agents: The three R's and beyond. *Education, 111,* 100–104.

Willis, P. (1981). *Learning to labor: How working class kids get working class jobs.* New York: Columbia University Press.

Wong, S. (1991). Evaluating the content of textbooks: Public interests and professional authority. *Sociology of Education, 64,* 33–47.

Wong, S.-Y. (1991). The evolution of social science instructions (1900–1986): A cross-national study. *Sociology of Education, 64,* 33–47.

World list of universities. (1969). Paris: International Association of Universities.

World list of universities. (19th ed.). (1995). New York: Stockton Publishng.

Young, M. (1961). *The rise of the meritocracy, 1870–2023: An essay on education and equality.* London: Thames and Hudson.

CHAPTER 9

Comparative and Historical Patterns of Education

RANDALL COLLINS

We usually take for granted that we know what a school is. There are a series of grade levels through which students progress, promoted by their scores on examinations. Schooling is limited, at least initially, by a pupil's age, and there is a fixed number of years for each level of study. More advanced schools take students who have completed the preceding level of schooling. Additionally, how far one advances in the educational sequence has consequences for one's adult career in the hierarchy of social stratification, as well as being influenced by it. This picture of education, although conventional for the 20th century, is not found throughout history; it was constructed by social processes in relatively recent times.

Today, it is one of the cliches of conversation with children to ask, "How old are you? What grade are you in?" This age-grading would not have been important in most previous societies; many children could not have answered the first question, let alone the second. Our omnipresent age consciousness was developed in large part because of the construction of bureaucratically age-graded schools. In a school in medieval Europe, the classroom would have contained pupils ranging in age from below 10 to over 20, all reciting the same lessons. In such a context, one could not take for granted that schooling starts with elementary education, then continues with secondary education, and is finally completed with higher education at the university; in fact, as a formal structure, the university or highest level of education was invented before secondary schools, and in a sense, even before elementary schools. As we shall see, different kinds of schools competed with each other before the modern sequence of schooling was established. It is conceivable in the future that variant forms of education will again compete and upset the sequence that we have come to think of as natural.

RANDALL COLLINS • Department of Sociology, University of Pennsylvania, Philadelphia, Pennsylvania 19104-6299

Handbook of the Sociology of Education, edited by Maureen T. Hallinan. Kluwer Academic/Plenum Publishers, New York, 2000.

The construction of schooling has been a historical process in its own right. Sociologists of education are right in seeing education as deeply implicated in the structure of the entire society, especially its stratification and even its ethnic divisions. The most popular view is that education reflects and reproduces social class inequality (Bourdieu & Passeron, 1977). Historical comparisons show that this is only partly correct. Educational organization has its own autonomous dynamic. It has shaped and reshaped social stratification, as well as vice versa. Educational dynamics have shaped the distinctive patterns of virtually every complex society. The Indian Brahman caste, the Confucian scholar–bureaucrat, and the Roman lawyer/speechmaker were all products of their own educational institutions; so were the Jewish rabbi and the Muslim *ulama* who still blends theology with legal authority in Islamic states like contemporary Iran. We ourselves go through a lengthy process of acquiring educational degrees that determine what jobs we can get because of a series of changes in school organization that started in the Christian Middle Ages and have recently spread around most of the world. Max Weber argued that the different world societies have taken unique paths because of their religions; we could just as well say that their distinctive forms of social stratification have been created by their forms of education.

Historical comparisons are crucial because there have been a number of different kinds of education, not a single evolutionary progress from primitive to modern forms. Because things do not develop in a straight line, we need to skip back and forth in time and in space, looking for key similarities and comparisons that reveal the main types of educational dynamics. In a brief overview, here are some of the main alternatives:

Schools might consist of the entire community of a particular age group, such as the adolescent cohorts undergoing initiation rites as in tribal societies and in early Greece; our own age-graded compulsory public schooling revives and extends this pattern and thereby creates a social definition of childhood encompassing everyone. A completely different pattern is apprenticeship that takes places within sharply divided enclaves such as families, households, and guilds; such education is often secret, and as such systems of training become more elaborate, it builds up status distinctions of exclusivity, which may even take a religious or ethnic form. In this way Brahman educational monopoly shaped the Indian caste system, and the learned rabbi shaped Jewish ethnicity. A third type of structure is the licensed profession, occupations like the lawyer or the physician that have acquired elite public status because their education gives them a recognized license to practice, in conjunction with their monopoly over teaching and hence admitting others to practice. This third type differs from the second type, the private apprenticeship in the family or household, because the profession is part of the public community. Professional licensing is connected with formal degree-granting institutions and thus grows up along with formal government-sanctioned schools, reaching its strongest development with the highly formalized university corporation.

The fourth type, bureaucratic schools with a hierarchy of grades, examinations, and degrees, often combines with the third type. The four kinds of educational organization are ideal types and thus can be found in various mixtures; there is a sense in which modern mass education has incorporated aspects of two of the others (excepting the second, private household education, which is antithetical to the bureaucratic form). We can see the dynamics of educational bureaucracy most clearly by looking outside the orbit of Western professions to the growth of the Chinese imperial examination system. Asian educational history is not very well known in the West, but it ought to be; among other reasons, it shows us the dynamics by which bureaucratic systems of formal examination not only stratify society into social classes but also foster competition that leads to both school expansion and inflation of educational credentials. These dynamics can take place no matter what kind of contents the schools teach as requirements for degrees: it happens with the literary texts of the Confucian schools, as well as with Buddhist certificates of religious enlightenment and with the Japanese martial arts; it has happened in the philosophical scholasticism of the medieval Christian universities and in the wide variety of topics taught in European-influenced universities since the 19th century. These comparisons warn us that it is not merely the rising sophistication of modern science and technology that makes modern students spend more and more years in schools taking examinations and earning degrees; the organizational dynamic of credential inflation has a rhythm of its own, no matter what cultural contents may be. The conclusion of this chapter considers why there have been boom-and-bust cycles of educational expansion and contraction in the past, and applies what we have learned from history to the possibilities of schooling in the future.

THE INVENTION OF THE SCHOOL

If we take the term broadly enough, education in some sense has always existed. Adults have always inculcated the younger generation with the skills and practices of their society. School may be taken in a more explicit sense, as a formal institution: an activity taking place in special places and times, under the direction of a specialized teacher. The school in this sense simultaneously constructs a social identity for pupils; that is, a group singled out as occupying a special probationary status in society: neither children naively at play, nor adults involved in the serious activities of work, but in between in a kind of social limbo. Even where schooling becomes normal for groups of adults (such as graduate students in modern universities), it structures a social identity outside of normal social life (sometimes jocularly referred to as "the real world").

Adolescent Age Groups and Initiation Rites

Schools are something like the institution of initiation rites at puberty found in many tribal societies (Eisenstadt, 1956). In these, youths typically undergo a period of ordeals in ritual seclusion, at the end of which they become members of the adult order. Such initiation rituals are most common in tribal societies with a sharp structural separation between men and women, especially where men live, or at least spend most of their time, in a men's house or a warrior's house, hedged round with religious secrets and taboo to women. Here we see one element that is shared with the formal school: the institution provides a Durkheimian ritual separation, marking out membership in a distinctive group, segregated from other groups in society. In tribal initiation rites, we see a double separation: the temporary segregation of the group of youths undergoing their ordeals, and the permanent segregation of adults (e.g., into warriors and women) that this initiation brings about. We can broadly draw a parallel to Bourdieu's model (Bourdieu & Passeron, 1977), that the ritual generates symbolic status, and this in turn promotes and reinforces the stratification of the adult social order. The reverse causal link stressed by Bourdieu does not necessarily operate; the elaboration of schooling was not usually brought about by a society's stratification patterns, but followed its own organizational dynamic. Historically, one might argue that developing educational organization has contributed more to the forms of stratification than vice versa.

In ancient Greece, circa 700 to 400 B.C.E. (Before Common Era), we see an institution resembling tribal initiation rites. Adolescent boys were segregated into a group, sometimes called *ephebes*, who underwent training, in the earlier period primarily in military drill, and then later increasingly in athletics, in singing, in playing musical instruments, and in reciting Homeric poetry (Marrou, 1964; see also, and for further elaboration and sources on the historical comparisons throughout this chapter, Collins, 1998). Only after completing the *ephebia* were young men allowed into the adult activities of the army, the gymnasium, and political life. Early Greek city–states such as Athens (on which most of our information is based), were ceasing to be tribal societies and were becoming coalitions of tribes or clans, in the process of creating a more universalistic structure transcending kinship connections. The *ephebia* or protoschool was thus an institution for creating a collective identity that cut across and united youths outside of clan membership and loyalty, and in considerable degree replaced it. In Sparta, one might say that the *ephebia* model was extended into the entire social structure, so that all males remained members of the collectivity, living and training for warfare together for the rest of their lives. The Spartan version of the *ephebia* was no mere school, no transitional status, but the collective order of male adult society itself.

There is another respect in which the Greek *ephebia* should not be taken as the full-scale creation of the school in the modern sense. This was not our elementary education, for it apparently did not include training in literacy or in numeracy. The *ephebia* did pioneer some key characteristics of the school: public recognition and the sense of social obligation to take part in it, rewarded by (or in case of failure to do so, penalized by loss of) social status as a proper citizen. The education of the *ephebe* was not practical, but ceremonial: it passed on, or indeed created, cultural capital in the sense of the highest prestige symbolic activities. The educated Greek was one who knew the forms of music for specific occasions and who could recite Homer's account of the deeds of the noble Achilles, the idealized standard of the Greek man.

Schools of Philosophy and Rhetoric in Ancient Greece

The advanced "school" crystalized in the generation of Plato (ca. 400–365 B.C.E.), and Plato's Academy is our best known example of such a school. However, Plato was only one of some half-dozen famous pupils of Socrates, all of whom founded formally organized schools. The social role of the philosopher and the mathematician, as specialists in knowledge, crystalized more-or-less simultaneously with the invention of the advanced school. The creation of these institutions built up over a period of several generations. There were two components, initially separate: the school itself as a collective organization of adults rather than of youths, and the professional teacher. The first of these was pioneered by religious brotherhoods, the second by the Sophists.

Around 500 B.C.E. there appeared religious brotherhoods, living in common or at least possessing their own houses or meeting places. The most famous of these was the Pythagoreans, a secret cult that venerated its founder, Pythagoras, as a sage teaching reincarnation, food taboos, and other ritual prohibitions, as well as a philosophy of numbers as constituents of the universe. There were other brotherhoods of this sort, such as the school at Abdera (on the northern coast of the Ionian sea), where the philosophy of atomism was taught; out of this school later (300 B.C.E) was created the Epicurean communities. The Epicureans continued this model of the school as a lifelong brotherhood down until their disappearance about 200 C.E. (Common Era; equivalent to the Christian A.D.). The Epicurean type of organization could be innovative as an intellectual center for lectures and publications, but it remained institutionally conservative; it was not a school as a place of transition into full adult life, but a community of withdrawal and refuge from ordinary life (Frischer, 1982). The Pythagorean brotherhood, too, had this character of a lifelong brotherhood, but its extreme social closure was broken down in the late 400s B.C.E., where a wave of popular revolts took place in southern Italy against aristocratic control supported by the Pythagoreans. Plate's utopian society depicted in *The Republic*, in which "philosopher–kings" rule over uneducated people, looks back nostalgically to these Pythagorean oligarchies. At this time their secret mathematical doctrines began to circulate in the public community of intellectual debate, and Plato incorporated Pythagorean mathematics into the curriculum of his Academy. The slogan over the Academy's gate, "Let no one ignorant of mathematics enter here" has been interpreted as the first formal entrance requirement.

The religious brotherhoods had intellectual content and collective identity; the Sophists (in the late 400s B.C.E.), on the other hand, provided the role of the professional teacher in a specialized, temporary relationship with students. Sophists had a bad reputation among the conservative Greek elite, whose idea of education was the citizen–*ephebia*; our image of the Sophists comes through the words of their enemy, Socrates. However, precisely what was considered immoral and low status about the Sophists was what would be sociologically crucial for the future of education: they were professionals who lived by taking fees from pupils. In return, they taught techniques for how to argue. The Sophists were not necessarily amoral relativists; they were also, in an important sense, the first pure intellectuals, concerned with the standards of argument. It was in the circles of Sophists, who travelled from city to city giving lectures and debates, that formal mathematics was invented: the concept of proof emerged in puzzle-solving contents, including such famous mathematical problems as squaring the circle.

The Sophists began the role of the rhetor, the teacher and practitioner of rhetoric. In societies such as the Greek and the Roman city–states, where laws were made by assemblies of citizens and law cases were argued before these same assemblies, the professional speaker or arguer became the advocate or lawyer. The most influential of the schools founded by the pupils of Socrates was not Plato's Academy, but its principal rival: the school of rhetoric founded by Isocrates. This school, along with the philosophical schools (the Academy, similar schools at Megara, Cyrene, Elis, a little later Aristotle's Lyceum, the Stoa, and others) became the institutional basis for higher education. These organizations survived for varying lengths of time; most of the post-Socratic foundations lasted about a century, although some of the Athenian philosophical schools, and their offshoots at Alexandria, survived through intermittent revivals down to 500 C.E. By around 200 C.E., the largest municipalities of the Roman Empire had taken over financial support of higher schooling, paying large salaries to a small number of official lecturers. At Constantinople in the 400s, for example, there were 31 chairs at the Imperial Academy, all but one of which were in grammar and rhetoric, that carried a monopoly over teaching in the city (*Cambridge History*, 1967, pp. 274, 483–484; Jones, 1986, p. 999). In this way, training of lawyers and public officials came to dominate Hellenistic and Roman education, a pattern characterizing Mediterranean education virtually ever since.

The first formal schools involving literate skills and professional teachers thus were created for adults, not for children. What we retrospectively call "higher" education in Greece did not grow from elementary schools to secondary schools to a crowning level but was the first self-conscious educational institution invented. The schools of philosophy and rhetoric set a pattern that spread downward, eventually shaping the lives of young children. The professional teachers, most of whom could find no clients at the prestigeous higher schools, became the *pedagogues,* low-paid instructors of children in the rudiments of literacy, displacing an earlier pattern in which a smattering of literacy had apparently been spread by home instruction (Havelock, 1982; Marrou, 1964). The elementary school became established in Hellenistic Greece, eventually displacing the military–athletic emphasis of the adolescent *ephebia*, which decayed with the passing of the independent city–state. We should bear in mind that the Hellenistic pattern of differentiated elementary and advanced schools did not generally survive in the European Middle Ages. As elsewhere in the world, the rudimentary skills of literacy might be learned in the same place where more advanced pupils studied religious texts. In the Buddhist monasteries of Asia, and in the cathedral schools of Christian Europe, pupils of all ages typically recited the same lessons, those who had been there longer becoming more advanced in memorization and eventually in textual interpretation. Such a school was intended for professional training in religious knowledge; an elementary education consisted, not of specialized training in the rudiments of literacy, but in participating for a few years while a smattering of learning sunk in. Those pupils who were not going on to become monks or priests would attend for a few years and would then return to lay life. It was only when still more elaborate forms of education, such as universities, were organized that the elementary school became recognized as distinctive; in Christian Europe, these were called "grammar" schools, appropriating a part of what in the Hellenistic and Roman world had been an honored adult training by "grammarians" who taught the forms of public discourse (Kaster, 1988). Here again we find that "higher" education led the way, and elementary schooling branched off from it.

FAMILY, GUILD, AND STATUS-GROUP CLOSURE OF EDUCATION

Apprenticeship in the Patrimonial Household

There is another, even older form of education, not necessarily recognized as such, because it is embedded in everyday life. This is education by apprenticeship, learning by working under a practitioner, helping, or simply observing by being close at hand. Such education still exists today; it is the way most girls learn how to cook, for example, or how teenage boys learn to repair cars. Such education might occur in the home, without formal sanctions; or it might become elaborated into a formal structure, as groups of practitioners form an association for ceremonial purposes, as well as to control the market for their products; such a guild could also make use of its formal structure to regulate the conditions of entry and thus decree formal steps of training and admission to practice. Education by apprenticeship automatically produces social closure: those who are present in the home or the workplace are included in the community of knowledge and in whatever social identity surrounds them; those who are not present are automatically excluded.

In these structures, there is no separate school, no distinctive place or organization where training takes place, apart from where the mature activity is itself done. It does not matter whether what is learned is a utilitarian skill, or an aesthetic accomplishment of cultivated leisure, or religious/ceremonial procedures. In the modern sociology of education, we tend to think of the ritualistic aspect of education as explicitly promoting group identity and closure, whereas utilitarian education, lacking in status honor, is merely acquired on an open market. This is one reason why repairing cars, although practically very important, has no status honor. However, this was not the case in apprenticeship structures, before (or running alongside of) the invention of the school. Both utilitarian and nonutilitarian training generated sharply bounded social enclaves.

Social boundedness of this kind tends to make knowledge secret. Medieval European guilds generally treated their lore as secret knowledge, sometimes even designated as "mysteries"; the ceremonial structure survives, without the skills, in the fraternal organization of Masons. Similar guild secrecy existed in the Islamic world and elsewhere. In tribal societies, crafts such as metalworking typically had the same structure of secrecy as the witch doctor, hedged round with ideologies and rites of magic. In agrarian civilizations, the number of specialists grew, and literate and other high-status and nonutiliarian specialties became differentiated from the more practical work skills. Astronomy in medieval India, for example, was practiced by families who taught their mathematical texts within the household lineage. As a result, there were a number of different systems of astronomy in India existing parallel with one another; this was not the social system of public science familiar from modern Europe, which brought diverse knowledge claims together into a single arena where they competed for recognition. There was not one body of knowledge that constituted Indian astronomy, but separate astronomies, the private property of each family of hereditary astronomers. A similar plurality of parallel systems of astronomy existed in medieval China (Needham, 1959; Pingree, 1981).

The apprenticeship structure of education was typically a household-based structure; the workplace was the same as the home, and the authority of the master was also that of the head of household, supporting children, servants, and apprentices out of the common pot, and subjecting them to household discipline and loyalty. This patrimonial household, in the Weberian term (Weber, 1968, pp. 1006–1069), gave a degree of flexibility beyond purely family inheritance; it was not necessary that a child should take over the family knowledge, because nonkin could be integrated as apprentices, as disciples, or even as adopted kin.

I have depicted this patrimonial/guild/apprenticeship structure as essentially conservative and static, but this was not necessarily so. New skills might be developed; particular teacher-households might acquire widespread reputations, bringing an influx of pupils and disciples. A competitive market might emerge, in which famous teachers were compared with one another by a public seeking their skills; at the same time, the closure of the household would be maintained so that the pupil had to enter into a relationship of personal loyalty to the teacher, even swearing to maintain the secrets of the house. Education in Tokugawa Japan often had this character. This was especially prominent in the late 1600s, when a flourishing urban society grew up in Edo, in Osaka, and in Kyoto, and schools proliferated teaching both textual and ceremonial knowledge (Dore, 1965; Moriya, 1990; Rubinger, 1982). There was an outburst of Confucian schools, offering new interpretations of imported Chinese texts, but also schools that taught haiku poetry (e.g., the famous haiku poet Basho operated one of these schools); still other schools, distinctively for the samurai class, taught swordsmanship. These sword schools are particularly revealing of the social dynamics of the period, for the samurai had been effectively pacified by strict political controls over military activities, and swordfighting was made ceremonial, a lifelong honorific training rather than a practical skill. Instead of fighting on the battlefield, samurai vaunted their status by displaying sword etiquette and collected certificates of proficiency that amounted to educational credentials (Ikegami, 1995). Here we see particularly clearly how sword schools promoted the status closure of the samurai group, a pattern of all such guild-structured education.

Confucian Scholar–Gentry, Brahman Caste and Jewish Rabbis

The patrimonial/household structure of education could expand in two directions. A certain style of knowledge could overflow the household, eventually becoming something like a social movement or a profession; in another direction, educationally cultivated households might become linked into an ethnoreligious identity. The former development is exemplified by Confucianism; the latter by Brahmanism and by diaspora Judaism.

The Confucian movement began in China around 500 B.C.E. as disciples of a famous teacher. The Confucians acquired their distinctive identity as *ju*, "scholars"; this did not mean that they were the only literate persons in Chinese society but that they were custodians of the ancient books; the chief tenet of their philosophy was that social life could best be organized by respecting the ancient texts. This claim involved considerable interpretation because the old texts were a miscellany including poetry, histories of old dynasties, and eventually incorporating old divination texts. What made the Confucians a rationalistic movement rather than merely promoters of archaizing magic was that their practice promoted literate administration: they became a political movement whose ideology was that government should be carried out by textually schooled officials. In the first strongly centralized dynasty, the Han, Confucians around 130 B.C.E. succeeded in establishing a protobureaucracy, staffed in principle (although not always in fact) by textual scholars trained at an elite school, sometimes referred to as the Imperial University. Until this time, the Confucian lineage had remained at least partly patrimonial, as indicated by the fact that descendents of Confucius were leaders of one branch of the school down through 200 B.C.E. When they succeeded in getting substantial control of the Han administration, the Confucians transformed from a patrimonial organization of group closure into the prototype of bureaucratic selection by formal schooling; they pass out of our present categorization, and are taken up again later in the chapter.

Restrictedly local closure at the level of the patrimonial teacher–household could be widened in another direction, one that remained compatible with familistic organization. This ethnoreligious development is illustrated in the history of the Brahmans. In ancient India (ca. 800 B.C.E.), Brahmans were priests, specialists in the sacrificial rites that were the chief ceremonies of the numerous petty kingdoms. The Vedas were created as collections of texts, containing materials that were recited at the ceremonies; several guilds of Vedic priests specialized in different parts of the ceremony (such as the musical part); it appears that guilds of magicians also incorporated themselves along Vedic lines and were eventually accepted as one of the orthodox guilds. When the sacrificial cult decayed and rival religions (such as Buddhism and Jainism) emerged around 500 B.C.E., the priest–guilds transformed themselves from ritual practitioners into teachers. The growing commentaries (the *Brahmanas* and *Upanishads*) attached to the old ritual texts became objects of learning in their own right; there are descriptions of boys learning from their fathers, or apprenticing themselves for a lengthy period with an eminent teacher. Those who underwent this training were becoming socially recognized as a distinctive caste, the Brahmans. Technically, a Brahman still had the right to officiate at rituals, but most typically they were landowners; they had expanded from a priest–guild into a status group with a strong emphasis on endogamy and on the pollution of contact with lower castes.

Caste in this sense was not primordial in India, but it developed in the centuries around the beginning of the Common Era. Education was a key to both formation and closure of this status-group structure. Once again, we see that education does not merely reflect stratification but shapes it. Above all, Brahmans became keepers and interpreters of law and hence arbiters of property transactions; rules of pollution, of marriage, and of inheritance were entwined with property and authority. The prestige of the Brahmans was not simply a matter of perpetuating cultural distinction arising from primordial tradition; the Vedic priests had lost much of their original function, and their cultural tradition was successfully attacked by reformers in the Upanishadic period. Instead, the Brahmans parlayed the structure of education monopolizing the expanded body of texts that accreted around the old Vedas into a social position where they dominated as arbiters of the legal order.

Confucians and Brahmans are similar in their origins. Both were so-to-speak *ju*, scholar–custodians of the ancient texts, in societies that had changed beyond the old conditions of ritualized support for public authority in petty kingdoms. However, Confucians became an educated stratum, open in principle to whoever was educated, a meritocracy allied with centralized bureaucracy; Brahmans became a hereditary caste, a network of intermarrying families that ritually excluded other marriage networks. The crucial difference in surrounding conditions was the political trajectories of China and of India. In China, key periods of centralized government promoted an opportunity for specialists in bureaucracy and thus broke the seams of patrimonial closure of education. In India, despite occasional periods of centralization (usually allied to Buddhist or to Jaina religions hostile to Brahmanism), states were weak, volatile, and fragmentary. Brahmanism developed in symbiosis with the weak Indian states, in which military rulers allowed Brahmans to monopolize the practice of law and hence control the property system, receiving ideological legitimation in return. In a caste system, it might appear that everything is hereditary and hence fixed by birth. However, caste, like everything else, must be enacted in everyday practice; a Brahman could not fall back on his birthright, but had to undergo extensive education. It was the Brahman as student of his father, and as teacher of his sons, that made the hereditary principle a living structure. Brahmanism is in effect an "educationocracy" of a distinctive kind: the extreme of social and economic status built on monopolization of education in an ethnoreligious form.

Another variant on this structure is the rabbinical Judaism that developed in the diaspora of the early centuries C.E. (Segal, 1986). In Jewish communities cut off from the state cult at Jerusalem, religious leadership was taken over by lay teachers, that is, by rabbis; this dominance was made definitive after the destruction of the temple at Jerusalem by the Romans. At this time appeared the dietary regulations and ritual centered on the everyday routine of the household, which served to keep Jews socially distinct from alien communities amidst which they lived. The rabbi was not a specialized occupation, unlike the earlier priest–guild of the Hebrew kingdoms, but simply an educated man who knew both the traditional sacred scriptures (Torah) and the body of scriptural interpretations (Mishnah) that expanded to encompass the conditions of life in exile. Jews now became not a geographically localized nationality but an ethnoreligious status group, living within pagan Roman, Christian, Persian/Zoroastrian, or later Muslim societies. The core organizing principle of the Jewish community was the educational practice of the rabbis. The convocation of men to read and to discuss the meaning of scriptures had the character of a school, a law court for deciding community matters, and the arbiter of community identity. Education became lifelong, an institution not merely for socializing the young but for maintaining and shaping the group's identity. In the case of diaspora Judaism, lifelong education became a key structural basis for ethnicity.

PROFESSIONAL LICENSING AND UNIVERSITY DEGREES

A profession may be defined sociologically as an occupation that has a strong corporate identity and closure enforced through licensing and through formal education monopolizing admission into practice. It is its formal education that raises a "profession" above the status of a mere craft, in explicit contrast to the familistic or guild structure of on-the-job training by apprenticeship. This is an ideal type rather than an absolute contrast, and historically there are gradations between the two types. The profession has high social prestige largely to the degree that it is not merely utilitarian but has an ostentacious symbolic training, not as mere practical lore but in the "higher" realms of allegedly pure principles of knowledge and ideals of conduct. A profession is an occupation raised into the realm of a Durkheimian sacred object. It is the history of educational systems that has determined where and how the prestigeous monopolistic professions have appeared in world history.

Lawyer-Rhetors, Physicians, and Lawyer-Theologians in Greece, Rome, and Islam

In Greece, the high-status, educated professions were rhetors (the politician/speechmaker and lawyer) and physicians; as we have seen, these professions became organized through the invention of the formal school around 400 B.C.E. We have already discussed the origins of the rhetoric schools, which trained the citizen–elite to argue before the Greek city assembly or the Roman senate. The distinctively Western role of the lawyer grew up by a combination of two new institutions: the formal school and democracy. Because citizenship was a restricted, closely guarded status, the right to argue before the public assembly became the basis of the first rudimentary licensing of professional practice.

In the case of medicine, there was no such politically enforced restriction. Ancient medicine was not a legally conferred monopoly; it acquired its exclusivity and its prestige gradually by alliance with high-status formal schooling. Prior to the development of the philosophical schools, medicine was partly folk practice, partly an apprenceticeship-structured cult of magician/physicians; such practitioners continued as a low-status stratum alongside the emerging medical elite as in many other societies of the world. The early Greek medical–religious cult of the Asclepiads became allied with the philosophical schools, initially in the school of Hippocrates, a contemporary of Socrates, and thereafter connected with Aristotelean, with Epicurean, and with other schools. The most prestigious form of medicine became not to practice at all, but to give lectures on the principles underlying medicine. In the Hellenistic and Roman periods, famous physicians like Galen lectured in the honorific and well-paid municipal schools on subjects such as logic; the philosophical movement of Skeptics for a long period was carried along by a faction of medical teachers, who argued that there were no medical cures. Ancient medicine was not technically very effective, and a practicing physician was not likely to acquire high prestige through success. Probably physicians proved their worth through their display of learning; if they could do little to cure, they could at least explain illnesses. Comparing ancient medicine with modern medicine shows us the importance of an elite educational institution for giving high social prestige apart from the technical content of the knowledge.

The Greeks and the Romans carried to an extreme the elevation of teaching over practice. Contempt for practical work went along with its relegation to slaves or to exslaves, whereas the respectable propertied classes devoted themselves to politics or to the higher life of the mind. The elite schools whose ideology was enunciated by Plato and by Aristotle provided a justification for stratification between slave-owners and slaves and thus helped legitimate the social order of the Greco–Roman world. However, the schools did more than this. The Greeks invented an institution that was to have influence long after the disappearance of slavery: an educational organization ostentaciously turned inward to its own discussions, upholding an ideal of pure knowledge transcending practice. Education proclaimed itself as producing an elite culture, equivalent to contemplation of religious truth. Pure knowledge became a status ideal that raised the impressiveness of whatever occupation became associated with it. In this sense, the professions were born as occupations whose prestige did not depend merely on their practical effectiveness, but on their high intellectual level.

In the medieval Islamic world, medical scholars were excluded from the dominant educational institutions, which emphasized theology and law. What kept medicine from falling back into folk practice and magic was the fact that physicians became the main specialists in importing and in translating Greek texts. Court physicians became the basis of an alternate intellectual network to the orthodox Muslim theologians, patronized by wealthy rulers who were involved in a power struggle against theological influence. Many of the most famous Muslim and Jewish intellectuals (such as Avicenna, Averroës, and Maimonides) of this period were physicians, whose chief cultural capital was knowledge of old Greek medical texts and of their surrounding systems of philosophy. Again we see that what prestige the medical profession had was based on the social prestige of its intellectual connections rather than on its practical effectiveness.

The most important learned Muslim profession was the *ulama*, in effect a combination of rhetor and rabbi. Because of the political developments of the Islamic state, there was no distinct category of priests; every man (but not women) could learn the holy scriptures and could carry out daily rites. Those who specialized in learning and interpreting the scripture, and the body of materials that became codified from the oral traditions (*hadith*, parallel to Jewish *Mishnah*) surrounding the practical decisions made by Muhammad, became simultaneously the core transmitters of community tradition, that is, teachers and jurists. As in Brahman India and in rabbinical Judaism, the learned layman rather than the government official became the interpreter of the law. This gave all three of these religions a character that was both culturally conservative and oriented toward preserving past traditions but was also socially participatory and to some extent relatively democratic in the sense that a wide and decentralized stratum of the populace held judicial power.

The lineages of *hadith* teachers into which the *ulama* became organized were patrimonial organizations, oriented toward loyalty to predecessors; legitimation was passed along personally through a chain of teachers and pupils, rather than by the licensing procedure of a body of practitioners. A more collective and impersonal form of educational institution, the *madrasa*, was created around 1050; these were specialized buildings and teachers supported by state (or sometimes by private) endowments. Previously the *ulama* taught in the mosque, and a new faction of disciples might break away simply by a teacher moving to another column that upheld the vault of the mosque. Now there was specialized training separate from the mosques. In the *madrasas* developed a formal curriculum, including preliminary studies in Greek logic, culminating in legal studies; as time went on, doctrines of Sufi mysticism were also routinized and added to the curriculum. The *madrasa* taught a compendium of Muslim learning, becoming the standard education for the cultivated man of the higher classes (Huff, 1993; Makdisi, 1981; Nakosteen, 1964). Theology and law thus became part of the status culture of the upper classes; the fact that they were tied together and were taught in the same schools that catered to pupils interested in general cultivation made these professions less specialized and less sharply separated from lay people than the licensed professions that emerged in western Europe.

THE CHRISTIAN UNIVERSITY CORPORATION

The monopolistic profession with its corporate powers of self-governance reached its fullest form in the West. The most powerful and idealized professional identity was developed along with the emergence of the university. A university, in the strict sense of the term, is an autonomously self-governing organization of teachers who hold legal rights to confer degrees of membership in their own rank. The key organizational difference from earlier schools such as the Hellenistic schools or the Islamic *madrasas* was that the university was a legal corporation, a collective body of teachers who had acquired monopolistic rights to teach and license certain professions. In medieval Christian Europe (around 1200 C.E.) , the university was a guild of teachers (the term *universitas* originally meant guild) of the three recognized professions: law, medicine, and theology, along with the "artists," that is, professional teachers of the liberal arts, which were a preliminary study leading to the advanced professional faculties. These faculty guilds became united into a corporate organization, which collectively upheld its monopolistic rights in the same way that a craft guild would have upheld its exclusive right to make silver, leather goods, or any other item. The difference was that whereas a craft guild had its monopoly backed up by a local city, the university acquired monopolies that were, in principle, universal throughout Christendom because they were backed up by the highest political authorities. Moreover, although the craft guilds crumbled in the later Middle Ages, the universities and their system of degrees survived and expanded into modern times.

The organizational core of the university was the collective body of teachers, giving publically recognized degrees, backed up by the official sanction of the pope, the emperor, or the king. The 1200s was the time when the papacy was at the height of its power, operating as a virtual theocracy, claiming the right to crown kings and to raise armies against pagans and heretics. The papacy was also creating the most effective legal system in Europe, adjudicating property cases through its system of canon law. In licensing universities, the pope thus dispensed a valuable monopoly right; university degrees conferred licenses to practice and to teach professional skills throughout the Christian domain, while putting teeth into the regulation by prohibiting those without licenses. The pope also gave charters, or licenses, to found universities themselves, in effect franchising out its degree-granting power. During the medieval centuries, as the pope struggled over power with the Holy Roman Emperor, both sought to add allies to their causes by granting charters to found more universities. Later, as national kings became more powerful, they too entered the competition and founded universities in their domains.

As the result of this political competition among rival sources of power, the system of chartered universities offering formal degrees became pervasive throughout western Europe. The degree-holding, licensed professions became a distinctive part of the occupational structure, an elite standing just below the hereditary aristocracy, while claiming official status and public prestige above what was regarded as the mere money-grubbing and practical activities of merchants and craftsmen. In this sense, we can say that the monopolistic pattern of controlling occupations expanded. At the same time, more people were brought into the system of professions; the monopolistic structure was quantitatively stretched, making the monopolies looser.

In the following centuries, down to our own times, this system of formal degrees and professional licensing has gone through many changes (Burrage & Torstendahl, 1990). At times, the professions have become separated from university education and have even reverted to apprenticeship; this was the case, for example, in the United States after the Revolution, down through the mid-1800s. At other times, many other occupations besides the classic professions of medicine, law, and theology have attempted to raise their status, and to restrict competition, by attaching themselves to the sequence of formal academic degrees. These vicissitudes of professional licensing will best be understood after we examine one more kind of educational dynamic, bureaucratization.

BUREAUCRACY, EXAMINATIONS, AND CREDENTIAL INFLATION

Large-scale formal organization typically involves rules and a division of labor among circumscribed positions coordinated by hierarchic channels of authority. The origins of bureaucracy requires the existence of at least some education because the key to controlling a large number of specialized workers is the use of written records. The very impersonality of the organization comes from the fact that written rules are treated as taking precedence over the human judgment of individuals, and official actions are supposed to be recorded, so that subordinates know what they must do and superiors can check on their behavior. Power struggles and organizational growth usually result in expanding the volume of written rules and records. Bureaucracy grows by its own momentum. Ever since the early developments of bureaucracy in Chinese government, in the closing centuries of imperial Rome, in the medieval Christian church, and in secular modern Europe, it has been recognized that bureaucracy is both formally "rational" and substantively "irrational"; Chinese writers satirized bureaucracy just as Europeans later would. It has been less appreciated that this is a classic dilemma of social organization, not a foible of individuals; the large organization owes its very existence to the network of written documents and deals with every problem by producing more documents; it is easy for the formal documents to be out of step with practical realities and for career-making officials to place emphasis on the proper use of documents as an end in itself.

The Chinese Imperial Examination System

The growth of bureaucracy, both inside schools and in the organizations that most typically hire educated persons, is the most important sociological theme of education in the modern West. It will give us perspective to examine this process sociologically by looking at the growth of the formal examination system in China. Because the Chinese had a different ideological justification for the growth of bureaucratic credentialism, the comparison will help to keep us from seeing bureaucratic growth through the lens of our own ideology that justifies educational bureaucracy as technical expertise.

The history of bureaucracy, in the sphere of government, of church, or of private business, is inseparable from the history of educational institutions providing bureaucrats. For the earliest period, we might regard this as simply a matter of literacy; in societies in which most persons, including the aristocracy, were illiterate, a recordkeeping officialdom was only possible if they were scholars, in the minimal sense of literate persons. However, administration is not the only use of literacy; small-scale merchants and craftsmen might also acquire literacy and numeracy for their own practical needs, without either their business or their schooling taking on a bureaucratic form. This comparison shows us that there is a crucial element of power and prestige in bureaucratic education. The early Confucians, the first Chinese bureaucrats, had an organizational culture stressing their genteel status above the level of mere utilitarian practice. "A gentleman is not a tool" is one of Confucius' most famous sayings. Conversely, it is possible that the government administrator could learn his (because ancient administrators were exclusively male) writing skills on the job, by apprenticeship; it appears that ancient Egyptian scribes learned their skills in this way. However, the mere scribe was limited to quasi-menial social status; status–prestige for the official depended on adding something to the bare utilitarian accomplishment. It was this claim of cultivation, of participating in ritualistic knowledge of a higher order, that allowed Confucians to claim positions not merely as menial servants of the palace but as men of dignity who could correct and even, at the extreme of their influence, direct the policy of the state.

As we have seen, the apprenticeship style of education was socially inappropriate for producing this kind of status culture, as well as structurally incompatible with the purer forms of bureaucratic organization. The independently organized school was the vehicle for the status honor of the trained official. By analogous processes, the school itself became bureaucratized. The administrative bureaucracy of the state, and the bureaucratization of the school system, grew in tandem.

Confucian bureaucracy became established about the third generation into the Hen dynasty [i.e., around 130 B.C.E.). Its development was not lineal but was limited and vacillating in a number of ways. Within the Han, and to a certain extent in subsequent dynasties, not all government positions were allocated by educational credentials. There continued to be positions reserved for Imperial relatives and for noble families. Another rival to the Confucians were the eunuchs who staffed the private chambers of the palace, sometimes constituting factions of behind-the-scenes court politicians. Confucian officials struggled against the influence of palace eunuchs as "corruption," whereas the latter often intrigued to have particular officials condemned for insubordination. In addition, Chinese dynasties underwent periodic crises of geopolitical weakness, internal rebellion, and fiscal crisis; there were several periods of breakdown into patrimonial/feudal regimes and fragmentation into multiple states. Ethnically alien rulers from the north or the west typically eliminated the Confucian officialdom in the early part of their reign, while allowing them to return later as their administrative organization proved attractive. A third limitation on Confucian bureaucracy was the rivalry of Taoist and Buddhist religious organization; under favoring regimes, these provided not only court ceremonial and legitimation but sometimes an alternate source of specialized officials. On occasion, Taoist or Buddhist texts were made into an official canon, paralleling the Confucian textual canon, and examinations were instituted in these alternate educational channels.

For the most part, Confucians maintained their hold over the predominant educational pathway to public office. Across their lengthy historical ups and down, an examination system for administrative office gradually expanded to encompass more and more of government and became the main activity in the lives of men of the gentry class. The state university established in 124 B.C.E. grew in the latter years of the Han dynasty (after 100 C.E.) to some 30,000 students, although its size varied greatly in subsequent dynasties. Admission however was not by competitive examination but by patronage of notables. Conversely, there were occasional Taoist and Buddhist intrusions into government administration. Buddhist theocracy under the Empress Wu and her successor flourished briefly between 690 and 710; the next emperor, reversing course, built Taoist temples in all cities and required all noble families to have a copy of the *Tao Tê Ching*. In 741 Taoist works were made official classics, an alternate basis of civil service examinations alongside the Confucian texts, but this lapsed with the crisis of the empire in 755 (Needham, 1956, pp. 31–32 Twitchett, 1979, pp. 411–412).

The Sung dynasty (960–1268) built up the formal examination system as a device to keep government free of military dominance. As the gentry class competed over educational qualifications, the size and elaborateness of the examination system developed enormously. In the T'ang dynasty (618–907), there had been one examination, open to candidates recommended by prefectural officials or to students at the schools in the capitol for relatives of officials (Chaffee, 1985, pp. 15–23). In the Sung, a sequence of more openly competitive examinations developed. The most important route went from local prefectural examinations (conferring the degree of *chü-jen*) to the metropolitan examinations, from whose graduates (*chin-shih*) officials were selected.

Competitiveness accelerated drastically. At the prefectural qualifying examinations, there were 20,000 to 30,000 candidates in the early decades after 1000 C.E.; 80,000 around 1100

C.E.; burgeoning to 400,000 near the end of the dynasty around 1250 (Chaffee, 1985, pp. 35–36, 50–53). At the narrow end of the funnel, the numbers of *chin-shih* who were recruited in each round of examinations averaged less than 200 (Chaffee, 1985, p. 16). Quotas were set for the lower examination as well, and these became increasingly restrictive. In the years between 1005 and 1026, 40% to 50% of candidates were awarded the *chü-jen* (lower) degree; the ratio began to drop sharply in the 1030s and 1040s, falling to 10% in 1066. Reforms increased competitiveness still further; by the Southern Sung, ratios had fallen another quantum leap, to 1% in 1156 and to 0.5% in 1275. This enormous competitiveness was to continue in the Ming (1368–1644) and the Ch'ing (1644–1911) dynasties, making preparation for repeated examinations virtually a lifetime pursuit of the gentry class.

Growth of the system fed on itself, as scholars who had not passed the final examination or who were out of office due to politics became private teachers. There was a large increase in the number of schools, including local Confucian temples, Buddhist schools, and the private academies of well-known scholars. Some schools were official, notably the Imperial University and other schools in the capital; initially for sons of officials, they began to be opened to others in the 1040s (Chaffee, 1985, pp. 30, 73–80). Local government schools were also promoted, with the height of schoolbuilding during 1020 to 1060, the time when the Neo-Confucian movement began in a protest against the examination system.

During 1100 to 1120, yet another twist of factional reforms brought a radical effort to replace the examination system with a hierarchy of government schools. These comprised primary, county, and prefectural schools, each divided into three grades; promotion from rung to rung in this ladder was based on internal examinations, leading finally to selection for the Imperial University and thence to the *chin-shih* degree for officials. Private schools and "unorthodox" books were banned. These government schools enrolled 200,000 students. The expense of supplying them with room and board brought the system to an end in 1121, and private and locally controlled education dominated thereafter. This episode was the earliest effort in the world at a comprehensive public school system, and it adumbrates the school reforms of 19th century Germany, France and the United States.

In the Ming dynasty (1368–1644), the older two-level system of local and metropolitan examinations was complicated still further into three levels by adding a provincial examination and subdividing the first, prefectural examination into three consecutive steps (Chaffee, 1985, pp. 23, 183). Competition had become enormous, as alternate routes to office were closed, while a huge number of candidates struggled for a tiny set of positions. The system provoked occasional egalitarian attacks on it. Among the most famous was the movement of Wang Yang-Ming and his followers in the early 1500s, attacking the standard of literary compositions and rote memorizations: "learning before they can act, they never get to the end of it" (Chan. 1963, p. 678). Yet even Wang regarded the grind of examination study as a necessary step for an official career, which would allow one to put one's ideals into action. Revolts against the examination system ended up giving still further importance to the educational establishment.

Inflation of Buddhist Certificates in China and in Japan

The dynamics of credential inflation also appeared in an unexpected place, in the training and promotion of Buddhist monks. After the failure of Empress Wu's theocracy in the 690s, Buddhism was made subject to increasing government regulation. In 747, people wishing to become monks were required to get an ordination certificate from the Bureau of National Sacrifices. During a crisis of military rebellion in 755, the practice began of selling these certificates to raise revenue, because ordination carried economic advantages such as exemption from taxation and from corvée labor. The system became very corrupt. Local officials began to sell ordination certificates for their own benefit; many ordinations were purely nominal (Weinstein, 1987, pp. 59–61). During the period of disintegration (ca. 900–960) after the collapse of the T'ang, entry examinations for monasteries were administered not by monks but by government officials. These exams were similar to the Confucian ones, consisting of composing an essay and a commentary, plus reciting a sutra and practicing meditation.

After 1000, Chinese Buddhism was strangled slowly by government regulation, instituted for the most part as fiscal measures. Sale of ordination certifications was revived under the Sung dynasty in 1067. This soon gave rise to market manipulations as individuals bought certificates not for their own use but for resale, speculating on future rises in price (Ch'en, 1964, pp. 241–244, 391–393). The long-term result was an inflationary spiral reducing the value of the certificates. The Sung government also began to raise money by selling the higher monastic ranks, and in the 1100s it added a series of monastic titles to spur further purchases. Eventually the status appeal of Buddhist culture for the upper classes faded. Earlier, members of the educated gentry or the court nobility might have frequented the Ch'an (Zen) sect, or might have even pursued careers as abbots of the wealthier monasteries. Now there was a massive pull on the cultivated classes from the expansion of a government examination system and of Confucian schools connected with it. The iconoclastic Ch'an Buddhists, who had begun by rebelling against the formalities of court Buddhism, became routinized and scholastic. Stories of the classic paradoxes and repartees of the great Ch'an masters were now collected. The later Ch'an masters added successive layers of poetic commentaries and metacommentaries. In place of the live experiences they depicted, these stories of six or eight generations past were now used as cases (Japanese: *koan*) on which students were tested in monastic exercises. Scholarly eminence now passed to the editors who added layers of cryptical remarks and poetic lines to *koan* collections. The metacomments themselves are repetitions of the *koan* style, showing mastery by adding yet further twists of insight (Dumoulin, 1988; McRae, 1986).

In Japan, the transplanted Zen lineages, especially of the Rinzai sect, became associated with the feudal aristocracy. Unlike China, centralized government was on the decline, and Buddhist institutions prospered. Education in the elite monasteries became the highest status culture. The material expansion of the Zen lineages brought problems of organizational control and status legitimation. Buddhist enlightenment was not only a personal religious experience; it was a socially recognized rite of passage. When accompanied by a certificate of enlightenment from an authenticated master, it entitled one to become head of one's own monastery. Organizational expansion thus went along with the increasing commonness of enlightenment (Dumoulin, 1990). By the late 1400s, an inflation of enlightenment certificates set in; pupils traveled from master to master collecting as many as possible. Buddhist organizations from 1200 through the 1500s proliferated throughout Japan. As the temples became rich, a superordinate market arose in sale of offices; by the 1380s, abbots and senior monks paid fees for their appointments. The shogun began to rake off fees from certificates of appointments and in the 1400s was inflating the turnover to maximize its income from the monastic sector.

The material success of Japanese Buddhism and its "corruption" were part of the same process. Spiritual careers blended with careerism in the pursuit of power and of status, even with material wealth that was concentrated in the great monasteries even more than in lay society. Even those monks who were most inwardly turned toward pure religious experience were caught up in an organizational dynamic that required competing in terms of inflationary criteria of advancement. Enlightenment was becoming structured by an expanding marketplace. In the elite Rinzai monasteries, where lay aesthetes merged with religious virtuosi, *koan* practice in effect became a literary practice, based on the texts of the *koan* collections that became prominent in Japan in the mid-1200s and 1300s. (Dumoulin, 1988, pp. 248–251; 1990, pp. 30–31, 47) The *koan* and their commentaries, written in elegant and paradoxical form so as to comprise meta-*koan* in their own right, were very close to poetry; they became marks of membership in an aristocracy of culture, no longer exclusively religious.

In the period of the "country at war" (1467–1580), when central political authority in Japan had collapsed, the worldly power of Buddhism became so great that it provoked a reaction similar to the Protestant Reformation in Europe. The military lords who finally reimposed secular control by a quasi-centralized state crushed the monasteries' power and confiscated their economic base. In the Tokugawa regime Zen was subjected to increasing government regulation. It became an administrative branch of the state church, used for enrolling the populace under approved religious practices. In 1614, Buddhism was made the official state religion; every household was required to register as members of one of the recognized Buddhist sects. Every temple was made a branch subordinate to its headquarters, and that in turn to government oversight. Tokugawa Zen underwent a crisis of bureaucratization, arising from the responsibility for vast numbers of purely nominal adherents, along with control by an unsympathetic secular administration. In 1627 a new regulation was imposed that abbots of the elite Rinzai temples should master the entire corpus of 1700 *koan* despite protests that such enforced study would vitiate the spirit of Zen enlightenment. High religious status, and along with it an honorable career ending as abbot in one's own right, became a largely formal process of seeking of certificates of legitimation.

Credential inflation arising from the jostling for organizational position now penetrated the religious curriculum itself. *Koan* practice became increasingly bureaucratized. In the early 1700s Hakuin, the last famous Rinzai master, sought to reinvigorate Zen as a meditative practice that could be carried on in everyday life; to this end he systematized *koan* into sequences of progressive difficulty. This led to another layer of routinization. Hakuin's successors categorized *koan* by form and by content, making them into an educational curriculum that could be pursued throughout one's career. The conception of enlightenment changed with these external changes in monastic careers. The old undifferentiated conception of enlightenment was increasingly refined. Distinctions were made between "little" and "Great" enlightenment. (Dumoulin, 1990, pp. 139, 373). Even for lower ranking monks, now a series of *koan* must be passed. The original Ch'an masters in medieval China had become honored after a single enlightenment experience; organizationally, this had given them the prestige to succeed one's master as head of a lineage or to found one's own monastery. With the expansion of career competition in the massive Zen establishment in Japan, it now took a lengthy series of tests to secure one's reputation and receive invitations to head important temples.

Although the contents of the Buddhist education system are remote from those of Western education, and from Confucian education as well, they all share an organizational dynamic: the elaboration of formal examinations for advancement. As competition increases for cultural credentials leading to material and honorific rewards, the sequence of examinations lengthens. In principle, there is no limit to how far the standard can be raised; whether it is called cultivation by the Confucian official, or enlightenment by the monk, the goal of infinite perfection corresponds to the degree of social competition driving its candidates.

Rise and Fall of University Credentialling in Medieval Europe

Similar developments took place in Europe. There have been several episodes of expansion of universities, with accompanying formalization of examination sequences, interspersed with periods when the demand for education collapsed in favor of informal alternatives to schooling. Guilds of teachers at Paris, at Oxford, at Bologna, and at a few other places in the late 1100s acquired formal monopolies over granting degrees. As the number of students increased, sequences of degrees were established from Master of Arts, to Bachelor and Doctor of Laws, of Medicine, and of Divinity. The main employer of advanced degree-holders, especially in theology and in canon law, was the church; reformers used educational credentials for the more highly preferred clerical posts both to raise the spiritual level of the clergy and to wrest control over appointments away from local aristocracies. Expansion of centralized papal control and of universities went in tandem; the papacy became the first bureaucracy in the West, the cutting edge of legal, educational, and administrative institutions that were later adopted by modern government and business organizations (Berman, 1983; Southern, 1970).

In the later Middle Ages, the church and universities underwent crises together: the papacy because of its increasing financial demands and increasing resistance from lay rulers; the universities because of inflationary consequences of the accelerating growth of the university system as a whole. By the end of the 1200s, there were 18 universities, 12 of them major in size and importance. By 1400 there were 34 universities, 18 of them major; by 1500 there were 56. Even more universities were founded, but many of them failed. The failure rate went up during these centuries; between 1300 and 1500, about half of all university foundations were failures. The market for educational credentials was expanding explosively, but at the same time such credentials were flooding the market, raising risks of failure and losing its former prestige.

The universities of the later Middle Ages were shrinking. Paris at its height around 1280 to 1300 had some 6,000 to 7,000 students; the number began falling in the early 1300s and fell below 3000 by 1450. Bologna rivalled Paris' size in the early 1200s but fell behind thereafter. Oxford may have had a maximum of 3000 students in the 1200s; there were an estimated 1500 in 1315 and fewer than 1000 in 1438; by 1500–1510, the yearly average was down to 124. Toulouse may have had 2000 students at its height; this fell to 1380 teachers and students in 1387 and below 1000 in the 1400s. The smaller French and Italian universities never had more than a few hundred students at their height, and they often closed for lack of students.

Proliferation of universities was especially rapid in Italy and in Spain, and here the failure rates were highest; Italy had an overwhelming 80% failure rate in the 1300s and the 1400s. France too experienced considerable numbers of foundings; it reached a failure rate of at least 78% in the 1400s. Expansion in Germany and in central and far northern Europe was more successful because this was a region where university expansion started centuries later, and there was less initial competition over students. The first university in the region was founded at Prague in 1347, which carried on successfully with some 1500 students until the early 1400s. Vienna, Cologne, and Leipzig succeeded to the leadership, with as many as 1000 students at various times in the 1400s. The smaller German universities varied from 80 to 400 students, hitting their peaks around 1450 to 1480 and declining thereafter.

As the "international" or Christendom-wide educational system of the High Middle Ages was broken up by the consolidation of national states, the cycles of educational expansion and inflation became desynchronized. England had a mini-cycle of expansion of university enrollments after the Reformation, but it was followed by deflation of numbers in the late 1600s and 1700s (Stone, 1974). Spain, which became the geopolitical hegemon of the emerging capitalist world system, underwent the most spectacular educational boom and bust (Kagan, 1974; Wallerstein, 1974). Spanish universities of the Middle Ages had been modest in number and size; in the 1400s the rate of new foundations picked up and reached a deluge in the 1500s and the early 1600s. Of the 32 Spanish universities of this period, three were overwhelmingly dominant. Salamanca alone had 6000 students most years between 1550 and 1620—a figure matched by no previous university except Paris in the 1200s, and by none subsequently until the late 1800s in Germany. Alcala at its height had 2500 to 3500 students, Valladolid had 2000. At the height in the late 1500s, approximately 3% of young Spanish males were attending universities, and perhaps half of them took degrees. The immensity of this educational movement in a relatively small population needs to be appreciated. The United States, the modern pioneer of mass higher education, did not pass this ratio until 1900; England did not pass it until 1950.

The underlying dynamic was a market for educational credentials. By the late 1500s, the lower arts faculty had largely dropped out, having been displaced by the mushrooming Jesuit colleges. The universities now consisted almost entirely of theology and of law students, seeking places in church and in state; Spain is the first society in history to be swamped by doctorates. This is a case of genuine credential inflation; the arts degrees were displaced by advanced degrees after 1550, with increasing emphasis on legal degrees as a ticket to administrative positions in the government. The big three universities monopolized the market. Graduates of Salamanca, of Alcala, and of Valladolid held a majority of top clerical and secular positions in the Habsburg administration, and they held a complete monopoly in royal councils and in provincial courts of justice. Poorer provincial nobility flocked to the universities, resulting in enormous expansion and an escalation of degree requirements, but without breaking the monopoly of the wealthy aristocrats holding favored connections. The result was a large floating population of penurious petitioners, living on hopes of patronage. After 1620, the system went into decline. By 1660 student numbers had fallen by a half, with decline continuing into the early 1800s. The great outburst of foundations came to an end, and no new universities were founded after 1620 until 1830. Of those 25 or more founded in the 1500s, half failed and many of the others limped into the 1700s with 30 students or fewer.

By the Enlightenment period of the 1700s, in the eyes of self-consciously progressive intellectuals and educators all over Europe, the university system was a medieval anachronism best left to die on the vine. Even in the Catholic world of the Counter-Reformation, the prestigeous form of education had become not the university but the Jesuit college, organized on quite different principles and holding a different position in the class and status structure of society. The Jesuit movement began as a reform of monastic life, abolishing choir, prayers, seclusion and distinctive uniforms, along with magic, legends and the worship of saints. Because universities were undergoing a boom in Spain, the founder Ignatius Loyola sought recruits at the elite Spanish universities of Alcala and Salamanca, and then at Paris, where in 1534 he organized the Society of Jesus. By Loyola's death in 1556 it had 1000 members; in the next century it had over 600 colleges and academies and was the largest educational institution in Europe. (Heer, 1968. pp. 26–27; O'Malley, 1993, pp. 200–242)

The Jesuits grew by exploiting a niche resulting from the reorganization of the medieval educational system. The medieval universities had been guilds of teachers, licensing the higher professions of law, medicine, and theology, and giving a formal degree structure to the arts course that prepared one for these. It was a two-tiered system, with universities as the top rung, whereas elementary literacy and grammar was provided in local schools attached to churches and to monasteries. We have already seen the crisis of the universities that set in after 1300, as universities proliferated, enrollments dropped, institutions failed, and the licensing monopolies over the professions tended to break down. Especially in England and in France, the core of the old system, the universities now shifted toward becoming collections of colleges, that is to say boarding schools for undergraduate students, taking away instruction from the arts faculty. In the 1500s, these university colleges began to expand downward to incorporate the elementary Latin curriculum as well, taking over the territory of the lower, grammar schools. Medieval schools never had any strict age grading, and the colleges now had an age range from 8 to 20. Most students were day students, most of whom attended for only a few years; the only remaining link to the old university structure was that if a student did persevere all the way to the end of the course, he could take the old M.A. degree; but the value of this credential was now disappearing. The medieval two-tiered system was now divided along a different line: instead of grammar schools and universities with teenagers and young adults in the latter, there were now colleges and professional faculties, with the former extending down to children (Aries, 1962, pp. 195–237; Grendler, 1989; Simon. 1966).

As many towns set up colleges independently of the universities, the status advantage of university education disappeared. The Jesuits made their success by pushing this tendency to an extreme. Their colleges were free and were open to all social classes: in the 1600s, 50% to 60% of students were sons of artisans and of the lower middle class. Although the emphasis remained on Latin, the old high-status language of the educated, the Jesuits incorporated the newer culture offering science, literature, and the latest modes of philosophy and of theologi-cal argumentation. The Jesuit curriculum became the model for textbooks in secondary schools, spreading widely in the new Calvinist middle schools that grew up, especially in Germany and in England, as an alternative to the traditional universities. The Jesuits paralleled on the Catholic side the organizational reforms opening up among Protestants with the collapse of the medi-eval system of religious education.

Against these "modern" forms of schooling, the revival of the universities and their link-ing into the system of formal credentialling that dominates modern life was a great surprise. The fact that it happened suggests that expansion of education goes in waves, with each peak followed by disillusionment over bureaucratization and credential inflation, and by actual decline as educators and students flow away to alternate forms of schooling. Then the dy-namic of competitive growth sets in again, leading to another wave of system expansion, usually with an even more comprehensive set of links in the sequence of schooling.

TRIUMPH OF THE MODERN UNIVERSITY-CENTERED CREDENTIALLING SEQUENCE

The German University Revolution

The academic revolution pioneered in Germany around 1800, and adopted by other economi-cally advanced societies in the following century, was a revival and a reform of the medieval organization of higher education. The medieval university was a bastian of the church, train-ing priests and theologians, combined with guilds monopolizing the teaching of law and medi-cine under the legitimation and control of the church. By the time of the Enlightenment, the church had lost its monopoly on the production of culture. In the 1700s the university was nearly abolished. Self-consciously progressive intellectuals regarded universities as outdated and as intellectually retrograde. Leibniz in 1700 had proposed that universities be replaced by government-regulated professional schools, with government-sponsored Academies taking over the production of science and high culture. The same proposal was made by the Prussian reform minister in 1806. This is in fact what the French did in 1793, replacing universities with a system of academies together with government Écoles for engineers, for teachers, and for other specialists.

To abolish the university would not have meant abolishing education. The 1700s was a period of expansion in what we call "secondary" schools; in Germany, *Gymnasia* for classical subjects and *Ritterakademie* for aristocratic manners; in France, the Jesuit colleges that spread widely to serve the middle or even lower classes; and in England, the elite Public Schools. As usual, we must guard against anachronism. In the 20th century we take it for granted that there is a sequence, that a student attends secondary school in order to prepare for the university. Before the German university reform, however, these two types of schooling were alternatives or rivals; the age range of the students tended to be similar in each (Aries, 1962, pp. 219–229). The "secondary" schools taught a largely secularized curriculum, appealing to the cultural aspirations of its clientele. This made them much more popular than the universities, whose curricula and credentialing sequence had been built up during the Middle Ages in connection with theology and careers within the church.

In Germany, the growing sense of crisis in the later 1700s was enhanced by a career problem for university graduates. The church, deprived of its property in the Reformation, was no longer a lucrative career. Parsons had low status and pay, and they served as minor functionaries of the state. Theology and its preparatory subject, philosophy, attracted mainly sons of peasants, petty shopkeepers, and clergy. The higher part of the middle class, the sons of urban patricians, the wealthier merchants, and the civil servants, studied law, a more costly course of study. A new structural attraction came from involvement of the bureaucratic state in education. (Mueller, 1983; Rosenberg, 1958) Enrollments in the leading universities rose after 1740, drawn by prospects of government employment at several levels. The bureaucratic administration of the numerous Absolutist states of Germany were expanding. Educational requirements became increasingly important for these posts; in some states, the proportion of government appointees who had some university education rose from 33% to 75% during the 18th century. At a lower level, new employment possibilities for teachers were created by the establishment of compulsory, state-supported elementary schools: first by a Prussian decree of 1717, which was largely unenforced, and then by a stronger decree in 1763, which specified schools teaching in the German language rather than the old medieval Latin schools run by the church.

The numbers of university students increased sharply by the 1770s, but competition in the expanding educational market produced both winners and losers. A population of the educated underemployed accumulated. The old medieval university of Cologne, one of the biggest in the early 1700s, had lost half its students by the late 1770s; Jena dropped from 1500 to 400. With the political crisis of the 1790s, the university crisis came to a head. Numbers fell to tiny levels: Königsberg in 1791 had only 47 students; Erfurt in 1800 had only 43; Kiel in one year had 8. During the crisis period of the Napoleonic wars and their aftermath (1792–1818), 22 of 42 the German universities were abolished. The traditionalistic Catholic universities, about one third of the total, were hit particularly hard; only one survived. In the early 1700s, there had been about 9000 students in the 28 universities then existing; in the 1790s, with more universities competing, the total was down to 6000 (McClelland, 1980, pp. 28, 63–64; Schelsky, 1963, pp. 22-3).

It would have fitted the cultural ethos of the time to abolish the old religious universities entirely and to replace them with a new system of "high schools" for general cultural status, together with professional schools for more specialized training. This did not occur because a movement of teachers in the Philosophical Faculty, emphasizing their opportunities for innovative research in an autonomous institution of academic freedom, revived the prestige of the university. The movement succeeded because it meshed with a structural trend in the German educational system. In the early 1700s, Prussia had already pioneered in state-mandated elementary schooling; bureaucratic centralization now moved toward formalizing credential requirements and hierarchizing the competing segments of the older educational system. In

1770, an examination was established for employment in the Prussian bureaucracy. In 1804, this was strengthened to require 3 years of study at a Prussian university for all higher offices. With the foundation of the University of Berlin in 1810 and an accompanying series of official examinations, university legal study became rigorously required for government employment; Prussia became the first Western society to establish something like the Chinese Imperial examination system.

Together with another Prussian reform initiated in 1788, and strengthened by 1810 to 1812, these regulations linked the entire educational system into a credentialling sequence (Mueller, 1987, pp. 18, 24–26). In an effort to limit the number of university students, the government established the *Abitur* examination for admission to the universities. This put a premium on study at a classical *Gymnasium*, which prior to this point had been more of an alternative to university education than a preparation for it; indeed in 1800 the director of the Berlin *Gymnasium* had proposed that the universities be abolished in favor of his institution. Now it became part of the state-controlled sequence, but at a preliminary level; conversely, after 1812 to 1820, to teach in a secondary school that prepared students for the university one needed a university degree. The university became locked into the apex of the credentialling sequence that, since the worldwide spread of the German model, we have come to take for granted.

Linking of University and Mass Public Education

German education was the magnet that drew educators and aspiring intellectuals to visit during the 19th century; eventually most modern societies adopted a version of the German university system. British reformers carried this out in the 1850s and the 1860s, abolishing the requirement that academics had to be in clerical orders and reclaiming the power to set professional credentials that had been lost. The establishment of free and compulsory public schooling at the lower levels moved more slowly in Britain, and the full sequence of the educational institutions was not in place until the early 20th century. Italy and Japan adopted the German system at the end of the 19th century; in both cases, there was a struggle of declericalization to eliminate religious control (Catholic and Buddhist, respectively) of popular education at the elementary levels. France adopted aspects of the German system after defeat in the war of 1870; the first task in Emile Durkheim's career was to visit German universities on behalf of the ministry of education to find the secrets of German success. The French system thus blended two different reforms: the first had taken place in the Revolutionary/Napoleonic period, when the medieval universities had been abolished outright, in favor of technical schools for an elite; thereafter the reconstituted "University" was in fact a bureau of the central state making appointments to secondary schools and controlling a uniform curriculum throughout the country. In the 1880s the research-oriented German university was grafted onto this centralized structure, but professors still had obligations to act as inspectors of secondary schools, and they typically made their career by teaching at these *lyceés* before making their way back to the apex at Paris (Fabiani, 1988; Ringer, 1987, 1992; Verger, 1986). French education became the most bureaucratically centralized system at the state level, whereas the German model, widely adopted elsewhere, allowed more autonomy to the individual university faculties and more competition among the various schools for students and for eminent professors. In France it was the students who did the most competing through a highly selective set of examinations administered at the national level that controlled access to the elite schools, as well as the awarding of degrees.

Education in the United States had started out along the English path: that is to say, it was the medieval system of religious colleges collapsed into local establishments. The unique feature of the United States was its political decentralization and its lack of a state church; a result was an early proliferation of schools of all kinds: elementary schools controlled at the local and state (not the federal) level; religious colleges put up by the competing denominations; and eventually, secondary schools in the mold of the cultivated German *Gymnasium*, as well as imitations of the upper class English Public Schools, which were known in America as private schools or as "prep schools" (Collins, 1979; Cookson & Persell, 1985) In the 19th century these did not comprise a credentialling sequence; much as in 18th century Germany, the more elite secondary schools overlapped in age with "college" students and taught much the same curriculum: indeed, given the religious traditionalism of the colleges, some high schools prided themselves on giving a more modern education. A further weakness of the colleges was that they had become largely undergraduate institutions, having lost the old medieval "higher" faculties that gave degrees in law, in medicine, and in theology. American political decentralization and religious pluralism had eroded these monopolies; in the period from the Revolution to the Civil War, there was a democratizing movement attacking the old elite professions, leaving professional training to apprenticeship or to independent schools; the latter often operated with narrowly commercial standards and disdained the more theoretical curriculum of the universities.

After the mid-19th century, there was a crisis of competition on many levels. Numerous college foundations failed, and others scraped along with small numbers of students. The professions came under attack for lack of ethical and intellectual standards, and movements arose to impose stricter licensing requirements and to close the commercial schools. Publically supported and compulsory elementary schools and high schools spread for other reasons, including efforts to control or to assimilate non-Anglo immigrants, as well as to provide cultural capital in a democratic form. The different kinds of education overlapped and competed with one another for students and for support; most of them suffered from lack of legitimation.

The solution to this crisis was structurally similar to what happened in Germany a century earlier. The various forms of schooling became organized into a sequence, with universities at the center of the chain. Universities, adopting the German model, in effect became two-tiered structures, comprising our now familiar undergraduate and graduate training. The lower B.A. degree or its equivalent became required to enter the graduate faculties, which around 1900 began to acquire the monopoly on training leading to licenses in the elite professions. The undergraduate colleges, in turn, brought order into secondary education by requiring a completed high school degree for admission. Together with the bureaucratization of state education departments and the elaboration of formal requirements for schooling (developed in part by symbiosis with reform political parties concerned with immigrants, in part by trade union movements restricting child labor), this eventually led to the standard sequence on 12 years of primary and secondary schooling as prerequisite for 4 years of undergraduate college, which in turn was prerequisite for advanced degrees and professional licensing through graduate training.

This structure was in place by the 1920s, and subsequent change has been quantitative, not qualitative, as the sheer numbers of students have expanded within this framework at the middle and higher levels of the system (Brown, 1995). The standards of minimal educational respectability as an adult member of American society have gradually risen, and in the process these standards have become part of hiring and promotion procedures for jobs throughout the labor force (Collins, 1979, pp. 4–7). In 1910, a high school diploma was held by only 9% percent of the population and was an acceptable credential for managerial positions; only 2%

had a B.A. or their first professional degrees. By 1960, 65% had graduated from high school and 14% from college; the high school diploma was now barely middle class, and college was becoming the requisite for managerial positions. In the 1990s, as high school graduation encompasses 84% of the adult population (figure for 1992: National Center for Education Statistics, 1995, p. 74), it has become a bare admission to working-class jobs; its principal value has become as a staging ground for further steps in the educational sequence. The same has been happening to the undergraduate degree. One can see a trend toward undergraduate degrees becoming as common as high school degrees were in the mid-20th century; this has fueled a drive toward advanced and specialized degrees: MBA's for business careers, as well as specialized degrees in the professions.

The United States, along with Japan (to a somewhat lesser degree), pioneered the mass education system, which might better be called the competitive–inflationary mass educational marketplace. In the 1950s and the 1960s, western European states generally launched a move in the direction of the American structure. Secondary schools in Europe typically had been divided into those channeling students directly into the labor force and into a small number of elite schools for those students going on to university training. Now the opportunities for admission to the universities were drastically expanded. Large numbers of new universities were founded: still below the 3000 institutions of higher education in the United States the 1000 in Japan, but mushrooming from some 20 universities in Germany to over 100, with similar growth in France, in England, and elsewhere. The proportions of the youth cohort attending universities jumped, from 5% to 10% in European societies around 1960, to 25% or more around 1990 (U.S. figures went from 35% to 52%; Collins, 1979; National Center for Education Statistics, 1995, p. 72) in this period. The national distinctiveness of educational organizations has remained to a certain extent. However, in general we can say that the German university system of the early 1800s and its sequence of credentials was adopted throughout the West; now, the twentieth century American version of mass competition within this system has been adopted virtually worldwide (Bourdieu, 1988; Dore, 1976: Ramirez & Boli-Bennett, 1982).

CONCLUSION: LIMITS AND DRAGS ON EDUCATIONAL EXPANSION

Can we expect that educational expansion and credential inflation will continue its upward trajectory into the foreseeable future? Can we imagine a world of the future in which janitors will need to have Ph.Ds in waste management, and managerial and professional careers will demand training at levels not yet imagined? Today's proliferation of specialized degrees and mid-career retraining programs suggest something of the pathway that we are to follow. Additionally, there is historical precedent, on a much smaller scale, in the Chinese would-be mandarins of the Sung, Ming, and Ch'ing dynasties who spent their entire lives (or at least well into their 30s and 40s) studying for the examinations. At the same time, the historical record shows us two limitations on straightforward expansion of credential hierarchies and concomitant bureaucratization of the regulations of schooling and of employment. One limitation is indicated in the periodic crises of highly competitive and expansionary school systems; there are waves or cycles of boom and bust, visible since the medieval period in China, in Japan, and in Christian Europe. We can expect periodic disillusionment with the grind of degree seeking and its tendency to erode the substance of cultural standards while placing the emphasis on the outward formalities of accomplishment. Highly expansionary school systems suffer crisis on the organizational level as well; too many credential suppliers tend to make life difficult for each other by saturating the market. Thus in highly expanded periods many schools have trouble finding enough students or sources of revenue, and they go out of existence.

A second limitation is manifest in the recent round of expansion of European education in the 1950s and the 1960s. By the 1970s and the 1980s there was a reaction in many European states—in part because the expansion of higher schooling had taken place so rapidly that the job market had little time to adjust, in part because it fed into a general fiscal crisis of state revenues. Given that the demand for school expansion was organized politically, the burden of economic support fell on public funding, with little taken up by private or mixed sources of economic support. In the Unites States, the latter pattern has mitigated state fiscal constraints on higher education because private schools and the greater legitimacy of private tuition even in public universities have made funding by students and by their families a larger portion of education's economic base.

The expansion of education can contribute, under certain conditions, to the aggregate economic well-being on the population. In the dynamic of economic growth, educational expansion can operate as a kind of Keynesian pump-primer, putting money into the system along with willingness to invest in the future; in economic downturns, it can act as a Keynesian device for keeping people out of the labor force and as a way of sustaining these nonworkers by hidden transfer payments. As long as education retains its legitimacy as cultural emblem of democratically contested career opportunities, it may continue to operate in this way even as other forms of government welfare come under attack. I couch the argument in these terms, stressing the indirect contribution of education to employment, to welfare, and to growth, rather than the more conventional ideology that assumes that education promotes economic growth through providing technical skills. Elsewhere I have marshalled evidence on why this technical–function view of education is largely inaccurate and why the dynamic of educational growth should be seen as primarily that of credential inflation that drives standards of employability higher as more degree-holders are produced (Collins, 1979), and I have seen nothing in the continued credential inflation since the late 1970s to make me alter my position on the basic mechanism.

Nevertheless, the inflation of educational credentials is not costless. Even as education acts as a hidden Keynesian mechanism of reinvestment and of hidden transfer payments, it also costs material inputs, for teachers, for the physical plant, and for student support. Whether these inputs come from government, from family, or from self-funding and borrowing by students, an expansionary educational system also drives up aggregate costs. At some point, the curve of educational credential inflation (i.e., the amount of schooling socially required to enter jobs that offer various levels of material rewards) intersects with the rising costs of education. At these points, the educational system is economically unable to expand further. Such a limiting point may have been approached during the rapid European expansion of mass higher education around 1970. This is a respect in which the inflation of educational credentials differs from inflation of a monetary currency; printing more money is relatively cheap, but minting new degree-holding persons requires a huge apparatus of teachers, administrators, testers, and buildings, as well as provisions for students' daily living. The government that inflates its monetary currency can just as easily print bills denoting 1,000,000 dinars (or pesos or marks or dollars) as those denoting 1,000 or 100, but the educational system that inflates its credentials so that students must spend 16 years in school, or 20, instead of 10 or 12, incurs material costs that dwarf the normal economic connotations of "transaction costs."

The fact that such economic crisis points occur, indeed are built into the structure of expansionary dynamics, does not mean that education will plateau out, reaching permanent stability at some time in the future. Quite possibly the long-term pattern of educational waves of boom and bust is due to repeatedly reaching the point where the budgetary expense of credential inflation becomes insupportable. Plateaus and downturns allow the competitive struggle for cultural credentials that bestow social advantage to turn in another direction, and eventually the upward dynamic begins again. The two limitations on growth to which I have referred would thus make up aspects of the same dynamic. Cultural disillusionment with the substantive aspects of bureaucratization and examination-itis can go along with the material strains of credential inflation. The two are not necessarily synchronized, although we know little as yet about how these patterns may operate. A good deal more historical and comparative research is needed to refine our theoretical understanding of these long-term patterns of educational systems.

REFERENCES

Aries, P. (1962). *Centuries of childhood.* New York: Random House.

Berman, H. (1983). *Law and revolution: The formation of the Western legal tradition.* Cambridge, MA: Harvard University Press.

Bourdieu, P. (1988). *Homo academicus.* Stanford, CA: Stanford University Press.

Bourdieu, P., & Passeron, J.-C. (1977). *Reproduction: In education, society, and culture.* London: Sage.

Brown, D. (1995). *Degrees of control. A sociology of educational expansion and occupational credentialism.* New York: Columbia Teachers College Press.

Burrage, M., & Torstendahl, R. (1990). *Professions in theory and history.* London: Sage.

Cambridge history of later Greek and early Medieval philosophy (1967). Cambridge, England: Cambridge University Press.

Chaffee, J. W. (1985). *The thorny gates of learning in Sung China.* Cambridge, England: Cambridge University Press.

Chan, W.-T. (1963). *A sourcebook in Chinese philosophy.* Princeton, NJ: Princeton University Press.

Ch'en, K. (1964). *Buddhism in China.* Princeton, NJ: Princeton University Press.

Collins, R. (1979). *The credential society: An historical sociology of education and stratification.* New York: Academic Press.

Collins, R. (1998) *The sociology of philosophies: A global theory of intellectual change.* Cambridge, MA: Harvard University Press.

Cookson, P. W., Jr., & Hodges Persell, C. (1985). *Preparing for power. America's elite boarding schools.* New York: Basic Books.

Dore, R. P. (1965). *Education in Tokugawa Japan.* Berkeley, CA: University of California Press.

Dore, R. P. (1976). *The diploma disease: Education, qualification, and development.* Berkeley, CA: University of California Press.

Dumoulin, H. (1988). *Zen Buddhism: A history. Vol. 1. India and China.* New York: Macmillan.

Dumoulin, H. (1990). *Zen Buddhism: A history. Vol. 2. Japan.* New York: Macmillan.

Eisenstadt, S. N. (1956). *From generation to generation: Age groups and social structure.* New York: The Free Press.

Fabiani, J.-L. (1988). Les philosophes de la république. Paris: Éditions de Minuit.

Frischer, B. (1982). *The sculpted word. Epicureanism and philosophical recruitment in ancient Greece.* Berkeley, CA: University of California Press.

Grendler, P. F. (1989). *Schooling in Renaissance Italy. Literacy and learning, 1300–1600.* Baltimore: Johns Hopkins University Press.

Havelock, E. A. (1982). *The literature revolution in Greece and its cultural consequences.* Princeton, NJ: Princeton University Press.

Heer, F. (1968). *The intellectual history of Europe.* New York: Doubleday.

Huff, T. E. (1993). *The rise of early modern science. Islam, China, and the West.* Cambridge, England: Cambridge University Press,

Ikegami, E. (1995). *The taming of the samurai. Honorific individualism and the making of modern Japan.* Cambridge, MA: Harvard University Press.

Jones, A. H. M. (1986). *The later Roman Empire, 284–602. A Social, economic, and Administrative Survey.* Baltimore, MD Johns Hopkins University Press.

Kagan, R. L. (1974). Universities in Castile, 1500–1800. In R. Stone, *The University in Society.* Princeton, NJ: Princeton University Press.

Kaster, R. A. (1988). *Guardians of language. The grammarian and society in late antiquity.* Berkeley, CA: University of California Press.

Makdisi, G. (1981). *The rise of colleges. Institutions of learning in Islam and the West.* Edinburgh, Scotland: Edinburgh University Press,

Marrou, H. I. (1964). *A history of education in antiquity.* New York: New American Library.

McClelland, C. E. (1980). *State, society, and university in Germany. 1700–1914.* Cambridge, England: Cambridge University Press.

McRae, J. R. (1986). *The northern school and the formation of early Ch'an Buddhism.* Honolulu, HI: University of Hawaii Press.

Moriya, K. (1990). Urban networks and information networks. In C. Nakane & S. Oishi (Eds.), *Tokugawa Japan. The social and economic antecedents of modern Japan.* Tokyo: University of Tokyo Press.

Mueller, D. K. (1987). The process of systematization: The case of German secondary education. In D. K. Mueller, F. Ringer, & B. Simon (Eds.), *The rise of the modern educational system.* Cambridge, England: Cambridge University Press .

Mueller, H -E. (1983). *Bureaucracy, education, and monopoly. Civil service reforms in Prussia and England.* Berkeley, CA: University of California Press.

Nakosteen, M. (1964). *History of Islamic origins of western education.* Boulder, CO: University of Colorado Press.

National Center for Education Statistics (1995). *The condition of education, 1995.* Washington DC: U.S. Department of Education.

Needham, J. (1956). *Science and civilization in China. Vol. 2. History of Scientific thought.* Cambridge, England: Cambridge University Press.

Needham, J. (1959). *Science and civilization in China. Vol. 3. Mathematics and the sciences of the heavens and the earth.* Cambridge, England: Cambridge University Press.

O'Malley, J. W. (1993). *The first Jesuits.* Cambridge, MA: Harvard University Press.

Pingree, D. (1981). History of mathematical astronomy in India. *Dictionary of Scientific Biography* (Vol. 15), pp. 533–633). New York: Scribners.

Ramirez, F., & Boli-Bennett, J, (1982). Global patterns of educational institutionalization. In P. Altbach (Ed.), *Comparative education.* New York: Macmillan.

Ringer, F. (1987). On segmentation in modern European educational systems: The case of French secondary education, 1865–1920. In D. K. Mueller, F. Ringer, & Brian Simon, *The rise of the modern educational system. Cambridge,* England: Cambridge University Press.

Ringer, F. (992). *Fields of knowledge. French academic culture in comparative perspective, 1890–1920.* Cambridge, England: Cambridge University Press.

Rosenberg, H. (1958). *Bureaucracy, aristocracy, and autocracy.* Cambridge, MA: Harvard University Press,

Rubinger, R. (1982). *Private academies in Tokugawa Japan.* Princeton, NJ: Princeton University Press.

Schelsky, H. (1963). *Einsamkeit und Freiheit. Idee und Gestalt de deutschen Universitat und ihrer Reformen.* Reinbek bei Hamburg, Germany: Rowohlt.

Segal, A. F. (1986). *Rebecca's children. Judaism and Christianity in the Roman world.* Cambridge, MA: Harvard University Press.

Simon, J. (1966). *Education in Tudor England.* Cambridge, England: Cambridge University Press.

Southern, R. W. (1970). *Western society and the church in the Middle Ages.* Baltimore, MD: Penguin.

Stone, L. (1974). *The university in society.* Princeton, NJ: Princeton University Press.

Twitchett, D. (1979). *The Cambridge history of China. Vol. 3 Sui and T'ang China, 581–906.* Cambridge, England: Cambridge University Press.

Verger, J. (1986). *Histoire des universités en France.* Toulouse: Bibliotheque historique Privat.

Wallerstein, I. (1974). *The Modern world–system* (Vol. 1). New York: Academic Press.

Weber, M. (1968). *Economy and society.* New York: Bedminster Press.

Weinstein, S. (1987). *Buddhism under the T'ang.* Cambridge, England: Cambridge University Press.

CHAPTER 10

The Limits of Growth

School Expansion and School Reform in Historical Perspective

Pamela Barnhouse Walters

INTRODUCTION

The history of schooling in the United States is marked by continual growth—albeit of an uneven nature—and by episodes of deliberate interventions to change the distribution of educational opportunities. Sociologists of education have studied the growth of schooling under the rubric of "school expansion." The structure and distribution of educational opportunity has been studied, on the other hand, by sociologists interested in school reform and in stratification. These two lines of research isolate the two key sources of variation in the structure of educational opportunities: the size of the educational "pie" can change, and the way the pie is divided among individuals or groups may change, respectively. As such, both lines of research speak to questions at the core of the sociology of education about the part education plays in the reproduction or transformation of social and economic inequalities. Schools cannot serve as a means of widespread social mobility if only a small portion of children are educated, but growth of enrollments—or school expansion—does not in and of itself necessarily lead to greater social mobility via education. Similarly, the effect of changes in the distribution of educational opportunities on social inequalities in educational advancement may depend in part on whether the system is expanding, contracting, or holding constant in size.

In the sociology of education, expansion of the size of the educational system and changes in the educational opportunity structure, defined here to mean change in either the shape of the

Pamela Barnhouse Walters • Department of Sociology, Indiana University, Bloomington, Indiana 47405

Handbook of the Sociology of Education, edited by Maureen T. Hallinan. Kluwer Academic/Plenum Publishers, New York, 2000.

system or the distribution of individuals within that system, have generally been treated as two distinct and largely unrelated phenomena. In this chapter, I argue that they must be seen as intertwined phenomena, as essentially two sides of the same coin. This is particularly true when the question at hand concerns the degree to which formal education has provided and provides equality of opportunity. Political decision-makers have used the dual-policy interventions of expanding access to formal education (or allowing formal education to expand) and instituting structural changes in the organization of schooling to increase educational opportunities for groups that have historically been educationally disadvantaged.

The literature on American school expansion has largely treated the growth of enrollments as a demand-driven process, determined almost exclusively by the decisions of students and their families about whether to send their children to school. The availability of schooling is taken for granted and is defined as either nonproblematic (e.g., school officials somehow managed to keep the availability of schooling at least one step ahead of enrollment demands) or as outside the scope of inquiry. The social reforms that created sufficient school spaces receive scant attention. In this view, the relevant social actors are individuals and families; decisions of various corporate actors to provide sufficient educational opportunities are rendered invisible. The literatures on southern and non-U.S. school expansion do take into account constraints on enrollment growth posed by the educational opportunity structure, but they nonetheless treat the educational opportunity structure as fixed. In other words, the opportunity to explore the dynamic relationship between enrollment pressures and deliberate attempts to reform or remake the educational opportunity structure is missed.

The literatures that deal with changes in the educational opportunity structure, on the other hand, do not investigate the ways in which the aggregate of decisions made by individuals and families to send their children to school or not interfaces with changes in the educational opportunity structure. Additionally, these literatures do not theorize how the sheer expansion of the educational system, manifested in, for example, increased proportions of children and youth enrolling in school, affects the distribution of educational opportunities. The stratification literature focuses on the association between social origins and educational experiences or outcomes. Although some work in this tradition has examined the effect of specific school reforms on this association, as I describe more fully in the following paragraphs, few if any studies have investigated how the growth of the system affects the distribution of educational opportunities.

In this chapter I argue that school officials' decisions to allow the expansion of schooling, either in response to or in anticipation of enrollment pressures, is an example of "school reform," even though it is not usually viewed that way. Further, I argue that the gradual expansion of the educational opportunity structure, which has allowed more and more students to stay in school for longer and longer periods of time, is the most significant school reform that has taken place in advanced industrial societies since the establishment of public educational systems. Most basically, the continual expansion of the system has allowed school officials and elites to accommodate pressures for greater access to education by disadvantaged groups and to satisfy social demands for equity, for fairness, and for greater social mobility via education without fundamentally jeopardizing the benefits that the educational system has conferred on more advantaged social groups. Furthermore, I argue that we can better understand the role of education in reinforcing or reducing social inequalities if we pay attention to the dynamics of growth as well as to the shape and distribution of educational opportunities.

In this view, school expansion has served as a sort of safety valve for advantaged groups by allowing them to maintain educational advantages in the face of state policies designed to close the gap in educational opportunities between advantaged and disadvantaged groups. It is not the only means advantaged groups have used, consciously or unconsciously, to maintain their educational advantages in the aftermath of state-adopted egalitarian reforms. In recent decades, for example, reforms of American education designed to equalize opportunities for Whites and for Blacks have been undermined by the departure of large numbers of middle-class and affluent Whites from public school systems with relatively high minority enrollments (James & Walters, 1990). In this chapter, however, I focus on school expansion because historically in the United States it is the safety valve that has been most consistently available by state policy and most consistently used by elites to maintain their relative educational advantages.

The next section of this chapter reviews theoretical and empirical work on school expansion in the United States, highlighting three general classes of explanation for why the proportion of children and youths choosing to attend school has steadily increased: because they were preparing themselves for economic or occupational roles, which were changing; because the alternate ways in which they could spend their time were diminishing; and because schooling was increasingly seen as a mark of political modernity or because it was embraced as a social right of citizenship, which in turn was extended to increasing proportions of the population. I then argue that the school-expansion literature has paid insufficient attention to the process by which the educational opportunity structure was created and to how the availability of opportunities to attend school affected the growth of enrollments. In this discussion I draw especially on research on Europe and on the American South that shows that enrollment growth was conditioned and limited by the availability of schools. Additionally, I discuss the implications of those findings for school systems that have few structural barriers to increased enrollments, which has been the most common case in the United States. The final section has two goals. The first is to briefly review recent research on the consequences for educational mobility of structural changes intended to decrease social inequality in education. The second is to present twin arguments about the relationship between the growth of enrollments and this type of school reform: that school expansion is a form of educational reform in its own right that must be considered in tandem with reforms intended to change the distribution of educational opportunities and that there are inherent limits to the reform policy of unchecked expansion—limits that we are approaching in the United States.

SCHOOL EXPANSION

The growth of schooling since the mid-1850s in the United States, as well as in most other countries in the world, has been nothing short of phenomenal. The United States was among the earliest countries in the world to see near-universal primary schooling, in the 19th century, and it was the first in which higher education became a mass institution, in the decades following the Second World War. School enrollments in the developing world since the 1970s and the 1980s have increased far more rapidly than did school enrollments in the United States and in other industrialized countries in periods in which schooling was at similarly low levels, however. The rapid convergence of primary and secondary school enrollment rates throughout the world since the 1970s and the 1980s has led some scholars to treat it as the worldwide institutionalization of mass education (see, e.g., Boli, Ramirez, & Meyer, 1985; Meyer, Ramirez, & Soysal, 1992; Ramirez & Boli, 1987).

The theories of education that pertain to questions of why schooling expanded generally see education responding to either economic or political change. Traditionally, attention has focused on education's role in preparing children and youths for adult economic roles. Three of the major theories of education focus on this link, although they differ radically in how they define the nature of the link. Technical–functionalist explanations hinge on the link of increasing technical and skill demands of jobs. Neo-Marxist accounts argue that capitalism requires a form of social control of workers that formal schooling provides. Status–competition theorists argue that once schooling started to expand, and once educational credentials became a "ticket" to powerful and high-status jobs (regardless of whether education provides valuable and valued job skills), a cycle of ever-escalating credentials expansion was set up whereby social groups with the most education had to keep getting more in order to stay ahead of challengers. A different take on the way in which education responds to economic change is provided by scholars who see schooling as an alternative to work and to other adult roles and responsibilities. In this view, children and youths became more likely to attend school as alternate ways for them to spend their time became more restricted. Finally, some scholars locate the primary dynamic of school expansion in processes of political change, either political modernization or changes in citizenship and the social rights that follow from it.

Education as Occupational Preparation

Functionalist accounts view the expansion of schooling as a natural societal response to technical innovation and development, and to the corresponding increased demand for skilled labor in the workplace (e.g., Bell, 1972; Parsons, 1975, 1977). In this view, schools perform two essential functions for the economy: they rationally sort people into occupational slots so that the most talented and motivated attain the most desirable positions, and they teach the type of cognitive skills required to perform occupational roles in our technologically complex society (Hurn, 1985). School expansion is explained as a logical response to the increasing need for skilled labor in the economy. Trow (1961) made a clear statement of this argument to explain secondary school expansion from the late 19th century to mid-20th century:

> Since the Civil War, and especially in the past fifty years, an economy based on thousands of small farms and businesses has been transformed into one based on large bureaucratized organizations characterized by centralized decision-making and administration carried out through coordinated managerial and clerical staffs . . . The growth of the secondary school system after 1870 was in large part a response to the pull of the economy for a mass of white collar employees with more than an elementary school education.

In parallel to the motivation for "society" to expand schooling, according to the functionalist account, children and youths have stayed in school for longer and longer periods of time because they use education as a way to prepare for the increases in skill they anticipate will be required of them in the workplace. Functionalist accounts do not theorize education as a state institution and thus do not speak to the political processes that allowed school expansion. The anticipation of skill needs that could be met by schooling is considered to be sufficient motivation for individuals and for families to get more education.

    One of the tenets of functionalist theory is that the transition from "traditional" to "modern" society is associated with more meritocratic forms of social selection, which is accomplished in part by incorporating ever-greater proportions of children and youths into systems of formal schooling. Contrary to this expectation, one of the most consistent findings in the school-expansion research is that neither urbanization nor industrialization, standard indicators of "modernization," accounts for school expansion (see, e.g., Fuller, 1983; Greene & Jacobs, 1992; Guest & Tolnay, 1985; Kaestle & Vinovskis, 1980; Meyer, Ramirez, Rubinson, & Boli-Bennett, 1977; Meyer, Tyack, Nagel, & Gordon, 1979; Richardson, 1984; Walters &

O'Connell, 1988). More specifically, during the period of most rapid expansion of primary and secondary school enrollments, the late 19th century and early 20th centuries, school enrollment rates were higher in rural than urban areas in the United States.*

Neo-Marxist accounts, in contrast, attribute the expansion of schooling to the needs of capitalists and other elites for socialization of a docile workforce, social control of subordinate groups, and political acquiescence (see, e.g., Bowles & Gintis, 1976; Katz, 1968; Nasaw, 1979; Schultz, 1973; Spring, 1972). Social control and socialization to capitalist–industrial work discipline were particularly pressing needs given the reliance on immigrants—cultural aliens—as cheap labor in the early stages of industrialization in the United States. Capitalists wanted to ensure that future workers were properly socialized into the work discipline expected of them in the wage economy (e.g., punctuality, deference to authority, rule following), and immigrants were seen as particularly lacking in these habits. Whereas in the functionalist accounts schooling expanded in response to the "needs" of the industrial economy, in the neo-Marxist accounts schooling expanded in response to the "needs" of capitalism. According to these accounts, capitalists and their allies were the main proponents of the growth of public educational opportunities, and the state did their bidding. Neo-Marxists make no assumption that expanding education would reduce class inequality. In fact, they assume it was intended to reproduce class inequality.

Whereas it seems fairly clear that capitalist elites did promote the type and form of schooling charged by neo-Marxists, it is much less clear that they were successful in achieving the educational ends they desired. Among other things, the neo-Marxist social control accounts pay little attention to the political efforts of the working class and other disadvantaged groups to get their own educational interests met—interests that often were at odds with capitalists' and with other elites' interests (see, e.g., Katznelson & Weir, 1985; Raftery, 1992; Ravitch, 1974; Reese, 1986; Wrigley, 1982). Perhaps more important, in order for education to serve a social control function the groups that are the object of the social control efforts have to be brought into the schools, and the social control theories do not explain how elites attempted to do so nor do they document that elites were successful in doing so. Moreover, the available evidence does not identify a mechanism that elites used to "corral" the working class into schools. Compulsory schooling legislation was notoriously ineffective, in part because it was not enforced and in part because it was largely passed after the rise of mass schooling (Landes & Solman, 1972). Additionally, a large proportion of the working-class immigrants who were the objects of social control efforts were Catholics, and they had an escape route in the form of the private Catholic mass educational system (Baker, 1992; Ravitch, 1974). The limitations of the neo-Marxist accounts highlight the degree to which attempts to establish new forms of distribution of educational opportunities—whether to reinforce or to ameliorate extant social inequalities—may succeed or fail depending on how willing students are to patronize the schools.

Because immigrants, especially Catholic immigrants, were a clear target of elites' efforts to control and Americanize the working class via education, some scholars have attempted to test the neo-Marxist social control arguments by examining the association between immigration rates, the proportion of immigrants in the population, or the proportion of Catholics in the population on the one hand and school enrollment rates on the other. Ralph and Rubinson (1980) found that yearly immigration flows had a negative 5-year effect on public secondary

---

*Note, however, that there is some evidence of an effect of urbanization on school enrollments in the late 19th and early 20th centuries when Catholic enrollments are added to public school enrollments, because the majority of (Catholic) immigrants were located in cities and many of them went to parochial schools (Baker, 1999).

enrollment expansion in the United States from 1890 to 1924, the worrisome (from the perspective of Protestant elites) period of "new" immigration when immigrants came predominantly from southern, central, and eastern Europe. The negative effect of immigration is consistent with the finding that immigrants had lower enrollment rates than native-born Americans early in the 20th century (Lieberson, 1980; Perlmann, 1988). Similarly, Walters and O'Connell (1988) found that the proportion of the population that was Catholic had a negative effect on school enrollment rates early in the 20th century.

The status–competition account directly addresses the question of why ever-increasing proportions of school-age youths opted to enroll in school once the school-expansion process got off the ground. The starting assumption is that the best and most powerful jobs are reserved for those who have the most (or "best") educations; this association is rooted in stratification practices from earlier periods. School expansion causes an "inflation" in the educational credentials required for given jobs, and in response to this students prepare themselves for jobs by staying in school longer than they would have had to in earlier years (Boudon, 1974; Collins, 1979; Thurow, 1974). As long as access to the most desirable occupations depends on high educational attainment, students seeking to maximize their competitive advantage must play the educational game and secure the requisite credentials. According to this logic, what matters is a student's educational attainment relative to his or her peers, not his or her absolute level of education. In Boudon's terms, those at the top of the education queue get the best jobs; an overall increase in educational credentials simply serves to up the ante for the amount of education required for the best jobs, regardless of the jobs' skill requirements. Perhaps most important, given the fact that children of elites tend to persist in school longer than children of the disadvantaged, the status–competition account of ever-increasing educational levels explains how elites can retain their educational competitive advantage over challenger groups at the same time as educational opportunities are improved for challengers. This has important political consequences. Challengers seem to focus on the fact that they are getting more (better?) educational opportunities than their parents did rather than the fact that elites are still ahead of them in the educational competition. This account explains how school expansion can leave social inequality in educational opportunity intact by establishing that growth in the absence of interventions that change the relative positions of social groups within the educational system will not alter patterns of relative social advantage.

Evaluation of the status–competition argument requires attention not only to historical increases in the years of schooling attained by successive cohorts of students but also to the linkage between family background and educational attainment. According to status–competition accounts, the most privileged social groups should manage to stay on top of the less privileged in terms of acquiring the most highly valued educational credentials. At first blush, the empirical fact that the association between family socioeconomic status and years of schooling completed has declined over successive cohorts in the United States would appear inconsistent with the status–competition process in that it suggests that educational attainment has, over time, become less consistently sorted by family background. However, in a path-breaking article Mare (1981) showed that when one analyzes the effects of family background on transitions from one level of education to another (e.g., movement into secondary school, graduation from high school, entry into college) the effect of family background on the probability of making the higher level transitions has increased over time in the United States. This important finding provides partial support for the status–competition perspective because what matters according to this perspective is the level of schooling completed (that is, credentials attained), not the number of years of schooling attained. Mare showed that at the same time as the number of years of schooling completed has increased in the United States, children of the most elite social groups have increasingly come to dominate at the highest levels of education (and thus have garnered an increasing share of the most valued educational credentials). Similar findings have also been reported for Britain (Halsey, Heath, & Ridge, 1980), for the Phillipines (Smith & Cheung, 1986), and for Israel (Shavit & Kraus, 1990).

The Warehousing Function

A different view on why schooling expands is that education functions as a kind of holding place for school-age youths. By extension, the growth of the system would have no necessary effect on social inequality in education.

One possibility is that school enrollments expand when youths are pushed out of the labor market (Grubb & Lazerson, 1982; Osterman, 1979). Allowing the schools to absorb otherwise unemployed youths may seem like an attractive policy option to elites interested in limiting social unrest during periods of economic contraction (O'Connor, 1973, p. 11). Possible examples of this kind of policy response include the G.I. Bill, which funded veterans' college educations following the Second World War and thus helped avert a potential crisis of large numbers of unemployed ex-G.I.s (Piven & Cloward, 1971), and the expansion of 2-year colleges during the 1960s, when unemployment started to rise (Grubb & Lazerson, 1982).

Although school enrollments have historically risen, this argument allows for the possibility that, net of other factors, school enrollments decrease during periods with relatively attractive employment opportunities for the relevant age group. That is, in some cases the expansion of work opportunities may draw students out of school. In fact, the expansion of job opportunities for youths in the emergent manufacturing and commercial sectors of the 19th century economy appears to have depressed the rate of growth of secondary school enrollments in the United States (Fuller, 1983; Katz, Doucet, & Stern, 1982); in the first half of the 20th century, secondary school enrollments expanded in response to increases in the unemployment rate (Walters, 1984). Similarly, schooling may prove attractive to adolescents and to young adults when other activities besides work in the formal economy that have generally occupied their time, and have conflicted with schooling, diminish. For example, Walters (1986) found that women's enrollments in higher education in the post-World War II period were positively related to increases in the mean age at marriage and to increases in the mean age at which women bore their first child.

A final part of the picture concerning how changes in the concurrent alternatives to schooling affect school enrollment concerns the organization of the family economy (Rury, 1985; Walters & O'Connell, 1988). In earlier periods in U.S. history (and in many developing countries at present—see, e.g., Buchmann, 1996), many families depended on the labor contributions of multiple family members for economic survival (Hall et al., 1987; Hareven, 1982; Tilly & Scott, 1978). Given the economic uncertainty that confronted (the many) families living at the edge of subsistence in the early 20th century, the family's welfare necessarily took priority over the welfare of individual family members, at least with respect to whether children went to school or to work. "Work," however, may not necessarily consist of formal participation in the wage labor market (which is what arguments about "warehousing" and the expansion of schooling in response to increases in unemployment speak to). Work may consist of unpaid labor in the household, as in the case of family agricultural workers or girls assuming unpaid domestic responsibilities, or work outside of the formal sector of the economy, as in the case of street peddlers, newspaper hawkers, and the like. Unlike work as a formal wage-laborer, unpaid family work or work in the informal economy may be seasonal or otherwise cyclical and/or may not occupy the bulk of a person's time. Thus unpaid family workers and workers in the informal economy are more likely to be able to work and to attend school than are workers in the formal wage economy, either because they can work part of the day and still attend school or because they can work part of the year and attend school part of the year. A number of other studies have shown that children's employment interfered with schooling (Fuller, 1983; Horan & Hargis, 1991) and, moreover, that school and work were less likely to be mutually exclusive for children who worked in agriculture than for children who worked in industry (Greene & Jacobs, 1992; Walters & Briggs, 1993; Walters & James, 1992; Walters, McCammon, & James, 1990).

Citizenship and the State

Although the accounts described previously acknowledge that public schools are funded and operated by the government, and sometimes analyzed the effects of political conflicts or decisions on education, there has been surprisingly little attention given to the ways in which schools are state institutions and/or the ways in which the growth of education or the distribution of educational opportunities are embedded in the logic and structure of the state (see James & Walters, 1990). Two lines of argument have developed concerning the growth of education and the development of the state: one that focuses on political culture and one that views education as a social right of citizenship.

John Meyer, Francisco Ramirez, John Boli, and their colleagues have argued that the establishment and growth of mass schooling is a consequence of changing political culture. In brief, one society after another, starting in Western Europe and in North America in the 19th century and spreading throughout the globe by the middle of the 20th century, attempted to establish a strong nation–state, to participate as a legitimate member of the interstate system, and to develop and promote a distinctly Western model of the individual–citizen by promulgating an expanded and Western model of schooling (Boli, 1989; Boli et al., 1985; Meyer, 1980; Meyer, Boli, & Thomas, 1987; Meyer et al., 1992; Ramirez & Boli, 1982, 1987; Ramirez & Rubinson, 1979). This particular type of political culture became the dominant worldwide political culture by the middle of the 20th century. From this perspective, the key social fact to be explained is why patterns of participation in schooling throughout the world have converged in recent decades despite important variation among states in key societal characteristics. The answer lies in something shared among all nation–states in the modem era: a commitment to a Western political model that values the individual, sees the nation as an aggregate of individuals, celebrates progress, identifies childhood experiences and socialization as the key to adult development, and grants legitimate control of society to the state (Ramirez & Boli, 1987). As Meyer et al. (1991) explained, the collective standardization of mass education (including the gradual incorporation of ever-increasing proportions of the school-age population into state [public] schools)

> celebrates the unified sovereignty and purposiveness of the collectivity (the state), its individual focus and universality enact the integrated and universal character of society (the nation of citizens), and its secularized culture defines the character of the nation–state as an enterprise that is designed to attain progress. (p. 131)

Research in this tradition has pursued three strategies. First, it has shown that national characteristics do not account for variation in national rates of school enrollment (Boli et al., 1985; Meyer et al., 1977; Ramirez & Boli, 1987). Second, it has shown that enrollment growth in most countries has followed an S-shaped pattern, which is taken to indicate that expansion is endemic to the modern interstate system, and that the timing of rapid expansion coincides with the intensification of the nation–state model (Meyer et al., 1992). Third, it has shown that ideological support for mass education and for the citizenship project embodied by it is encoded in virtually all national constitutions and is promoted and spread by influential international organizations (Boli-Bennett & Meyer, 1978; Fiala & Lanford, 1987; McNeely, 1995).

The argument that mass education—achieved by a process of school expansion—is intimately linked with a "modern" political culture that values universality implies, by extension, that a transformation of public education to a mass system would result in a more equal distribution of educational opportunities among social groups. After all, equality is one of the core values of Western culture. In this light, it is surprising that work in this tradition has paid little attention to patterns or processes of the distribution of educational opportunities within societies.

Others have located the connection between education and citizenship in the organizational and political foundations of the welfare state. Education can be seen as a right of social citizenship (Marshall, 1950), as a social good that the modern welfare state extends to those who are entitled to the benefits of citizenship (the development of the modern welfare state itself and the link between extension of citizenship rights and that development is beyond the scope of this chapter). Citizenship in the modern state also implies a degree of equality of social rights. Marshall, for example, argued that civil rights, including freedom of mobility, free speech, and the right to justice, are precursors of political rights, such as voting; political rights, in turn, determine access to social rights, such as education. It follows from this argument that schooling would expand and the educational opportunity structure would become more open as full citizenship rights were extended to increasing proportions of the population and/or as citizenship rights themselves became more extensive.

An expansion of citizenship rights could affect schooling in two ways. First, some scholars have argued that it encourages elites to expand educational opportunities because fledgling citizens need to be socialized to the citizen role. This argument has been used to explain the earlier expansion of mass educational opportunities in the United States than in Western Europe (Katznelson & Weir, 1985; Rubinson, 1986): The working class had the franchise earlier in the United States than in Western Europe, and thus American elites had a greater incentive to incorporate the working class into public schools to properly socialize them to the responsibilities of citizenship. It is also consistent with the many historical analyses of American education that argue that public education was promoted for purposes of citizenship in the 19th century, not for purposes of individual material advancement (see, e.g., Cremin, 1980; Kaestle, 1983; Spring, 1980).

Second, it encourages children and youths to enroll in school in greater proportions because those who are newly incorporated as citizens are more likely to feel entitled to the social right of education or because it provides them with greater political resources to obtain the educational opportunities they desire. Walters (1999), for example, argued that at the turn of the 20th century southern Blacks, who were only a generation removed from slavery, and Southern and Eastern European immigrants to the North, many of whom had enjoyed only restricted citizenship rights in their countries of origin, were strongly committed to the right of access to public education, even if limited family resources made it difficult for them to take advantage of that right. Southern Blacks' commitment to educational access—or, put differently, entitlement to one of the key social rights of citizenship—was particularly strong, given the long shadow cast by slavery. Anderson (1988, p. 17), for example, argued that for ex-slaves reading and writing was valued as a contradiction to oppression; Jones (1980) argued that having access to schooling was an act of "individual and collective defiance to white authority" (p. 49)—in other words, the right of a free person.

In the American context, the starkest case of the effect of citizenship rights on educational rights, including basic access to education as well as the structure of educational opportunities above and beyond access, is that of southern Blacks in the period between Reconstruction and the Civil Rights movement. Largely between 1890 and 1910, one southern state after another enacted legislation and adopted electoral practices that stripped virtually all Blacks and many poor Whites of the vote (Ayers, 1992; Kousser, 1974). Following the loss of the vote and other political rights, and probably as a consequence of it, racial inequalities in southern educational opportunities increased dramatically (Anderson, 1988; Bond, 1934, 1939; Harlan, 1958; Kousser; 1980; Margo, 1982, 1990; Myrdal, 1944). The increase in the funding disparity for Black and White schools was especially dramatic. Moreover, Walters, James, and McCammon (1997) found that disfranchisement changed the determinants of the distribution of educational opportunities to Whites and to Blacks, and that racial inequality in educational enrollments would have been much smaller had educational opportunities been more racially equal (on the latter, also see Margo, 1987). Among other things, this line of research suggests the importance of the interplay between the expansion of schooling and the rules that govern the allocation of schooling when studying historical change in social inequality in education.

School Expansion and Social Advancement

My purpose in discussing theories and research on school expansion has been to consider the relationship between the remarkable growth of schooling in the United States and in other industrial countries and the degree to which education has met one of its core societal expectations: breaking down social barriers to achievement and mobility. The major theories of education have offered mixed expectations. Functionalism associates expanded schooling with an increased societal emphasis on merit, talent, and skill, which in turn should reduce the association between social origins and educational processes. Contrary to some of the core expectations of functionalist theory, however, the effect of social origins on the probabilities of making key educational transitions has remained relatively constant over time. Moreover, research has shown that some of the key indicators of modernization, industrialization, and urbanization do not predict school expansion. Neo-Marxist accounts imply that school expansion should reinforce existing class inequalities, but there is little evidence that elites were able to mold schooling to meet these goals. These accounts do not see the state as an independent actor, nor do they attend to the actions and behaviors of individuals and families—both in terms of schooling decisions they make and attempts to affect educational policy. The available evidence on the association of social origin and educational transitions is consistent with the claims of status—competition theory, but the extant research has not successfully sorted out effects that are due to decisions of individuals and to families and to structural changes that result from political processes and decisions. Theory and research that consider schooling as an alternative to work focus primarily on decisions of individuals and families, but imply that to the degree to which schooling expands because students do not find more appealing ways to spend their time, school expansion should not necessarily affect the relationship between social origins and educational attainment.

Theory and research on schooling, citizenship, and the state speak more directly to state decisions and actions rather than to decisions made by individuals and by families. These theories see the right to education as a core component of a "legitimate" modern state and modern citizenship. Work in the institutionalist perspective, however, has focused on overall patterns of growth rather than on patterns of the distribution of schooling among social groups. Research on education and citizenship rights does suggest that school expansion, under conditions of expanding citizenship rights, should be accompanied by a reduction of social inequalities in education.

The school expansion research as a whole, then, offers only partial evidence about the relationship between school expansion and social advancement. As I discuss more fully in the next section, one limitation of the body of research is that little of it has fully accounted for the fact that school expansion is jointly determined by political decisions made about the way that educational opportunities are distributed and by decisions made by individuals and by families about whether to send their children to school.

OPPORTUNITY STRUCTURES AND ENROLLMENT GROWTH

Schools in the United States accommodated all comers, or so most of the literature on the growth of American schooling assumes, without exploring further. By focusing almost entirely on the influence of factors that would induce ever-increasing proportions of children and youths into schools and virtually ignoring the process by which sufficient opportunities to attend school were provided (see, e.g., Fuller, 1983; Katz & Davey, 1978; Meyer et al., 1979; Walters & O'Connell, 1988), the empirical research on American school expansion assumes that the growth of schooling was what Rubinson (1986) called a demand-driven process. Indeed, the absence of political decisions, political conflict, or political process from these accounts is striking.

There are two problems with this assumption. The first is that it does not accurately characterize American education in that it does not hold for the American South, for either Blacks or Whites.* In the South, insufficient educational opportunities almost certainly prevented some children who wished to go to school, and who would otherwise have been able to go to school, from attending public schools. The structural limitations on enrollment growth were particularly acute for African Americans. I return to this point in the following section.

What's more important, the literature on nonsouthern American schooling takes for granted the reasonableness, the normalcy, perhaps even the inevitability of having a public school system that expands in (immediate and unproblematic?) response to increases in demand. The very important questions of how that situation came to be and what political processes produced it go unasked. This lack of attention to the question of how and why public schools in the Unites States, outside the South, have accommodated all comers is all the more remarkable when one considers how unusual it is. It was not the case in the South, and it was not the norm among other advanced, industrial countries either. In Western Europe, for example, states carefully limited access to state-supported schools in the 19th century, when public schooling in the United States expanded rapidly. Only in very recent decades have practices such as competitive exams for entry into academic (college-prep) high schools and careful limits on the number of places made available at higher and more elite levels of public education been eliminated in most Western European countries. Unlike the United States, Japan tightly controls access to higher education through a rigorous and highly selective examination system. (See Brint, 1998, ch. 2, for an overview.)

To understand these key—and very consequential—differences in educational policy

---

*Relatedly, it may not hold for other politically disadvantaged groups in other geographic areas, such as Mexican–Americans in the Southwest or Asians on the West Coast.

between the United States and Western Europe, it is important to consider the development of the welfare state in the United States and Western Europe. One aspect of American "exceptionalism" in terms of social welfare policies is, of course, that at present, as in the past, we are a far less developed "welfare state." How ironic that in one area, the provision of public educational opportunities for the masses, we had a generous and universal welfare policy long before the countries that are generally considered the leaders in welfare–state development. American educational welfare–state exceptionalism, then, has two important elements: the United States is distinguished from most other advanced, industrial democracies by its early provision of generous educational opportunities, and the generosity of educational policy in the United States diverges sharply from overall American welfare programs, which have offered less generous benefits.

All this is by way of saying that scholars interested in the growth and development of American education must problematize the seemingly unremarkable: the policy decision to provide public schooling to virtually anyone who sought it. I use the term "policy decision" deliberately: The situation has to be understood as the result of a political process, as a state outcome. Local, state and federal policymakers made the myriad policy decisions that allowed public schools to absorb all comers, such as decisions about school funding, school construction, teacher preparation, hiring, educational content, licensing and certification, educational curriculum, and educational selectivity. In doing so, they either responded to public pressure to do so or they received sufficient public support for these decisions.

The practice of unrestrained growth, of providing schools and teachers and a seemingly appropriate course of study on demand, may be the most consequential educational policy decision—the single most important "school reform," albeit of an ongoing nature—in American history. It is the policy decision that allowed the growth of enrollments in the United States to fluctuate as a result of variation in factors that made individuals more or less likely to choose to go to school or to continue in school once enrolled, unchecked and unrestrained by structural limitations. It is the context within which school expansion in the United States can be modeled as a demand-driven process.

We can gain a better understanding of how and why the policy decision to allow unchecked enrollment growth was made and implemented by comparing the key instance of this policy decision, the nonsouthern United States, to situations in which the state did not provide sufficient educational opportunities to accommodate all comers. The main examples here are the American South and Western Europe.*

The American South

The American South was slower than the rest of the country to create a publicly funded and controlled system of mass education. Whereas states and localities in the rest of the country established "common" schools in the first third of the 19th century, public education was not established in the South until after the Civil War, even for Whites. By the end of Reconstruction, southern states and localities had incorporated the right to a public education into their constitutions and had established separate educational systems for Black and for White chil-

---

*I focus here on examples in which the state was apparently unwilling to provide more generous educational opportunities for the masses, rather than examples in which the state lacks (or lacked) the fiscal capacity to do so, as is the case today in many third world countries (Fuller, 1991). The political outcome of insufficient educational opportunities is created by very different political processes in cases where the state cannot afford better opportunities versus cases where the state has the financial capacity but chooses not to exercise it.

dren. However, southern educational opportunities were limited, especially for Black children, and differences in educational opportunities provided by the state to Black and to White children increased dramatically following disfranchisement in the late 19th and early 20th centuries (Bond, 1934, 1939; Harlan, 1958; Kousser, 1980; Margo, 1982, 1990; Myrdal, 1944). More important for the question at hand, school enrollments for both Black and White children were constrained by insufficient educational opportunities in the late 19th and early 20th centuries (Walters et al., 1997), although Black children's enrollments were more severely constrained by a lack of educational opportunities than were White children's enrollments. (On the restrictions on Black enrollments due to insufficient educational opportunities, also see Margo, 1990; Walters & Briggs, 1993; Walters & James, 1992.) Walters (1992) argued that northern school policies can be characterized as a politics of inclusion, whereas southern school policies were governed by a politics of exclusion.

Walters and associates (1997) further found that disfranchisement in the South, a process by which virtually all Blacks and many poor Whites were deprived of the vote in the late 19th century, changed the process by which educational opportunities were distributed to White and Black children. For both Black and White children, school board decisions about the allocation of teachers, schools, and the like appear to have been less responsive to enrollment pressures, or demands, following disfranchisement. In addition, disfranchisement appears to have allowed school boards and other state officials to exercise a freer hand in discriminating against blacks in the provision of educational opportunities. They have explained their findings in terms of citizenship rights, especially access to the vote. Groups without the vote—without full citizenship rights—are less able to pressure the state to provide adequate educational opportunities. In addition, state officials have less of an incentive to provide "good" schooling opportunities to groups without citizenship rights: They do not have to curry political support from these groups, and they do not have to worry about these groups making "irresponsible" electoral choices.

Western Europe

Educational opportunities in Western Europe have historically been far more restricted than in the United States,* although since the 1970s and the 1980s various school reforms in Western Europe have eliminated some important barriers to the growth of schooling. In many Western European countries, the growth of schooling above the primary level was (and to some degree still is) checked by school fees, by rigid tracking, by entrance and placement examinations into special curricula or differentiated secondary schools, and by the close control of the number of places available at higher level and more prestigious schools (Archer, 1979; Brint, 1998, ch. 2; Heidenheimer, Heclo, & Adams, 1983; Organization of Economic Cooperation and Development [OECD], 1996; Ringer, 1979). In some respects, differences between Western Europe and the (nonsouthern) United States parallel differences between the South and the rest of the United States: In the former cases, access to education was controlled and a "politics of exclusion" prevailed, whereas in the latter case schools generally accommodated all comers and a "politics of inclusion" prevailed (Walters, 1992).

A series of empirical studies of school expansion in various Western European countries

---

*A few other advanced industrial countries have open systems similar to the American one, such as Canada. Others, such as Australia, bear a stronger similarity to the model of restricted access common in western Europe (Brint, 1998).

showed clearly that enrollments in Western Europe were constrained and limited by the relatively closed opportunity structure (Garnier, Hage, & Fuller, 1989; Hage & Garnier, 1992;
Hage, Garnier, & Fuller, 1988). Garnier, Hage, and Fuller contrasted this to the American
case, in which school expansion is driven by demand, and argued that the more closed nature
of Western European public education is due to the more rigid class structures in Western
Europe, to strong central states, and to the more limited nature of the franchise. Rubinson
(1986) and Katznelson and Weir (1985) made similar points when they explained the relative
absence of class conflicts over education in the United States as the intersection of class
structure and the franchise: because the franchise was extended to the working class early on,
with little conflict, elites found it in their interest to make education relatively available to the
working class so that they could be socialized to democratic values and taught to make "proper"
political choices.

SCHOOL REFORM, EXPANSION, AND EQUALITY

Growth of enrollments represents an expansion of educational opportunities in some important respects, especially relative to older cohorts. Nonetheless, the expansion of schooling has
not reduced the relative educational advantage that children of elites enjoy over less privileged children. As described previously, this finding has been documented for the United
States (Mare, 1981), for Britain (Halsey et al., 1980), for the Phillipines (Smith & Cheung,
1986) and for Israel (Shavit & Kraus, 1990). Consistent with Boudon's (1974) arguments, this
occurs because expansion in and of itself does not necessarily change the relative position of
social groups in the "education queue." That is, elites manage to stay at the top of the education queue by getting more education (or more of the most valued type of education) than their
competitors. Boudon's arguments highlight the need to consider separately the effects on educational equality of an overall increase in the size of the educational system (i.e., school expansion) and changes in the rules by which educational opportunities are allocated. (Also see
Mare, 1981, who established the importance of separating the effects of increases in mean
educational attainments from the effects of changes in rates of entrance into or completion of
various levels of education by social group when studying intergenerational educational mobility.) If school expansion does not produce greater equality, how about reforms intended to
modify directly the allocation of educational opportunities? Equally important, how do school
expansion and school reform work together to produce greater educational equality (or not)?

School reforms intended to promote greater educational equality generally have been no
more effective in closing overall class or other social differentials than has school expansion.
The most striking evidence on this score is an edited book by Shavit and Blossfeld (1993) that
reports the results of comparable analyses of the effects of family background on educational
attainment over time in 13 different industrialized countries. In 11 of the 13 countries, inequalities in educational attainment among students of different social classes were remarkably stable over the several decades, despite the institution in some countries of apparently
far-reaching reforms to equalize educational opportunities, including Czechoslovakia, Hungary, and Poland. The two counter-examples, Sweden and the Netherlands, are equally illumi-
nating. In both cases, the authors attributed the decline in educational inequality to social–
welfare policies that created greater social equality outside the educational system. In other
words, the changes that produced a more egalitarian distribution of educational opportunities
were located outside the schools.

Other studies of specific school reforms intended to promote greater educational equality have produced similar results: little change in social differentials in educational attainment. For example, the elimination of secondary school fees, among other reforms, in Ireland in 1967 did not significantly alter the working-class disadvantage in education (Raftery & Hout, 1993). Despite attempts to directly change the rules of allocation of educational opportunity in socialist era Hungary—the reservation of a large portion of seats in academic high schools and in universities for students from working-class backgrounds—class-based inequalities in secondary and in higher education persisted (Hanley & McKeever, 1997). Among Eastern European countries, Czechoslovakia had the most consistently applied "reverse discrimination" policy governing access to education, yet here too family status remained associated with children's educational opportunities (Wong, 1998). In England and in Wales a dual system of secondary education, consisting of separate schools for students being prepared for higher education and those who would not advance beyond secondary education ("grammar schools" and "secondary modern schools," respectively), gave way to comprehensive secondary schools serving students of all abilities between the mid-1960s and the mid-1970s. This reform, however, did not reduce the association between social origins and educational attainment (Kerckhoff, Fogelman, & Manlove, 1997). An important educational reform in 1968 in the Netherlands did not disrupt the association between family background and transitions among levels of schooling (Dronkers, 1993).

There are a number of reasons why the previously mentioned school reforms did not produce their intended egalitarian results. Whether by default or by design by the state, none of these reforms closed off all possible means by which elites could circumvent the reforms, in whole or in part. On this point the socialist cases are particularly interesting, because the socialist states tried not only to increase educational opportunities for historically disadvantaged groups but also to limit educational advantages for historically advantaged groups. In other words, state educational policy was designed to more thoroughly limit (or eliminate) elites' safety valves in the socialist states than in the capitalist states. In Hungary, elites used bribes, favors based on personal ties, and other extralegal means to secure their children's educational places (Szelenyi & Aschaffenburg, 1993). Additionally, the greater cultural capital possessed by children of administrators and by children of professionals—especially those who were Party members—apparently helped them overcome limitations on the number of seats allocated to them at secondary and at tertiary schools (Hanley & McKeever, 1997). In Czechoslovakia, Party membership supplemented but did not replace class-based patterns of intergenerational educational inequality, which Wong (1998) attributed to the persistent effects of family capital.

There was a good deal of variation from country to country in the means available to or created by elites to blunt the effects of egalitarian school reforms, depending on the structure of the educational system, the resources on which elite advantage was based, and the nature of the reforms themselves. However, one structural opportunity to circumvent reforms intended to reduce elites' educational advantages was a constant. In all of these cases, school enrollments were expanding before and after the reforms in question. Additionally, school expansion allowed absolute educational attainments to improve for disadvantaged groups (compared to the same groups' educational attainments in earlier cohorts) without eliminating the relative educational advantages enjoyed by elites (relative, that is, to the attainments of disadvantaged groups of the same cohort).

Raftery and Hout (1991; also Hout, Raftery, & Bell, 1993) argued that a process they call "maximally maintained inequality" (MMI) accounts for the seeming puzzle that so many sweeping reforms intended to make education more egalitarian—to loosen the association between social origins and educational attainment—have not accomplished their purpose. They illustrate their argument with the case of Ireland and its elimination of secondary school fees in 1967. As expected, this reform increased the proportion of working-class students who attended secondary schools, but it did not alter the effect of social background on transitions from one level of education to the next. As Raftery and Hout explained it, this seemingly anomalous finding can be accounted for by two processes. First, the elimination of school fees resulted in an increase in secondary school attendance rates for all students, not only for those with working-class origins. Second, class effects on the likelihood of entering secondary school remained large—larger than for subsequent transitions (such as entry to higher education). As they put it,

> Together these trends and differentials imply that educational developments independent of social class passed students of all classes over the first big hurdle in the educational system—the one with the highest class barriers. By advancing to secondary education many who might otherwise have been mustered out on the basis of class, expanding schools reduced class differences in the overall distribution of educational attainments without affecting the class selectivity at any particular transition point. (p. 60)

One of the keys to maximally maintained inequality is that expansion at the secondary level had the effect of pushing to higher education the crucial sorting of students by class background.

There are two examples of school reform that, on the surface, appear counter to the general finding that school reforms do not reduce educational inequalities: Post's (1994) study of the establishment of free and compulsory secondary education in Hong Kong, and Gamoran's (1996) study of curriculum reform in Scottish secondary education. Post found that after the reforms, family income was less of a factor in access to secondary education in Hong Kong, and Gamoran found that curricular standardization at the secondary level in Scotland reduced social inequality in achievement (measured by standardized exams) within secondary schools. Note that both of these studies, however, focused on the secondary level rather than transitions throughout the entire educational system and thus do not account for the possibility that the educational sorting of consequence may have been displaced, either to probabilities of secondary school completion or to probabilities of entry to higher education.

What do these studies of school reform tell us about the joint effect of expansion and reform on educational equality? Hout and associates (1993) argued for a link between the two processes: One of the basic points of the "MMI thesis" is that "in the absence of growth in educational systems, there will be no redistribution of educational opportunity among social classes" (p. 48). In other words, it is school expansion that may loosen the effect of class on access to education. What their discussion misses, however, is the parallel point that it is school expansion that simultaneously allows elites to increase their participation at the highest levels of the educational system and, consequently, to retain their overall competitive advantage in the educational credentials game. I believe that the evidence from the studies of school reform leads to an important qualification: We can expect school reforms intended to reduce social advantages in access to secondary or higher education to have no overall effect on social advantages conferred by education unless the state anticipates and closes off means by which elites can circumvent the reforms. (Whether it is politically feasible, or indeed even desirable, to do so is another question entirely.) The enormous expansion of education, the most important school reform of the 20th century, has provided the most important means by which elites can maintain their relative educational advantage.

School expansion may, therefore, function as a sort of counter-reform to interventions designed to reduce social inequalities by changing the rules of access or allocation. In this view, the process of unfettered educational growth—the operation of a free market in education—is not the result of an absence of state intervention. Rather, it is a deliberate state policy, at least for the relatively powerful states we are considering here. Unfettered growth allows elites to retain their competitive educational advantage while simultaneously appearing to offer increased educational opportunities to the working class, thus "buying" the political support of both groups. The working class can focus on the fact that they are getting a larger piece of educational pie than they used to—current cohorts get more education than older cohorts did. Additionally, elites can focus on the fact that this is accomplished by increasing the total size of the pie rather than by reducing the relative size of elites' piece of the educational pie, thus allowing elite students to stay ahead of the game. However politically appealing it may be to simultaneously expand schooling and allow elites to stay one step ahead of the game, unchecked school expansion works at cross-purposes to school reforms intended to promote social equality.*

This is one of the "limits of growth" to which I refer in my title: By allowing unfettered growth in enrollments, states provide elites with a way of escaping the intent of egalitarian reforms—and thus the reforms do not significantly reduce class educational differentials. When social equality is achieved at the level of the school system that was formerly the place of consequence (for example, secondary education), expansion just pushes the consequential sorting to the next higher level (for example, higher education). What matters in the educational competition is not absolute level of attainment, but relative attainment. In this, elites still win.

There is another limit of growth. At some point, either the state or families may become unable to bear the cost of further expansion or may become unwilling for other reasons to encourage or to allow students to stay in school for long periods of time. The transformation of higher education to a mass system in the United States, for example, may be the limit of school growth. In this volume, Collins (Chapter 9) argues that in both the ancient and modern worlds higher educational systems have expanded as a result of status competition over credentials and subsequently have collapsed under the weight of too many irrelevant and costly credentials. If we run out of levels, elites will likely find other ways to retain their educational advantage, perhaps by patronizing different types of schools at the level of consequence (e.g., elite universities instead of state schools).

CONCLUSIONS

Education is the institution that, more than any other in modern society, holds the promise of social advancement and equality of opportunity. In the United States and in virtually all other industrial countries, educational institutions have expanded dramatically in the past several decades as a consequence of actions and commitments on the part of policymakers to expand the "carrying capacity" of schools and on the part of individuals and families to take advantage of the opportunities provided by the enlarged capacity of schools. Throughout the same period, we have witnessed a myriad of school reforms intended to reduce socioeconomic barriers to progress through school and to make the distribution of schooling opportunities

---

*Note that the policy of unchecked school expansion, which was a characteristic of American education long before it was the norm elsewhere, has been successfully exported throughout the world (remember, many of the controls over unfettered growth in schooling formerly exercised by, for example, Western European states have been eliminated in recent decades), making it more likely now than in the past that school reforms will be undermined by expansion.

more neutral with respect to social origins. Both types of institutional change—the increase in the size of the system (e.g., increasing enrollments, increasing attainments) and the changes in the rules of allocation of educational opportunity—were expected by policymakers and by scholars to reduce or remove social inequalities in students' progress through the educational system. The evidence suggests that neither form of institutional change has significantly altered the relationship between social origins and advancement through schooling.

I have suggested in this chapter that we need to simultaneously direct our attention to the dual processes of the growth of the system and the distribution of opportunities within the system. Most of the extant literature has focused on one process to the exclusion of the other. I argue that we can not understand fully either the factors that produce school expansion or the effects of school expansion without also focusing on the distribution of opportunities within schools. Conversely, I do not think we can understand the apparent puzzle that virtually all of the major reforms that were intended to reduce social inequalities in progress through school have had little or no effect on the association between social origins and educational attainment without considering the degree to which schools were expanding—that is, without considering school expansion as a possible counter-reform.* Some of the research on mobility has attempted to control for the growth of the system in modeling the determinants of the distribution of opportunities (e.g., Mare, 1981 and others following his lead), but that is not the same as investigating the dynamic interplay between school expansion and school reform.

ACKNOWLEGMENTS: The author gratefully acknowledges the support of the Spencer Foundation and the National Science Foundation (SES 93-10585 and SBR 95-11835).

REFERENCES

Anderson, J. D. (1988). *The education of Blacks in the South, 1860–1935.* Chapel Hill, NC: University of North Carolina Press,

Archer, M. (1979). *Social Origins of Educational Systems.* Beverly Hills, CA: Sage.

Ayers, E. L. (1992). *The promise of the new South: Life after reconstruction.* New York: Oxford University Press.

Baker, D. P. (1992). The politics of American Catholic school expansion, 1970–1930. In B. Fuller & R. Rubinson (Eds.), *The political construction of education* (pp. 189–206). New York: Praeger.

Baker, D. P. (1999). Schooling all of the masses: Reconsidering the origins of American schooling in the postbellum era. *Sociology of Education, 72,* 197–215.

Bell, D. (1972). *The coming of post-industrial society.* New York: Basic Books.

Boli, J. (1989). *New citizens for a new society: The institutional origins of mass schooling in Sweden.* Oxford, England: Pergamon Press.

Boli, I., Ramirez, F. O., & Meyer, J. (1985). Explaining the origins and expansion of mass education. *Comparative Education Review, 29,* 145–170.

Boli-Bennett, J., & Meyer, J. W. (1978). The ideology of childhood and the state: Rules distinguishing children in national constitutions, 1870–1970. *American Sociological Review, 43,* 797–812,

Bond, H. M. (1934). The education of the Negro in the American social order. New York: Octagon Books.

Bond, H. M. (1939). *Negro education in Alabama: A study in cotton and steel.* New York: Octagon Books,

Boudon, R. (1974). *Education, opportunity, and social inequality: Changing prospects in western society.* New York: Wiley.

Bowles, S., & Gintis, H. (1976). *Schooling in capitalist America: Educational reform and the contradictions of economic life.* New York: Basic.

Brint, S. (1998). *Schools and societies.* Thousand Oaks, CA: Pine Forge Press.

Buchmann, C. (1996). *Family decisions and social constraints: The determinants of educational inequality in contemporary Kenya.* Unpublished doctoral dissertation, Department of Sociology, Indiana University.

*It is also important to consider other situationally-specific means by which elites have been able to circumvent school reforms intended to reduce their relative educational advantages.

Collins, R. (1979). *The credential society: An historical sociology of education and stratification.* New York: Academic Press.

Cremin, L. A. (1980). *American education, the national experience, 1783–1876.* New York: Harper & Row.

Dronkers, J. (1993). Educational reform in the Netherlands: Did it change the impact of parental occupation and education? *Sociology of Education, 66,* 262–277.

Fiala, R., & Lanford, A. (1987). Educational ideology and the world educational revolution. *Comparative Education Review, 31,* 315–333.

Fuller, B (1983). Youth job structure and school enrollment, 1890–1920. *Sociology of Education, 56,* 145–156.

Fuller, B (1991). *Growing up modern: The western state builds third world schools.* New York: Routledge.

Gamoran, A. (1996). Curriculum standardization and equality of opportunity in Scottish secondary education: 1984–90. *Sociology of Education, 69,* 1–21.

Garnier, M., Hage, J., & Fuller, B. (1989). The strong state, social class, and controlled school expansion in France, 1881–1975. *American Journal of Sociology, 95,* 279–306.

Greene, M., & Jacobs, J. (1992). Urban enrollments and the growth of schooling: Evidence from the U.S. 1910 Census Public Use sample. *American Journal of Education, 101,* 29–59.

Grubb, W. N., & Lazerson, M. (1982). Education and the labor market: Recycling the youth problem. In H. Kantor & D. Tyack (Eds.), *Work, youth, and schooling* (pp. 110–141). Stanford, CA: Stanford University Press.

Guest, A. M., & Tolnay, S. E. (1985). Agricultural organization and educational consumption in the U.S. in 1900. *Sociology of Education, 58,* 201–212.

Hage, J., & Garnier, M. (1992). Strong states and educational expansion: France versus Italy. In B. Fuller & R. Rubinson (Eds.), *The political construction of education* (pp. 155–172). New York: Praeger.

Hage, J., Garnier, M., & Fuller, B. (1988). The active state, investment in human capital, and economic growth: France, 1825–1975. *American Sociological Review, 53,* 824–837.

Hall, J. D., Leloudis, J., Korstad, R., Murphy, M., Jones, L. A., & Daly, C. B. (1987). *Like a family: The making of a southern cotton mill world.* Chapel Hill, NC: University of North Carolina Press.

Halsey, A. H., Heath, A. F., & Ridge, J. M. (1980). *Origins and destinations: Family, class, and education in modern Britain.* Oxford, England: Clarendon Press

Hanley, E., & McKeever, M. (1997). The persistence of educational inequalities in state–socialist Hungary: Trajectory versus counterselection. *Sociology of Education, 70,* 1–18.

Hareven, T. (1982). *Family time and industrial time: The relationship between the family and work in a New England industrial community.* Cambridge, England: Cambridge University Press.

Harlan, L. R. (1958). *Separate and unequal: Public school campaigns and racism in the southern seaboard states 1901–1915.* Chapel Hill, NC: University of North Carolina Press.

Heidenheimer, A. J., Heclo, H., & Adams, C. T. (1983). Education policy. In A. J. Heidenheimer, H. Heclo, & C. T. Adams (Eds.), *Comparative public policy* (pp. 21–51). New York: St. Martin's Press.

Horan, P. M., & Hargis, P. G. (1991). Children's work and schooling in the late nineteenth-century family economy. *American Sociological Review, 56,* 583–596.

Hout, M., Raftery, A. E., & Bell, E. O. (1993). Making the grade: Educational stratification in the United States, 1925–1989. In Y. Shavit & H.-P. Blossfeld (Eds.), *Persistent inequality* (pp. 25–50). Boulder, CO: Westview Press.

Hum, C. H. (1985). *The limits and possibilities of schooling* (3rd ed.). Boston: Allyn and Bacon.

James, D. R., & Walters, P. B. (1990). The supply side of public schools: Local state determinants of school enrollment patterns in the U.S. *Research in Sociology of Education and Socialization, 9,* 81–110.

Jones, J. (1980). *Soldiers of light and love: Northern teachers and Georgia Blacks, 1865–1873.* Chapel Hill, NC: University of North Carolina Press.

Kaestle, C. F. (1983). *Pillars of the republic: Common schools and American society, 1780–1860.* New York: Hill and Wang.

Kaestle, C. F., & Vinovskis, M. A. (1980). *Education and social change in nineteenth-century Massachusetts.* Cambridge, England: Cambridge University Press.

Katz, M. B. (1968). *The irony of early school reform: Educational innovation in mid-nineteenth-century Massachusetts.* Cambridge, MA: Harvard University Press.

Katz, M. B. (1971). *School reform: Past and present.* Boston: Little, Brown.

Katz, M. B., & Davey, I. E. (1978). Youth and early industrialization in a Canadian city. *American Journal of Sociology, 84*(suppl.), S81–S119.

Katz, M. B., Doucet, M., & Stern, M. (1982). *The social organization of early industrial capitalism.* Cambridge, MA: Harvard University Press.

Katznelson, I., & Weir, M. (1985). *Schooling for all: Class, race, and the decline of the democratic ideal.* New York: Basic Books.

Kerckhoff, A. C., Fogelman, K., & Manlove, J. (1997). Staying ahead: The middle class and school reform in England and Wales. *Sociology of Education, 70,* 19–35.

Kousser, J. M. (1974). *The shaping of southern politics: Suffrage restriction and the establishment of the one-party South, 1880–1910.* New Haven, CT: Yale University Press.

Kousser, J. M. (1980). Progressivism—For middle-class Whites only: North Carolina education, 1880–1910. *Journal of Southern History, 46,* 169–194.

Landes, W., & Solmon, L. (1972). Compulsory schooling legislation: An economic analysis of law and social change in the nineteenth century. *Journal of Economic History, 32,* 54–97.

Lieberson, S. (1980). *A piece of the pie: Blacks and White immigrants since 1880.* Berkeley, CA: University of California Press.

Mare, R. D. (1981). Change and stability in educational stratification. *American Sociological Review, 46,* 72–87.

Margo, R. A. (1982). Race differences in public school expenditures: Disfranchisement and school finance in Louisiana, 1890–1910. *Social Science History, 6,* 9–33.

Margo, R. A. (1987). Accounting for racial differences in school attendance in the American South: The role of separate-but-equal. *The Review of Economics and Statistics, 4,* 661–666.

Margo, R. A. (1990). *Race and schooling in the South, 1880–1950: An economic history.* Chicago: University of Chicago Press.

Marshall, T. H. (1950). *Citizenship and social class.* Cambridge, England: Cambridge University Press.

McNeely, C. (1995). *Constructing the nation state: International organization and prescriptive action.* Westport, CT: Greenwood Press.

Meyer, J. W. (1980). The world polity and the authority of the nation–state. In A. Bergesen (Ed.), *Studies of the modern world system* (pp. 109–138). New York: Academic Press.

Meyer, J. W., Boli, J. & Thomas, G. (1987). Ontology and rationalization in the western cultural account. In G. Thomas, J. W. Meyer, F. O. Ramirez, & J. Boli (Eds.), *Institutional structure: Constituting state, society, and the individual* (pp. 11–38). Newbury Park, CA: Sage.

Meyer, J. W., Ramirez, F. O., Rubinson, R., & Boli-Bennett, J. (1977). The world educational revolution, 1950–1970. *Sociology of Education, 50,* 242–258.

Meyer, J. W., Ramirez, F. O., & Soysal, Y. N. (1992). World expansion of mass education, 1870–1980. *Sociology of Education, 65,* 128–149.

Meyer, I. W., Tyack, D., Nagel, J., & Gordon, A. (1979). Public education as nation-building in America: Enrollments and bureaucratization in the American states, 1870–1930. *American Journal of Sociology, 85,* 591–613.

Myrdal, G. (1944). *An American dilemma: The Negro problem and modern democracy.* New York: Harper and Brothers.

Nasaw, D. (1979). *Schooled to order: A social history of public schooling in the United States.* New York: Oxford University Press.

O'Connor, J. (1973). *The fiscal crisis of the state.* New York: St. Martin's Press.

Organization for Economic Cooperation and Development. (1996). *Education at a glance: OECD indicators.* Paris: OECD.

Osterman, P. (1979). Education and labor markets at the turn of the Century. *Politics and Society, 9,* 103–122.

Parsons, T. (1975). Social structure and the symbolic media of interchange. In P. Blau (Ed.), *Approaches to the study of social structure.* New York: The Free Press

Parsons, T. (1977). *Social systems and the evolution of action theory.* New York: Free Press.

Perlmann, J. (1988). *Ethnic differences: Schooling and social structure among the Irish, Italians, Jews and Blacks in an American city, 1880–1935.* Cambridge, England: Cambridge University Press.

Piven, F. F. & Cloward, R. A. (1971). *Regulating the poor: The functions of public welfare.* New York: Vintage.

Post, D. (1994). Educational stratification, school expansion, and public policy in Hong Kong. *Sociology of Education, 67,* 121–138.

Raftery, A. E., & Hout, M. (1993). Maximally maintained inequality: Expansion, reform, and opportunity in Irish education, 1921–75. *Sociology of Education, 66,* 41–62.

Raftery, J. (1992). *Land of fair promise: Politics and reform in Los Angeles schools, 1885–1941.* Stanford, CA: Stanford University Press.

Ralph, J. H., & Rubinson, R. (1980). Immigration and the expansion of schooling in the United States, 1890–1970. *American Sociological Review, 45,* 943–954.

Ramirez, F. O., & Boli, J. (1982). Global patterns of educational institutionalization. In P. Altbach, R. Amove, & G. Kelley (Eds.), *Comparative education* (pp. 15–38). New York: Macmillan.

Ramirez, F. O, & Boli, J. (1987). The political construction of mass schooling: European origins and worldwide institutionalization. *Sociology of Education, 60,* 2–17.

Ramirez, F. O., & Rubinson, R. (1979). Creating members: The political incorporation and expansion of public education. In J. W. Meyer & M. T. Hannan (Eds.), *National development and the world system* (pp. 72–84). Chicago: University of Chicago Press.

Ravitch, D. (1974). *The great school wars, New York City, 1805–1972: A history of the public schools as battlefields of social change.* New York: Basic Books.

Reese, W. (1986). *The power and the promise of school reform. Grassroots movements during the progressive era.* Boston: Routledge & Kegan Paul.

Richardson, J. G. (1984). Settlement patterns and the governing structures of nineteenth-century school system. *American Journal of Education, 92,* 178–206.

Ringer, F. (1979). *Education and society in modern Europe.* Bloomington, IN: Indiana University Press.

Rubinson, R. (1986). Class formation, politics, and institutions: Schooling in the United States. *American Journal of Sociology, 92,* 519–548.

Rury, J. L. (1985). American school enrollment in the progressive era: An interpretive inquiry. *History of Education, 14,* 49–67.

Schultz, T. (1973). *The culture factory: Boston public schools, 1789–1860.* New York: Oxford University Press.

Shavit, Y., & Blossfeld, H.-P. (Eds., 1993). *Persistent inequality: Changing educational attainment in thirteen countries.* Boulder, CO: Westview Press.

Shavit, Y., & Kraus, V. (1990). Educational transitions in Israel: A test of the industrialization and credentialism hypotheses. *Sociology of Education, 63,* 133–141.

Smith, H. L., & Cheung, P. L. (1986). Trends in the effects of family background on educational attainment in the Phillipines. *American Journal of Sociology, 91,* 1387–1408.

Spring, J. (1972). *Education and the rise of the corporate state.* Boston: Beacon Press.

Spring, J. (1980). *Educating the worker–citizen: The social, economic, and political foundations of education.* New York: Longman.

Szelenyi, S., & Aschaffenburg, K. (1993). Inequalities in educational opportunities in Hungary. In Y. Shavit & H.-P. Blossfield (Eds.), *Persistent inequality: Changing educational attainment in thirteen countries* (pp. 273–301). Boulder, CO: Westview Press.

Thurow, L. C. (1974). *Generating inequality: Mechanisms of distribution in the U.S. economy.* New York: Basic Books.

Tilly, L., & Scott, J. (1978). *Women, work and family.* New York: Holt, Rinehart and Winston.

Trow, M. (1961). The second transformation of American secondary education. *International Journal of Comparative Sociology, 2,* 144–165.

Walters, P. B. (1984). Occupational and labor market effects on secondary and postsecondary educational expansion in the United States: 1922 to 1979. *American Sociological Review, 49,* 659–671.

Walters, P. B. (1986). Sex and institutional differences in labor market effects on the expansion of higher education, 1952 to 1980. *Sociology of Education, 59,* 199–211.

Walters, P. B. (1992). Who should be schooled? The politics of class, race, and ethnicity in the turn-of-the-century U.S. In B. Fuller & R. Rubinson (Eds.), *The political construction of education: The state, school expansion, and economic change* (pp. 173–187). New York: Praeger.

Walters, P. B. (1999). Education and advancement: Exploring the hopes of Blacks and poor Whites at the turn of the century. In M. Lamont (Ed.), *The cultural territories of race: Black and White boundaries* (pp. 268–290). Chicago: University of Chicago Press and New York: Russell Sage Foundation.

Walters, P. B., & Briggs, C. M. (1993). The family economy, child labor, and schooling: Evidence from the early twentieth-century South. *American Sociological Review, 58,* 163–181.

Walters, P. B. & James, D. R. (1992). Schooling for some: Child labor and school enrollment of Black and White children in the early twentieth-century South. *American Sociological Review, 57,* 635–650.

Walters, P. B., James, D. R., & McCammon, H. J. (1997). Citizenship and public schools: Accounting for racial inequality in education in the pre- and post-disfranchisement South. *American Sociological Review, 62,* 34–52.

Walters, P. B., McCammon, H. J., & James, D. R. (1990). Schooling or working? Public education, racial politics, and the organization of production in 1910. *Sociology of Education, 63,* 1–26.

Walters, P. B., & O'Connell, P. J. (1988). Schooling and the family economy: The effects of industrialism, race and religion on American educational participation, 1890–1940. *American Journal of Sociology, 93,* 1116–1152.

Wong, R. S.-K. (1998). Multidimensional influences of family environment in education: The case of socialist Czechoslovakia. *Sociology of Education, 71,* 1–22.

Wrigley, J. (1982). *Class politics and public schools: Chicago, 1900–1950.* New Brunswick, NJ: Rutgers University Press.

PART III

THE STUDY OF ACCESS
TO SCHOOLING

CHAPTER 11

Equitable Classrooms in a Changing Society

Elizabeth G. Cohen

The concept of equality of educational opportunity lies at the juncture of two sets of inequalities: the unequal distribution of power, economic, and educational resources across society and unequal possibilities for successful educational outcomes. Therefore, it is necessary to study the processes of the larger society and the institution of education along with processes that produce inequalities of outcome. Research on equality of educational opportunity at the societal or regional level alone will neglect the experiences of students within classrooms and schools. These experiences are the most proximate causes of educational success or failure. At the level of the larger society, one can document how the physical location of social classes and social change in the makeup of the population affect the composition of schools, of tracks, and of classrooms. This documentation, however, will not explain precisely how the resulting differences in opportunities to learn for individual students produce major differences in school success.

Similarly, work with the concept of equal opportunities only at the level of the classroom will neglect the big picture of the social location of that classroom in relationship to inequalities in the larger society and in the organization of the school. Moreover, inequalities at the societal level interpenetrate inequalities at the classroom level in complex ways. Stratification of the larger society has indirect effects on status orders that develop among the students. These effects combine with the power of the social system of the classroom to generate a new set of inequalities and to block access to learning for some students. This chapter attempts to show how blending of individual and contextual analysis is the most fruitful approach to the study of equality of educational opportunity.

ELIZABETH G. COHEN • School of Education, Stanford University, Stanford, California 94305-3084

Handbook of the Sociology of Education, edited by Maureen T. Hallinan. Kluwer Academic/Plenum Publishers, New York, 2000.

In discussing equality of educational opportunity, Coleman (1990) distinguished between equality of input and equality of outcome. In this chapter, I add to this distinction while at the same time making the definition more complex. Because the social context of an individual's family, neighborhood, and school varies sharply with location in the system of social stratification, there are indeed differences in input to the educational process that represent inequality in educational opportunity. However, if one wants to understand the process by which inequality of educational outcome arises, it is not enough to simply consider inputs to the process at the level of family, neighborhood, and school characteristics. The formulation of inputs and outcomes leaves the school and the classroom as a black box with unknown internal features. Instead, I propose to include in the concept of equality of educational opportunity various contextual sources of inequality that have their origin within the school and the classroom. These sources of inequality include internal organizational arrangements such as tracking and ability grouping that lead to unequal treatment in instruction, unequal access to peers who represent resources of academic achievement, and status orders that arise in the classroom and lead to unequal status interaction among peers. All of these sources of inequality bear some relationship to the societal input variables, but the relationship is not always a direct one. Inequalities in individual educational outcomes show direct and indirect effects of these inequalities in social context.

OVERVIEW OF THE CHAPTER

The chapter has three parts. The first deals with the inequality of opportunity that stems from the location of the classroom in particular schools in particular social contexts. Some students will never experience grade-level curricula and an academically demanding environment because of events over which they, their teachers, or their parents have little control. Such students may live in neighborhoods with other poor families and with members of racial and linguistic minorities and may attend segregated "high-poverty" schools. The technology for a successful public school under these conditions is not well developed nor understood. In addition to inequalities arising from the school that the student attends, schools have internal ways of structuring inequality. Students may find themselves in classrooms within schools that do not offer grade-level curricula and that demand little of the student academically. Whole classrooms that do not offer grade-level curricula represent a contextual factor affecting every student within that classroom, regardless of individual characteristics.

The second part of the chapter presents the sources of inequity and unequal opportunity that arise within classrooms. In the earliest work in the sociology of education, researchers focused on the academic difficulties of students of lower socioeconomic status as a major source of unequal outcomes. In other words, inequalities of outcome arose from inequalities in the human capital characteristics of individual students. More recently, the focus has shifted from the student to a contextual variable—for example, the professional preparation of the teacher affects every individual in the classroom. Instead of the teacher, I have selected as a contextual factor features of the social system of the classroom that mediate the effects of the teacher on the achievement and the effort of the students. For example, the status orders that develop in the classroom are an important feature of the social system; differences in academic status and in peer status within the classroom are a major source of inequity among the students. Having low academic status can inhibit participation and learning. For children entering school without a middle-class repertoire, the typical school curriculum presents additional sources of inequity. Because of their difficulty with the curriculum, such children not only fail to grasp basic skills in the early elementary years, but they are likely to take up places on the bottom of the academic status order in the social system of the classroom. As a result of this interaction between individual repertoire, the typical curriculum, and the status order of the classroom, too many children are never able to catch up with their more successful peers.

The third and final section of the chapter reports on a body of research conducted by my colleagues and myself using a sociological approach to the creation of equitable classrooms. This research is a conscious attempt to alter the social system of the classroom along with the curriculum in order to defeat the process by which educational outcomes mirror the social inequalities among individuals, both those with which they enter school and those that develop within the classroom. Increasing heterogeneity of classroom populations greatly heightens the challenge of creating equitable classrooms. Working toward equity in the heterogeneous classroom requires a change in curriculum materials, a change in instructional strategies, and a direct attempt to change differential expectations for competence that lead to status differences. We have studied both the implementation and the effect of a combination of these changes on students' participation and achievement. I summarize the outcomes of this research.

UNEQUAL SCHOOLS AND CLASSROOMS

Let us start with the contextual factor of classrooms where all the pupils do not have the same opportunities to learn as students in more fortunate circumstances. In order to locate these sources of inequality, one should ask questions such as these: Is this classroom in a school filled with students from poverty-stricken homes and marked by a poor academic and disciplinary climate? Does this classroom contain many students who are English language learners and who come from minority groups in the society with a history of discrimination? Is this a lower track classroom where the nature of the curriculum is significantly watered down in comparison to higher track classrooms? And finally, are the reading scores of most of the students in this classroom far below grade level so that there are few students who can serve as academic resources among the classmates?

Segregated High-Poverty Schools

The most problematic schools in the United States are in segregated areas where the poorest people live—in isolated rural communities and in poor central city neighborhoods (Cohen, 1996). A report from Harvard's Project on School Desegregation (Orfield, Bachmeier, James, & Eitle, 1997) showed that the racial and ethnic segregation of African–American and Latino students has produced a deepening isolation from middle-class students and from successful schools. Latino students now experience more isolation from Whites and more concentration in high-poverty schools than any other group of students (Orfield et al., 1997, p. 2).

The analyses of the Harvard report (Orfield et al., 1997) also demonstrate that this pattern of segregation is not simply racial separation, but it is segregation by class and by educational background of the family and the community as well. Whereas 5% of the nation's segregated White schools face conditions of concentrated poverty among their students, more than 80% of segregated African–American and Latino schools are high-poverty schools. The investigators reported that the correlation between the percentage of African–American and Latino enrollment and the percentage of students receiving free lunches is .72. Thus, racially segregated schools are very likely to be economically segregated as well.

According to the Harvard report (Orfield et al., 1997) high-poverty schools, quite aside from the educational characteristics of the students in such schools, face important differences at an organizational level. These schools have to devote far more time and resources to family and to health crises, to children who come without proficiency in English, to seriously disturbed children, to children with no educational materials in their homes, and to many children with weak educational preparation. These schools tend to draw less qualified teachers and to hold them for shorter periods of time. In urban secondary schools where more than 50% of the students are eligible for free lunch, *Education Week*, in a special supplement called *Quality Counts* (1998), reported that 45% of the mathematics teachers did not major or minor in mathematics while in college.

In urban districts of the United States, 53% of the students are in high-poverty schools, whereas in nonurban districts the figure is 22% (*Quality Counts*, 1998) Academic achievement in high-poverty inner-city schools is lower than that in high-poverty schools in nonurban settings. Using data from the National Assessment of Educational Progress (NAEP) test of 1994, *Education Week* (*Quality Counts*, 1998) illustrated how something about the high-poverty school in the urban setting seems to drag performance down. Only 23% of students in high-poverty urban schools met the basic criterion in reading as compared to 46% of students in high poverty schools in nonurban districts. The parallel comparisons for mathematics are 33% versus 61% and for science, 31% versus 56%. By the simple expedient of visiting schools in places like East St. Louis and Camden, New Jersey, Kozol, in his widely read book, *Savage Inequalities* (1991), did much to bring out the terrible inequities of some inner-city schools.

Research on the National Education Longitudinal Study (NELS; Horn & Hafner, 1992) database revealed specific deficiencies in some rural schools that have clear implications for opportunities to learn in science. An analysis of eighth-grade mathematics and science instruction found that 24.9% of rural eighth-grade students have science classes where experiments are never conducted. The equivalent figures are 17% for suburban students and 20.6% for urban students (Horn & Hafner). Rural students are more likely to have a science teacher with neither a major nor a minor in science (21.3%) in comparison to suburban students (12.8%) or urban students (19.9%; Horn & Hafner, p. 29).

In review, school context is more than the sum total of the characteristics of the individual learners. Differences in social context include differences in the preparation of teachers, very different physical facilities, and different allocation of staff time and attention, as well as compositional effects arising from the total makeup of the school population.

Linguistic Segregation

The total number of English learners has rapidly increased in the K–12 population since 1990. August and Hakuta (1997) reported that in 1991, the number of English-language learners in grades k–12 was 2,314,079. These students represent more than 100 language groups who come to school each year unable to speak or to understand the language of instruction. For many of these students, failure to learn English promptly and thus to master content in science, in mathematics, and in social studies leads to detrimental educational outcomes.

Although the educational literature treats this problem most frequently as if it were a deficiency of the individual student, English learners are much more concentrated in the problematic schools just described. Most English learners are in early elementary grades and they are overwhelmingly from disadvantaged backgrounds of low socio-economic status. A large percentage of English-language learners attend schools where a high proportion (75%–100%)

of the students are in poverty (August & Hakuta, 1997). Moreover, there is an increase in linguistic segregation over time, especially among Hispanics (Donato, Menchaca, & Valencia, 1991) so that many young students are in classes where there are no native English speakers except for possibly the teacher. The lack of peers who speak English well, who could serve as linguistic models, constitutes a contextual barrier to the learning of English. Eugene Garcia (1991) concluded from a review of research on second language acquisition that highly segregated Chicano classrooms deprive English learners of a critical mode of language learning—natural conversations in which the learner receives the necessary input and structures that promote second language acquisition. When English learners are placed in English as a Second Language (ESL) classes, they fall behind in academic subjects because the focus is on language acquisition without content. This combination of linguistic and socioeconomic segregation leads to marked reduction in the quality and quantity of instruction in school subjects, a factor that affects every child in the class.

Tracking and Classroom Inequalities

Classroom inequalities also arise as a result of tracking or streaming within schools. Sociologists of education have been prominent in demonstrating that students in low-track classes do worse than equivalent students in mixed-achievement settings (Kerckhoff, 1986; Cakes, 1985; Vanfossen, Jones, & Spade, 1987). Sociologists of education see these effects of school structure as a major mechanism by which schools reproduce in the next generation the inequalities in power and resources of the adult generation.

A number of studies have documented differences in curriculum and in instruction occurring between tracks. Braddock and Williams (1996) summarized some of this research:

> At present, different curricula are provided to different students as a way to deal with the diversity of student abilities, especially in the middle and high school grades. . . . This often means that below average students are not offered as many courses in science and foreign languages or are enrolled in math and English classes that deemphasize key units in algebra and writing that are prerequisites for advanced work in later grades. (p. 104)

Gamoran (1989) argued that the primary link between school stratification and achievement are the contextual variables of differential instruction in stratified classrooms. Grouping itself does not produce achievement—teaching does. Once students are in different groups and tracks, they experience different curricula and a different quality of instruction (Gamoran & Berends, 1987; Nystrand & Gamoran, 1988; Oakes, 1985). However, Gamoran (1989) also pointed out that tracking does not necessarily lead to curriculum differentiation; he described research on counterexamples, particularly in Catholic schools, in which tracking does not lead to lower academic standards.

It is one thing to document differences in curriculum and in instruction between tracks or schools, but it is much more difficult to demonstrate that these differences affect the achievement of students in classrooms while holding constant the individual characteristics of those students. Hoffer and Gamoran (1993) were successful in demonstrating at the classroom level the effects of differences in instruction in specific high-ability and low-ability middle school classrooms. They used longitudinal data on middle school achievement in mathematics and in science as well as multiple controls on early achievement. The use of "inquiry-based" instruction, lectures, and small-group projects in high-track classes accounted for the largest part of the effect of track in science on achievement. The instructional variables that accounted for the largest part of the effects of tracking on mathematics achievement included emphases on problem solving and on understanding principles (as opposed to computational mechanics), the pacing of the course, and the use of lectures. These instructional features were more common in high-track classes. Altogether, instructional variables in the achievement models accounted for 75 % of the high-ability group effects on science achievement, and from 17% to 33% of the effects on mathematics achievement.

Composition of the Classroom

Still another contextual source of classroom inequalities is the lack of academic resources available among the students. Dar and Resh (1986) showed with Israeli data that the composition of the class, as measured by the distribution of achievement, was a powerful predictor of the individual's achievement, holding constant characteristics of the individual learner. For these investigators, the achievement of members of the classroom (the composition) represents the richness of the learning environment. Reviewing recent studies that are more theory oriented, including studies using hierarchical linear modeling (HLM) procedures, Dar and Resh (1997) found that classroom composition consistently affects student performance. In other words, the presence of students who can act as academic resources for their classmates is an important factor in improving achievement.

Sociologists have found it very difficult to document the compositional effects of schools and of classrooms made up of low achievers. Disentangling the effects of individual characteristics from these contextual effects presents a major methodological problem. Dar and Resh (1997) provided an excellent treatment of the limitations of using the composition of the classroom as a predictor variable in an analysis of achievement at the individual level (p. 200). This same methodological problem at the school level was probably responsible for the failure of early research that used the composition of the school as a predictor of achievement. Additionally, this failure no doubt led to the abandonment of the attempt to document the contextual effects of attending a segregated inner-city school independent of the effects of most of the individual students having a low-SES or a minority background.

HLM analysis shows great promise in disentangling individual effects from classroom and school compositional effects. For example, Lee and Croninger (1996) carried out an HLM analysis with NELS data of between-school variance in the proportion of students who feel safe at their school. Schools with low average SES and schools with high enrollments of minority students were particularly likely to have large proportions of students who did not feel safe in school, holding constant the propensity of individuals of this background to report feeling unsafe. The results suggest that the social stratification process in U.S. schools whereby minority and low-SES students are "packed" into high schools with students similar to themselves has serious negative effects on feelings of personal safety. Safety in schools would seem like a minimum necessary condition for successful educational achievement.

This section began with a series of questions one might ask to locate sources of inequality that are based on the location and composition of the classroom and the school. If the answer to any of these questions is "yes," then there are negative educational outcomes that are associated with each of these conditions: high-poverty schools (especially those in the inner city), linguistic segregation, curriculum differentiation in lower track classrooms, and lack of academic resources in the composition of the classroom. Future research in the sociology of education should explicate and study a *process* by which contextual variables are translated into individual educational success and failure. For example, what is it about high-poverty urban schools that makes them so much more problematic than high-poverty nonurban schools? Exactly which features of low-track classrooms lead to depressed rates of academic achievement and how do these features operate? Sociologists of education have done very little to study the phenomenon of linguistic segregation and the segregation of English learners into ESL classes. How and why do these practices retard educational achievement?

INEQUALITY AND THE SOCIAL SYSTEM OF THE CLASSROOM

To understand what happens to individuals in the schools, it is necessary to consider multiple levels of social context ranging from societal stratification to the social system of the classroom. In addition to the direct effects of the stratification system on the school one attends, inequity in the larger society has an indirect effect on opportunities *within* the classroom. Powerful social systems of the classroom mediate the effects of social stratification on achievement.

Task and Evaluation Practices

The task and evaluation practices of a classroom help to build inequity through a process of social comparison in which students see each other arrayed on a single dimension of ability in schoolwork. Students form ideas about their own ability by comparing themselves to each other as they complete tasks and when they hear teachers make public evaluations (Rosenholtz & Simpson, 1984). Standardized tasks encourage a process of social comparison in which students evaluate how well they are doing in completing assignments rapidly and successfully. Emphasis on marking and on grading has the same effect, giving students objective grounds for deciding where each person stands on academic ability and on achievement. The net result of this process of social comparison is a rank order agreed upon by teachers and by students on the relative "smartness" of each member of the class. The high level of agreement among peers and between students and teachers on ranking of reading ability or academic ability illustrates the consensual nature of this construct of intellectual ability (Rosenholtz & Wilson, 1980; Simpson, 1981).

Rosenholtz and Simpson (1984) stressed the "dimensionality" of classroom organization. Unidimensional organization of instruction establishes conditions that facilitate "ability formation." In unidimensional classrooms, daily activities encourage comparison, and they imply a single underlying dimension of ability. Thus, students' perceptions of ability become one-dimensional.

The first feature of unidimensional classrooms is an undifferentiated academic task structure. All students work on similar tasks or with a narrow range of materials and methods. For example, unidimensional classes require reading for successful performance of most tasks and rely mostly on paper-and-pencil tasks. A second feature of unidimensional classrooms is a low level of student autonomy, reducing the variety of tasks and preventing students from using their own evaluations of performance. Third, unidimensional classrooms use whole-class instruction or clear-cut ability groups. A final feature is the emphasis on grading to convey clear-cut, unidimensional evaluation by teachers.

In contrast, the multidimensional classroom has varied materials and methods, a higher degree of student autonomy, more individual tasks, varied grouping patterns, and less reliance on grading. In a comparison of these two types of classrooms, researchers have found that students' self-reported ability levels have a greater variance in unidimensional classrooms (S.

J. Rosenholtz & Rosenholtz, 1981; Simpson, 1981). In multidimensional classrooms, fewer children will define themselves as being "below average" thus restricting the distribution of self-evaluations. Students' reports of their peers' ability levels are also more dispersed and more consensual (as measured by a coefficient of concordance) in unidimensional classes, and perceptions of individual ability are much more closely related to ratings by teachers and by peers.

There are also connections between classroom tasks and the creation of hierarchical peer status. Many classrooms exhibit an unequal number of sociometric choices; a few sociometric stars receive many choices whereas social isolates receive few or no choices. When students have more opportunity to walk around, to talk with others, to choose seats and activities, and to work in small groups, the pattern of peer status changes (Cohen, 1994; Epstein & Karweit, 1983; Hallinan, 1976). There is a less hierarchical distribution of choices and fewer social isolates and sociometric leaders.

Academic and Peer Status Orders

Some task and evaluation structures help to create clear hierarchies of academic and peer status. These status characteristics have a strong influence on behavior within groups of students working together. According to status characteristic theory (Berger, Cohen, & Zelditch, 1966; Webster & Foschi, 1988), once the socially agreed-upon rank order has formed, it is a major source of inequity. There are high expectations of competence for those who hold high rank and correspondingly low expectations of competence for those with low rank. Differential expectations become self-fulfilling prophecies, producing differential effort, participation, and performance on the part of high-ranking and low-ranking students (Cohen, 1997b). In a process of status generalization, expectations for competence attached to states of the status characteristic are activated and form the basis of expectations for competence on new collective tasks. Through the process of status generalization, the social context of the status system of the classroom affects the behavior of individuals.

The effects of peer status and academic status on interaction have appeared repeatedly in studies of classrooms using small groups working on collective tasks. Within classroom groups of students working cooperatively, those students who had higher academic and peer status were more active on the task than those who had lower academic and peer status (Cohen, 1997b).

Theoretically, it is clear why academic status has such a strong effect. It has a direct path of relevance to the academic tasks of the classroom and will thus be more powerful than other status characteristics that are not directly relevant. It is less clear why peer status is so powerful, especially in the middle school when it begins to operate independently of academic status in many classrooms. The correlation of peer and academic status measures is often close to zero in middle school classrooms, whereas the relationship between the two dimensions of status is highly positive in elementary schools (Cohen, 1997b).

The issue of academic status and peer status orders within the classroom is a very serious one with respect to the equality of opportunity. Those who hold low status will put out less effort and participate less. As a result, they will have less access to interaction with their classmates and less access to any shared materials. Access to interaction is critical in a classroom featuring cooperative learning. Because cooperative learning leads to an increase in friendliness and in trust, it is the most common recommendation for instruction in multiracial and in multilingual classrooms. However, as we have just seen, cooperative learning can activate status problems, and status problems lead to differential interaction and influence among the students that affect achievement. Those who talk more learn more. The net result of the process of status generalization is observable in tests of achievement.

In studies of classrooms using open-ended group tasks, the amount of interaction whether at the individual level or at the classroom level is a powerful predictor of learning outcomes. For students engaged in true group tasks involving ill-structured problems, this proposition holds at the elementary and the middle school levels and for a variety of subject matters. True group tasks are those tasks that an individual working alone could not complete successfully. Ill-structured problems are open-ended tasks where there are no standard procedures. At the elementary school level, the more students in a classroom talked and worked together, the higher were their gains on the standardized achievement test in mathematics ($r = .72, p < .05$ for 1982–1983 and $r = .52, p < .05$ for 1984–1985; Cohen, Lotan, & Holthuis, 1997). In Israel, Ben-Ari (1977) found that the process of students talking and working together on challenging group tasks even leads to significant gains on a measure of intellectual ability, a standardized test of reasoning. At the middle school, the higher the percentage of and working together, the greater were the gain scores on a social studies test ($r = .50, p < .01$).

These findings are at the classroom level, but the relationship between lateral communication and achievement also holds at the individual level. Those who talk more in small groups working on true group tasks that require exchange of ideas learn more (Cohen, 1997a). Leechor (1988) found that the student's average rate of task-related talk was a significant predictor of posttest score, holding constant pretest score and student status (p. 119). In a study of 56 students in sixth-grade science classes using challenging group tasks (Bianchini, 1995), the correlation between the average rate of talk and a gain score summed over several unit tests was $r = .453, p < .001$).

Effects of Race, Ethnicity, and Gender

Academic status and peer status are only two of the status characteristics that affect interaction and influence in small groups. Race, gender, and ethnicity are diffuse status characteristics that have the same effects on small-group interaction as do local status characteristics such as peer status and academic status. When a mixed-status group undertakes a collective task Whites, Anglos, and males are more influential than African–Americans, Latinos who look visibly different, and females (Cohen, 1982; Ridgeway & Diekma, 1992).

Diffuse status characteristics would seem to have the greatest potential for affecting small-group interaction in the classroom. However, inequity in the larger society has no simple and direct reflection in student interaction in classrooms with diverse populations. Classroom social systems generate their own inequities and can mediate the effects of the larger society. Although Whites dominate African–Americans economically, politically, and socially in U.S. society, White students will not necessarily dominate African–American students in the classroom.

Although gender acts as a status characteristic in adult society, Lockheed, Harris and Nemceff (1983) and Leal-Idrogo (1997) found that gender has no effect on interaction in collective tasks at the elementary school ages. There are many contemporary scholars who will argue that girls and boys do not experience equal opportunities in the classroom. It should be noted that I am discussing the specific operation of gender as a diffuse status characteristic in the context of peer interaction. This finding does not contradict the well-documented empirical generalization that teachers interact more frequently with boys than with girls.

There is some evidence that dialects spoken by the student act as a diffuse status characteristic, activating low expectations for competence by teachers. Research by Harrison cited in Garcia (1993, p. 58) indicates that dialects spoken by students influence teachers' perceptions of their academic ability, the students' learning opportunities, evaluations of their contributions to the class, and the way they are grouped for instruction.

In heterogeneous middle school classrooms on a combined sociometric measure of peer and academic status, African–Americans, Latinos, and young women were just as likely to be high status as Anglos, Asians, and young men (Cohen, 1997b). The effects of gender and ethnicity on interaction only appeared for those young women and minority students who were already low on peer and academic status. Among students who were low on the measure of peer and academic status, the female, African–American, and Latino students were less active than the Angles and the males. The least active in interaction were the minority females who were low on academic and peer status.

Social Background and Achievement

One of the oldest and most reliable findings in the sociology of education is the relationship between SES of the family, race, ethnicity, and academic achievement. Clearly, there is some mechanism by which differences in family background translate into individual success and failure in the classroom, starting in the early grades.

To solve this classic problem, I believe that it is necessary to turn to two areas of research in the sociology of education. The first of these has to do with human capital characteristics of the individual and stems from preschool preparation of students from different social classes and the linguistic, academic, and cultural repertoire of the child on entering school. The second area is contextual and has to do with the conventional curriculum and the success of students with different repertoires in acquiring basic skills in the early grades.

When children from parents with little formal education enter school, they do not come with the same repertoire of preliteracy and prenumeracy skills or of other types of cultural capital as do children of parents with more schooling. The repertoire of middle-class students is a much closer match to the school's curriculum than the repertoire of lower class students.

These differences in repertoire are evidently more complex than the presence or absence of preschool coaching in letters, in numbers, in vocabulary, and in literacy given by most well-educated parents. Laosa and Henderson (1991) found that parents with little formal education, whether they are recent immigrants from Mexico or native-born non-Hispanic whites, tend to teach their children with demonstration and physical modeling rather than with conversation and positive verbal reinforcement. They concluded that children of the more highly schooled parents learn to master in their homes the form and dynamics of teaching and learning processes that "take after" those of the school classroom, thereby gaining a decided academic advantage over the children of the less-schooled parents (p. 171).

George Farkas (1996) studied early cognitive skills of African–American, Latino and Anglo children in Dallas, Texas and was able to demonstrate the connection between exposure to mainstream English among African–American children and success in learning to read. The entry in a regression of early cognitive skill measures of auditory processing—the ability to fluently comprehend patterns among auditory stimuli—apparently accounted for the effect of race on early reading achievement. The two auditory processing variables measure the ability to extract standard English words from audiotape sounds. They are likely to be strongly affected by the extent to which the child has been immersed in standard English.

Curriculum as a Source of Inequity

Differences in repertoire translate into differential readiness to learn reading and arithmetic. Thus, what begins as an individual difference in repertoire associated with social class, race, and ethnicity translates into a difference in achievement in the primary grades. The curriculum with its emphasis on reading skills in every subject contributes to the growing inequity. Students who have not mastered basic skills in reading and computation in the early grades are very likely to compile a record of academic failure as they advance through the school system.

The cumulative impact of weak reading skills was shown in a study of middle school students in Dallas. Farkas (1996) used as a dependent variable a content-referenced test that measured coursework mastery in social studies. A test of basic skills given in the middle school was the most powerful predictor of coursework mastery in the middle school. Using a detailed measure of reading skill in a regression, he was able to eliminate the negative effects of being African–American or Latino on coursework mastery. From this work, Farkas concluded that an early attack on the development of reading skills is the single best intervention.

Insofar as differences in social background result in differences in achievement within a classroom, students from lower socioeconomic backgrounds are somewhat more likely to have low academic status than students from higher socioeconomic backgrounds. Because elementary curriculum relies so heavily on reading skills, those who are slower to master reading are seen as less able in schoolwork. Classmates have low expectations for their competence at a wide variety of school tasks. Failure to master basic skills not only handicaps the student's academic performance but is likely to place that student on the bottom of the academic status order.

Still another source of inequity arises from the response of educational decision-makers to students whom they perceive to be more and less "able." Teachers do not expect students who are weak in the basic skills to be able to grasp more advanced concepts at the same pace as their classmates. They often report that such students have a general deficiency in abstract thinking. They may place them in low-ability groups where the curriculum is presented at a slower pace. As a result, the student is unable to catch up and perform at grade level. Once students from poorer backgrounds achieve at a lower level in the basic skills, teachers respond directly to differences in academic achievement rather than to class, race, or ethnicity (Mercer, Iadacola, & Moore, 1980).

In review, children enter school with differential preparation for academic success. Differences in repertoire interact with conventional curricula and with academic status systems to produce academic failure for many children from low-SES backgrounds. I have painted a picture of a hypothetical process. I have presented evidence suggesting many of the links in this series of hypothesized, causal connections, but researchers have still to explicate and document the multistage, multivariate process of school achievement.

CREATING EQUITY IN HETEROGENEOUS CLASSROOMS

The moves to eliminate tracking (particularly in some middle schools), to foster inclusion of previously segregated special education students, and to eliminate curriculum differentiation in order to teach to statewide standards have increased the academic heterogeneity within classrooms. Creating an equitable classroom with students who represent a wide academic range is especially challenging for teachers. If teachers want to set high standards and teach at a high level, they run the risk of having a large number of low-achieving students fail. If teachers "dumb down" the curriculum in order to reach the low-achieving students, the high-achieving students are restless and bored and their parents are understandably angry. If teachers compromise and teach to an "average-achieving" student, they neither challenge the high achiever nor successfully reach the low achiever.

From their studies of the negative effects of low tracks, sociologists of education have recommended doing away with curriculum differentiation. However, this can leave teachers facing heterogeneous classrooms with the dilemma just described. The status systems that were supposedly eliminated with the abandonment of tracking can easily be reconstituted in heterogeneous classrooms. The wider the academic range in the classroom, the more severe will be the status problems (Cohen & Lotan, 1997, p. 84).

Defining an Equitable Classroom

Creating an equitable classroom requires more than simple elimination of the various sources of inequity discussed previously. It is necessary to develop a model of the observable features of the desired goal (Cohen, 1997a). In an equitable classroom, teachers and students view each student as capable of learning both basic skills and high-level concepts. All students have equal access to challenging learning materials; the teacher does not deprive certain students of tasks demanding higher order thinking because they are not ready; classmates do not block access to instructional materials or prevent others from using manipulatives. Students who cannot read or understand the language of instruction have opportunities to complete activities and to use materials. The interaction among students is "equal-status," that is, all students are active and influential participants and their opinions matter to their fellow students.

Finally, the achievement of students does not vary widely between the academically stronger and weaker students. Whereas the more successful students continue to do well, the less successful students are much more closely clustered around the mean achievement of the classroom rather than trailing far out on the failing end of the distribution. Thus there is a higher mean and a lower variance of achievement scores in more equitable classrooms as compared to less equitable classrooms.

A Working Model of an Equitable Classroom

In the previous section, I reviewed the theory and research connecting the development of status orders in the classroom to the way the teacher organizes instruction. I also pointed out the role of the conventional curriculum in aggravating the effects of social stratification on educational achievement. Using this theoretical base, the creation of an equitable classroom requires changes in the task and the evaluation structure and changes in the curriculum, as well as a direct treatment of status problems.

There are actually two reasons why the task and the evaluation structure must change. The first lies in the power of task and evaluation structure to create strong academic status orders. By changing the simple task structure of the unidimensional classroom so that groups of students carry out noncomparable tasks, there will be fewer invidious comparisons. As in the multidimensional classroom conceptualized by Rosenholtz and Simpson (1984), the students have more autonomy if the tasks are open ended and permit the students to choose how they will attack and solve problems. Evaluation can include much more feedback than is available through marks and grades. Groups can make formal presentations of their products that provide an occasion for feedback from the teacher and from the rest of the class. Students can write individual reports on questions they discussed in the group, and these also can be a rich source of feedback.

If the objective is to provide all students with access to intellectually challenging tasks, there is a second reason for changing the task structure. If the learning tasks are challenging, but the students represent very different levels of achievement, it will be necessary for students to use each other as resources. By assigning tasks to groups rather than to individuals, the group as a whole can function at a higher level than each of its members can manage individually.

To create an equitable classroom, it is also necessary to do something about the ordinary curriculum. Without neglecting basic skills, one can broaden the curriculum so that a wider variety of skills and abilities will be relevant. Curriculum can reflect the view of human intelligence as multidimensional (Gardner, 1983). If the groups work on challenging tasks that require both basic skills and a wide variety of human intellectual skills and abilities, then different students will be able to make different contributions. The low-achieving student will not be barred from access to higher level thinking by difficulty in reading or in computing. At the same time, that low-achieving student may be able to make an important contribution to a group product such as a role play, a physical model, or a mural.

Theoretically, a mixed-status group working on a collective task, no matter how many skills and abilities it requires, will activate the process of status generalization. Even in classrooms with carefully designed multiple-ability tasks there are marked status effects among students working on such tasks (Cohen, 1997b). Unless the teacher intervenes, one will not see equal-status interaction in the heterogeneous classroom. It is necessary to treat different competence expectations for low-status and for high-status students directly. The use of rich multiple-ability group tasks as part of the curricula is a necessary but not a sufficient condition for raising expectations for competence for low-status students.

My colleagues and I have developed several treatments for this problem, derived from Status Characteristic Theory. One is the Multiple Ability Treatment in which the teacher convinces the students that many different intellectual abilities are required by the task. Moreover, the teacher explains that no students will excel at all these abilities and that each student will excel on some of the abilities. If the teacher is successful in convincing the students that this is the case, then each student develops a *mixed set of expectations* for competence rather than a uniformly high or low set of expectations. Because people aggregate all expectations for competence in assigning expectations for a new collective task (Berger & Conner, 1974), the net result is everyone's holding a set of mixed expectations, thereby lessening the difference in expected competence between high-status and low-status students.

Another treatment, "Assigning Competence to Low-Status Students," requires careful observation of the low-status students as they work on group tasks requiring multiple abilities. The teacher observes the low-status student when he or she makes a contribution to the task, demonstrating some intellectual skill or ability. Generally, these are very concrete and specific abilities such as "keen observation of the experiment," "figuring out how the model will fit together," or "understanding how a character in the story really felt." The teacher publicly comments on the ability or skill that has been demonstrated by the low-status student, making sure the other students understand that the low-status student has shown an important ability. Because the status problem resides not only in the lack of expectations for competence held by the low-status students themselves, but in the same lack of expectations for competence held by other students for the low-status students, it is necessary to treat everyone's expectations. The teacher must also make the ability relevant to the task at hand, so that everyone understands that the ability demonstrated is an important resource for the group. Theoretically, the teacher is using his or her standing as a high-status source of evaluation to assign to the low-status student a high level of competence on a specific status characteristic. By making the competence directly relevant to the task, the teacher strengthens the assignment of competence (for more detailed explications of these treatments, see Cohen, 1994; Cohen & Lotan, 1997).

In a lengthy program of research and evaluation, a working model of these changes, called "Complex Instruction," has been implemented in many heterogeneous classrooms in the United States, in Israel, and in Europe. Complex instruction is an umbrella label for a set of propositions on creating equitable classrooms. Using these basic sociological ideas, we have created a workable model that can be adapted to a wide range of school conditions. So that students working in small groups can use each other as resources, it has been necessary to change the organization of the classroom. Teachers learn how to delegate authority to groups while holding individuals and groups accountable for their performance. Student groups are heterogeneously composed and stay together for a unit during which time they move through most if not all of the group tasks, typically completing one during each class session.

It has also been necessary to develop model curricular units that embody multiple abilities and permit students to grasp difficult central concepts by rotating through multiple group tasks, each providing a different way to understand the central concept. At any given moment, different groups are working on different and noncomparable tasks. These curricula have been developed for the elementary school in mathematics and in science and for the middle school in human biology, in social studies, and in mathematics. Each unit is based on a central concept or "big idea" and includes activity cards and individual report forms for approximately six groups of five students each (Lotan, 1997).

Finally, it has been necessary to teach teachers the sociological theory and research on the organization of the classroom and the design of the status treatments (Ellis & Lotan, 1997). The teacher's grasp of the underlying concepts clearly predicts the quality of implementation. Attaining a good understanding of the underlying principles, in turn, requires repeated classroom observations and systematic feedback from and discussion with a staff developer.

Findings

If opportunities have been equalized, then there should be a significant gain in achievement. In an evaluation of complex instruction in the elementary school in 1982 to 1983, a standardized test of mathematics achievement was administered before and after the children experienced *Finding Out/Descubrimento* (FO/D), a bilingual curriculum designed to develop thinking skills, employing concepts in mathematics and science (Cohen, Bianchini, et al., 1997). In addition, the tests were administered to a set of comparison students who were also in bilingual education classrooms in the same schools but who did not experience complex instruction. For Total Math scores and for the score on the computation subscale, FO/D students moved from the 25th percentile of a nationally normed population to grade level or 50th percentile. Comparison students also gained relative to the nationally normed population, but the FO/D students showed significantly greater gains in Math Computation and in Total Math scores.

In 1992 to 1993, a set of social studies classrooms using specially constructed multiple-ability units and complex instruction strategies was compared to other classrooms in the same schools that were covering the same period in the textbook but did not have access to the special curricular units or to training in the instructional strategies of complex instruction (Cohen, Bianchini, Cossey, Holthuis, Morphew, and Whitcomb, 1997). Before and after the units, students took a content-referenced test including only those items that the students in the comparison classrooms could have learned from a study of the required textbook. Being in a complex instruction classroom versus a comparison classroom had significant favorable effects on test items requiring higher order thinking. The two sets of classrooms showed no difference in gains on the more factual items.

There is no conflict between the acquisition of basic skills and a curriculum focused on higher order thinking and problem-solving skills. In the FO/D curriculum, multiple evaluations revealed that the gains in computation were among the largest and always accompanied the gains in word problems and in math concepts. In social studies, the complex instruction classrooms did just as well on factual items as the comparison classrooms but performed better on items that involved analogies, a challenging example of higher order thinking.

Equitable classrooms should show favorable achievement gains in a wide variety of subjects and across different age groups. The early elementary students working with FO/D made significant gains in the mathematics and science scales on standardized achievement tests (Cohen et al., 1997). Middle school students in complex instruction classrooms using multiple-ability units made significant gains in social studies in mathematics, and in human biology (Cohen et al., 1997).

If an equitable classroom has been created, there should be a change in the distribution of achievement over time in which the average performance improves and the variance declines. The previous evidence attests to the increase in average performance. For two data sets of elementary school children who had experienced complex instruction, Cohen, Lotan, and Leechor (1989) calculated a measure of the reduction in the variance of test scores from fall to spring using coefficients of variation for the two data sets. Using standardized tests as a measure of achievement, there was one calculation for Math Concepts and Application and another for Computation. In all classrooms, the coefficients of variation were smaller for the posttest scores than for the pretest scores. In other words, there was a consistent decrease in the variance of achievement scores over time. Moreover, the change in the distribution of achievement is linked to changes in task structure and in student interaction. In this same study, the percentage of students talking and working together predicted a reduction in the coefficient of variation in the posttest scores on math concepts and applications.

As the curriculum is broadened to include multiple abilities, formerly low-achieving students will gain access to both factual and conceptual material. Evidence for this proposition comes from Bowers' (1997) classroom experiment. Working with secondary school social studies teachers, Bower developed two types of units covering the same topics. One set of units featured use of primary historical sources and utilized abilities that were primarily linguistic (reading, writing, and discussion). The other set of units featured multiple intellectual abilities. Students prepared skits, dialogues, and pantomimes. They analyzed political cartoons and also prepared multimedia presentations. Each teacher acted as his or her own control and taught the contrasting treatments in different classes. All students were carefully prepared for cooperative learning; all students heard the same introductory lectures (although the multiple-ability treatment used slides in connection with the lectures); and all students studied the same textbook chapters and worked with the same concepts and guiding questions. Bower measured achievement with a content-referenced test of mastery of knowledge of U.S. history in the period from 1919 to 1930. The test was administered before and after the experimental units.

Results showed a significantly higher mean gain for the multiple ability treatment than for the linguistic treatment. The linguistic treatment resulted in a statistically significant gap in achievement on the posttest between high-status and low-status students, whereas the multiple ability treatment did not produce such a gap. Thus the linguistic treatment exacerbated achievement differences by status, whereas the low-status students in the multiple-ability treatment did particularly well. The possibility of multiple ways to understand and to demonstrate knowledge of historical concepts was of particular advantage to the low-achieving students. Nonetheless, they were able to demonstrate their increasing knowledge on a paper-and-pencil test with multiple-choice items and in their written essays.

With a measure of the rate of direct supervision by the teacher (a negative measure of delegation of authority), three different studies found a negative relationship between direct supervision and the percentage of students talking and working together (Cohen, Lotan, & Holthuis, 1997). In other words, when teachers failed to delegate authority to groups, the result was a decreased level of interaction and weaker achievement gains in three different studies.

Finally, in an equitable classroom, a direct attempt to boost competence expectations of low-status students will provide low-status students with more access to interaction. In 13 elementary classrooms in 1984 to 1985 where complex instruction was implemented, Lotan and I (Cohen & Lotan, 1995) measured the frequency with which teachers used the two status treatments described previously. This design focused on the natural variation in the extent to which trained teachers implemented status treatments. The more frequently the teachers used these treatments, the higher was the rate of participation of low-status students in their small groups.

For each classroom we calculated an index of status problems by correlating each student's status score with his or her observed rate of interaction in small groups. The status score was based on the number of choices each student received on a questionnaire as being the best in math and science and on the number of friendship choices received. After standardizing the percentage of choices received according to quintiles of the classroom distribution, each student was given a score of 5 (*high*) to 1 (*low*), indicating the relative percentage of choices received for each of the two status characteristics. For a single measure of status, we added the two status scores together to form a single "costatus score" ranging from 2 to 10. We added them together because, according to the theory, participants aggregate status information (Berger & Conner, 1974).

The index of status problems was related to the standard deviation of reading achievement for each classroom; the wider the range on reading achievement, the more severe were the observed status problems. Holding this variable constant, the rate at which the teacher used the status treatments was *negatively* related to the index of status problems. Those teachers who implemented the status treatments more frequently had classrooms where a student's status was more weakly related to his or her interaction in the group. In classrooms where teachers failed to implement status treatments with any frequency, there was a statistically significant relationship between a student's costatus score and the frequency with which the observers scored his or her task-related participation in a group.

CONCLUSION

We have experienced some success in creating equitable classrooms by altering the social system of the classroom. With these changes in context, we are able to do much to equalize educational outcomes in the short term. However, these changes in classroom context do not, by themselves, alter the larger social context of the school that I have argued is also a major source of inequality.

One cannot pick a school at random and find success in altering the social system of the classroom. Research has shown the importance of a supportive principal for introducing innovation. Moreover, large urban school districts present a number of special difficulties in implementing equitable classrooms. First, they often do not have a wide academic range in their classrooms. Most of the students may read far below grade level. Without academic resources in each group, it is difficult to implement a demanding curriculum with academic as well as other intellectual requirements. Second, there are more classrooms (and even whole schools) with discipline problems where it is not possible to introduce delegation of authority to groups. Third, there is more rapid turnover of both principals and teachers that can vitiate innovations soon after they are implemented. Lastly, many large urban school districts are quite resistant to working with innovations that do not arise from their own internal political processes.

These limitations illustrate a central theme: although it is possible to create equality of opportunity within classrooms containing many students from low-SES backgrounds, there is no panacea that will eliminate inequalities of educational opportunity in all schools under all conditions. To improve the educational outcomes for children in difficult settings will require a concerted effort to explicate the complex social processes operating in our changing society. For example, to understand what is happening to performance in high-poverty urban schools will require a conceptualization of the interplay between the working of the schools and the classrooms and the bureaucratic difficulties faced by very large urban districts in communities with a high concentration of unemployed families struggling to survive. Only in this way will we have sufficient knowledge to make recommendations concerning equality of educational opportunity in the inner-city classrooms.

Explicating these fundamental social processes will also require an integration of the contextual and individual level of analysis. For example, for those who study the effects of class and race on the comparative success of students in academically and socially heterogeneous settings, it will be necessary to understand more about the process by which success and failure develops for these children in the early elementary years. It is not enough to look at the "deficits of either lower class students or of teachers of these students. Rather, we must understand the interplay of the stratification system with the curriculum, the organization of the classroom, and the status orders within the classroom social system. The sociology of education has come a long way in understanding different sources of inequality of educational opportunity. As we move further into explanation as opposed to documentation, and as we move from theoretical research to applied research on intervention, we will discover the power and the potential of our theories and research tools.

REFERENCES

August, D., & Hakuta, K. (Eds., 1997). *Improving schooling for language-minority children: A research agenda.* Washington, DC: National Academy Press.

Ben-Ari, R. (1997). Complex instruction and cognitive development. In E. G. Cohen & R. A. Lotan (Eds.), *Working for equity in heterogeneous classrooms: Sociological theory in practice* (pp. 193–206). New York: Teachers College Press.

Berger, J. B., Cohen, B. P., & Zelditch, M., Jr. (1966). Status characteristics and expectation states. In J. Berger & M. Zelditch, Jr. (Eds.), *Sociological theories in progress. Vol. 1* (pp. 9–46). Boston: Houghton Mifflin.

Berger, J. B., & Conner, T. L. (1974). Performance expectations and behavior in small groups: A revised formulation. In J. Berger, T. L. Conner, & H. M. Fisek (Eds.), *Expectation states theory: A theoretical research program* (pp. 85–109). Cambridge, MA: Winthrop.

Bianchini, J. (1995). *How do middle school students learn science in small groups? An analysis of scientific knowledge and social process construction*. Unpublished doctoral dissertation, Stanford University, Stanford, California.

Bower, B. (1997). Effects of the multiple-ability curriculum in secondary social studies classrooms. In E. G. Cohen & R. A. Lotan (Eds.), *Working for equity in heterogeneous classrooms: Sociological theory in practice* (pp. 117–133). New York: Teachers College Press.

Braddock, J. H., II, & Williams, M. M. (1996). Equality of educational opportunity and the Goals 2000, Educate America Act. In K. M. Borman, P. W. Cookson, Jr., A. R. Sadovnick, & J. Z. Spade (Eds.), *Implementing educational reform: Sociological perspectives on educational policy* (pp. 89–109). Norwood, NJ: Ablex.

Cohen, E. G. (1982). Expectation states and interracial interaction in school settings. *Annual Review of Sociology, 8*, 209–235.

Cohen, E. G. (1994). *Designing groupwork: Strategies for heterogeneous classrooms* (rev. ed.). New York: Teachers College Press.

Cohen, E. G. (1996). An animal guide to opportunities-to-learn standards—Response and rejoinder. In K .M. Borman, P. W. Cookson, Jr., A. R. Sadovnick, & J. Z. Spade (Eds.). *Implementing educational reform: Sociological perspectives on educational policy* (pp. 111–126). Norwood, NJ: Ablex.

Cohen, E. G. (1997a). Equity in heterogeneous classrooms: A challenge for teachers and sociologists In E. G. Cohen & R. A. Lotan (Eds.). *Working for equity in heterogeneous classrooms: Sociological theory in practice* (pp. 3–14). New York: Teachers College Press.

Cohen, E. G. (1997a). Understanding status problems: Sources and consequences. In E. G. Cohen & R. A. Lotan (Eds.). *Working for equity in heterogeneous classrooms: Sociological theory in practice* (pp. 61–76). New York: Teachers College Press.

Cohen, E. G., & Lotan, R. A. (1995). Producing equal-status interaction in the heterogeneous classroom. *American Educational Research Journal, 32*, 99–120.

Cohen, E. G., & Lotan, R. A. (1997). Raising expectations for competence: The effectiveness of status interventions. In E. G. Cohen & R. A. Lotan (Eds.). *Working for equity in heterogeneous classrooms: Sociological theory in practice* (pp. 77–91). New York: Teachers College Press.

Cohen, E. G., Lotan, R. A., & Holthuis, N. C. (1997). Organizing the classroom for learning. In E. G. Cohen & R. A. Lotan (Eds.). *Working for equity in heterogenous classrooms: Sociological theory in practice* (pp. 31–43). New York: Teachers College Press.

Cohen, E. G., Lotan, R. A., & Leechor, C. (1989). Can classrooms learn? *Sociology of Education, 62*, 75–94.

Cohen, E. G., Bianchini, J. A., Cossey, R., Holthuis, N. C., Morphew, C. C., & Whitcomb, J. A. (1997). What did students learn?: 1982–1994. In E. G. Cohen & R. A. Lotan (Eds.). *Working for equity in heterogeneous classrooms: Sociological theory in practice* (pp. 137–165). New York: Teachers College Press.

Coleman, J. S. (1990). *Equality and achievement in education*. Boulder CO: Westview Press.

Dar, Y., & Resh, N. (1986). Classroom intellectual composition and academic achievement. *American Educational Research Journal, 23*, 357–74.

Dar, Y., & Resh, N. (1997). Separating and mixing students for learning: Concepts and research. In R. Ben-Ari & Y. Rich (Eds.), *Enhancing education in heterogeneous schools: Theory and application* (pp. 191-213). Ramat Gan, Israel: Bar-Ilan Press.

Donato, R. L., Menchaca, M., & Valencia, R. R (1991). Segregation, desegregation and integration of Chicano students: Problems and prospects. In R. R. Valencia (Ed.), *Chicano school failure and success: Research and policy agendas for the 1990s* (pp. 27–63). London: Falmer Press.

Ellis, N., & Lotan, R. A. (1997). Teachers as learners: Feedback, conceptual understanding, and implementation. In E. G. Cohen & R. A. Lotan (Eds.). *Working for equity in heterogeneous classrooms: Sociological theory in practice* (pp. 209–222). New York: Teachers College Press.

Epstein, J. S., & Karweit, N. (1983). *Friends in school: Patterns of selection and influence in secondary schools*. New York: Academic Press.

Farkas, G. (1996). *Human capital or cultural capital? Ethnicity and poverty groups in an urban school district*. New York: Aldine de Gruyter.

Gamoran, A. (1989). Measuring curriculum differentiation. *American Journal of Education, 97*, 29–43.

Gamoran, A., & Berends, M. (1987). The effects of stratification in secondary schools: Synthesis of survey and ethnographic research. *Review of Educational Research, 57*, 415–435.

Garcia, E. E. (1991). Bilingualism, second language acquisition and the education of Chicano language minority students. In R. R. Valencia (Ed.), *Chicano school failure and success: Research and policy agendas for the 1990s* (pp. 93–118). London: Falmer Press.

Garcia, E. E. (1993). Language, culture, and education. *Review of Research in Education, 19*, 51–98.

Gardner, H. (1983). *Frames of mind: The theory of multiple intelligences*. New York: Basic Books.

Hallinan, M. (1976). Friendship patterns in open and traditional classrooms. *Sociology of Education, 49,* 254–265.

Hoffer, T., & Gamoran, A. (1993). *Effects of instructional differences among ability groups on student achievement in middle-school science and mathematics.* Madison, WI: Center on Organization and Restructuring of Schools. (ED363509).

Horn, L., & Hafner, A. (1992). *A profile of American eighth-grade mathematics and science instruction.* National Education Longitudinal Study of 1988. Washington, DC: National Center for Education Statistics.

Kerckhoff, A. C. (1986). Effects of ability grouping in British secondary schools. *American Sociological Review, 51,* 842–855.

Kozol, J. (1991). *Savage inequalities: Children in America's schools.* New York: Crown.

Laosa, L. M., & Henderson, R. W. (1991). Cognitive socialization and competence: The academic development of Chicano students. In R. R. Valencia (Ed.), *Chicano school failure and success: Research and policy agendas for the 1990s* (pp. 164-199). London: Falmer Press.

Leal-Idrogo, A. (1997). The effect of gender on interaction, friendship, and leadership. In E. G. Cohen & R. A. Lotan (Eds.). *Working for equity in heterogeneous classrooms: Sociological theory in practice* (pp. 92–102). New York: Teachers College Press.

Lee, V. E., & Croninger, R. G. (1996). The social organization of safe high schools. In K. M. Borman, P. W. Cookson, Jr., A. R. Sadovnick, & J. Z. Spade (Eds.), *Implementing educational reform: Sociological perspectives on educational policy* (pp. 359-388). Norwood, NJ: Ablex.

Leechor, C. (1988). *How high and low achieving students differentially benefit from working together in cooperative small groups.* Unpublished doctoral dissertation, Stanford University, Stanford, California.

Lockheed, M. E., Harris, A., & Nemcef, W. P. (1983). Sex and social influence: Does sex function as a status characteristic in mixed-sex groups of children? *Journal of Educational Psychology, 75,* 877–866.

Lotan, R. A. (1997). Principles of a principled curriculum. In E. G. Cohen & R. A. Lotan (Eds.), *Working for equity in heterogeneous classrooms: Sociological theory in practice* (pp. 105–116). New York: Teachers College Press.

Mercer, J., Iadacola, P., & Moore, H. (1980). Building effective multiethnic schools: Evolving models and paradigms. In W. G. Stephan & J. R. Feagin (Eds.), *School desegregation: Past, present and future* (pp. 81–307). New York: Plenum.

Nystrand, M., & Gamoran, A. (1988, April). *A study of instruction as discourse.* Paper presented at the annual meeting of the American Educational Research Association, New Orleans, Louisiana.

Oakes, J. (1985). *Keeping track: How schools structure inequality.* New Haven, CT: Yale University Press.

Orfield, G., Bachmeier, M. D., James, D. R., & Eitle, T. (1997). *Deepening segregation in American public schools.* Cambridge, MA: Harvard Project on School Desegregation.

Quality Counts, (1998, January). *Education Week, No. 17.* Washington, DC: Editorial Projects in Education.

Ridgeway, C. L., & Diekema, D. (1992). Are gender differences status differences? In C. L. Ridgeway (Ed.), *Gender, interaction, and inequality* (pp. 157–180). New York: Springer-Verlag.

Rosenholtz, S. J., & Rosenholtz, S. H. (1981). Classroom organization and the perception of ability. *Sociology of Education, 54,* 132–140.

Rosenholtz, S. J., & Simpson, C. (1984). The formation of ability conception: Developmental trend or social construction. *Review of Educational Research, 54,* 31–63.

Rosenholtz, S. J., & Wilson, B. (1980). The effect of classroom structure on shared perceptions of ability. *American Educational Research Journal, 17,* 175–182.

Simpson, C. (1981). Classroom structure and the organization of ability. *Sociology of Education, 54,* 120–132.

Vanfossen, B., Jones, J., & Spade, J. (1987). Curricular tracking and status maintenance. *Sociology of Education, 60,* 104–122.

Webster. M. Jr., & Foschi, M. (1988). Overview of status generalization. In W. Webster, Jr. & M. Foschi (Eds.), *Status generalization: New theory and research* (pp. 1–20). Stanford, CA: Stanford University Press.

CHAPTER 12

Connecting Home, School, and Community

New Directions for Social Research

Joyce L. Epstein
Mavis G. Sanders

INTRODUCTION

Sociologists' attention to schools, to families, and to communities has changed dramatically since 1950. Then, most studies of families, of schools, or of communities were conducted as if these were separate or competing contexts. In the late 1960s and 1970s, researchers argued heatedly about whether schools or families were more important. There was clear agreement about the importance of families, disagreements about the effectiveness of schools, cursory attention to communities as purveyors of children's education, and little attention to whether or how these contexts worked together (Coleman et al., 1966; Jencks, 1972).

The topic of parent involvement gained prominence in the 1960s with the implementation of federal Head Start, Follow Through, and Title I programs in preschool and in the early elementary grades (Gordon, 1979; Keesling & Melaragno, 1983; Zigler & Valentine, 1975). These programs legislated the involvement of low-income parents to prepare their very young children for successful entry to school. Other personal and demographic factors were at work that increased the involvement of middle-income and high-income parents in their children's education. Since the 1960s, for example, more women graduated from college and entered

JOYCE L. EPSTEIN AND MAVIS G. SANDERS • Center on School, Family, and Community Partnerships, Johns Hopkins University, Baltimore, Maryland 21218

Handbook of the Sociology of Education, edited by Maureen T. Hallinan. Kluwer Academic/Plenum Publishers, New York, 2000.

and stayed in the work force. Highly educated and employed parents became more active in decisions about early care and schooling for their children. There were, then, pressures and opportunities for families with more and less formal education to increase their participation in their children's education. These experiences made parents less inclined to simply turn their children over to the schools or to accept without question all decisions by educators for and about their children.

In the 1970s, the effective schools movement captured the attention of educators and researchers interested in improving schools for traditionally underserved students (Edmonds, 1979). Parents' involvement was one topic in an expanding list of components that research and practice suggested would improve schools and increase students' success. Community involvement also became a central issue in school reform during this period. The New York City community control movement in the late 1960s and early 1970s challenged educators, policy leaders, and researchers to understand new concepts and practices of community participation in decisions about the education of minority and low-income youths (Fantini, 1970; Lutz & Merz, 1992).

Since the mid-1980s, the importance of improving schools for all children gained urgency with a recognition of the need to maintain U.S. leadership and competitiveness in a global economy (National Commission on Excellence in Education, 1983). Concerns have increased about the quality of students' skills and abilities for occupations that will determine this nation's success in the 21st century. Also, researchers and educators have drawn attention to the growing social and economic problems faced by families in this country (Children's Defense Fund, 1997; Jencks, 1995). Compared to the 1950s, now there are more two-parent homes with both parents employed; more young, single parents who also are working outside the home; more children in poverty; more migrant, homeless, and foster children and families; and more family mobility during the school year. Federal, state, and local social service and community programs, although numerous, are neither coordinated nor continuous, making it difficult for families to obtain the assistance they need for their children from birth through high school. These and other factors increase the importance of good school programs for students and the need to redesign policies and practices that link schools, families, and communities.

The simultaneous influence on children of schools, of families, and of communities is undeniable, but too often the connections across contexts are ignored in theory, in research, in policy, and in practice. Indeed, most social scientists who study one environment rarely give serious attention to another. For example, sociologists who study schools rarely examine how school practices affect family attitudes or influence on children or how families and communities affect the schools. Similarly, sociologists who study families rarely examine features of children's preschools, elementary, middle, and high schools or conditions in communities that affect family life.

This chapter reviews the progress of a field of study that expressly explores the overlapping spheres of influence on children's learning and development. It summarizes results from studies that have created a strong knowledge base on partnerships, and it presents some issues that need attention in basic and in applied research. The topics and questions should capture the interest, expand the concepts, improve the methods, and extend the knowledge of sociologists and others who study education, families, children, work, attainment, social psychology, and related topics.*†

*This research was supported by grants from the U.S. Department of Education, Office of Educational Research and Improvement, OERI, and the DeWitt Wallace-Reader's Digest Fund. The opinions expressed are the authors' and do not represent the policies or positions of either funding source.
†This chapter draws from, updates, and extends Epstein (1996b) and Epstein and Sanders (in press).

THEORETICAL AND EMPIRICAL ADVANCES

The first frameworks to explain the concept of parents' involvement focused mainly on parents' roles and responsibilities, not on the work that schools need to do to organize programs to involve all families and engage communities in children's education. In the 1980s, studies began to clarify terms and recast the emphasis from parents' involvement (activities left up to parents) to school and family partnerships (programs that include school and family responsibilities). Discussions also turned to the many ways that communities influence the quality of family life, school programs, and the prospects for students' futures. It is now generally agreed that school, family, and community partnerships are needed in order to improve the children's chances for success in school. Advances in theory and in research helped to shape the field.

Theory of Overlapping Spheres of Influence

The results of early empirical studies (Becker & Epstein, 1982; Epstein, 1986) could not be explained by established sociological theories that stated that social organizations are most effective if they set separate goals and unique missions (Waller, 1932; Weber, 1947). Rather, a social organizational perspective was needed that posited that, in education, the most effective families, schools, and communities had shared goals and a common mission concerning children's learning and development. This view recognized that the three contexts—home, school, and community—act as overlapping spheres of influence on children and on conditions and relationships in the three contexts (Epstein, 1987). The model includes external and internal structures.

The external structure of the model of overlapping spheres of influence can, by conditions or by design, be pulled together or apart by important forces (e.g., the background and practices of families, schools, and communities, developmental characteristics of students, historical and policy contexts). These forces create conditions, space, opportunities, and incentives for more or for fewer shared activities in school, family, and community contexts. The internal structure of the model specifies institutional and individual lines of communication, and it locates where and how social interactions of participants occur within and across the boundaries of school, home, and community. The theory integrates and extends several ecological, educational, psychological, and sociological perspectives on social organizations and relationships (e.g., Bronfenbrenner, 1979; Comer, 1980; Elder, 1997, Leichter, 1974; Lightfoot, 1978; Litwak & Meyer, 1974; Seeley, 1981; and a long line of sociological research on school, family, and community environments and their effects).

Shared responsibilities and overlapping influence mean that parents do not bear the entire burden of figuring out how to become and remain involved in their children's education across the years of schooling. Rather, schools share this burden and must create programs and conditions that inform, consult, assist, and involve all families in their children's education and development every year. Also, community groups, agencies, and individuals are not left to operate in geographic or in social isolation. Rather, educators, parents, and members of communities combine efforts to create a coherent program to help students succeed.

Other concepts contribute to the usefulness of this perspective. For example, the model of overlapping spheres of influence helps place the concept of social capital (Coleman, 1988) in a broader theoretical context. In this view, the results of interactions of family, school, and community members are accumulated and stored as social capital within the internal structure of the model of overlapping spheres of influence. Social capital is increased when well-designed partnerships enable families, educators, students, and others in the community to interact in productive ways.

Social capital may be spent, invested, or reinvested in social contacts or in activities that assist students' learning and development, strengthen families, improve schools, or enrich communities. For example, a parent may contact a teacher to obtain extra work or extra help for a child who is at risk of failing; a teacher may contact a community health service professional in the community to assist a family in need; or a parent may contact another parent to get the name of an after-school sports or tutorial program for a child. If well invested, social contacts and social skills may help improve the experiences of children and families, the climate of the school, the effectiveness of teachers, and other school, family, or community conditions. The model of overlapping spheres of influence helps locate and explain where and how processes making social ties and acquiring and investing social capital occur, along with other processes of school–family–community partnerships.

The theory also alters how to understand family, school, and community influences on very young children. An early view was that family influence in infancy and in the early years of childhood is followed in a fixed sequence by the influence of the school and, then, the community (Piaget & Inhelder, 1969). Recent syntheses of many studies indicate, however, that infants, toddlers, and their families do not exist in isolation but are linked to informal and formal networks of neighborhoods, communities, and schools. Very young children's growth, development, learning, health, and other qualities are simultaneously, not sequentially, influenced by multiple contexts (Morisset, 1993; Wasik & Karweit, 1994; Young & Marx, 1992). Similarly, older students are influenced by home, school, peers, and community concurrently, not in defined sequence.

Research Summary

Results of research conducted in the United States and in other nations confirm the usefulness of the theory of overlapping spheres of influence (Davies & Johnson, 1996; Organization for Economic Cooperation and Development [OECD], 1996; Sanders & Epstein, 1998a, 1998b). Researchers from many disciplines are applying various methodologies to study the implementation and effects of connections of schools and communities with families of various backgrounds and cultures, and with students at different age and grade levels. (See Booth & Dunn, 1995; Chavkin, 1993; Christenson & Conoley, 1992; Fagnano & Werber, 1994; Fruchter, Galletta, & White, 1992; Rioux & Berla, 1993; Ryan, Adams, Gullotta, Weissberg, & Hampton, 1995; Schneider & Coleman, 1993 for a few collections of studies and programs that illustrate the interdisciplinary nature and growth of the field.) Studies from the United States and from countries as diverse as Chile, Cyprus, and Australia confirm four general findings that provide a base on which to build new studies.

One general finding is that teachers, parents, and students have little understanding of each other's interests in children and in schools. Most teachers do not know most parents' goals and high aspirations for their children, what parents do to help their children, how they would like to be involved at school and at home, and what information parents want in order to be more effective in their interactions with their children about schoolwork. Most parents do not know much about the programs and opportunities that are available in their children's schools, the plans for school change and improvement, course offerings and consequences for their children and their family goals, or what teachers require of their children each year in school. Similarly, neither parents nor teachers fully understand what students think about family–school partnerships, about their schoolwork, or future plans. Studies point to the need to measure and compare teachers', parents', and students' views to identify gaps in knowledge that each has about the other, and to identify their common interests in good communications, good schools, and in children's success in school (Coleman, Collinge, & Seifert, 1992; Dauber & Epstein, 1993; Epstein & Dauber, 1991; Useem, 1992).

Another finding confirmed in national and in international studies is that school and classroom practices influence family involvement. Presently, on average, families with more formal education and higher incomes are more likely to be partners with their children's schools (Baker & Stevenson, 1986; Lareau, 1989; Useem, 1991). However, families with less formal education and lower incomes become involved if schools successfully implement programs of partnership.

Studies in the United States and in other nations show that teachers' practices to involve families are as important as or more important than family background variables such as race, ethnicity, social class, marital status, or mother's education or work status for determining whether, how, and which parents become involved in their children's education. Also, family practices of involvement are as important as or more important than family background variables for determining whether and how students progress and succeed in school. At the elementary, middle, and high school levels, surveys confirm that if schools invest in practices to involve families, then parents respond by conducting those practices. This includes parents with less formal education or lower incomes who might not have otherwise become involved on their own (Ames, deStefano, Watkins, & Sheldon, 1995; Cairney & Munsie, 1995; Comer & Haynes, 1991; Dauber & Epstein, 1993; Epstein, 1986; Griffith, 1998; Johnson, 1994; Kilmes-Dougan, Lopez, Nelson & Adelman, 1992; Palanki, Burch, & Davies, 1995; Sanders, Epstein & Connors-Tadros, 1999; Swap, 1993).

A third corroborated result in the research literature is that teachers who involve parents in their children's education rate parents more positively and stereotype families less than do other teachers. Teachers who frequently involve families in their children's education rate single and married parents, and more and less formally educated parents, as equally helpful with their children at home. By contrast, teachers who do not frequently involve families give more stereotypic ratings to single parents and to those with less formal education, marking them lower in helpfulness and in follow-through than other parents (Becker & Epstein, 1982; Epstein, 1990b). Parents and principals, in turn, give higher ratings to teachers who communicate frequently with families (Epstein, 1985).

A fourth major finding on which to build future studies is that specific outcomes are linked to different types of involvement. The results of many studies and activities in schools, in districts, and in states contributed to the development of a framework of six major types of involvement that fall within the overlapping spheres of influence model (Epstein, 1992, 1995). Briefly, the six types are as follows:

1. Parenting—helping all families understand child and adolescent development and establish home environments that support children as students
2. Communicating—designing and conducting effective forms of communication about school programs and children's progress
3. Volunteering—recruiting and organizing help and support for school functions and activities
4. Learning at home—providing information and ideas to families about how to help students at home with homework and curriculum-related activities and decisions
5. Decision-making—including parent representatives and all families in school decisions
6. Collaborating with the community—identifying and integrating resources and services from the community to strengthen and support schools, students and their families

Each type of involvement requires two-way connections so that schools know and can support their families, and families know and can support their schools.

The six types of involvement may be operationalized by hundreds of practices from which schools choose to develop their programs. Each of the six types poses specific challenges to schools in the design and implementation of activities. The challenges must be met to move an ordinary program of partnerships to an excellent one. Finally, different types of involvement lead to different results for students, for parents, and for teachers (Epstein, Coates, Salinas, Sanders, & Simon, 1997).

The most immediate effects of family and of community involvement should be outcomes that are theoretically linked to the design and focus of the practice. For example, subject-specific practices that encourage parent–child interactions in reading at home should initially affect students' skills and achievement in reading. Interactions in other academic subjects or on specific content will have specific results (Border & Merttens, 1993; Cairney, 1995; Epstein, 1991; Epstein, Jackson & Salinas, 1994; Epstein, Simon, & Salinas, 1997; Sanchez & Baguedano, 1993; Silvern, 1991; Topping, 1995). Similarly, practices to involve families in improving school safety should positively affect the school climate and students' learning environment (Sanders, 1996).

To summarize, school, family, and community involvement and effects have been studied with increasing insight, specificity, and sophistication since 1950. Researchers across countries and across disciplines have employed many methodologies including surveys, case studies, experimental and quasi-experimental designs, longitudinal data collections, field tests, program evaluations, and policy analyses. Studies have grown from focusing mainly on preschools to elementary, middle, and high schools, and from focusing on what parents do on their own to what schools, families, and communities do in partnership. Studies have expanded from small, local samples to national and purposive samples of students and families with diverse racial and cultural backgrounds in urban, in rural, and in suburban locations.

As research proceeds and improves, researchers must continue to ask deeper questions, employ better samples, collect useful data, create more fully specified measurement models, and conduct more elegant analyses to more clearly identify the results of particular practices of partnership. An added challenge is to continue to conduct research that helps improve educational policies and school practices of partnership. Studies are needed at all grade levels, in differently organized schools, in varied locations, and with students and families with diverse racial, cultural, and linguistic backgrounds.

TOPICS FOR NEW STUDIES

Four major topics that have emerged from recent research open many questions for new studies on partnerships. These topics are transitions; community connections; students' roles in partnerships; and the results of school, family, and community connections.

Transitions

In the theory of overlapping spheres of influence, it is assumed that time and the transitions it brings affect the nature and extent of family–school–community connections. Students and their families experience regular transitions from year to year and unscheduled or unexpected transitions such as family moves, school closings, redistricting, student suspension, or other activities and policy changes that affect school or class assignments. Research examining these transitions is needed.

Research is needed on regular transitions across the grades to learn how school, family, and community partnerships change or remain the same from birth through high school; the challenges that families meet at each stage of their children's development; and the results of partnerships across the grades for students, for parents, for teachers, and for schools. Studies of continuity and change are demanding because they require longitudinal data or innovative retrospective data and appropriate quantitative or qualitative methods. New questions also are emerging about the annual transitions that students and their families make from the summer to the fall of the school year (Alexander & Entwisle, 1996). We need to know much more about the design and implications of summer transitions for improving school, family, and community connections. For example, How might teachers collect information from families about their children each year and periodically during a school year? How do families learn about each new teacher's criteria for success in their classrooms? What are the best designs for summer learning opportunities for students with their families and peers at home and in the community? Should summer activities be organized for students and their families as part of the concluding school year or as part of the oncoming school year? Whose responsibility is it to design and follow up summer activities?

Other regular transitions take students and families to new levels of schooling. Many studies report dramatic declines in family involvement when children move to the next school level (Baker & Stevenson, 1986; Eccles & Harold, 1995; Epstein & Dauber, 1991; Epstein & Lee, 1995; Lee, 1994). Research is needed on alternate designs and effects of activities to help students and their families make successful transitions from preschool to elementary, elementary to middle, middle to high schools, and high schools to postsecondary settings. How can educators maintain appropriate and active family involvement across school levels? What do families need to know about changes that their children will experience when they move to new schools? Should feeder schools, receiver schools, or both, conflict these activities?

There have been fewer studies of school, of family, and of community partnerships in high schools than in lower grades, although research is increasing due to the availability of the National Education Longitudinal Study of 1988 (NELS:88) surveys and other unique regional data (Bauch, 1988; Brian, 1994; Clark, 1983; Conners & Epstein, 1994; Dornbusch & Ritter, 1988; Epstein & Conners, 1994; Keith, 1991; Lee, 1994; Sanders & Epstein, 1998c; Sanders et al., 1999). More research is needed on the transition to and through high school on such questions as the following: Which practices of partnerships are important for students, for families, and for schools at the high school level? How should practices to inform and involve families change from the freshman to senior years in high school? What are the results of partnerships for high school students, parents, and teachers? What steps should be taken each year for students and families to successfully plan for postsecondary education and for work?

Other questions should be addressed to understand various unscheduled transitions in schooling due to family moves, migrancy, homelessness, student suspensions, expulsions, and other circumstances that affect children, families, and their connections with schools. For example, mobility is a serious problem in inner-city, migrant farm, military, and other communities. Research is needed on the organization and effects of various approaches to partnerships in schools and in communities with high rates of mobility where many students and families move in and out throughout the school year. We need better information on which practices of school, family, and community partnerships reduce the negative effects of mobility on students' attendance, achievement, and behavior, especially in single-parent in stepparent, and in blended families (Tucker, Marx, & Long, 1998). What might schools do to welcome new students and their families with useful information on school policies and parent involvement? Can partnership activities reduce the stress caused by moving by integrating families new to the community with other families?

Community Connections

Community is a venerable and vast term in sociology (Dewey, 1916; Tonnies, 1963/1887) that demands new and focused attention in modern times (Etzioni, 1993), and, particularly, in studies of school, family, and community partnerships. The community is one of the spheres of influence that affect students' learning and development (Epstein, 1990a). Schools, families, and students are part of, but do not fully define the community (Mawhinney, 1994). The community also includes businesses, organizations, neighborhoods, peer and friendship groups, and other organizations, associations, and individuals who have a stake in the success of children in school and who serve children and families as a matter of course or in times of trouble. Community laws, regulations, resources, services, and programs may bring schools, families, and communities together, or they may separate and segregate these groups. Partnerships must be organized to enable educators, families, and other members of the community to help each other and to assist children.

In the past, many sociologists identified and categorized communities using census data such as the distribution of education, income, race, or other descriptors of a population. Such data do not address the inherent powers that exist within all communities. Studies are beginning to identify the human and social resources that represent the strengths of people, of programs, and of organizations in all communities. More than low or high rankings on demographic characteristics, the qualities within communities may predict and explain the success of students, the strength of school programs, and the capacities of families and community groups to guide and to assist their children.

Families and communities have untapped funds of knowledge (Moll, Amanti, Neff, & Gonzalez, 1992) that are used in everyday activities including skills and knowledge for repairing the home, gardening, butchering, cooking, making things, using transportation routes, gaining access to programs, and other skills. Adults in communities may share their talents with children by coaching youngsters in such things as public speaking, chess, sports, music, dance, art, science, and other interests (Nettles, 1992, 1993). It is important to ask the following: How might local communities identify, organize, and study the effects of available resources to help students, families, and schools? In what ways might adult knowledge be shared in coaching strategies and with what results for students; for the adults involved, or for the schools? What new methodologies are needed to identify these qualities, processes, and results?

Active engagement in religious groups or in other community organizations also are potentially powerful influences on students and on families. In a study of urban African–American youths, Sanders (1998) found that students' involvement in Black churches has significant positive effects on achievement through its influence on school-related attitudes and behavior. Specifically, regular attendance and participation in church services and programs influence students' academic self-concept. Students report that within the church they find guidance, support, and encouragement from congregational members with whom they develop strong ties and whom they view as extended family. Similarly, drawing on biographical and on interview data, Galindo and Escamilla (1995) found that the church was a supportive and influential context for literacy learning among educationally successful Hispanic students.

Other studies of community partnerships focus on the effects of programs to increase parenting skills, to help parents increase the skills of infants and toddlers, and to train parents for occupations in child care (Conners, 1994; Kagan, Neville, & Rustici, 1993; Morisset, 1994). Some researchers are beginning to look across generations to study effects of programs to help adolescent parents stay in school and become involved in their own children's care and education (Scott-Jones, 1996) or to explore factors such as the mobility of extended family members that affect the rate of teen pregnancies and the meaning of community in multigenerational families (Burton, 1995).

There is growing interest in integrating services across governmental agencies and community organizations to support families, to provide health, recreation, training, and other services, and to increase students' success in school (Dryfoos, 1994; Wynn, Costello, Halpern, & Richman, 1994). Studies of interagency connections still are mainly anecdotal. A few studies have shown that interagency collaboration requires restructuring responsibilities and sharing resources (Burch, Palanki, & Davies, 1995; Connors-Tadros, 1996; Dolan, 1995; Mawhinney, 1994). More information is needed on such questions as the following: What are the effects on students' learning, on parental behavior, and on school programs of alternate approaches of interagency collaborations in health, in recreation, in job training, in child care, and in other services? What decisions and actions are required for two, three, or more organizations to collaborate and to integrate services and with what effects for students and families?

Other researchers are exploring the strengths of families and communities with diverse racial, ethnic, and cultural characteristics. Resources are inherent in rituals, in traditional values, in family dreams and aspirations for children, in cultural norms for student behavior, in racial identity development, in family involvement in the schools, and in formal and informal community organizations that support families (Bright, 1994; Siu & Feldman, 1996; Swap, 1994). A few studies indicate that the culture of home and community—including languages, patterns of discourse, values, behaviors—may be different from the school, but that these differences will not be barriers to students' success unless they are treated as deficits (Hidalgo, 1994; Ferry, 1993). These and other studies confirm that families in diverse cultural groups believe that education is important for children, involvement is important for parents, and that they need better information from their schools in order to help their children succeed. Families are more similar than different on these issues (Hidalgo, Bright, Siu, Swap, & Epstein, 1995).

Within all cultural groups, families vary in their ideas about their linkages to schools and to communities. For example, one study of Puerto Rican families in Boston suggests that immigrant families who aim to retain cultural identities and ties in their local communities desire and require schools to change more than do immigrant families who aim to assimilate in the mainstream community (Hidalgo, 1994). The former group wishes to be recognized and respected by the schools for their differences and to be assisted in unique ways. The latter group wishes to avoid attention by or special services from the schools. Studies are needed on such topics as the following: How do partnership programs build on family and community strengths? How do schools learn about and respond to the diverse backgrounds, cultures, philosophies, talents, and goals of families in ways that help students? How are families from different communities integrated in one school community?

Delgado and Rivera (1996) identified the potential strengths of natural support systems in Puerto Rican communities. Natural support systems are networks of extended families, religious groups, merchants, social clubs, and other individuals or groups that people contact for assistance instead of or in addition to seeking help from formal institutions such as hospitals, health centers, and schools. Their study revealed that urban families had limited natural support systems and placed heavy importance on their connections with their children's schools.

This finding revises the view that schools are distant from or avoided by immigrant families, and it suggests that schools are important for families' sense of community and connectedness. Studies are needed to determine how schools can best help immigrant families connect with others in their community. New questions include the following: How are community support systems developed, strengthened, and renewed? What are the effects of formal and informal community support systems on students, on families, and on the schools?

New research also is needed to define and explore what is meant by a sense of community. A common distinction in school improvement contrasts strong academics and a caring community, as if one precluded the other. Shouse (1996) found that a sense of community, indicated by shared beliefs and supportive activities can, indeed, coexist with high academic standards and expectations for high academic achievement. Most studies of the school community focus on the norms, the values, the beliefs, and the interactions of administrators, teachers, and students, with little or no attention to connections and interactions with families and with others in the geographic community. The theory of overlapping spheres of influence suggests that definitions and measures of a sense of community need to include the extent of shared values for academic success and for caring behavior of the home, the school, and the community. This could help identify how a school community develops over time and how far a sense of community extends.

Further, research is needed on community participation in school decision making and community control, which is returning in new forms in local school councils, as in Chicago's program for school improvement (Ryan, et al., 1997). The new efforts, still threatening to some and puzzling to others, support local decision making and the participation of family and community members in school decisions that affect their children. School councils have been mandated in South Carolina since the early 1980s, and councils, improvement teams, site-based decision-making teams, and other structures have been instituted in many states and school districts in this and in other countries. Common "guidelines to councils usually confuse policymaking with program development. The councils usually include parents with important responsibilities who often represent only themselves and who do not collect or identify the views of other parents. It is becoming clear that school councils are one component in a much broader program of school, family, and community partnerships, and that schools, districts, and states need to understand the big picture in order for councils to be more effective (McKenna & Willms, 1998).

New directions for studies about community start from the inside out, with attention to the traditions and talents of families and other individuals and groups. Basic questions include the following: How do schools identify, understand, and utilize the resources in their communities to assist students, to engage families, and to improve schools? How do communities (e.g., individuals, groups, businesses, other organizations, and agencies) encourage student learning, reinforce schooling, and recognize accomplishments? Which communications and exchanges are needed to create a unified school community that also accepts and celebrates diversity?

Students' Roles

Students are the center of the model of overlapping spheres of influence because they are the main actors in their own education, and because families, schools, and communities share an interest in and responsibility for children's success and well-being. Indeed, the main reason that educators, parents, and students communicate is to help students succeed in school and in life. Although everyone is concerned about students' happiness, safety, school success, and personal development, students often are excluded from family–school communications. They may be informed later by teachers, by administrators, or by parents about decisions that affect them. Most often, students feel acted on rather than like actors and done to rather than like doers in their education.

Bronfenbrenner (1979) advised that socialization and education should be organized so that, over time, the balance of power is given to the developing person. Epstein (1983) found that age-appropriate decision-making opportunities at school and at home increased students' independence and other positive school outcomes. Without question, students are responsible for their own education, but they can be helped or hindered in their attainments by their schools, families, and communities, and by the connections or lack of connections across contexts.

Research is needed to define, to design, and to study students' roles and responsibilities in school, family, and community partnerships across the grades from preschool through high school. Some studies have asked students directly for their views on home–school–community connections and how they participate as partners (Ames, et al., 1995; Dornbusch & Ritter, 1988; Montandon & Perrenoud, 1987). When asked, adolescents express an overwhelming desire to participate in parent–teacher conferences and on school committees, to have their families better informed about and involved in their education and extracurricular activities, and to communicate more with their families about schoolwork and school decisions (Conners & Epstein, 1994).

When they believe that their families are involved in their education, students say that their schools and families are more similar, that their teachers and parents know each other, that they do more homework on weekends, and that they like school better (Coleman, et al., 1992; Epstein, in press). In high school, students who report that their families are involved in many different ways at school and who discuss school and their futures at home have more positive attitudes about school, better attendance, and better grades than other students, even after accounting for their scores on these measures in the middle grades (Lee, 1994; Pryor & Favorini, 1994).

Homework is a particularly important topic that connects students, families, and schools. Most studies indicate that, regardless of their starting skills, students who do their homework improve their skills and do better in school than similar students who do not do their homework. Not all students complete their homework, however, and not all homework is designed to encourage completion. Research on where students do their homework (Keith, 1998), how motivated they are about homework and learning (Corno & Xu, 1998), and the connections of students and family members in interactive homework (Epstein, 1998; Hoover-Dempsey, Bassler, & Burow, 1995) are beginning to extend knowledge of students' roles in increasing parents' involvement at home.

Many new questions should be asked about students' roles in education and in partnerships. For example: How should education be organized for students to take appropriate leadership for their learning at all grade levels? How should school, family, and community partnership activities be designed to ensure that students participate in these interactions? How much guidance and support, rules and regulations, and independence and self-direction do students need across the grades? What are the results of high or low student participation in activities for the six major types of involvement?

Results of Partnerships

One of the most persistent oversimplifications that must be corrected for researchers, for policy leaders, for educators, and for the public is that any family or community involvement leads to all good things for students, for parents, for teachers, and for schools. As discussed earlier, studies show that not all school–family–community partnership learning, to better report card grades, or to higher standardized test scores. Rather, results should be theoretically linked to different types of involvement (Epstein, 1995). For example, some family, school connections, such as interactive homework in specific subjects, affect students' skills and scores in those subjects (Epstein, Simon, & Salinas, 1997). Other activities are more likely to influence attendance, students' attitudes, family's confidence about parenting, or teachers' respect for families (Epstein, in press).

Research at all grade levels is needed on the effects of specific partnership activities on the attitudes, behaviors, and skills of students, of parents, and of schools. Studies of results also are needed on the three topics discussed previously to learn the effects of alternate designs for activities partnership practices at times of transition, of connections with community, and on students' roles in partnerships. We still know relatively little about which practices produce positive or negative results, for whom, under what conditions, and in what sequence or combination.

A trickier, persistent question is whether and how it is possible to separate the effects of particular partnership practices from the effects of other school improvement activities that occur simultaneously. Indeed, this question pertains to and perplexes research on the effects of any component of school and classroom organization. Although it is virtually impossible to account for all possible conditions, structures, processes, and activities in schools, in homes, and in communities, it is possible to learn more about effects of partnership practices with rigorous, multiple methods and data.

Detailed longitudinal studies would help increase an understanding of the sequences and patterns of effects of partnership practices over time. For example, workshops for parents on child development (e.g., parent education programs), or membership in the PTA are many steps away from parental influence on students' achievement test scores, a greater distance from the student's demonstration of achievement, and even further from changing the achievement levels of a classroom, a grade level, or a school. By contrast, daily parent–child interactions about reading, writing, or math may directly affect the student's reading, writing, and math activities at home, completion of homework, classwork, class tests, report card grades, and ultimately achievement test scores. Longitudinal studies also help researchers take a two-step approach to evaluation, with attention to the implementation of practices before studying effects (Epstein, Herrick, & Coates, 1996). Research on the influence of family and of community involvement on students' learning also must account for the quality of classroom teaching—the main influence on students' achievement in specific subjects.

Although positive results of family involvement on various student outcomes have been given the most attention (Henderson & Berla, 1994), many studies report negative correlations of some types of involvement with students' achievement, behavior, and parental attitudes. For example, teachers telephone and conference with parents of students who need help to improve their academics or behavior more often than they do with other parents. Also, parents are more likely to call or to initiate a meeting with a teacher or a school if they are concerned about their children's attitudes, relationships at school, or academic progress. Parents report spending more time helping low-achieving elementary school children with homework, and teachers report asking these parents to help more often (Epstein, in press).

Not surprisingly, on average, the number of home–school communications (including phone calls, conferences) and the minutes of help with homework are negatively correlated with students' achievement and behavior (Catsambis, 1998; Catsambis & Garland, 1997; Epstein & Lee, 1993; Lee, 1994). Also, parents who receive more phone calls or have more conferences with teachers are more likely to rate the school lower in quality than do other parents because they are less satisfied with the school if their children are frequently in trouble or are failing academically (Epstein & Jacobsen, 1994).

The negative correlations are provocative because they could be misinterpreted to mean that home–school communications cause academic and behavioral problems, and that there is a negative effect (implying direct impact) of home–school communications on students' achievement or attitudes. In fact, these correlations usually indicate that, presently, schools and families contact each other mainly when students have academic and behavior problems. Outreach is usually a sign that teachers or parents know they need to work together to help a student correct a serious problem. As our field studies indicate, any partnership practice can be well-timed or poorly timed and implemented. Thus, activities that are poorly designed and implemented, or that are theoretically detached from the desired results could, fail to address and, in some cases, even increase students' academic or behavior problems.

What's more, the negative correlations and statistical effects decline, disappear, or fail to appear when schools develop comprehensive programs of partnership that include positive phone calls, parent–teacher–student conferences, and other positive communications with all families, and not just those whose children are in trouble. The association of home–school communications and students' achievement changes from a negative to a null or a positive relationship if a school effectively implements a well-designed partnership program. The program should include regular, positive home–school communications with all families along with targeted contacts to help students solve problems.

To further explore this topic, longitudinal studies are needed on whether and how communications of home and school help students improve over time. There are several related questions to address. These include the following: Which contacts and follow-up activities are most successful in helping students stay or return to successful pathways? How do parent–teacher–student communications about academic and behavioral problems change across the grades, and with what results? What are the results of students' participation in family–school communications about academic and behavior problems or successes?

Patterns are emerging that suggest different connections among the six types of involvement. For example, the structure of an activity and the results of the activity may relate to two or more types of involvement. In practice, programs such as food cooperatives or clothing swap-shops run by parent volunteers (Type 3—Volunteering) are designed to assist many parents with their basic parenting responsibilities to feed and clothe their children (Type 1—Parenting).

Although activities for each type of involvement lead to some distinct results (Epstein, 1995), some activities for different types of involvement contribute to the same result. For, example, analyses of national data and of field studies showed that several home–school–community connections influence students' attendance (Epstein & Lee, 1993; Roderick, 1997). When schools set specific goals—such as improving or maintaining good attendance, school safety, or achievement—they need good information on which activities for all or some of the six types of involvement will help produce the desired results. For example, students' success in science may be influenced by Type 2—communications about science courses, Type 4—learning activities at home in student–parent discussions about science homework, and Type 6—collaborations in the community in weekend and summer science programs and activities for students and for families, as well as other activities.

Connections of the six types of involvement are different in extensive and in limited data sets. Because there is an underlying construct of involvement, single-item indicators of two or more types of involvement may be strongly correlated. Richer data, however, with many questions for each type of involvement show how different types of involvement are separable. For example, volunteering at school (Type 3) and attending PTA meetings (Type 5) are correlated, and if there are only one or two items, these types of involvement may be treated as one construct (Rumberger, 1995). When there are many items about school and classroom volunteers and many items about PTA membership, meetings, participation, and decision-making opportunities, the two types of involvement emerge as separate factors or types of involvement that require different kinds of parental talents and commitments (Epstein, 1995; Epstein & Dauber, 1991).

All surveys are necessarily limited by the number and content of questions that are asked. For example, the National Education Longitudinal Study of 1988 (NELS:88) Base-Year and Follow-up Surveys have only a few items on Type 6—collaborating with the community. When NELS:88 was designed, Type 6 was in its early stages of development in the model of school, family, and community partnerships. Now, with more attention to the components, challenges, and results of Type 6 (see the previous discussion of community), new surveys can study this type of involvement more informatively than in the past.

DISCUSSION

It is essential to understand home, school, and community connections in order to understand the organization and improvement of schools, the influence of families and communities on children, and the academic and developmental progress or problems of students. Interdisciplinary and international research on school–family–community partnerships is increasing knowledge about the nature and effects of connections among the major contexts in which children learn and grow. Studies conducted in the United States and in other countries confirm several general tendencies.

The first of these tendencies is that schools can be assisted by thoughtful federal, state, district, and school leadership and policies to develop strong and responsive programs of partnerships with families and with communities. Second, more parents become involved when schools establish good programs, which include activities for the six types of involvement. Third, teachers are more positive about family involvement when they try and frequently use practices that involve all families in their children's education and when they see that their principal and colleagues also support family involvement. Fourth, all communities possess resources to promote students' social and intellectual development. Finally, students are more positive about and do better in school if their families and communities are involved in particular and productive ways.

Extending the Research Agenda on Partnerships

Despite advances in understanding school, family, and community partnerships, there still is much to learn. In addition to the four major topics for future research discussed in this chapter, inquiries also are needed in many other areas.

Studies are needed on partnership policies and their effects. Federal, state, and local policies promote partnerships, but there are few rigorous studies of the separate and combined effects of policies across levels on the design of programs or results at the school and the classroom levels. We need to know more about the kinds of procedural enactments that must accompany policy statements in order for schools, districts, or states to develop and sustain high quality programs of school, family, and community partnership. Also, states, districts, and schools respond differently to federal laws and mandates for school–family partnerships (e.g., Title I, Goals 2000, Even Start). Comparative studies are needed on the effects of decisions about staff responsibilities, allocations of funds, and program designs for developing partnerships.

Another area requiring further study is the role of fathers' involvement. Most studies have been conducted with data from mothers, but we need to know much more about the nature and effects of the involvement of fathers (Nord, Brimhall, & West, 1997). For example: How does the involvement in children's education of fathers and mothers differ at home and at school? What effects does this have on students' attitudes, behaviors, and achievements? What school and nonschool factors influence fathers' involvement in children's learning, including resident or custodial status? Additional research could be conducted on the nature and effects on students of the involvement of siblings and of extended family members (e.g., aunts, uncles, grandparents) across the grades and in varied socioeconomic, geographic, racial, and ethnic groups.

Studies also are needed on the nature and results for practice of course content on partnerships. College courses are increasing that prepare teachers and administrators to involve families and communities in children's education, but there still are relatively few such courses required for all professionals who will work with children, with families, with schools, or with communities (Epstein, Sanders, & Clark, 1999; Shartrand, Weiss, Kreider, & Lopez, 1997). Studies are needed on whether and how partnership topics are addressed in the sociology of education, the sociology of family, the introduction to sociology, and all education courses.

For example, although social class and family structure are important variables that help explain the involvement of some parents in some ways (Lareau, 1989; Zill, 1996), studies indicate that school practices of partnership help equalize the involvement of families in their children's education (Epstein, 1990b; Sanders et al., 1999). This kind of information should help to refocus sociology of education's emphasis from ascriptive variables (e.g., social class and marital status) to alterable variables (e.g., school and classroom organization and school and family practices) for explaining and enhancing students' success and failure in school.

This kind of information also should influence the attitudes and practices of teachers, administrators, counselors, social workers, other professionals, and parents. Studies are needed to determine whether those who learn only that parents' social class determines parental involvement have measurably different attitudes and practices from those who learn that comprehensive programs of partnerships make a difference in which parents and how parents become involved.

Finally, the field would benefit from studies of the design and effects of university–school collaborations. Sociologists should be aware of emerging forms of university–school collaborations (Epstein, 1996b; Goodlad, 1988; Harkevy & Puckett, 1990). Most of the progress since the late 1980s in understanding school, family, and community partnerships has been made by researchers, by educators, and by parents working together to define questions that are important for improving school practice and sharing expertise so that new approaches are implemented, documented, analyzed, and improved.

Studies are needed on how research-based approaches developed in collaborative demonstration sites work in other locations (Schorr, 1997). Initiatives designed to improve programs and practices of school, family, and community partnership (e.g., National Network of Partnership Schools at Johns Hopkins, the National PTA standards, the U. S. Department of Education's Partnerships for Family Involvement in Education) open many opportunities to assess the quality of implementations and the effects of well-implemented programs on student, on families, and on schools (Sanders, 1999).

School, family, and community partnerships are one of many topics on most school improvement agendas. Studies are needed on whether and how partnership topics are linked with other components of school improvement. Do good home–school–community connections increase the likelihood that other components of school improvement (e.g., curriculum, innovative instruction, new assessments) will succeed? What combinations of school and classroom organizational innovations have the greatest positive effects on students' attendance, achievement, behavior, or other desired results?

Sociologists of education, family, community, occupations, and organizations have important contributions to make to the field of school–family–community partnerships (Epstein, 1990a; 1996a). Opportunities for new and exciting research are enhanced by the availability of national data that can be used to address many of the questions raised in this chapter, such as the National Education Longitudinal Study (NELS), the Panel Study of Income Dynamics (PSID), or the Early Childhood Longitudinal Study (ECLS–K), starting with a kindergarten cohort in the fall of 1998 and ECLS–B starting with a birth cohort in 2000.

Despite the importance of these large-scale data sets, general surveys often are limited in concepts and in items on school, family, and community partnerships. Researchers' well-designed local, regional, state, and other national data collected in surveys, in case studies, in experimental, and in other action research studies still will be needed for in-depth analyses of the design and effects of partnerships at all levels of schooling, in diverse communities, and for students and for families with varied cultural, economic, social, and educational backgrounds.

CONCLUSION

In an important exchange about the core of sociology in the January 1998 issue of *Contemporary Sociology*, several sociologists discussed how the discipline focuses on studies to explain social life. Offering a different view, Sprague (1998) suggested that "support for informed social action" unifies the subdisciplines of sociology (p. 24). This opinion reflects Coleman's (1993) impassioned call for sociologists to participate in the reconstruction of society using research to make social institution more humane. Using the topic of school, family, and community partnerships as one example, Epstein (1996b) suggested that research in the sociology of education can and should do more to promote the improvement of educational policy and practice. Research-based school improvements would, in turn, broaden the field for new studies, which would, in turn, lead to continued school improvements, and so on.

This chapter presents an overview of research and new developments in the practices of school, family, and community partnerships and identifies several sets of questions that need attention. Sociologists of education and researchers in other disciplines who study schools, family structures and processes, the life course, cultural diversity, attainment processes, and communities can contribute new and important knowledge on partnership topics. Specifically, studies are needed on partnerships at times of students' transitions; the organization of community resources for education; students' roles in school, family, and community partnership; the results of school, family, and community connections on participants and contexts; the organization and effects of policies; the impact of new content in courses on partnerships; fathers' involvement in children's education; and new school–university collaborations. These topics, by design, support the implementation of and research on school, family, and community partnerships in ways that will explain social life, support social action, and contribute to the school improvement process.

REFERENCES

Alexander, K. L., & Entwisle, D. R. (1996). Schools and children at risk. In A. Booth & J. Dunn (Eds.), *Family–school links: How do they affect educational outcomes* (pp. 67–88). Mahwah, NJ: Lawrence Erlbaum Associates.

Ames, C., deStefano, L., Watkins, T., & Sheldon, S. (1995). *Teachers' school-to-home communications and parent involvement: The role of parent perceptions and beliefs.* Report 28. Baltimore, MD: Center on Families, Communities, Schools and Children's Learning, Johns Hopkins University.

Baker, D. P., & Stevenson, D. L. (1986). Mothers' strategies for children's school achievement: Managing the transition to high school. *Sociology of Education, 59,* 156–166.

Bauch, P. A. (1988). Is parent involvement different in private schools? *Educational Horizons, 66,* 78–82.

Becker H. J., & Epstein, J. L. (1982). Parent involvement: A study of teacher practices. *Elementary School Journal, 83,* 85–102.

Booth, A., & Dunn, I. (Eds., 1995). *Family–school links: How do they affect educational outcomes.* Hillside, NJ: Lawrence Erlbaum Associates.

Border, R., & Merttens, R. (1993). Parental partnership: Comfort or conflict? In R. Merttens & J. Vass (Eds.), *Partnerships in math: Parents and schools IMPACT project.* London/Washington, DC: Falmer Press.

Brian, D. (1994). *Parental involvement in high schools.* Paper presented at the annual meeting of the American Educational Research Association, New Orleans, Louisiana.

Bright, J. A. (1994). Beliefs in action: Family contributions to African–American student success. *Equity and Choice, 10*(2), 5–13.

Bronfenbrenner, U. (1979). *The ecology of human development: Experiment by nature and design.* Cambridge, MA: Harvard University Press.

Burch, P., Palanki, A., & Davies, D. (1995). *From clients to partners: Four case studies of collaboration and family involvement in the development of school-linked services.* Report 29. Baltimore, MD: Center on Families, Communities, Schools and Children's Learning, Johns Hopkins University.

Burton, L. M. (1995). *Urban survival in the Black community: A multi-generational perspective.* Paper presented at the annual meeting of the American Sociological Association, Washington, DC.

Cairney, T. H. (1995). Developing parent partnerships in secondary literacy learning. *Journal of Reading, 38*(7), 520–526.

Cairney, T. H., & Munsie, L. (1995). Parent participation in literacy learning. *Reading Teacher, 48,* 392–403.

Catsambis, S. (1998). *Expanding knowledge of parental involvement in secondary education: Social determinants and effects on high school academic success.* CRESPAR Center Report. Baltimore, MD: Johns Hopkins University.

Catsambis, S., & Garland, J. (1997). *Parent involvement in students' education: Changes from the middle grades to high school.* CRESPAR Center Report. Baltimore, MD: Johns Hopkins University.

Chavkin, N. (Ed., 1993). *Families and schools in a pluralistic society.* Albany, NY: State University of New York Press.

Children's Defense Fund. (1997). *State of America's children.* Washington, DC: Author.

Christenson, S., & Conoley, J. (Eds., 1992). *Home and school collaborations: Enhancing children's academic and social competence.* Colesville, MD: National Association of School Psychologists (NASP).

Clark, R. M. (1983). *Family life and school achievement: Why poor black children succeed or fail.* Chicago: The University of Chicago Press.

Coleman, J. S. (1988). Social capital in the creation of human capital. American *Journal of Sociology, 94,* 95–120.

Coleman, J. S. (1993). The rational reconstruction of society. *American Sociological Review, 58,* 1–16.

Coleman, J. S., Campbell, E., Mood, A., Weinfeld, E., Hobson, C., York, R., & McPartland, J. (1966). *Equality of educational opportunity.* Washington, DC: U. S. Government Printing Office.

Coleman, P., Collinge, J., & Seifert, T. (1992). *Seeking the levers of change: Participant attitudes and school improvement.* Paper presented at 5th Annual International Congress on School Effectiveness and Improvement, Victoria, British Columbia.

Comer, J. P. (1980). *School power: Implications of an intervention program.* New York: The Free Press.

Comer, J. P., & Haynes, N. (1991). Parent involvement in schools: An ecological approach. *Elementary School Journal, 91,* 271–277.

Conners, L. J. (1994). *Small wins: The promises and challenges of family literacy.* Report. 22. Baltimore, MD: Center on Families, Communities, Schools and Children's Learning, Johns Hopkins University.

Conners, L. J., & Epstein, J. L. (1994). *Taking stock: The views of teachers, parents, and students on school, family, and community partnerships in high schools.* Report 25. Baltimore, MD: Center on Families, Communities, Schools and Children's Learning, Johns Hopkins University.

Connors-Tadros, L. J. (1996). *Effects of Even Start on family literacy: Local and national comparisons.* Report 35. Baltimore, MD: Center on Families, Communities, Schools and Children's Learning, Johns Hopkins University.

Corno, L., & Xu, J. (1998). *Homework and personal responsibility.* Paper presented at the annual meeting of the American Educational Research Association, April, San Diego, California.

Dauber, S. L., & Epstein, J. L. (1993). Parents' attitudes and practices of involvement in inner-city elementary and middle schools. In N. Chavkin (Ed.), *Families and schools in a pluralistic society* (pp. 53–71). Albany, NY: State University of New York Press.

Davies, D., & Johnson, V. R., (Eds., 1996). Crossing boundaries: Family, community, and school partnerships. *International Journal of Education Research, 25*(1), Special Issue.

Delgado, M., & Rivera, H. (1996). *Use of Puerto Rican natural support systems as a bridge between community and schools.* Report 34. Baltimore, MD: Center on Families, Communities, Schools and Children's Learning, Johns Hopkins University.

Dewey, J. (1916). *Democracy and education.* New York: Macmillan.

Dolan, L. J. (1995). An evaluation of social service integration in six elementary schools in Baltimore. In L. Rigsby & M. Wang (Ed.), *School/community connections.* San Francisco, CA: Jossey-Bass.

Dornbusch, S. M., & Ritter, P. L. (1988). Parents of high school students: A neglected resource. *Educational Horizons, 66,* 75–77.

Dryfoos, J. (1994). *Full-service schools.* San Francisco, CA: Jossey-Bass.

Eccles, J. S., & Harold, R. D. (1995). Family involvement in children's and adolescents' schooling. In A. Booth & J. Dunn (Eds.), *Family–school links: How do they affect educational outcomes* (pp. 3–34). Hillside, NJ: Lawrence Erlbaum Associates.

Edmonds, R. R. (1979). Effective schools for the urban poor. *Educational Leadership, 37*(2), 15–24.

Elder, G. H., Jr. (1997). The life course and human development. In R. M. Lerner (Ed.), *Handbook of child psychology, Vol. 1: Theoretical models of human development* (pp. 939–991). New York: Wiley.

Epstein J. L. (1983). Longitudinal effects of family–school–person interactions on student outcomes. In A. Kerckhoff (Ed.), *Research in sociology of education and socialization, Vol. 4* (pp. 101–128). Greenwich, CT: JAI Press.

Epstein, J. L. (1985). A question of merit: Principals' and parents' evaluations of teachers. *Educational Researcher, 14*(7), 3–10.

Epstein, J. L. (1986). Parents' reactions to teacher practices of parent involvement. *Elementary School Journal, 86,* 277–294.

Epstein, J. L. (1987). Toward a theory of family-school connections: Teacher practices and parent involvement. In K. Hurrelman, F. Kaufmann, & F. Losel (Eds.), *Social intervention: Potential and constraints* (pp. 121–136). New York: DeGruyter.

Epstein, J. L. (1990a). School and family connections: Theory, research, and implications for integrating sociologies of education and family. In D. Unger & M. Sussman (Eds.), *Families in community settings: Interdisciplinary perspectives* (p. 99–126). New York: Haworth.

Epstein, J. L. (1990b). Single parents and the schools: Effects of marital status on parent and teacher interactions. In M. Hallinan (Ed.), *Change in societal institutions* (pp. 91-121). New York: Plenum.

Epstein, J. L. (1991). Effects on student achievement of teacher practices of parent involvement. In S. Silvern (Ed.), *Advances in reading/language research: Literacy through family, community, and school interaction, Vol. 5* (pp. 261–276). Greenwich, CT: JAI.

Epstein, J. L. (1992). School and family partnerships. In M. Adkin (Ed.), *Encyclopedia of educational research* (6th ed., pp. 1139–1151). New York: MacMillan.

Epstein, J. L. (1995). School/family/community partnerships: Caring for the children we share. *Phi Delta Kappan, 76,* 701–712.

Epstein, J. L. (1996a). New connections for sociology and education: Contributing to school reform. *Sociology of Education, 69* (Special issue), 6-23.

Epstein, J. L. (1996b). Perspectives and previews on research and policy for school, family, and community partnerships. In A. Booth & J. Dunn (Eds.). *Family–school links: How do they affect educational outcomes* (pp. 209–246). Hillside, NJ: Lawrence Erlbaum Associates.

Epstein, J. L. (1998). *Interactive homework: Effective strategies to connect home and school.* Paper presented at the annual meeting of the American Educational Research Association, San Diego, California.

Epstein J. L. (in press). *School and family partnerships: Preparing educators and improving schools.* Boulder, CO: Westview Press.

Epstein, J. L., Coates, L., Salinas, K. C., Sanders, M. G., & Simon, B. S. (1997). *School, family, and community partnerships: Your handbook for action.* Thousand Oaks, CA: Corwin Press.

Epstein, J. L., & Conners, L. J. (1994). *Trust fund: School, family, and community partnerships in high schools.* Report. 24. Baltimore, MD: Center on Families, Communities, Schools and Children's Learning, Johns Hopkins University.

Epstein, J. L., & Dauber, S. L. (1991). School programs and teacher practices of parent involvement in inner-city elementary and middle schools. *Elementary School Journal, 91,* 289–303.

Epstein, J. L., Herrick, S. C., & Coates, L. (1996). Effects of summer home learning packets on student achievement in language arts in the middle grades. *School Effectiveness and School Improvement, 7*(3), 93–120.

Epstein, J. L., Jackson V., & Salinas, K. C. (1994). *Manual for teachers: Teachers involve parents in schoolwork TIPS language arts, science/health, and math interactive homework in the middle grades.* Baltimore, MD: Center on Families, Communities, Schools and Children's Learning, Johns Hopkins University.

Epstein, J. L., & Jacobsen, J. (1994). *Effects of school practices to involve families in the middle grades: Parents' perspectives.* Paper presented at the annual meeting of the American Sociological Association, Los Angeles, California.

Epstein, J. L., & Lee, S. (1993). *Effects of school practices to involve families on parents and students in the middle grades: A view from the schools.* Paper presented at the annual meeting of the American Sociological Association, Miami, Florida.

Epstein, J. L., & Lee, S. (1995). National patterns of school and family connections in the middle grades. In B. A. Ryan, G. R. Adams, T. P. Cullota, R. P. Weisberg, & R. L. Hampton (Eds.), *The family–school connection* (pp. 108–154). Thousand Oaks, CA: Sage.

Epstein, J. L., & Sanders, M. G. (in press). School, family, and community partnerships: Overview and new directions. In D. L. Levinson, A. R. Sadovnik, & P. W. Cookson, Jr. (Eds.), *Education and sociology: An encyclopedia.* New York: Garland.

Epstein, J. L., Sanders, M. G., & Clark, L. A. (1999). Preparing educators for school–family–community partnerships: Results of a national survey of colleges and universities. Report 34. Baltimore, MD: Center for Research on Education of Students Placed at Risk (CRESPAR), Johns Hopkins University.

Epstein, J. L., Simon, B. S., & Salinas, K. C. (1997). Effects of teachers involve parents in schoolwork (TIPS) language arts interactive homework in the middle grades. *Research Bulletin, #18*(September). Bloomington, IN: Phi Delta Kappa/Center for Evaluation, Development, and Research.

Etzioni, A. (1993). *The spirit of community: The reinvention of American society.* New York: Simon and Schuster.

Fagnano, C. L., & Werber, B. Z. (1994). *School, family, and community interaction: A view from the firing lines.* Boulder, CO: Westview Press.

Fantini, M. D. (1970). *Community control and the urban school.* New York: Praeger.

Fruchter, N., Galletta, A., & White, J. L. (1992). *New directions in parent involvement.* Washington DC: Academy for Educational Development.

Galindo, R., & Escamilla, K. (1995). A biographical perspective on Chicano educational success. *Urban Review 27*(1), 1–29.

Goodlad, J. (1988). *School–university partnerships in action.* New York: Teachers College Press.

Gordon, I. J. (1979). The effects of parent involvement in schooling. In R. S. Brandt (Ed.), *Partners: Parents and schools* (pp. 4-25). Alexandria, VA: ASCD.

Griffith, J. (1998) The relation of school structure and social environment to parent involvement in elementary schools. *The Elementary School Journal, 99,* 53–80.

Harkevy, L., & Puckett, J. L. (1990). *Toward effective university–public school partnerships: An analysis of three contemporary models.* University of Pennsylvania Graduate School of Education, Philadelphia.

Henderson, A. T., & Berla, N. (1994). *A new generation of evidence: The family is critical to student achievement.* Washington, DC: National Committee of Citizens in Education.

Hidalgo, N. M. (1994). Profile of a Puerto Rican family's support for school achievement. *Equity and Choice, 10*(2), 14–22.

Hidalgo, N. M., Bright, J., Siu, S., Swap, S., & Epstein J. (1995). Research on families, schools, and communities: A multicultural perspective. In J. Banks (Ed.), *Handbook of research on multicultural education* (pp. 498–524). New York: MacMillan.

Hoover-Dempsey, K. V., Bassler, O. C., & Burow, R. (1995). Parents' reported involvement in students' homework: Strategies and practices. *Elementary School Journal, 95,* 435–450.

Jencks, C. (1972). *Inequality: A reassessment of the effects of family and schooling in America.* New York: Basic Books.

Jencks, C. (1995). *Did we lose the war on poverty?* Paper presented at Seminar on Poverty and Social Policy, Department of Sociology, Johns Hopkins University, Baltimore, Maryland.

Johnson, V. R. (1994). *Parent centers in urban schools: Four case studies.* Report 23. Baltimore, MD: Center on Families, Communities, Schools and Children's Learning, Johns Hopkins University.

Kagan, S. L., Neville, P., & Rustici, J. (1993). *Family education and training: From research to practice—Implementation plan.* Report 14. Baltimore, MD: Center on Families, Communities, Schools and Children's Learning, Johns Hopkins University.

Keesling, J. W., & Melaragno, R. J. (1983). Parent participation in federal education programs. In R. Haskins & D. Adams (Eds.), *Parent education and public policy* (pp. 230–254). Norwood, NJ: Ablex.

Keith T. (1991). Parent involvement and achievement in high school. In S. Silvern (Ed.) *Advances in reading/language research: Literacy through family, community, and school interaction, Vol. 5* (pp. 125–141). Greenwich, CT: JAI Press.

Keith, T. (1998, April). *Homework in and out of school.* Paper presented at the annual meeting of the American Educational Research Association, San Diego, California.

Kilmes-Dougan, B., Lopez, J. A., Nelson, P., & Adelman, H. (1992). Two studies of low-income parents' involvement in schooling. *Urban Review, 24*(3), 185–202.

Lareau, A. (1989). *Home advantage: Social class and parental intervention in elementary education.* Philadelphia: Falmer Press.

Lee, S. (1994). *Family–school connections and students' education: Continuity and change of family involvement from the middle graded to high school.* Baltimore. MD: Unpublished doctoral dissertation, Department of Sociology, Johns Hopkins University.

Leichter, H. J. (1974). *The family as educator.* New York: Teachers College Press.

Lightfoot, S. L. (1978). *Worlds apart: Relationships between families and schools.* New York: Basic Books.

Litwak, E., & Meyer, H. J. (1974). *School, family, and neighborhood: The theory and practice of school–community relations.* New York: Columbia University Press.

Lutz, F. W., & Merz, C. (1992). *The politics of school–community relations.* New York: Teachers College Press.

Mawhinney, H. B. (1994). Institutional effects of strategic efforts at community collaboration. *Educational Administration Quarterly, 30*(3), 324–341.

McKenna, M., & Willms, J. D. (1998). The challenge facing parent councils in Canada. *Childhood Education, 74,* 378–382.

Moll, L. C., Amanti, C., Neff, D., & Gonzalez, N. (1992). Funds of knowledge for teaching: Using a qualitative approach to connect homes and classrooms. *Theory into Practice, 31*(2), 132–141.

Montandon, C. & Perrenoud, P. (1987). *Entre parents et enseignants un dialogue impossible?* Berne, Switzerland: Lang.

Morisset, C. E. (1993). *Language and emotional milestones: On the road to readiness.* Report 18. Baltimore, MD: Center on Families, Communities, Schools and Children's Learning, Johns Hopkins University.

Morisset, C. E. (1994). *School readiness: Parents and professionals speak on social and emotional needs of young children.* Report 26. Baltimore, MD: Center on Families, Communities, Schools, and Children's Learning, Johns Hopkins University.

National Commission on Excellence in Education. (1983). *A nation at risk: The imperative for educational reform.* Washington, DC: National Government Printing Office.

Nettles, S. M. (1992). *Coaching in community settings.* Report 9. Baltimore, MD: Center on Families, Communities, Schools, and Children's Learning, Johns Hopkins University.

Nettles, S. M. (1993). *Coaching in communities: A practitioner's manual.* Baltimore, MD: Center on Families, Communities, Schools, and Children's Learning, Johns Hopkins University.

Nord, C. W., Brimhall, D., & West, J. (1997). *Fathers' involvement in their children's schools.* Washington, DC: National Center for Education Statistics (NCES 98–091).

Organization for Economic Cooperation and Development (OECD). (1996). *What works in innovation in education: Parents as partners in schooling.* Paris, France: Center for Educational Research and Innovation/Organization for Economic Cooperation and Development.

Palanki, A., Burch, P., & Davies, D. (1995). *In our hands: A multi-site parent–teacher action research project on family–school–community partnerships.* Report 30. Baltimore, MD: Center on Families, Communities, Schools and Children's Learning, Johns Hopkins University.

Perry, T. (1993). *Toward a theory of African American school achievement.* Report 16. Baltimore, MD: Center on Families, Communities, Schools and Children's Learning, Johns Hopkins University.

Piaget, J., & Inhelder, B. (1969). *The psychology of the child.* New York: Basic Books.

Pryer, C., & Favorini, A. (1994). *Youth, parent, and teacher views of parent involvement in schools.* Department of Education, Wayne State University, Detroit, Michigan.

Rioux, W., & Berla N. (Eds., 1993). Innovations in parent and family involvement. Princeton Junction, NJ: Eye on Education.

Roderick, M. (1997). *Habits are hard to break: A new look at truancy in Chicago's public high schools.* Research brief: Student life in high schools project. Chicago: University of Chicago School of Social Service Administration.

Rumberger, R. W. (1995). Dropping out of middle school: A multilevel analysis of students and schools. *American Educational Research Journal, 32,* 583–626.

Ryan, B. A., Adams, G. R., Gullotta, T. P., Weissberg, R. P., & Hampton, R. L. (Eds., 1995). *The family–school connection.* Thousand Oaks. CA: Sage

Ryan, S., Bryk, A. S., Lopez, G., Williams, K. P., Hall, K., & Luppescu, S. (1997). *Charting reform: LSC—Local leadership at work.* Chicago: Consortium on Chicago School Research.

Sanchez, R. P., & Baguedano, M. M. (1993). *Curriculum of the home and mathematics achievement.* Paper presented at Fifth Annual International Roundtable on Family, Schools, and Children's Learning, Atlanta, Georgia.

Sanders, M. G. (1996). School–family–community partnerships focused on school safety: The Baltimore example. *Journal of Negro Education, 65*(3), 369–374.

Sanders, M. G. (1998). The effects of school, family, and community support on the academic achievement of African–American adolescents. *Urban Education, 33,* 385–410.

Sanders, M. G. (1999). School membership in the national network of partnership schools: Progress, challenges and next steps. *The Journal of Educational Research, 92*(4), 220–230.

Sanders, M. G., & Epstein, J. L. (Eds., 1998a). International perspectives on school, family and community partnerships. In *Childhood Education, 74* (International Focus Issue on School, Family, and Community Partnerships: International Perspective).

Sanders, M. G., & Epstein, J. L. (1998b). School–family–community partnerships and educational change: International perspectives. In A. Hargreaves, A. Lieberman, M. Fullan, & D. Hopkins (Eds.), *International handbook of educational change* (pp. 482–502). Hingham MA: Kluwer.

Sanders, M. G., & Epstein. J. L. (1998c). School–family–community partnership in middle and high schools: From theory to practice. CRESPAR Report 22. Baltimore, MD: Center for Research on the Education of Students Placed at Risk (CRESPAR), Johns Hopkins University.

Sanders, M. G., Epstein, J. L., & Connors-Tadros, L. C. (1999). *Family partnership with high schools: The parents' perspective.* CRESPAR Report. Baltimore MD: Center for Research on the Education of Students Placed at Risk (CRESPAR), Johns Hopkins University.

Schneider, B., & Coleman, J. S. (Eds., 1993). *Parents, their children, and schools.* Boulder, CO: Westview Press.

Schorr, L. (1997). *Common purpose: Strengthening families and neighborhoods to rebuild America.* New York: Doubleday.

Scott-Jones, D. (1996). *Social relationships, sources of support, and educational aspirations of adolescent childbearers.* Baltimore, MD: Center on Families, Communities, Schools and Children's Learning, Johns Hopkins University.

Seeley, D. S. (1981). *Education through partnership: Mediating structures and education.* Cambridge, MA: Ballinger.

Shartrand, A. M., Weiss, H. B., Kreider, H. M., & Lopez, M. E. (1997). *New skills for new schools: Preparing teachers in family involvement.* Cambridge, MA: Harvard Family Research Project.

Shouse, R. C. (1996). Academic press and sense of community: Conflict, congruence, and implications for student achievement. *Social Psychology of Education, 1,* 47–68.

Silvern, S. (Ed., 1991). Advances in reading/language research: Literacy through family community, and school interaction. Vol. 5. Greenwich, CT: JAI Press.

Siu, S., & Feldman, J. (1996). *Patterns of Chinese American family involvement in young children's education: Final report.* Report 36. Baltimore, MD: Center on Families, Communities, Schools and Children's Learning, Johns Hopkins University.

Sprague, J. (1998). (Re)making sociology: Breaking the bonds of our discipline. *Contemporary Sociology, 27,* 24–28.

Swap, S. M. (1993). *Developing home–school partnerships: From concepts to practice.* NY: Teachers College Press.

Swap, S. M. (1994). Irish–American identity: Does it still have meaning in supporting children's school success? *Equity and Choice, 10*(2), 33–41.

Tonnies, F. (1963/1987). [*Gemeinschaft und Gesellschaft*]. Community and society (C. P. Loomis, Trans). New York: HarperCollins.

Topping, K. J. (1995). Cued spelling: a powerful technique for parent and peer tutoring. *The Reading Teacher, 48*(5), 374–383.

Tucker, C. J., Marx, J., & Long, L. (1998). "Moving on": Residential mobility and children's school lives. *Sociology of Education, 71,* 111–129.

Useem, E. L. (1991). Student selection into course selection sequences in mathematics: The impact of parent involvement and school policies. *Journal of Research on Adolescence, 1,* 231–250.

Useem, E. L. (1992). Middle school and math groups: Parents' involvement in children's placement. *Sociology of Education, 65,* 263–279.

Waller, W. (1932). *The sociology of teaching.* New York: Russell and Russell.

Wasik, B. A., & Karweit, N. (1994). Off to a good start: Effects of birth-to-three interventions on early school success. In R. Slavin, N. Karweit, & B. Wasik (Eds.), *Preventing early school failure* (pp. 13–57) New York: Longwood.

Weber, M. (1947). *Theory of social and economic organization* (A. M. Henderson and T. Parsons trans.) New York: Oxford University Press.

Wynn, J., Costello, J., Halpern, R., & Richman, H. (1994). *Children, families, and communities.* Chapin Hall Center for Children, University of Chicago.

Young, K. T., & Marx, E. (1992). *What does learning mean for infants and toddlers? The contributions of the child, family, and community.* Report 3. Baltimore, MD: Center on Families, Communities, Schools and Children's Learning, Johns Hopkins University.

Zigler, E., & Valentine, J. (Eds., 1975). *Project Head Start: A legacy of the war on poverty.* New York: The Free Press.

Zill, N. (1996). Family change and students' achievement: What we have learned, and what it means for schools. In A. Booth & J. Dunn (Eds.), *Family–school links: How do they affect educational outcomes* (pp. 139–174). Hillside, NJ: Lawrence Erlbaum Associates.

CHAPTER 13

The Variable Construction of Educational Risk

John G. Richardson

INTRODUCTION

In this chapter I explore educational risk as a professional motivation and as a strategy for policy reform and intervention. I do so by way of a comparison of two educational practices: curricular tracking and special education placement. Both tracking and special education placement exhibit a number of common features, such as organizational and pedagogical similarities. However, they diverge in a critical way. Despite evidence showing the disproportionate assignment of minority and low socioeconomic students to lower tracks, the practice of tracking has never fully developed a consensual discourse of educational risk. In contrast, the evidence of racial overrepresentation, revealed for educable mentally retarded (EMR) classes in the 1960s, and continuing for learning disability (LD) classes currently, promoted a discourse of risk within special education and impelled it toward broader challenges that helped to shape a program of full inclusion into public education.

By maximizing the features tracking and special education share in common, I hope to isolate the factors that provide the best explanation for this difference. I argue that the main source is the strategic roles played by school psychology and by counseling, the former linked to special education and the latter to tracking. Although this difference in strategic practice is a necessary element, the sufficient condition was prompted by a professional crisis within school psychology that led to a reflection on its knowledge base and its authoritative standing within public education. This reflection focused on special education and has had important

JOHN G. RICHARDSON • Department of Sociology, Western Washington University, Bellingham, Washington 98225

Handbook of the Sociology of Education, edited by Maureen T. Hallinan. Kluwer Academic/Plenum Publishers, New York, 2000.

implications for general education as a whole. As a consequence, the original discourse relating minority students and inappropriate placement broadened in ethical scope and in legal jurisdiction, causing a maturation in curricular content that tracking has not shared. Tracking, on the other hand, has remained an obdurate practice that is resistant to a cohesive discourse of educational risk as well as to reform efforts to detrack.

Conditions for a Discourse of Educational Risk

Two conditions are necessary for the emergence of a motivation that would give form to a discourse of educational risk. The first is a change in the social organization of schooling, such as a change in the size or the composition of school participation. The change need not be dramatic; indeed, incremental changes can become magnified and defined as evidence of circumstances that expose children to some risk (Cuban, 1989).

Second the changes in school organization must assume a broader political and cultural resonance. They must take on a meaning that transcends the educational. For example, leaving school before receiving a diploma has always occurred, yet dropping out assumes a larger symbolic meaning. Those at risk of dropping out take on symbolic proportions that exceed their actual statistical size. Indeed, the rate of school leaving may be declining, as it has over the past several years (Loveless, 1997, pp. 143–144), yet dropping out takes on a symbolic life of its own. Rather than being contained within the boundary of routine educational practice, it becomes a significant symbol that reverberates beyond schools. Independent of the size of the population that drops out of school, the collective behaviors constitute a phenomenon that departs from prevailing expectations.

The mechanism that elevates organizational changes to assume a broader political resonance is nearly always a legal or legislative decision with such scope that it ties local school problems to national issues. Decisions such as *Brown v. Board of Education* (1954) or *PL 94–142* (The Education for All Handicapped Children Act, 1975) qualitatively redefine how school practices are to be seen. As I show, a court decision of national import was instrumental to the initial problematization of tracking and special education placement and to the stimulation of an at-risk motivation.

The Stratification of Educational Risk

For urban schools during the years following WWII, the postwar optimism seemed to overshadow the organizational vulnerability of earlier decades. Economic prosperity and a wish for normalcy certainly contributed to this optimism. Yet, due in large part to this very prosperity and optimism, social and organizational changes bearing a strong resemblance to those of the first decades of the 20th century were underway.

Among the major changes was the migration of Blacks out of southern states to northern and western cities. Throughout the 1950s and into the 1960s, the composition of major urban school systems was significantly altered, for some in a matter of a few years. Without question, the impact of *Brown v. Board of Education* in 1954 accentuated this demographic trend by striking at the traditional authority of schools at the local level. Yet just as special education reform was built in stages, this demographic trend may not have had the organizational impact it did without prior changes internal to schools.

The key internal change was what Martin Trow aptly called the "second transformation of secondary education (Trow, 1973). By 1945, American secondary schools had reached a mass, universal level of participation and were no longer simply a terminal level. The second transformation, in Trow's terms, was the necessity of high school curriculum and instruction reorganization as preparatory to higher education. This reorganization of secondary education tightened the tracking structure, with a main dividing line drawn between the college preparatory track and the general, noncollege-bound track. Whereas the comprehensive high school had once been promoted as the model distinguishing American secondary education, now track placements were closely linked to higher education. Estimates for the late 1960s claimed that 85% of students in college preparatory curriculum enrolled in college compared to only 15% for those in other curricular placements (Jencks et al., 1972, pp. 33–34).

At about the same time that surveys explored the statistical prevalence of tracks and their implications (see National Education Association, 1968), state surveys made evident the statistical overrepresentation of minority students in special education classes for the mentally retarded. In California, students with Spanish surnames comprised 15% of the statewide public school population but represented 28% of the EMR classes. Likewise, Black students comprised 9% of the statewide population but made up 26% of California's EMR classes (Memorandum, 1970). In Tempe, Arizona, it was reported that "while 17.8% of the district's school children [are] Mexican–American, 67.7% of the children assigned to EMR classes and 46% of the children assigned to classes for the trainable mentally retarded are Mexican–American" (Kirp, 1973, p. 760). Like tracking, which "almost inevitably means [students] are segregated, albeit to a lesser extent, in terms of social class and race" (Jencks et al., 1972, p. 34), such statistical evidence revealed that special education placement was deeply implicated in the curricular segregation of students along racial and ethnic lines.

The organizational change in secondary schooling might have passed as a routine but challenging transformation in curriculum and instruction. Moreover, district and state survey data on tracking and on special education might simply have been interpreted as local and particular to each case. Instead, significant court decisions elevated both programs into national view, conferring enormous political resonance onto the educational consequences of school tracking and on special education placement.

In a sweeping decision handed down in 1967 and relating to a host of school practices in the Washington D.C. school system, the U.S. District court Judge J. Skelly Wright concluded that "the tracking system must simply be abolished" (*Hobson v. Hansen*, 1967). The tracking system in Washington, D.C. was implemented in the high schools in 1956 and in the junior high and elementary schools in 1959. The timing of its implementation is significant, for in large measure it came in response to *Brown v. the Board of Education* (1954) and the specter of desegregating what was a dual school system founded on race. When *Brown v. Board of Education* was issued, there were some 64,000 Black students and 41,000 White students who were each educated in separate schools. Policies set by the Board of Education unified the city's schools, producing racially mixed classes in 116 schools, which constituted 73% of the total number of schools. Based on citywide test results that demonstrated the comparative weakness of the schools, a four-track system was soon instituted. The tracks consisted of honors, college preparatory, general, and basic tracks (Hansen, 1964). The timing of the four-track system with the federal mandate to desegregate became transparent with evidence that Black students were assigned to the basic track in disproportionate numbers. When efforts were made to evaluate these assignments by psychological testing, it was revealed that nearly two thirds of the 1,272 students were improperly classified.

The brunt of the challenge focused on the use of standardized aptitude tests that were argued to produce inaccurate and misleading test scores. In contrast to achievement tests, which are designed to measure competence in a given subject, and can thus be used to group students for shorter periods of time, aptitude tests are employed to track students for longer periods. Although admittedly a strong case, the focus by *Hobson v. Hansen* (1967) on the deficiencies of aptitude tests and the discrepancies between initial and later assessments left open a more complex question. *Hobson v. Hansen* identified the use of aptitude tests as the root cause of racial and class discrimination and concluded that the tracking system as a whole must be abolished.

Although it brought constitutional issues to bear on the outcomes of student grouping, the real effects of *Hobson v. Hansen* (1967) may have been more symbolic than organizational. In spite of the declaration to abolish the tracking system, the responses of school systems have sustained the very outcomes that this court challenge sought to alter. As Judge Wright foresaw, a name change from Basic track to Special Academic was largely a euphemistic change.

Special education was also the cause of strenuous complaint. In just months after *Hobson v. Hansen* (1967) one of the first class action suits against minority overrepresentation in EMR classes was filed in California. In *Diana v. Board of Education* (1970), the fundamental argument was that Mexican–American children placed in EMR classes were not legally mentally retarded because they were not tested in their primary home language. The settlement was confined to this specific challenge, enjoining state schools to test in both English and Spanish where necessary and to produce norms based on Mexican–American students in the school population.

Coming soon after *Diana v. Board of Education* (1970) was the most significant challenge to the overrepresentation of Black students. In *Larry P. v. Riles* (1972), the class action suit filed on behalf of Black children in San Francisco, the scope of challenges was broadened with the claim that the IQ test was culturally biased and that inaccurate tests violated the constitutional right to equal protection when used to assess Black students. Low socioeconomic status students, Black students, and Hispanic students, and males as well, were the groups that were most at risk for referral to special education and for potential misclassification. The demand for an immediate moratorium was granted and won, initiating a decade-long debate over test bias and special education placement.

Both tracking and special education placement share these organizational and legislative events. Both were rendered problematic by evidence that minority and low socioeconomic groups were disproportionately at risk of inappropriate assignment to a low track or to placement in special education. Yet there was an important difference. Tracking did not go on to fully develop either a cohesive professional discourse or a reform effort of national scope that successfully generalized the impact of *Hobson v. Hansen* (1967). In contrast, special education strengthened its stature and broadened its professional jurisdiction, advancing a vision of full inclusion into public education as a national objective and an attainable policy.

Before returning to this critical difference, I first review the mutual lines of agreement that tracking and special education placement share. Against their several commonalties, the failure of tracking to develop a generalized discourse of educational risk becomes all the more salient against the inclusive discourse of special education.

LINES OF AGREEMENT

Selection and Placement: Common Processes, Similar Outcomes

Empirical research yields similar findings about how tracking and special education function and about their effectiveness and resilience. Both are procedurally similar. Track assignments and special education placements are social processes that initiate from referrals and from recommendations coming from teachers and counselors, from school psychologists, and from related staff (cf. Hallinan, 1992, p. 115; Skrtic, 1995, p. 246). Amidst this process is parental involvement, intruding at various points and with varying resources.

SCHOOL TRACKING.   The empirical study of tracking has undergone a discernible maturation. In the "first generation" of studies published during the mid- and late 1970s, the focus was almost wholly on the secondary level. In the analysis of track assignment, empirical results disputed the relative influence of students' background characteristics or prior achievement. A number of studies found that although students' background characteristics were associated with track placement, the factors most directly responsible were students' ability and academic performance differences (Davis & Haller, 1981; Rehberg & Rosenthal, 1978; Schafer & Olexa, 1971). However, these meritocratic and functionalist interpretations were challenged by studies that emphasized how race and social class exerted their influence prior to and beyond initial track recommendations (Alexander, Cook, & McDill, 1978; Alexander & McDill, 1976; Rosenbaum, 1976, 1980). The confounding of race and class background with measures of students' ability seemed an inescapable dilemma.

One apparent exit from this impasse appeared to be the role played by high school counselors in the advising process (Cicourel & Kitsuse, 1963; Erickson, 1975; Heyns, 1974, p. 1445). As gatekeeper, the counselor was the key intervening variable. Higher social class and advantaged racial background may influence track assignment by influencing the distribution of relevant information and advice. That is, a counselor might be more inclined to advise a wealthier student to try for a college-bound track. The strategic role of counseling seemed to break the logjam between merit and background.

In spite of this important and mutual recognition, the empirical study of track assignment turned elsewhere, growing lengthwise by extending the temporal boundary to grades before the secondary level. In their re-examination of the curriculum process model, Alexander and Cook (1982) included a measure of "the very *raison d'etre* of the differentiated high school curricula (p. 626)," that is students' prior academic records. Their results helped to disentangle the impasse on track assignments, doing so by reinterpreting curriculum effects as reflecting "pre-high school differences in academic experiences and resources" (p. 636). The surprise ending in Alexander and Cook's study was to focus the study of track assignment onto earlier grades, thereby conceiving of eventual track placements as carrying along "differences in achievement trajectories set in motion years earlier" (p. 637). Track placement becomes just one point among many that constitute an educational trajectory begun much earlier than high school.

With the singular notion of trajectory, the earlier dilemma of entangled effects seemed to quickly recede. By conceiving of track assignment more as a career than as a curricular place, the relative contribution of status characteristics, ability, or prior achievement records is also reconceived as patterns of interactions that change over time (Dauber, Alexander, & Entwisle, 1996; Oakes, 1990; Stevenson. Schiller, & Schneider, 1994) and that structure learning opportunities (Oakes, 1985, Chapter 5; 1987, p. 140; Gamoran, 1987; Hallinan, 1991, 1992; Lee & Bryk, 1988; Oakes, Gamoran, & Page, 1992). Earlier claims that parental background variables were weak or insignificant are also revisited, now asking when race or social class influences enter into the shaping of educational careers.

As Dauber and associates (1996) found, the transition to the sixth grade is an especially critical point, for students' academic records are "weakly articulated" here, allowing for "extra-schooling factors to affect the placement process" (p. 301). With this insight, earlier studies claiming weak or irrelevant effects of social background were cast in a different light: when this critical time in the trajectory of a student's career is included in analyses, strong effects are revealed for social background. For example, at this critical point higher socioeconomic parents may exert their pressure on their children to study and on the school to track their children appropriately. With the higher academic performance of their children ensured, school achievement is linked to school track (Baker & Stevenson, 1986; Finley, 1986, p. 236; Lareau, 1987; Useem, 1991; Vanfossen, Jones, & Spade, 1987, p. 108).

The research that extended the study of track assignment along temporal dimensions paralleled research that enlarged the measurement of organizational constraints on placement. Much of this research can be traced to the early formulations by Barr and Dreeben (1983) and by Sørensen (1970). The former conceived of instructional groups as outcomes of intentional decisions made by teachers to regulate the pace of instruction. Instructional groups that are purportedly homogeneous in students' ability and achievement are formed in response to the class distribution of these differences.

In contrast to this view, Sørensen's likening of ability groups to a vacancy competition allowed for the separation of student, ability distributions and instructional group formation. Ability groups and tracks are closed-position systems that are filled by ranking procedures, much like promotion schedules fill job vacancies (Hallinan & Sørensen, 1983). Teachers may refrain from altering the size of groups because they anticipate organizational disturbances that may elicit resistance from parents as well as alter their own expenditure of instructional effort. Thus, within the constraints of limited resources and facing a range of student abilities, teachers form groups not in full cognizance of instructional goals but in response to the practical limitations of resources and the requirement that groups survive through time. Independent of the stated intentions of teachers, instructional groups remain constant in size, and once formed, remain stable over time as well.

Misassignments may go undetected or become increasingly difficult to correct, because to the extent that ability groups are both invariant in size and stable over time, the potential for movement across groups is diminished. Although initial group formation indeed inaugurates a trajectory, these trajectories are not certain outcomes. The risks associated with tracking vary and feature departures from expected inequities. In their analysis of secondary tracking using *High School and Beyond* data, Gamoran and Mare (1989) found that tracking widens differences in achievement between high- and low-socio-economic status students, but the assignment process "favors blacks and females over non-blacks and males who are equal on other characteristics (p. 1172), "a finding they interpret as compensating for preexisting differences. However, with the same data, Jones, Vanfossen, and Ensminger (1995) have found that higher SES students in tracking systems that are high in electivity (the ability of students to choose) are more likely to be in the general than in the academic track; and in lower electivity schools, where students are assigned by school personnel, lower SES students are more likely to be in the academic track. In support of Gamoran and Mare, they found Blacks to be more likely than non-Blacks to be in the academic track, but the probability of being in the vocational track increases "if students are Black or female and have lower educational expectations and grades" (Jones et al., 1995, pp. 294-295).

Thus, whether race or SES will be misassigned to lower tracks depends on the particular configuration of variables, a configuration that arises, in part, from the microeconomic decisions made by teachers. As Brown and Saks (1981) aptly noted, by sorting students, teachers do indeed regulate the pace of learning, but pace is a property of the group so formed. These group properties, in turn, affect the broader context of the school, for "the decision about pace is also a decision about the mean and variance of outcomes" (Brown & Saks, p. 241). The difference between the mean and the variance of outcomes is at the core of ability groups as a tracking structure. At the same time, the contrast between the mean and the variance of outcomes is at the core of the relationship between tracking and special education placement. The two are not separate structures dealing with different student populations. Rather, they are dynamically similar and organizationally interdependent, linked by way of the population of low-achieving students.

SPECIAL EDUCATION PLACEMENT.   Much like tracking, the empirical study of special education placement has undergone a maturation. Fueled by revelations of minority overrepresentation in EMR classes (Dunn, 1968; Mercer, 1973), the early focus was preoccupied with questions of the efficacy of special class placement, a question that was shadowed by claims of test bias and inaccurate diagnosis of students from minority and from low-socioeconomic-status backgrounds.

The division between individual ability characteristics and nonintellectual factors has strongly shaped the course of empirical research on special education placement. The first generation of studies occupied with the efficacy of special class placement reported largely negative findings (Christoplos & Renz, 1969; Jones, 1972). However, in the course of such assessments, attention turned to the factors that accounted for the decision-making phase (Gerber & Semmel, 1985, p. 20). Educational risk was greatest at this point, for evidence showed that IQ was not the determining factor in special education placement (Garrison & Hammill, 1971; Mercer, 1973; Rubin, Krus, & Balow, 1973).

Like track assignment, special education placement is the culmination of a series of interchanges between teachers, psychologists, and parents. As Mehan, Hertweck, and Meihls (1986) demonstrated, the result is a socially constructed "discourse of persuasion" (pp. 109–138) that legitimizes the initial referral. This discourse becomes persuasive, in large part as the technical expertise of school psychologists is elevated above the lay observations of teachers and of parents. Yet the elevation of technical expertise is influenced by parental resources (Christenson, Ysseldyke, & Algozzine, 1982) and knowledge (Brantlinger, 1987): parents with higher status intrude at the point of referral, shaping the trajectory or terminating special class placement altogether. The point of referral is akin to the critical sixth grade in tracking. For both it is the point of opportunity when parental status and resource differences define what become long-term educational trajectories in schools.

A number of studies have demonstrated that the decision-making process for special education is only minimally guided by objective data (Johnson, 1980, p. 199; Yssledyke, Algozzine, & Allen, 1981; Ysseldyke, Thurlow, et al., 1983). Damaging is evidence that teachers are poor judges of candidates for special education (Ysseldyke, Algozzine, Shinn, & McGue, 1982; Ysseldyke & Foster, 1978) and that teachers and psychologists cannot reliably differentiate between students labeled as LD from low-achieving students (Algozzine & Ysseldyke, 1983; Epps, Ysseldyke, McGue, 1984; Ysseldyke, Algozzine, Richey, & Graden, 1982), nor from students identified as at risk (Hocutt, Cox, Pelosi, 1984). Such evidence reinvigorated claims that nearly half of the students in LD classes may be inappropriately classified (Shepard, 1987), unjustifiably "burgeoning the masses" (Algozzine, Ysseldyke, & Christenson, 1983).

Like tracking, special class placement can be viewed as a vacancy competition. The number of positions in special classes is closed and vacant slots are filled less by the true instructional needs of handicapped students than by the timing of referral and of district policy. Evidence of the unreliability of assessment and professional judgments, evidence that reveals the sources of inaccurate diagnosis and improper placement, underscores the organizational context of special education placement and weakens the empirical and logical rationale for the classification of students with disabilities (Ysseldyke, 1987, p. 261; Ysseldyke, Algozzine, & Epps, 1983). The studies that demonstrate a failure by teachers and by psychologists to reliably distinguish low-achieving students from students classified in special education illustrate the constraints that Mehan and associates (1986) called practical circumstances, the "sedimentation from actions of several individuals, some of which are taken in concert, some autonomously" (p. 52). At a minimum, the number of students who are low achieving typically exceeds the number of students who are referred for and placed in special education. Once a student was referred, the probability was nearly 80% that he/she would be placed. Similar to track assignment, once referred, a trajectory is defined that is difficult to alter.

Even apart from school climate or from formal policy, the mere existence of placements separate from regular classes bears on the allocation of time by teachers. As Gerber and Semmel (1985) noted, "classroom teachers' behavior is fundamentally oriented toward maintaining the *forward flow of activity* in classrooms" (p. 23), a force that constrains teachers to relinquish responsibility for low-achieving students onto more specialized, but separate, instructional arrangements. Teachers must make decisions that influence the allocation of their instructional effort and time. Thus, insofar as low achievement is a central reason for referral and for placement, the class distribution of achievement is defining, not only of an individual student's ranking but also of a teacher's allocation of instructional time.

The microeconomics of special education referral (Gerber & Semmel, 1985) are determined by the prevailing orientation of the school generally and constrained in particular by the organizational relation between general and special education in particular. If the orientation of the school is to enhance the academic performance of able and achieving students, the allocation of time by teachers is more rationally directed toward higher tracked students and away from low-achieving students. If, on the other hand, policy constraints promote the integration of low-achieving students and students with disabilities into the mainstream of instruction, the behavior of teachers would be toward reducing the variance in the overall student ability distribution. Overrepresentations in special education need not imply insensitivity or discriminatory referral; they can arise as unintended consequences generated by particular organizational features of a school. A consequence, albeit unintended, is that "erroneous classification of students as mildly handicapped is a function of, and is encouraged by, many of the structural limitations imposed upon schooling" (Gerber & Semmel, 1985, p. 24).

The longitudinal research of the School Environment Project (Semmel, Gerber, & Abernathy, 1993) demonstrates just how intricate the nexus can be that joins special to general education. This research takes the school and not the classroom as the unit of analysis and examines the impact of general education achievement gains on the variation in achievement measures among special education students. Empirical results find no positive relationship between general school achievement and the enhanced performance of special education students. The findings revealed that schools with gains in general education are not necessarily the same schools with gains in special education. More revealing, however, is the finding that gains experienced in a school's general education may be detrimental to special education:

> As schools respond to pressures of the most recent school improvement reforms for increasing academic achievement, under conditions of diminishing resources, they may adaptively develop strategies for increasing school means—to the detriment of their nonmodal special education pupils. (Semmel, Gerber, & MacMillan, 1995, p. 54)

Legal Challenges: Similar Evidence, Similar Records

The agreements between tracking and special education placement are matched by striking parallels in their mutual legal careers. Both have been subject to court challenges over evidence of minority disproportion, in lower tracks and in classes for the mildly handicapped. Yet, following *Hobson v. Hansen* (1967) and *Larry P. v. Riles* (1972), the record of legal challenges has been checkered for both tracking and special education. With essentially similar claims, founded on comparably similar statistical evidence, subsequent cases have not been granted favorable opinions. Although some cases have followed the precedents set by *Hobson v. Hansen* and *Larry P. v. Riles*, others have failed to affirm their conclusions. Indeed, they have set their own precedents.

The legal challenges surrounding tracking carry with them the legacy of racial segregation. Challenges to current outcomes of tracking may seek to demonstrate that such outcomes are continuations of earlier policies of segregation by arguing that "districts used tracking to undermine the intent of the original desegregation orders" (Welner & Oakes, 1996, p. 456). Recent successful challenges have indeed linked evidence of racial disproportion in ability groups and in tracks to the vestiges of past segregation, demonstrating both discriminatory intent and disparate impact on minority students (cf. *Coalition to Save Our Children v. State Board of Education,* 1995; *People Who Care v. Rockford,* 1994; *Vasquez v. San Jose Unified School District,* 1994). What's important, the challenges to racial disproportion in ability groups included similar challenges to special education placement. Successful challenges demonstrated the inseparable relation between tracking and special education, for as stated in *People Who Care v. Rockford,* "a finding of intentionally segregative school board conduct in a meaningful portion of a school system creates a presumption that other segregated activity within the school system is not coincidental" (p. 931).

Yet, in contradistinction to these successful challenges, essentially the same claims resulted in different outcomes in *Georgia State Conference of Branches of NAACP v. Georgia* (1985) and in *Quarles v. [Oxford] Municipal Separate School District* (1989). In the former case, the Appeals Court Judge found that achievement grouping of students in fact "remedied consequences of prior segregation" (p. 1403). This interpretation nullified "any resulting numerical racial disproportionality." The racial disparity in lower achievement groups was not disputed; rather, it was fully acknowledged. Yet, the claim that these disparities were continuations of earlier practices of segregation was rejected, for contemporary grouping practices were found to be remediating. The rejection of racial disproportionality in achievement grouping extended to special education. In its rejection of statistical evidence showing racial overrepresentation in EMR classes, the court argued that this evidence was "insufficient to establish a prima facie case of disparate impact" (p. 1421). This rejection was bolstered by the court's claim that "the number of white children assigned to EMR programs through the same impermissible application of the procedural regulations was not examined by the plaintiffs" (p. 1421–1422). Thus, statistical evidence of racial disproportion in tracking and in special education does not by itself imply inequity, for "practices which detrimentally affect all groups equally do not have a discriminatory effect" (p. 1422).

Likewise, in *Quarles v. Oxford Municipal Separate School District* (1989) the court asserted frankly that "achievement or ability grouping has been recognized by both courts and educators as an acceptable and commonly used instruction method" (p. 753). Although presented with statistical evidence that showed accelerated classes were composed predominantly of White students, the district countered that it did not strictly impose the state's cut off for entrance into these classes. The court agreed and rejected any claim of discrimination, for "all classes truly are open to all students" (p. 754). Similarly, for allegations of discriminatory disciplinary treatment, the court found that the publication of race-neutral and uniform rules and regulations erased discriminatory intent. Equalities of risk nullified disparities in outcomes.

In the legal tempest over racial overrepresentation in special education, the arguments framed by *Larry P. v. Riles* (1972) composed the model for subsequent challenges. Yet, much like the confrontations over tracking, statistical patterns of overrepresentation did not by themselves demonstrate discriminatory intent. The outcome of *PASE v. Hannon* (1980) stands in sharp contrast to *Larry P. v. Riles*. Whereas Judge Peckham declared the IQ test to be culturally biased in *Larry P. v. Riles*, Judge Grady expressed no such agreement in *PASE v. Hannon*. With most of the issues strikingly the same, *PASE v. Hannon* nonetheless critiqued the claim that poverty was a source of IQ deficits and downplayed the significance of adaptive behavior for the measurement of intelligence. As Elliot (1987) summarized: "Judge Grady was interested in the tests at a far more microanalytical level than Judge Peckham" (p. 199).

Similarly, in *Marshall et al. v. Georgia* (1985) first filed in 1982, plaintiffs argued that the overrepresentation of Black students arose from violations of procedural protections and improper interpretation of federal and state standards and guidelines. Although many of the claims drew on *Larry P. v. Riles* (1972) as precedent, the decision was, like *PASE v. Hannan* (1980), strikingly opposite. The claims of misclassification were rejected, turning away the argument that overrepresentation arose from discriminatory intent. With affinities to *GANAACP* (*Georgia State Conference of Branches of NAACP v. Georgia* (1985) statistical disparity in EMR placement was nullified as resulting from procedural violations, for such occurrences were found for White students as well. Moreover, the court emphasized the beneficial outcomes from the grouping of low-achieving Black and White students, a departure from the reasoning in *Hobson v. Hansen* (1967) (Reschly, Kicklighter & McKee, 1988, p. 18).

The cumulation of these contrasting decisions for tracking and special education brought both to a critical juncture. For tracking, the decision in *McNeal v. Tate County School District* (1975) opened the way for the modification of desegregation orders by declaring that school districts were "free to use ability grouping . . . in an otherwise unitary system" (p. 1017–1018). Convincing a court that a unitary system had been essentially achieved would render statistical evidence of racial disparities across tracks more difficult to challenge. The practice of ability grouping was neither inherently wrong nor constitutionally forbidden (*Castaneda v. Pickard*, 1981). If equality of access to courses was flexible and if procedures were published in a uniform manner, statistical disparities arose more from student choice, neglect, or underachievement, not from discriminatory intent.

Like tracking, the discrepant outcomes in special education cases weakened contentions that overrepresentation was prima facie evidence of discriminatory intent. Discrepant court decisions contributed to a declining consensus about what caused racial overrepresentation and about its meaning as well. The national panel on overrepresentation, Panel on Selection and Placement of Students in Programs for the Mentally Retarded, commissioned by the National Academy of Sciences (Heller, Holtzman & Messick, 1982) reflected this by signaling a shift in focus. The commission changed the question from why overrepresentation occurred to why it was a problem all (see also Prasse & Reschly, 1986; Reschly, 1984). The panel confirmed the national presence of minority overrepresentation; yet just as quickly it demoted the statistical disparities as not by themselves implying inequity.

POINTS OF DIFFERENCE

The Difference of Organizational Response

In spite of the similarities in judicial histories, tracking and special education placement took different paths. Special education progressed toward a broader conceptualization of educational risk and was the agent for significant change in the professional role of school psychology itself. In contrast, challenges against tracking have been stalled. In spite of forceful efforts to detrack a school system (Oakes, 1992), or of innovative efforts to untrack single schools (Mehan, 1997; Mehan, Villanueva, Hubbard, & Lintz, 1996;), such efforts remain largely isolated from each other. Although significant organizations are on record as opposing tracking (Oakes, 1992, p. 16–17; Welner & Oakes, 1996, pp. 452–453), such declarations await a national-level focus akin to the panel in special education, and federal legislation akin to PL 94–142.

The initial contribution of minority overrepresentation to the broadening of the discourse of special education was moral. In spite of the evidence that more is spent on programs for the mildly handicapped and that student–teacher ratios are smaller, special education placement had become associated with the stigma of disability (Reschly, 1988a, p. 27). The moral dimension overshadowed the empirical and contributed to an ever-widening conceptualization of educational risk.

Fueled by the moral characterization of special class placement as segregationism (Wang & Walbert, 1988), calls were voiced for a Regular Education Initiative (REI), a partnership between special and general education (Will, 1986), and more forcefully, for the dismantling of special education itself and the construction of a unitary system (Lipsky & Gartner, 1989). Yet, these initiatives and bold proclamations distracted attention from serious divisions within school psychology that expressed a sense of diminished power, and they evoked fears about the future of the profession. Soon after the passage of The *Education for All Handicapped Children Act* in 1975, Ysseldyke (1978) expressed in frank terms that "while school psychologists have sat around arguing their role and function, the courts, the legislature, and special education administrators have determined the destiny of their profession" (p. 373–374). Likening the profession to a football team behind in points late in the game, school psychology was "in a state of crisis and confusion," vulnerable to the intrusion of many and conflicting views (p. 374).

The vulnerability of school psychology was exacerbated by the legalization of its occupational field. The potential for teacher and parent distrust of school psychology was always a structural liability, for school psychologists "serve twin masters, the profession and the bureaucracy" (D. L. Kirp & Kirp, 1976, p. 84). However, in addition, Supreme Court decisions that extended due process rights to students (*Goss v. Lopez,* 1975; *Wood v. Strickland,* 1975) introduced the threat if not the actuality of legal sanction into the process of assessment and special education placement. Although this increased legal formalism surrounded the role of school psychologist, exposing the potential risks of assessment and placement decisions, the crisis in professional authority presented a unique challenge, an opportunity to break from its twin masters, by redirecting assessment efforts long designed to have "institutional payoff" to ones that promoted "individual payoff" (Ysseldyke, 1978, p. 377).

By the mid-1980s, school psychology began to reflect on its history, its knowledge base, and its professional training. However, prompted by the challenges and reforms in special education, school psychology viewed a fractured past and a threatened present. Its reflection was centered on the risks and inequities of overrepresentation in special education, not on the evidentiary similarities in school tracking. Such a reflection contributed to a broadened ethical scope (Ysseldyke, 1982, p. 551). However, a technical narrowing of the freedom to exercise professional inference enabled this broadening, for the ability to retain jurisdictional power is intertwined with the relations linking diagnosis and inference (Abbott, 1988, p. 49).

The scope of ethical concern was broadened by the attachment of procedural due process rights to special education referral, assessment, and placement decisions. The ethical focus reached beyond diagnostic classifications, endorsing alternatives to current categorical systems (National Association of School Psychologists/National Coalition of Advocates for Students [NASP/NCAS] 1985), and defining "Rights Without Labels" (NCAS, 1987; see also NCAS, 1985). The broadened ethical scope for school psychology was closely tied to the cumulative history of risk faced by minority students and by disadvantaged students. Among the lessons learned was the awareness that school psychology had an "unfortunate tradition of high levels of inference whereby fairly simple behaviors are attributed to highly complex underlying dynamics" (Reschly, 1988b p. 469). The conceptual broadening of the at-risk population led to the technical reduction in levels of inference, in turn, altering the scene of professional practice (Ysseldyke, Reynolds, & Weinberg, 1984).

As rules of inference tightened within school psychology, it allowed its scope to link issues across diverse groups and to offer some resolve to the vexing matter of minority overrepresentation. A consequence of a disjunctured view of professional history and a weakened professional authority was a paradigmatic shift in school psychology (Reschly & Ysseldyke, 1995). The shift centers on system reform, the core of which is an emphasis on outcomes rather than on interventions. The knowledge base and assessment technology of school psychology should focus on outcomes reached in natural settings, neither confined to nor measured against categorical labels.

SCHOOL COUNSELING VERSUS SCHOOL PSYCHOLOGY.   Throughout the 20th century, the expansion of special education has been a barometer of the change in the formal rules that have regulated admission into general education. Insofar as special education is linked to these rules of access, it is the manifestation of the American ideal of inclusion in a common schooling. Yet once included, the rules change, becoming ones of passage through a sequentially tracked curriculum (Richardson, 1999). Thus, with some irony, tracking becomes identified with the manifest purpose of public education, the advancement of students who will proceed on to higher education. Although it is identified with the ideal of participation in public schooling, special education has remained implicated in the latent dilemmas of mass education—the containment of students who fail by the curricular standards of the current time and school. Insofar as track placement based on achievement tests is seen as "more equitable than other sources of inequality" (Heyns, 1974, p. 1450), ability grouping emerges as pedagogically sound and legally defensible. Indeed, it has been the symbol of progress (Oakes, Gamoran, & Page, 1991, p. 579).

This difference in historical function carries over into the contrast in practice between counseling and school psychology. Unlike school psychology, school counseling is rooted in vocational guidance (Armor, 1969, p. 149), developed as a mediator between the curricular choice of students and their future goals (Cicourel & Kitsuse, 1963; Erickson & Shultz, 1982; Lee & Ekstrom, 1987). Within the social encounter between student and counselor, status characteristics shape the "comembership" between the student and the counselor (Erickson & Shultz, 1982, p. 38, *passim*). High comembership between student and counselor arises from shared status characteristics, a condition that furthers the trajectory of track assignments. The counselor's dilemma of having to uphold universalistic norms while negotiating the leakage of particularistic information is intensified by the social immediacy of the encounter. Yet, as a result, the leverage of the counselor is broader, or more diffuse. In turn, the sources of risk to the student can be more easily obscured, for "both gatekeeping and advising behavior can be used by counselors to advocate students' interests or to promote the interests of school and society at the students' expense" (Erickson, 1975, p. 46).

For special education, the procedural model developed differently. Because it is linked to school psychology, the initiations by classroom teachers are validated by "psychometry-based identification procedures" (Gerber & Semmel, 1984, p. 137). A student's future goals outside the school are of marginal consideration, although profoundly affected. There is no social encounter comparable to counseling that can give form to particularistic comembership and which can so personally sanction curricular choice. For special education, the jurisdiction of the school psychologist is more delimited and detached, increasingly removed from the initial time of referral. With distance from initial referral, the gap widens between the ideal model of decision making and the bounded rationality of actual practice—the pressures to narrow or to ignoring competing alternatives (Mehan et al., 1986, p. 113). With distance from initial referral, the discourse of risk and intervention indeed becomes persuasive.

Yet, paradoxically, the sources of the risk to the student may be rendered more visible and reformable. Through such options as prereferral discussions or pullout programs, the sequence from referral to psychometric validation can be interrupted structurally, replacing a categorical system with "continuous-progress" models (Madden & Slavin, 1989, p. 70). By altering the psychometry-based procedures, the goal of participation can be enhanced and the professional stature of school psychology can be redefined and strengthened. The discourse of risk in special education can be broadened not only by challenging racial overrepresentation but also by defining as an inequity the failure to extend services to students in need as well.

CONCLUSIONS

The comparison of tracking and special education provides the opportunity to examine both the similar conditions that enable each to arise as a reform motivation and the conditions that distinguish their contrasting directions. The comparison reveals strong similarities with respect to enabling conditions. Both have been accentuated by organizational changes in public schooling, and these changes were elevated into national resonance by means of a court decision of broad and timely importance. Yet from these common roots their directions have been different.

The explanation of their divergent paths focuses on two conditions that are sequentially related. The initial, triggering condition is a threat to the professional role and stature of the school agent that is central to the educational practice of tracking or special education. The second condition is an ethical content that moralizes educational risk that, in turn, broadens the jurisdiction of the school agent. The capacity of the professional group to emerge from the threat in a way that preserves or strengthens its role in schools is not a direct or predictable outcome. In this comparison of tracking and special education, the critical difference is traceable to the contrast between school counseling and school psychology. Both tracking and special education share the empirical evidence of discriminatory assignment and placement; yet, school psychology was least able to insulate itself from legal challenges to this evidence. However, its weakness was historically momentary, for its response to legal and professional challenges contributed to a broadened conception of educational risk and enhanced its own professional standing.

The relation between the reflection on professional history and defining the scope of ethical concerns may be informed by Mead's interpretation of romanticism (Mead, 1936). The romantic movements of the 19th century shared the common property of looking back, yet what distinguished them was the variable way in which they returned from this nostalgia to their own time and problems. However, it is only the realization that the past cannot be retrieved or relived, that it is incongruous with the present that provides the (romantic) movement with a collective, self-consciousness. In the comparison explored here, it is school psychology that most poignantly experienced a sense of discontinuity with its past professional history. Out of this emerged a broader awareness, one that enjoined professional practice to wider ethical obligations. This is, after all, what is meant by paradigmatic shift.

The theoretical reply is an extension of professional practice. However, the content of this reply is dependent on the way that school counseling and school psychology are situated concretely in the organization of public schooling. The contingencies that distinguish school counseling and school psychology are subtle but no less consequential for what is defined as educational risk. Whereas school counseling is more ethnographically embedded in the relations and the culture of students, school psychology is more removed, peripheral to the interpersonal dynamics that inform curricular choice and assignment. One consequence, explored in this chapter, is that such organizational remove gave to school psychology the opportunity to expand its conception of educational risk in ways that strengthened its own professional role in schools. The directional fate of special education was, in turn, redefined. From a long history of organizational dependency, special education has assumed the high road of pedagogical innovation and legal reform.

REFERENCES

Abbott, A. (1988). *The system of professions*. Chicago: University of Chicago Press.

Alexander, K. L., & Cook, M. A. (1982). Curricula and coursework: A surprise ending to a familiar story. *American Sociological Review, 47,* 626–40.

Alexander, K. L., Cook, M., & McDill, E. L (1918) Curricular tracking and educational stratification. *American Sociological Review, 43,* 47–66.

Alexander, K. L., & McDill, E. (1976). Selection and allocation within schools: Some causes and consequences of curriculum placement. *American Sociological Review, 41,* 963–80.

Algozzine, B., & Ysseldyke, J. (1983). Learning disabilities as a subset of school failure: The over-sophistication of a concept. *Exceptional Children, 50,* 242–246.

Algozzine, B., Ysseldyke, J. E., & Christenson, S. (1983). An analysis of the incidence of special class placement. *The Journal of Special Education, 17,* 141–147.

Armor, D. J. (1969). *The American school counselor, a case study in the sociology of professions.* New York: Russell Sage Foundation.

Baker, D. P., & Stevenson, D. (1986). Mothers' strategies for children's school achievement: Managing the transition to high school. *Sociology of Education, 59,* 156–166.

Barr, R., & Dreeben, R. (1983). *How schools work*. Chicago: University of Chicago Press.

Brantlinger, E. (1987). Making decisions about special education placement: Do low-income parents have the information they need? *Journal of Learning Disabilities, 20,* 94–101.

Brown v. Board of Education, 347 U.S. 483 (1954).

Brown, B. W., & Saks, D. H. (1981). The microeconomics of schooling. *Review of Research in Education, 9,* 217–254.

Castenada v. Pickard, 648 F.2d 989, 996 (5th Cir. 1981).

Christenson, S., Ysseldyke, J. E., & Algozzine, B. (1982). Institutional and external pressures influencing referral decisions. *Psychology in the Schools, 19,* 341–345.

Christoplos, F., & Renz, P. (1969). A critical examination of special education programs. *Journal of Special Education, 3,* 371–380.

Cicourel, A. V., & Kitsuse, J. I. (1963). *The educational decision makers*. Indianapolis, IN: Bobbs-Merrill.

Coalition to Save Our Children v. State Board of Education, et al., 901 F. Supp. 784 (D. Del. 1995).

Cuban, L. (1989). The "at-risk" label and the problem of urban school reform. *Phi Delta Kappan, 70*(10), 780–784, 799–801.

Dauber, S. L., Alexander, K. L., & Entwisle, D. R. (1996). Tracking and transitions through the middle grades: Channeling educational trajectories. *Sociology of Education, 69,* 290–307.

Davis, S. A., & Haller, E. J. (1981). Tracking, ability and SES: Further evidence on the "revisionist–meritocratic" debate. *American Journal of Education, 89,* 283–303.

Diana v. Board of Education, C-70-37 RFP (N.D. Cal.1970).

Dunn, L., M. (1968). Special education for the mildly retarded—Is much of it justifiable? *Exceptional Children, 35,* 5–22.

Elliott, R. (1987). *Litigating intelligence, IQ tests, special education, and social science in the courtroom.* Dover, MA: Auburn House.

Epps, S., Ysseldyke, J. E., & McGue, M. (1984). Differentiating LD and non-LD students: I know one when I see one. *Learning Disability Quarterly, 7,* 89–101.

Erickson, F. (1975). Gatekeeping and the melting pot: Interaction in counseling encounters. *Harvard Educational Review, 45*(1), 44–70.

Erickson, F., & Shultz, J. (1982). *The counselor as gatekeeper: Social interaction in interviews.* New York: Academic Press.

Finley, M. K. (1984). Teachers and tracking in a comprehensive high school. *Sociology of Education, 57,* 233–43.

Gamoran, A. (1987). The stratification of high school learning opportunities. *Sociology of Education, 60,* 135–155.

Gamoran, A., & Mare, R. D. (1989). Secondary school tracking and educational inequality: Compensation, reinforcement, or neutrality? *American Journal of Sociology, 94,* 1146–1183.

Garrison, M., & Hammill, D. D. (1971). Who are the retarded? *Exceptional Children, 38,*13–20.

Georgia State Conference of Branches of NAACP v. Georgia, 775 f 2d 1403 (11th Cir. 1985).

Gerber, M. M., & Semmel, M. I. (1984). Teacher as imperfect test: Reconceptualizing the referral process. *Educational Psychologist, 19*(3), 137–148.

Gerber, M. M., & Semmel, M. I. (1985). The microeconomics of referral and reintegration: A paradigm for evaluation of special education. *Studies in Educational Evaluation, 11,* 13–29.

Goss v. Lopez, S. Ct. 729 (1975).

Hallinan, M. T. (1991). School differences in tracking structures and track assignments. *Journal of Research on Adolescence, 1,* 251–275.

Hallinan, M. T. (1992). The organization of students for instruction in the middle school. *Sociology of Education, 65,* 114–127.

Hallinan, M. T., & Sørensen, A. B. (1983). The formation and stability of instructional groups. *American Sociological Review, 48,* 838–851.

Hallinan, M. T., & Sørensen, A. B. (1986). Student characteristics and assignment to ability groups: Two conceptual formulations. *Sociological Quarterly, 27,* 1–13.

Hansen, C. F. (1964). *The four-track curriculum in today's high schools.* Englewood Cliffs, NJ: Prentice-Hall.

Heller, K., Holtzman, W., & Messick, S. (Eds., 1982). *Placing children in special education: A strategy for equity.* Washington, DC: National Academy Press.

Heyns, B. (1974). Social selection and stratification within schools. *American Journal of Sociology, 79,* 1434–51.

Hobson v. Hansen, 269 F. Supp. 401 (D.D.C. 1967), aff'd sub nom. Smuck v. Hobson, 408 F.2n 175 (D.C. Cir. 1969).

Hocutt, A. M., Cox, J. L., & Pelosi, J. (1984). An exploration of issues regarding the identification and placement of LD, MR, and ED students. In *A policy oriented study of special education's service delivery system,* Phase 1: Preliminary study (RTI Report No. RTI/2706-06/OIES). Durham, NC: Research Triangle Institute, Center for Educational Studies.

Jencks, C., Smith, M., Acland, H., Bane, M. J., Cohen, D., Gintis, H., Heyns, B., & Michelson, S. (1972). *Inequality.* New York: Harper Colophon Books.

Johnson, V. M. (1980). Analysis of factors influencing special educational placement decisions. *Journal of School Psychology, 18,* 191–202.

Jones, R. L. (1972). Labels and stigma in special education. *Exceptional Children, 38,* 553–564.

Jones, J. D., Vanfossen, B. E., & Ensminger, M. E. (1995). Individual and organizational predictors of high school track placement. *Sociology of Education, 68,* 287–300.

Kirp, D. L. (1973). Schools as sorters: The constitutional and policy implications of student classification. *University of Pennsylvania Law Review, 121,* 705–797.

Kirp, D. L., & Kirp, L. M. (1976). The legalization of the school psychologists' world. *Journal of School Psychology, 14,* 83–89.

Lareau, A. (1987). Social class differences in family–school relationships: The importance of cultural capital. *Sociology of Education, 60,* 73–85.

Larry P. v. Riles, 343 F. Supp. 1306 (N.D. Cal. 1972).

Lee, V. E., & Bryk, A. S. (1988). Curriculum tracking as mediating the social distribution of high school achievement. *Sociology of Education, 61,* 78–94.

Lee, V. E., & Ekstrom, R. B. (1987). Student access to guidance counseling in high school. *American Educational Research Journal, 24*(2), 287–310.

Lipsky, D. K., & Gartner, A. (1989). *Beyond separate education, Quality education for all.* Baltimore, MD: Paul H. Brookes.

Loveless, T. (1997). The structure of public confidence in education. *American Journal of Education, 105,* 127–159.

Madden, N. A., & Slavin, R. E. (1989). Effective pullout programs for students at risk. In R. E. Slavin, N. L. Karweit, & N. A. Madden (Eds.), *Effective programs for students at risk* (pp. 23–72). Boston: Allyn and Bacon.

Marshall et al. v. Georgia. U.S. District Court for the Southern District of Georgia, CV482-233, June 28, 1984; Aff'd (11th cir. No. 84-8771, October 29, 1985).

McNeal v. Tate County School District, 508 F. 2d 1017 (5th Cir. 1975).

Mead, G. H. (1936). *Movements of thought in the nineteenth century.* Chicago: University of Chicago Press.

Mehan, H. (1997). Tracking untracking: The consequences of placing low-track students in high-track classes. In P. M. Hall (Ed.), *Race, ethnicity and multiculturalism: Policy and practice* (pp. 115–150). New York and London: Garland Press.

Mehan, H., Hertweck, A., & Meihls, J. L. (1986). *Handicapping the handicapped. Decision making in students' educational careers.* Stanford, CA: Stanford University Press.

Mehan, H., Villanueva, I., Hubbard, L., & Lintz, A. (1996). *Constructing school success, The consequences of untracking low-achieving students.* Cambridge, England: Cambridge University Press.

Memorandum, State Department of Education. (1970). *House resolution 444 relative to mentally retarded minors.* Sacramento, CA: Part 3.

Mercer, J. R. (1973). *Labeling the mentally retarded.* Berkeley, CA: University of California Press.

National Association of School Psychologists/National Coalition of Advocates for Students (NASP/NCAS, 1985). *Advocacy for appropriate educational services for all children.* Washington, DC: Author.

National Coalition of Advocates for Children (NCAS, 1985). Barriers to excellence: *Our children at risk.* Boston: Author.

National Coalition of Advocates for Students (NCAS, 1987). *Rights without labels.* Washington, DC: Author.

National Education Association (NEA), Research Division. (1968). *Ability grouping.* Research Summary, 1968–S3. Washington, DC: National Education Association.

Oakes, J. (1985). *Keeping track: How schools structure inequality.* New Haven, CT: Yale University Press.

Oakes. J. (1987). Tracking in secondary schools: A contextual perspective. *Educational Psychologist, 22*(2), 129–153.

Oakes, J. (1990). *Multiplying inequalities: The effects of race, social class, and tracking on opportunities to learn mathematics and science.* Santa Monica, CA: Rand.

Oakes, J. (1992). Can tracking research inform practice? Technical, normative, and political considerations. *Educational Researcher, 21*(4), 12–21.

Oakes, J., Gamoran, A., & Page, R. (1991). Curriculum differentiation: Opportunities, consequences, and meaning. In P. Jackson (Ed.), *Handbook of research on curriculum* (pp. 570–608). New York: Macmillan.

PASE v. Hannon, 74C 3586 (N.D. Ill., 1980).

People Who Care v. Rockford Board of Education School District No. 205, 851 F. Supp. 905 (N.D. Ill. 1994).

Prasse, D. P., & Reschly, D. J. (1986). Larry P.: A case of segregation, testing, or program efficacy? *Exceptional Children, 52,* 333–346.

Quarles v. Oxford Municipal Separate School District, 868 F. 2d 750 (5th Cir. 1989).

Rehberg, R. A., & Rosenthal, E. R. (1978). *Class and merit in the American high school.* New York: Longman.

Reschly, D. J. (1984). Beyond IQ test bias: The national academy panel's analysis of minority EMR overrepresentation. *Educational Researcher, 13*(3), 15–19.

Reschly, D. J. (1988a). Minority mild mental retardation overrepresentation: Legal issues, research findings, and reform trends. In M. C. Wang, M. C. Reynolds, & H. J. Walberg (Eds.), *Handbook of special education: Research and practice: Vol. 2, Mildly handicapped conditions* (pp. 23–41) . Oxford, England: Pergamon Press.

Reschly, D. J. (1988b). Special education reform: School psychology revolution. *School Psychology Review, 17*(3), 459–475.

Reschly, D. J., Kicklighter, R. H., & McKee, P. (1988). Recent placement litigation, part I: Regular education grouping: Comparison of *Marshall* (1984, 1985), and *Hobson* (1967, 1969). *School Psychology Review, 17,* 9–21.

Reschly, D. J., & Ysseldyke, J. E. (1995). School psychology paradigm shift. In A. Thomas & J. Grimes (Eds.), *Best practices in school psychology—III* (pp. 17–31). Washington, DC: National Association of School Psychologists.

Richardson, J. G. (1999). *Common, delinquent and special: The institutional shape of special education.* New York: Falmer Press.

Rosenbaum, J. E. (1976). *Making inequality: The hidden curriculum of high school tracking.* New York: Wiley.

Rosenbaum, J. E. (1980). Track misperceptions and frustrated college plans: An analysis of the effects of tracks and track perceptions in the National Longitudinal Survey. *Sociology of Education, 53,* 74–88.

Rubin, R. A., Krus, P., & Balow, B. (1973). Factors in special class placement. *Exceptional Children, 39*(7), 525–532.

Schafer, W. E., & Olexa, C. (1971). *Tracking and opportunity.* Scranton, PA: Chandler.

Semmel, M. I., Gerber, J., & Abernathy, T. (1993). *The relationships between school environment variables and educational outcomes for students with mild disabilities* (SERL/SEP Research Report). Santa Barbara, CA: University of California, Special Education Research Laboratory.

Semmel, M. I., Gerber, M., & MacMillan, D. L. (1995). A legacy of policy analysis research in special education. In J. M. Kauffman & D. P. Hallahan (Eds.), *The illusion of full inclusion* (pp. 39-57). Austin, TX: Pro-ed.

Shepard, L. A. (1987). The new push for excellence: Widening the schism between regular and special education. *Exceptional Children, 53,* 327–329.

Skrtic, T. M. (Ed., 1995). *Disability & democracy.* New York: Teachers College Press.

Sørensen, A. B. (1970). Organizational differentiation of student and educational opportunity. *Sociology of Education, 43,* 355–356.

Stevenson, D. L., Schiller, K. S., & Schneider, B. (1994). Sequences for opportunities for learning. *Sociology of Education, 67,* 184–198.

Trow, M. (1973). The second transformation of American secondary education. In S. D. Sieber & D. E. Wilder (Eds.), *The school in society, studies in the sociology of education* (pp. 45–61). New York: The Free Press.

Useem, E. L. (1991). Student selection into course sequences in mathematics: The impact of parental involvement and school policies. *Journal of Research on Adolescence, 1*(3), 231–250.

Vanfossen, B. E., Jones, J. D., & Spade, J. Z. (1987). Curriculum tracking and status maintenance. *Sociology of Education, 60,* 104–22.

Vasquez v. San Jose Unified School District, C-71-2130, (N.D. Cal. 1994).

Wang, M. C., & Walbert, H. J. (1988). Four fallacies of segregationism. *Exceptional Children, 55,* 128–137.

Welner, K. G., & Oakes, J. (1996). (Li)Ability grouping: The new susceptibility of school tracking systems to legal challenges. *Harvard Educational Review, 66,* 451–470.

Will, M. C. (1986). Educating children with learning problems: A shared responsibility. *Exceptional Children, 52,* 411–415.

Wood v. Strickland, 95 S. Ct. 922 (1975).

Ysseldyke, J. E. (1978). Who's calling the plays in school psychology? *Psychology in the Schools, 15,* 373–378.

Ysseldyke, J. E. (1982). The Spring Hill symposium on the future of psychology in the schools. *American Psychologist, 37*(5), 547–552.

Ysseldyke, J. E. (1987). Classification of handicapped students. In M. C. Wang, M. C. Reynolds, & H. J. Walberg (Eds). *Handbook of special education: Research and practice, Vol. I. Learning characteristics and adaptive education.* (pp. 253–271). Oxford, England: Pergamon.

Ysseldyke, J. E., Algozzine, B., & Allen, D. (1981). Regular education teacher participation in special education team decision making. *Elementary School Journal, 82,* 160–165.

Ysseldyke, J. E., Algozzine, B., & Epps, S. (1983). A logical and empirical analysis of current practice in classifying students as handicapped. *Exceptional Children, 50,* 160–165.

Ysseldyke, J. E., Algozzine, B., Richey, L., & Graden, J. (1982). Declaring students eligible for learning disability services: Why bother with the data? *Learning Disability Quarterly, 5,* 37–44.

Ysseldyke, J. E., Algozzine, B., Shinn, M. R., & McGue. M. (1982). Similarities and differences between low achievers and students classified learning disabled. *Journal of Special Education, 16,* 73–85.

Ysseldyke, J. E., & Foster, G. (1978). Bias in teachers' observations of emotionally disturbed and learning disabled children. *Exceptional Children, 45,* 613–615.

Ysseldyke, J. E., Reynolds, M. C., & Weinberg R. A. (1984). *School psychology: A blueprint for training and practice.* Minneapolis, MN: National School Psychology Inservice Training Network, University of Minnesota.

Ysseldyke, J. E., Thurlow, M. L., Graden, J. L., Wesson, C., Algozzine, B., & Deno, S. L. (1983). Generalizations from five years of research on assessment and decision making. *Exceptional Education Quarterly, 4*(1), 75–94.

PART IV

THE STUDY OF SCHOOL ORGANIZATION

CHAPTER 14

School Size and the Organization
of Secondary Schools

Valerie E. Lee

SCHOOL SIZE: AN IMPORTANT
STRUCTURAL FEATURE OF SCHOOLS

The size of any school is a defining dimension of its structure. The number of students a school serves has a profound influence on many elements of its organization. A large amount of recent empirical research (some of which is described in this volume) documents how features of a school's academic and social organization influence its members, namely teachers and students. The actual mechanisms through which school size influences these members is unclear. However, it is reasonable to assume that size helps define elements of any school's academic and social organization and that these organizational elements in turn influence outcomes. This suggests that the major way in which school size actually influences outcomes is indirect. However, research on school size generally investigates direct effects.

The major focus of this chapter is on the size of secondary, rather than elementary, schools. Elementary schools are often small, based on an interest in providing intimate relations and a supportive environment for young children. The purpose of many elementary schools was, and still is, to provide relatively simple and relatively undifferentiated educational programs to the children of a socially homogeneous neighborhood clientele. On the other hand, secondary schools—particularly public comprehensive schools—need more students in order to accomplish their more complex purposes. Typically, secondary schools draw from larger areas with more heterogeneous populations. The historical development of public high schools is instructive in understanding their purpose and in understanding how growing enrollments

VALERIE E. LEE • School of Education, University of Michigan, Ann Arbor, Michigan 48109

Handbook of the Sociology of Education, edited by Maureen T. Hallinan. Kluwer Academic/Plenum Publishers, New York, 2000.

helped define that purpose. These explanations are closely tied to the high school curriculum.

During the American republic's early decades, the purpose of high schools (both public and private) was to prepare their students with classical training for entry into the university. At the end of the 19th century, very few adolescents attended high school. Because of their singular focus, early high schools were small, and they offered a narrow focus on academics (mostly classics). At the beginning of the 20th century, however, the demand for secondary schooling burgeoned, especially in cities. This was caused by migration to urban areas, immigration from abroad, and new laws restricting child labor (Cremin, 1988). These new students had much more varied backgrounds, goals, and agendas. What did these students want from high school? What should the high school offer them? Debates over the form of the public high school curriculum polarized around two alternatives: either a common core of courses that was appropriate for all, or a diversified set of offerings to accommodate a variety of students. The debate was settled in favor of the latter, and the comprehensive high school was born (Conant, 1959; Oakes, 1985; Tyack, 1974).

Besides offering courses to prepare their traditional clientele for advanced academic learning, public high schools increasingly took on the burden of training other students in personal care (home economics, health, child care), vocational skills (industrial arts, business skills), and remediation for basic skills (English as a second language, basic reading, functional mathematics). By providing a wide array of options, "high schools would serve democracy by offering usable studies to everyone, rather than dwelling on academic abstractions that would interest only a few.' (Powell, Farrar, & Cohen, 1985, p. 260) An important objective of the comprehensive curriculum was, and still is, to keep students in school until graduation. In order to serve what may be seen as a basic democratic purpose—to provide differentiated programs to students with varying backgrounds, interests, and skills—high schools must enroll large numbers of students.

Defining the optimal size of a school has been an enduring issue for educational policy, for educational research, and for school district staff who have to make decisions about drawing district lines and building schools. Researchers would begin the task of studying school size by defining a theoretical model to link school size with outcomes (particularly student outcomes). Policymakers and schoolpeople would probably approach the issue more instrumentally. Reflecting these different aims, optimal size historically has been defined using two potentially conflicting criteria: how organizational size affects group members (a sociological criterion) and the best school size for optimum economic efficiency (an economic criterion). Although these goals are certainly related, some researchers have suggested that maximizing performance can lead away from efficient functioning, and vice versa (Goss, 1994; Morrison, 1993). At least since the end of World War II, the topic of the best size for a school has been hotly debated in policy circles. Such discussions, often motivated by either expanding populations or a need to consider school consolidation, have focused more on the economic than the sociological criteria. These discussions have a decidedly bureaucratic bent.

The issue of high school size has received much recent attention in theoretical and in popular writings about education, as well as in reports spelling out ideas for reforming schools. A broader range of writings than is typically considered by scholars centers on this issue. Some of these writings, although quite influential in defining important educational issues and solutions, do not draw their conclusions directly from empirical analyses. One example is James Bryant Conant, acknowledged as the father of the comprehensive high school. In his influential 1959 book about the American high school, Conant indicated that a school with a graduating class of 100 should be sufficiently large to implement his recommended curriculum (although he favored schools somewhat larger than this). Quite obviously, contemporary comprehensive high schools are considerably larger than Conant's minimum.

Goodlad (1984) wrote about high schools almost three decades after Conant. In *A Place Called School*, he commented: "The burden of proof, it appears to me, is on large size. Indeed, I would not want to face the challenge of justifying a senior . . . high of more than 500 to 600 students (unless I were willing to place arguments for a strong football team ahead of arguments for a good school, which I am not)" (p. 310). In an essay about size and adolescent development, Garbarino (1980) argued for the particular importance of school size for marginal students. Echoing Barker and Gump's (1964) study, he described a threshold effect whereby advantages from increases in high school size over about 500 students were minimal. Neither Conant (1959) Goodlad, nor Garbarino provided any evidence for their recommended numbers.

Reflecting the theme of differential effects of size for students of varying backgrounds, Bryk, Lee, and Holland (1993) presented evidence that school size has more influence on social equity than on achievement in Catholic and in public high schools. Without making a specific size recommendation, they concluded, "Quite simply, it is easier to create a more internally differentiated academic structure in a larger school" (p. 270). Although the Coalition for Essential Schools also makes no specific recommendations about high school size, Theodore Sizer (1984), in *Horace's Compromise*, included "keep[ing] the structure simple and flexible" among the five "imperatives for better schools" (p. 214).

The Carnegie Foundation sponsored two very influential reports on school reform since 1989. Their 1989 report, *Turning Points*, spelled out policies for changing schools serving the middle grades. The first recommendation was to "create small communities for learning" (Carnegie Council on Adolescent Development, 1989. p. 9). The report gave no explicit guidelines for middle school size, but listed such elements as "schools-within-schools or houses" as key. Carnegie's most recent policy statement on school reform is the 1996 report, *Breaking Ranks* (National Association of Secondary School Principals [NASSP], 1996). Using the word *personalization,* terminology identical to a major element in the Coalition for Essential Schools, the first of the report's six major themes recommended: "[h]igh schools must break into units of no more than 600 students so that teachers and students can get to know each other" (p. 5). A recent and popular book described a school reform effort in Philadelphia, where 90 small charter schools were created within the city's 22 comprehensive high schools (Fine, 1994). Although the small Philadelphia schools were specialized in some sense (as charters typically are), the tenor of the book definitely favored small high schools and emphasized the communal environment fostered within them.

These writings draw out a consistent theme: high schools should be smaller than they are. A major assumption underlying suggestions for reducing high school size is that human relations in smaller schools will be more personalized. The consistency of the recommendations for an ideal size (600 seems very popular) is striking, although in these writings little empirical support for that specific recommendation is provided. Not every policy recommendation requires specific evidence to support it (some rest on solid moral ground). The fact is that reformers are out in front of researchers on the issue of high school size. Particularly in large urban districts, many small high schools are being created. However, there is little empirical data to support the decisions that are being made. The chapter now turns to a review of empirical studies of school size.

RESEARCH BACKGROUND ON SCHOOL SIZE

Arguably the seminal study of high-school size is Barker and Gump's 1964 book, *Big School, Small School*. Prefacing multilevel considerations common in later research on this topic, these authors recognized that the ecological environment in which human behavior occurs is bounded by "variegated but stable patterns in the behavior of people en masse" (p. 9). This study, grounded in a well-developed theory of human behavior, focused on behavior settings in several Midwest high schools of varying sizes (fewer than 20 to over 2,000 students). The behavior settings they studied included classes, activities, and community events. Using a multitude of simple quantitative analyses, their research explored the hypothesis that individuals in smaller settings (communities and high schools) would be presented a wider range of activities, and would expend more effort, than in larger settings. The behaviors they explored did not include achievement.

Their investigations of relationships between school size, school settings, and students' participation resulted in conclusions that favored smaller settings consistently. Although there is an obvious (but illusory) authority to large schools that derives from "an implication of power and rightness" (Barker & Gump, 1964, p. 195), according to these authors, students in smaller schools were more engaged with their educational experiences—through relatively more frequent opportunities for participation and a strong social press to do so. The Barker and Gump book has provided good theoretical grounding for the subsequent research on the topic of school size, although it is not often cited. For example, the authors recognized that decisions about how large a school should be frequently recognize the need to balance students' versatility of experiences (which favor small schools) with opportunities for specialization (which favor large schools). They suggested several different responses to expanding school populations, including "the campus school, an arrangement by which students would be grouped in semiautonomous units for most studies but are actually provided a school-wide extracurricular program" (p. 201). This suggestion (and the justification for it) has an almost identical current manifestation—schools-within-schools.

Most recent studies on high school size fall into two separate research traditions that reflect the need for a social and specialization balance posed by Barker and Gump (1964). One tradition reflects an economy-of-scale argument. Writings on this theme focus on the potential for savings through less redundancy and more resource strength as schools get bigger. The second tradition, and the one that attracts more attention from sociologists, investigates how size influences other properties of schools as organizations. As schools grow, they become more formal and bureaucratic. Certain consequences flow from these changes, one of which is typically a more specialized curriculum. Conclusions from the two traditions go in opposite directions: the efficiency argument suggests benefits from increased size, whereas the organizational argument favors smaller schools.

The issue of economy of scale is one of efficiency. Increasing the numbers of persons served in a service-production organization can generate greater efficiency under two criteria (Buzacott, 1982). First, more recipients means that a given service is delivered more economically. For example, if one goal of a high school is to provide a curriculum tailored to particular aptitude levels (i.e., advanced, average, or basic), then more students would help maximize the delivery of this curriculum by increasing the numbers of students of similar ability who would need or want any particular program. This argument applies to curriculum goals targeted to different student interests, to special needs, or to other selection criteria. Based on the importance of these goals, meeting them efficiently means that the school must have enough students to sustain separate programs or classes with separate teachers. As the number of students with common needs increases, schools can create more specialized programs.

The second criterion is the efficient use of physical resources. Supplies and materials needed to deliver services are more economically obtained through larger purchases (Buzacott,

1982). If the cost of supplies (such as paper) is reduced when purchased in greater amount or if other costs (such as lighting or heat) can be sustained at a relatively flat level regardless of the numbers served, then spreading the relatively lower per-person cost over a larger base reduces overall spending on core costs.

An economy-of-scale argument, applied to the cost of producing a given level of achievement, would lead to conclusions favoring school consolidation and larger size (Kenny, 1982). The logic is that savings that accrue as core costs are spread over a large pupil base can be applied toward strengthening (or expanding) the school's academic offerings in response to individual differences in interest and in ability among students. This shift should result in either a general increase in resource strength, greater program specialization, or both. Program specialization is seen as an advantage within this research.

This argument assumes that greater size results in an economically more efficient operation (Guthrie, 1979; Michelson, 1972). However, savings projected by proponents of school consolidation have not materialized (Chambers, 1981; Fox, 1981). As schools get larger, they typically expand their support and administrative staffs to handle the greater bureaucratic demands. Especially in rural locations, where consolidation continues to be a big issue, higher costs for distributing materials and transporting students offset any savings (Chambers, 1981).

Evidence that size and academic outcomes are positively related is weak, although Bidwell and Kasarda (1975) offered evidence of an indirect relationship. They showed that the availability of resources is indirectly related to achievement, with the effect mediated through hiring better trained teachers and more staff to support students' special needs. School and district size are often confused, particularly for high schools (as many districts operate a single high school). The relationship between school district size and resource availability is inconsistent across communities, contingent on the socioeconomic status of the community (Friedkin & Necochea, 1988). Although larger districts in low-income areas typically have access to more resources than small districts, the higher incidence of exceptional problems in such populations introduces constraints in such schools that contribute to lower achievement.

The second research tradition concerns academic and social organization. Basic sociological theory would hold that as an organization grows, human interactions and ties become more formal (Weber, 1947). As organizations grow, they typically create new bureaucratic structures that are based on hierarchical positions and roles. These structures, in turn, can inhibit the personal ties that characterize a community (Bryk & Driscoll, 1988). This hypothesis has been supported in the research studies that identify the organizational characteristics of effective schools. In much literature on school climate, for example, size operates as an ecological feature of a school's social structure, part of the physical or material environment that influences the nature of social interactions (Anderson, 1982; Barker & Gump, 1964; Bryk & Driscoll, 1988; Garbarino, 1980; Morocco, 1978).

A relationship between organizational size and program specialization is documented in recent research. Larger schools, in principle, have more students with similar needs, and thus are better able to create specialized programs to address those needs. Small schools, on the other hand, must focus resources on core programs, with marginal students (at either end of a distribution of ability or interest) either excluded from programs or absorbed into programs that may not meet their needs as well (Monk, 1987; Monk & Haller, 1993). But is curriculum differentiation good or bad? Research on tracking suggests that extensive differentiation in schools' curricular offerings and students' academic experiences has debilitating consequences for some students (Gamoran, 1989; Oakes, 1985). Increasing size promotes curriculum specialization, resulting in differentiation of students' academic experiences and social stratification of student outcomes (Lee & Bryk, 1989).

A specialization model fits the aims of the comprehensive high school, where a major goal is to cater to individual differences among students. However, an alternate perspective focuses attention on the more communal aspects of learning. From this vantage point, which values students' common experiences, specialization is less appealing. This perspective has motivated some recent empirical work on curriculum effects that links differences in students' academic experiences to stratification in academic outcomes (Garet & DeLaney, 1988; Lee & Bryk, 1988, 1989; Lee, Burkam, Smerdon, Chow-Hoy, & Geverdt, 1998; Lee & Smith, 1995). Private and public schools alter course offerings differently with a change in size. Catholic schools add academic courses as they grow bigger, whereas public schools typically add courses in personal development and in other nonacademic areas (Bryk et al., 1993). The more constrained curriculum in small high schools is typically composed of academic courses, resulting in virtually all students following the same course of study, regardless of their interests, abilities, or social background. This results in both higher average achievement and achievement that is more equitably distributed (Lee & Bryk, 1988, 1989; Lee et al., 1998). Thus, small school size appears to serve as a facilitating factor for creating organizational conditions that foster student achievement that is both higher and more equitably distributed.

There are at least three organizational consequences that flow from increasing the size of a school. Although these consequences accrue to all school members, the effects are especially important for teachers. First, the more formal division of labor that accompanies larger size leads to a static set of roles for individuals at every level in the organization. Members' loyalties are, by virtue of more specialized roles, turned away from the larger organization to some subunit (in high schools, this is often the department; see Barker & Gump, 1964; Gottfredson & Daiger, 1979; Neufeld, 1984; and Newmann, 1981). Second, the transmission of information in the school is more complex, which increases the distance between any individual and the source of information. This results in a more formalized communication system (Anderson, 1982; Bridges & Hallinan, 1978). The third consequence is a more formalized set of cultural beliefs, developed to counteract the effects of large numbers of people holding conflicting goals. Group cohesion is thus diminished. Because individuals' tacit beliefs are not engaged, they are not integrated into the school's organizational life. Disagreements instead reside beneath the surface and become a potential oppositional force.

These consequences of increasing organizational size on students and on teachers are multifaceted, whereby size influences social relations that, in turn, influence outcomes. Thus, size effects depend on the link between the structure of social relations in a school and the academic development of its students. The direct effects on school members of changes in school size are, unsurprisingly, social or affective—isolation, alienation, or social engagement (Chambers, 1981; Fowler & Walberg, 1991; Newmann, 1981; Wehlage, Rutter, Smith, Lesko, & Fernandez, 1989). Extant research suggests that efforts on the margin of the organization to mitigate the negative social effects of size, such as schools within schools or house systems, have been only partially successful (Goodlad, 1984; Newmann, 1981).

In a review article focused on the organization of secondary schools, Lee, Bryk, and Smith (1993) categorized school size as one of three "external influences on school organization" (the other two were school social composition and parental involvement—p. 175). Summing up their review, these authors recommended that research findings about school size be "seen with a balanced eye. Schools should be neither too large to inhibit a strong sense of community nor too small to offer a full curriculum and adequate instructional facilities" (p. 189). The focus of this chapter now shifts from a summary of the findings of existing research about school size to a discussion of methodological issues that are important to consider in conducting and evaluating research on this topic.

METHODOLOGICAL CONSIDERATIONS

Conceptual writings about school organization have a long and illustrious history, beginning with the seminal work of Waller (1932) and enriched by Weber's (1947) theoretical contributions about organizations. However, empirical/analytic studies of schools as organizations are more recent. Past quantitative research on how the organization of schools affects the individuals within them has been plagued by substantial analytic problems (Burstein, 1978, 1980). Because such serious problems as misestimated standard errors and aggregation bias were, until recently, almost endemic in this type of research, findings from earlier quantitative research that investigated the influence of organizational characteristics of a group (e.g., a school) on its members may be suspect. Recently there has been an enormous expansion of research on how the organization and structure of schools influences how school members fare, which is often called school effects research. Studies of school size typically fall within this category.

Almost by definition, school effects studies are multilevel. That is, typically they are driven by research questions defined at more than one unit of analysis. The variables included in such analyses are measured at more than one level. The units of analysis that define a study of school effects would logically be schools and students (or schools and teachers, if organizational effects on teachers were the topic under investigation). The research community is fortunate that, since the late 1980s, a new statistical methodology—Hierarchical Linear Modeling, or HLM—has become available, providing researchers with a valuable tool for exploring research questions with a multilevel structure (see Bryk & Raudenbush, 1988, for a general review of the development of this statistical methodology; Bryk & Raudenbush, 1992, for a general text on how to conduct such studies). Therefore, researchers who conduct quantitative studies that investigate the influence of school size on outcomes for individual students or teachers should seriously consider using multilevel statistical methods.

Although the statistical underpinnings of multilevel analysis are quite complex, the conceptualization behind this approach is not. There are several reasons for spelling out in some detail the structure of conceptual models that might be used to investigate these questions. One reason is to alert researchers interested in quantitative research on this topic to the problems that are inherent in this type of research. A second is to assure them that the statistical solutions to such problems are at hand. Finally, a third is to provide a brief framework for how analyses using it may be structured.

A simple example may be useful. A reasonable hypothesis is that the size of a high school would influence the frequency and character of its teachers' interactions with one another. A researcher interested in exploring this hypothesis would usually measure the frequency and type of such interactions by surveying individual teachers in a number of schools of different size. The first step in an HLM analysis of this type would be to partition the variance in the dependent variable (in this case, teachers' reports of their interactions) into two components and then' determine the proportion of overall variance in that variable that lies between and within schools (i.e., among teachers in a single school, pooled over the several schools in the sample). It is only variance in an outcome that lies systematically between schools on which school size effects may be estimated. If the between-school variance in the outcome is very small, identifying school effects of any sort is likely to be unsuccessful. Let's assume here that the between-school variance is substantial.

The second step in an HLM of this structure is to estimate a within-school model. This model is estimated among individual teachers in each school. For example, we may want to take into account characteristics of teachers that could influence the frequency and character of their interactions—such factors as gender, subject-matter specialization, the types of students taught, and teaching experience. The within-school model would adjust the dependent variable for these factors. Once the researcher arrives at a within-school model that is conceptually and analytically satisfactory, he or she moves to the third step in the HLM: the between-school model. At this level, the researcher estimates how school size influences teachers' interactions (adjusted for personal characteristics of teachers). In estimating the effects of school size, the researcher might want to take into account structural and demographic characteristics of schools that could bias these effects (e.g., whether it is private or public, whether it enrolls economically affluent or disadvantaged students, the degree of departmentalization in the school). Such school-level control variables could be included at this level. School effects are estimated in this third step. It is also possible in this type of HLM model to estimate how school characteristics might influence the social distribution of these outcomes. Bryk and Raudenbush (1992), have offered a full exposition of the methodology.

In sum, researchers interested in school-effects questions are fortunate in having the HLM methodology on which to draw. Published studies using this methodology in several fields of social science research are by now quite common, and training in its use is widely available though universities and through workshops. HLM allows researchers to estimate school effects—in this case the effects of school size—on the attitudes, well-being, or accomplishment of individuals within the school.

Although investigations of how school size influences individual school members are typically multilevel, not all quantitative research that has focused on the effects of school size has been (or should be) of this form. For example, the statistical software for conducting multilevel analyses has only been available since the late 1980s, but research addressing the topic of school size and its effects on students has been of interest for much longer.

Earlier in the chapter, I discussed several consequences of increasing school size, including changes in the social organization of schools. Empirical/analytic studies can ascertain how school size (a structural dimension) influences schools' organizational dimensions—I listed role structure, communication structure, and group cohesion as possibilities. Research that investigates questions of this type would quite appropriately be restricted to a single unit of analysis: the school. Thus, such studies would make use of such common single-level analytic techniques as linear regression, analysis of variance, or structural equation modeling. I do not mean to imply that the only methodological approach that should be used in quantitative research on school size is multilevel. Nor do I wish to suggest that investigations of the effect of school size that was conducted before multilevel methods should be discounted. Rather, I suggest that researchers' choice of methodology should be driven by the research questions they pose and by the unit(s) of analysis that are appropriate to address those questions.

In the type of studies described previously with representative samples and quantitative data on representative school members in a relatively large number of secondary schools, the researcher would be able to evaluate whether school size had an influence on outcomes measured on students or on teachers. Alternate, single-unit studies might investigate whether school size influences organizational characteristics of schools. Obviously, these types of studies are quite useful. Given the current interest in school size in educational policy circles, having evidence from well-designed studies that school size matters is important. However, once we felt confident that size was important, we would probably want to understand the process through which school size influences are manifest in particular high schools. That is, we would be interested in how school size influences play out.

Although it might be possible to design surveys to learn about the complexities of organizational conditions in small and in large high schools, it seems reasonable that this kind of information is best obtained by more intensive study in a relatively small number of schools.

Further, we might want to select our sample of schools to study based on variation in school size. In field-based studies of schools that employ qualitative methods (e.g., observation, interviews, document analysis), we might want to learn about the mechanisms through which school size plays out. Such studies could take a variety of forms. One useful form would be comparative. Under this approach, the researcher would select several schools to study in some depth. However, how would researchers using field-based methods decide which (and how many) schools to study?

Although quantitative studies value large and randomly selected samples to increase the generalizability of their findings, this approach is not feasible when sample sizes are quite small. Michael Patton's (1990) suggestions about purposive sampling may be useful here. For example, a comparative study might use what Patton called "maximum variation sampling" (pp. 172–173). Here, the researcher might want to compare a few small and a few large high schools that are similar on some other dimensions. Beyond the comparative approach, another field study of school size might focus on a more intense study of a single school (either very large or very small). This might involve what Patton called "extreme or deviant case sampling" (pp. 169–171), where cases are sampled because they are unusual or special in some way. The major criterion in selecting a school to study is to select cases from which there is the most to be learned. The logic here is that the lessons to be learned by studying a particular phenomenon in a single setting would be relevant in more typical settings.

The purpose of field-based studies of school size is to understand well how issues of size play out in schools. To do this, researchers would either select a relatively small number of schools (based on size) and compare them, or it could also be useful to study a single school with intensity over some period of time. In this type of research, the selection of the school sample and the length of time in which the schools are studied are both determined by the resources available for the study. This type of research is intensive in terms of time and resources (mostly human resources).

The point here is a simple one: the type of methodological approach should meet the purpose of the study. Some evaluations want to answer such questions as, "Does a particular structural characteristic of high schools, such as the number of students they enroll, influence particular outcomes for school members?" For those studies, large and diverse samples of school members and schools are desirable, and multilevel statistical methods are recommended. In other studies, researchers might want to know, "How do school structural characteristics play out in particular settings?" For those studies, a focus on a smaller number of schools, usually selected purposely rather than randomly, makes sense. Field methods are required for such studies.

RECENT EVIDENCE ON THE EFFECTS OF SCHOOL SIZE

Thus far, this chapter has been devoted to a discussion of theoretical issues surrounding research on school size, including a summary of the research base of the topic. Some of the methodological issues surrounding the study of this topic have been discussed. This section provides some detail about three studies of school size that I have recently conducted, mainly to provide a closer look at this type of research from a vantage point I know well. Because more detail is available on these studies elsewhere, I provide few technical details.

The first two are school-effects studies, within the quantitative mode, both of which use multilevel methods with large and representative samples. The third is a field-based study, in the comparative mode, conducted in a modest number of large and small high schools. My purpose in describing these studies is to contrast two generic models of research about school size cast within a sociological and a policy perspective.

In a recent study, Smith and I investigated the relationship between high school size and students' learning (Lee & Smith, 1997). In an earlier study, we had reported positive effects of small school size on students' learning (Lee & Smith, 1995). However, the structure of the analysis in the earlier study had not allowed us answer important questions that were posed to us frequently by many school practitioners, such as the following: "What do you mean by small schools?" and "Exactly what size works best?" Together with these questions, two additional research questions drove the study: "Does an ideal size, defined in terms of maximal learning, also support an equitable social distribution of learning in the same school?" and "Do size effects vary by the types of students enrolled in the school?"

We used multilevel methods to explore these questions with three waves of longitudinal data drawn from the National Educational Longitudinal Study of 1988 (NELS:88). Our sample, which was nationally representative, included 9,812 high school graduates attending 789 public, Catholic, and elite private schools. We defined learning as the change in students' scores on the same tests of mathematics and reading comprehension over the course of high school (i.e., between 8th and 12th grades). As school size is also related to other characteristics of students and of schools, we took into account several measures that might provide alternate explanations for our results. We created eight categories of schools divided by enrollment. Using multilevel methods, we estimated the relative score differences attributable to these different enrollment sizes in students' achievement in reading and math over the 4 years of high school.

The findings were clear. In response to the question, "Which size works best?" we found that students learned more, in both reading and mathematics, in middle-sized high schools (600–900 students) compared to smaller and especially to much larger schools. Size effects on learning were somewhat stronger in mathematics than in reading. However, learning was more equitably distributed (our second question), in mathematics and particularly in reading, in smaller high schools, and it was particularly inequitable in very large schools. In response to our third research question, we found that although size effects were strongest in the range of 600 to 900 students for schools enrolling different types of students (defined by average school socioeconomic status and school minority concentration), the effects of school size on learning were strongest in schools enrolling more students from lower SES families and more minority students.

We summarized the findings of this study with four conclusions that we suggested have policy implications for secondary schooling: high schools should generally be smaller than they are; high schools can be too small; the ideal size of a high school is unrelated to the types of students who attend; and school size is an especially important factor in determining learning in schools enrolling higher proportions of socially disadvantaged students. As I mentioned earlier, an assumption underlying a study with this structure is that school size has a direct effect on students' learning. However, it also seems reasonable that a school's size would influence learning indirectly through an impact on other dimensions of the organization. The next study to be discussed focuses on one element of school social organization: teachers' attitudes about students' learning.

In a recent two-part multilevel study (Lee & Loeb, in press), we investigated the effects of the size of Chicago's public elementary schools (which typically enroll grades K–8). We investigated these questions with data from over 20,000 sixth and eighth graders, almost 5,000 teachers, and the 254 Chicago elementary schools that offered those grades (these samples are close to the population of Chicago students, teachers, and schools). The data were collected in 1997 through surveys conducted by the Consortium for Chicago School Research.

We were interested in exploring whether school size influences teachers' attitudes about their students. In addition, we explored both direct and indirect effects of school size on students' learning (measured by one-year gains in scores on standardized tests of math achievement). In the first part, we investigated whether teachers' attitudes about their students (in this case, their willingness to take responsibility for students' learning) was related to the size of the schools in which the teachers taught. We found that it was: teachers in smaller schools (fewer than 400 students) were more willing to take responsibility for learning than those in either medium-sized schools (400–750 students) or especially in larger schools (over 750 students).

The study's second part focused on students' learning. Here we focused on two school effects: school size (the same categories as described previously) and the effects of teachers' attitudes (a school-level aggregate of the measure explored in Part one—called *collective responsibility for learning*). Both size and collective responsibility were related to one-year gains in mathematics achievement, but in opposite directions. Size effects again favored smaller schools. We concluded that in Chicago elementary schools, school size influences students' learning both directly and indirectly—through teachers' attitudes about their students. Both for Chicago's students and for teachers, smaller schools were favored.

My colleagues and I pondered the larger implications of the findings from the Lee and Smith (1997) study. We concluded that we needed a smaller scale study to explore more directly how school size plays out inside schools. We pursued this question in a field-based study in a small number of high schools. In the study, our research team focused on the academic and social organization of high schools, particularly the curriculum and social relations, and how these organizational features were defined by high school size (Lee, Smerdon, Alfeld-Liro, & Brown, 1996). We studied these themes in nine high schools—five small schools and four large schools—in a single Midwestern state. We defined small schools as those enrolling fewer than 500 students, whereas large schools were those that enrolled more than 1,500. Our sample was also stratified by urbanicity and by sector; we selected a small and a large urban, suburban, and rural public school, a small and a large Catholic high school, and a small public school of choice. Thus, our sample contained six regular public high schools (we tried to avoid special purpose schools, although many small high schools are of this sort), and three schools of choice (two Catholic, one public). The range in size was considerable, from a small urban Catholic school with fewer than 200 students to a suburban public high school enrolling over 4,000 students.

We thought that we could best learn about the impact of school size on curriculum and on social relations by talking with school members. Using structured interview protocols, we interviewed the principal, a guidance counselor, two teachers in specified subjects, and a focus group of six to eight students meant to be representative of the school's student body. The study's data consisted of transcriptions of all interviews, extensive field notes, and documents supplied by the school (typically mission statements and descriptions of course offerings circulated to students and to parents). We visited each school three or four times.

Because almost all of our respondents considered their school's size to be a very important definitional feature of the school, they spoke about it freely. In most of the small schools, students were seen through a financial lens, as state funding (close to half of the school budget in that state) was drawn directly from head counts. Therefore, almost all the small-school personnel (except for the public school of choice) wanted the school to be larger than it was. Many members of large public schools, both teachers and students, talked of anonymity, specialization, and a lack of close personal relations with anyone outside of their immediate circle. Many school members in these schools wanted a smaller size.

Before entering the field, we posed two hypotheses, based on the literature and our own research findings from previous studies. The first concerned social relations. We expected (and mostly confirmed) that social relations would be more intimate and more positive in small schools. Our second hypothesis concerned the curriculum. We expected that curriculum would be more specialized and differentiated in large high schools, whereas in small schools we expected that schools—almost by default—would follow the Catholic school curriculum model: a small set of courses, mostly academic in nature, that were followed by all students. Although we found what we expected about the curriculum of the large public high schools, our hypotheses about curriculum structure were generally not confirmed in the small high schools.

Two findings were surprising, the first of which concerns social relations. Although we confirmed our hypotheses that more personalized and intimate relationships (particularly between teachers and students) were more common in small high schools, in those same schools there were some students who did not think intimate social relations were always an advantage. Unflattering family reputations followed some students who would have preferred more anonymity (alcoholism, welfare status, and a troublemaking older brother were mentioned). Moreover, if some students and teachers did not get along—which is to be expected—there was no alternative to their being together (often for several years). For example, the small rural school employed only a single mathematics teacher. Students who didn't like that teacher didn't take mathematics courses beyond their requirements.

Not surprisingly, the Catholic school curriculum model was solidly in place in the two Catholic schools we studied (although the types of students the two schools enrolled differed markedly). Even the large Catholic school followed this model. However, the structure of the curriculum in the small public schools was not like this. In the three small regular public schools, teachers and administrators tried hard to offer the type of curriculum of a comprehensive high school—but they could not. They felt that a differentiated curriculum was the best way to serve their students' needs, and they were well aware of the diverse academic preparations of the study body. The curriculum we found in these schools was constituted of unusual and illogical course sequences. For example, each spring the small rural school would prepare a list of courses the faculty could offer. Students would indicate which they wanted, and the courses with the most votes became next year's curriculum. As a result, students might begin a foreign language (Spanish) but never get a followup course. Students might be in nonacademic English but in advanced mathematics. Many seniors were taking physics, but few took advanced mathematics. "Why?" we asked. "We like the science teacher, but we don't like the math teacher," some students told us. Many teachers in these schools (which all had very small faculties) were teaching courses outside of their areas of interest or expertise.

Despite its low enrollment (small by design), the small public school of choice could offer a very broad curriculum, because students who didn't find courses they wanted at the school could go to the town's other two public high schools (with transportation provided), they could take courses at the local university (and many did), or they could find adults in the community to provide them with educational experiences they wanted and for which they received credit. The small urban school was especially disadvantaged by its size, which resulted largely from declining public confidence in the school (many families sent their children across city lines to other schools by declaring false addresses). The school appeared to be quite orderly, but this was mostly because of very high daily absenteeism.

The major conclusion we drew from this field-based study in a modest number of small and large high schools focused on social policy. In fact, we found that the majority of the small schools we studied didn't want to be so small. The low enrollments in several schools we studied seemed to reflect decline in some way: declining population, declining demand, a decline in public confidence, and this resulted in a severe decline in resources. Of the five small schools we studied, only the public school of choice really wanted their enrollment to be as small as it was. Because enrollments are the major determinant of funding in that state (or tuition base), small enrollments resulted in very constrained resources. We cautioned against the current reform recommendations about reducing the size of high schools. "The nation cannot expect that the generally perceived problematic nature of contemporary U.S. high schools is going to be solved just by making them smaller" (Lee et al., 1996, p. 29).

NEW DIRECTIONS FOR RESEARCH ON SCHOOL SIZE

Schools-within-Schools

One of the conclusions from our multilevel study of the effects of high school size on students' learning is that, in general, high schools should be smaller than they are. In practical terms, how does the nation change the size of its schools? One approach would be to create brand new schools (or smaller schools within the walls of larger existing schools). This approach is now underway in New York City, with generous support from the Annenberg Foundation for School Reform. The results from the two studies reported on previously suggest that this approach, however—opening many very small schools—might not be wise. In fact, several problems have been described in these small New York high schools. Given the present fiscal environment and modest public support for investment (financial or psychic) in social betterment, it seems unlikely that we could expect that America's public school districts would embark on a new building campaign to create many new smaller high schools in the near future. This is especially unlikely in our largest cities, where schools are largest but where financial resources are particularly problematic.

A reasonable alternative to building new schools (and one suggested by Barker and Gump [1964] and Goodlad [1984]) is a movement to create a set of smaller schools within schools inside larger high schools. In fact, this movement is now flourishing. This policy appears to be a reasonable approach to breaking up large school units, which our studies have shown are especially problematic places for learning. However, policymakers should be cautious as they adopt the schools-within-schools approach to reducing unit size. One consideration is related to overall structure. In an exploration of the Coalition of Essential Schools' use of schools-within-schools, Muncie and McQuillan (1991) described several difficulties of this type of school restructuring, where a single small unit was created within a larger school. Their work suggests that the schools-within-schools plan should involve the entire school, rather than being restricted to a single small unit. Another consideration should be the actual size of the resulting units. The studies described earlier in this chapter suggest that very small units may be problematic. Attention should be directed to an ideal size; our study has suggested that there is one.

A third consideration is the theme of the smaller schools. Both sociologists and policymakers should be cautious that a decision to go with a schools-within-school reform might be used to create a number of "specialty shops" (Powell et al., 1985). Several approaches to specialization come to mind: by ability, by vocational/career focus, by grade level, by deviant behaviors, or by any other organizational means to differentiate students and their high school experiences. Many chapters in this volume describe both the difficulties and the prevalence of social stratification in the U.S. educational system. Were this type of specialization explicit among smaller units within a large school, the schools-within-schools option could have the side effect of exacerbating social stratification in educational opportunities and outcomes. It would seem to be more reasonable that each small unit should reflect the demographic and academic diversity of the school as a whole.

Is Small Always Better?

In this chapter, I have argued that the relationship between school size and positive outcomes for school members (students and staff) is more complex than the approach that most research on this topic has taken. In the three studies described in some detail in this chapter, we found large high schools to be particularly problematic in several ways: students learn less mathematics and reading in very large schools, teachers are less willing to take responsibility for their students' learning in larger schools, social relations are more formalized and less personalized in large schools, and it is much easier to differentiate the curriculum according to students' skills, interests, and future plans in large schools.

However, these studies also found difficulties in very small high schools: lower levels of learning, unusual decisions about curriculum that often added to disjointed educational experiences for students, and in some cases social discrimination based on knowledge of some children's family background. The results of the studies described here also suggest that very small high schools may not always be favorable places for adolescents to develop, either intellectually or socially.

It seems reasonable that high schools should be large enough to offer a rational curriculum to high school students who intend to continue their education after graduation and large enough to employ teachers who are well prepared to offer the courses in such a curriculum. Research by my colleagues and me in Catholic high schools suggested that it is possible to offer a solid curriculum in a relatively small school if the curriculum is academic in nature, if all students are expected to master substantially the same skills and engage in the same intellectual activities, and if remediation for struggling students is intended to lead them eventually to succeed in this type of curriculum rather than in a separate remedial track throughout their high school career (Bryk et al., 1993). However, in the field-based study of small and of large high schools described in this chapter we found that this was not the approach to curriculum used in the small regular public high schools we studied. There would seem to be a good balance point—large enough to offer a solid curriculum and small enough that each child is known well—and our own research suggested that this balance point fell into the 600 to 900 student range.

Size and Social Disadvantage

The study that explored school size and students' learning demonstrated the special importance of school size for economically disadvantaged and for minority students (nationally and in Chicago). Historically, U.S. policy and custom about which students attend which schools has relegated such decisions to the local level. Usually access to schools is determined by residential location. We also know that residential segregation in the United States is increasing rather than decreasing over time (Farley & Frey, 1994). De facto school segregation by race and by class is now common and seemingly acceptable to the American public. Secondary school students of color, and those who come from low-income families, tend to be concentrated in large U.S. public schools with others quite like themselves (at least demographically). Very many of these schools are located in our nation's largest cities.

Our results (Lee & Loeb, in press; Lee & Smith, 1997) demonstrated that size is especially important for learning in schools with high concentrations of disadvantaged students. Our results favored moderate-sized high schools that are neither so small that the curriculum students experience is inadequate nor so large that some students are neglected or have socially stratified learning experiences. Students most likely to be overlooked and assigned to inappropriate courses are those with an economic or an ethnic disadvantage. Our studies indicate that these are exactly the students for whom school size is most important. Consequently, large school size is particularly problematic in schools enrolling large proportions of disadvantaged students.

WHAT WE STILL NEED TO KNOW

As I have tried to describe throughout this chapter, the research base on school size is neither large nor is it distinguished by many well-designed studies. Therefore, I suggest that there is much we still do not know about how school size influences important outcomes for students and for teachers. Several areas for research seem particularly promising: understanding the mechanism through which school size plays out throughout schools; expanding the range of outcomes to be linked to school size and to the school members who might be affected; learning more about how school size influences school organization; exploring and evaluating efforts to reduce school size, such as the schools-within-schools reform; or more exploration of school size effects in elementary and in middle schools. Perhaps most pressing is our lack of knowledge about the mechanisms by which school size influences school members. Both large-scale quantitative studies and smaller-scale field studies are useful ways to explore these mechanisms.

I suggested early in this chapter that it is unlikely that school size really *causes* students to learn more, even though the structure of our studies of enrollment size on students' learning would imply this. Rather than a direct causal link between the number of students a high school serves and how much students learn in school, I suggest that size acts as a facilitating or debilitating factor for other organizational forms or practices that, in turn, promote children's well-being. Although our study of size effects on teachers' attitudes about their students suggests one such organizational form, there are dozens of other possibilities. Thus, a fruitful line of inquiry would explore how size influences organizational structures (social and academic). We have some evidence that large size facilitates a more specialized curriculum, but we know much less about size and school social organization. Therefore, this is another fruitful area of research.

School size can influence many outcomes, and it seems reasonable that different sizes might be optimal for different outcomes. Throughout the chapter, I have mentioned that a major theoretical focus of school size writings is on social relations. This theory favors small schools; social relations between school members are likely to be more collegial (among teachers or between teachers and administrators) and more personalized (between teachers and students; among all school members). We need to understand these links better. In substantial opposition to the notion of small schools and intimate social relations is a policy issue raised by Goodlad (1984) that is important to people within schools and within communities served by schools: sustaining winning sports teams. Despite its importance to many constituents of U.S. high schools, I am hesitant to raise this concern to the level of theory. Perhaps more useful would be an expansion of the outcomes explored to include the extracurriculum in any high school and students' participation in it. This is an important element in the high school experience that is surely influenced by school size.

In fact, it is reasonable to hypothesize that school size influences many other student outcomes beyond cognitive development (e.g., social relations, students' engagement with learning, self-esteem, sense of belonging, participation in extracurricular activities, leadership roles). Moreover, the ideal size may be quite different for other outcomes. There are almost no studies that link school size to teacher outcomes of obvious interest to sociologists of education: school versus subgroup loyalty (e.g., to departments, grade-level groupings, or schools within schools), shared decision making, professional community, reflective dialogue, satisfaction, or self-efficacy. Exploring links between size and teacher outcomes of this sort is, thus, another useful area for research. Collecting data useful for exploring such outcomes is important to consider.

Because the schools-within-schools reform policy is spreading so rapidly, there should be more research on this reform that is specifically directed to reducing school size. Although the schools-within-schools movement is most common in secondary schools, it would be interesting to know if there is a move to create smaller schools within large elementary schools. How prevalent is the schools-within-schools option? In which types of schools (enrolling which types of students) has it been adopted? For what reasons did school or district staff decide to adopt this practice? What are the disadvantages? How are the smaller schools organized? How are students and teachers mapped to the smaller units? Has the schools-within-schools organization solved the problems it was meant to address, or has it created others?

The fact that the very large majority of research about school size has focused on secondary schools is understandable. For several decades, researchers have had available excellent data collected by the U.S. Department of Education about high schools—longitudinal, nationally representative, and large samples (*High School and Beyond*, NELS:88). The range in size among U.S. high schools is also dramatic, and the varying educational and social needs that schools need to serve for adolescents are numerous and complex. However, there are many very large elementary schools, especially in the nation's largest cities. Exploring issues of school size in elementary and middle-level schools is a wide open area of research on this topic.*

Knowing more about how school size influences school organization, and how it influences important outcomes for students and teachers, is one area in the sociology of education that is directly connected to educational policy. Reformers are very interested in school size, and many are acting on it quickly. However, important decisions are often made with little empirical support. The fact that many schools are making changes in their size (or in the size of instructional units) without research that either supports or discourages them suggests that empirical work on this topic is very much needed. It also suggests an unusual receptivity among practitioners to research results that offer post-hoc support for their decisions (the changes often occur before research results are known). I suggest that the issue of school size is one about which scholars do not have to argue for the importance of research to mobilize school professionals toward reform. In this case, reform efforts are in full gear.

---

*By the year 2000, it is anticipated that researchers will have access to public-use data that includes large samples of elementary students and schools. Data collection by the U.S. Department of Education for the Early Childhood Longitudinal Study (ECLS) began in fall 1998 on the kindergarten class. These children will be followed longitudinally throughout their elementary school years. The first portion of the ECLS will provide longitudinal data (including several cognitive measures) on about 25,000 children in 1,000 elementary schools, as well as information about their parents, schools, classrooms, and teachers, collected at the beginning and end of their kindergarten and first-grade years. For more information about ECLS, contact Dr. Jerry West at the National Center for Education Statistics, U.S. Department of Education.

REFERENCES

Anderson, C. S. (1982). The search for school climate: A review of the research. *Review of Educational Research, 52*, 368–420.

Barker, R., & Gump. R. (1964). *Big school, small school: High school size and student behavior.* Stanford, CA: Stanford University Press

Bidwell, C., & Kasarda, J. (1975). School district organization and student achievement. *American Sociological Review, 40*(1), 55–70.

Bridges, E. M., & Hallinan, M. T. (1978). Subunit size, work system interdependence, and employee absenteeism. *Educational Administration Quarterly, 14*(2), 24–42.

Bryk, A. S., & Driscoll, M. E. (1988). *The school as community: Theoretical foundations, contextual influences, and consequences for students and teachers.* Madison, WI: Center on Effective Secondary Schools, University of Wisconsin.

Bryk, A. S., Lee, V. E., & Holland, P. B. (1993). *Catholic schools and the common good.* Cambridge, MA: Harvard University Press.

Bryk, A. S., & Raudenbush, S. W. (1988). On heterogeneity of variance in experimental studies: A challenge to conventional interpretations. *Psychological Bulletin, 10*(1), 147–158.

Bryk, A. S., & Raudenbush, S. W. (1992). *Hierarchical linear models: Applications and data analysis methods.* Newbury Park, CA: Sage.

Burstein, L. (1978). Assessing differences between grouped and individual-level regression coefficients: Alternate approaches. *Sociological Methods and Research, 7*(1), 5–28.

Burstein, L. (1980). The analysis of multi-level data in educational research and evaluation. *Review of Research in Education, 8*, 158–233.

Buzacott, J. A. (1982). *Scale in production systems.* New York: Pergamon.

Carnegie Council on Adolescent Development. (1989). *Turning points: Preparing American youth for the 21st century.* New York: Carnegie Corporation of New York.

Chambers, J. G. (1981). An analysis of school size under a voucher system. *Educational Evaluation and Policy Analysis, 3*, 29–40.

Conant, J. B. (1959). *The American high school today.* New York: McGraw-Hill.

Cremin, L. A. (1988). *American education: The metropolitan experience. 1876–1980.* New York: Harper and Row.

Farley, R., & Frey, W. H. (1994). Changes in the segregation of Blacks and Whites. *American Sociological Review, 59*(91), 23–45.

Fowler, W. J., & Walberg, H. J. (1991). School size, characteristics, and outcomes. *Educational Evaluation and Policy Analysis, 13*(2), 189–202.

Fox, W. F. (1981). Reviewing economics of size in education. *Journal of Education Finance, 6*, 273–296.

Fine, M. (Ed., 1994). *Chartering urban school reform: Reflections on public high schools in the midst of change.* New York: Teachers College Press.

Friedkin, N. E., & Necochea, J. (1988). School size and performance: A contingency perspective. *Educational Evaluation and Policy Analysis, 10*(3), 237–249.

Gamoran, A. (1989). Measuring curriculum differentiation. *American Journal of Education, 97*, 129–143.

Garbarino, J. (1980). Some thoughts on school size and its effects on adolescent development. *Journal of Achievement and Engagement for Early Secondary School Students, 68*(4), 271–290.

Garet, M. S., & Delaney, R. (1988). Students' courses and stratification. *Sociology of Education, 61*, 61–77.

Goodlad, J. (1984). *A place called school: Prospects for the future.* New York: McGraw-Hill.

Goss, D. (1994). *Principles of human resource management.* New York: Routledge.

Gottfredson, G. D., & Daiger, D. (1979). *Disruption in six hundred schools (Report 289).* Baltimore, MD: Johns Hopkins University, Center for the Social Organization of Schools.

Guthrie, J. (1979). Organizational scale and school success. *Educational Evaluation and Policy Analysis, 1*(1), 17–27.

Kenny, L. (1982). Economies of scale in schooling. *Economics of Education Review, 2*(1), 1–24.

Lee, V. E., & Bryk, A. S. (1988). Curriculum tracking as mediating the social distribution of high school achievement. *Sociology of Education, 61*, 78–94.

Lee, V. E., & Bryk, A. S. (1989). A multilevel model of the social distribution of high school achievement. *Sociology of Education, 62*, 172–192.

Lee, V. E., Bryk, A. S., & Smith, J. B. (1993). The organization of effective high schools. In L. Darling-Hammond (Ed.), *Review of research in education 19* (pp. 171–267). Washington, DC: AERA.

Lee, V. E., Burkam, D. T., Smerdon, B. A., Chow-Hoy, T., & Geverdt, D. (1998, August). *High school curriculum structure: Effects on course taking and achievement in mathematics for high school graduates.* Working Paper No. 98–09. Washington, DC: U.S. Department of Education, Office of Educational Research and Improvement, National Center for Education Statistics.

Lee, V. E., & Loeb, S. (in press). School size in Chicago's elementary schools: Effects on teachers' attitudes and students' achievement. *American Educational Research Journal.*

Lee, V. E., Smerdon, B. A., Alfeld-Liro, C., & Brown, S. L. (1996). *Inside large and small high schools: Curriculum and social relations.* Paper presented at the annual meeting of the American Sociological Association, August 1996, New York, New York.

Lee, V. E., & Smith, J. B. (1995). The effects of high school restructuring and size on gains in achievement and engagement for early secondary school students. *Sociology of Education, 68*(4), 271–290.

Lee, V. E., & Smith, J. B. (1997). High school size: Which works best, and for whom? *Educational Evaluation and Policy Analysis, 19*(3), 205–227.

Michelson, S. (1972). Equal school resource allocation. *Journal of Human Resources, 7,* 283–306.

Monk, D. (1987). Secondary school size and curriculum comprehensiveness. *Economics of Education Review, 6,* 137–150.

Monk, D., & Haller, E. J. (1993). Predictors of high school academic course offerings: The role of school size. *American Educational Research Journal, 30,* 3–21.

Morocco, J. C. (1978). The relationship between size of elementary schools and pupils' perceptions of their environment. *Education, 98,* 451–454.

Morrison, C. (1993). *A microeconomic approach to the measurement of economic performance: Productive growth, capacity utilization, and related performance indicators.* New York: Springer-Verlag.

Muncie, D. E., & McQuillan, P. J. (1991, May). School-within-a-school restructuring and faculty divisiveness: *Examples from a Study of the Coalition of Essential Schools.* Report Number 6, the School Ethnography Project. Providence, RI: Annenberg Institute for School Reform, Brown University.

National Association of Secondary School Principals (NASSP, 1996). *Breaking ranks: Changing an American institution.* Reston, VA: Author, in partnership with the Carnegie Foundation For the Advancement of Teaching.

National Center for Education Statistics (1982). *High School and Beyond 1980. Sophomore cohort first followup (1982). Data file users' manual.* Washington, DC: National Center for Educational Statistics.

National Center for Education Statistics (1995). *National Educational Longitudinal Study of 1988*: Psychometric report for the NELS-88 base year. Second follow-up (NCES-95-382). Washington, DC. U.S. Department of Education, Office of Educational Research Information.

Neufeld, B. (1984). *Inside organization: High school teachers' efforts to influence their work.* Unpublished doctoral dissertation, Harvard University, Cambridge, Massachusetts.

Newmann, F. M. (1981). Reducing student alienation in high schools: Implications of theory. *Harvard Educational Review, 51,* 546–564.

Oakes, J. (1985). *Keeping track: How schools structure inequality.* New Haven, CT: Yale University Press.

Patton, M. Q. (1990). *Qualitative evaluation and research methods* (2nd ed.). Newbury Park, CA: Sage.

Powell, A. G., Farrar, E., & Cohen, D. K. (1985). *The shopping mall high school: Winners and losers in the educational marketplace.* Boston: Houghton-Mifflin.

Sizer, T. R. (1984). *Horace's compromise: The dilemma of the American high school.* New York: Houghton-Mifflin.

Tyack, D. (1974). *The one best system.* Cambridge, MA: Harvard University Press.

Waller, W. (1932). *The sociology of teaching.* New York: Russell and Russell.

Weber, M. (1947). *Theory of social and economic organization* (Trans. by A. M. Henderson & T. Parsons). New York: MacMillan.

Wehlage, G., Rutter, R. A., Smith, G. A., Lesko, N. & Fernandez, R. R. (1989). *Reducing the risk: Schools as communities of support.* Philadelphia: Falmer Press.

CHAPTER 15

Comparative Sociology of Classroom Processes, School Organization, and Achievement

DAVID P. BAKER
GERALD K. LETENDRE

INTRODUCTION

The study of the schooling process and associated outcomes, such as cognitive achievement, is central to the sociology of education. Similarly, perspective gained from cross-societal, comparative research is central to sociology in general and is a well-established tradition in the intellectual study of society (e.g., see essays by M. Weber in Gerth & Mills, 1991). However, the combination of the two—examining schooling and its outcomes comparatively—has had a peculiar history in the development of modem sociology of education: peculiar in several important ways. First, most of the concepts and methods used in the comparative sociological study of schooling and outcomes were developed initially for specific questions about American education. Second, there has been a less-than-tight connection between the sociology of education and the broader field of comparative research. Third, because this general comparative study on school processes is heavily motivated by utilitarian, policy-related questions, and is thus undermotivated by explicitly theoretical questions, sociological theory in this area is not fully developed. Last, more nonsociologists than sociologists routinely undertake research in this area, and their research is published in journals that most sociologists do

DAVID P. BAKER AND GERALD K. LETENDRE • College of Education, Pennsylvania State University, University Park, Pennsylvania 16802

Handbook of the Sociology of Education, edited by Maureen T. Hallinan. Kluwer Academic/Plenum Publishers, New York, 2000.

not routinely read (e.g., *Comparative Education Review, Anthropology and Education Quarterly, Educational Policy*). Nevertheless, there is an emerging set of important sociological studies in this area all employing standard methods that are generating a useful empirical perspective on education.

This chapter weaves through the development of this subfield of the sociology of education and in doing so reviews its basic findings and arguments. We do not limit our review to purely sociological work because this field is a blend of both theoretically grounded comparative research and a large volume of atheoretical comparative studies. Overall the literature is not a concise and well-aligned body of research where central theories have been tested in clashing studies, thereby driving a series of empirical breakthroughs. Although many other sociological subfields also do not enjoy a tight alignment between theory and empirical study, this weakness is particularly pronounced in this subfield of the sociology of education. This diverse literature is far more a catch-all: a pot into which many things—explicit sociological inquiry and otherwise—have been mixed together and have been called on to do service in various capacities such as supporting or contradicting educational reform and justifying policy, as well as advancing sociological theory. Consequently, the story here is neither exhaustive nor neatly organized by competing theories of schooling and achievement.

All research designs are comparative at some conceptual level, and what is really comparative is mostly a judgement call. Because "comparative" has chiefly come to mean cross-national, we limit our review to cross-national comparative work on schooling and achievement outcomes. However, it is noted that by doing so we do not review other streams of comparative research, such as historical comparisons in one society or even historical comparisons across societies. Additionally, there are some very useful historical works on classroom processes and school organization, particularly in American schools, which have affected the way in which some cross-national work is done. See for example, the historical comparison of teaching styles, teaching work conditions (Cuban, 1983, 1992), and the historical development of organizational coeducational arrangements in American schools (Tyack & Hansot, 1988a, 1988b). Unfortunately there is far less historical work on cognitive outcomes of schools (see Stedman, 1997, for a review of some relevant material).

Also, to write this review we divide up the large field of comparative education and focus on the young subfield of the comparative study of school processes and outcomes. Because of the considerable challenge of generating either quantitative or qualitative comparative micro-data on schooling, this kind of research has developed more slowly than traditional macrocomparative endeavors where large sets of cross-national and historical data on school enrollments, school structure, and even school policy are readily available. The review, then, does not directly examine the origins of the general comparative study of schooling because most of this has evolved from the macrocomparative perspective of education's role in national development (e.g. Fägerlind & Saha, 1989). Much of the work on cultural capital that has been carried out in the United States and in other nations (usually single-nation studies), as well as the large stratification literature, has also been set aside. Furthermore, there is a generous literature on the expansion of schooling and the institutionalization of Western schooling practices in many nations around the world that we do not summarize, as these studies rarely attempt to analyze what goes on in classrooms (see Benavot, Cha, Kamens, Meyer, & Wang, 1991 for a notable exception). Finally, although considerable work has been done on the effects of schooling on economic development, especially work on modernization and the school's role in modernizing economies, we do not review this literature here.

We begin with a historical sketch about how several strands of American sociological inquiry have come to shape the comparative study of schooling and achievement. This is followed by a review of important comparative studies of school effects that have shaped central questions about cross-national variation in the way schools and families produce achievement. Next, we describe some of the political processes that have propelled the comparative study of schooling into the policy arena and discuss what this means for the future of sociological inquiry in this area. After this is a brief discussion about what role a comparative sociology of schooling might play in the main sociological line of inquiry about social stratification in modem society. In the final section we speculate on what the future looks like for this subfield in the sociology of education. Throughout all of these sections we integrate a literature review with some critical commentary on this evolving field, its current status as a research endeavor, and various challenges that lie before it. Such a critical review offers a way to put this diverse field's numerous accomplishments into intellectual perspective, as well as to offer some speculation on what important territory remains to be explored.

AMERICANIZED COMPARATIVE SOCIOLOGY OF EDUCATION

An essential thing to know in order to understand what this subfield has done and has not yet done is that most studies in the comparative sociology of education of schooling or of outcomes were shaped to a considerable degree by American intellectual questions. In part this is because sociological approaches applied to schooling in the United States have enjoyed considerable academic success since 1950 (Dreeben, 1994). The United States has the largest set of sociologists of education in the world producing research that has been shown to have measurable scientific impact worldwide.[*] Further, American sociologists of education are themselves embedded within the world's largest, and arguably most influential, national community of scholars and researchers of education from all disciplines (American Educational Research Association [AERA], 1992). Lastly, as a purely domestic field, American sociology of education has been successful in placing sociologists within the national education establishment and in weaving sociological issues into some key American educational agenda (McCartney, 1971). Additionally, to the degree to which U.S. political interests increase opportunities for international study of education, this intensifies the overlap between American topics and comparative research (Meyer & Baker, 1996; see also the discussion of International Association for the Evaluation of Education Achievement (IEA) studies that follow).

This Americanization of educational research sustains an imbalance between purely American sociology of schooling and a more comparative approach (Baker, 1994; Ramirez & Meyer, 1981). Unintentionally, the former tends to dictate the tenor of the latter. For better or for worse, a large part of the methods, theoretical concerns, and research topics found in the comparative sociology of education have evolved first in the more dominant sociology of American schooling. Some argue that this imbalance retards comparative education research in general, maybe even slowing the incorporation of comparative findings back into American sociology of education (Ramirez & Meyer). This is particularly the case for the comparative study of school and classroom processes and their associated outcomes. One way to read this review is to note the considerable degree to which comparative research on schooling and its outcomes is an extension of essentially American questions into a cross-national framework. This is perhaps best illustrated by the development of American school-effects research and the effect this line of inquiry had on its comparative counterpart.

---

[*]See Baker (1994) for specific bibliographic analyses of the journal *Sociology of Education* relative to other education research journals.

From American School-Effects Research to the Heyneman/Loxley Effect

As is well known, the 1966 *Equality of Educational Opportunity* (EEO, Coleman et al., 1966) both in technique and in concept, defined the idea of a sociology of school effects (see Riordan, 1997, for a rich description of EEO and its impact on sociological research). Although the study was initiated to answer policy questions generated by the American government about school funding, poverty, and race, the basic findings staked out several key sociological questions that the field of the sociology of education has been addressing ever since. The most lasting and comprehensive sociological question the report generated was, "What effect does schooling have on achievement?"

This question surfaced from the unexpected finding that the amount of variation in achievement among students accounted for by their nonschool background (family Socioeconomic status SES, ability, etc.) substantially exceeded a set of school qualities in explaining achievement differences. In the parlance of school-effects research, within-school differences in achievement are greater than between-school differences. Even though similar findings would be reported some 5 years later in a British study (Peaker, 1971), EEO (Coleman et al.) was a uniquely American study in its questions, its design, and its ultimate intellectual impact.

The notion behind the larger political agenda leading up to EEO (Coleman et al., 1966) was conceived out of the Johnson administration's War on Poverty and Great Society, essentially political legacies of the New Deal. The assumption then was the following: improving and equalizing public services such as schooling would help solve many problems of the modem industrial society. This is why the basic findings of the report troubled educators and the public alike. In the mid-1960s these findings seemed to fly in the face of the basic utilitarian notion of schooling—namely, that if schools educate, differences in school quality should produce differences in outcomes. The startling, yet oversimplified, message taken from EEO (Coleman et al.)—that school processes had little direct effect on achievement—is what caught the public's attention, and, as a result of heavy media coverage of the report, may have been the conclusion that influenced most education policymakers.

For much of American sociology of education, the flip side of this finding proved to be the most intriguing. Schools appeared to pass on family socioeconomic status differences into their outcomes (Jencks et al., 1972). Schools, by translating social factors into achievement differences, work to amplify social inequality. Taken together with findings from another 1960s sociological development—status attainment research—that showed how pivotal educational attainment is in translating social position into adult occupational status (e.g. Blau & Duncan, 1967; Duncan & Hodge, 1963), the EEO (Coleman et al., 1966) report findings opened up a whole set of inquiries into the way schools reproduce social inequalities. These include the main research literatures on subtler within-school process such as curricular tracks and ways in which parents influence the schooling process in the United States (e.g., Baker & Stevenson, 1986; Epstein, 1998; Lareau, 1987).

Not until a decade and a half later did sociologists turn directly to the question of comparative school effects. There are several important findings from this comparative analysis of schooling and achievement—all of which shed light on the nature of school effects. Contrary to what many took away from EEO (Coleman et al., 1966), namely, that schools have little effect beyond family background, these studies show otherwise. Stephen Heyneman and William Loxley, who were working to expand The World Bank's lending policy agenda to include educational development, undertook EEO-type school-effects analyses in 29 countries. Their findings have greatly expanded our understanding of the sociological functions of schools (Heyneman & Loxley, 1982, 1983; see also Fuller & Heyneman, 1989; Heyneman, 1976).

There are two main findings from these studies. First, using the same test to evaluate similar curriculum in mathematics and in science, there are clear school effects across economic level of countries. Heyneman and Loxley (1983) reported that about 30% of the variation across countries in achievement is accounted for by variation among countries in wealth (i.e., per capita GNP, see also Comber & Keeves, 1973; Thorndike, 1973). Second, the relative effects of school factors and socioeconomic family factors vary by the economic development level of the country. Just as EEO (Coleman et al., 1966) and Plowden (Penker, 1971) studies had shown before, in developed countries (i.e., high per capita GNP) family factors significantly outweigh school factors in predicting between students' variation in achievement. However, in less developed countries the reverse is true—school factors outweigh family factors. Both of these comparative findings illustrate the effects of schooling on a societal level and they indicate that social forces at the national level set the context for achievement patterns. This extends considerably the initial EEO (Coleman et al.) findings by first doing away with the notion that schools universally have only modest effects, and second, by demonstrating an inseparable link between the two institutions of family and school that is conditioned by larger social contexts such as national development (e.g., Katsillis & Rubinson, 1990).

What specifically produces the Heyneman/Loxley effect is still debated, but Heyneman and Loxley (1983) themselves have offered two explanations for the findings. First is the notion that in developing countries schooling is a scarce good, and this scarcity motivates students, regardless of family background. Second is the notion that the size and importance of public labor sectors, such as the civil service, in developing countries tend to tighten the connections between school achievement at all levels and future employment opportunities. Both of these factors, they argued, could yield larger school effects in poorer countries. In point of fact, there are other reasons one could make for the Heyneman/Loxley effect. One is that the ability of wealthier countries to fund a deeper institutionalization of schooling in their society yields a significantly higher minimum level of school quality. Even though there is always variation within countries in school quality, marginal school effects on achievement may fall off after a certain basic threshold has been reached throughout the system in terms of basic resource inputs, and hence a large share of achievement differences are produced by variation in nonschool inputs. However, in poorer countries variation in school quality spans further down below these threshold levels and, hence, many schools would be significantly less effective even after controlling for family background. For example, teaching without textbooks or other basic resources happens far more in some schools in developing countries than in developed ones.

This notion is partially illustrated by detailed analyses of which educational resources have the largest impact on achievement. Fuller (1987) reviewed some 60 school-effects studies completed in developing countries to determine which resources may be most responsible for the Heyneman/Loxley effect. The studies, many of which were done by comparative sociologists of education, showed that both basic school resources, as well as school and classroom management factors, generate school effects in these countries. In keeping with a threshold argument, these studies found that a lower end of resources in systems often includes schools with little basic educational resources. For example, among studies of schooling in developing countries that focus on between-school variation in the availability and adequacy of instructional material, there are clear effects after controlling for family background. This holds true when using measures such as whether or not there are textbooks and also in experimental studies with control groups. These kinds of textbook effects have been reported for countries such as Uganda, Egypt, El Salvador, Paraguay, Bolivia, Brazil, India, Chile, Nicaragua, Malaysia, Ghana, the Philippines, and Thailand (Armitage, Batista, Harbison, Holsinger,

& Helio, 1986; Comber & Keeves, 1973; Haron, 1977; Heyneman, 1976; Heyneman & Jamison, 1980; Heyneman & Loxley, 1983; Jamison, Searle, Galda, & Heyneman, 1983; Lockheed, Vail, & Fuller, 1986; Smart, 1978). More complex factors such as teacher quality, teaching practices, and school leadership also are shown to be part of the school effect in developing countries. Variation in basic primary and secondary schooling for teachers has an effect in India, in Uganda, in Bolivia, in Chile, in Botswana and in Paraguay (Armitage et al., 1986; Heyneman & Loxley, 1983; Husen, 1967). Additionally, so does basic literacy and numeracy provided by in-service training and by teacher selection mechanisms and principal training (e.g., Egypt—Hartley & Swanson, 1984; Kenya—Thias & Carnoy, 1973; Botswana—Loxley, 1984). Similar positive effects on achievement in developing countries are reported in these studies for a number of other school and classroom factors, including expenditures on schooling, specific material inputs, quality of teaching stock, classroom practices, pedagogic approach, and school management. Across a large number of methodologically sound studies, Fuller's review shows considerable evidence that variation among school, classroom, and teacher factors that tend to have either small or no effects in developed countries are significantly related to variation in students' achievement in developing countries.[*]

Heyneman and Loxley's (1983) original speculations on what produced their findings ended up moving away from the central notion of functional school effects, for which there is now considerable evidence from poorer countries. Although their own explanations about school scarcity and connections to the labor market are still viable, these explanations—as well as the ones we propose—remain to be adequately tested. Nevertheless, taken as a whole this set of cross-national research dramatically demonstrates the functional power of schooling as a cognitive transforming process (Meyer, 1977). With its extreme focus on inequality production, American sociology of school outcomes (and related work in other developed countries) has not fully appreciated the implications of functional qualities of education that are so clearly demonstrated cross-nationally (Meyer & Baker, 1996).

School versus No-School

An intriguing comparative question raised by the Heyneman/Loxley effect considered from a functional perspective on the role of schooling in the production of achievement is the following: What effect does schooling large portions of children have on cognitive functioning in the general population? In other words, does the act of schooling shape how most people think and not just how much they might know or how they are sorted according to academic ability? Additionally, what might this mean for modem societies?

It is clear from cohort studies of school achievement that participation in schooling over time yields knowledge accumulation in populations and, regardless of persistent fanning of achievement levels across cohorts, all of the schooled cohort increases in learning (e.g., Ralph, Keller, & Crouse, 1994). Similarly, cross-national studies of literacy in adults have shown that within a relatively narrow band of cognitive functioning, exposure to schooling corresponds to adult abilities (Office and Economic Cooperation and Development [OECD], 1997). We also know much about the sorting functions of schools (e.g., Riordan, 1997). Yet to really show the cognitive impact of schooling on society at large it is necessary to compare the schooled with the unschooled. This is difficult, however, because the widespread expansion

---

[*]It is interesting to note that there is no one clear pattern of exactly which resources produce school effects across all developed countries examined; see Fuller (1987) for discussion of this point.

of schooling for all children took place well before any inquiry of this type could take place; almost all of the work on the cognitive effects of education has been limited to studies of marginal effects of varying amounts or quality of schooling. Consequently, comparing students with slightly different levels of education often finds less than dramatic cognitive differences that are hard to separate from confounding factors.

In most developed countries there are no significant-sized populations of completely unschooled people that do not suffer various physical and psychological handicaps and social stigmas with which to undertake this kind of analysis. However, in some developing countries there are large unschooled populations. One of the few studies to quantitatively compare schooled children with unschooled children is by Harold Stevenson and his colleagues (Stevenson, Parker, Wilkinson, Bonnevaux, & Gonzalez, 1978). In short, formal schooling leads to a different way for children to cognitively organize their world in comparison to the unschooled. Stevenson's team traveled to isolated rural areas of Peru and administered a battery of tests to children ages 5 and 6, as well as to children living in Lima. The researchers reported finding "pervasive and strong positive influences of attending school on all of the memory and cognitive tasks used in this study" (p. 64). This study documented that on many cognitive tasks, school attendance (sometimes as brief as a year) had measurable effects on children's cognitive orientation to a variety of tasks compared to unschooled children. From a sociological perspective, the attainment of education credentials and the production of achievement are often seen solely to be part of the larger social stratification process. Thinking about schooling as an institution that also (and maybe primarily) transforms cognitive perspectives of whole schooled populations, and the effect that this transformation might have on society at large, illustrates the potential benefit of the comparative study of schooling to broader sociological questions about the makeup of modern society.

Nevertheless, there is a knowledge gap in our comparative understanding of how schools might produce these cognitive effects and what that might mean for modern society. Related, of course, is the older work on modernity (e.g., Inkeles & Smith, 1974), but this strand of functional analysis stopped as more Marxist theories of education interested primarily in explaining class reproduction and national development became dominant. Very few studies in the comparative sociology of schooling have focused on the functional outcomes of teaching and classroom processes aside from social class sorting and inequality analyses. Although some research on developing countries reviewed previously does this, this has not been fully developed comparatively. This is true of noncomparative sociology as well; other than a few notable American sociological studies (Boocock, 1978; Cohen, 1986), this area has been dominated by psychologists, who in turn have been critically attacked by various groups such as linguistic anthropologists (e.g., Mehan, 1979). Thus, beyond achievement as either a stratifying property, or as a utilitarian property to be maximized through organizational change, the entire central technical operation of schooling and its effects on the cognitive domains of humans and societies has not received attention by comparative sociologists of education.

Comparative Research on Family, on Community, and on Schooling

For many sociologists of American education one popular and useful research activity leading out of the EEO (Coleman et al., 1966) is considering how family socioeconomic status (SES) and the process of schooling interactively reproduce social status, often through effects on achievement and on attainment (e.g., Epstein, 1998; Lareau, 1987; Schneider & Coleman, 1993). Far less has been done on this central American question from a cross-national perspective. There is some work on how different features of schooling in selected countries have produced different kinds of family effects. Some examples are Oswald, Baker, and Stevenson's (1988) work on the effect of the structure and charter of German secondary streams on parental involvement in activities to enhance achievement, and Stevenson and Baker's (1992) study of family SES, shadow education (tutoring, private exam classes, etc.) and university examinations in Japan.

The EEO's (Coleman et al., 1966) main message resonated with another significant, if less prominent, line of inquiry in sociology, and that is the qualitative analysis of how family SES and the larger community's social structure articulated with schooling and with students' lives. This line of work in the United States (e.g., Hollingshead, 1975; Lynd, 1959; Stinchcombe, 1964) has clearly influenced the analysis of schooling in other countries as a way to understand how the process of schooling replicates social class for an American audience. Three of the most widely read qualitative works on family social status reproduction in schools are MacLeod's (1987) study of low-income youths in an urban U.S. high school, Willis' (1991) ethnographic study of working-class youths in British schools, and Rohlen's (1983) ethnography of life in Japan's high schools. Although investigating a common topic, these three works draw on very different theoretical and disciplinary literatures. Such qualitative investigations (see also Okano, 1993) are richly descriptive and offer a window for sociological readers into the interaction of culture and schooling.

These studies usually describe, but do not necessarily test, the hypothesis that schools transmit social status. Similar to U.S. studies of tracking (e.g., Oakes & Guiton, 1995), qualitative studies of social status reproduction often are influenced by general notions of French theorists of education and inequality (e.g., Bourdieu, Passeron, & Boudon), particularly Bourdieu's formulation of cultural capital (Lareau, 1987). Because of this, and also because the works are not explicitly comparative, they have yet to develop a sustained line of comparative research.

Finally, another related and emerging line of research is on how large-scale demographic change (something that can vary greatly cross-nationally) influences the way family SES and school effects are structured. Working mostly on developing countries, Pong showed that demographic effects across national populations (e.g., changes in average sibship size, divorce and remarriage rate, and school completion rates of parenting generations) can restructure how families and schools interact to create schooling inequalities that can influence achievement and attainment (Pong, 1997; Post & Pong, 1997). This demographic approach has also been applied to thinking about patterns of national achievement among U.S. students as well (Grissmer, Kirb, Berends, & Williamson, 1994; Pong, 1997).

THE POLITICAL INCORPORATION OF CROSS-NATIONAL ACHIEVEMENT DATA

What is known simply as the IEA (International Association for the Evaluation of Educational Achievement) is the international organization most responsible for establishing the most basic resource required for the comparative quantitative study of schooling and achievement data. Usually such an organization playing this role would not warrant much discussion in a review of research, except that this particular organization's development and the political reaction to the publication of its studies have shaped the comparative study of schooling and achievement. The IEA has been a primary actor in organizing comparative research, and its organizational history is critical to understanding many aspects of the field in general as well as to assessing future capacity for comparative research on schooling. Perhaps most important is the increasing political incorporation of IEA and its studies into the workings of educational policymaking in many countries.

In some ways the IEA's role is analogous to that played by the U.S. Department of Education's National Center for Educational Statistics (NCES) in producing large-scale, microdata sets that in addition to answering specific policy questions have become the mainstay for secondary analysis done by sociologists of education. However, unlike the production of the American data sets, such as *High School and Beyond* or *National Education Longitudinal Study* (U.S. Department of Education) which were shaped through the exceptionally high involvement of sociologists of education working either in the U.S. government or in influential agencies closely tied to the government, the IEA has historically not been heavily influenced by sociologists or by their research paradigms. Many IEA studies draw on a range of scholarly expertise, which often form competing groups of experts, and have been organized around producing basic data on achievement in various subject areas that do not necessarily reflect sociological questions.

Further, it is important to consider that the size and scale of the average IEA study is immense. At a minimum these studies require valid achievement assessments on relatively large probability samples of students, information on school factors often collected from multiple actors (e.g., teachers, principals), and information on family background. To produce this on a large cross-national scale requires international cooperation and significant amounts of resources. The IEA has in large part met this challenge by mounting increasingly larger and more ambitious studies of schooling and achievement, but this was not always the case.

Up until its most recent study, the Third International Mathematics and Science Study (TIMSS), IEA studies were fielded by decentralized networks of academics from various countries who were connected through professional activities around curricular interests such as science, math, civics, or reading. Heavy involvement on the part of curricular specialists in the design of these comparative data sets has given many IEA studies their distinct focus on curriculum and on related issues such as opportunity-to-learn and instruction. For example, both math and science specialists have generated large-scale studies starting in the 1960s (Comber & Keeves, 1973; Husen, 1967; Travers & Westbury, 1989), and these have been useful to comparative sociologists of schooling (see studies reviewed earlier on developing countries and the Heyneman/Loxley effect Heyneman and Loxley, 1983; Comber and Keeves, 1973; Thorndike, 1973.).

Although the IEA data on comparative effects of schooling are a major resource, research using these data does not tend to be well integrated into the broader field of comparative education. Because comparative education in general is at best a loose confederation of theories, methods, and literatures, incorporation of IEA studies into this framework has tended to be piecemeal. For example, a review of the annual meeting proceedings since the late 1980s of the most prominent comparative education scholarly association—the Comparative and International Education Society (CIES)—finds sessions on IEA studies, but they are segregated from other more central topics in the CIES, such as, for example, interpretations of the educational legacy of the colonialist period. Rarely are there joint discussions of the study of schooling process and outcomes from IEA data and of other more traditional topics found in the CIES. Even though IEA studies produce data that are central to the comparative study of schooling and achievement, they have tended to be isolated in the larger field of comparative education (see Baker, 1994; Torney-Purta, 1987, for related discussions).

At the same time, however, IEA studies have had considerable impact on American education policy and research (Schmidt, McKnight & Raizen, 1997). Additionally, these studies have been the cornerstone of numerous widely publicized and politicized comparative reports about school outcomes and quality in the United States; the most salient example being the *Nation at Risk* report (see Baker, 1998, for a discussion of the politics of IEA studies and U.S. education policymaking). Like other large data sets with high policy relevance, IEA data have been used and have created many debates in the United States about educational reform, but there has also been substantial misuses of the data along with a remarkable lack of secondary analysis of the many facets of these large studies (Torney-Purta, 1987).

TIMSS, the current 40-country IEA study on math and science, continues some of this legacy, but it also makes a significant break with the past IEA studies. First, its size is unique even for the IEA in both its curricular scope (two subject areas) and its ambitious design, including innovative videotaping and ethnographic study in selected countries. Second, and perhaps most revolutionary, is that TIMSS was not a product of a confederation of academics as in the past, but rather was the product of several national governments (the United States and Canada) who underwrote the main infrastructure of the study.* Although governments have always been involved in the past, TIMSS is completely a cross-governmental undertaking that has affected the field.

This comes with some consequences. First, the initial TIMSS results have been far more publicized both in the United States and in other countries than past IEA studies. In the United States, this coverage has resulted in an intense debate about how valid comparative studies are, and how (or if) they should be incorporated into the debate on U.S. educational policy (for a review see Stedman, 1997). Second, past IEA studies had always been a combination of the latest psychometric techniques in assessment of academic knowledge, curricular assessments, and survey technology, but TIMSS, under the influence of the American and Canadian federal statistical services, has taken methodological innovation to new heights. The combination of advanced Item Response Theory technology with an elaborate curricular analysis in roughly a school-effects design offers exciting opportunities. At the same time, however, the more innovative data collected remains underanalyzed several years after collection (i.e., the videotape studies and ethnographic studies of three countries). The impact of this has been to emphasize descriptive aspects of the data, not theory testing, as researchers have yet to devise ways to link different types of data together in a coherent analysis.

TIMSS could be a new breed of comparative data collection: large, multifaceted, complex, and highly integrated into the operation of nation–state governments around the world, and thus publicly financed. If these data prove to have clear and assessable payoffs for major nation–states, it is likely to become a standard source of comparative data. However, if TIMSS proves too large and too complex, with too few payoffs from the investment, future studies of this scope are unlikely. Governments could only invest in relatively inexpensive, simpler, indicator comparative studies that just provide achievement assessments instead of the information needed to undertake causal, explanatory analyses (see OECD, 1997, for an example of this alternative to causal data sets).

By incorporating, and thus making obsolete an older model of comparative data collection, governments have pushed the IEA to a new technical level. This means that future studies will now be even more permeated by education politics of nation–states. The capacity to collect some of the best data in this subfield will increasingly be subject to political interests of governments. Although this may mean, as was the case with TIMSS, significant improvements in resources, it does come at some cost. The potential for negative impact of such

---

*The U.S. government paid about 50 million dollars and only a small fraction of that was for collecting American data.

politicization of the research process can already be seen in the case of research on Japanese schooling and its relation to American educational crises.

Who's First: Hegemonic Politics and Educational Crises

Intensive political incorporation of cross-national achievement studies has had a significant impact on the way international comparisons are used in American education policy. The politicization of cross-national achievement comparisons has also affected which countries sociologists of education select to study and how they go about studying the schooling process. The case of Japan and the latest two rounds of IEA studies of mathematics and science are particularly illustrative of this point.

As early as the late 1960s, studies of Japanese education began to appear in research publications on international and comparative issues. The 1980s saw a virtual explosion of literature on Japanese education: whole issues of *Comparative Education* (1986) and *The Journal of Japanese Studies* (1989) were devoted to educational issues in Japan. Several important studies were conducted that explicitly linked classroom processes and the production of achievement (e.g. DeVos, 1973; Peak, 1989; Schaub & Baker, 1991; Shimahara, 1979; White, 1987). During the same period, the Japanese school became a standard topic in American mass media. This American fascination with Japanese schooling has had as much to do with reactions to Japanese economic success in the 1980s as with Japanese educational success, and media reports emphasized the idea that Japan, as a nation–state, was somehow setting a standard with which the United States or individual U.S. states should compete. This trend may have reached its zenith in such publications as the National Educational Goals volumes wherein individual U.S. states are compared with Japan in math and science achievement (National Educational Goals Panel [NEGP], 1995).

Japan (and to a lesser extent other Asian nations with high average test scores in math and in science) now plays a key role in various arguments about how to interpret comparative test-score data and its implications for U.S. education. Much of this has an overt economic competition bent to it, with a vague underlying notion of human capital investment. To improve the United States' economic competitiveness in the world, the idea was to somehow copy school features of Japan. In the debate about public school quality in the United States, references are often made to comparisons with Japan, and there has been a lively discussion of the appropriate way to incorporate these studies into the American educational reform movement (Baker, 1993, 1997; Bracey, 1996, 1997; Stedman, 1994, 1997; Westbury, 1992; 1993).

Nevertheless, in all of this discussion of Japanese schooling within an American context, scholarly studies of the multiple facets of Japanese education are rarely reviewed or cited. Japanese schooling takes on mythical portions, both good and bad depending on the particular politics of the American writer (e.g., Bracey, 1997). What results is a unidimensional stereotype conveniently packaged for different American policy positions (see Baker, 1997 for a critique of this trend).

Japanese achievement data are thus divorced from studies that emphasize theoretical aspects. Comparative qualitative studies of schooling and instruction, including some from a sociological perspective, reveal a complex picture about Japanese education and its relevance to education policy in the United States that is not picked up in the current debate on TIMSS. An illustrative example of this is the paradoxical view of Japanese classroom instruction held at different times in recent U.S. policy debates. In the early 1980s, the aftermath of Second International Math Study (SIMS) and Second International Science Study (SISS) motivated

American commentators to soothe the public's concerns about low U.S. scores with descriptions of Japanese rote learning. The argument went that rote learning, as it was assumed to be practiced in Japan, was only good for increasing test scores, but creative learning, assumed to be taking place in U.S. schools, was better for life. With the advent of several studies in the early 1990s, these earlier descriptions have been forgotten and much the reverse is now offered to the American public—Japan engages in creative learning and the United States is mired down in rote skill production (see Lewis, 1995).

In reality, both kinds of approaches may be present in Japanese education depending on the level of the class. The child-centered nature of Japanese classrooms has been documented in the literature on preschools and on elementary schools showing that nationwide, teachers de-emphasize rote learning and emphasize hands-on activities, problem solving, higher order questioning, and the creative application of materials learned (Hendry, 1986; Lewis, 1995; Peak, 1989; White, 1987). Elementary school teachers in Japan, as explicitly compared to U.S. classrooms, place more emphasis on student reasoning and allow for more creative problem solving on the part of students, and this approach was consistent across types of students and communities (Lee, Graham, & Stevenson, 1996; Sato & McLaughlin, 1992; Stigler, Fernandez, & Yoshida, 1996; Tobin, Wu & Davidson, 1989). Further, and what is often missed in more cursory accounts of instruction in Japan, is that the nature of instruction changes toward more drill-oriented learning over the course of schooling, and there is considerable tracking of students by ability in the later grades. The pressure to perform well on college entrance exams has now moved downward so that middle school students are increasingly under pressure to perform well on the high school entrance exam.

Several key studies conducted in Japan have addressed central sociological issues in a comparative perspective. In Bowman's (1981) work on class background and educational decisions, Brinton's work on gender and educational stratification (Brinton, 1988), Rosenbaum and Kariya's work on educational achievement and occupational status (1989; 1991), and Ishida's (1993) study of the role of school in social mobility in Japan, the United States and Britain have significantly advanced our understanding of the ways in which cultural parameters impact the effects of school on social status attainment. Additional studies (Stevenson & Baker, 1992; Treiman & Yamaguchi, 1993) have employed more complex theoretical and statistical models to further analyze the institutional forces that construct the multiple ways in which schools and cram schools impact social status attainment.

Although these studies have advanced sociological knowledge, regrettably, the more nuanced messages have not had much of an impact on the way future international achievement studies are to be designed. In both the case study and the survey portions of TIMSS, for example, there was no explicit focus on the differential impact of types of shadow education (outside school achievement preparation)—a feature of schooling that is very prevalent in some countries. The consequences can be significant when analysts attempt to compare systems with very different mechanisms for promoting achievement, such as shadow education, high-stakes tests, and employment of teachers as private tutors (see Eckstein & Noah, 1993).

Lastly, all of this attention on schooling in front-runner nations needs to be put into context. Those nations that attract the attention of the U.S. public, media, education establishment, and comparative sociologist of education tend to be those that are typically identified with a host of noneducational issues such as economic competition, fascination with the exotic, and perhaps even some extreme stereotyping (e.g., Bennett, 1988; Higham, 1955). The interesting counterexample to the use of Japanese and other Asian nations' school systems as focal points in American policy and intellectual debates is Finland. Finland scored the highest in the latest IEA Reading and Literacy study in the mid-1980s, but Finland as an educational example hardly was mentioned in the United States. Granted, the United States scored very high on this test (just behind Finland in some subtests), but certainly a case could be made that some examination of the world's best reading country would have been useful. The broader effects of international achievement studies have become very political, but the politics are often simplistic, using cultural issues in a limited, nearly stereotypic fashion.

The Rising Focus on Culture in Achievement Studies

Since the mid-1980s, major journals in the field of comparative education have seen more articles that draw on critical and postmodern theory to analyze the culture of schooling,[*] especially the contested meanings that school has for various groups. A representative example of this is Taylor's (1996) discussion of education for democracy and aboriginal Australians. Further, the 1998 theme of the CIES was "Bringing Culture Back In." Although many comparative scholars of education profess an interest in culture, the fact that culture is something that needs to be brought back into the field shows the ambivalence about this concept. Whether or not there is a revival of culture as an organizing concept in the comparative study of schooling is still unclear, but it is clear that more scholars are using some version of this concept to guide their work.

The importance of culture in explaining the schooling process, or more basically, in identifying the boundaries of school as an institution, have played an increasing role in the IEA's studies. As in TIMSS, the use of cross-national surveys and international assessments of achievement are now contextualized by case studies or video studies that examine the culture of schooling. This is a significant addition to the contextless study of national systems often encouraged by IEA data (e.g., Olmstead & Weikert, 1989). However, it does not appear that the images of school culture that are being interjected into international assessment studies have relied much on knowledge from either comparative sociological or anthropological studies.

Returning briefly to Japan as an illustrative case, many scholars have attempted to understand how Japanese culture affects the educational system. In Japanese culture, tests are given high social status; tests and test taking are viewed, generally, as more positive and as imbued with more creativity than in our own culture. The sociocultural role of tests in Japan has been extensively analyzed (see Amano, 1990, and most recently Zeng, 1996). Conversely, the creativity of traditional Japanese arts that so mesmerizes many cursory visitors to Japan has been argued to be rooted in a culture that emphasizes a pattern of slow learning that begins in a foundation of repetitive tasks (Hare, 1996; Singleton, 1989).

In more explicit cross-cultural studies of schools, researchers have made advances both in methods for studying the impact of culture and in theoretical formulations of just what culture is. For example, Tobin, Wu, and Davidson's (1989) *Preschool in Three Cultures* is widely read as a model for comparative case studies of schooling. Extensive detail is given to outlining the basic cultural concepts at play in preschools in each nation, and verbatim selections of teacher and administrator's interviews are used to show points of consensus and disagreement. Cross-cultural reflection, stimulated by showing videotapes of schools in other countries, was used to elicit further information about what specific aspects of culture (i.e., the

---

[*]Like qualitative research, the term culture has many contested meanings. Louise Spindler (1984), in her work *Cultural Change and Modernization*, provides a succinct description: "Culture . . . refers to shared designs for living. It is not the people or things or behaviors themselves. Culture can be equated with the shared models people carry in their minds for perceiving, relating to, and interpreting the world about them. . . . these models are not replicas of each other. Every individual has his or her version." (p. 4).

teacher's expected roles, norms for classroom interaction, ideals of individuality) were most salient in determining how classrooms and schools in the three nations were organized and operated.

Yet, this fertile field has been largely ignored in terms of comparative/international achievement studies. The TIMSS study incorporated video and ethnographic description but only as an adjunct to the scores. Moreover, rather than presenting the qualitative data in ways that highlight areas of conflict and consensus about schooling in each of the target nations, the use (to date) of the video and ethnographic data have been to provide actual depictions of typical classrooms or of students' lives.

This means that although there is renewed interest in bringing culture back into international test comparisons, culture is still largely formulated as the black box. Culture in international studies is still undertheorized and repeatedly overused as a scapegoat in explaining mean differences in student achievement data. Rather than trying to understand how the logic of schooling situations (such as classrooms) can be directly linked to educational policies or to school structures (e.g., Rohlen, 1983), there is great interest in finding models that work. However, the fact that high-quality cultural analysis rarely makes its way into the cross-national achievement debates means that any models identified will be difficult to emulate in practical reforms.

MISARTICULATION BETWEEN STRATIFICATION
AND THE SOCIOLOGY OF EDUCATION

The accomplishments of the comparative analysis of school outcomes and classroom processes potentially have much to offer stratification research, but it is not clear if this opportunity will be realized in the future. Paradoxically, the central intellectual pursuit of American sociology—social stratification research—tends not to incorporate findings from the sociology of education on school processes and outcomes and this extends to comparative findings as well. This is particularly evident in status attainment research. Even though formal schooling is conceptualized as a major sorting mechanism in attainment models, the school and what happens there remains a black box.* Stratification research appreciates academic achievement as only an individual (or family enhanced) property that plays into the attainment of adult status, but rarely does it include sociological analysis of the production of achievement itself in schools. The image of academic achievement in stratification research appears limited and at times devoid of all substances other than family effects on ability and on other related processes such as cultural capital (e.g., Dimaggio, 1982; Robinson & Garnier, 1985). Achievement is either a product of some prematriculation ability that somehow schooling does not greatly influence (e.g., Crouse, Mueser, & Jencks, 1979), or it is a by-product of the mechanical reproduction of class by formal mass schooling (e.g., Bowles & Gintis, 1976). The sociology of how schools produce achievement, the dynamics of achievement, and any notion of a social construction of achievement are left out (e.g., Rosenholtz & Simpson, 1984). The same can also be said about closely related classroom processes, curriculum, and instruction.

This is further evident by the fact that as a field, stratification research more routinely incorporates comparative studies into its literature than does the sociology of education (Baker, 1994; Burton & Grusky, 1992). Even the most sophisticated comparative research on educa-

---

*The notable exception is research on curricular tracking in the American school, but this is just one portion of the wide functions of schooling that is the domain of the sociology of education.

tional stratification tends not to deal explicitly with the schooling process (e.g., Shavit & Blossfeld, 1993).

The comparative analysis of schooling may be very useful to further balance stratification research. In addition to the school-effects studies in many developing countries reviewed earlier, there are other studies that shed some light on how the production of achievement fits within the stratification process. A good example is Katsillis and Rubinsons' (1990) study of Greek senior high students that finds reproduction of social status in Greece occurring through schooling processes and through student ability as applied to schooling. Examples of this include the formation of shadow education of private tutoring schools and cram schools that are nationally distributed, unequally bought, and significantly affect the academic achievement of large portions of the school-age populace (LeTendre, 1996; Stevenson & Baker, 1992; Tsukada, 1991). Additionally, these products of the stratification elements of modern schooling also have effects on the way teachers and students interact and produce achievement within the formal school itself (LeTendre, 1996). A related example is how the institutional structure of schools can influence other processes known to influence achievement such as family–school interactions. Oswald and associates (1988) showed that various qualities of the school charter in different German secondary schools can influence the patterns of family involvement in achievement-related processes in school.

THE FUTURE OF COMPARATIVE STUDY
OF SCHOOLING AND ACHIEVEMENT

This subfield of the sociology of education has made a number of important contributions to the understanding of schooling and academic outcomes. At the same time, our review illustrates the fact that there is some distance to go before the comparative sociology of school processes and outcomes is a mature research venture. Even though the logic of the comparative study of these topics has proved beneficial, the field has not developed as much as it could, given the robustness of the sociology of education in general. This is probably a result of a mixture of reasons. In part, this is because the main producer of the sociology of education in general—the American research community—has not easily looked beyond studies of the United States (Baker, 1994). At the same time, the comparative study of schooling outside the sociology research community is itself underdeveloped and therefore does not offer much institutional support for comparative sociology of education (Ramirez & Meyer, 1981). Lastly, the comparative study of school processes and outcomes requires considerable resources, and until very recently available resources have been very slim. It is still too early to determine whether or not the political incorporation of TIMSS will change the abundance of resources for the better.

Even though all of this is true, it is also true that the comparative study of schooling and achievement benefits from emerging areas of intellectual vitality. Much like the broadening of American stratification research through its incorporation of comparative work, the sociology of education has been enriched by even a modest level of comparative study. As this review shows, the work on school effects in developing countries, educational effects of rapid demographic changes across countries, the social construction of culture and schooling, and research resulting from IEA data on classroom production of achievement are all examples of fertile areas of comparative sociological inquiry.

Finally, a sustained and maturing literature on the comparative study of schooling and achievement may offer the sociology of education some important theoretical advantages. For example, a classical theoretical challenge in sociology in general is how to integrate social phenomena at more microlevels with phenomena at more macrolevels in order to unify sociological theory (e.g., Tilly, 1984). As in many subfields of sociology there can often be an unproductive split between work on microlevel and on macrolevels. The same is true in the sociology of education; even though the subfield is not very large, there is some Balkanization of microwork and of macrowork without much thinking about how to combine them. For example, research on curricular tracking in the United States has rarely considered work on the historical organizational development of school streams in European systems (see Kerckhoff, 1974, for a notable exception). Similarly, work on the expansion of formal schooling has rarely considered implications of expansion for the social construction of achievement and the development of classroom processes (see Benavot et al., 1991 for a notable exception, as well as Stevenson & Baker, 1991). Finally, rarely have we been able to go beyond a rather stilted and mechanical reductionist's vision of the connection between any of our best theories about how schools develop as institutions (i.e., Marxist conflict theory, status conflict theory, or various functionalist theories) and our best empirical descriptions of the microprocesses in schools (i.e., teaching, learning, curriculum, sorting). Comparative studies can help to bridge these gaps and to move us toward more unified theoretical positions.

Another theoretical payoff awaiting this field is to broaden our ability to test complex theories of schooling. For example, in 1977, John Meyer published a provocative theoretical argument about schools, their functions, and what institutional effects those functions can have on society at large (Meyer, 1977). Although not explicitly comparative, Meyer's argument lends itself to greater emphasis on a comparative approach to fully develop and test a more integrated theory of schooling. Simply stated, the argument is that as formal schooling is more institutionalized into nation–states and into modern culture (a macroprocess), schooling will have greater effects on a variety of microprocesses such as the sorting and socializing of students, the development of curricular topics (e.g., valid knowledge), and creation of new status categories throughout society. This kind of integrated argument about schooling and modern society needs comparative study to begin to test and explore its validity. As has been well documented from the sociology of school expansion and the historical development of mass education (see Walters' chapter [10] in this volume), institutionalization happens at different rates in different places throughout the world. Further, it is clear that not all cultures and nation–states end up with exactly the same institutional arrangement of mass schooling, and there can be considerable organizational variation in how schools perform modern functions cross-nationally. All of this is ripe theory-testing territory for the comparative study of schooling and its outcomes.

The comparative study of schooling and its outcomes provides far more than a view of the exotic; it offers real opportunities to broaden the empirical and theoretical base of the sociology of education. For that reason alone, it should be supported and encouraged. However, it is also very clear that in the United States, and perhaps elsewhere, policy discussions are increasingly interjected with reference to schooling and to outcomes of other notable national competitors. If, as it has in the past, the sociology of education wishes to continue to be relevant to U.S. policy discussions, a broader cross-national comparative perspective in research is essential.

REFERENCES

Amano, I. (1990). *Education and examination in modern Japan* (W. Cummings & F. Cummings, Trans.). Tokyo: University of Tokyo Press.

American Educational Research Association. (1992). *American Educational Research Association Membership Record.* Washington, DC: Author.

Armitage, J. Batista, J., Harbison, R. W., Holsinger, D. B., & Helio, R .(1986). *School quality and achievement in rural Brazil.* Washington, DC.: The World Bank, Education and Training Department.

Baker, D. (1993). Compared to Japan, the U.S. is a low achiever . . . Really: New evidence and comment on Westbury. *Educational Researcher, 22*(3), 18–20.

Baker, D. (1994). In comparative isolation: Why comparative research has so little influence on American sociology of education. *Research in Sociology of Education and Socialization, 10,* 53–70.

Baker, D. (1997). Good news, bad news, and international comparisons: comment on Bracey. *Educational Researcher, 26*(3), 16–18.

Baker, D. (1998, December). Surviving TIMSS. Or, everything you blissfully forgot about international comparisons. *Phi Delta Kappan,* 295–300.

Baker, D., & Stevenson, D. (1986). Mothers' strategies for children's school achievement: Managing the transition to high school. *Sociology of Education, 59,* 156–166.

Benavot, A., Cha, Y., Kamens, D., Meyer, J., & Wong, S. (1991). Knowledge for the masses: World models and national curricula, 1920–1986. *American Sociological Review, 56,* (February), 85–100.

Bennett, D. (1988). *The party of fear: From nativist movements to the new right in American history.* Chapel Hill, NC: University of North Carolina Press.

Bennett, W. (1987). Implications for American education. *NASSP Bulletin, 71*(499), 102–108.

Blau, P., & Duncan, O. D. (1967). *The American occupational structure.* New York: Wiley.

Boocock, S. (1978). The social organization of the classroom. *Annual Review of Sociology, 4,* 1–28.

Bowman, M. J. (1981). *Educational choice and labor markets in Japan.* Chicago: University of Chicago Press.

Bracey, G. (1996). International comparisons and the condition of American education. *Educational Researcher, 25,* 5–11.

Bracey, G. (1997). On comparing the incomparable: A response to Baker and Stedman. *Educational Researcher, 26*(3), 19–26.

Brinton, M. (1988). The social–institutional bases of gender stratification: Japan as an illustrative case. *American Journal of Sociology, 94*(2), 300–334.

Burton, M., & Grusky, D. (1992). A quantitative history of comparative stratification research. *Contemporary Sociology, 21,* 623–631.

Cohen, E. (1982). Expectation states and interracial interaction in school settings. *Annual Review of Sociology, 8,* 209–235.

Cohen, E. (1986). On the sociology of the classroom. In J. Hannaway & M. Lockheed (Eds.), *The contributions of the social sciences to educational policy and practice: 1965–1985* (pp. 127–162). Berkeley, CA: McCutchan.

Coleman, J. S., Campbell, E., Hobson, C., McPartland, J., Mood, A., Weinfall, F., & York, R. (1966). *Equality of educational opportunity.* Washington, DC.: Department of Health, Education, and Welfare.

Comber, L., & Keeves, J. (1973). *Science Education in nineteen countries.* New York: Halsted.

Crouse, J., Mueser, P., & Jencks, C. (1979). Latent variable models of status attainment. *Social Science Research, 8,* 348–368.

Cuban, L. (1983). How did teachers teach, 1890–1980. *Theory into Practice, 22*(3), 159–165.

Cuban, L. (1992). What happens to reforms that last? The case of the junior high school. *American Educational Research Journal, 29* (2), 227–251.

DeVos, G. (1973). *Socialization for achievement.* Berkeley, CA: University of California Press.

Dimaggio, P. (1982). Cultural capital and school success: The impact of status culture participation on the grades of U.S. high school students. *American Sociological Review, 47,* 189–201.

Dreeben, R. (1994). The sociology of education: Its development in the United States. *Research in Sociology of Education and Socialization, 10,* 53–70.

Duncan, O., & Hodge, R. (1963). Education and occupational mobility: A regression analysis. *American Journal of Sociology, 68,* 629–644.

Eckstein, M., & Noah, H. (1993). *Secondary school examinations: International perspectives on policies and practices.* New Haven, CT: Yale University Press.

Epstein, J. L. (1998). *School & family partnerships, preparing educators & improving schools.* Boulder, CO: Westview Press.

Fägerlind, I., & Saha, L. (1989). *Education and national development.* Oxford, England: Butterworth-Heinemann.

Fukuzawa, R. (1989). *Stratification, social control, and student culture: An ethnography of three junior high schools.* Unpublished doctoral dissertation, Department of Anthropology, Northwestern University.

Fuller, B. (1987). What school factors raise achievement in the third world. *Review of Educational Research, 57*(3), 255–292.

Fuller, B., & Heyneman, S. (1989). Third world school quality: Current collapse, future potential. *Educational Researcher, 18*, 12–19.

Gerth, H. H., & Mills, C. W. (Eds., 1991). *From Max Weber: Essays in sociology.* New York: Routledge.

Grissmer, D., Kirb, S., Berends, M., & Williamson, S. (1994). *Student achievement and the changing American family.* Santa Monica, CA: Rand.

Hare, T. (1996). Try, try again: Training in noh drama. In T. Rohlen & G. LeTendre (Eds.), *Teaching and learning in Japan* (pp. 345–368). New York: Cambridge University Press.

Haron, I. (1977). *Social class and educational achievement in a plural society: Peninsular Malaysia.* Unpublished doctoral dissertation, University of Chicago.

Hartley, M., & Swanson, E. (1984). *Achievement and wastage: An analysis of the retention of basic skills in primary education.* Washington, DC: The World Bank, Development Research Department.

Hendry, J. (1986). *Becoming Japanese: The world of the pre-school child.* Manchester, UK: Manchester University Press.

Heyneman, S. (1976). Influence on academic achievement: A comparison of results from Uganda and more industrialized and more industrialized societies. *Sociology of Education, 49*, 200–211.

Heyneman, S., & Jamison, D. (1980). Student learning in Uganda: Textbook availability and other factors. *Comparative Education Review, 24*, 206–220.

Heyneman, S., & Loxley, W. (1982). Influences on academic achievement across high and low income countries: A re-analysis of IEA data.1982. *Sociology of Education*, 55(1), 13–21.

Heyneman, S., & Loxley, W. (1983). The effect of primary-school quality on academic achievement across twenty-nine high-and low-income countries. *American Journal of Sociology, 88*(2), 1162–1194.

Higham, J. (1955). *Strangers in the land: Patterns of American nativism, 1860–1925.* Brunswick, NJ: Rutgers University Press.

Hollingshead, A. (1975). *Elmtown's youth and Elmtown revisited.* New York: Wiley.

Husen, T. (1967). *International study of achievement in mathematics: A comparison of twelve countries.* (2 vols.) Stockholm: Almquist & Wiksell.

Inkeles, A., & Smith, D. (1974). *Becoming modern.* London: Heinemann.

Ishida, H. (1993). *Social mobility in contemporary Japan.* London: Macmillan.

Jaeger, R. (1992, October). Weak measurement serving presumptive policy. *Phi Delta Kappan,* 118–128.

Jamison, D., Searle, B., Galda, K., & Heyneman, S. (1983). Improving elementary mathematics education in Nicaragua: An experimental study of the impact of textbooks and radio on achievement. *Journal of Educational Psychology, 73*(4), 556–567.

Jencks, C., Smith, M., Acland, H., Bane, M. J., Cohen, D., Gintis, H., Heyns, B., & Michelson, S. (1972). *Inequality: A reassessment of the effect of family and schooling in America.* New York: Harper Colophon Books.

Katsillis, J., & Rubinson, R. (1990). Cultural capital, student achievement, and educational reproduction: The case of Greece. *American Sociological Review, 55*, 270–279.

Kerckhoff, A. (1974). Stratification process and outcomes in England and the U.S. *American Sociological Review, 39*, 789–801.

Lareau, A. (1987). Social class differences in family–school relationships: The importance of cultural capital. *Sociology of Education, 60*, 73–85.

Lee, S., Graham, T., & Stevenson, H. (1996). Teachers and teaching: Elementary schools in Japan and the United States. In T. Rohlen & G. LeTendre (Eds.), *Teaching and learning in Japan* (pp. 157–189). New York: Cambridge University Press.

LeTendre, G. (1996, July). Constructed aspirations: Decision-making processes in Japanese educational selection. *Sociology of Education, 69*, 193–216.

Lewis, C. (1995). *Educating hearts and minds.* New York: Cambridge University Press.

Lockheed, M., Vail, S., & Fuller, B. (1986). How textbooks affect achievement in developing countries: Evidence from Thailand. *Educational Evaluation and Policy Analysis, 8*, 379–392.

Loxley, W. (1984, March). *Quality of schooling in the Kalahari.* Paper presented at the annual meeting of the Comparative and International Education Society, San Antonio Texas.

Lynd, R. (1959). *Middletown: A study in American culture.* New York: Harcourt Brace.

MacLeod, J. (1987). *Ain't no makin' it.* Boulder, CO: Westview Press.

McCartney, J. (1971). The financing of sociological research: Trends and consequences. In E. Tiryakian (Ed.), *The phenomenon of sociology: A reader in the sociology of sociology* (pp. 383–397). New York: Appleton-Crofts.

Mehan, H. (1979). *Learning lessons: Social organization in the classroom.* Cambridge, MA: Harvard University Press.

Meyer, J. (1977). The effects of education as an institution. *American Journal of Sociology, 83*(1), 55–77.

Meyer, J., & Baker, D. (1996, Extra). Forming American educational policy with international data: Lessons from the sociology of education. 1996. *Sociology of Education*, 123–130.

National Educational Goals Panel. (NEGP, 1995). *Data volume for the National Educational Goals Report.* Washington, DC: U.S. Government Printing Office.

Oakes, J., & Guiton, G. (1995). Matchmaking: The dynamics of high school tracking decisions. *American Educational Research Journal, 32*(1), 3–34.

Office of Economic Cooperation and Development. (OECD, 1997). *Literacy skills for the knowledge society: Further results from the International adult literacy survey.* Paris: OECD.

Okano, K. (1993). *School to work transition in Japan.* Philadelphia: Multilingual Matters Ltd.

Olmstead, P., & Weikert, D. (Eds., 1989). *How nations serve young children: Profiles of child care and education in 14 countries.* Ypsilanti, MI: The High/Scope Press.

Oswald, H., Baker, D., & Stevenson, D. (1988). School charter and parental management in West Germany. *Sociology of Education, 61,* 255-265.

Peak, L. (1989). Learning to become part of the group: The Japanese child's transition to preschool life. *Journal of Japanese Studies, 15*(1), 93–124.

Peaker, G. (1971). *The Plowden children four years later.* London: National Foundation for Educational Research in England & Wales.

Pong, S. (1997). Trends in achievement: What do we know? *Teachers College Record, 99,* 23–29.

Post, D., & Pong, S. (1997). Intra-family educational inequality in Hong Kong: The Waning effects of sibship composition. *Comparative Education Review, 42,* 99–117.

Ralph, J., Keller, D., & Crouse, J. (1994). How effective are American schools? *Phi Delta Kappan, 76,* 2.

Ramirez, F., & Meyer, J. (1981) Comparative education: Synthesis and agenda. In J. Short (Ed.), *The State of Sociology: Problems and Prospects* (pp. 215–238). Beverly Hills, CA: Sage.

Ravitch, D. (1986). Japan's smart schools. *The New Republic, 194,* 13–15.

Riordan, C. (1997). *Equality and achievement: An introduction to the sociology of education.* New York: Longman.

Robinson, R., & Garnier, M. (1985). Class reproduction among men and women in France: Reproduction theory on its home ground. *American Journal of Sociology*, 91, 250–280.

Rohlen, T. (1983). *Japan's high schools.* Berkeley, CA: University of California Press.

Rosenbaum, J., & Kariya, T. (1989). From high school to work: Market and institutional mechanisms in Japan. *American Journal of Sociology, 94*(6), 1134–1165.

Rosenbaum, J., & Kariya, T. (1991). Do school achievements affect the early jobs of high school graduates in the United States and Japan? *Sociology of Education, 64,* 78–95.

Rosenbaum, J., Kariya, T., Settersten, R., & Maier, T. (1990). Market and network theories of the transition from high school to work. *American Review of Sociology, 16,* 263–299.

Rosenholtz, S., & Simpson, C. (1984) . The formation of ability conceptions: Developmental trend or social construction? *Review of Educational Research, 54*(1), 31–63.

Sato, N., & McLaughlin, M. (1992). Context matters: Teaching in Japan and in the United States. *Phi Delta Kappan, 73*(5), 359–366.

Schaub, M., & Baker, D. (1991). Solving the math problem: Exploring mathematics achievement in Japanese and American middle grades. *American Journal of Education, 99*(4), 623–642.

Schmidt, W., McKnight, C., & Raizen, S. (1997). *A splintered vision.* Dordrecht, the Netherlands: Kluwer Academic Publishers.

Schneider, B., & Coleman, J. S. (1993). *Parents, their children, & schools.* Boulder, CO, Westview Press.

Shavit, Y., & Blossfeld, H. (1993). *Persistent inequality, changing educational attainment in thirteen countries.* Boulder, CO: Westview Press.

Shimahara, N. (1979). *Adaptation and education in Japan.* New York: Praeger.

Shimahara, N., & Sakai, A. (1995). *Learning to teach in two cultures.* New York: Garland.

Singleton, J. (1967). *Nichu: A Japanese school.* New York: Holt, Rinehart and Winston.

Singleton, J. (1989). Japanese folkcraft pottery apprenticeship: Cultural patterns of an educational institution. In M. Coy (Ed.), *Apprenticeship: From theory to method and back again* (pp. 13–30). Albany, NY: State University of New York Press.

Smart, M. (1978). The Denzu Times: Self-made literacy. *Development Communication Report, 21,* 51–73.

Stedman, L. (1994). Incomplete explanations: The case of U.S. performance in the international assessments of education. *Educational Researcher, 22*(7), 24–32.

Stedman, L. (1997). International achievement differences: An assessment of a new perspective. *Educational Researcher, 26*(3) 4–15.

Stevenson, D., & Baker, D. (1991) State control of the curriculum and classroom instruction. *Sociology of Education, 64,* 1–10.

Stevenson, D., & Baker, D. (1992). Shadow education and allocation in formal schooling: Transition to university in Japan. *American Journal of Sociology, 97*(6), 1639–1657.

Stevenson, H., Parker, T., Wilkinson, A., Bonnevaux, B., & Gonzalez, m. (1978). Schooling, environment, and cognitive development: A cross-cultural study. *Monographs of the Society of Research in Child Development, 43*(3), #175). Chicago IL: University of Chicago Press.

Stigler, J., Fernandez, C., & Yoshida, M. (1996). Cultures of mathematics instruction in Japanese and American elementary classrooms. In T. Rohlen & G. LeTendre (Eds.), *Teaching and learning in Japan* (pp. 213–247). New York: Cambridge University Press.

Stinchcombe, A. (1964). *Rebellion in a high school.* Chicago: Quadrangle Books.

Taylor, A. (1996). Education for democracy: Assimilation or emancipation for Aboriginal Australians. *Comparative Education Review, 40*(4), 426–438.

Thias, H., & Carnoy, M. (1973). *Cost benefit analysis in education: A case study of Kenya.* Baltimore, MD: Johns Hopkins Press.

Thorndike, R. (1973). *Reading comprehension in 15 countries: An empirical study.* Stockholm: Almquist & Wiksell.

Tilly, C. (1984). *Big structures, large processes, huge comparisons.* New York: Russell Sage Foundation.

Tobin, J., Wu, D. Y., & Davidson, D. H. (1989). *Preschools in three cultures: Japan, China and the United States.* New Haven, CT: Yale University Press.

Torney-Purta, J. (1987). The role of comparative education in the debate on excellence. In R. Lawson, V. Rust, & S. Shafer (Eds.), *Education and social concern: An approach to social foundation.* Ann Arbor, MI: Prakken Publications.

Travers, K., & Westbury, I. (1989). *The IEA Study of mathematics I: International analysis of mathematics Curricula.* Oxford, England: Pergamon.

Treiman, D., & Yamaguchi, K. (1993). Trends in educational attainment in Japan. In Y. Shavit & H. Blossfeld (Eds.), *Persistent inequality: Changing educational attainment in thirteen countries* (pp. 229–249). Boulder, CO: Westview Press.

Tsukada, M. (1991). *Yobiko life: A study of legitimation process of social stratification in Japan.* Berkeley, CA: Institute of East Asian Studies.

Tyack, D., & Hansot, E. (1988a). Gender in American public schools: Thinking institutionally. *Signs: Journal of Women in Culture and Society, 13*(4), 741–760.

Tyack, D., & Hansot, E. (1988b). Silence and policy talk: Historical puzzles about gender and education. *Educational Researcher, 17*(3), 33–42.

Westbury, I. (1992). Comparing American and Japanese achievement: Is the United States really a low achiever. *Educational Researcher, 21*(5) 18–24.

Westbury, I. (1993). American and Japanese achievement . . . Again: A response to Baker. *Educational Researcher, 22*(3), 18–20.

White, M. (1987). *The Japanese educational challenge.* New York: Kodansha.

Willis, P. (1991). *Learning to labour.* Farnbourough, England: Saxon House.

Zeng, K. (1996). Prayer, luck, and spiritual strength: The desecularization of entrance examination systems in East Asia. *Comparative Education Review, 40*(3) 264–279.

CHAPTER 16

Social Systems and Norms

A Coleman Approach

Barbara Schneider

James S. Coleman clearly emerged as one of the most important American scholars of the 20th century to have examined empirically the social organization of education from the disciplinary perspective of sociology. Although researchers have often seen Coleman's work in education as primarily policy driven, few recognize that his interest in education developed from concepts deeply rooted in sociological theory. In their tribute to Coleman, James Heckman and Derek Neal concluded that, for Coleman, the high school was a laboratory for the study of social systems (Heckman & Neal, 1996). Essentially, Heckman and Neal viewed Coleman's work in education as motivated by theoretical issues that lie at the core of sociology, one of these being the creation of social norms in social systems. How norms are formed in social systems was one of the theoretical ideas and methodological issues Coleman was working on at the time of his death in the spring of 1995.

Theoretically, Coleman was interested in the conditions under which stable and effective norms, with particular content, can be brought into existence. He assumed that knowledge of these conditions would be extremely valuable in the design of organizations such as schools. For example, students typically develop norms regarding how much effort they are willing to expend on their schoolwork. Sometimes these norms are in opposition to putting forth considerable effort and working hard. Under such circumstances, these negative norms can act to suppress the students' efforts. However, sometimes the norms can operate in the other direction, encouraging students to expend considerable effort toward high achievement. This raises the question of what conditions determine the strength and the direction of norms.

BARBARA SCHNEIDER • National Opinion Research Center, Chicago, Illinois 60637

Handbook of the Sociology of Education, edited by Maureen T. Hallinan. Kluwer Academic/Plenum Publishers, New York, 2000.

Coleman saw the problem of understanding the creation of norms not only in schools but in organizations more generally. Citing earlier work on organizations, conducted by researchers such as Roethlisberger and Dickson (1939), Coleman noted that it is commonly known that workplace norms can be so strong that their direction may increase or decrease output in the plant production process. Even though research on norms in noneducational organizations has been conducted for more than 50 years, Coleman asserted that theoretically, the field of sociology has yet to sufficiently investigate how to create norms in schools and in the workplace that would encourage production rather than discourage it (see Coleman, 1966a, in Clark, *A Vision of Sociology*).*

Norms, Coleman maintained, are the engine that drives production. Without them, standards of performance, redesign of instruction, or revision of curricular content would do little to improve education. This chapter examines Coleman's interest in understanding norms in schools and attempts to explain why he argued that developing a comprehensive theory of norm emergence would inform the design of organizations and improve the effectiveness and productivity of education and the economy. In reviewing several of his major studies on schools, as well as his last unpublished paper, this chapter explores how norms were a fundamental part of his theoretical conceptions of social capital and his practical plans for improving schools.

COLEMAN'S EARLY CAREER

Coleman's intellectual career did not begin with the study of educational problems. His first venture into education came after he received his Ph.D. in sociology from Columbia University in 1955. Coleman's path to Columbia University, and sociology, is particularly interesting, and in his autobiography he provides the details and explanations of why he embarked upon such a life course (see Coleman, 1985a, *Autobiographical Sketch. I–II*).† Education was an interest of the Coleman family, and both of Coleman's parents were high school teachers. Shortly after Coleman's birth, his father became a football coach at the College of the Ozarks in Arkansas. The coaching job did not last long. When Coleman was 2 years old, the family moved north to Cincinnati, where Coleman's father became a tire salesman, a job for which Coleman believed he was ill-suited. Moving several more times, the family settled in Louisville, Kentucky in 1941, where Coleman attended the town's vocational technical high school—

---

*In April, 1994 James S. Coleman was the first recipient of the Phoenix prize from the Social Sciences Division of The University of Chicago. The prize was awarded in recognition of his career achievements in expanding the research horizons of the social sciences. The presentation of this award was made at a 2-day conference honoring Coleman. "A Vision for Sociology" (Coleman, 1994a) was Coleman's response to that award, although he never delivered it. By the end of the second day, the time had moved near to the reception hour and Coleman, in his unique Coleman style, came to the podium and said, "Instead of giving this paper, I think I would rather just sit back and hear all these people say nice things about me." Given his very controversial career, it undoubtedly was, for him, a rare event to have people he respected deeply complementing him rather than attacking him and asking him to explain his findings and conclusions. A very slightly revised version of "A Vision for Sociology" (Coleman, 1996a) appears in *James S. Coleman,* edited by Jon Clark (1996).

†In various publications, Coleman has discussed his career, beginning with his family's orientation to him as an only child and continuing through the controversial events of his academic life, including the debates over his findings in the Coleman Report, the racial effects of mandatory school busing, and private and public schools. I find that it is in some of his earlier unpublished biographies that his dedication and commitment to the study of sociology is the most evident—and the most humorous. I have chosen to rely on these unpublished works because the stories, in my opinion, highlight Coleman's passion for the study of sociological problems. Parts of these unpublished materials appear in "Columbia in the 1950s" in B. Berger (Ed.), *Authors of Their Own Lives,* Berkeley, CA: University of California Press (Coleman, 1990a), and in "Interview: James S. Coleman," in R. Swedberg (Ed.), *Economics and Sociology*, Princeton, NJ: Princeton University, pp. 47–62 (Coleman, 1990d).

the Manual Training High School. The only other high school in the town was an academic one.

Coleman graduated from high school and entered the Navy in June, 1944. While in the Navy, he spent a year studying engineering at Emory University. A boxer and a football player, Coleman turned down a football scholarship to college after being discharged from the service. Instead of pursuing football, Coleman decided to attend Indiana University to study chemistry. Once at Indiana, he was unsure about whether his occupational choice to become a chemist matched his interests. A close friend suggested that he transfer to Purdue University, where he could study chemical engineering, allowing him to combine his interests in both chemistry and engineering. Coleman followed his friend's advice and transferred from Indiana to Purdue at the end of his freshman year.

Soon after college graduation, Coleman accepted a job at Eastman Kodak as a chemical engineer, but he delayed his start at the company to spend the summer on a belated honeymoon bicycling through France. The experience in France had a profound effect on Coleman. At the time, several novels were banned in the United States, but were easily available overseas. Coleman, a voracious reader, eagerly read these censored books and learned French in the process. On returning to the Kodak company in New York, Coleman was sent to work on developing the substratum coating that is applied to film backing to make the film emulsion adhere. Quickly growing dissatisfied intellectually with this type of work, and having concerns about career advancement, Coleman at first considered returning to graduate school to obtain an advanced degree in physical chemistry. However, after joining a Great Books club and reassessing his career directions, Coleman realized that, for him, the most interesting subject matter of all was people, their relationships, and their social organizations.

Despite being discouraged by his colleagues at Kodak, Coleman decided to make a major career shift. Being warned that changing careers so late in life—he was 25 at the time—could have disastrous results for job stability and advancement, Coleman made a decision that few in chemical engineering could have foreseen. He applied to sociology programs at the University of Michigan, Harvard University, and Columbia University. He never heard from Harvard University, a letter from the University of Michigan recommended that he take undergraduate classes in sociology and reapply, but Columbia accepted him. In the spring of 1951, Coleman left Kodak to enter summer school in sociology at Columbia University. He was one of 100 students who entered the program.

Coleman's intellectual acumen for the study of sociology was almost immediately recognized by the most eminent sociologists at Columbia University. As Robert Merton (1996) wrote,

> Paul Lazarsfeld and I spotted Jim as a sociological talent within months after he came to the Department. Indeed, in fairly short order, we were at first unwittingly and then quite overtly competing for his attention. At least, we came dangerously close to such rivalry. The question was: which one of us had rightly identified the quintessential Jim? Paul confidently claimed that Jim was of course destined to be a methodologist and mathematical sociologist of the first rank, while, with equal assurance, I claimed that he was destined to be a phenomenal theorist who would draw upon his systematic empirical research to greatly deepen and extend out basic sociological understanding. I don't recall when it came to pass that Paul and I finally saw the light and recognized that we were both right: Jim was bound to be all that—and more. Plainly, he would be both an extraordinary sociological theorist and an extraordinary methodologist, endowed with a keen sense of the practical and policy implications of sociological inquiry. (p. 351)*

---

*The quote referenced here appears in "Teaching James Coleman" by Robert K. Merton (1996). Appendix 1 in Jon Clark's *James S. Coleman*. An earlier version was presented by Robert K. Merton at The University of Chicago, in April, 1994, at the festivities honoring Coleman's receipt of the Phoenix Prize.

Coleman's dissertation was based on work that was part of a project initiated by Martin Lipset, who was then an assistant professor in sociology at Columbia. Martin Trow, a graduate student, also collaborated on the project. Lipset's project focused on a substantive macrosocial problem in political sociology—the social bases of political democracy—that had a rich history in sociological theory. Lipset began the project with an idea about the importance of a particular occupational community—New York printers, and their political participation in the union. The project was unusual for the time because it used quantitative data based on new sample survey techniques to study a theoretical issue in sociology. But, as Coleman (1985) wrote, "macro-social problems and sample survey techniques do not mix well in social research" (p. 37). From Coleman's perspective, what made this work successful was " . . . the rich store of knowledge that Lipset had about the printer's union and the rich fund of social and political theory bearing on the problem that he had at his fingertips. The result was that the problem was central and the data subordinate" (p. 37). The resulting publication from this effort was *Union Democracy* (Lipset, Trow, & Coleman, 1956).

One cannot leave this formative period of Coleman's life without recognizing how he viewed the influence of Merton, Lazarsfeld, and Lipset on his career. Coleman dedicated *Foundations of Social Theory* (Coleman, 1990c), which he considered his most significant work, to his teacher Robert Merton. From Merton came not only the vision of sociology as a calling but also a focus on the sociological determinants of individual behavior. From Lazarsfeld came his orientation to mathematical sociology. Finally, from Lipset, who invited him onto the team of *Union Democracy* (Lipset et al., 1956), and with whom he worked most continuously, he gained the experience of conducting collaborative empirical research. Reflecting on the research and discussions around *Union Democracy*, Coleman (1985) wrote, "I have co-authored books with others; but the interaction over the course of the two years 1952–53 and 1953–54 was unlike any other" (p. 46).

In *Autobiographical Sketch II*, Coleman (1985a) also described other professors at Columbia and other people—including theorists such as Emile Durkheim, Adam Smith, and Max Weber—who influenced his sociological thinking. However, it was the Columbia experience that Coleman saw as significantly shaping his orientation to sociology and to the study of the problems of social systems. For him, sociology offered a set of disciplinary interests that allowed him to study social theory empirically and to apply it to social policy. As he would later write, the study of sociology should "have the social system (whether a small system or a large one) as its unit of analysis, rather than the individual; but it should use quantitative methods" (Coleman, 1996a, p. 345).

Coleman linked his work on *Union Democracy* (Lipset et al., 1956) with the ideas that led him to write a proposal for a study of high schools. He observed that the study of *Union Democracy*

> . . . was consistent with and reinforced my interest in political pluralism, the social sources of political diversity, and the structural bases for opposition to an incumbent authority. . . . I wanted to study the effects of monolithic vs. pluralistic status systems on the behavior of adolescents, and the sources of these variations in status systems (Coleman, 1985a, p. 39).

Coleman argued that his proposed study of adolescents was different from other work on educational policy at the time in that it viewed educational institutions as distinctively sociological. Its design was constructed to characterize the school as a social system and the behavior of the students within those systems. He received funding from the U.S. Office of Research to pursue these ideas in a study at The University of Chicago in 1957 to 1958 that later was published as *The Adolescent Society: The Social Life of the Teenager and its Impact on Education* (Coleman, 1961).

ADOLESCENT SOCIETY: A STUDY OF SOCIAL STATUS

The American high school in the 1950s was in many ways a different place than the schools of today (Schneider & Stevenson, 1999).* These institutions, which drew primarily from neighborhood communities, were for the most part closed social systems. Adolescents and their teachers lived in a world where certain activities, such as athletics and school clubs, were highly valued and others were less so. The college-going rate was approximately 30%, and most students left high school for the labor force (Farley, 1995; Kosters, 1991). Both boys and girls hoped to marry soon after high school, and the average marriage age for females was 20 years old (Farley, 1996).

In contrasting high schools with other social institutions at the time, Coleman (1996a) wrote

> ... high schools seemed to be one of the few social contexts in modern society that constituted largely self-contained social systems. Most adolescents directed their attention inward. Status among the adolescents in the school was more important than status outside. The youth could not easily leave the system and choose a different one. This meant that the processes which generate norms, systems of status, cleavage and conflict, in short the community's functioning, were first of all internally generated (though with influences from school staff, parents, and community), and second, they were effective in shaping the behavior of the members of the system. (p. 345)

Reflecting on Coleman's focus on the development of norms in an interactive context, it seems reasonable that he would choose to examine an institution such as the high school, where the students had some choice of activities to pursue. In elementary schools, by contrast, students were seen as needing more nurturing care and attention, especially in the lower elementary grades. Grade school students were allowed few freedoms with respect to selecting courses or school activities—quite unlike the middle schools of today.

In the spring of 1957, Coleman began his study of adolescent society by selecting ten high schools in diverse types of communities in northern Illinois that had apparent differences in their status systems. The schools were selected not to be representative of Illinois, but rather to be representative of the various types of communities in the nation (see Coleman, 1961, p. ix on this point). The data collection plan involved obtaining student achievement test scores and administering student questionnaires in the fall of 1957, and again in the spring of 1958. In the spring of 1958, informal interviews with students were also conducted, and information was obtained from school records. At the time, the team also administered teacher and parent questionnaires; these data, however, were minimally analyzed in the study.

Coleman viewed the high school of 1957 as segregated from the rest of society and believed that certain social and familial conditions reinforced this separateness. He noted that the entertainment industry had begun to develop films for teenage audiences and that adolescents also had their own music. Having their own entertainment industry helped to facilitate the development of separate teenage language, dress, and norms of acceptable behavior distinct from adult society. In this context, Coleman argued, families no longer had the major responsibility for socializing their children toward adulthood. Rather, more formalized institutions such as schools, where students existed apart from society for longer periods of time, were taking on socialization roles that had been traditionally performed by the family. He concluded that " . . . society was confronted no longer with a set of individuals to be trained

---

* The rates for college-going, marriage, and employment from the 1950s through the present are discussed in Schneider and Stevenson (1999). In this book the authors compare growing up in the 1950s with growing up in the 1990s. See chapters 1 and 2 specifically.

toward adulthood, but with distinct social systems, which offer a united front to the overtures made by adult society" (Coleman, 1961, p. 4).

Citing the responses of students to questions about whose disapproval would be most difficult to accept—parents', teachers', or friends—Coleman suggested that

> Adolescents today are cut off, probably more than ever before, from the adult society. They are still oriented toward fulfilling their parents' desires but they look very much to their peers for approval as well. Consequently, our society has within its midst a set of small teen-age societies, which focus teen-age interests and attitudes on things far removed from adult responsibilities and which may develop standards that lead away from those goals established by the larger society. (Coleman, 1961, p. 9)

In describing his findings on the values and attitudes of the adolescent community, Coleman (1961) observed that the occupational aspirations of boys and girls, irrespective of the communities in which they lived, seemed to reflect the dominant themes and heroes in the mass media far more than the heroes their teachers would have them emulate. It may be that the most impressive contacts adolescents have with the adult culture are through the distorted lens of the mass media and its "newsworthy" events. When boys and girls were asked how they wanted to be remembered in school, boys most frequently said that they wanted to be remembered as athletes; girls preferred to be remembered as popular and as involved in school activities such as cheerleading. Few boys or girls wished to be remembered as brilliant students.

When Coleman asked similar questions of parents, he found that their professed values and those of the students were seemingly divergent. However, even in the 1950s, Coleman suspected that although parents hoped their children would be good students, they also wanted their teenagers to be successful in high school. At the time, success in the high school society translated into playing a sport for boys and making the cheerleading squad for girls. Thus, he concluded, "even the rewards a child gains from his parents may help reinforce the values of the adolescent culture—not because his or her parents hold those same values, but because parents want their children to be successful and esteemed by their peers" (Coleman, 1961, p. 34).

In Coleman's high school, to be popular was to exhibit qualities valued by the culture of the school. Being popular for boys meant being an athlete and being in the leading crowd—what it took to "rate" in these schools. For girls, popularity was first achieved by being in the leading crowd, followed by being a leader in activities, having nice clothes, coming from a family with more than perceived average economic and social resources, getting good grades, and being a cheerleader. Although the teenagers were fairly consistent in how they rated popularity, each school contained a somewhat distinctive culture.

Among the ten schools that were studied, there were variations in the importance given to scholastic achievement, family background, popularity with the opposite sex, and athletics or cheerleading. At one end of the continuum were schools that were oriented to scholastic success. Also, in one school this emphasis on academics was not coupled with participation in other school activities such as athletics or school clubs. Among the remaining schools, some emphasized athletics and academic performance, whereas others emphasized family background and scholastics. However, as Coleman pointed out, these schools were more alike than they were different. The relative positions of the various dimensions along which status was measured were similar in all of the schools (see Coleman, 1961, p. 93). In most instances, academic performance did not confer status at the individual level, nor was it valued as highly important at the school level.

The values, norms, and customs of schools are used to identify certain activities as important, and they help to define social status by according greater prestige to students who participate in valued activities. However, the perceived popularity of students who participate in an activity may also influence students' evaluations of an activity's importance. In schools where students who are seen as very popular participate in activities such as organizing a school dance, these activities may acquire a higher status because of the students who participate and how they spend their time. Even in this early work, Coleman was interested in the associations among the actors who compose the system and how they allocate their resources. From his perspective, "These associations help reinforce certain values, undercut others; pull energies in the direction of some activities and away from others; strengthen the prestige of some persons, and weaken that of others. They are, in part, a source of the culture, and in part are determined by it" (Coleman, 1961, p. 173).

In reflecting on *The Adolescent Society* (Coleman, 1961), one cannot help but be struck by Coleman's deep concern that academics were not as important to students as other activities. Yet, in looking at the lives of young people, it is hardly surprising that schoolwork was not highly valued because only one fourth of them would matriculate to college. Moreover, it was possible to obtain a well paying job without a postsecondary degree or some specialized training. Among girls, what was valued was finding a mate. Correspondingly, if one realizes the importance placed on marriage immediately after high school, it follows that social success, in the form of being popular and well liked, would be highly valued attributes for girls, especially those looking for someone with whom to spend the rest of their lives. Coleman was concerned that the norms of the high school were not achievement oriented, but, in retrospect, they were probably more consistent with the adult lives these young people were soon to pursue.

However, we need to recognize that *The Adolescent Society* (Coleman, 1961) was a study of social systems, and it sought to determine what was valued within those systems and how these values differed across communities. Even though he would have preferred different norms, what Coleman found were norms that were highly valued at the time. It is important to stress that *The Adolescent Society* (Coleman, 1961) is about social relationships. Status and norms are formed not by individuals but through social systems. Coleman's intent was to learn how social systems function and how individuals' actions are shaped in these systems. The concepts of norms and social status that are typical of adolescent societies continued to be a central research problem for him throughout his career.

SCHOOLS AND ADOLESCENT ACHIEVEMENT

The next major education project that Coleman undertook after *The Adolescent Society* (Coleman, 1961) was *Equality of Educational Opportunity*, often referred to as The Coleman Report (Coleman, et al., 1966). In 1965 he received a telephone call from Alexander Mood, then the Assistant Commissioner of Education and Director of the National Center for Education Statistics (NCES), asking him to direct a study mandated in the Civil Rights Act of 1964. The Act specified that

> The Comrmssioner shall conduct a survey and make a report to the President and the Congress, within two years of the enactment of this title, concerning the lack of availability of equal educational opportunities for individuals by reason of race, color, religion, or national origin in public educational institutions at all levels in the United States, its territories and possessions, and the District of Columbia. (U.S. Congress, 1964)

Coleman was not the first or perhaps even the second choice for conducting the study, but after considerable discussion he agreed to direct the work (personal conversation with James S. Coleman, Spring 1993).

For the study, students in Grades 1, 3, 6, 9, and 12, as well as teachers and principals, were surveyed. Of the 645,504 instruments that were fielded, 639,650 were processed (Coleman et al., 1966, Appendix 9.2: Sample Design). In addition to the major quantitative study, 10 case studies of the educational experiences of minorities were also conducted in 10 American cities. The magnitude of this undertaking was certainly daunting, especially for the time. The study set out to examine the relationship between students' achievement, as measured by standardized tests, and school resources, as measured by a series of organizational and contextual indicators such as per pupil expenditures, teachers' postsecondary degrees, and school facilities. There were two major policy findings from this report: First, school resources showed little relation to achievement in schools when students of similar backgrounds were compared. Students' family backgrounds, however, did show a significant relation to achievement. Second, minority children benefited academically by attending high schools with White students. Although a similar benefit was not found for White students who attended racially mixed schools, their academic performance did not decline when they attended schools with Black students.

The controversy over the findings from the Coleman Report (Coleman et al, 1966) was intense, and severe criticisms were launched by groups ranging from politicians to academicians. Harvard University organized a year-long faculty seminar to review the findings; the reviews were published in a volume edited by Frederick Mosteller and Daniel Moynihan (1972).* Reanalyses of the data confirmed Coleman's findings. As a result, the findings on students' academic performance in relation to like and unlike racial peers were used to support movements toward school integration and busing (see Kandel, 1996).

From Coleman's perspective, the Coleman Report (Coleman et al., 1966), in contrast to *The Adolescent Society* (Coleman, 1961), grew from the interests of policymakers and consequently did not begin with the lives of children. Because the work was administratively driven, the social system of the school and how children were affected by it were largely ignored. As Coleman wrote, the report " . . . did not ask what was the school experience for black children and for white children in the varying school settings in which they found themselves" (Coleman, 1996b, p. 20). It is important to underscore what Coleman, over 30 years later, believed was problematic with the questions asked in the study and with the study's design. The Coleman Report (Coleman et al., 1966) did not start with a conception of the school as a social system. Consequently, one could not learn how the norms of that system were able to influence the students' investments of effort both in academics and in their social lives. A study that approached the school as a social system would have to use

> . . . information from students (based on interviews, questionnaires or observations) to reconstruct
> conceptually the functioning of the social system of the school, by determining the norms, the bases
> of popularity, the positive or negative status conferred by various activities, and the social location
> of each child in the system. (Coleman, 1996b, p. 20)

Coleman argued that if such a study had been undertaken, the process of racial integration would be far more advanced.

After the Coleman Report (Coleman et al., 1966), two other major educational projects were undertaken by Coleman, although neither directly spoke to the influence of social sys-

---

*Other critical reviews of the Coleman Report can be found in Bowles and Levin (1968) and in Cain and Watts (1970).

tems and norms *per se.* In the early 1970s, Coleman served as a member of the President's Science Advisory Committee and organized a Panel on Youth which produced the report, *Youth: Transition to Adulthood* (Coleman, 1973). At the time of the report, the baby boomers were in school and the educational system was coping with young people who were overtly challenging societal norms. In the context of this review of Coleman's work, it is important to realize that although the report was designed to deal with questions of transitions into adulthood, focusing on the discontinuity between school and work, the topic forced Coleman to once again revisit the adolescent society and its norms nearly 15 years after writing *The Adolescent Society* (Coleman, 1961)—this time, during a period of macrosocietal change.

In looking at the recommendations of the report, it is clear that Coleman continued to see adolescents as occupying a world whose norms were in conflict with those of their teachers. He viewed the youth rebellion of the late 1960s and early 1970s as an expression of youth searching for autonomy by challenging authority. Coleman believed that youth in the 1970s, " . . . now see themselves more as a specific group with specific interests than in earlier times. It results in part from an increased deviation of norms of youth from those that adults in their homes and schools and colleges encourage them to hold" (Coleman, 1971, p. 119). This deviation from adult norms, Coleman suggested, has led American youth to champion the rights of the underdog and to reject competition and academic performance. Although in later writings on the norms of adolescents, Coleman dropped his argument regarding teenagers' concern with the interests of the underdog, he still maintained that adolescent norms are in conflict with achievement and competition (see Coleman, 1994b). It may be that, in his earlier writings, Coleman relied on classic explanations of youth rebellion to interpret the behavior of the youth of the 1970s. A study of the social system of the high school in the early 1970s, much like the one he conducted in the 1950s, would no doubt have provided a more comprehensive picture of the orientation of youth toward the norms of both adolescent and adult society.

The next education study that Coleman undertook examined trends in the racial integration of schools. As Coleman commented, the results of this study ". . . led to another period of controversy, which made the earlier controversy over EEO [The Coleman Report] pale by comparison" (Coleman, 1996b, p. 21).* He found that one unintended result of desegregation policies was that in large urban cities Whites were moving out to the suburbs. This "White flight" effect was more prevalent in cities where desegregation policies were the strongest (Coleman, Kelly, & Moore, 1975, reprinted in Coleman 1990b). Similar to the Coleman Report (Coleman et al., 1966) this project was designed and carried out with an administrative goal as opposed to one in the tradition of intensive examination of the social system. However, this project and the Coleman Report both focused on societal norms centering on equality of educational opportunity.

Although Coleman differentiated the intent of *The Adolescent Society* (Coleman, 1961) from his EEO project (Coleman et al., 1966), a recent book of Coleman reprints on *Equality and Achievement in Education* (Coleman, 1990b) begins with a chapter, initially published in 1985, entitled "Norms of Equal Opportunity: When and Why Do They Arise?" (Coleman, 1985b). Even though the EEO study may not have been designed to examine social systems, the underlying administrative intent became grist for Coleman's later discussions of norms in social systems. This relatively short paper raises issues that are addressed more extensively in

---

*Coleman discusses the criticisms he received at the time and why some may have had the reactions they did, including the activities of the then-president of the American Sociological Association, who proposed to have him censored by the association (See Coleman, 1990b, pp. 165–168.)

his later work, *Foundations of Social Theory* (Coleman, 1990c), concerning social capital and the transmission of norms.

In this 1985 paper, Coleman (1985b) argued that for sociologists interested in a norm such as equal opportunity, the focus should not be on defending its merits or attacking its intent. Instead, he believed that norms arise in certain times and places, and that it is the sociologist's role to examine what characterizes those times and places (reprinted in Coleman, 1990b, p. 9). For a norm such as equal opportunity to emerge, it must be the case that among all persons holding such a norm, each person must be able to easily imagine themselves exchanging positions with anyone else covered by the norm. The second condition for a norm's emergence relates to the structure of the macrosociety. Norms of equal opportunity are achievable in a democracy but not in a system stratified by rank, for in such a system each member cannot easily imagine changing places with anyone else in the society. In associations or organizations where the members are not subject to the same authorities, it is also difficult to achieve a norm of equal opportunity.

Relating this line of argument to an educational issue, Coleman provided the example of public school funding. Prior to the 1960s, schools were typically financed through local property taxes. In such situations, norms of equal educational opportunity were limited to local school districts. However, as states have increased their funding of schools, lawsuits have been brought to create financial equalization across school districts within states. Coleman's argument regarding unequal authority and its consequences for achieving similar norms could also be examined within particular schools. Parents, teachers, and principals do not necessarily answer to the same authorities; they do not share equal power in determining what actions in the school should be taken to increase equality of educational opportunity. However, they can be convinced that if such a norm were in place then the collectivity would be improved.

This leads us to the third condition of norm emergence—the individualistic orientation of the society. Suppose that by imposing a norm of equal opportunity, a member stands to lose his or her advantaged position in the society. Then there is a disincentive for him or her to support a change in norms. Individuals who stand to benefit by a change in equal opportunity norms are of course more likely to endorse such a change. When a change in norms carries the potential for a loss of status, incentives must be offered to offset the potential costs to someone who stands to lose if the new norm is fully endorsed. Such incentives need not be monetary; they could be ideological and could appeal to individuals' sense of what is fair and good for the collectivity.

Coleman argued that although some members stand to lose by endorsing a norm of equal opportunity, potential opposition can be overcome by appealing to the needs of the collectivity. This can even occur in social systems that are highly individualistic and where members see themselves as able to change status positions with others. In such systems, though, a norm would not be endorsed if most members stood to lose something. In societies that are highly collective, on the other hand, individual rights are viewed as secondary. In such societies, norms of equal opportunity are likely to be subordinated to communal norms.

These three conditions for the emergence of a norm of equal opportunity prefigure Coleman's later emphasis on the importance of incentives and rewards for creating new, and modifying existing, norms. The issue of authority is also important, for it emphasizes how difficult it is to create norms when individuals are not subject to the same authorities. For example, if there is no external authority determining what is an acceptable academic performance, students may try to negotiate with their teachers to change their grades (see Coleman et al., 1997, on this point). These ideas of collective responsibility and functional communities were more fully developed in Coleman's next major education study.

PUBLIC AND PRIVATE SCHOOLS: FUNCTIONAL COMMUNITIES

The questions of norms and schools as social systems grew in importance in the 1980s with the national study, *High School and Beyond* (*HS&B*). In 1979 the National Center for Education Statistics decided to conduct a new longitudinal survey of 10th and 12th graders in different types of high schools across the United States. This longitudinal study, designed somewhat similarly to the National Longitudinal Study of 1972 (NLS–72), was conducted to learn what students' experiences were in high school, what factors contributed to high schoolers' cognitive performance and social development, and how students' experiences, individual achievement, and social development influenced later educational and career choices (Coleman, Hoffer, & Kilgore, 1982). The topics for specific analyses were very broad, and Coleman submitted to NCES a list of ten possible topics. NCES approved five of these. In meeting with the research team, Coleman asked his colleagues to select the topics on which they wanted to work. Differences between public and private schools was not selected by members of the team, so Coleman decided to take on this question (personal communication with James S. Coleman). Coleman, along with his two research assistants at the time, Thomas Hoffer and Sally Kilgore, wrote two books that analyzed the data on this question: *High School Achievement: Public, Catholic, and Private Schools Compared* (Coleman, et al., 1982), and *Public and Private High Schools: The Impact of Communities* (Coleman & Hoffer, 1987).

In examining the base-year data from the 10th and 12th graders, Coleman and colleagues (1982) found that degree of racial segregation in private schools was not greater than that in public schools, and that for students of comparable family background, achievement was higher in private versus public schools. Controversy once again erupted, and Coleman's results were reanalyzed (see Report Analysis: Public and Private Schools, *Harvard Educational Review,* 1981; *Sociology of Education,* 1982; *Sociology of Education,* 1985). This time the findings raised questions about selection bias among students who chose to attend private schools, a condition that some argued could not be sufficiently controlled. The magnitude of effect sizes between public and private school student test results was also called into question.

When the longitudinal sample of *HS&B*—that is, 10th-grade students who were included in the initial sample and who had progressed to 12th grade after 2 years—was examined, the findings regarding Catholic schools appeared more robust than those of public schools and of other private schools. Of particular interest was the finding that Catholic schools were more successful at increasing their students' chances of graduating from high school and going on to attend some type of postsecondary school. The second wave of analyses undertook several different techniques to control for selection bias, and gains in achievement for Catholic students were higher than those for public school students with similar background characteristics (Coleman & Hoffer, 1987).

For Coleman, the importance of the *HS&B* study was not in finding that one type of school outproduced another, but rather in discovering the conditions within schools that helped to create norms that supported academic achievement and school success. Looking more intensively inside Catholic schools, Coleman identified a new set of actors that were encouraging positive achievement norms—the parents of students in the Catholic schools. When adult networks in the school community were strong, as was more often the situation in Catholic schools, they provided a resource (which he termed *social capital*) that was important for students' achievement and for their commitment to staying in high school until graduation. In reflecting on these results, Coleman wrote

> This research again focussed attention on the point suggested in Adolescent Society, that educational outcomes are not merely independent consequences of institutional treatments or delivery

services but can be understood only as a complex consequence of the functioning of social systems
of which the formal school activities are merely a part. (Coleman, 1996b, p. 22)

Some have argued that Coleman's notion of a functional community is somewhat spe-
cious in that the members of the schools he examined did not live in the neighborhoods in
which the schools were located. I would argue that there is another interpretation that is perhaps more consistent with Coleman's views of schools as social systems. Much as he had in
The Adolescent Society (Coleman, 1961), Coleman perceived the Catholic schools in *HS&B*
as closed social systems. It is the strong social ties among parents, teachers, and students in the
school that facilitate the creation of norms. The norms in the school grow from a common
purpose—quality education for the child; consequently, parents of children in the school are
more likely to relate to one another around issues of education. It is the interrelationship of
individuals, held together through social ties, that Coleman saw as the conduit through which
norms could be transmitted and sanctions imposed. These ideas are more fully developed in
Foundations of Social Theory (Coleman, 1990c), and in Coleman's articles on social capital
(Coleman, 1987, 1988).

SOCIAL CAPITAL AND SUSTAINING NORMS

When Coleman was analyzing data from *HS&B* (Jones et al., 1981) he also was very much
engaged in other sociological and mathematical issues, many of which are comprehensively
discussed in *Foundations of Social Theory* (Coleman, 1990). This book took over 10 years to
complete and contained many problems Coleman had visited and revisited over the course of
his sociological career. Although Coleman had looked at norms at several points during his
career, it is in this book that he begins to articulate a formal conception of the emergence of
social norms (see Chapters 10 and 11 in *Foundations of Social Theory*, Coleman, 1990). The
formation of social norms is fundamental to understanding Coleman's definition of social
capital.

Formation of Norms

According to Coleman, sociological theory tends to view social norms as given and rarely
raises the question of why and how norms come into existence. In *Foundations of Social
Theory*, Coleman (1990c) gives a functional and explicit definition of social norms. The functional definition describes norms as those "actions [that are] regarded by a set of persons as
proper or correct or improper or incorrect. They are purposively generated, in that those persons who initiate or help maintain a norm see themselves as benefitting from its being observed or harmed by its being violated" (p. 242). Norms are enforced by sanctions, and individuals either receive rewards for actions seen as positive or are punished for behaviors regarded
as negative (or incorrect). Individuals who hold a norm can claim the right to apply sanctions.
Persons whose actions are subject to norms, but who may not endorse them, will nonetheless
take them into account when making decisions about what actions to take. In Coleman's explicit definition of norms in social systems the right to control actions—whether formally or
informally defined—must be held by others within those systems.

According to Coleman, "Norms are macro-level constructs, based on purposive actions
at the micro level but coming into existence under certain conditions through a micro to macro
transition. Once in existence, they lead, under certain conditions, to the actions of individuals"

(Coleman, 1990c, p. 244). In developing his theory of norms, Coleman also made other distinctions about who benefits from certain types of norms and the conditions under which such benefits occur. A considerable part of Coleman's analysis of norms is related to game theory, but for purposes of this chapter, I have abstracted those concepts that seem most directly related to social capital and have focused on how Coleman applied these concepts to families, to schools, and to communities.

Formation of Social Capital

Coleman traced the conception of social capital to Loury (1977), who introduced the term to describe how individuals use resources that accrue through social relationships in the family and the community for their own benefit. Coleman defined social capital as a set of relational ties that facilitate action. These sets of relational ties are viewed as networks of social relations among individuals (see Coleman, 1990c, p. 302). This network conception of social capital fits closely with his desire to develop concepts that can be used to characterize social systems rather than attributes of individuals. The social capital that comes through relational exchanges helps to generate trust by establishing expectations and by creating and enforcing norms.

Coleman's conception of social capital as a set of relational ties that help to establish norms can be traced to earlier sociological work by Park and Burgess (1921) and by Mead (1934). Park, Burgess, and Mead referred to social institutions as communities of mutual interests that form mores and values of social control. Through common understandings that emerge from discourse and activities, such institutions define socially responsible patterns of conduct. Janowitz (1975) argued that the task of empirical social research is to investigate the forms and consequences of social control that enable a social group to regulate itself in terms of a set of legitimate moral principles.

Social capital, from Coleman's perspective, is especially useful for describing the actions of actors in social systems, regardless of whether those systems are families, schools, or communities. Like other forms of capital, such as human and physical capital, social capital makes possible the achievement of certain ends that would be impossible without its presence. The denser and closer the relational ties in the system, the greater the likelihood that information that provides a basis for action will be communicated. For example, in small, closed communities, information about which teachers are the best teachers is often widely discussed. Parents who are privy to this information often try to move their child to the preferred classrooms where instruction is perceived to be of high quality, which typically translates into higher student achievement.

Exchanging useful information is only one aspect of social capital. The more critical component is its ability to foster normative behavior that enhances the productivity of the system. This is accomplished through the fulfillment of expected obligations that are reciprocal and that engender trust. From Coleman's perspective, the value of social capital is its ability to provide a mechanism of social control through the creation of voluntary norms. These norms are based on clearly understood obligations and shared expectations. Obligations require action; expectations are assumptions about others' behaviors. The concepts of obligation and expectation are often overlooked in interpreting Coleman's formulation of social capital. Obligation and expectation assume a pre-existing value system that each individual has that affects his or her actions. For social capital to effectively operate as a mechanism of social control these obligations and expectations of individuals must become shared by the collectivity.

The presence or absence of social ties helps to establish and to define links among members in the network. In communities where these ties have been developed across generations, the social capital is even stronger, for all individuals within the system have some link to other members in the system. Coleman hypothesized that such intergenerational ties can provide a mechanism not only for maintaining effective norms but also for creating trustworthiness. It is this trustworthiness that makes possible the establishment of obligations and expectations—and of sanctions, when such obligations and expectations are not fulfilled. In structures that are open, trustworthiness can provide the same types of sanctions that exist within structures that have more closure.

In social structures where individuals have clear expectations of how they are supposed to act and how others are expected to act, this information is shared throughout the system. Obligations of action are a resource unto themselves, and they can be made tangible by their availability to others when needed. For example, in a school community that values high academic success, teachers can call on parents to help them in implementing new policies, such as introducing stricter rules regarding the completion of homework. The more social capital in the system, the greater the number of parents and students who will follow these new rules regarding homework completion. In this example, the teachers assume that parents and students will fulfill their obligations to the principles endorsed by the school. For the parents, this may mean that they have to more carefully monitor their child's time, which requires them to take attention away from other interests. In order to comply with these rules, the students will also have to forego time they might have spent watching television or visiting with friends. Both parents and their children have to forego spending time on other preferred activities and act in the interests of the collectivity, in this instance, the school. Coleman argued that a norm of this sort—reinforced by status, by honor, and by other rewards—constitutes a powerful source of social capital (see Coleman, 1988, pp. 104–105).

Looking back to the 1985 norm paper, we can elaborate on some of Coleman's ideas on how norms of equal opportunity might be brought about. In our example, the students and their parents are giving something up for the interests of the collectivity—in this instance, higher educational performance. Students would rather spend their time on other interests as would their parents, who now have responsibility for monitoring their children's school assignments. Both the students and their parents are under the authority of the school. What is missing is the exchange. However, we could imagine that even if students do not endorse the homework policies, the sanctions imposed might be so strict—such as lower grades or suspension of special privileges—that they would comply with the norm to avoid such consequences, despite their lack of support for the policies.

In addition to these broad principles of social capital Coleman also specifically defined social capital within the family and the community. With respect to the family, he viewed social capital as the number of adults in the family and the quality of attention they give to the children within the home. Coleman defined social capital in the community in terms of the social relationships that exist among parents and the closure exhibited by the parents' ties to other parents and to the institutions within the community. Social capital in the community depends greatly on the stability and strength of the community's social structure.

Coleman maintained that even where the social structure of neighborhoods has deteriorated, social capital can be created through functional communities. These social institutions, which may or may not be neighborhood-based, can provide a functional linkage among parents. Coleman uses the religious community surrounding parochial schools as an example of a functional community that increases the social capital among its members. He conceded that other institutions may play a similar role for some public schools. Coleman asserted that his analysis of HS&B data, which compares the low dropout rates in religious schools with public and secular private schools, demonstrates the important benefits of social capital created by such functional communities (Coleman, 1991; Coleman & Hoffer, 1987).

Coleman argued that closer connections between parents and their children—for example, schools organized around the parents' workplace—can strengthen social ties between teachers and families; this would particularly be the case in neighborhood schools where most parents work outside of their own neighborhoods. Coleman argued that one way to improve schools is to create close ties among parents and their child's school, where parents, teachers, and students share a common set of standards that social norms help to bring about and maintain.

The role of social capital in the family and the community was the question that drove the analyses of the base-year data of the National Education Longitudinal Study of 1988. Once again, Coleman used a national data set to examine the activities parents engage in with their children—at home, in school, and in the community—that actually improve school performance. Findings from these analyses were presented in *Parents, Their Children, and Schools* (Schneider & Coleman, 1993). Unlike other family studies at the time, this edited volume of empirical large-scale quantitative analyses focused on the processes through which some families support and create opportunities for learning among students. The analyses in this book were directed toward determining what norms and sanctions families impose that either encourage or discourage learning in school. Also examined was the question of what other social institutions families rely on, beside schools, to socialize their children and reinforce their learning.

In contrast to other studies, the analyses in this volume focused on what parents do at home to help their children learn—regardless of whether this learning is school-related or independent of school. Some parents, for example, may enroll their child in music classes outside of school. The discipline and time involved in learning an instrument may in turn have positive spillover effects on academic work. The actions parents take at home with children can be seen as a measure of their responsiveness to the availability of certain resources. Parents' decisions to spend time talking to their children about school, or enforcing rules about television viewing and homework, are means through which parents can positively influence children's learning. Both time and communication help to strengthen social relations between parents and their children.

The results from the analyses presented in *Parents, Their Children, and Schools* (Schneider & Coleman, 1993) suggested that family activities outside of school were more beneficial for children's academic performance than parents' involvement in activities at the school, such as joining the PTA or volunteering. It was found that parents' contact with the school was often closely related to students' misbehavior; more positive forms of parent contact, such as seeking academic help for children, were less common. When this project started, the investigators hoped to find a closer relationship between family and school activities. This hope was not realized. Families who invested their resources in activities at home, and who had high expectations and norms for their children's academic performance, were more likely to have children who did well in school. In these cases, family norms were consistent with academic norms. What was not examined was whether the activities families engaged in at home had an independent positive effect beyond positive school norms, and whether they were effective in counteracting negative achievement norms held by other students in the schools. A multilevel school comparison looking at the interaction between family norms and school norms would have been more consistent with Coleman's notions of schools as social systems. Such an analysis would undoubtedly provide a deeper understanding of the relationships between families, schools, and the creation of norms.

NORMS FOR RAISING ACHIEVEMENT

Coleman's interest in norms continued, and while on a Fulbright Senior Scholarship at the European University Institute in 1993, he returned to one of his primary interests in education—how to form norms in schools that could enhance students' social development and improve their academic performance. Coleman believed that strengthening the social ties among teachers and students would facilitate the creation of norms that would motivate students to learn. He argued that the relational ties among teachers and students in public elementary and secondary schools had become increasingly detached and indifferent, to the point where teachers often compromised their own professional standards in order to maintain social control in their classrooms. Instead of a classroom where teacher and students were working toward a common set of performance goals, both parties were negotiating with each other to advance their own self-interests. Students, Coleman (1997) suggested, were interested in obtaining higher grades for less effort, whereas teachers, who needed measures to enforce social control in the classrooms, were willing to assign less homework and accept lower standards of performance for high grades in exchange for students' willingness to behave in the classroom.

The problem identified by Coleman was moving classrooms from an individual self-interest model to a model where norms of high performance were collectively shared by both teachers and students. Returning to the earlier discussion of the conditions for achieving norms of equal opportunity, we see that, for Coleman, this was an achievable condition, provided that the teacher's authority as an evaluator was removed and that incentives were available for both students and teachers if performance improved.

Today, one problem that many teachers have is determining what is a reasonable expectation regarding students' performance from the beginning to the end of the school year. The wide authority that individual states, districts, or schools have to determine their own policies often results in teachers being sent inconsistent and confusing messages about what constitutes acceptable levels of student performance. These sometimes conflicting and ambiguous expectations leave many teachers with the task of creating their own standards of classroom performance. Externally based standards could help to reshape the system and to create enabling conditions for improving classroom instruction.

In essence, Coleman wished to place teachers and students under a single authority that would establish standards for teachers' and for students' performance and that would operate independently of local school interests. Shifting the authority to an external agency would make it easier to monitor and to ensure compliance at the local level. Although standards would be established externally, Coleman (1997) maintained that the work in classrooms should be left to the discretion of the teacher. Thus, although local schools would retain autonomy over instructional methods, the basic content of what should be taught, and what students should know and be able to do, would be determined by external standards. By placing responsibility for standards and assessment with an external agent, the basis for the teacher's authority in the classroom changes, and the teacher has greater responsibility for ensuring that students achieve academically. In such situations, the role of the teacher changes to one of academic coach. Changing the function of the teacher's role in the classroom in turn aids in the establishment of norms directed at students' learning.

Coleman realized that the teacher alone cannot be totally responsible for setting classroom norms because they are shaped in part by the actions and attitudes of students in the class and by their parents. However, he recognized that the disorganization of many communities, and parents' focus on noneducational aspects of their children's lives, make it difficult for them to reinforce academic goals for high achievement. Thus the primary responsibility for enforcing such goals rests with the teacher and the students in the class. To ensure that this occurs, Coleman suggested offering incentives and rewards. The incentive plan Coleman (1997) designed was based on a student achievement value-added model. Instead of being linked to absolute levels of achievement, the determination of a teacher's success is based on the amount of progress individual students, and the class as a whole, make over the entire year. Teachers are evaluated not only by the numbers of their students performing academically at grade level, but also by the amount of progress individual students make during the academic year. Teachers who are able to advance the most deficient or most challenging students would receive extra compensation. In addition, students who make the most relative progress would have greater choice in the educational market—that is, they would be given a chance to select high quality schools, programs, and teachers. Coleman referred to these reforms as an output-driven model of education. This model recognizes that most student academic learning occurs in the classroom, and that the key to raising academic productivity is to develop strong norms that stress student achievement.

These concepts were described in Coleman's last book, *Redesigning American Education* (Coleman, et al., 1997). In contrast to his other work, Coleman actually wrote a plan of what an output-driven model would encompass and then, using the base year and first follow-up of the National Education Longitudinal Study of 1988–92 (NELS:88–92), he and his research team set out to determine if any of the principles he believed were responsible for changing norms actually affected academic performance. Although clearly limited by the variables in the NELS:88–92 study, the researchers were able to determine that students' performance is likely to increase when academic values and incentives are central to a school's organizational culture. Students in schools that direct their activities toward the pursuit of academic excellence have higher levels of performance than students in schools that do not share this emphasis. This achievement effect is especially strong in schools where the majority of students are from poor families or have parents with low levels of education. Results also showed that limiting the control teachers have over curricular content, while granting teachers a high level of autonomy in determining teaching techniques, is beneficial in raising students' achievement.

As for external standards, the data set did not allow us, at the time, to determine which of the U.S. states had external standards. Instead, the Scholastic Aptitude Test (SAT) was used as a proxy for an externally controlled exam with high-stakes results. The mathematics test scores of students who planned to take the SAT as sophomores were nearly 10% higher than those of seniors who did not have such plans as sophomores. Students with considerable family and school resources were the most informed about SAT preparation, but activities offered by the school to assist in that preparation did not affect their performance. This was not the case for students with limited family and school resources. For these students school information and preparation had significant effects on their performance.

Coleman's plans for redesigning American schools had many components that have been advocated by a variety of educational reformers. He never expected that others would adopt his recommendations fully in their school systems and recognized that the piecemeal adoption of some of his recommendations could, in the end, result in unintended effects that would defeat their purpose. However, what gave this scheme for reform a decidedly Coleman-like character was its explicit focus on norms and on the need for strong social ties between the teacher and students to facilitate the development of norms. Such norms would help to define the roles of teacher and student and to clarify what was expected of each. However, these norms could not be sustained without incentives and rewards.

A NEW STUDY

In "Transcripts of Drafts for a Concluding Chapter, by James S. Coleman with a Commentary by Zdzislawa Coleman" (Z. A. Coleman, 1996), Zdzislawa observed that Jim was working until just days before he died. In the spring of 1995 he was working on the syllabus for his Mathematical Sociology Seminar and rewriting and reorganizing his concluding chapter for the Clark (1996) volume. On March 21st he discussed the chapter with Zdzislawa. She noted that "He was sitting in an armchair with his writing on his lap as usual. He felt good about it, and said: 'Now I know what to write.' On Thursday morning, I took him to the hospital and on Saturday, 25 March 1995 at 12:15 p.m. Jim died" (Z. A. Coleman, 1996, p. 359).

Coleman never had a single research and scholarly agenda. The scope of his interests was enormous and the range and depth of his intellectual pursuits could only be described as staggering. One of the projects Coleman was working on in the winter of 1995 was a new study of high schools. He decided to return to *The Adolescent Society* (Coleman, 1961)—"this time to do it right." Coleman had always been fascinated by the fact that nearly all the boys in his high school went out for football at the beginning of their freshman year, even though most of them had no talent for playing the game. He would often ask why young boys would subject themselves to competing for something at which they were sure to fail. (The question of talent was always an issue for him, particularly because he had considerable prowess in the game.) Was the social status of being a football player so important that boys would risk physical harm and personal defeat just on the chance that they might be selected to play a sport highly valued in the school?

The study he planned to undertake was titled "What Goes On In School: A Student's Perspective" (Coleman, 1994b). Coleman intended to show how the interests of individual students, as well as their abilities, can determine the value of different activities in a school and the status or power of different students in the school. In the first stages of this work, Coleman simulated six students in a high school and estimated the effects on their achievement of the esteem of significant others such as teachers, coaches, and parents. Employing a series of mathematical formulae, he then calculated the effect of different student abilities, talents, and investments of time in activities valued by significant others.

As expected, students invest their time in those activities in which achievement is rewarded by the persons whose esteem they want. However, the students' academic achievement differs as a consequence of their differences in potential. One could adjust a student's time investment in a given activity by modifying the esteem he or she expects to get from significant others. Coleman had just begun this work in collaboration with Huayin Wang, a graduate student in sociology with a specialization in mathematical sociology, and he saw this type of modeling as a way to determine what goes on in schools by examining students' interests in significant others and the rewards given by those significant others. The difficulty for some students may be that they have high potential in activities for which significant others do not give rewards, which results in low self-esteem. In such situations, the principal of the school may be able to modify the reward structure so that more students can achieve rewards. Coleman used the example of a sports-oriented high school where the principal generates new activities for students who do not excel at sports. Another modification would be to attempt to increase the potential of students in certain activities for which significant others provide high rewards.

Coleman ends the unpublished paper for the study with the following example:

> . . . in my high school, one friend showed some improvement in football the first year, even though he was on the junior varsity team, and still was on the JV team in the second year, but still improv-

ing. He worked hard and made the varsity team and his letter in football in his senior year. Achievement in football had the potential for producing a lot of rewards for him, and his improving ability made this potential a likelihood, so by working hard he increased the potential, finally getting the achievement and the rewards. There were a lot of others in the same boat: For others, either the lack of improvement or the lack of potential rewards [quote includes the notation "y_{ji}"] made them quit after a first try. (1994b, p. 17)

THINKING ABOUT SOCIAL SYSTEMS AND NORMS

Although Coleman had a central interest in social systems, how they function, and how social norms are created within them, this is not the only theoretical problem that held his interest throughout his career. His work on rational choice, exchange theory, and incentive structures was also fundamental to his attempts to describe social systems. This review focuses on schools as social systems, the emergence of norms in these systems, and on the relevant studies and written text Coleman produced on these topics. Although it attempts to cover this work comprehensively, some papers were undoubtedly overlooked. The mathematical formulations on some of the topics were excluded because of the audience. For the mathematical constructions of different types of norms and their consequences, see *Foundations of Social Theory* (Coleman, 1990c). The last paper discussed previously (Coleman, 1994b) is unpublished but is available by request.

Coleman has been criticized on the grounds that the only school norms that he viewed as worthy of attention were those related to academic performance. Certainly, he was very interested in achievement norms, but I would argue that this interest did not stem from a narrowness or an insensitivity to the other outcomes of schooling. Instead, he attempted to analyze an organization whose primary function was seen by most as academic learning. Coleman viewed schools as social systems, in much the same way that he viewed law firms and other organizations as social systems. The goal of schools is academic achievement, just as the goal of law firms is to settle disputes and the goal of auto manufacturers is to produce cars. What held his interest was that although academic performance was the main activity of schools, the value placed on learning, and on instruction related to achievement, was less than one might expect. In the extreme, it would be as if the lawyers in a firm decided to offer their clients psychological therapy rather than focusing on resolving their disputes. This is not to say that some clients might not need counseling or that counseling would not be helpful to them in resolving their disputes but that counseling is not a service that a lawyer's clients expect to receive or spend their resources on.

Coleman saw schools as having other roles, such as the socialization of youths into adulthood. This, however, he saw primarily as the function of the family, although as families became increasingly disorganized, and the socialization of youth was passed off to other institutions, Coleman became more interested in having teachers assume a greater role in teaching students the values that would lead them to successful school careers and ultimately to stable, well-paying jobs. The role of the teacher in *Redesigning American Education* (Coleman, et al., 1997) is central, and Coleman advocated having the same teachers stay with their students for several years, especially in the early grades.

Coleman was concerned about the eroding role of the family in the socialization of children. He was interested in incentives and rewards as a mechanism for drawing parents back toward focusing on their children's education, and he sought ways to make the quality of education a primary concern of parents, of teachers, and of students. Positive social norms that carried sanctions imposed by external agents would help to strengthen relational ties among parents, their children, and their teachers. Having clear and shared norms that are widely upheld, and that are reinforced in the home, in the classroom, and in the community, can instill a stronger sense of institutional purpose among students, parents, and staff. To accomplish this, he argued, we need to understand more fully why families, their children, and schools do not have norms that support achievement.

It is in Coleman's last educational work that we find a more systematic attempt to uncover students' interests, whose opinions matter to them, and how those interests can be changed. In *The Adolescent Society* (Coleman, 1961), the students valued athletics, popularity, and, to a much lesser extent, being a good student. Some might argue that the values of today's adolescents are not the ones described in *The Adolescent Society*, in Coleman's 1970s Panel Report, or the ones held by students who attended the public or private schools Coleman examined in the 1980s. If this is the case, then we are left with the question that Coleman himself asked in his final paper: What do America's young adults today value in school, whose interests matter to them, and what effect is it having on how they spend their time?

Coleman's methodological approaches, driving interest in matters of educational policy, and the single-mindedness with which he interpreted the norms of schooling have often been criticized. This review has attempted to place his work on social systems and norms in a broader context by tracing through his scholarly work how he came to think about values, norms, and incentives, and how they operate in social systems, primarily schools. What critics often have failed to recognize is how Coleman's empirical work on schools is linked to his theoretical and mathematical work on social systems and on norms. Although Coleman's policy findings and arguments for school choice may be historically specific and have limited application, the theoretical underpinnings of his work remain central to the field of the sociology of education.

REFERENCES

Bowles, S., & Levin, H. (1968). The determinants of scholastic achievement—An appraisal of some recent evidence. *Journal of Human Resources, 2*(1).

Cain, G., & Watts, H. (1970). Problems in making inferences from the Coleman Report. *American Sociological Review, 35*, 228–242.

Clark, J. (Ed., 1996). *James S. Coleman*. London: Falmer Press.

Coleman, J. S. (1961). *The adolescent society: The social life of the teenager and its impact on education*. Glencoe, IL: The Free Press.

Coleman, J. S. (1971). Collective decisions. In H. Turk & R. L. Simpson (Eds.), *Institutions and social exchange: The sociologies of Talcott Parsons and George C. Homans*. New York: Bobbs-Merrill.

Coleman, J. S. (Ed., 1973). *Youth: Transition to adulthood*. Chicago: University of Chicago Press.

Coleman, J. S. (1985a). *Autobiographical sketch, I–II*. Unpublished manuscript. Second draft. Partly published as "Columbia in the 1950's," in B. M. Berger (Ed.), *Authors of their own lives*. Berkeley, CA: University of California Press, 1990.

Coleman, J. S. (1985b). Norms of equal opportunity: When and why do they arise? *Angewandte Soziaforschung* (Vienna), *13*(1), 55–60. Reprinted in J. S. Coleman, (1990b), *Equality and achievement in education* (pp. 8–16).

Coleman, J. S. (1987). Microfoundations and macrosocial behavior. In J. C. Alexander, B. Giesen, R. Munch, & N. S. Smelser (Eds.), *The micro–macro link*. Berkeley, CA: University of California Press.

Coleman, J. S. (1988). Social capital in the creation of human capital. *American Journal of Sociology, 94*, 95–120.

Coleman, J. S. (1990a). Columbia in the 1950's. In B. M. Berger (Ed.), *Authors of their own lives*. Berkeley, CA: University of California Press.

Coleman, J. S. (1990b). *Equality and achievement in education*. Boulder, CO: Westview Press.

Coleman, J. S. (1990c). *Foundations of social theory*. Cambridge, MA: Harvard University Press

Coleman, J. S. (1990d). Interview: James S. Coleman. In R. Swedberg (Ed.), *Economics and sociology* (pp. 57–62). Princeton, NJ: Princeton University Press.

Coleman, J. S. (1991). Changes in the family and implications for the common school. *The University of Chicago Legal Forum,* 153–170.

Coleman, J. S. (1994a). A vision for sociology. *Society, 32*(1), 29–34.

Coleman, J. S. (1994b). What goes on in school: A student's perspective. Unpublished manuscript, The University of Chicago.

Coleman, J. S. (1996a). A vision for sociology. In J. Clark (Ed.), *James S. Coleman* (pp. 343–349). London: Falmer Press.

Coleman, J. S. (1996b). Reflections on schools and adolescents. In J. Clark (Ed.), *James S. Coleman* (pp. 17–22). London: Falmer Press.

Coleman, J. S., Campbell, E. Q., Hobson, C. J., McPartland, J., Mood, A. M., Weinfeld, P. D., & York, R. L. (1966). *Equality of educational opportunity.* Washington, DC: U.S. Government Printing Office.

Coleman, J. S., & Hoffer, T. (1987). *Public and private high schools: The impact of communities.* New York: Basic Books.

Coleman, J. S., Hoffer, T., & Kilgore, S. (1982). *High school achievement: Public Catholic, and private schools compared.* New York: Basic Books.

Coleman, J. S., Kelly, S., & Moore, J. (1975). *Trends in school segregation, 1968–73.* Washington, DC: The Urban Institute. Reprinted in J. S. Coleman (1990b), *Equality and achievement in education* (pp. 169–197).

Coleman, J. S., Schneider, B., Plank, S., Schiller, K. S., Shouse, R., Wang, H., & Lee, S. A. (1997). *Redesigning American education.* Boulder, CO: Westview Press.

Coleman, Z. A. (1996). Commentary on 'Transcripts of drafts for a concluding chapter by James S. Coleman.' Appendix 2 in J. Clark (Ed.), *James S. Coleman* (pp. 357—359). London: Falmer Press.

Farley, R. (Ed., 1995). *State of the union: America in the 1990s.* Vol. I. New York: Russell Sage Foundation.

Farley, R. (1996). *The new American reality: Who we are, how we got here, where we are going.* New York: Russell Sage Foundation.

Heckman, J. J., & Neal, D. (1996). Coleman's contributions to education: Theory, research styles, and empirical research. In J. Clark (Ed.), *James S. Coleman* (pp. 81–102). London: Falmer Press.

Janowitz, M. (1975). Sociological theory and social control. *American Journal of Sociology, 81,* 82–108.

Jones, C., Clarke, M., Mooney, G., McWilliams, H., Crawford, I., Stephenson, B., & Tournangeau (1983). *High school and beyond senior cohort, Data file user's manual.* Chicago: National Opinion Research Center.

Kandel, D. B. (1996). Coleman's contributions to understanding youth and adolescence. In J. Clark (Ed.), *James S. Coleman* (pp. 33–45). London: Falmer Press.

Kosters, M. H. (1991). *Workers and their wages: Changing patterns in the United States.* Washington, DC: AEI Press.

Lipset, S. M., Trow, M., & Coleman, J. S. (1956). *Union democracy.* New York: The Free Press.

Loury, G. (1977). A dynamic theory of racial income differences. In P.A. Wallace & A. LeMund (Eds.), *Women, minorities, and employment discrimination.* Lexington, MA: Lexington Books.

Mead, G. H. (1934). *Mind, self and society.* Chicago: University of Chicago Press.

Merton, R. K. (1996). Teaching James Coleman. Appendix 1 in J. Clark (Ed.), *James S. Coleman* (pp. 351–356). London: Falmer Press.

Mosteller, F., & Moynihan, D. P. (Eds., 1972). *On the equality of educational opportunity, papers deriving from the Harvard University faculty seminar on the Coleman Report.* New York: Random House.

Park, R. E., & Burgess, E. W. (1921). Social control and schools of thought; Control of the collective mind; Social control defined; Classification of the materials. In *Introduction to the science of sociology* (pp. 27–42, 783–799). Chicago: University of Chicago Press.

Report Analysis: Public and Private Schools. (1981). *Harvard Educational Review, 51,* 481–545.

Ricobson, J., Henderson, L., Burkeheimer, G., Place, C., & Levinsohn, J. (1981). *National longitudinal study: Base Year (1972) through fourth follow-up (1979).* Chapel Hill, NC: Center for Educational Research and Evaluation, Research Triangle Institute.

Roethlisberger, F. J., & Dickson, W. J. (1939). *Management and the worker; an account of a research program conducted by the Western Electric Company, Hawthorne Works, Chicago.* Cambridge, MA: Harvard University Press.

Schneider, B., & Coleman, J. S. (1993). *Parents, their children, and schools.* Boulder, CO: Westview Press.

Schneider, B., & Stevenson, D. (1999). *The ambitious generation: America's teenager, motivated but directionless.* New Haven: Yale University Press.

(April–July, 1982). Special two-volume series on the debate surrounding Public and Private Schools (1981). *Sociology of Education, 55.*

(April, 1985). Third special issue devoted to public and private school debate. *Sociology of Education, 58.*

U.S. Congress. (1964). Section 402 of the Civil Rights Act.

CHAPTER 17

Values, Control, and Outcomes in Public and Private Schools

Caroline Hodges Persell

A new stream of educational reform arguments has emerged since the late 1970s suggesting that public and private schools differ in their effectiveness and efficiency, that the differences in their outcomes are due to differences in the dominant values and control that operate within the sectors, and that other features that vary by sector (such as characteristics of families and students using private schools, curriculum, tracking, and school size) are not responsible for the greater educational success of the private sector. This argument has been used to support requests for more privatization of education and for increased choice, which usually include the idea of using public monies for private schooling.

In order to analyze this argument, we need to consider several questions:

1. What is distinctive about the public and private school sectors and what types of schools exist in each sector?
2. What sectoral differences in educational outcomes occur?
3. How do educational values and controls vary?
4. Does sector or something else explain differences in values and controls?
5. What affects variations in the operations and outcomes of public and private schools?

DISTINCTIONS BETWEEN PUBLIC AND PRIVATE SECTORS

A public school is one managed by a state or by some other public authority, whereas a private school is one that is not managed by a state or a public authority (Anderson, 1994, p. 4826).

Caroline Hodges Persell • Department of Sociology, New York University, New York, New York 10003
Handbook of the Sociology of Education, edited by Maureen T. Hallinan. Kluwer Academic/Plenum Publishers, New York, 2000.

Private schools may or may not receive government monies. In European countries and in Australia, private education is generally confined to nonprofit forms (although this was not always the case) and often receives state subsidies. In the United States, for-profit schools and educational programs are expanding in both the public and the private sectors (see Ascher, Fruchter, & Berne, 1996), alongside nonprofit religious and nonreligious private schools.

Public schools encompass urban, suburban, and rural school systems that vary widely across states and with respect to size, student composition, teacher characteristics, and curricula, among other things. Although most public schools are run on a not-for-profit basis, some have agreed to for-profit programs or to being run by for-profit corporations, such as The Edison Project and Channel One of Whipple Communications and Education Alternatives, Inc.'s contract with the Baltimore City Public Schools in 1992. Private schools include Catholic, nonprofit; other religious, nonprofit; nonsectarian, nonprofit; nonprofit elite private schools (religious and nonreligious); and for-profit educational programs such as proprietary schools. Clearly there are significant variations within both public and private sectors.

Worldwide, at the primary level, 12% of students are in the private sector. At the secondary level, 28% of students in the developing world are in the private sector as are 14% of students in the developed world (Anderson, 1994, p. 4824). In the United States, the proportion of students in private schools declined slightly from 12% in 1987 to 11% in 1997 (U.S. Department of Education, 1997, pp. 5–6). There are some 26,093 private elementary and secondary schools in the United States, enrolling an estimated 5.8 million students in 1997 (U.S. Department of Education, Tables 2 and 59). About 46.4 million students attend public schools.

The wide variations within the public and private sectors notwithstanding, a number of researchers in recent years have suggested that there are systematic sectoral differences in school outcomes.

OUTCOME DIFFERENCES IN PUBLIC AND PRIVATE SCHOOLS

Several researchers in recent decades have suggested that student outcomes are more positive in private schools compared to public schools. They have considered such outcomes as students' achievement, retention, college attendance, and desegregation. Of course the very choice of relevant outcomes is itself highly value-loaded. Is one's score on particular standardized multiple choice tests an adequate measure of cognitive learning and development? Such tests have very limited capacity for predicting employment, earnings, or other important life consequences (Haertel, James, & Levin, 1987, p. 3).

Student Achievement

Students' achievement frequently appears higher in private schools than in public schools. For example, Coleman and Hoffer (1987) found that students in Catholic schools showed greater growth in verbal skills and in mathematics compared to students in public schools, although there were no differences in the growth of their science or civics knowledge (p. 92). Others have challenged Coleman and Hoffer's conclusions on several grounds with respect to the significance of the difference and its causes. Researchers differ, for example, on whether the achievement gain from sophomore to senior years should be expressed as a fraction of a standard deviation (which makes it look negligible) or as a fraction of a year's growth (which makes it look large [Haertel et al., 1987, p. 5]). As Willms (1987) pointed out, compared to four other types of educational intervention (cross-age tutoring, cooperative learning, improved reading and study skills, and reinforcement) the Catholic school effect per year is minuscule (p. 129). Others have pointed out that whatever average differences exist in the achievement of comparable students in public schools and in private schools, "these differences are dwarfed by the variability within each sector from one school to another" (Haertel et al., p. 2).

Alexander and Pallas (1987) have noted that the tests used by Coleman and Hoffer may not be the best measure of how effectively schools are teaching and students are learning. Most researchers agree that one of the single biggest factors in achievement differences is curricular track (academic or general), as well as the number of math courses that a student has taken. A big debate is whether curricular track structure (i.e., the percent in an academic curriculum) is a school characteristic or an indicator of the characteristics of students and their families who opt for such schools. If it's the latter, it reflects selectivity bias rather than a school effect.

Even Coleman and Hoffer, who believe there is a Catholic school effect, noted that public schools making the same demands (in terms of curriculum, homework, and discipline) produce comparable achievement (Hoffer, Greeley, & Coleman, 1987, p. 87). This conclusion suggests that it is not sector, *per se*, but organizational practices that may be related to sector that contribute to students' achievement. "The difference in average scores is the result of the fact that many public schools do not make such demands" (Hoffer et al., 1987, p. 87). One of the questions we want to consider is why it is that many public schools fail to make as many academic demands as some private schools. Do marketlike conditions within some public schools operate to suppress academic demands in any way? To address this question, we need to examine the interplay of sector, values and control, organizational practices, and outcomes. Insights from such an examination could have important implications for the school choice debate currently raging in U.S. public policy. Before turning to these issues, however, it is worth considering how public and private schools compare on several other outcomes.

Retention

Coleman and Hoffer also found that public and other private high school students drop out at higher rates than Catholic school students (Coleman & Hoffer, 1987, p. 116). The probability of dropping out of school between spring of the sophomore year and spring of the senior year was 14% for public high school students, 12% for other private high school students, 3% for Catholic high school students, and virtually zero for high-performance private high school students (Coleman & Hoffer, p. 99). Even among students with academic, disciplinary, or attendance problems, dropout rates were lower in Catholic schools than in public or other private schools (Coleman & Hoffer, p. 105). Differences in dropout rates across the sectors were greater than were achievement differences.

College Attendance

Private school high school graduates (whether Catholic or other private) are much more likely to attend 4-year colleges and slightly more likely to attend 2-year and 4-year colleges than are public high school graduates (Coleman & Hoffer, 1987, p. 175; Persell, Cookson, & Catsambis, 1992, pp. 12–18). Private school and especially elite private school graduates are also much more likely than other high school graduates to attend private colleges and highly selective colleges (Persell et al., 1992).

Persell and associates (1992) compared all *High School and Beyond* (*HSB*) public high school seniors with elite boarding school seniors. Considering public school students whose families earned $38,000 or more per year (the top category in 1983), whose mothers and fathers both wished them to attend college, who were enrolled in an academic high school program, and whose grades and achievement scores were one standard deviation above the average value of the sample, the predicted probabilities of elite boarding school seniors attending a highly selective college or university were 61%, compared to 39% for the *HSB* sample. These authors suggested that it was impossible to separate the relative contribution of school and family background but that both operated conjointly to transmit educational advantages from one generation to the next.

Segregation

School segregation is another outcome considered by researchers, because greater racial segregation has been suggested as a potentially negative result of private education. Coleman, Hoffer and Kilgore (1982) suggested that "private schooling does not affect the overall racial segregation in American schools" (cited in Taeuber & James, 1982). Although fewer minority students attend private school compared to public school, those who do attend are highly desegregated there (Crain, 1988, p. 270). Taeuber and James argued that there are four serious flaws in Coleman, Hoffer and Kilgore's argument that "render their analysis meaningless and their conclusion improper" (p. 133). Taeuber and James indicated that the "only unflawed portion of their analysis is their confirmation of the fact that private schooling, nationwide, tends to separate white students from the racially more diverse public sector" (p. 133).

Crain (1988) also challenged Coleman, Hoffer and Kilgore's (1982) optimistic conclusions, finding that private schools do contribute to racial segregation but also may offer ways of overcoming racial isolation. Analyzing data on Catholic schools from Cleveland and from Chicago, Crain found that the elementary schools in both cities are highly segregated, although the Catholic high schools are less segregated than the public high schools were when traditional neighborhood school assignments were used (Crain, 1988, p. 271). He concludes that "not enough data are available to draw the more complicated conclusion which is probably the correct one: private schools further the segregation of schools under certain conditions and encourage racial integration of either schools or residential neighborhoods in others" (Crain, 1988, p. 292).

Who attends what type of school is strongly affected by cost and by the sources of funding. Catterall (1988)

> compares such things as family income and racial balance between the two sectors, finding that private school participation increases with family income and that there are proportionately more whites in private schools than blacks or Hispanics. The implication is that public subsidies (of private education) are likely to bring greatest benefit to those groups that are now participating disproportionately in private schools" (James & Levin, 1988, p. 11).

Studying Minnesota, a state where public support of private school choices exists on a small scale, Darling-Hammond and Kirby (1988) found that "race, income and the extent to which people know about the (tax) deduction have little relation to schooling choices, but that attitudes, tastes and the availability of free transportation are important influences on the choices that parents make in educating their children" (p.14).

Economic Efficiency

Another proposed difference between public and private schools is their cost. In the 1979–1980 school year based on reports by school administrators, the average expenditure per public school pupil was $2,016, compared to $1,353 in Catholic schools, $2,777 in other private schools, and $4,648 in high-performance private high schools (Coleman & Hoffer, 1987, p. 35). In public and in Catholic high schools, expenditures tend to cluster around these means, but in other private schools the variation in costs is greater. About 60% of students in other private schools attend schools with much lower than average expenditures, whereas others attend schools with much higher than average costs. Thus, there is much greater diversity in expenditures in the private, non-Catholic sector than in either the public or the Catholic sector. In the 1980s, high-performance private high schools cost more than three times what Catholic schools cost, whereas elite boarding schools cost nearly nine times what Catholic schools did (Persell et al., 1992, p. 8). There is no reason to believe that these ratios are different today. Catholic schools appear to be less expensive because classes are larger, there are fewer administrative personnel, and teachers are generally paid less.

In sum, although there is some disagreement about the existence of different outcomes in public schools and in private schools, the biggest disagreements occur with respect to the significance and interpretation of the small differences that occur and with respect to the posited causes of sectoral outcome differences. Chubb and Moe (1990), virtually alone, argued that outcome differences are due to sectoral differences in values and in control. Building on Bidwell, Frank, and Quiroz (1997), I see organizational conditions, namely school size, client power, and revenue sources as affecting values and control, educational activities, and outcomes. Although sector is correlated with all three, it is these variables rather than sector that affect educational practices and outcomes. Before considering the relationships between sector, values and control, and outcomes, values and control themselves warrant closer scrutiny.

VALUES AND CONTROLS IN EDUCATION

Values are strongly held ideas about what is desirable and what is undesirable. In education, this includes ideas about the goals or purposes of education and ideas about appropriate ways to achieve those goals. Values relate closely to the outcomes deemed important, including the impact of education on students, how schooling shapes their thinking (is it rote or creative?), their values (are they democratic, participatory, innovative?), their competencies (such as problem solving, inventing, discovering, being curious, questioning received knowledge), their interpersonal skills (being able to work effectively with a wide variety of others), and their character.

At least three important realms of influence or control are noteworthy. The first is the articulation of values and goals, and the second is the development of a legitimate system of authority for conducting activities designed to accomplish agreed-on values and goals. These include such things as the hiring, retention, and promotion of teachers; teachers' pedagogical beliefs and practices; curriculum; tracking structures and practices, text selection; class size; discipline; amount and type of homework assignments and projects; instructional guidance and monitoring; and the allocation of time across activities such as academic subjects, music, art, physical education, recess, and vocational subjects. The third is the existence of legitimate procedures for debate, dissent, and due process.

Two ways that control may be exercised were well noted by Hirschman (1970), namely exit and voice. Participants may leave an organization or decide not to enter it, or they can express their concerns to authorities within an organization in the hope of changing or shaping what they dislike about it. Whereas many may possess the exit option (although not all equally), market governed organizations may have less clearly articulated ways for participants to exercise voice compared to political organizations. As a result, the opportunity to exercise voice may be less available in market organizations than it is in political organizations. Both exit and voice have costs and benefits. The costs of exit include its zero-sum nature; you're either in or out. This means that you may wait a long time to leave and suffer some damage in the meanwhile. For organizations, exit has the cost that organizations may be short-lived. In the absence of means for self-correcting, they may fail. In the case of business firms producing a product that is readily available from another firm, this is not serious for consumers. However, what does a family do if their child's school suddenly closes in the middle of the term and there are no alternatives available or open? The most serious cost of the exit option is that its presence "can therefore tend to atrophy the development of the art of voice" (Hirschman, p. 43). This means that people stop trying to influence or improve educational practices and simply opt out of the public system. Some of the costs of voice include open dissent and conflict, time, and a multiplicity of competing goals.

Hirschman (1970) concluded that although both exit and voice provide useful forms of reaction and feedback, it is extremely difficult to maintain an optimal mix of the two. Thus, he suggested that

> organizations that rely primarily on one of the two reaction mechanisms need an occasional injection of the other. Other organizations may have to go through regular cycles in which exit and voice alternate as principal actors. Finally, an awareness of the inborn tendencies toward instability of any optimal mix may be helpful in improving the design of institutions that need both exit and voice to be maintained in good health. (p. 126).

Thus, Hirschman suggested that both exit and voice may contribute something to the viability of organizations.

The acknowledgment of the value of both forms of reaction is consistent with the view among at least some economists that there are many situations where pure markets are not the optimal form. Relatively pure markets may work in situations where economic efficiency is appropriate as a sole objective. Perhaps the supermarket (although even there health and safety standards are relevant, as well as labeling standards) is such a situation. Many arenas where goods and services are exchanged have clear social objectives as well as purely economic ones. For example, health care and education both have social goals as well as efficiency goals. If health care were allowed to operate as a pure market, efficiency-driven, for-profit firms would avoid sick people like the plague and would only offer health care services to generally healthy groups of people. They would also choose not to invest in public health measures, like vaccinations, that have no immediate positive impact on their bottom line. Clearly the system of health care needs to have other goals besides maximizing the profits of private vendors. Two economists, Richard Lipsey and Kelvin Lancaster (1956), recognized this in what they called "The General Theory of the Second Best." They suggested that

> when a particular market departs significantly from a pure market and yields an outcome that is not "optimal" in market terms, attempts to make it more marketlike in some, but not all, respects will have indeterminate results for economic efficiency—and sometimes perverse ones. (cited in Kuttner, 1997, p. 19).

Kuttner (1997) continued:

> The Second Best theorem suggests that when there are multiple "distortions" in the price and sup-
> ply disciplines of a given market, the removal of one distortion in the attempt to create a purer
> market will not necessarily improve the overall outcome. A second-best market typically has sec-
> ond-best forms of accountability—professional norms, government supervision, regulation, and
> subsidy—to which market forces have adapted. For example, if the health-care system is already a
> far cry from a free market on both the demand side and the supply side, removing one regulation,
> and thereby making the health system more superficially marketlike, may simply increase oppor-
> tunism and inefficiency. (p. 14)

In Kuttner's view, the "second-best" market outcome may be the best for many economic
realms. In health care, for example, efforts to achieve a pure free market may "lead to third-
best outcomes" (p. 19). Of course, second-best here is in terms of economists' values. In terms
of society's values and goals, alternate systems of control may be far preferable to economic
ones. What is noteworthy in this discourse is the way the market metric sets the standard
against which institutional arrangements are measured. This is an indication of the extent to
which market ideology has permeated our discussion of public policy and issues, including
education. Clearly education, like health care, has social goals as well as efficiency goals. In
the quest to privatize and marketize education, social values and goals may be ignored. One of
the potential casualties of such an oversight is the erosion of legitimate educational authority.
Goldstone (1998) noted a similar threat to the authority structure of prisons if they are run on
a for-profit basis.

Systems of values and control may operate at the level of school systems and within
individual schools. The conduct of activities requires delegation of the means of control to
authorities deemed legitimate and presumed to be appropriate. At both of these levels, different configurations of values and control may operate within education, including the following: home-based values, market principles, political authority, administrative values, professional values, and ideas.* These clusters may articulate different values, exercise control through
different means, and locate authority in different sources. For each it is worth considering
their predominant values and the rationale for them, the ways they exercise control, potential
pitfalls in their operation, and dilemmas or contradictions within them. The first option/deci-
sion families face is whether or not to participate in some form of organized educational
system. Legally in the United States families lack the option of not educating their children.
This issue of public policy reflects the general consensus that education is a social good as
well as an individual good.

Home-Based Values and Control

The growth of home-based schooling since the 1960s represents a rejection of both political
and market control of education and an assertion of the primacy of the family for education
and socialization. It also represents a negation of professional authority (at least to a considerable extent) and of administrative authority (to the extent possible within state laws). State
laws regarding home instruction take three forms. The first accepts home instruction only if
the home can qualify as a private school. The second implicitly allows home instruction through
such language as "equivalent education elsewhere." The third specifically provides for home
instruction (Richardson & Zirkel, 1991). States vary widely with respect to required procedures for approving home instruction programs, degrees of curricular conformity, the exist-

---

*Weiss (1990) identified five of these types of control, to which I add home-based values and control.

ence of state achievement tests, and mandated teacher characteristics.* Home schooling may save a state and/or a locality money. Some families decide to do this because they dislike what they see as the lack of values, standards, or discipline in public schools, some because they wish to teach more overt religious values to their children, and some because they see schools as cramping the intellectual growth, individuality, and creativity of their children (See Gladin, 1987; Gustafson, 1988; Wartes, 1988). Because the families using home schooling are disproportionately White (Lines, 1991), some critics suggest they may also do it to avoid racial integration. Estimates of the number of children receiving home schooling in 1988 ranged from 150,000 to 300,000 children (Lines 1991). Institutional supports for parents conducting home schooling include national home schooling associations, correspondence courses, curricula provided by some public and private schools, and local or state education authorities.

Although there may be some guidance or framework required by the state, such as curricular guides or achievement tests, the relatively homogeneous views of a few people (most likely a child's relatives) may govern the educational process. Neither states nor markets exercise control over daily educational activities. Thus control rests to a very large extent with parents and/or with other family members. To the degree that parents control the process, they have direct accountability to themselves but much less to state authorities who are infrequently involved. Even in formal schools, educational practices and behavior are rarely observed. In home-based schooling, such practices are even less observable. The result is that accountability, like control, rests with the family.

Some pitfalls may reside in the conjoining of family and educational authority. If children are resistant to parental authority in the family, that resistance may infuse their educational relationship as well. There is no countervailing power to which children might appeal. When schools are separate from families, children have at least the potential of appealing to their parents for support in the face of what is seen as an unjust exercise of authority by a school or a school official. (Of course, parental willingness to do this varies widely.) Similarly, in some cases schools may serve as lifelines for children facing abuses of parental authority.

Other pitfalls may arise from the social conditions of education. For example, some argue that schooling involves more than cognitive learning, and that the social aspects of schooling are important features of the educational experience—learning to give and take, learning to deal with other forms of authority besides that of one particular family, and learning to deal with ideas that differ from their own and those of their family, and learning to get along with others and to work in groups. Some of this social learning may be less likely to occur in home-schooling experiences. Many parents conducting home schooling consciously involve their children in various group experiences, whether they be athletic teams, 4-H, scouting, religious activities, or other group enterprises.

To some degree home schooling minimizes the public purposes of education and may formulate education more as a private good. Home schooling epitomizes the exit option for expressing dissatisfaction with existing institutions. As such, it pulls parents out of public debates over educational issues and reduces their support for public education. This dilemma arises with private schooling as well. Another potential dilemma is whether parents should be paid by the state for educating their children at home. If they were, would that increase the state's authority and weaken parental control? This dilemma is similar to one that private schools would face if they were to accept significant public monies.

---

*Michigan and Iowa, for example, require parents conducting home schooling to be certified teachers. However, Lines (1991) noted that few are.

Home schooling raises several sociological questions. Is the phenomena more prevalent in areas with fewer educational alternatives in either the public or the private sectors? Is it more likely among college-educated parents? Would other parents feel qualified to provide it? Would they be allowed to do so by the states? At least 17 states specify some form of educational requirement or certification for home school instructors (Richardson & Zirkel, 1991).

Market Principles and Controls

Schools organized around market principles are thought to exhibit greater effectiveness, greater efficiency, lower costs, greater competition, and enhanced parental freedom to choose. Market theory suggests that schools that do not succeed will be eliminated, and in an open market, schools will be more responsive to their clientele. In market-grounded organizations, greater control is exercised by those with more economic resources and options. This includes some parents and prospective parents, students and former students, and teachers and prospective teachers. If the state supplies any economic resources, some control may also reside with legislators at state and local levels who regulate the flow of funding into schools.

In market systems, patterns of social behavior are determined by the interaction of many autonomous parties who exchange resources in pursuit of their self-interest, which determines the flow of resources into schools or within schools to various teachers. These exchanges are not deliberately designed to influence behavior (Weiss, 1990, p. 110). Thus, markets represent an extreme version of a loosely coupled system (Weick, 1976). Because the opportunity to exercise voice may be less available in market organizations than it is in political organizations, the mechanisms for exercising voice are frequently unclear and accountability tends to occur, in the final analysis, through participants' decisions to stay or to leave. Such an option assumes full knowledge and capacity to judge the relative merits of various educational offerings, an open market with many choices open to all, and frequent and easy transactions within that market.

Schools governed by market principles may be too responsive to certain clientele such as those who pay full freight or who donate a lot. (For an example, see George Orwell's discussion of Crossgates, in Walzer, 1983, pp. 211 and 332). They may also become overly focused on measurable outcomes such as test scores or college admissions and less focused on more intangible consequences, such as higher order mental processes, tolerance, democratic participation, and civic values. Limited resources may be devoted to activities that support unmeasurable goals, such as extracurricular activities and functions, even though they seem to be related to staying in school and to the development of civic values (Persell & Wenglinsky, 1999).

When market values predominate, education may be conceptualized as more of a private good rather than a public good. In fact, education has elements of being both a public and a private good (see Levin, 1987). The wealthy are advantaged in markets compared to the poor, and as Weiss (1990) noted, markets tend to amplify rather than to equalize initial inequalities in the distribution of resources (p. 115). Heavy reliance on market principles may subvert teaching and learning. Some observers have suggested that when market principles become more operative within higher education, for example, when schools or departments compete fiercely for students, grade inflation escalates. In for-profit postsecondary proprietary schools, virtually everyone receives A grades, regardless of their performance (Persell & Wenglinsky, 1993).

Market values rest on the assumption of rational behavior by all the actors involved.

Within the parameters of this assumption, competition is assumed to work to keep an organization responsive and effective. However, markets are sensitive to networks of personal relationships that distort efficiency criteria (noted by Granovetter and cited in Weiss, 1990, p. 113), suggesting that the assumption of total rationality is not always realized. In decentralized markets with multiple buyers and sellers in frequent interaction, better services at lower prices may be likely (Weiss, 1990, p. 126). However, in the absence of such a situation, it is hard for buyers to make informed decisions, and it is hard for them to evaluate quality (Weiss, p. 114). Education is not something like milk that people buy regularly and whose quality can be immediately assessed.

Market controls may produce several contradictions. For example, some advocates of market control argue for government subsidies of private schools, which ironically would reduce their potentially greater sensitivity to their clientele. Thus, proposals for greater public subsidies of private education in the United States might lead to greater regulation by public authorities, as noted by James and Levin (1988, p. 7). Similarly, although the value of tolerance is supported by providing choice, the creation of relatively more homogeneous schools because of choice may make it harder to teach tolerance in the schools (Anderson, 1994, pp. 4829).

Political Authority and Control

Because children represent the future of a society, government has a long-standing interest in education. Government seeks to provide equal opportunities for all children, regardless of their family backgrounds, and aims to help diverse members of a society learn a common language, culture, and history to strengthen their identification with a national society. At the same time, government should have an interest in developing tolerance for diverse groups in society and for instilling civic-mindedness. As Dewey noted, democratic societies rely on schools that will provide an education, making it possible to change those societies in a democratic fashion (cited in Levin, 1990, p. 251). Schools may help young people learn the principles and practices of participatory democracy and of self-governance.

Within systems based on political principles, mechanisms for expressing voice exist. They may be complex, highly bureaucratic, perhaps even Byzantine, but they exist, and they are based on the assumption of equality: one person gets one vote. There is competition among many elected authorities who may proffer numerous competing goals, at least in the United States, and the mechanisms for exercising control on a daily basis may be weak. Mechanisms for the exit option are less clear in systems where political values and control predominate. If education is required by state laws (and it is mandated through at least some of the teen years in virtually every U.S. state) and if families have no options within the state system, then the opportunities for exit are limited to private schools or to home schooling. The growth of school choice programs within the public sector increases exit options from particular schools.

In politically grounded systems, accountability is exercised through the electoral process. This assumes broad levels of participation (which seldom occurs in school board elections), evenly distributed across all segments of the population. Accountability to the community is widely regarded as desirable (Chubb & Moe, 1990; Tyack, 1974), if cumbersome (Cohen, 1982). The front line of political control operates through elected local boards, but other elected officials (federal, state, or local) and their designates (such as federal or state education agencies) also obtain control by virtue of their mandate from the voters, as Weiss noted (1990, p. 105).

Political control contains several potential pitfalls. Control resides outside the schools, in people who do not teach children. It is also likely that schools will be held responsible for multiple, perhaps contradictory, goals. There are potential problems associated with getting school staff to comply with the directives of elected officials. Political actors and educators face different incentives, with educators usually supporting professional values and norms (see the text that follows). Legal reasoning and potential or actual litigation may shape responses in other directions, thus creating educational problems.

Political control faces the risk of being captured by groups pursuing narrow interests; for example, those pursuing fundamentalist or creationist agendas, teachers' unions, or book publishers. Some constituents (e.g., organized groups and/or members of the middle class) have greater political clout than more diffuse clienteles (Weiss, 1990, p. 108). Generally voter turnout in school elections is low, candidates do not have party affiliations and therefore their political positions are unclear to many voters (Weiss, p. 109). This may result in special interests being much more likely to vote in such elections. Given the low levels of participation in school elections, and questions about how representative the political process is, confidence in its legitimacy and in its accountability may be low. Political control may also contain the potential for political patronage in hiring, in promotion, and in assignment decisions, which undermines merit criteria in staffing schools, suggested Weiss (p. 109). Assuming that merit criteria are more efficient, political patronage risks lower educational effectiveness and legitimacy.

Political control poses several dilemmas. Multiple jurisdictions may contribute to highly fragmented and competing authority systems operating within education, with the result that there is no agreement on goals or on priorities. Thus one dilemma is how to balance multiple competing goals while maintaining effectiveness and efficiency in their pursuit. Another dilemma is how to give school administrators at least some control over personnel matters while avoiding patronage.

Administrative Values and Control

The rationale for administrative values rests on the way all organizations need some predictability and coordination in order to function, some accountability with respect to their predominant values, and need to use finite resources carefully and effectively. Administrative control tends to be exercised through rational–legal or through bureaucratic authority, through the management of employees, and through the internal allocation of resources. Control is exercised by individual administrators, by organizational arrangements (for example, budgets allocating resources, incentives, rules, and procedures), and by interorganizational networks (involving relations with other organizations in the environment, often resource-supplying organizations or membership in an institutional sector that provides support and legitimacy while requiring some conformity to institutional practices) as Weiss noted (1990, pp. 97–102).

Within an administrative system, efforts to achieve accountability include observing whether rules and procedures are being followed, sometimes by specifying input and output controls, and sometimes by efforts to standardize teaching practices (see Rowan, 1990, pp. 359–368). Many of the most important activities within schools are difficult to observe directly, however. Furthermore, there are persistent tensions between administrative control and professional values. By stressing predictability and order, administrative control reduces the flexibility and discretion that professionals need to do their work, noted Weiss (1990, p. 103).

If the rational–legal and bureaucratic models of organization prevail, that may dampen the development of a school community, suggested Talbert (1988, p. 184). Religious private schools tend to be based on traditional authority, whereas nonreligious private schools are organized around the authority of specialized goals (Talbert, p. 173). Relative uniformity between goals and forms of control promote program and social system integration, suggested Talbert (p. 184). This integration may be more difficult in systems where administrative values predominate.

When administrative values predominate, learning may diminish. McNeil (1986), argued that "when the school's organization becomes centered on managing and controlling, teachers and students take school less seriously" (cited in Weiss, 1990, p. 103). In McNeil's study of four high schools, Weiss (1990) noted, "administrators who focused on minimum standards and social order achieved minimum standards and social order, but little learning or thinking" (p. 103). Administrative values appear to represent one means toward achieving an end, but they themselves cannot be an end goal. Undue stress on administrative control may undermine institutional legitimacy.

Professional Values and Control

The work of teachers is not standardized because students are highly variable. Therefore, teaching requires the application of professional judgment, developed through specialized education and experience. Professionals seek autonomy from political, market, and even administrative requirements so they may perform their work with discretion in the best long-term interest of their clients. As Weiss (1990) noted, "Like other professionals, teachers defer to one another's professional judgment and prefer not to interfere (with) or evaluate one another's work" (p. 94). Teachers expect professional standards to govern key aspects of their work, including daily instructional practices, student evaluation, and maintaining order, and they resist supervision or control by nonprofessionals (Weiss, p. 94). Teachers know more about how to teach reading, writing, or arithmetic, for example, than do state legislators or marketing consultants. Teachers are part of a large profession that transcends any particular school, district, or state, and that offers new ideas and teaching models (Weiss, p. 95). When teachers are tenured, that increases their autonomy in relation to other forms of control.

Professional values and control assume that accountability can be maintained through the existence of professional associations and standards, through professional training and/or certification, through accreditation visits, and to some degree through professional peers who may question or challenge actions they consider unprofessional. There is evidence, however, that members of professions are reluctant to police their members (Freidson, 1987), one dilemma that professional values must address. A second dilemma in education is how to preserve a reasonable degree of professional autonomy while preventing that autonomy from being subverted for personal ends. Yet another dilemma is how to balance professional judgments with client concerns, cost factors, and administrative considerations.

Professional training teaches teachers what they should do and how they should do it. Hence, they are suspicious of administrative efforts to reduce costs or to improve productivity. They may resist other changes as well (Weiss, 1990, p. 96). Professional autonomy can lead to failure as well as to success and to few chances for constructive feedback or for professional development. Efforts to control the supply and training of teachers through restrictive credentialing requirements may limit the number of able and motivated teachers (Weiss, p. 96).

Ideas and Control

Education is not (hopefully) a mindless activity. How people think about their work may affect their behavior and their commitment. Idea-driven educational systems may include ones based on traditional authority as well as ones rooted in charismatic authority. In schools where traditional values predominate, for example, heavy emphasis is placed on transmitting religious or cultural values and identity and on doing things the way they have always been done. Traditional values may be manifest in a strong head of school, who may be a priest, a monk, or a nun. The head obtains additional authority from a (usually) hierarchical religious, military, or other traditional body (see, for example, Hays, 1994).

Values may influence daily practices and pedagogy, curricular design, and evaluation. Although akin to professional control, the control exercised through values and ideas can affect all the participants in a situation, not just the professionals. As Weiss (1990) noted, "social values, good and bad, control the organization of schooling" and they also "constrain schools from venturing outside the mainstream conventional wisdom" (p. 115). In a tradition-centered school, control rests heavily in the office of the leader, supported by a board of trustees. If it is a religious institution, the board may be heavily composed of members (and perhaps even leaders) of the religious denomination. Education is thought to be about values and character at least as much as about academic achievement, and therefore the character and behavior of all participants—school head, teachers, and students—is closely monitored and disciplined.

Schools governed by charismatic authority and control, such as some alternative schools, may value authentic personal relationships and personal trust above all else. When authenticity is the predominant value, control (or more likely influence) is based on personal bonds, on allegiance, or on charisma. Such bonds may be developed by sharing inner thoughts and feelings. The exercise of authority depends on the emotional attachments of students to teachers and on those of teachers to leaders. The primary means of exercising authority (or influence) is through the withholding of love, friendship, or social interaction, because there are few institutionalized supports for authority, such as formal sanctions.

There is not always a direct link between a particular set of values and the mechanisms of control. Entry is one means of control, but it can play only a very limited role in systems that are open to all. Expulsion is another means of control, which is also limited in open systems. If the predominant values in a school are not to the participants' liking, those with options may try to construct an alternative, organized around different values. Thus, Lines (1988) argued that the progressive secularization of public schools has influenced the growth of private schools that focus on particular religious or philosophical values.

In an idea-driven system, accountability is exercised through superiors' or through peers' assessments of whether a participant's statements and behaviors are consistent with a particular set of values or ideas. For example, in a school valuing tradition, accountability occurs through the judgment of selected members of the tradition who decide whether the tradition is being properly upheld. The exercise of voice tends to be limited to designated authorities, and exit is an option for participants with alternatives.

Idea-driven schools face a number of pitfalls. Thought control has dangerous potential and is difficult to conduct, there are limited sanctions for encouraging conformity, uniformity may be difficult to obtain, conflicting ideas may be operating, and ideas can lag changes in conditions, noted Weiss (1990, p. 118). Traditional or charismatic values may clash with political, economic, market, and professional values. Without mechanisms for participation by those with competing values and with opportunities for compromise, organizations may become increasingly rigid and unchanging. Thus, it may be difficult for traditional institutions to adapt to change. One result might be relatively homogeneous communities that fail to prepare young people for a heterogeneous world. Depending on how uniform and hierarchical a traditional system is, there may be varying opinions about what the tradition is and how to interpret it. For example, there might be generational differences within a community. There may be few mechanisms for those with alternate interpretations to exercise voice. Their only recourse in the face of differences may be exit. If many dissenting voices leave, that further reduces the chances for change or for adaptation. Moreover, with exit as participants' primary mechanism for expressing dissent, there may be greater risk of organizational failure and death.

In schools based on charismatic authority, teachers with the highest level of commitment and success may tend to "burn out" and withdraw from teaching because they lack the support of formal authority (Swidler, 1979). Because students and teachers in such schools are about equal but students outnumber teachers, there is the possibility that students may have more authority and control than teachers, a condition that might affect learning goals and teacher satisfaction. The process of extensive discussion and/or negotiation is often extremely time consuming, as Rothschild-Witt (1979) found in the democratic–collectivist organizations, including free schools, that she studied. Thus, the process may divert effort from more traditional educational endeavors.

DO SECTORAL DIFFERENCES EXPLAIN DIFFERENT OUTCOMES?

Efforts to link sector, values and control, educational practices, and outcomes face a number of problems. First, there is an absence of pure cases. Although it may be possible to characterize a school with respect to its predominant values and control, no school is unidimensional, that is, no school perfectly displays only one type of values and control. Although the private sector may achieve greater clarity of vision and purpose compared to the public sector, because political control may be more muted and there are fewer competing goals and authorities, competition over goals and purposes remains. In elite private schools, for example, ambitious parents may be most concerned about where their child gets into college, whereas school officials may be more concerned about the child's character and intellectual development. These goals are not necessarily perfectly compatible.

Second, much of the writing about sector, different forms of values and control, and their possible consequences takes an advocacy position rather than an analytical stance. For example, Chubb and Moe (1990) and Salganik and Karweit (1982) discussed the disadvantages of political and/or administrative authority but failed to consider its strengths. Similarly, they considered the advantages of market-based values and controls without considering their potential pitfalls. Finally, theoretical discussions of differences in operative values and controls by sector often fail to distinguish between ideal types of values and control and the reality of those values and control in practice.

An important article by Bidwell, Frank, and Quiroz (1997) specifically aimed to relate modes of control to teacher styles. They identify four modes of control and four modal teacher types (Figure 17.1). Their four modal types are congruent with the values and control of ideas, administration, markets, and professionalism defined previously. Furthermore, they show that these modal types are generated by the organizational conditions of school size and degree of client power. In this chapter, I suggest that these two social conditions, plus a school's sources of revenue, are more important for educational practices (such as curriculum, tracking, and teaching styles) and for outcomes than is sector.

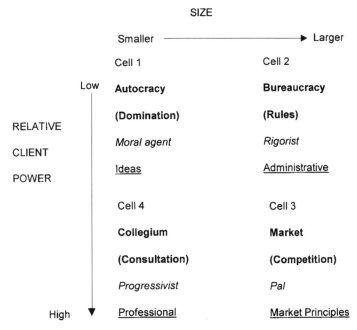

FIGURE 17.1. School size, relative client power, workplace control, and dominant values. The mode of control (in bold face) and the modal teacher type (in italics) are from Bidwell et al., 1997, p. 288. The dominant values (underlined) have been added.

One of the key differences between public and private schools in the United States is the source of their revenues, with public schools being supported heavily by local taxes, then by state taxes, and to a much lesser extent by federal taxes. A few public schools also have small endowments and/or receive foundation and other grants. Private schools obtain their revenue from tuition, from endowment, from bonds (for capital expenses), and possibly from corporate or foundation grants and/or from a religious authority such as a church parish or diocese.

Both public and private schools can be found in all four locations of the attribute space that Bidwell and associates (1997) articulated. For example, in Cell 1 of Figure 17.1, one could find small, economically marginal, private religious schools as well as small rural public schools in conservative communities. In Cell 2, one could find large, urban public schools, but also large, private boarding schools where client power is reduced somewhat because the parents are remote. In Cell 3, when market considerations are significant, private schools may take more students either than they have room for or than they want (whether for behavioral or disciplinary reasons). Within public schools, market competition for parental and for student support may create situations described by Sizer in *Horace's Compromise* (1984) where teachers and students make an informal pact, with the teacher tacitly agreeing not to make too many demands and the students agreeing to be orderly. Similarly, *The Shopping Mall High School* (Powell, Farrar, & Cohen, 1985) suggested that an open curricular marketplace for students facilitates their taking less demanding programs and fewer rigorous courses. In Cell 4 one could find small, so-called alternative public schools organized around a particular educational philosophy as well as small private schools centered on a particular educational approach.

Sector is related to the three key variables of school size, client power, and sources of revenue (Figure 17.2). Most private schools are smaller than public schools. The average

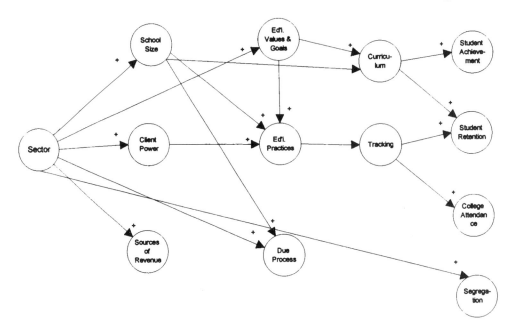

FIGURE 17.2. Proposed model of sector, key variables, manifestations of values and control, and educational outcomes.

enrollment in public elementary schools in the United States is 476, and less than 1% of schools enroll 1500 or more students. Almost 60% enroll fewer than 500 students. The average public secondary school enrolls 703, but one third enroll 1500 or more students, with 3% containing more than 3,000 students (U.S. Department of Education, 1997, Table 95). The average secondary prep school enrollment in 1987 to 1988 was 298 (Powell, 1996, p. 207). Many experienced school administrators have told me that once a school exceeds 500 students, it is no longer possible for them to know all the students in it by name. More face-to-face and personal control is possible in a school when teachers and administrators know the students by name.

Sector is variably related to client power. Catholic schools represent 70% of private school enrollment, and the parent bodies are similar to public school parents with respect to educational level, occupation, and income (Persell et al., 1992). In most other private schools where tuition is higher, client power is greater. Students attending all kinds of private schools, and especially those attending college preparatory schools, are considerably more likely to be White, are more likely to have two parents, are less likely to have mothers who work full-time, are more likely to have much higher levels of parental education, and are more likely to have considerably higher levels of income (Coleman & Hoffer, 1987, p. 30; Persell et al., 1992, pp. 4–5). Clearly student background and client power varies within sectors. In some affluent suburban communities, for example, client power may be high in the public sector.

Sector is definitely related to sources of revenue in the United States. Source of revenue is also undoubtedly related to client power. Accountability tends to focus toward revenue source. A question to ask of both public and private schools is whether revenue is importantly tied to per capita enrollment. Another question is, does the school have other potential enrollees if they lose the ones they have?

I am unable to find evidence that sector affects educational values, practices, and outcomes independently of these three key variables. Moreover, several kinds of evidence and argument support the conclusion that sector is insignificant once these three variables are taken into consideration. First, as Hoffer, Greeley, and Coleman (1987) noted, "those public schools which make the same demands as found in the average Catholic school produce comparable achievement" (p. 87). Second, although the primary focus of the Bidwell and associates (1997) paper was not the effect of sector, they do perform one analysis showing that sector (Catholic vs. public) is not significantly related to one modal teacher type, namely rigor, when school size and client power are controlled. Even Chubb and Moe (1990) acknowledged that it is possible for public schools to develop "effective," that is, nonbureaucratic, school organizations when there is social homogeneity in a community leading to broad agreement on educational policy and when there is an absence of serious problems in the school (pp. 62–63). Thus, sector is not a necessary condition for achieving nonbureaucratic schools.

Finally, we can conduct a thought experiment to ascertain the plausibility of our proposed model. Suppose that private schools received public monies. This would affect their sources of revenue and weaken client power. Private schools might even become bigger in the face of increasing demand. Is it plausible that they wouldn't become more bureaucratic under such circumstances? They might also have to temper their religious values, or at least become more diverse.

In short, school size, client power, and revenue sources affect the organizing values and ways of running schools, which in turn are related to such educational practices as teaching styles, curriculum and tracking, and extracurricular activities. These educational practices affect educational outcomes such as achievement, graduation, and college attendance. Thus it becomes plausible that other explanations lie behind observed differences by sector.

OTHER EXPLANATIONS

Although Bidwell and associates (1997) showed that school size and client power are related to modal teacher styles, they do not relate these teacher styles to students' achievement or to other outcomes. My view is that effective learning can occur with a variety of teaching styles. Teacher commitment does appear to vary by sector, but the correlation may be spurious. Only about one fourth of school principals in public high schools say they have no problem with teacher lack of commitment or absenteeism, compared to 50% to 60% of Catholic high school principles, and 70% to 90% of private high performance high school heads (Persell et al., 1992, p. 9). There is reason to believe that such indicators of commitment are related to teacher fatigue, to students' effort, and to the level of administrative support (McNeil, 1986, p. 176), which may be related to school size. Although I am willing to assume that teacher commitment is related to students' achievement, I don't know of research that shows this.

Curriculum and tracking vary by school sector and are related to students' achievement and dropout rates (Gamoran & Mare, 1989; Oakes, 1985; Persell, 1977). In various types of private schools, 70% or more of high school students are enrolled in academic curricula, whereas in public school only about 36% are, with another third in a general curriculum, and slightly less than one third in some kind of vocational program (Coleman & Hoffer, 1987, p. 43). Half or more of the students in various kinds of private high schools are enrolled in specialized academic programs, compared to only 3.3% of public high school students (Coleman & Hoffer, p. 44). The vast majority (77%) of public high school students are enrolled in comprehensive school programs (Coleman & Hoffer, p. 44). Compared to public high school students, Catholic high school students take more mathematics, English, and foreign language courses even when the family and academic backgrounds of students are held constant (Coleman & Hoffer, p. 49). Students in other private high schools take only more English and foreign language courses than public high school students, once controls for background are introduced (Coleman & Hoffer, p. 49). In short, students' background explains little of the differences in coursework in Catholic high schools, but quite a bit in other private schools (Coleman & Hoffer, p. 50).

Regarding ability grouping, Catholic and public high schools are about equally likely to use it (nearly two thirds in both sectors), whereas only 43% in other private and 10% in "high performance" private schools use ability grouping (Coleman & Hoffer, 1987, p. 45). The degree of tracking is strongly related to school size and also to the diversity of the student body and the curriculum. Lee and Bryk (1988, 1989) suggested that Catholic school achievement advantages were largely explained by differences in their academic organizations and their normative environments (Marks & Lee, 1994). Similarly, Gamoran (1992) suggested that differences in the structure of tracking in Catholic schools compared to public schools explains part of their lower inequality and higher productivity in mathematics achievement (p. 824). Tracking as a practice is strongly related to school size and to the ethnic and socioeconomic diversity of the student bodies within schools (Persell, 1977).

Students in public and Catholic high schools are about equally likely to participate in various extracurricular activities, whereas students in other private and high performance private high schools have higher participation rates (Coleman & Hoffer, 1987, p. 52). The differences appear to be due more to client power and school size than to sector *per se*. For average academic achievers especially, outside activities provide an important alternate source of achievement and self-esteem (Murtaugh, 1988). This may be why extracurricular activities have been found by other researchers, such as McNeal (1995), to be related to school retention, an important educational outcome.

There is more student-centered discussions, more writing, more individualized instruction, and more time spent on homework weekly in high performance private high schools, somewhat more writing, and more hours spent on homework in Catholic schools compared to public schools (Persell et al., 1992, p. 13), but to some degree educational demands are influenced by class size. Time spent writing and doing homework is correlated with students' achievement. The presence of such educational demands appears to depend on parental support for them (or at least on noninterference by the parents), on administrative support for teachers making such demands, and on commitment by teachers to high professional learning standards. Thus, high educational expectations would appear to depend on the insulation of teachers from undue market, political, and administrative pressures. These conditions are more likely in smaller schools with high client power, assuming that the clients support such demands. They may also be more likely in schools with value homogeneity and with relatively less diversity. Thus, they might be more possible in schools with private rather than public sources of revenue. Public schools must educate all the students in their district, whether handicapped, bilingual, gifted, or disadvantaged, and those from many different religious and political backgrounds (James & Levin, 1988, p. 8). Private schools, however, may choose to focus on a more homogeneous subset of students.

Not only family background, but parental behavior differs by sector. "Parents of private school students are more likely to attend parent–teacher conferences, PTA meetings, and to do volunteer work for the schools. In contrast, public and private school parents are about equally likely to phone the school when their children have problems and to visit classes." (Coleman & Hoffer, 1987, p. 53). Public school officials are less likely than private school officials to feel that parents are interested in their children's education and are more likely to have hostile confrontations with parents (Coleman & Hoffer, p. 54). Constructive parental involvement is positively related to achievement and to other outcomes. Parental involvement that schools perceive as constructive is highly related to client power (Lareau, 1987).

Organizational complexity and linkages also vary by sector but may be explained by other organizational characteristics. James and Levin (1988) noted that Scott and Meyer found

> that the environment of public schools is more complexly organized but also more fragmented than is the environment of private schools . . . [and] that the governance of public education is more elaborate, largely because it is more interconnected with external influences above the level of the individual school, than is the governance of private education. The result is both more complexity in administration and less coherence in programs among public schools (James & Levin, 1988, p. 12).

Relatively less program coherence may be negatively related to school achievement and to other positive outcomes. However, it is hard to believe that complexity is not a direct result of size and of multiple revenue sources.

What other organizations schools are linked with may depend heavily on client power. For example, Persell and Cookson (1985) found that elite private boarding schools had much more closely developed linkages with elite private college admissions offices than did public high schools, a factor that seemed to affect where their graduates attended college.

In sum, a number of educational practices that vary by sector and that seem to be related to school achievement are also related to school size, client power, and/or revenue sources. Therefore, we cannot conclude that sector operates independently of these key organizational factors. Nor can we conclude that markets are good for education whereas political or administrative control is bad. The picture appears to be considerably more complex than such a forced choice captures. Various forms of values and controls exist in both the public and the private sector. They appear to be more strongly influenced by school size, by client power, and/or by revenue sources than by sector. Moreover, there are advantages and disadvantages in all configurations of values and control. Proponents of privatization who see it as a panacea for all of education's ills are as misguided as proponents of public education who refuse to vary school or system size and client power. Those clamoring for public monies to support private education should be aware that changing the revenue sources will very likely reduce client power and increase political and administrative values and control. In short, we need more light and less heat in the analysis of public and private schools. Further research is needed on organizational factors that appear to influence values and control and school effectiveness with respect to achievement, participation, completion, and continuance.

REFERENCES

Alexander, K. L. & Pallas, A. M. (1987). School sector and cognitive performance. In E. H. Haertel, T. James, & H. M. Levin (Eds.), *Comparing public and private schools: Volume 2: School achievement* (pp. 89–111). Philadelphia: Falmer Press.

Anderson, D. S. (1994). Public and private schools: Sociological perspectives. In T. Husen & T. N. Postlethwaite (Eds.), *The international encyclopedia of education, 8* (2nd ed., pp. 4824–4831). Oxford, England: Pergamon Press.

Ascher, C., Fruchter, N., & Berne, R. (1996). *Hard lessons: Public schools and privatization.* New York: The Twentieth Century Fund Press.

Bidwell, C. E., Frank, K. A., & Quiroz, P. A. (1997). Teacher types, workplace controls, and the organization of schools. *Sociology of Education, 70,* 285–307.

Catterall, J. S. (1988). Private school participation and public policy. In T. James & H. M. Levin (Eds.), *Comparing public and private schools: Volume 1: Institutions and organizations* (pp. 46–66). New York: Falmer Press.

Chubb, J. E., & Moe, T. M.. (1990). *Politics, markets, and America's schools*. Washington, DC: Brookings.

Cohen, D. (1982). Policy and organization: The impact of state and federal educational policy on school governance. *Harvard Educational Review, 52*, 474–499.

Coleman, J. S., & Hoffer, T. (1987). *Public and private high schools: The impact of communities*. New York: Basic Books.

Coleman, J. S., Hoffer, T., & Kilgore, S. (1982). *High school achievement: Public and private schools compared*. New York: Basic Books.

Crain, R. L. (1988). Private schools and black–white segregation: Evidence from two big cities. In T. James & H. M. Levin (Eds.), *Comparing public and private schools: Volume 1: Institutions and organizations* (pp. 270-293). New York: Falmer Press.

Darling-Hammond, L., & Kirby, S. N. (1988). Public policy and private choice: The case of Minnesota. In T. James & H. M. Levin (Eds.), *Comparing public and private schools: Volume 1: Institutions and organizations* (pp. 243–269). New York: Falmer Press.

Freidson, E. (1987). *Professional powers*. Chicago: University of Chicago Press.

Gamoran, A. (1992). The variable effects of high school tracking. *American Sociological Review, 57*, 812–828.

Gamoran, A., & Mare, R. D. (1989). Secondary school tracking and educational inequality: Compensation, reinforcement or neutrality? *American Journal of Sociology, 94*, 1146–1183.

Gladin, W. E. (1987). *Home education: Characteristics of its families and schools*.Unpublished doctoral disertation, Bob Jones University, Greenville, South Carolina.

Goldstone, J. (1998, March 27). Prison riots as revolutions: A test of theories of social order. Presentation given in the Power, Politics, and Protest Workshop, Department of Sociology, New York University.

Gustafson, S. K. (1987). A study of home schooling: Parental motivations and goals. *Home School Researcher, 4*, 4–12.

Haertel, E. H., James, T., & Levin, H. M. (1987). Introduction. In E. H. Haertel, T. James, & H. M. Levin (Eds.), *Comparing public and private schools: Volume 2: School achievement* (pp. 1–8). Philadelphia: Falmer Press.

Hays, K. (1994). *Practicing virtues: Moral traditions at Quaker and military boarding schools*. Berkeley, CA: University of California Press.

Hirschman, A. O. (1970). *Exit, voice, and loyalty: Responses to decline in firms, organizations, and states*. Cambridge, MA: Harvard University Press.

Hoffer, T., Greeley, A. M., & Coleman, J. S. (1987). Catholic high school effects on achievement growth. In E. H. Haertel, T. James, & H. M. Levin (Eds.), *Comparing public and private schools: Volume 2: School achievement* (pp. 67-88). Philadelphia: Falmer Press.

James, T. & Levin, H. M. (Eds.), (1988). *Comparing private and public schools: Volume 1: Institutions and organizations*. Philadelphia: Falmer Press.

Kuttner, R. (1997). *Everything for sale: The virtues and limits of markets*. New York: Knopf.

Lancaster, K., & Lipsey, R. G. (1956). The general theory of the second best. *Review of Economic Studies, 24*, 11–32.

Lareau, A. (1987). Social class differences in family–school relationships: The importance of cultural capital. *Sociology of Education, 60*, 73–85.

Lee, V. E., & Bryk, A. S. (1988). Curriculum tracking as mediating the social distribution of high school achievement. *Sociology of Education, 61*, 78–94.

Lee, V. E., & Bryk, A. S. (1989). A multilevel model of the social distribution of high school achievement. *Sociology of Education, 62*, 172–192.

Levin, H. M. (1987). Education as a public and private good. *Journal of Policy Analysis and Management, 6*, 628–641.

Levin, H. M. (1990). The theory of choice applied to education. In W. H. Clune & J. F. Witte (Eds.), *Choice and control in American education, Vol. 1: The theory of choice and control in education* (pp. 247–284). New York: Falmer Press.

Lines, P. (1988). Treatment of religion in public schools and the impact on private education. In T. James & H. M. Levin (Eds.), *Comparing public and private schools: Volume 1: Institutions and organizations* (pp. 67–94). New York: Falmer Press.

Lines, P. (1991). Home instruction: The size and growth of the movement. In J. V. Galen & M. A. Pitman (Eds.), *Home schooling: Political, historical, and pedagogical perspectives* (pp. 9–41). Norwood, NJ: Ablex.

Marks, H. M., & Lee, V. E. (1994). Public vs. private schools: Research controversies. In T. Husen & T. N.

Postlethwaite (Eds.), *The international encyclopedia of education, Volume 8* (2nd ed., pp. 4839–4845). Oxford, England: Pergamon Press.

McNeal, R. B., Jr. (1995). Extracurricular activities and high school dropouts. *Sociology of Education, 68*, 62–80.

McNeil, L. (1986). *Contradictions of control.* New York: Routledge.

Murtaugh, M. (1988). Achievement outside the classroom: The role of nonacademic activities in the lives of high school students. *Anthropology and Education Quarterly, 19*, 382–395.

Oakes, J. (1985). *Keeping track: How schools structure inequality.* New Haven, CT: Yale University Press.

Persell, C. H. (1977). *Education and inequality: The roots and results of stratification in America's schools.* New York: The Free Press.

Persell, C. H., & Cookson, P. W., Jr. (1985). Chartering and bartering: Elite education and social reproduction. *Social Problems, 33*, 114–129.

Persell, C. H., Cookson, P. W., Jr., & Catsambis, S. (1992). Family background, high school type, and college attendance: A conjoint system of cultural capital transmission. *Journal of Research on Adolescence, 2*, 1–23.

Persell, C. H., & Wenglinsky, H. (1993, August). Privatization, market logic, and educational experiences: The case of proprietary schools. Paper presented at the American Sociological Association annual meeting in Los Angeles, California.

Persell, C. H., & Wenglinsky, H. (1999). The civic consequences of attending public and for-profit post-secondary schools. Manuscript in preparation.

Powell, A. G. (1996). *Lessons from privilege: The American prep school tradition.* Cambridge, MA: Harvard University Press.

Powell, A. G., Farrar, E., & Cohen, D. K. (1985). *The shopping mall high school.* Boston: Houghton Mifflin.

Richardson, S. N., & Zirkel, P. A. (1991). Home schooling law. In J. V. Galen & M. A. Pitman (Eds.), *Home schooling: Political, historical, and pedagogical perspectives* (pp.159–210). Norwood, NJ: Ablex.

Rothschild-Witt, J. (1979). The collectivist organization: An alternative to rational–bureaucratic models. *American Sociological Review, 44*, 509–27.

Rowan, B. (1990). Commitment and control: Alternative strategies for the organizational design of schools. In C. B. Cazden (Ed.), *Review of research in education 16* (pp. 353–389). Washington, DC: The American Educational Research Association.

Salganik, L. H., & Karweit, N. (1982). Voluntarism and governance in education. *Sociology of Education, 55*, 152–161.

Sizer, T. R. (1984). *Horace's compromise: The dilemma of the American high school.* Boston: Houghton Mifflin.

Swidler, A. (1979). *Organization without authority: Dilemmas of social control in free schools.* Cambridge, MA: Harvard University Press.

Taeuber, K. E., & James, D. R. (1982). Racial segregation among public and private schools. *Sociology of Education, 55*, 133–143.

Talbert, J. E. (1988). Conditions of public and private school organization and notions of effective schools. In T. James & H. M. Levin (Eds.), *Comparing public and private schools, Volume 1: Institutions and organizations* (pp. 161–189). New York: Falmer Press.

Tyack, D. (1974). *The one best system.* Cambridge, MA: Harvard University Press.

U.S. Department of Education. National Center for Education Statistics. (1997). *Digest of education statistics, 1997,* NCES 98–015, by T. D. Snyder. Production Manager, C. M. Hoffman. Program Analyst, C. M. Geddes. Washington, DC: U.S. Department of Education, Office of Educational Research and Improvement.

Walzer, M. (1983). *Spheres of justice: A defense of pluralism and equality.* New York: Basic Books.

Wartes, J. (1988). The Washington home school project: Quantitative measures for informing policy decisions. *Education and Urban Society, 21*, 42–51.

Weick, K. E. (1976). Educational organizations as loosely coupled systems. *Administrative Science Quarterly, 21*, 1–19.

Weiss, J. A. (1990). Control in school organizations: Theoretical perspectives. In W. H. Clune & J. F. Witte (Eds.), *Choice and control in American education, Volume 1: The theory of choice and control in education* (pp. 91–134). London: Falmer Press.

Willms, J. D. (1987). Patterns of academic achievement in public and private schools: Implications for public policy and future research. In E. H. Haertel, T. James, & H. M. Levin (Eds.), *Comparing public and private schools: Volume 2: School achievement* (pp. 113–134). Philadelphia: Falmer Press.

PART V

THE STUDY OF SCHOOL OUTCOMES

CHAPTER 18

Interactions between High Schools and Labor Markets

JAMES E. ROSENBAUM

STEPHANIE ALTER JONES

INTRODUCTION

Recent high school graduates have great difficulty entering the labor market. Youths have high unemployment, high turnover, and low pay (Borman, 1991; Rosenbaum & Kariya, 1989; Veum & Weiss, 1993), these early problems hurt their careers many years later (D'Amico & Maxwell, 1990; Lynch, 1989), and they persists longer in the United States than in other nations.[*] In addition, young workers' wages have dropped even more than those of adults since the late 1970s (Katz & Murphy, 1992; Levy & Murnane, 1992).

Although youth unemployment, job instability, and low pay are usually blamed on youths' deficiencies or on labor market rigidities, poor networks are a possible explanation. Research indicates that social contacts are important for getting jobs, especially better jobs (Granovetter, 1995), yet low-income and minority youths often lack contacts to people with jobs, especially good jobs (Wilson, 1996). In other nations, youths get jobs through national systems of school job placement, which do not exist in the United States.

Although functionalist theory and some economic theories assume that schools and labor markets are mutually responsive, these theories are vague about specific mechanisms that

---

[*]Among males aged 35 to 39, the percentage of workers with short job tenure (less than 5 years) is 40% in the United States, but it is only 28% in Germany, 24% in the Netherlands, 22% in France, and 17% in Japan (Organization for Economic Cooperation & Development, 1993, Tables 4.3 and 4.4).

JAMES E. ROSENBAUM AND STEPHANIE ALTER JONES • Institute for Policy Research, Northwestern University, Evanston, Illinois 60208

Handbook of the Sociology of Education, edited by Maureen T. Hallinan. Kluwer Academic/Plenum Publishers, New York, 2000.

make them responsive. In contrast, network theory contends that labor markets require social relationships to convey needed information. Without good information, labor markets cannot operate effectively. Specifically, poor information prevents students from having appropriate plans and preparation, prevents employers from using available information, and prevents school staff from having incentives to help employers.

This chapter examines the interactions between high schools and labor markets and the information problems that hinder these interactions. The chapter begins with studies of Japan and Germany that illustrate how school–employer interaction works in nations with formal systems. In contrast, American procedures lack clarity and have some puzzling features. We examine three puzzles: Why are most work-bound students unidentified in high school? Why don't employers use school information for hiring? and How do schools help students get jobs? Although schools lack formal job placement procedures, we find that some teachers create informal relationships with employers to provide the kinds of information employers need. These informal linkages operate somewhat similarly to the formal systems in Japan and in Germany. Finally, we examine what kinds of students get jobs from school placement—are these students who might otherwise have difficulty getting jobs?

These theoretical issues have practical implications. In other nations, school contacts help youths to get good jobs and to have incentives for school effort. In the United States, we find that some teachers act as informal intermediaries for conveying information between students and employers, and, as a result, some employers hire applicants whom they might not have hired otherwise, including females, minorities, and youths with other disadvantages. These previously unnoticed linkage activities have theoretical implications for understanding schools' potential for creating social charters and increasing the social capital available to work-bound youths, and they have policy implications for creating dependable career pathways for disadvantaged youths.

THE FUNCTIONALIST MODEL

According to the functionalist model, school "functions to allocate human resources within the role-structure of the adult society" (Parsons, 1959, p. 130). Although noting the influence of social background, Parsons contended that in recent decades

> Selection . . . [largely] takes place on a single main axis of achievement . . . "earned" by differential performance of the tasks set by the teacher, who is acting as an agent of the community . . . There is a relatively systematic process of evaluation of the pupils' performances . . . in the form of report card marks [which function both to provide incentives to students, and to enable the] school system [to act] as an allocating agency . . . for future status in society. (p. 135)

Grades are based on skill attainments and on "moral" qualities, like "deportment, . . . responsible citizenship, . . . work-habits, . . . leadership, and initiative" (p. 137). Consequently, this educational process is highly beneficial to the operation of the economy: it provides incentives for all students to gain appropriate skills and work habits, and it provides a selective mechanism for assigning youths to appropriate roles in society.

In economics, the functionalist view is reflected in human capital theory, which contends that schools respond to labor market needs by developing students' productive capabilities (human capital). Ironically, functionalism is even advocated by Marxist writers Bowles and Gintis (1976), who contended that schools serve employers' needs. Again, economic functionalism portrays a smooth interface between schools and the economy in which youths' school programs, credentials, and grades predict economic profits.

The functionalist view also supports economists' assumptions that markets work well on their own and that intermediaries are unneeded, and these assumptions are widely held. School–business partnerships rarely provide job placement; they mostly provide mentoring or donations. Even school guidance counselors, the officials responsible for career guidance, unapologetically stated that they do not help students with job placement because youths should find jobs on their own (Rosenbaum, Miller, & Krei, 1996). The functionalist assumption that markets work smoothly on their own is widely believed in the United States.

Challenging functionalism's contention that employers really need greater skills, Berg (1971), Squires (1979), and Attewell (1992) found that workers are overqualified for their present job tasks. However, Rosenbaum and Binder (1997) suggested that such findings may occur because employers use these jobs for portals to higher jobs that do require these advanced skills. Studies find that even after controlling for educational level, cognitive skills have strong effects on earnings 6 or more years after high school (Altonji & Pierret, 1996), and these effects have increased over time (Murnane, Willett, & Levy, 1995). In addition, Kane and Rouse (1995) found that college effects on earnings are not just from degrees; individual courses have incremental effects on earnings, and some subject areas may have greater effects than others (Grubb, 1995). Other studies have concluded that employers do in fact have unmet skill needs, which have increased since the late 1970s (Boesel, Hudson, Deich, & Masten, 1994; Gamoran, 1994; Ray & Mickelson, 1993; Rosenbaum & Binder, 1997; Zemsky, 1994), since Berg's and Squire's data were collected. Therefore, this challenge to functionalism no longer seems as compelling as it once did.

NETWORK THEORY OF SIGNALING

Another challenge to functionalism comes from network theory. Whereas functionalist theory assumes that schools automatically respond to society's needs, network theory contends that such responsiveness is not automatic; it requires enabling mechanisms—social relationships that convey information. Network theory asserts that information is crucial to the operation of markets, that labor markets often lack ways to convey information, and that social contacts often provide a way to convey appropriate information.

Network theory focuses on the problematics of information. Employers need ways to learn about job applicants, and they do not trust much of the information that they do receive (Miller & Rosenbaum, 1997). On the other hand, work-bound youths face two problematic issues. First, how can youths with poor contacts convey their value to employers? The youths who seek jobs after high school tend to be from low-income backgrounds, so their relatives may not provide them with good information about work or with contacts to people who make hiring decisions. Second, how can youths with poor school achievement signal positive value to employers? The youths who seek full-time jobs after high school have generally done poorly in school and lack basic literacy skills (Murnane et al., 1995). How can such youths get positive signals of their value?

The importance of trusted signals is increasingly recognized by economic and sociological theories (Althauser & Kalleberg, 1981; Altonji & Pierret, 1995; Dore, 1992), and the new institutional economics considers the efficiencies of institutional relationships (Lazear, 1979; Rosen, 1982). Sociological models contend that labor markets often "depend on the nature of personal relations and the network of relations between and within firms" (Granovetter, 1985, p. 502). These models note that information is given meaning and credibility through social contacts. "People prefer to deal with individuals of known reputation, or, even better, with individuals they have dealt with before. Social relations ... are mainly responsible for the production of trust in economic life" (Granovetter, 1985, pp. 490–491).

Thus, functionalist "need" may not be enough to make appropriate behaviors emerge. Social relationships are needed to make the functional model work. Rather than specifying vague labor market needs, network theory urges that we instead focus on the specific kinds of information employers need, whether schools respond to these needs, and what social mechanisms enable this responsiveness to operate.

What Kinds of Information Are Conveyed in the Japanese and German Systems?

The formal school–work systems in other nations provide a good model for illustrating how enabling mechanisms can operate. Perhaps the best indication that poor information may cause youths' labor market problems in the United States is that these problems are less common in some nations where institutional networks provide employers with trusted signals of youths' value. Compared with the United States, both Germany and Japan have lower youth unemployment and turnover (Organization for Economic Cooperation & Development, 1993), and youths are more likely to get jobs with advancement possibilities (Reubens, 1974; Rosenbaum, Kariya, Settersten, & Maier, 1990).

In Germany, a national employment agency evaluates students (based in part on school performance) and certifies which youths will best fit the better apprenticeships, which, in turn, prepare and certify them for later jobs. In Japan, employers ask high schools to nominate students for jobs. Employers in both nations view these procedures as giving trusted certifications of students' capabilities. As a result, whereas American youths have difficulty providing trusted signals of their value to employers (Miller & Rosenbaum, 1997), German and Japanese youths have little difficulty doing so.

Analysts have noted three elements that make the Japanese and the German job placement systems effective (Hamilton, 1990; Rosenbaum et al., 1990). First, teachers give employers hard-to-assess information about students. In both nations, employers believe that teachers' ratings offer information about students' work habits and behavior, which employers cannot easily assess for themselves.

Second, employers feel that their systems give relevant information. Japanese employers believe that school ratings are good indicators of youths' work habits, and teachers give ratings accordingly (Rosenbaum & Kariya, 1989). German employers select workers based on their performances in relevant contexts (apprenticeship programs). Even if the apprenticeship trains skills that an employer does not need, it instills work habits that have general value in other jobs (Berryman, 1992). Therefore, while half of German apprentices get jobs in areas that do not use their specific apprenticeship skills, employers still pay a premium for out-of-area apprenticeships (Witte & Kalleberg, 1994), presumably because apprentices learn generalizable competencies. For instance, doing well in auto mechanics apprenticeships helps youths get jobs in other production jobs where knowledge of machinery and good work habits are needed.

Third, Japanese teachers develop trusted reputations with employers. They build trust through their professional reputation, history of transactions with certain employers, and actions to preserve their reputation into the future (Kariya & Rosenbaum, 1995).

Thus, the formal mechanisms in Japan and in Germany confirm the predictions of network theory. These systems are premised on the assumptions that employers have information needs and that schools can provide this information. Both nations have formal systems that give youths dependable pathways to good jobs by conveying information with three properties—hard to assess, relevant, and trustworthy.

THREE PUZZLES

Functionalist theory assumes that the interaction of school and society works well on its own and that formal procedures like those of Japan and Germany are unnecessary. In contrast, network theory suggests that the lack of social contacts might create problems in conveying information. As we examine specifics, we discover three puzzles that seem related to the kinds of information problems noted by network theory. First, whereas functionalists assume that work-bound students can be identified and given job preparation, we have found that most work-bound students are unidentified in high school. Second, whereas functionalist theory assumes that employers would use school information about job applicants, we find that most employers do not use this information. Third, whereas schools lack procedures to help students get jobs, we find that some employers hire through high schools and some students get jobs through high schools. How do these puzzles occur?

Why Are Most Work-Bound Students Unidentified in High School?

When we try to figure out how many students are work-bound, we discover the first puzzle—why do so few high school students realize that they are work-bound? Since 1960, the percentage of high school graduates enrolling in college has increased from 45% to 65% (National Center for Education Statistics [NCES], 1997, Table 184), and the number of students planning to take full-time jobs after high school has declined. However, half of 12th-grade students lack basic 9th-grade math and verbal skills (Murnane & Levy, 1996), so many "college-bound" students have no realistic chance of completing any college degree. After they fail to get a degree (often with zero college credits), youths will enter the labor market with the same educational credentials as students who were "work-bound" in high school, but without the vocational preparation that many of those students received.

In fact, only about half of college entrants complete a college degree (Resnick & Wirt, 1996). Since the 1960s, most of the growth in college enrollment has been in 2-year colleges, where completion rates are even worse. For example, for the 1980 graduates enrolled full-time in 2-year public colleges in October 1980, fewer than 40% completed any degree (AA or higher) by 1986, and the rates were only 15.2% for the large number (about 25%) enrolled part-time (NCES, 1992, Table 287).

Moreover, as enrollments increased in the 1970s, the dropout rate from public 2-year colleges also increased sharply (from 36.0% to 49.6% between 1972 and 1980; Grubb, 1992, Table 2). Rather than acting as gatekeepers as they did in earlier decades (Rosenbaum, 1976), guidance counselors now urge all students to attend college, but they rarely warn poorly prepared students that they will have difficulty completing a degree (Rosenbaum et al., 1996). Rather than hurting students by posing obstacles to their plans, counselors now may be hurting students by not informing them of potential obstacles they will face in the future.

Furthermore, many of these failures are predictable. In 1982, of the high school graduates who planned to get a college degree, only about 40% achieved a college degree (AA or higher) 10 years later. However, for students with poor high school grades (C or lower), only

20% got a college degree (Rosenbaum, 1998a, Table 2). In other words, counselors could predict that these students would fail, yet counselors say they "do not want to discourage students' high hopes."

So the question of the number of "work-bound" students turns out to be complex. If "work-bound" refers only to those who do not plan to earn a college degree, then only 30% of high school seniors are work bound. However, this is a gross underestimate. About 60% of college planners (seniors who plan to get a postsecondary degree) fail to get any degree within 10 years after graduating high school. These "college-planning" seniors are effectively work-bound—they will ultimately have only their high school diplomas when they enter the labor market. If we define work-bound students as including those who actually end their schooling with no degree above a high school diploma, then a large majority of high school graduates are work-bound in that they will enter the labor market with no degree above their high school diplomas.*

Although Kane and Rouse (1995) contended that isolated college courses give economic benefit, this may be true for only certain courses (Grubb, 1993, 1995). Regardless, many college-entrants get no college credits. In the class of 1982 *High School and Beyond* (*HSB*) data, 31% of all students who entered college (or other postsecondary schools) obtained zero college credits within the next 10 years (Rosenbaum, 1998b).†

Thus, over half of college planners are likely to get no economic benefit from college. These students will therefore end up having only their high school diplomas to bring to the labor market. Of course, in high school, students do not anticipate that this will happen (even though it is highly predictable), so these work-bound students are "unidentified." As such, they are less likely to prepare themselves for their subsequent risk of failure, to have back-up plans, to get back-up preparation, or to get help in finding jobs from their high schools (Rosenbaum, 1998a).

Why Don't Employers Use Information from Schools?

We next turn to the second puzzle—Why don't employers use students' information from schools? Although functionalist theory makes a reasonable assumption that schools provide information and employers use it, these assumptions are contradicted by research.

First, the literature suggests that schools do not encourage teachers to give information to employers. Studies have found that teachers view their responsibilities as confined to the classroom (Lortie, 1975). Teachers rarely know employers, they tend to mistrust them, and they do not want to interact with them (Useem, 1986). Ironically, even vocational teachers,

*One-year certificates are not college degrees, and their economic value varies greatly. Including one-year certificates improves the ratios a little—48.5% of 1982 seniors planning to get a certificate or degree succeeded in doing so over the next 10 years.

†Of the 11223 students who entered college (or other postsecondary schools) from the class of 1982, 1822 (16.2%) got zero credits and another 1669 (14.5%) reported attending college, but have no transcript reported. Grubb (1995) concluded that "no transcript" probably indicates that these students did not attend college long enough to get any credits. Grubb's inference is supported by our finding that "no transcript" students have even lower high school grades than students with zero college credits (low high school grades [below B-] were held by 74.5% of students with zero credits and by 82.3% of students who had no transcripts, but only by 46.4% of other students). Thus, if we consider those students with no transcript to have zero credits, 31.1% (1669 + 1822) of students who enter college get zero college credits to bring to the labor market. (Even if these students had credits, they may not get any benefit from them if their colleges do not send out transcripts.)

who are responsible for preparing youths for work, report that job placement is not one of their duties, that they do not receive extra rewards or resources for providing job help, and most denied that incentives of any kind exist, aside from personal gratification (Rosenbaum & Jones, 1995).

Second, research suggests that employers often do not use information from schools. First, despite indications that employers need academic skills (Bailey, 1989, 1994; Bills, 1992; National Academy of Sciences, 1984; National Center on Education & the Economy, 1990; Ray & Mickelson, 1993), employers' hiring decisions do not use the primary information that schools generate—school grades or test scores. The functionalist model posits that employers care about how students perform in school, and Parsons (1959) explicitly stated that employers use high school grades in their hiring decisions. This may have been true at the time of Parsons' paper, but he cited no evidence. In any case, much recent research contradicts that assertion. Most employers ignore students' grades and test scores when they hire new high school graduates. Grades and test scores have no influence on the earnings, job status, or employment of recent high school graduates (Bishop, 1988; Daymont & Rumberger, 1982; Kang & Bishop, 1986; Meyer, 1982; Meyer & Wise, 1982; Miller, 1998; Rosenbaum & Kariya, 1991; Willis & Rosen, 1979). These school indicators of youths' human capital do not influence employers' hiring decisions.

Moreover, the evidence is mixed on whether employers use the vocational programs that schools create for them. Research indicates that, true to its mission, vocational education increases youths' employment and earnings after high school. Although critics claim that vocational programs only offer preparation for low-skill jobs, most research shows strong job benefits from vocational courses. Studying the 1983 National Longitudinal Survey on 6953 youths, Campbell, Basinger, Dauner, and Parks (1986) found that vocational graduates were 8.2% more likely to be in the labor force and their pay was 5.6% higher than academic program graduates, after controlling for test scores and for enrollment in higher education. In another sample, the 6098 youths in the HSB, Campbell et al. (1986) found that vocational graduates were 14.9% more likely to be in the labor force and were paid about 9% more than academic graduates, after controlling for test scores and for college attendance. Analyses that focused on *HSB* seniors who did not attend college full time found similar results, with male vocational graduates getting 8% higher hourly wages, working 10% to 12% more, and earning 21% to 35% more in 1981, the first calendar year following graduation. For females, vocational graduates got 8% higher hourly wages, worked 18% more, and earned 40% more during 1981 than academic graduates (Kang & Bishop, 1986). Similar benefits have been found for postsecondary vocational programs (Kerckhoff & Bell, 1998; Wirt, Muraskin, Goodwin, & Meyer, 1989), and other recent analyses have confirmed the economic benefits (Lewis, Hearn, & Zilbert, 1993).

On the other hand, although vocational education graduates get significantly higher earnings on average, many vocational students get little benefit because employers give them jobs unrelated to their training. Research indicates that the "economic benefits [of vocational education] are zero if a training-related job is not obtained . . . Unfortunately, less than one-half of [vocational] graduates . . . work in occupations that match (very broadly defined) their training" (Bishop, 1988). The National Assessment of Vocational Education (NAVE) concluded that "the largest single influence [on low payoff to vocational education] in most analyses was unrelated placements. In the first three years after graduation, unrelated placements . . . accounted for 25–31% of the underutilization [of vocational training] for men, and 37–44% for women" (Wirt et al., 1989, p. 73). Students with 'low' amounts of job matched vocational credits earn an average of $6.59 per hour, while similar students with a 'high' number of credits matching their job earn $8.00 (Wirt et al., 1989, p. 108). Both Bishop (1988) and NAVE concluded that high schools should devote more attention to helping students with job placements and to getting employers more involved. As network theory indicates, vocational training is not sufficient to assure better earnings if employers do not recognize the value of students' training and respond to it.

Thus, contrary to functionalist theory, employers do not necessarily use high school information. They rarely use school grades, and they often do not respond to students' vocational skills. This casts serious doubt on functionalist theories, including human capital theory in economics. If employers ignore school information about students' human capital, then are employers really interested in human capital?

Network theory may explain why employers do not respond to school information. It suggests that employers may indeed care about human capital, but they may not realize that the information they get from schools is valuable. If employers believe that school information adds little to what they can easily assess themselves, if it is irrelevant to their needs, or if it is untrustworthy, then employers might ignore this information even though they are very concerned about assessing students' human capital. Thus, the key questions are whether employers believe that school-provided information is hard-to-assess, relevant, and trustworthy.

How Do Employers Hire through School Help?—The Hidden Link

We next turn to the third puzzle. Although the United States lacks a job placement system and schools do not provide job placement procedures, how do some employers hire through schools and some students get their first jobs through high school help? Two surveys of employers indicate that about 5% of employers have continuing contacts with school staff (Bishop, 1993; Holzer, 1995), and employers report that these contacts are a good source of productive workers. Bishop (1993, Table 7) found that workers recruited through vocational teachers add to profitability and that "references from people who have recommended previous successful hires [add 7.7% to productivity]" (p. 369). Another employer survey found that workers who are recruited from schools get higher status occupations more often (professional/ managerial, clerical, or crafts) and get low-status occupations less often (operative, service, and laborer; Holzer, Table 3.4). In contrast, workers hired from state employment services have the opposite pattern, primarily getting low-status occupations.

Similarly, in the national HSB survey, 8% of graduating seniors got jobs through high school help (Rosenbaum & Roy, 1996), and these students get better paying jobs. Even after controlling for individual background, tracking, and grades, youth who get their first jobs through their high schools get 4% higher earnings in the year after high school than those who did not use contacts (Rosenbaum & Roy, 1996; Rosenbaum, Deluca, Miller, & Roy, 1999). Indeed, for youth without college degrees, schools are the best contacts for getting jobs that lead to future earnings gains. Compared with students who did not use contacts, high school contacts lead to over 17% higher earnings by age 27, whereas relatives' contacts lead to only 9% higher earnings, and employment services lead to 8% higher earnings. School help also leads to lower unemployment rates (Arum, 1998).

Apparently, some high school graduates get jobs through high school help, employers place such students in better occupations, and these students have improving earnings over their first 9 years in the labor market. Why and how is this happening? The following sections seek to answer these questions by returning to the central issues posed by network theory—do employers have difficulty getting some kinds of information and do teachers take actions to meet those needs?

DO AMERICAN EMPLOYERS HAVE UNMET INFORMATION NEEDS AND DO TEACHERS CREATE INFORMAL INFRASTRUCTURES?

In the absence of a formal system in the United States, do employers have difficulty getting appropriate information, and do teachers respond to these needs? Ironically, we know more about what information employers get about youths in Germany and in Japan than in the United States. If network theory is correct that effective markets require intermediaries, and the United States lacks formal intermediaries, we may wonder whether any school staff become informal intermediaries.

Someone in schools must be taking such actions because 5% of employers say they hire new workers through schools, and 8% of graduating seniors get jobs through high school help. We suspect that vocational teachers are the agents, because vocational students are twice as likely to get high school job help than other students getting jobs, and vocational teachers often worked in a trade or business before becoming teachers. Therefore, our inquiry focuses on vocational teachers.

The following sections review evidence on employers' needs and vocational teachers' actions. Although studies have examined representative samples of employers, studies of schools' efforts to help students get jobs have usually examined atypical school reforms. Given the paucity of research on ordinary teachers' efforts at job placement after high school, this review focuses on the results of a new study of 110 vocational teachers in 12 diverse high schools (8 comprehensive high schools; 4 vocational high schools, see Appendix). Although a single study is not definitive, these findings indicate previously undiscovered processes that deserve further study.

Of course, even if teachers have ties to employers, the key questions for employer–school interaction are whether employers have certain information needs and whether teachers are aware of these needs and are able to provide such information. The following sections examine whether American employers have difficulty getting information that is hard to assess, relevant, and trusted, and whether teachers provide these three kinds of information.

Employers Need Hard-To-Assess Information, which Teachers Can Provide

Contrary to the functionalist assumption that employers automatically get the information they need, employers report that they actually have difficulty getting detailed, useful information about applicants and that they only get it through social relationships (Miller & Rosenbaum, 1997). Consistent with network theory, research has also found that some vocational teachers have reported that they have contacts to employers, and they act as intermediaries to convey appropriate information to employers. These teachers know what information employers need, they believe they possess it, and they provide it in the references they give to employers.

Popular stereotypes often envision confident employers who know just what they want and know how to get it and diffident teachers who know little about the world and remain detached from it. Like all stereotypes, both are partly wrong. In hiring recent high school graduates, employers' highest priority is work habits, and employers have reported that they have great difficulty inferring work habits from available information (Bishop, 1993). Interviews are employers' primary method for assessing applicants (Wanous, 1992), but research indicates that interviews are not very effective for telling employers whether a job applicant will be honest, hard-working, cooperative, or trainable (Miller & Rosenbaum, 1997). Some employers are aware of the problems of interviewing. They have reported that "You never really know 'til you get somebody in," and "if a person has any skill . . . in being deceptive or a good actor, you can learn next to nothing in an interview" (Miller & Rosenbaum, 1997, p. 512).

Research has confirmed their suspicions; interviewing does give biased and invalid information (Arvey & Faley, 1988; Wanous, 1992). Decades of studies suggest that the popularity of interviewing is not justified by its accuracy in predicting future performance (Wanous, 1992). For example, J. E. Hunter and Hunter (1984) found the validity correlation between interviewer ratings and subsequent job performance is only .14, and Arvey and Faley (1988) found interviews to be unfair to racial minorities. Yet employers overwhelmingly choose to make their decisions based on the 15 minutes they spend interviewing candidates.

Few schools have formal procedures to help employers hire students or to help students get jobs. A survey of U.S. high schools found that although 56% of schools offered counseling services, only 37% offered job placement services, and schools reported that they were increasing the former more than the latter (Stern, Finkelstein, Stone, Latting, and Dornsife, 1994, p. 54). Even when they offer job placement help, they usually offer in-school training (reading want-ads, filling out job applications, and interviewing skills), and they rarely offer formal outreach procedures to develop job openings. In a report that reviewed hundreds of programs, Stern et al. (1994) found one high school (Duncan Polytechnical, Fresno, CA) that explicitly created "a 'job developer' position . . . responsible for reviewing want-ads, calling on local businesses, attending job fairs, and informing students of job opportunities" (p. 55). When this large report by the National Center for Research on Vocational Education can only find one such program, one must conclude that formal activities to generate job options are rare. This is confirmed by the study of 110 vocational teachers that found few formal programs to generate job options.

In contrast to employers' lack of information, research has found that some vocational teachers are confident that they know what information employers need, they believe they possess it, and they provide it in the references they give to employers. Teachers learn employers' needs through a variety of informal activities. In the study of 110 vocational teachers, 95% entered teaching after having careers in their industry, and 86% have made special efforts to learn the specific needs of local employers. Many still have ties; they attend industry or union meetings and visit former colleagues at work or after work. Others build new contacts with employers by having advisory programs to their vocational program, by visiting students' co-op learning field sites, or just by visiting to learn about employers' current practices and needs. Some teachers say that when employers call seeking students to hire, they use these calls as a chance to learn employers' specific needs and to build a relationship with them.

Most vocational teachers (82%) reported that their recommendations give employers information about students' work capabilities that employers would have difficulty assessing by themselves (Rosenbaum & Jones, 1998). Indeed, some teachers asserted that employers would be foolish to try to make selections without them. They reported that they know better than employers which students should be hired, and their detailed knowledge about students gives them a special advantage in informing employers' hiring decisions. A teacher in an urban school noted,

> I've done the screening already. If they've gotta do the screening, employers have got some serious problems, because there's no way in an interview [that an employer] can come up with what's going on. I don't care how well you do this or how many years you do this, you can't call it that good. You don't know until you get the person under the gun how he's gonna handle it. (T12 in Rosenbaum & Jones, 1998)

Another urban teacher reported, "a teacher can give [information about] things like quality, . . . honesty, dependability, and helpfulness and that kind of thing. I think it would be very hard [for employers] to get that from another source" (T15).

Teachers get to know students over the course of a year or more, and this detailed knowledge is just what employers need for predicting youths' work performance and is what they cannot get from other sources. As a teacher in the urban business school said, "My advantage is in knowing the student well . . . I can give [employers] more specific measures of skills as well as attitudes" (T74). Another added, "I can give [employers] some insight into the students' academic or personal [qualities] that they probably would have a hard time getting" (T75).

Teachers noted that their evaluations are based on extensive information that employers cannot obtain on their own. A teacher at the suburban vocational school said, "I would have had the opportunity to see students in the classroom for at least a year. I would have evaluations from at least one or more employers based on the experiences that students have in the field. And I would make my recommendation based on that" (T24).

Thus, whereas employers' interviews poorly predict job performance (Wanous, 1992), and some employers realize these limitations, vocational teachers have detailed information about youths' work habits exhibited on a daily basis over the course of a year and sometimes based on the evaluations of co-op employers. Employers cannot get this kind of information on their own, but teachers' references provide just this kind of hard-to-assess information to employers.

Employers Need Relevant Information, which Teachers Can Provide

Second, contrary to the functionalist assumption that employers automatically get useful information from schools, we have found that employers doubt that most school-provided information is relevant to their needs. However, consistent with network theory, some vocational teachers realize employers' needs, and they take actions to enhance the relevance of information they provide to employers.

American employers doubt that most of the information they get about job applicants is relevant to their work demands (Miller & Rosenbaum, 1997). That is why employers were initially enthusiastic about apprenticeships (Lerman & Pouncy, 1990), although their enthusiasm cooled once they realized the high costs of apprenticeships (Harhoff & Kane, 1993). A variety of school reforms try to make school instruction more relevant to work, but a survey of U.S. high schools estimates that few high schools offer tech-prep programs (7%), school-to-apprenticeship programs (6%), or youth apprenticeships (2%; Stern et al., 1994, p. 7).

Vocational education was originally designed to provide relevant training and evaluations (Wirt et al., 1989). Although this is often interpreted to mean relevant skills, employers rarely stress specific job skills in hiring entry workers, and they often prefer to train specific job skills themselves (Osterman, 1980, 1994). Rather, employers stress work habits as the most relevant attributes—attendance, discipline, initiative, persistence, attention to quality, and the ability to work with others (National Center on the Educational Quality in the Workforce [NCEQW], 1994).

Vocational teachers believe they are in a good position to assess students' work habits. In the study of 110 vocational teachers (Rosenbaum & Jones, 1998), most felt they could assess students' likely performance in work settings (65%) and this was even more true for the 46 teachers in the four vocational schools (85%). In addition, vocational teachers increase the relevance of their evaluations in two ways: they create "quasi-apprenticeships" in their classrooms, and they make their student evaluations address attributes that are relevant to employers' needs.

Teachers Assess Students in Relevant Contexts—Quasi-Apprenticeships.   Work-based experience is one way to offer training in relevant contexts. Roughly half of American high schools offer co-op programs that give students a chance to learn about work in actual work sites and about 8% of juniors and seniors take part in co-op experiences (General Accounting Office, 1991; Stern et al., 1994, p. 7). Co-op programs allow employers to evaluate students, and if the employer is satisfied with the student, then research finds that "former co-op students who kept working for their co-op employers did experience significantly higher earnings" (Stern & Stevens, 1992, p. 7). However, some co-op jobs do not offer much training. They only give co-op youths routine, unchallenging tasks.

Because work-based co-op experience is practical, but not always educational, school-based experience is another way to combine practical elements with education. Some vocational teachers design their classrooms to include work simulations that are relevant to employers' needs. Having come from industry and having continuing contacts with employers, vocational teachers often know how the local employers in their field operate, and they have constructed classroom tasks to develop, monitor, and assess students' workplace capabilities. Although not as thorough as German apprenticeships, which occur over several years in actual workplaces, classroom work simulations resemble apprenticeships—they give students a chance to learn to perform at joblike tasks, which teachers can monitor, evaluate, and certify. Teachers view their classroom work-simulations as quasi-apprenticeships (Jones & Rosenbaum, 1995; Rosenbaum & Jones, 1995, p. 252). As one suburban teacher said,

> I think a lot of what we do here is very similar to [the training provided in business or industry apprenticeships]. Primarily the hands-on experience. Most apprenticeship programs, be it for an electrician or a plumber, involve some classroom work. . . . So the academics is important, but the ability to perform, to do the work is even more important . . . [being able to] apply what they know. (T24)

Another teacher expressed the same idea, "Our graduates really are like first or second year apprentices when they leave here" (T35). Teachers noted that the similation includes responsibility:

> We try and operate the on-board technology department as close as possible to a dealership. We use repair orders, we have a parts and service director, students are responsible for completing repairs. If the repair comes back, they are responsible for repairing it a second time, like a dealership would. (T29)

Teachers tell students that they must be able to see what tasks need to be done and to do them on their own. Teachers also monitor students' behaviors and help them progress to the point where they no longer need the teacher's supervision. While his students worked on their projects, a suburban drafting instructor remarked, "I give them confidence that they know that skill . . . You can see now, a student is plotting a drawing by himself. I mean, I didn't give him any instructions. They know what to do, and that's important to me, because it's a simulation of what's in the real world" (T20). Thus, just as some employers value the work-site student performances they see in co-op programs, vocational teachers believe their classes allow them to see behaviors that are relevant to work demands.

Teachers' References Convey Relevant Information to Employers.   Vocational teachers also make their recommendations relevant to employers' needs, and they match students with employers on a number of dimensions. Teachers see the particular needs of each employer, and they give employers information about relevant student attributes. In an urban vocational school, the broadcast media teacher stated, "I send kids to the cable systems, my best kids. Not necessarily best, that's wrong. My most responsible kids. Kids who can work independent-ly . . . They're gonna be sent out with expensive [camera] equipment and told, 'Shoot this.' Well, they have to be able to work independently" (T16).

The quasi-apprenticeship structure of many vocational classes allows teachers to see students' qualities that are relevant to employers' needs. As a result, many vocational teachers feel that classroom experiences enable them to provide distinctively valuable evaluations. As one noted,

> I have a better insight as to the work habits [than do teachers] in the traditional classroom. . . . Here, I can see the motivation and [self-direction] . . . Will a student do something on their own? Will they think on their own? Will they problem solve on their own, or are they asking me every two minutes how to do something? (T30)

A teacher at the suburban vocational center reported, "I think I can tell employers about those job transferable skills more than a regular high school teacher could, because I've seen 'em in action. I see how they work, . . . their motivation, initiative, cooperation" (T33).

In turn, teachers' demands for worklike performances show students new dimensions of their own capabilities. As one teacher in an urban vocational school said, "The employer is really interested in what they can do, not just what they know" (T83). Focusing on work demands in academic classes also provides relevant information to employers, for, as one teacher noted (Rosenbaum & Jones, 1998), "I tell them [students] that good academics indi-cates to an employer that you can show discipline, so even if they don't get stellar grades, students' efforts are important" (T83).

The process of tailoring evaluations to employers' needs makes students see that their classroom behaviors are relevant to work. Students realize that their class performances are an opportunity to show what they can do in workplaces. As one teacher reported, "I try to give them the self-evaluation thing—you know, such as 'Do you really believe that you would want me to give a recommendation for you based on what you do in this class?' You tell the kid that they have to make you want to give them a job" (T81).

Indeed, many teachers let students know that their behavior is important and that there are incentives to demonstrate appropriate performances. Teachers say they cannot help stu-dents who perform poorly in class. Even if teachers want to help their students, they must report the truth about their class performance. "When I help a kid get a job, my reputation is at stake as well. If I put some 'dork' in there who's going to screw up, then the next time that the employer is looking for someone to fill a job, then is he really going to call me again?" (T81) When students ask "Do I have to do that? It's so difficult," one teacher responds, "Don't do it for me. But the employers I know who offer good jobs in this field require these skills, and I can't recommend you to those employers if you don't master these skills" (T12). Thus, stu-dents learn that their own performances are relevant and that they constrain whether teachers can help them get jobs.

Most vocational teachers believe that they are helping students and employers see alter-nate kinds of capabilities besides the academic ones that are evaluated in other classes. One teacher stated this particularly clearly in the way he described his grading scale: "An 'A' student has a good attitude, and works well with his mind and his hands. A 'B' student works well with his hands and has a good attitude . . . A 'C' student maybe has just a good attitude" (T83). This teacher presented a range of capabilities for students to show which ones are tailored to employers' needs.

Our classroom observations revealed how teachers could assess work readiness. A graphics class was run like a print shop. Students were assigned a whole project, they solved problems themselves, and they kept busy and on task, even when the teacher was out of the room. In other schools, business students dressed and acted as they would in offices. The machinist, sheet-metal, and carpentry programs were taught on a project basis with considerable autonomy and self-direction. Students often performed work-related tasks on their own, without close supervision. Students performed lengthy tasks without getting teachers' comments, they solved problems that arose, they prepared equipment and materials for the next operation, and they organized the work site for the next person to use it. Students stopped and talked occasionally, but the chats were brief and often work-related.

Having designed classes that simulate work demands, teachers can assess students in relevant contexts on relevant dimensions. Work simulations permit teachers to assess the ways students work—their perseverance, initiative, responsibility, problem solving, and ability to learn—and to do so on tasks that resemble real work tasks. This is the kind of information that employers desperately want and cannot get in job interviews (Miller & Rosenbaum, 1997). Vocational teachers can certify students' work readiness because they have seen them doing the same tasks that are done in workplaces.

Employers Need Trusted Information, which Teachers Can Provide

Trust is the most overlooked component of infrastructure. Although weak ties give job seekers more information about possible job openings (Granovetter, 1995), employers report that they do not need more information, they need trusted information (Miller & Rosenbaum, 1997). Consistent with network theory, research indicates that employers lack trusted information and vocational teachers take steps to make the information they provide trustworthy.

Employers' mistrust of information may explain why students only benefit from co-op programs if hired by their co-op employer (Stern & Stevens, 1992), but not if they are hired by other employers (Bishop, Blakemore, & Low, 1985; Lewis et al., 1993; Stern et al., 1994). Apparently, employers trust their own evaluations of co-op students, but they may not trust the evaluations of other co-op employers or teachers.

Employers report that they do not trust teachers to be candid about students' shortcomings. In the words of one employer, "teachers are trying to help their own students, Heaven bless them . . . but that doesn't make them very useful to me" (Miller & Rosenbaum, 1997). However, employer surveys indicate that about 5% of employers recruit new workers through school contacts, so they presumably have overcome this mistrust (Bishop, 1993; Holzer, 1995). How is this trust formed?

Japan provides a clue. Although Japan's system confers formal authority to teachers to nominate students for jobs, this does not force an employer to contact a particular school. Japanese teachers believe their job placement effectiveness depends on building informal authority with employers, which comes from their school's reputation, the track record of their school's past interactions with employers, and the actions they take to preserve their reputation into the future (Kariya & Rosenbaum, 1995). In effect, these teachers turn ordinary recommendations into trusted certifications of students' quality by building trust into their relationship with employers.

Some American vocational teachers also build trusted relationships with employers. In the study of 110 vocational teachers, over one third (38%) said they have a good reputation with employers, and the proportion was much higher in vocational schools (70%).

How do teachers build this reputation? Whereas Japanese teachers focus on the school's reputation and interactions with employers, American teachers build a trusted personal reputation by stressing their previous work experience in the trade, their track record of placing students with employers, and activities to preserve their reputation into the future.

Experience in the Trade.   In Japan, teachers' authority is conferred by society and by the formal employment system. Although American teachers get less respect than teachers in Japan (Stevenson & Stigler, 1992), and employers do not value most teachers' recommendations (Miller & Rosenbaum, 1997), some vocational teachers have built a reputation from their previous work in a trade. Of the 110 vocational teachers, 95% had some work experience in their field, and 32% had 10 or more years of experience. Even after becoming teachers, most vocational teachers continue to identify with their trade, and 30% work in industry in summers. Whereas a few have formal contacts through advisory boards or co-op programs, many have continuing informal contacts, visiting former workplaces, attending union meetings, or informally socializing.

Many vocational teachers are confident that they have a trusted reputation from their years in industry. As a teacher in an urban vocational school noted, "Being in the trade, I think they accept your recommendation, that you know what they're looking for" (T42). A suburban teacher reported, "My opinion of one of my students . . . would have more of an impact . . . people would know me in the trade and know my level of performance and my expectations" (T24). Teachers' previous experience "in the trade" is a source of authority in recommending students for jobs (Rosenbaum & Jones, 1998).

Track Record of Placing Students with Employers.   Many vocational teachers have a continuing history of recommending students to employers. Teachers see their history of transactions with employers as an additional basis of their reputation. An urban teacher noted, "They know from their past experience with me what they're getting" (T12). A suburban teacher added, "[Employers] trust me because I continuously try to work with them and give them . . . the kind of student that they want" (T75).

Many teachers feel that this history of references leads to trust. A teacher at the urban business school reported, "Based on the relationships that I've developed over the years, the employers have confidence in what I tell them" (T65). Trust comes from an implicit or explicit promise in the relationship. Another urban teacher noted, "They get to know me, . . . and respect my position and who I'm gonna send them" (T73).

Vocational teachers see their relationships with employers as a valued "asset" that belongs to them personally, not to the school. Teachers were asked a hypothetical question: "If you took a job at a nearby school with a similar program, would the employers you've worked with in the past be more likely to deal with your former school or with you in hiring students?" Most teachers said their employers would keep working with them, not their former school.

Trust is especially salient to new teachers who are trying to build a reputation. Although most already have job experience in their field, they report that they have not yet attained a reputation for placing qualified students. Building a reputation takes time. As an urban teacher noted, "[Our business high school] has a real good reputation. [Employers] didn't of course, just trust me at the start"(T67). A new teacher at the urban business school reported, "[If older teachers] recommend a student, [employers] know they're gonna be a dynamite student. I don't know if I'm at that place yet [where employers automatically trust my recommendations]" (T73).

In Japan, reputation resides with the high school, and teachers work to maintain the school's reputation. In the United States, reputation resides with individual teachers, and, although a high school can help that, teachers feel that they must build their own reputations by their history of transactions with employers.

Activities to Preserve Reputation: Prescreening and Candid References. In Japan, teachers take two kinds of actions to preserve their schools' reputation. First, they prescreen students before nominating them for job openings, because they know that an employer who receives a poorly qualified student would not recruit from the school in future years. Second, teachers give candid references about students, even if they would like to help likable, poor-achieving students. Teachers feel they must be candid if they want to help capable students in future years. As one Japanese teacher stated, "Getting a job is only a one-time experience for individual students, but it is repeated year after year for schools" (Rosenbaum & Kariya, 1989). Teachers will not nominate a student if they think that student will not meet the employer's needs. Sometimes teachers will not fill all the job openings that employers offer because they do not have enough students who meet the employers' needs.

American vocational teachers boost their credibility with employers with similar strategies—they prescreen students, and they give candid references. Without employers asking them to do so, many vocational teachers have reported that they prescreen students when they make nominations for a job opening (32%). Teachers see prescreening as necessary for maintaining their credibility with employers in the future. As one teacher noted, "It would make me look bad, if I recommend someone (who would not do good work)" (T6).

Teachers also give candid recommendations to maintain their reputation with employers. Most vocational teachers (85%) reported that many students ask them for help in getting jobs, and virtually all of vocational teachers want to help their students. However, teachers report that they must be candid with employers about students' shortcomings. Very few teachers (4 of 110) said they would send a student with poor work habits to an employer they knew. A business teacher in the urban vocational school reported, "I've always told [employers] the truth about all my students, including . . . a student's deficiencies" (T74). Similarly, a teacher in the suburban vocational school noted, "[If students lack skills] I only feel it would be fair to tell the employer" (T36). Sometimes, teachers sacrifice program enrollment and rapport with students to preserve their reputation with employers. One teacher noted, "There is even some hard feeling over it, but that's too bad. . . . Some [students] left the program, simply left because they knew I wasn't going to recommend them for a job" (T24).

Teachers say that they can only be effective in helping students in future years if they have credibility, and that requires candor about their students' shortcomings. Echoing the view of many others, an urban business school teacher noted, "It is very difficult for students to understand that we have a reputation to maintain" (T69). Another teacher noted that a good reputation requires continuing efforts: "I've worked hard to build a good reputation, and . . . employers are aware of the caliber of students that we produce" (T22). Teachers guard their recommendations to preserve the idea that their word is solid. An urban business school teacher noted, "I go see people [employers] all the time. My success is personal, face to face. . . . You're selling them you, not the kid" (T72).

Like Japanese teachers, many of these vocational teachers saw themselves as effective only because they gave employers what they needed. Although there are no formal demands for such a commitment to employers' needs in the United States, these teachers feel that their credibility with employers is crucial to their effectiveness at helping their students in the future.

DO EMPLOYERS RESPOND TO TEACHERS' EFFORTS?

Meyer and Rowan (1977) contended that some universities have "charters" that confer trusted certifications of students' value, which encourage employers repeatedly to hire their graduates because these universities certify the desirability of their graduates. Similarly, management schools use specific strategies to build trusted relationships with employers (Burke, 1984), and some vocational institutes have trusted charters for training technicians in certain fields (Mills, 1977). Although some high school vocational programs have developed strong programs (Stern, Raby, & Dayton, 1992; Stern et al., 1994), studies have not examined whether vocational teachers create "charters" which confer trusted certifications and consistent placement of graduates.

As noted, national surveys indicate that some employers hire through schools (Bishop, 1993; Holzer, 1995), that "references from people who have recommended previous hires are . . . more profitable" (Bishop, 1993, p. 369), and that students who get jobs through school help get higher earnings (Rosenbaum & Roy, 1996). However, many programs that try to help youths get jobs do not improve outcomes (Basi & Ashenfelter, 1986; Lah et al., 1983), so one needs to examine what teachers do and why it has an impact.

Although the national surveys do not permit analysis of the hiring relationship, the study of 110 vocational teachers does (Rosenbaum & Jones, 1998). A majority of these vocational teachers (68%) said that some employers trust their recommendations. Many teachers report similar themes—"Some employers will even say, 'You just send me a student. You know what I want" (T74). "I have been here long enough that some [employers] have already said, 'Well, you know what I'm looking for,' . . . they take . . . my word, and it's worked out in the past" (T4). "[Some employers] say 'Send me somebody, and I know who you send, they have always worked out'" (T68). "Among my employers, they take my word for it . . . Employers who keep calling back . . . [They] know they can rely on my word" (T69). Employers trust these teachers' recommendations.

Indeed, when asked, "What percent of your work-bound students can you place in good jobs that use students' skills," most teachers report that they can consistently place large portions of their students in jobs. Even in 1991 to 1993, during a weak labor market when large layoffs were common, 58% of the teachers said they could place three fourths or more of their students in good jobs that use their skills.[*]

Although one might be skeptical about self-reports, these placement rates are credible, because the teachers who made these claims regularly attend professional association and union meetings, have employers on their program advisory boards, have former students who are workers and employers in the field, and could name five or more specific employer contacts in high-demand fields (administrative, clerical, sheet metal, heating, machining, etc.). As a check on teachers' reports, 51 employers in the vicinity of three of these schools were interviewed, and over 20% reported having contacts with one or more of these teachers, seven have strong long-term contacts, and these employers consistently hired highly recommended students from these teachers (Rosenbaum & Binder, 1997).

---

*This question was near the end of the survey and was not asked to all teachers.Of all of the teachers in the sample, 58% (40/69) and 66% of teachers in vocational schools (25/38) said they could place three fourths or more of their students in good jobs that use their skills. The labor market was even weaker in the city, yet many urban teachers were as confident as suburban teachers about their ability to place students.

Thus, some employers show confidence in teachers' selections, and teachers can place large portions of their students. Teachers' long-term relationships with employers become a dependable hiring channel for employers and thus a dependable career pathway for students.

Teachers Get Jobs for Some Youths Who Might Not Otherwise Be Hired

Do teachers only help students who would get jobs anyway? Minorities and females are generally disadvantaged in the labor market, yet the HSB survey indicates that these groups are more likely to get their first jobs from high school help. Although schools helped only 7% of White males get their first job after high school, they helped 9% of White females, 5% of Hispanic males, 10% of Black males, 10% of Hispanic females, and 15.6% of Black females (Rosenbaum & Roy, 1996). Indeed, although employers who recruit youths through advertisements complain about the quality of their applicants, employers who recruit through school links reported that they got many qualified applicants, including many minorities. As one noted "I do get a better quality of individual coming through school than through ads in the paper." (Rosenbaum & Binder, 1997).

Even when employers deny discriminatory intent, employers' reliance on interviews for making hiring decisions hurts minorities (Arvey & Faley, 1988). It is hard for a White employer to know if uncomfortable feelings in interviews come from astute assessment or from racial bias. As Neckerman and Kirschenman (1991) concluded, "however qualified they are for the job, inner-city black applicants are more likely to fail subjective 'tests' of productivity given during the interview."

Other hiring procedures might reduce bias. Indeed, although employment tests are often biased against minorities (National Research Council, 1989), employers who use them are more likely to hire minorities than employers who lack such tests (Neckerman & Kirschenman, 1991). Testing may be biased, but the alternatives to testing are worse.

Similarly, teacher ratings may be less biased than employer interviews. If prejudice is conceived as "prejudging," prejudice is more likely in employers' 15-minute interviews than when teachers judge their students' work over one or more semesters of daily interaction. Teachers probably cannot escape societal biases, and some teachers report being initially put off by the student qualities that employers reject in interviews (hair styles, T-shirt slogans, dialect). Yet over the course of a term, teachers come to see students' actual work capabilities. This may explain why minorities and females are more likely to get school job placement help than White males.

Like any third party trying to make a transaction happen, teachers sometimes act like brokers—getting buyers and sellers to modify their expectations to accommodate to reality. Just as real estate brokers try to get both sellers and buyers to reduce their expectations so a transaction will occur, some vocational teachers try to convince employers and students that the other meets their needs, even if neither exactly matches the other's ideal.

The ultimate indication of teachers' impact is in examples where teachers get students into jobs that they would not have gotten otherwise, and this is often done by brokering—shaping the expectations of students and of employers. First, teachers get students to have realistic expectations. They tell students what pay to expect, what tasks they will be doing, how to act, what skills will improve their careers, and the timetables for advancement. Students do not know how to tell whether a job will offer valuable skill training and the possibility of later advancements, but teachers can direct youths to such jobs and inform them regarding how to get those advancements. Without teachers' advice, students would refuse many promising entry jobs or would quit them soon after beginning.

Even more surprising, teachers shape employers' expectations of students. The teacher–broker can help employers to understand what students can and cannot do and the ways to help them progress. Teachers can tell employers to ignore their customary hiring criteria and rely on more relevant information that the teacher has observed.

Here we return to the question asked earlier—how can youths with poor school achievement signal positive value to employers? This is a key dilemma of the youth labor market. Students with academic or personal difficulties face the greatest difficulty showing their value to employers. These students look like high-risk workers.

Vocational teachers provide an answer to this dilemma. They report that students' work-relevant performances in vocational classes provide alternative opportunities to signal labor market value on alternative dimensions of value besides academic skills. Relying on their reputation with employers, some vocational teachers encourage employers to overlook superficial appearances for more work-relevant personal qualities. Vocational teachers' evaluations give otherwise poorly achieving students positive signals to take into the labor market.

For students with handicapping features or experiences, this sort of teacher brokering provides opportunity that the impersonal labor market cannot. Several teachers have offered anecdotes that illustrate this function. In one case, an urban business teacher recalled,

> I called the bank and asked them to give [a teenage mother] a chance, because she was much more mature than the other students . . . She had the desire and the motivation, and she could develop the skill level . . . So, on that recommendation, they took her. They probably would not have [otherwise]. . . . She's received three promotions. She's the youngest loan officer in the history of that particular branch, and she's going back to school. . . . Employers know that you don't stick your neck out for people that you know are not going to work out. (Rosenbaum & Jones, 1998, T2)

In another case, the construction teacher at the suburban vocational school related (Rosenbaum & Jones, 1998).

> A kid who's . . . got a speech impediment, and . . . if you had a job interview with him, [you're] not gonna hire this guy. But . . . he comes when he's supposed to . . . and if you [explain a task], he'll pick up anything. . . . I've already lined the kid up with a job, and I said, "You probably won't like this kid until after he's worked for you a month or two, but then you'll realize he'll probably be a lifelong employee." I'd hire the kid in a second, but I wouldn't have the first time I met him. (T25)

Similarly, teachers place students with limited English skills. At the urban business school, a teacher reported "[I tell employers] forget testing. I've got Hispanic kids with poor English skills, they won't test out, but they show up every day, they're reliable. I know what you're looking for. I've got what you want. . . . I tell them the inside scoop" (T72).

Teachers even place students with learning disabilities. A suburban teacher reported, "I've had LD students that maybe aren't gonna be tool-and-die makers or mold makers but they can definitely be trained to run a type of machine. They'll be very satisfied to run that machine the rest of their lives" (T23).

Some teacher–brokers even convince employers to make a hire when they do not have a vacancy. At the urban career school, a teacher recalled, "A year ago, I went to these people that I dealt with for many years, . . . and I said, 'I know you don't need anybody right now, but you can't pass this person up.' They hired him, and they're very happy" (T12).

In some cases, teachers convinced employers to hire females or minorities in jobs that had previously been only held by White males. One teacher gave the example of a female who did well in his sheet metal class. When an employer expressed reluctance because he had never hired a female, the teacher reassured him that she was "as good as the last five males I sent you." The employer hired her. Without his recommendation, no woman would have been hired.

Although teachers usually try to serve employers' needs as employers state them, teacher–brokering goes even further—teachers tell employers whom to hire. Employers are reluctant to give teachers authority to override their traditional hiring criteria. However, many employers realize the limitations of their established procedures, and, if a trusted teacher is enthusiastic about a student, employers may forego procedures that do not work all that well anyway. The fact that vocational teachers can provide a trusted source of information that is not available through other screening methods gives these teachers additional leverage. Trusted teachers offer numerous advantages over the ordinary labor-market gamble.

These examples contradict a common conception. Getting jobs through "contacts" is often viewed as "cronyism"—unmeritocratic and biased. However, minorities and females more often get jobs through school contacts than White males. The many minority, female, low-achieving students who get better jobs through teacher contacts than could otherwise may indicate a less biased, meritocratic quality to "contacts." Teachers sometimes use their employer links to convince employers to consider alternate criteria of merit that are more work-relevant and less biased. Hiring based on "contacts" may sometimes be more meritocratic than using objective "merit" criteria.

CONCLUSION

Does this chapter exaggerate the importance of signals? Good information is nice, but surely it is no substitute for good training. That is what the British thought when they set up the expensive Youth Training System (YTS) program to give apprenticeship training to youth. They found that the program worked, but not because it provided training. Indeed, program success predicted labor market failure! Youths who successfully completed the program were more likely to be labor market failures than program drop-outs. Looking more closely, it was found that employers used the program to identify promising workers, and once identified, employers immediately shifted them to real jobs, rather than wait for them to complete their training (Cappelli, 1991). Apparently, trusted information about youths is more important than training. Employers are so desperate for good information that, when they get it from apprentice programs, they steal workers from the programs without letting them finish. A similar process may explain why co-op students get economic benefits if hired by their co-op employers (Stern & Stevens, 1992).

This model also sheds light on other puzzling research findings. Random-assignment evaluations of job training programs sometimes find negative effects—job training graduates get lower earnings than a control group with no training (Bloom, Orr, Cave, Bell, & Doolittle, 1992; Cave & Doolittle, 1991). The most plausible interpretation of negative effects is that participation in such programs confers stigma and fails to confer positive signals to employers.

Unlike the usual view of teachers as operating in the closed world of the classroom (Lortie, 1975), this chapter finds that teachers in other nations have formal responsibilities to help place their students in the labor market. Although American vocational teachers lack such formal responsibilities, some improvise informal initiatives. They know that employers have difficulty assessing new high school graduates and that, as teachers, they possess the very information employers need. Contrary to labor-market models that ignore intermediaries, we have found that some vocational teachers play a pivotal role in helping their students get jobs and in helping employers get useful information about youths. Some vocational teachers have made themselves intermediaries for conveying information between students and employers, and some employers have authorized teachers to influence their hiring decisions, even for applicants they might not have hired otherwise.

Network theory has generally focused on the ways weak contacts help people get jobs (Granovetter, 1995). Indeed, many teachers use weak contacts. Of the 110 vocational teachers (Rosenbaum & Jones, 1998), 95% have casual employer contacts from jobs they held before teaching, 85% know the specific attributes that local employers value, 86% have made efforts to learn the specific attributes that local employers in their field value, and 82% believe that their references are of some value to employers.

Yet, some teachers have strong contacts: 30% still keep summer jobs in industry, 32% had ten or more years of experience in their field, 38% said they have a good reputation with employers, and 31% prescreen students for specific employers. These teachers have strong relationships with employers, and they use these relationships to get jobs for deserving students. Although such strong contacts are not recognized and are not in teachers' job descriptions, many teachers improvise informal placement transactions, which mirror those in more formal systems of Japan and Germany. In effect, teachers not only make contacts; they also actively construct linkages, which they strengthen by conveying hard-to-assess, relevant, and trusted signals to employers. By these activities, teachers make their contacts into strong linkages that convince employers to hire youths whom they might not have considered otherwise.

Japanese high schools have institutional charters for job placement similar to the institutional charters of prestigious colleges in the United States (Meyer & Rowan, 1977). American high schools generally lack such formal charters, but the present results suggest that American teachers build linkages that turn ordinary recommendations into trusted certifications of students' quality. Unlike theorists, teachers do not view youths' problems as merely due to youth deficiencies or to labor market rigidities. Teachers see employers' difficulties in trusting the information they get about young job applicants (as employers themselves have also reported; Miller & Rosenbaum, 1997), and students' difficulties in knowing what behaviors employers value. In response, teachers take steps to provide both sides with the information they need in the context of trusted relationships.

These findings have policy implications. Because many work-bound students come from low-SES families, their families may have poor links to employers. Teachers' links can provide options that these students cannot get otherwise. Research has found that students who get "skill relevant" jobs do considerably better in the labor market than other students (Grasso & Shea, 1979), but research has not described how students obtain these skill-relevant jobs. Teachers' contacts with employers may underlie such successes, giving students access to jobs with higher wages and better earnings trajectories years later (Rosenbaum & Roy, 1996). Whereas policy reforms have advocated expensive and cumbersome certification bureaucracies, the informal initiatives that teachers describe are likely to be inexpensive and easily implemented.

Giving signals of value to these students contradicts a common stereotype in our society. Vocational students are often viewed as academic underachievers with behavior problems, but, like all stereotypes, these are partly wrong. Although vocational students have lower academic skills than college-track students on average, their academic skills have high variation, and some have higher achievement than some college-track students. In addition, Wirt and associates (1989) found that some vocational courses increase academic skills more effectively than general track courses.

More important, academics is not employers' highest priority, despite the Sunday speeches of top executives at top corporations (which rarely hire youths). Small businesses are the main employers of new high school graduates, and their highest priority is work habits such as attendance, responsibility, initiative, perseverance, and attention to quality, as national surveys have shown (NCEQW, 1994). Vocational teachers are in a good position to evaluate and certify these attributes in their students.

These findings are also theoretically significant. Functionalist theory predicts a simple automatic responsiveness that rarely occurs. However, we have found support for the theory's assumptions that employers have functional needs that schools can meet and that schools will respond to those needs. Indeed, some teachers improvise actions that respond to the very information needs that employers express. Whereas functionalist theory is too complacent about expecting the social system to respond automatically, some individual actors do sometimes respond. These responses may be sporadic, idiosyncratic, and hard to see, yet they ratify some of the premises of functionalist theory, even though the theory's predicted outcomes occur for less than 10% of relevant youths. Even though these activities are not expected, encouraged, or even publicly recognized in schools, some teachers seem to discern the need for them. It is noteworthy that they are described similarly by some local employers and by many teachers who do not know each other across unrelated schools.

Besides finding that some teachers create strong ties, we have also found some properties of those ties. Interestingly, these are just the kinds of social processes that are evident in the formal infrastructures of Japan and of Germany. On their own, some vocational teachers enhance the signaling effectiveness of their recommendations by learning what information employers value, by conveying hard-to-get information, by conveying relevant information through quasi-apprenticeship activities, and by conveying trusted information. Teachers build trust by emphasizing their professional reputation, their history of transactions, prescreening, and other sacrifices to preserve their reputation. In effect, these teachers turn ordinary recommendations into trusted certifications of students' quality by giving students signals that employers value and cannot easily assess in other ways.

Here again, Parsons (1959) may be partly correct—schools help youths enter adult roles in society. However, what Parsons failed to note is the observation of network theory—adult roles are only conferred to youths who have acquired trusted signals of their value, and schools can only aid this process if teachers build trusted relationships with employers. This is not as automatic as Parsons assumed. This process is a new discovery, consisting of actions that no one realized existed. Although they only affect 8% of work-bound students, they could be more frequent if they were recognized and encouraged, and they could offer a valuable option to a higher percentage of work-bound students or even to those who hold jobs while attending college, especially if college does not work out for them. Such findings pose an agenda for further research and for social policy.

APPENDIX: RESEARCH STRATEGY AND SAMPLE IN THE STUDY OF 110 VOCATIONAL TEACHERS

Because vocational teachers are likely to be key agents in this process, vocational teachers were studied, and vocational schools, which emphasize jobs more than comprehensive high schools, were oversampled. The analysis is primarily qualitative, and it focuses on what vocational teachers do in ordinary schools, but the generalizability of quantitative results cannot be certain.

The study interviewed 110 vocational teachers in 12 public high schools across the Chicago metropolitan area, 6 in the city and 6 in suburbs. Four were vocational high schools, which strongly emphasized offering job help; eight were comprehensive high schools with several substantial vocational programs.

Eleven of these 12 schools are fairly typical in operation and resources. The six suburban schools have larger budgets than city schools, but most do not devote much to vocational programs. Three of the four vocational schools are urban, and none has a large budget for new equipment. The suburban vocational school is the only one with many programs and new equipment in most fields.

The four vocational high schools encourage vocational teachers to have contacts with employers to keep abreast of employers' current practices, but teachers are not expected to help students get jobs. In the comprehensive schools, vocational programs are not highly valued, and vocational teachers are not encouraged to contact employers. Instead, students are encouraged to have college plans. All vocational programs are not very selective; all primarily enroll students with below-average achievement.

The six urban schools had substantial minority populations, ranging from 30% to 100% Black. Although three of the suburban schools were mostly White and middle class, the other three were not: one was mostly lower middle-class White, and two had high proportions of low-income and minority students. Although no claims can be made about generalizability, these schools represent a wide spectrum.

Approximately one fourth of each school's vocational teachers in business and in trade–technical training were interviewed. These fields are the two largest vocational programs in the United States, and they have positive occupational benefits (Arum & Shavit, 1995). Focusing on teachers who taught seniors, one-hour interviews were conducted during school hours. Interviews were taped, transcribed, and coded into a computer-based qualitative data analysis program, Factfinder.

REFERENCES

Althauser, R., & Kalleberg, A. (1981). Firms, occupations and the structure of labor markets. In I. Berg (Ed.), *Sociological Perspectives on Labor Markets* (pp. 308–356). New York: Academic Press.

Altonji, J. G., & Pierret, C. (1995). Employer learning and statistical discrimination. Unpublished manuscript. Evanston, IL: Institute for Policy Research, Northwestern University.

Arum, R. (1998, July). *The significance of school–business institutional ties.* Paper presented at the annual meeting of International Sociological Association, Montreal, Canada.

Arum, R., & Shavit, Y. (1995). Secondary vocational education and the transition from school to work. *Sociology of Education, 68,* 187—204.

Arvey R. D., & Faley, R. H. (1988). *Fairness in selecting employees.* Reading, MA: Addison-Wesley.

Attewell, P. (1992). Skill and occupational changes in U.S. manufacturing. In P. S. Adler (Ed.), *Technology and the future of work* (pp. 46–88). New York: Oxford University Press.

Bailey, T. (1989). Changes in the nature and structure of work. (Technical Paper No. 9). New York: Teachers College, Columbia University.

Bailey, T. (1994, May). *Barriers to employer participation in school-to-work transition programs.* Paper presented at the seminar on Employer Participant in School-to-Work Transition Programs, Brookings Institution, Washington, DC.

Basi, L., & Ashenfelter, O. (1986). The effect of direct job creation and training programs on low-skilled workers. In S. H. Danziger & D. H. Weinberg (Eds.), *Fighting poverty: What works and what doesn't* (pp. 133–151). Cambridge, MA: Harvard University Press.

Berg, I. (1971). *Education and jobs: The great training robbery.* Boston: Beacon Press.

Berryman, S. E. (1992). Apprenticeship as a paradigm for learning. In J. E. Rosenbaum (Ed.), *Youth apprentice-*

ship in America: Guidelines for building an effective system (pp. 25–39). Washington, DC: William T. Grant Foundation Commission on Work, Family, and Citizenship.

Bills, D. (1992). A survey of employer surveys: What we know about labor markets from talking with bosses. Research in Social Stratification and Mobility, 11, 3-31.

Bishop, J. (1988). Vocational education for at-risk youth: How can it be made more effective? (Working Paper No. 88–11). Ithaca, NY: New York State School of Industrial and Labor Relations, Cornell University.

Bishop, J. (1993). Improving job matches in the U.S. labor market. In M. N. Bailey (Ed.), Brookings papers on economic activity: Microeconomics (pp. 335–400). Washington, DC: The Brookings Institution.

Bishop, J., Blakemore, A., & Low, S. (1985). High school graduates in the labor market: A comparison of the class of 1972 and 1980. Columbus: National Center for Research in Vocational Education, Ohio State University.

Bloom, H.S ., Orr, L. L., Cave, G., Bell, S. H., & Doolittle, F. (1992). The national JTPA study: Title II–A impacts on earnings and employment at 18 months. Bethesda, MD: Abt Associates.

Boesel, D., Hudson, L., Deich, S., & Masten, C. (1994). Participation in and quality of vocational education. National Assessment of Vocational Education, Vol. II., U.S. Dept. of Education.

Borman, K. M. (1991). The first "real" job: A study of young workers. Albany, NY: State University of New York Press.

Bowles, S., & Gintis, H. (1976). Schooling in capitalist America: Educational reform and the contradictions of economic life. New York: Basic Books.

Burke, M. A. (1984). Becoming an MBA. Unpublished doctoral Thesis. Northwestern University, Evanston, Illinois.

Campbell, P., Basinger, K.S., Dauner, M.B., & Parks, M.A. (1986). Outcomes of vocational education for women, minorities, the handicapped, and the poor. Columbus: National Center for Research in Vocational Education, Ohio State University.

Cappelli, P. (1991). Are skill requirements rising? (EQW Working Paper). Philadelphia: National Center on the Educational Quality of the Workforce, University of Pennsylvania.

Cave, G., & Doolittle, F. (1991). Assessing Jobstart: Interim impacts of a program for school dropouts. New York: Manpower Demonstration Research Corporation.

D'Amico, R., & Maxwell, N. (1990). Black-white employment differences during the school-to-work transition: An explanation for between- and within-race Differences. Palo Alto, CA: SRI International.

Daymont, T. N., & Rumberger, R. W. (1982). Job training in the schools. In R. Taylor, H. Rosen, & F. Pratzner (Eds.), Job training for youth: The contributions of the Unites States employment development system. Columbus: National Center for Research in Vocational Education, Ohio State University.

Dore, R. (1992). Goodwill and the spirit of market capitalism. In M. Granovetter & R. Swedberg (Eds.), The sociology of economic life (pp. 159–180). Boulder, CO: Westview Press.

Gamoran, A. (1994). The impact of academic course work on labor market outcomes for youth who do not attend college: A research review. Unpublished manuscript prepared for the National Assessment of Vocational Education.

General Accounting Office. (1991). Transition from school to work. Washington, DC: Author.

Granovetter, M. (1985). Economic action and social structure: The problem of embeddedness. American Journal of Sociology, 91, 481–510.

Grannovetter, M. (1995). Getting a job: A study of contacts and careers (2nd ed.). Chicago, IL: University of Chicago Press.

Grasso, J. T., & Shea, J. R. (1979). Vocational education and training: Impact on youth. A technical report for the Carnegie council on policy studies in higher education. New York: The Carnegie Foundation for the Advancement of Teaching.

Grubb, W. N. (1992). Postsecondary vocational education and the sub-baccalaureate labor market: New evidence on economic returns. Economics of Education Review, 11(3), 225-248.

Grubb, W. N. (1993). The varied economic returns of postsecondary education: New evidence from the class of 1972. Journal of Human Resources, 28(2), 265-282.

Grubb, W. N. (1995). Response to comment. Journal of Human Resources, 30(1), 222-228.

Hamilton, S. F. (1990). Apprenticeship for adulthood: Preparing youth for the future. New York: The Free Press.

Harhoff, D., & Kane, T. J. (1993). Financing apprenticeship training: Evidence from Germany. (Working Paper No. 4557). Cambridge, MA: National Bureau of Economic Research.

Holzer, H. (1995). What employers want: Job prospects for less-educated workers. New York: Russell Sage Foundation.

Hunter, J. E., & Hunter, R. F. (1984). Validity and utility of alternative predictors of job performance. Psychological Bulletin, 96(1), 72–98.

Jones, S. A., & Rosenbaum, J. E. (1995, April). Vocational teachers' linkages as quasi-apprenticeships. Presented at the annual meeting of the American Educational Research Association, San Francisco, California.

Kane, T., & Rouse, C. E. (1995). Labor-market returns to two- and four-year college. *American Economic Review*, *85*(3), 600–614.

Kang, S., & Bishop, J. (1986). Effects of curriculum on labor market success immediately after high school. *Journal of Industrial Teacher Education*, *23*(4), 15–29.

Kariya, T., & Rosenbaum, J. E. (1995). Institutional linkages between education and work as quasi-internal labor markets. *Research in Social Stratification and Mobility*, *14*, 99–134.

Katz, L. F., & Murphy, K. M. (1992). Changes in relative wages, 1963–1987: Supply and demand factors. *Quarterly Journal of Economics*, *107*(1), 35–78.

Kerckhoff, A. C., & Bell, L. (1998). Hidden capital: Vocational credential and attainment in the U.S. *Sociology of Education*, *71*(2), 152–174.

Lah, D., et al. (1983). *Longer-term impacts of pre-employment services on the employment and earnings of disadvantaged youth: A project of the private sector initiatives demonstration of public/private ventures.* Philadelphia: Public/Private Ventures. (ERIC Document Reproduction Service No. ED 245 000).

Lazear, E. P. (1979). Why is there mandatory retirement? *Journal of Political Economy*, *87*(6), 1261–1284.

Lerman, R., & Pouncy, H. (1990). The compelling case for youth apprenticeships. *Public Interest*, *101*, 62–77.

Levy, F., & Murnane, R. J. (1992). U.S. earnings levels and earning inequality: A review of recent trends and proposed explanations. *Journal of Economic Literature*, *30*(3), 1333–1381.

Lewis, D. R., Hearn, J. C., & Zilbert, E. E. (1993). Efficiencies and equity effects of vocationally focused postsecondary education. *Sociology of Education*, *66*(3), 188–205.

Lortie, D. (1975). *School teacher: A sociological study.* Chicago: University of Chicago Press.

Lynch, L. M. (1989). The youth Labor market in the eighties: Determinants of re-employment probabilities for young men and women. *Review of Economics and Statistics*, *71*(1), 37–45.

Meyer, J. W., & Rowan, B. (1977). Institutionalized organizations: Formal structure as myth and ceremony. *American Journal of Sociology*, *83*, 340–363.

Meyer, R. (1982) *The federal role in vocational education* (Special Report #39). National Commission for Employment Policy. Washington, DC: U.S. Government Printing Office.

Meyer, R. H., & Wise, D. A. (1982). High school preparation and early labor force experience. In R. B. Freeman & D. A. Wise (Eds.), *The youth labor market problem: Its nature, causes, and consequences* (pp. 277–347). Chicago: University of Chicago Press.

Miller, S. R. (1998). Short-cut: The effects of high school grades on earnings (Unpublished Manuscript). Evanston, IL: Institute for Policy Research, Northwestern University.

Miller, S. R., & Rosenbaum, J. E. (1997). Hiring in a Hobbesian world: Social infrastructure and employers' use of information. *Work and Occupations*, *24*(4), 498–523.

Mills, V. (1977, November). *From school to work: Matching graduates to careers.* Paper presented at the conference on Labor Market Intermediaries sponsored by the National Commission for Manpower Policy, Washington, DC.

Murnane, R. J., & Levy, F. (1996). *Teaching the new basic skills: Principles for educating children to thrive in a changing economy.* New York: The Free Press.

Murnane, R. J., Willett, J. B., & Levy, F. (1995). The growing importance of cognitive skills in wage determination. *Review of Economics and Statistics*, *77*(2), 251–266.

National Academy of Sciences. (1984). *High schools and the changing workplace: The employers' view.* Washington, DC: National Academy Press.

National Center for Education Statistics. (1992). *Digest of educational statistics.* Washington, DC: Author.

National Center for Education Statistics. (1997). *Digest of educational statistics.* Washington, DC: Author.

National Center on Education & the Economy. (1990). *America's choice: High skills or low wages!* Rochester, NY: Author.

National Center on the Educational Quality in the Workforce. (1994). *The EQW national employer survey: First Findings,* Issues Number 10. Philadelphia: University of Pennsylvania.

National Research Council. (1989). *Fairness in employment testing: Validity generalization, minority issues, and the general aptitude test battery.* Washington, DC: National Academy Press.

Neckerman, K. M., & Kirschenman, J. (1991). Hiring strategies, racial bias, and inner-city workers. *Social Problems*, *38*, 801–815.

Organization for Economic Cooperation & Development. (1993). *Employment outlook.* Paris: Author.

Osterman, P. (1980). *Getting started: The youth labor market.* Cambridge, MA: MIT Press.

Osterman, P. (1994, May). *Strategies for involving employers in school to work programs.* Paper presented at the Brookings Institution Conference, Washington, DC.

Parsons, T. (1959). The school class as a social system: Some of its functions in American society. *Harvard Educational Review, 29*(4), 297–318.

Ray, C. A., & Mickelson, R. A. (1993). Restructuring students for restructured work. *Sociology of Education, 66*, 1–20.

Resnick, L. B., & Wirt, J. G. (1996). The changing workplace. In L. B. Resnick & J. G. Wirt (Eds.), *Linking school and work: Roles for standards and assessment* (pp. 1–22). San Francisco, CA: Jossey-Bass.

Reubens, B. G. (1974). Foreign and American experiences with the youth transition. In E. Ginzberg (Ed.), *From school to work*. Washington, DC: National Commission Manpower Policy.

Rosen, S. (1982). Authority, control, and the distribution of earnings. *Bell Journal of Economics, 13*(2), 311–323.

Rosenbaum J. E. (1976). *Making inequality: The hidden curriculum of high school tracking*. New York: Wiley.

Rosenbaum, J. E. (1998a). College-for-all: Do students understand what college demands? *Social Psychology of Education, 2*, 55–80.

Rosenbaum, J. E. (1998b). Should low-achieving high-school graduates attend college? Unpublished manuscript.

Rosenbaum, J. E., & Binder, A. (1997). Do employers really need more educated youth? *Sociology of Education, 70*, 68–85.

Rosenbaum, J. E., & Jones, S. A. (1995). Creating linkages in the high school-to-work transition: Vocational teachers' networks. In M. Hallinan (Ed.), *Restructuring schools: Promises, practices, and policy* (pp. 235–258). New York: Plenum.

Rosenbaum, J. E., & Jones, S. A. (1998). Creation and maintenance of effective school–work linkages. Working Paper. Evanston, IL: Institute for Policy Research, Northwestern University.

Rosenbaum, J. E., & Kariya, T. (1989). From high school to work: Market and institutional mechanisms in Japan. *American Journal of Sociology, 94*, 1334–1365.

Rosenbaum, J. E., & Kariya, T. (1991). Do school achievements affect the early jobs of high school graduates in the United States and Japan? *Sociology of Education, 64*, 78–95.

Rosenbaum, J. E., DeLuca, S., Miller, S., & Roy, K. (1999). Pathways into work: Short and long-term effects of personnal and institutional ties. *Sociology of Education, 72*(3), 179–196.

Rosenbaum, J. E., Kariya, T., Settersten, R. & Maier, T. (1990). Market and network theories of the transition from high school to work: Their application to industrialized societies. *Annual Review of Sociology, 16*, 263–299.

Rosenbaum, J. E., Miller, S. R., & Krei, M. S. (1996). Gatekeeping in an era of more open gates: High school counselors' views of their influence on students' college plans. *American Journal of Education, 104*, 257–279.

Rosenbaum, J. E., & Roy, K. (1996, August). *Long-term effects of high school grades and job placements*. Paper presented at the annual meeting of the American Sociological Association, New York,.

Squires, G. D. (1979). *Education and jobs: The imbalancing of the social machinery*. New Brunswick, NJ: Transaction Books.

Stern, D., Finkelstein, N., Stone, J. R., Latting, J., & Dornsife, C. (1994). *Research on school-to-work transition programs in the United States*. Berkeley, CA: National Center for Research in Vocational Education.

Stern, D., Raby, M., & Dayton, C. (1992). *Career academies: Partnerships for reconstructing American high schools*. San Francisco, CA: Jossey-Bass.

Stern, D., & Stevens, D. (1992). *Analysis of unemployment insurance data on the relationship between high school cooperative education and subsequent employment*. Paper prepared for the National Assessment of Vocational Education, Berkeley: University of California: School of Education.

Stevenson, H. W., & Stigler, J. W. (1992). *The learning gap: Why our schools are failing and what we can learn from Japanese and Chinese education*. New York: Summit.

Useem, E. (1986). *Low-tech education in a high-tech world: Corporations and classrooms in the new information society*. New York: The Free Press.

Veum, J. R., & Weiss, A. B. (1993). Education and the work histories of young adults. *Monthly Labor Review, 116*(4), 11–20.

Wanous, J. P. (1992). *Organizational entry: Recruitment, selection, orientation, and socialization of newcomers* (2nd ed). Reading, MA: Addison-Wesley.

Willis, R., & Rosen, S. (1979). Education and self-selection. *Journal of Political Economy 87*(5, part 2), 527–536.

Wilson, W. J. (1996). *When work disappears: The world of the new urban poor*. New York: Vintage.

Wirt, J. G., Muraskin, L. D., Goodwin, D. A., & Meyer, R. H. (1989). *National assessment of vocational education*. Washington, DC: U.S. Department of Education.

Witte, J., & Kalleberg, A. L. (1994). Determinants and consequences of fit between vocational education and employment in Germany. In N. Stacey (Ed.), *School-to-work: What Does Research Say about it?* (pp. 3–32). Washington, DC: U.S. Office of Education.

Zemsky, R. (1994). What employers want. (Working Paper). Philadelphia: National Center on the Educational Quality of the Workforce, University of Pennsylvania.

CHAPTER 19

Vocational Secondary Education, Tracking, and Social Stratification

YOSSI SHAVIT
WALTER MÜLLER

INTRODUCTION

Most secondary school systems maintain a distinction between academic and vocational education. The specifics may vary from place to place, but in most countries academic education prepares students for college or for a university whereas vocational education prepares them for immediate entry into the labor market. Some sociologists consider such tracking an aspect of the social organization of education that differentiates the life chances of the various social classes. They argue that whereas middle-class and upper class children attend tracks that lead through higher education to the professions, lower class children are more likely to be placed in vocational tracks that reduce their chances to attend a university later on, and that divert them from the more desirable occupations in the labor market (e.g., Shavit, 1990b). Some proponents of this approach would support the abolition of vocational education at the secondary level altogether, arguing that it teaches skills that can easily be acquired on the job rather than through schooling.

This perspective ignores the positive role that vocational education can play in shaping the life chances of its graduates. By focusing primarily on the process by which people gain entry to the most prestigious occupations and on the admittedly negative role of vocational education in this regard, they fail to notice that vocational education can reduce the likelihood of unemployment and of employment in the least desirable jobs.

YOSSI SHAVIT • Department of Sociology and Anthropology, Tel Aviv University, Tel Aviv, Israel 69978
WALTER MÜLLER • Department of Sociology, University of Mannheim, Mannheim D-68131, Germany

Handbook of the Sociology of Education, edited by Maureen T. Hallinan. Kluwer Academic/Plenum Publishers, New York, 2000.

This chapter is based on the assumption that the role of education in general, and of vocational education in particular, in the stratification process varies in accordance with its institutional context. It is organized as follows. We first outline the theoretical debate concerning the role of tracking and of vocational secondary education. This is followed by a brief discussion of the literature on the labor market outcomes of vocational secondary education. We then summarize the recent literature on the institutional characteristics of educational systems in an attempt to identify those characteristics that determine whether vocational education is a diversion from rewarding occupations or is a valuable safety net that reduces the risks of unemployment and of employment as unskilled labor. Following that, we summarize the results of an international comparative study that shows that in countries where vocational education provides an effective safety net, it also diverts students from prestigious occupations and that in other countries it does neither. The final section provides a summary of the chapter and lists some prevalent methodological shortcomings of research in the area.

VOCATIONAL EDUCATION: A DIVERSION OR A SAFETY NET?

Many educational systems are faced with a dilemma: on the one hand, they wish to equalize the life chances of their students, whereas on the other hand, they are expected to prepare them for positions in a differentiated labor market. The equalization of life chances requires that students be taught similar curricula in integrated classrooms and schools and experience similar educational environments. By contrast, the preparation of young people for the differentiated labor market requires a differentiation of the educational experience. The labor market requires a multiplicity of specific occupational skills corresponding to the many occupations that must be manned by cohorts entering the labor market. The preparation of young people for the labor market requires that curricula be differentiated to suit the diverse occupational destinations of students. The dilemma stems from the fact that the differentiation of curricula by type of skill requires tracking, namely, the differentiation of the student body into distinct groups experiencing different educational environments and leading to different social destinations. Educational systems that offer both academic and vocational training are necessarily tracked.

Scholars are divided between those who view the phenomenon primarily as a matter of vocational training and labor market preparation and those who view it as "tracking," namely the hierarchical differentiation of students into qualitatively distinct groups. Members of the first group perceive vocational education primarily through the prism of human capital theory, which assumes that skills, whether they be vocational or academic in nature, improve one's economic prospects in the labor market (Becker, 1975). These authors (e.g., Bishop, 1989; Blossfield, 1992; Rumberger & Daymont, 1984) assume that vocational education equips students with skills that can enhance their productivity on the job. Therefore, vocationally trained workers are in demand and their chances of gaining employment and decent wages are enhanced, compared to the chances of untrained workers.

The second group of scholars (e.g., Oakes, 1985; Shavit 1990a) draw on theories of class reproduction (Bowles & Gintis, 1976) and social exclusion (e.g., Collins, 1979; Parkin, 1979) and argue that tracking is a mechanism for the reproduction of social inequality across generations. Studies in numerous countries have shown that tracking impedes equality of educational and occupational opportunity. Lower class students are typically placed in lower tracks that, in turn, reduces their chances of attending a university and of subsequently entering the professions and other high-prestige occupations (e.g., Gamoran & Mare 1989; Iannelli, 1997; Shavit, 1990b).

Vocational tracks inhibit further educational attainment in several ways. First, attending a class alongside highly motivated and academically successful students enhances ones own chances of success (Coleman, et al., 1966; Hallinan & Williams, 1990). Because vocational tracks are usually attended by academically weaker students, they are deprived of the beneficial effect of a more favorable milieu. Second, vocational tracks offer a more restricted curriculum (Gamoran, 1987; Oakes, 1985) and their students are less likely to take advanced courses. Third, in the less selective tracks, less time is devoted to actual instruction (Oakes, 1985), and instruction is conducted at a lower level of intellectual complexity (Metz, 1978). Consequently, students in the lower tracks learn less than those in the upper tracks and are less likely to succeed in college admission tests. Fourth, being placed in a lower track or ability group signals to students that they are less worthy, which in turn dampens both their expectations of what they can achieve and their aspirations for the future (Vanfossen, Jones, & Spade, 1987). Thus, vocational track placement at the secondary level reduces students' chances of continuing on to college.

Bowles and Gintis (1976) argued that tracking contributes to the reproduction of class inequality by differentiating the socialization of the different social classes. Students of working-class origins typically attend vocational tracks where they are socialized in accordance with the values that correspond to those that will shape their lives as members of the proletariat. Academic tracks, in contrast, socialize their predominantly middle-class students in accordance with the values of managerial and professional occupations.

Proponents of the critical approach to vocational education tend to downplay the relevance of school knowledge for job performance and argue that occupationally relevant skills are acquired primarily on the job. They often cite the Signaling Theory (Spence, 1974; Thurow, 1975), which alleges that schools are simply sorters and signalers, with school performance being an indicator of various characteristics of job applicants. Good students are assumed to be hard working, disciplined, intelligent and, most important, fast learners of new skills. In their attempt to cut training costs, employers hope to recruit fast-learning employees. Vocational qualifications may signal to them that the job applicant has a low aptitude, or is a troublemaker, for why else would he or she have attended a vocational track rather than an academic one?

It is important to point out that this critique of vocational education is presented from a decidedly middle-class perspective. It evaluates vocational education from the point of view of its effects on university attendance and on the chances of finding prestigious occupations when entering the labor market. However, the effect of vocational education on the opportunities of its students should also be evaluated by the extent to which it serves as a safety net that reduces the probability of unemployment and of employment in the lowest paying jobs (Arum & Shavit, 1995). From the point of view of working-class youths these are real risks, and educational alternatives should be evaluated according to their effectiveness in reducing them.

Several American studies evaluated the effects of vocational education on these and other labor market outcomes, and reported significant, if small, effects. Hotchkiss and Dorsten (1987) found statistically significant effects of vocational high school curricula on various early career outcomes such as unemployment, occupational prestige, and earnings. Similarly, Rumberger and Daymont (1984) found that the accumulation of both academic and vocational credits increases the chances of employment, reduces the duration of unemployment, and increases earnings. Bishop (1989) found that vocational courses increase the earnings and the chance of employment for men and women. Arum and Shavit (1995) found that although vocational education reduces the likelihood of students attending postsecondary education and subsequently of finding employment in the professions and in managerial occupations, it also reduces the risk of unemployment and increases the chances of employment as skilled workers.

The effects of vocational education on the future attainments of students appear to vary consistently between men and women, with women benefiting more from it than men. Analyzing the *High School and Beyond* data set, Lewis, Hearn, and Zilbert (1993) found that compared with secondary education, postsecondary vocational programs relatively enhance the mean future earnings of their students. However, the effects were much more pronounced for women than for men.

Using the same data set, Arum and Shavit (1995) examined the effects of various vocational programs on the occupational attainment of men and women. They found that vocational programs play a doubly important role for women. Vocational business programs, where women are largely concentrated, enhance the likelihood of finding routine nonmanual employment, whereas trade and technical programs, which have a smaller number of women enrolled in them, provide a path into skilled manual occupations, which are still sex-typed as masculine occupations.

In their exhaustive review of the empirical literature on vocational education and training in the United States, Boesel and his associates (Boesel, Hudson, Deich, & Masten, 1994; chapter 6) found consistent differences between men and women. Vocationally trained women had higher income and better employment chances than both their male counterparts and women who had attained comparable levels of academic education. The advantages are most pronounced for women who had attended vocational education in business, in health, and in home economics, the traditional fields of training for women. Because these are traditional fields of employment for women, training in them is often relevant to job requirements, and therefore, it enhances earnings.

The quality of training that vocational programs offer is another factor that accounts for the differences in the effects of vocational education. Arum (1997) showed that financial support for vocational programs varies greatly between states. Differences between states in the level of funding is strongly related to differences between them in the degree to which vocational education affects labor market outcomes such as income and the chances of being employed. In states such as California and New York, which invest less resources in these programs, enrollment in vocational programs decreases an individual's likelihood of doing well in the labor market. However, in states that spend more on these programs, such as Pennsylvania and Michigan, enrollment in vocational programs dramatically improves student outcomes.

The effectiveness of vocational education also varies by its specificity and relevance to employers', requirements. Boesel and his associates (1994) stated that

> [D]espite the mixed results regarding overall returns to secondary vocational education there is evidence of beneficial employment outcomes whenever students find jobs related to their field of study. The strongest, most consistent finding throughout the literature is that improved earnings do accrue in situations where vocational training is directly related to job tasks. (p. 137)

They also found that

> . . . Students who concentrate in a single area of course work have better economic outcomes than those who take courses in a variety of subjects . . . The effects of course concentration . . . appear to influence outcomes via the link between training and related jobs. That is, taking more courses in a major subject pays off only if work is in a related field. (p. 139)

These findings would put into question the view, cited earlier, that vocational education is of little relevance to job performance and is not rewarded in the labor market. In fact, they are consistent with the view that employers prefer workers who have specific vocational skills that are relevant to the requirements of their jobs, presumably because such workers require less on-the-job training and can be productive soon after they are hired. As we show in the following section, this view is also supported by the results of an international comparative research on the effects of vocational education on occupational outcomes.

INTERNATIONAL VARIATIONS

The literature cited previously suggests that the extent to which vocational education enhances the future attainments of its students varies. It tends to be greater for women than for men, and it is related to the specificity of the curriculum and to its relevance for job performance. It is also greater in states that invest more heavily in their vocational education programs. In the present section we focus on international differences in the effects of vocational education on occupational attainment.

In recent years, we have seen a new wave of comparative international studies on variations in the role of education in the process of stratification. (For an excellent review, see Kerckhoff, 1995.) This literature builds on, and extends, the agenda of an earlier wave of research that has been stimulated by Turner's (1960) typological distinction between the American and the British educational systems. Studies in the earlier wave (e.g., Kerckhoff, 1974; Treiman & Terrell, 1975) tested the hypothesis that in the British system of sponsored mobility, there is less equality of educational opportunity than in the American system of contest mobility. The hypothesis was refuted, but the premise, that the role of education in the stratification process is conditioned by its institutional context, stands fast. The new wave of research is based on a more elaborate typology of educational institutions and suggests that it does condition the attainment process in consistent ways (e.g., Allmendiger, 1989; Hannan, Raffe, & Smyth, 1997; Kerckhoff, 1995; Shavit & Müller, 1998a). In the present section we review some of this literature with specific reference to the issue of vocational secondary education and its role in the occupational attainment process.

Organization and Qualification Spaces

A very influential study in this new wave was Maurice, Sellier, and Silvestre's (1986) comparison of French and German firms and their labor practices. Through a detailed analysis of work organization, job recruitment, and mobility patterns in French and in German firms, the authors showed that the characteristics of the educational system in these countries have profound effects on the social organization and the management of labor.

The authors refer to the German system as a qualification space, whereas the French one is described as an organizational space. In Germany, most young workers begin their working life with an apprenticeship. These apprenticeships are organized as a "dual system," which combines on-the-job training with instruction in public vocational schools. Apprentices spend several days a week in the firm, performing various tasks through which they learn the practical aspects of the occupation for which they are trained. On other days they attend classroom instruction in which they are taught theoretical knowledge related to their occupational specialization and more general skills that cut across occupations. The apprenticeship system is maintained through a cooperation between three kinds of organizations: the State, business organizations (chambers of trade, industry, and commerce), and the trade unions. These organizations jointly design the training programs, negotiate the specific skills which are taught, negotiate the standards of instruction, determine the examination procedures, and attempt to meet the demand for both training opportunities and trained workers (Crouch, Finegold, & Sako, 1999, chapter 5).

This institutional structure leads to highly standardized qualifications in the German workforce. German employers know which skills are taught in the various apprenticeship programs and can rely on vocational qualifications to indicate mastery of these well-defined skills. Consequently, employers can organize work and production in accordance with the availability of skill pools.

Maurice, Sellier, and Silvestre (1986) label the German system as a qualification space because it is segmented by vocational qualifications. Qualified workers have a clearly defined occupational identity and as a result, mobility between occupations, which require different qualifications, is not very common. And yet, due to the standardization of vocational qualifications, qualified workers can move between firms with relative ease.

Furthermore, because training takes place before bona fide labor force entry, young workers already have well-defined occupational skills, and they can contribute to the firm from the start. As a result, they do not suffer a substantial disadvantage when compared with experienced workers and can find employment with relative ease. Indeed, youth unemployment rates in Germany are low.

Part of the corporatist agreements between unions and employers is that unskilled workers can not be hired for jobs that require vocational qualifications. Thus, workers without certified vocational qualifications, except university graduates, stand at a marked disadvantage in the labor market. Their unemployment rates are high and they are consigned to unskilled work.

By contrast, in France, as in many other countries, education is centered on the provision of general, rather than vocational, education. To the extent that vocational education is offered, it is given mainly in schools rather than in firms.* Vocational education has a residual character—it is intended for students who do not do well in school. The major shortcoming of school-based training is that it does not provide students with the same degree of hands-on experience as do apprenticeships. Graduates of school-based training often complain, when entering the workplace, that they had not been taught "what it's really like" (Blossfeld, 1992; Erbes-Seguin, Gilan, & Kieffer, 1990). Another problem of school-based training is that it tends to lag behind technological and other developments in the economy and is often obsolete. In a world of rapid change, it takes time to convert new technologies to training curricula and for schools to acquire the equipment necessary for their instruction.

Human capital theory (Becker, 1975) distinguishes between firm-specific and general skills. The former refers to skills that are useful only to a particular firm, whereas the latter are transferable between firms. In an economy where workers are free to move between firms, employers are reluctant to invest in workers' general skills because the investment is lost once workers move on to another firm. However, in a system such as the French one, employers cannot draw on ready-made skills and have no choice but to train their workers.

The ideas developed by Maurice et al (1986) are closely related to the literature on segmented labor markets (Doeringer & Piore, 1971) and, in particular, to the recent distinction between firm-internal and occupational labor markets (Marsden, 1990). In countries such as

---

*Although, in very recent years, there has been a growing involvement of French firms and of employer's organizations in the provision of vocational training and apprenticeships (Goux & Maurin, 1998; Crouch, Finegold, & Sako, 1999, chapter 4).

France, where vocational training is not well developed, firms that require substantial job-specific training for job performance create internal promotion ladders and tend to pay wages and salaries above the market rate, all in an attempt to reduce worker turnover. In such firm-internal labor markets young workers would find it difficult to enter the qualified jobs and will suffer from higher job instability and unemployment rates than older workers. However, once they gain entry, and are trained, at the expense of their employers, they are likely to remain in the organization for long periods. Hence the label "organizational space."

Other things being equal, the prevalence of occupational labor markets, such as in Germany, in an economy should grow as the vocational training is more occupationally specific. The more specific the training, the bigger the impact of vocational qualifications on the labor market prospects of workers. Indicators of occupational specificity are the number of occupational specializations that are taught and the proportion of cohorts who receive such occupationally specific training. Countries vary to a large degree in the characteristics of their educational systems. Some offer general education (e.g., Ireland or the United States); others offer specialized vocational training for hundreds of different occupations and for large proportions of each cohort (e.g., the German-speaking countries, the Netherlands, and Denmark); still others (such as Sweden) take an intermediate approach providing vocational education under broad headings, such as metalwork, and teach basic principles while avoiding narrow specialization.

Standardization and Stratification

Several recent comparative studies of educational systems have distinguished between different systems on the basis of their degree of stratification and standardization (e.g., Allmendinger, 1989; Blossfeld, 1992; Kerckhoff, 1995; Müller & Shavit, 1998). The term "stratification" refers to the extent and form of tracking that is pervasive in the educational system. In highly stratified systems (e.g., Germany and Switzerland), students are separated early on into tracks that differ greatly in their curricula and in the probability of students continuing to the tertiary level. In these countries there is also little or no mobility between tracks. By contrast, in less stratified educational systems, such as the American and the Irish ones, tracking begins at a later age, the curricula of the various tracks are less distinct, there is more intertrack mobiliy, and consequently, there are smaller differences between tracks in the probability of continuing to tertiary education.

Clearly, the stratification of an educational system is closely related to the specificity of its vocational education. Where vocational education is highly specific, as it is in qualification spaces, the curricula taught in the different tracks are very distinct from one another, and as a result, intertrack mobility is limited. Where stratification is high, credentials provide detailed signals about the educational achievements of job applicants and therefore serve as an important basis for hiring and for the occupational allocation of workers.

Standardization is defined as the degree to which the quality of education meets the same standards nationwide. Variables such as teacher training, school budgets, curricula, and the uniformity of school-leaving examinations are relevant in measuring standardization. Several authors have argued (Allmendinger, 1989; Blossfeld, 1992) that the coupling of educational qualifications and occupational attainment is stronger in highly standardized systems because employers can rely on credentials to represent skill content reliably. In systems with a low degree of standardization, employment decisions are less likely to be based on education because credentials are a less reliable indication of employee qualifications.

Linkages

Another characteristic of vocational education systems that determines their effectiveness in the occupational allocation of graduates is the extent to which they are "linked" to employers. Linkages can take a variety of forms (Hannan et al., 1997). As noted earlier, in some countries, most notably in Germany, in Switzerland, and in Austria, training is managed jointly by firms, by employers' organizations, and by the educational system. These institutions are jointly responsible for the training, and together they determine the skill requirements of specified occupations in the labor market. As noted, employers can rely on vocational qualifications to represent well-defined skills that are relevant to job requirements.

Another form of linkage between schools and the labor market is the involvement of teachers in the job placement process. In some countries, most notably Japan, schools serve as job placement offices. In a series of papers, Rosenbaum and his various associates (Rosenbaum & Kariya, 1991; Rosenbaum, Kariya, Settersten, & Maier, 1990) compared the school-to-work transition process in Japan and in the United States. They demonstrated that in Japan there is a strong institutional linkage between school and universities on the one hand and firms on the other. Schools and universities refer students to specific employers. These relationships have important implications for the role of education in job placement. Characteristically, Japanese employers rely on school grades in the same way that employers in other countries rely on letters of recommendation. Schools do not recommend students lightly because they have to maintain their credibility with the employers. Employers will continue the relationship because they value the screening that trusted partner–schools perform for them. In a very recent study Rosenbaum (1998) found a similar phenomenon in America. He showed that vocational school teachers in the Chicago area maintained very close ties with employers and played an important facilitating role in the job placement of their students, much like the Japanese teachers did. However, it seems that in the United States these schools are more the exception than the rule.

A Comparative Study

In the previous section we discussed some of the institutional characteristics of educational systems that may have an impact on the role of vocational education in the occupational attainment process. In the present section, we present comparative data on the relationship between vocational secondary education and various occupational outcomes and examine how they vary according to institutional context. Specifically, we were interested in identifying the institutional characteristics of educational systems that determine the extent to which vocational education diverts its students from prestigious occupations and in identifying those characteristics that enhance its role as a safety net. We also wanted to know in which countries vocational education is a diversion and in which it is a safety net.

We drew on data that was generated recently by our comparative study on educational qualifications and occupational destinations (Shavit & Müller, 1998a). The objective of that study was to examine a series of hypotheses concerning differences between countries regarding the way educational qualifications affect occupational attainment and employment. Research teams from 13 countries participated in the project: Australia, Great Britain, France, Germany, Ireland, Israel, Italy, Japan, the Netherlands, Sweden, Switzerland, Taiwan, and the United States. Each team studied the relationship between educational qualifications and occupational attainment early in the careers of men and women, as well as their labor force participation and unemployment rate. The 13 studies maintain a common research design, used similar operational definitions of variables, and employed similar data sets and statistical methods and are, therefore quite comparable.

We measured educational qualifications on the CASMIN (Comparative Analysis of Social Mobility in Industrialized Societies) educational schema (Braun, Müller, & Steinman, 1997; Müller, Luettinger, Koenig, & Karle, 1989). The schema was developed through intensive study of the educational systems in many countries and is now widely used in comparative studies of education and of social stratification. The schema, its categories, and their definitions are shown in Table 19.1. With some minor adaptations, it is applicable to a wide variety of educational systems. All educational systems are differentiated into primary, secondary, and tertiary levels, and virtually all systems distinguish between vocational and academic, or general, tracks. The CASMIN schema combines these two dimensions. It distinguishes between primary, secondary, and postsecondary education, and within each level, it also distinguishes between academic and vocational education. In the present discussion, we focused primarily on the occupational outcomes for persons with vocational secondary qualifications (2a), academic secondary qualifications that do not qualify for university admission (2b), and academic secondary qualifications that do grant access to universities (2c).

Occupational attainment early in the career was measured in two ways: first, on occupational prestige scales, or their equivalents, which are available for virtually all countries (see, e.g., Treiman, 1977). Each occupation is assigned a score, which represents its social standing or prestige relative to other occupations. In addition, we measured the odds ratio of entering the labor force as a skilled worker rather than an unskilled one.

The individual country studies estimated the effects of educational qualifications on the occupational prestige of first jobs, and on the odds of entering the labor force as skilled workers rather than unskilled workers rather than unskilled ones. Differences between countries in these effects were then related to differences between them in the institutional characteristics of their national educational systems.

Four characteristics of the education systems were considered, of which the first three were discussed in the previous section. These are as follows:

TABLE 19.1. The CASMIN Educational Schema

Qualification	Description
1ab	This is the social minimum of education. Namely, the minimal level that individuals are expected to have obtained in a society. It generally corresponds to the level of compulsory education.
1c	Basic vocational training above compulsory schooling. In Germany, in Switzerland, and in similar countries, this category corresponds to short apprenticeships that are taken after compulsory schooling. In most other countries this category does not exist.
2a	This category represents vocational secondary education or, where applicable, apprenticeships for teenagers, which combine firm-based training supplemented with school instruction.
2b	Academic tracks at the secondary level. In the American case, this category refers to the general track.
2c	Full matriculation diploma (e.g., the *Abitur*, Matriculation, *Baccalaureate*, A-levels). In the American study, this category was assigned to graduates of college preparatory tracks in high school.
3a	Lower level tertiary degrees, generally of shorter duration and with a vocational orientation (e.g., American junior colleges, technical college diplomas, social worker or, nonuniversity teaching certificates).
3b	The completion of a traditional, academically oriented college or university education.

1. The extent to which vocational students are taught specific occupational skills, as opposed to more general ones.
2. The extent to which the curricula, and certificates awarded in the systems, are standardized.
3. The degree of stratification of secondary education in the different countries.
4. The proportion of recent cohorts who attained postsecondary qualifications.

We found that the effects of education in the occupational attainment process were systematically related to some of the institutional characteristics. The effects of education on occupational outcomes were stronger in countries with a high degree of occupational specificity of vocational education, highly stratified secondary education, and standardized educational systems. In a related study (Shavit & Müller, 1998b), we found that in these countries there are also strong linkages between the educational system and labor market organizations.

We also found that the effects of education on labor allocation tended to be weaker in countries with a large sector of tertiary education. We suspect that the reason for this finding is the following: in countries, such as the United States, where vocational education is not well developed, there is a built-in incentive for young people to acquire more and more education so they can stay ahead in the competition for jobs, but as more people obtain diplomas, their value in the labor market declines. In contrast, in countries where vocational education is specific, the value of a diploma does not derive (solely or primarily) from its position in the hierarchy of credentials but also from the specific skills it represents. Thus, in such qualification spaces there is less pressure to attain ever higher certificates and diplomas. When comparing Switzerland and Germany, two typical qualification spaces, with the United States and Japan, two organization spaces, we found (Müller & Shavit, 1998, pp. 12–13) that in the former, only about 10% to 15% attain tertiary degrees, as compared with over 30% in the latter. Thus, organization spaces tend to produce an excessive supply of secondary and postsecondary graduates, thereby lowering the value of these credentials in the labor market. By contrast, in occupational spaces, the value of educational credentials is preserved because it is mediated by skill rather than by the relative ranking of workers in a quantitative educational queue.

Vocational Education as a Safety Net

Having discussed more general implications of institutional characteristics of school systems, we now turn to several more specific issues of the relationship between vocational secondary education and occupational attainment in early career. In Table 19.2 we present three indicators of that relationship. The first refers to vocational education as a safety net. The numbers in the first column show the log odds ratios for men with secondary vocational education, compared with the lowest educational category, of getting a first job as a skilled worker, rather than as an unskilled one.* The larger the number, the more beneficial is vocational education in the competition for employment as skilled workers. This variable measures the extent to which vocational secondary education serves as a safety net in the sense that it reduces the odds of entering the labor market in the least desirable occupation.

There are clear national differences in the magnitude of this safety-net effect. It is strongest in Germany, in Austria and in Switzerland, and weakest in Taiwan, in Sweden, and in

_____

*In order to save space, we have presented data for men only. The results for women are similar but not identical.

TABLE 19.2. Country Differences in the Effects of Vocational Secondary Qualifications on Men's Occupational Outcomes.

Countries	The effect of vocational secondary education, compared to no secondary education, on the log chances of entering the labor force as a skilled, rather than an unskilled worker. (1)	The effect of vocational secondary, compared to academic secondary education on the log chances of entering the labor market as a skilled, rather than an unskilled worker. (2)	The effect of vocational secondary education, compared to the matriculation diploma, on the occupational prestige of first job (in units of standard deviation). (3)
1. Australia (AUS)	2.53	2.57	0.04
2. Britain (GB)	1.72	0.62	−.15
3. France (F)	1.54	0.45	−.28
4. Germany (D)	3.05	n.a.	−.30
5. Ireland (IRL)	n.a.	n.a.	n.a.
6. Israel (IL	0.64	1.00	−.43
7. Italy (I)	1.11	0.22	−.16
8. Japan (J)	n.a.	n.a.	n.a.
9. Netherlands (NL)	1.14	1.10	−.36
10. Sweden (S)	0.59	0.52	−.51
11. Switzerland (CH)	2.35	0.32	−.34
12. Taiwan (TAI)	0.20	−.26	0.03
13. USA	0.71	0.20	−.11

Israel. It tends to be large in countries where vocational secondary education has a strong occupationally specific component and where the system of secondary education is highly stratified. It is weak in those where vocational education is more general and where stratification is low.

We now present a more stringent test of the benefits of vocational secondary education in the occupational attainment process. Rather than comparing its effects with those of elementary education, we compared it with the effects of academic secondary education, on the log odds of entering the labor market as a skilled worker rather than an unskilled one. The results are shown in Column 2 of Table 19.2. It is striking that in 9 out of the 10 countries for which data is available, vocational education is a more effective safety net than academic education of a comparable level. In all countries except Taiwan, the chances of entering the labor market in the lowest occupational class are greater for those with just a 2b qualification. This pattern is consistent with the rationale of vocational education, which is to improve the occupational prospects of those who are not likely to continue past the secondary level. It also underscores the risk involved in attending the academic track for students who, for various reasons such as low scholastic aptitude or motivation, are not likely to obtain a diploma of matriculation (or in the American case, to graduate from the college track). In virtually all countries, academic education without a diploma is associated with a greater risk of entering the labor force through the least desirable jobs.

The magnitude of the contrast between the effects of vocational and academic secondary education varies between the countries in our sample. It is greatest in Australia, followed by Great Britain, Israel, and the Netherlands, it is small in the United States and in Switzerland, and is negative in Taiwan. We were not able to identify any consistent covariation between the size of the contrast and the institutional characteristics of the national educational systems.

Vocational Education as a Diversion

As noted at the outset, the major criticism directed against vocational education is that it diverts students away from the more prestigious occupations. Studies in many countries have shown that vocational track placement lowers students' chances to attain higher education and prestigious occupations (e.g., Breen, Iannelli, & Shavit, 1998; Shavit, 1990a). However, we also know that many of those who turn to vocational tracks are unlikely to have continued on to college or to a university even if they had selected the academic track while in secondary education (e.g., Shavit, 1984). It is interesting, therefore, to compare the occupational costs and benefits associated with vocational secondary education with those secured by graduates of academic education who enter the labor market with a matriculation diploma (or its equivalent), but without any tertiary education.

In Column 3 of Table 19.2, we compare the effects of having a vocational secondary education or of having obtained a matriculation diploma (i.e., qualification 2c) on the occupational prestige of first jobs. Positive figures mean that the average prestige scores of first jobs are higher for graduates with vocational qualifications than for graduates from the academic route; negative figures indicate the contrary. In all but 2 of the 10 countries for which data is available, vocational education returned less prestigious jobs than a matriculation diploma, but the magnitude of this negative effect varies between countries. In Sweden, for example, the mean occupational prestige attained by graduates of vocational education is lower by about half a standard deviation than that attained by workers holding a matriculation diploma. The prestige difference between the two educational categories is lowest in the English-speaking countries in our sample: Australia, Great Britain, and the United States, as well as in Taiwan.

To sum, and this perhaps is an unexpected result, the disadvantage, in occupational prestige, associated with vocational secondary education tends to be large especially in those countries where vocational education provides the most effective safety net (e.g., Germany and Switzerland) and small in those with the least effective net (e.g., Taiwan and the United States).

SUMMARY AND DISCUSSION

This chapter is concerned with one of the more persistent debates in the sociology of education: What is the role of vocational education in the process of occupational attainment? Many scholars, especially neo-Weberians and neo-Marxists, subscribe to the position that the skills that are taught in most vocational tracks are of little value to employers and to employees and that vocational education is simply a diversion of working-class students from the high road leading to higher education and the professions. These scholars consider vocational secondary education as an organizational aspect of education, which serves to reproduce social inequality between generations. Human capital theorists, on the other hand, argue that vocational education can teach students skills that might be valuable to employers and can enhance employability and the attainment of both earnings and desirable occupations.

We began with the assumption that the role of vocational secondary education in the stratification process—a safety net or diversion—varies between countries in ways that are consistently related to the way these countries organize their educational systems. We have seen that the effects of vocational secondary education on labor market outcomes in the United States are generally small, especially for men, but that they vary in interesting ways. Vocational secondary education appears to be effective when it is well focused, occupationally specific, and relevant to the requirements of jobs. It is more effective for women than for men, probably because women are more likely to be trained in areas closely related to their future occupations.

Drawing on the recent international comparative literature on educational institutions, we identified four systemic variables that might determine the extent to which vocational education enhances or inhibits the occupational attainment of its students. Briefly, they are the following: the extent to which the national educational system is standardized; the extent to which secondary education in the different countries is stratified; the extent to which vocational secondary education teaches specific rather than general skills; and, finally, the extent to which there is a linkage between schools and firms, which facilitate the job placement of graduates. We hypothesized that these four variables affect the role vocational education plays in the occupational attainment process.

These hypotheses were examined using data on the relationship between educational qualifications and occupational attainment early in the careers of men in 11 countries that have diverse educational institutions. We found four interesting results. First, in all countries secondary vocational education reduced the chances of a worker entering the labor force as an unskilled worker. Vocationally trained workers were more likely than workers without secondary education to enter the labor force as skilled workers rather than as unskilled ones. Second, the advantages associated with vocational education were most pronounced in countries where vocational secondary education is specific rather than general, and where it is highly stratified. Third, in most countries, graduates of vocational secondary education attained lower occupational prestige than that attained by graduates of academic secondary education. Finally, this disadvantage of vocational education appears to be most pronounced in countries where vocational education also serves as an effective safety net. It was least pronounced in the United States and in Taiwan where it does not provide a safety net. This is an important finding because it suggests that both groups of scholars, human capital theorists as well as Neo-Weberians and Neo-Marxists, are correct. Vocational education and tracking can both provide a safety net and be a mechanism of social exclusion.

Clearly, the role of vocational education varies between countries in complex ways, which are not fully captured by the institutional variables that we have studied. And yet, a simplified picture of our results would distinguish between two ideal-typical worlds of educational institutions, closely corresponding to the distinction made by Maurice, Sellier, and Silvestre (1986) between qualification spaces and organizational spaces. The former includes countries such as Germany, Switzerland, and the Netherlands, in which secondary education is highly stratified, where vocational education offers occupationally specific training, and where institutional links between training institutions and employers are prevalent. The other includes countries in which there is little stratification, where vocational education is general rather than specific, and where links between the two kinds of institutions are not very common.

In the first world, vocational education seems to serve a dual purpose: on the one hand, it enhances the chances of students to find a job as skilled workers and reduces their chances of slipping to the bottom of the occupational ladder. On the other hand, it has a strong negative effect, compared with academic secondary education, on the chances of attaining a prestigious occupation early in one's career. In these countries vocational secondary education is a double-edged sword. It is both an effective safety net and an effective mechanism of diversion from desirable occupations.

By contrast, in the world of organizational spaces, the distinction between vocational and academic secondary education is less consequential either way. Vocational education is less valuable as a safety net because it is general rather than specific. However, it is also less effective as a mechanism of exclusion because stratification is less pronounced, and students are not locked into a trajectory early on.

Before concluding, we would like to discuss methodological shortcomings which seem to recur in the literature we reviewed. First, most studies on the labor market outcomes of vocational education focus on the career beginnings of young men and women (Boesel et al., 1994, chapter 6). Recent research has shown that the advantages of vocational training in the occupational and income attainment processes are short-lived (Grubb, 1996) and tend to disappear after several years in the labor force. This may be due to the following reasons: Academic education prepares students for a wide range of occupations in the labor market. This increases their flexibility and enables them to shift between occupations in search of a better job. In contrast, an emphasis on specific skills in the curriculum increases the probability that students will gain entry into related jobs but reduces their chances of mobility into better ones or of finding employment outside the band of their qualifications. This logic suggests that vocationally trained workers benefit from their specific skills in the early stages of their career but are then unlikely to move to better jobs. In contrast, those trained in general education may find it more difficult to gain entry into good jobs but can improve their occupations and earnings over time, as they shift between jobs and occupations (Keijke, Koeslag, & Van der Velden, 1997). Thus, future research should study the effects of vocational qualifications at several points during a career.

Second, most studies on the subject, ours included, distinguish between vocational and academic (or general) education but fail to identify distinct areas of specialization. Some studies differentiate between broad fields of study but do not identify individual programs. There is clear evidence, from a variety of countries, that different vocational programs affect the attainment process in distinct ways. For example, Kerckhoff and Bell (1998) compared the labor market outcomes for American graduates of vocational posttsecondary programs with the outcomes attained by those holding an associate's degree. They found that the status levels of the jobs held by those with vocational degrees were usually lower than the status levels of the jobs held by the associate's group. The exceptions were the jobs held by graduates of the vocational programs in computer-related occupations. These were higher status on the average than the status of the associate's group. Similar differences among distinct types of vocational programs in their effects on occupational and income attainments have also been shown by Dronkers (1993) in his description of vocational education systems in the Netherlands, and by Erikson and Jonsson (1998), who studied the school-to-work transition in Sweden. Future studies should try and use detailed classifications of education and training programs.

Finally, there is, as always, the general issue of definition—what counts as vocational education and/or training. Most studies on education and social stratification have focused on school-based education and ignore training in out-of-school settings. In some countries, especially in the German-speaking world, in the Netherlands, and in Denmark, out-of-school training is highly formalized and is therefore measured by students of stratification. However, in other countries practices vary. For example, American studies of stratification usually measure the traditional, school-based variety of education, despite the fact that since the 1960s more and more of it is taking place in community colleges, in technical institutes, and in area vocational schools. In addition, there has been a proliferation of job-training programs, which are often targeted at specific high-risk populations, such as the unemployed or recipients of welfare (Grubb, 1996, pp. 1–4). Clearly, future research on the labor market outcomes of education should take cognizance of all forms of formal education, whether in school or out of school, and at both the secondary and the postsecondary levels.

ACKNOWLEDGMENTS: This paper was prepared for the *Handbook of Sociology of Education* (Maureen T. Hallinan, Editor). Its preparation was supported by a grant from the Japan Foundation. We thank Richard Arum, Hanna Ayalon, Adam Gamoran, Alan Kerckhoff, Noah Lewin-Epstein, Susanne Steinmann, and Abraham Yogev for their helpful comments on an earlier draft. We also thank David Berkhoff for his editorial assistance.

REFERENCES

Allmendinger, J. (1989). Educational systems and labor market outcomes. *European Sociological Review, 5,* 231–250.

Arum, R. (1977, August). *The effect of resource investment on vocational student early labor market outcomes.* Paper presented at the 1997 Annual Meeting of the American Sociological Association, Toronto, Canada.

Arum, R., & Shavit, Y. (1995). Secondary vocational education and the transition from school to work. *Sociology of Education, 68,* 187–204.

Becker, G. (1975). *Human capital.* New York: Columbia University Press.

Bishop, J. (1989). Occupational training in high schools: When does it pay off? *Economics of Education Review 8,* 1–15.

Blossfield, H-P. (1992). Is the German dual system a model for a modern vocational training system? A cross-national comparison of how different systems of vocational training deal with the changing occupational structure. *International Journal of Comparative Sociology, 23,* 168–181.

Boesel, D., Hudson, L., Deich, S., & Masten, C. (1994). *National assessment of vocational education, Vol. 2: Participation in and quality of vocational education.* Washington, DC: U.S. Department of Education.

Bowles, S., & Gintis, H. (1976). *Schooling in capitalist America.* New York: Basic Books.

Brauns, H., Müller, W., & Steinmann, S. (1997, September). *Educational expansion and returns to education: A comparative study for Germany, France, the UK and Hungary.* Paper presented at the Dublin Workshop of the Network on Transitions in Youth. Dublin, Ireland.

Breen, R., Iannelli, C., & Shavit, Y. (1998). *Occupational returns to education in Italy: A consideration of rational action theory of university attendance.* Paper presented at the 14th World Congress of Sociology, Montreal, Canada.

Coleman, J. S., Campbell, E. Q., Hobson, C., McPartland, J., Mood, A., Weinfeld, F. D., & York, R. (1966). *Equality of educational opportunity.* Washington, DC: U.S. Department of Health, Education, and Welfare.

Collins, R. (1979). *The credential society: A historical sociology of education and stratification.* New York: Academic Press.

Crouch, C., Finegold, D., & Sako, M. (1999). *Are skills the answer? The political economy of skill creation in advanced industrial countries.* Oxford, England: Oxford University Press.

Doeringer, P. B., & Piore, M. J. (1971). *Internal labor markets and manpower analysis.* Lexington, MA: Heath Lexington Books.

Erbes-Seguin, S., Gilan, C., & Kieffer, A. (1990). *Building the employment market for young peoples. State and companies face to face in France and West Germany.* Paper presented at the 12th World Congress of Sociology, CNRS, Paris (MS).

Erikson, R., & Jonsson, O. (1998). Qualifications and the allocation process of young men and women in the Swedish labour market. Y. Shavit & W. Müller (Eds.), *From school to work: A comparative study of educational qualifications and occupational destinations.* Oxford, England: Clarendon Press.

Gamoran, A. (1987). The stratification of high school learning opportunities. *Sociology of Education, 60,* 135–155.

Gamoran, A., & Mare, R. (1989). Secondary school tracking and educational inequality: Compensation, reinforcement, or neutrality. *American Journal of Sociology, 94,* 1146–1183.

Goux, D., & Maurin, E. (1998). From education to first job: The French case. In Y. Shavit & W. Müller (Eds). *From school to work: A comparative study of educational qualifications and occupational destinations.* Oxford, England: Clarendon Press.

Grubb, N. W. (1996). *Learning to work: The case for reintegrating job training and education.* New York: Russell Sage Foundation.

Hallinan, M., & Williams, R. (1990). Students' characteristics and the peer-influence process. *Sociology of Education, 63,* 122–133.

Hannan, D., Raffe, D., & Smyth, E. (1997). Cross-national research on school to work transitions: An analytic framework. In P. Wequin, R. Breen, & J. Planas (Eds.), *Youth transitions in Europe: Theories and evidence.* Cereq, Document 120.

Hotchkiss, L. & Dorsten, L. (1987). Curriculum effects on early post-high school outcomes. *Research in the Sociology of Education and Socialization, 7,* 191–219.

Iannelli, C. (1997, May). *Tracking and its consequences in Italy.* Paper presented at the meeting of the Research Committee on Stratification, Tel Aviv.

Keijke, H., Koeslag, M., & Van der Velden, R. (1997). Skills, occupational domains and wages. In P. Wequin, R. Breen, & J. Planas (Eds.), *Youth transitions in Europe: Theories and evidence.* Cereq, Document 120.

Kerckhoff, A. C. (1974). Stratification processes and outcomes in England and the United States. *American Sociology, 15,* 323–347.

Kerckhoff, A. C. (1995). Institutional arrangements and stratification processes in industrial societies. *Annual Review of Sociology, 15,* 323–347.

Kerckhoff, A. C., & Bell, L. (1998). Hidden capital: Vocational credentials and attainment in the U.S. *Sociology of Education, 71,* 152–174.

Lewis, D., Hearn, J., & Zilbert, E. (1993). Efficiency and equity effects of vocationally focused postsecondary education. *Sociology of Education, 66,* 188–205.

Marsden, D. (1990). Institutions and labour mobility: Occupational and internal markets in Britain, France, Italy, and West Germany. In R. Brunetta & C. Dell'Aringa (Eds.), *Labour relations and economic performance.* London: Macmillan.

Maurice, M., Sellier, F., & Silvestre, J.-J. (1986). *The social foundations of industrial power: A comparison of France and Germany.* Cambridge, MA: MIT Press.

Metz, M. H. (1978). *Classrooms and corridors: The crisis of authority in desegregated secondary schools.* Berkeley, CA: University of California Press.

Müller, W., Luettinger, P., Koenig, W., Karle, W. (1989). Class and education in industrialized nations. *International Journal of Sociology, 19,* 3–39.

Müller, W., & Shavit, Y. (1998). The institutional embeddedness of the stratification process: A comparative study of qualifications and occupations in thirteen countries. In Y. Shavit & W. Müller (Eds.), *From school to work: A comparative study of educational qualifications and occupational destinations* (pp. 1–48). Oxford, England: Clarendon Press.

Oakes, J. (1985). *Keeping track: How schools structure inequality.* New Haven, CT: Yale University Press.

Parkin, F. (1979). *Marx's theory of history: A bourgeois critique.* New York: Columbia University Press.

Rosenbaum, J. E. (1998, July). *Vocational teachers' linkages with employers: Improving a work-entry infrastructure for low-achieving students.* Paper presented at the 14th World Congress of Sociology, Montreal, Canada.

Rosenbaum, J. E., & Kariya, T. (1991). Do school achievements affect the early jobs of high school graduates in the United States and Japan. *Sociology of Education, 64*(2), 78–95.

Rosenbaum, J. E., Kariya, T., Settersten, R., & Maier, T. (1990). Market and network theories of the transition from high school to work: Their application to industrialized societies. *Annual Review of Sociology, 16,* 263–299.

Rumberger, R., & Daymont, T. (1984). The economic value of academic and vocational training acquired in high school. In M. E. Borus (Ed.), *Youth and the labor market: Analysis of the National Longitudinal Survey.* Kalamazoo, MI: W. E. Upjohn Institute for Employment Research.

Shavit, Y. (1984). Tracking and ethnicity in Israeli secondary education. *American Sociological Review, 49,* 210–220.

Shavit, Y. (1990a). Segregation, tracking and the educational attainment of minorities: Arabs and Oriental Jews in Israel. *American Sociological Review, 55*(1), 115–126.

Shavit, Y. (1990b). Tracking and the persistence of ethnic occupational inequalities in Israel. *International perspectives on education and society*: Vol. 2. Greenwich, CT: JAI Press.

Shavit, Y., & Müller, W. (Ed., 1998a). *From school to work: A comparative study of educational qualifications and occupational destinations.* Oxford, England: Clarendon Press.

Shavit, Y., & Müller, W. (1998b, July). *Vocational secondary education, tracking and occupational attainment in a comparative perspective.* Paper presented at the Vienna Meeting of the Society for Socio-Economics.

Spence, M. (1974). *Market signaling.* Cambridge, MA.: Harvard University Press.

Thurow, L. C. (1975). *Generating inequality: Mechanisms of distribution in the U.S. economy.* London: Macmillan.

Treiman, D. J. (1977). *Occupational prestige in comparative perspective.* New York: Academic Press.

Treiman, D., & Terrell, K. (1975). The process of status attainment in the United States and Great Britain. *American Journal of Sociology, 81,* 563–582.

Turner, R. H. (1960). Sponsored and contest mobility. *American Sociology Review, 25,* 855–867.

Vanfossen, B., Jones, J., & Spade, J. (1987). Curriculum tracking and status maintenance. *Sociology of Education, 60,* 104–122.

CHAPTER 20

Transition from School to Work in Comparative Perspective

ALAN C. KERCKHOFF

The term *social stratification* refers to both a condition and a process. The stratified condition of industrial societies is defined in terms of a hierarchy of classes or of occupational positions within the labor force. Although there is some variation, the hierarchy of occupational levels of all industrial societies is essentially the same, ranging from professionals and managers at the top of the hierarchy to unskilled laborers at the bottom.

Social stratification as a process refers to the operation of the mechanisms through which each generation becomes distributed into those stratified occupational levels. Scholars who study social stratification processes in industrial societies all recognize the major role played by educational institutions in distributing new generations into the stratified labor force. In fact, educational institutions are sometimes referred to as a society's "sorting machine" (Spring, 1976).

The widely accepted conceptualization of the social stratification process in industrial societies attributes the resulting distribution of adults into the stratified labor force to the combined effects of the individual's family of orientation, educational institutions, and adult mobility within the labor force. Much, but not all, of the effect of the family of orientation is transmitted through its influence on the individual's educational attainment.

The most crucial linkage in the social stratification process is between educational attainment and occupational placement. This is a strong linkage in all industrial societies. The hierarchy of educational attainments is significantly correlated with the hierarchy of occupational positions, and some researchers have claimed that the education–occupation linkage is essentially the same in all industrial societies.

ALAN C. KERCKHOFF • Department of Sociology, Duke University, Durham, North Carolina 27708-0088

Handbook of the Sociology of Education, edited by Maureen T. Hallinan. Kluwer Academic/Plenum Publishers, New York, 2000.

One of the most ambitious attempts to date to compare societies' patterns of social stratification processes (Treiman & Yip, 1989) provided an analysis of the patterns in 21 countries. The authors concluded that there is much less variation in that relationship among industrial societies than between industrial societies and either socialist-bloc or developing societies. However, the very ambitious nature of the study made its conclusions more tentative than would be wished. Not all of the societies studied had all of the detailed data needed to conduct an in-depth comparison, so the measures used were somewhat rudimentary.

Ishida, Müller, & Ridge (1995) focused more narrowly on patterns of association among social origin, educational attainment, and class destination in 10 industrial societies for which more adequate data were available. They concluded that "the pattern of allocation to class positions given a specific level of education is highly similar in our 10 nations. The strength or extent of association, however, varies across nations" (p.179). They hypothesized that this variation reflects differences in the societies' institutional arrangements related to the use of educational credentials in the labor market.

An important element of those institutional arrangements is the set of mechanisms involved in a worker's initial entry into the labor force. Rosenbaum, Kariya, Settersten, & Maier (1990) reviewed several theoretical perspectives that can help to explain the education–occupation linkage in the transition from school to work as well as the intersocietal variation in its strength. They focused especially on signaling theory (Spence, 1974) and network theory (Granovetter, 1974).

Signaling theory recognizes that employers usually must make hiring decisions on very limited information about potential employees. Interviews can provide a basis for assessing the personal qualities of the potential employee, but they are a less adequate basis for judging the individual's job skills. In such a situation, educational credentials provide a better basis for judging skill. However, the value of the credentials in this regard varies depending on their specificity and their relevance to the job that is to be filled.

Credentials awarded by American schools tend to be less informative than those awarded in most European countries. Knowing that someone has a high school diploma tells the employer little about how the individual might perform on a job requiring specific kinds of quantitative or linguistic skills. In contrast, the more differentiated secondary school credentials awarded in Great Britain, and even more so in Germany, provide potential employers with much more useful information.

Network theory recognizes that the employment decision involves others besides the employer and the prospective worker. Not only family and friends, but also schools, labor unions, trade associations, and government agencies often provide access, evaluations and recommendations that assist in matching a worker's skills to the employer's needs. All of these help to insure a better fit between the skills of the worker and the requirements of the job. The school–employer linkage is not very strong in most industrial societies, although it is all-important in Japan. Unions, trade associations, and government agencies play more important roles in most European societies. None of these is a particularly strong part of the network linking prospective employees with employers in the United States. (But see Rosenbaum & Jones [Chapter 18] in this volume for U.S. examples of school-based networks assisting students' entry into the labor force.)

There are, thus, some important differences among societies in the nature of the education–occupation linkage and the processes involved in the transition from school to work. Industrial societies differ in many important ways. They vary in the clarity with which the educational credentials they award provide meaningful signals to both workers and employers. They also vary in the institutional context in which individuals move from positions in the educational attainment hierarchy to positions in the occupational hierarchy.

One way to appreciate the societal differences and their possible significance in shaping the education–occupation linkage is through an examination of the transition from school to work in societies that exhibit the differences. That is the purpose of this chapter.

DIMENSIONS OF SOCIETAL VARIATION

In addition to the varied meaningfulness of educational credentials and the involvement of school personnel, unions, trade associations, and government agencies, other societal differences can affect the transition from school to work. For instance, the general health of the society's economy may affect both the availability of entry-level jobs and students' decisions about leaving or staying in school (Furlong, 1992; Sorensen & Blossfeld, 1989). Also, the increasing proportion of young women in the labor force in recent decades has altered the youth labor market through both male–female job competition and increasing the proportion of gender-specific occupations (Jacobs & Lim, 1992; Müller, 1986).

In addition, even industrial societies vary greatly in the ages of those who make the transition from school to work. This is reflected in the proportions of age cohorts who obtain postsecondary, especially university level, credentials. For instance, nearly one fourth (24%) of American adults have a university level degree compared with only 13% of German adults and 9% of French adults (Organization for Economic Cooperation and Development, 1996). Level of educational attainment, in turn, is related to the kinds of jobs available to school leavers. However, the proportion who obtain university-level credentials is also related to the overall nature of the fit between the education and occupation hierarchies. Societies with large proportions with university degrees will probably recruit such highly educated people into jobs that would be filled by those with lower level credentials in societies having smaller proportions with university degrees.

Although all of these factors are undoubtedly important sources of intersocietal differences in the process of transition from school to work, the present discussion concentrates on three other sources of variation that are all features of the educational systems. These three have been generally viewed as the most important sources of variation in the nature of the transition from school to work. They are (1) the degree of stratification of the education system, (2) the degree of standardization of educational programs, and (3) the degree to which the educational credentials awarded are general academic ones or specialized vocationally relevant ones.

Rather than attempt to make general statements about all industrial societies, the present discussion focuses on four societies that vary on these three dimensions and that also vary in the nature of the transition from school to work. The four societies are France, Germany, Great Britain, and the United States.

The rest of this section reviews the nature of these three characteristics of educational systems and shows how these four industrial societies' educational systems vary in their degrees of stratification and standardization and in the kinds of credentials they provide for their students. The discussion then turns to an analysis of the ways in which these characteristics of educational systems affect the transition from school to work.

Educational Stratification

The use of the term "stratification" in the analysis of educational systems is generally intended to recognize that many systems have clearly differentiated kinds of schools whose functions are defined in terms of "higher" and "lower" levels of academic offerings. Allmendinger (1989a) says, "*Stratification* is the proportion of a cohort that attains the maximum number of school years provided by the educational system, coupled with the degree of differentiation within given educational levels (tracking)" (p. 233).

In the usual case, the levels of program offerings are also associated with different degrees of access to opportunities for additional, more advanced, schooling. Thus, stratification refers to both the varied prestige of kinds of educational programs and the varied chances of reaching high levels of educational attainment. Vocational programs have generally been viewed as "lower" than academic programs. Most European systems have historically reflected social class divisions and have usually been stratified into a restricted elite academic stream and one or more vocationally oriented mass streams (Archer, 1979; Ringer, 1979). The strata have usually been most salient at the time of transfer from primary to secondary school. Rubinson (1986, p. 521) described the traditional European system as one in which a small percentage of primary students is admitted to academic secondary schools that lead to universities and then to high-status occupations. However, most primary students enter secondary schools for vocational studies. These schools are terminal points, not linked to advanced education"

The selective system most familiar to American social scientists is the British one, which Turner (1960) referred to as a "sponsorship" system. In the traditional British system, students were separated at about age 11 into two kinds of secondary school—the grammar school and the secondary modern school. The grammar school provided a demanding academic curriculum intended to prepare students for possible university attendance. Students who were selected to go to grammar schools were "sponsored" by being provided with the opportunity to obtain skills and credentials that were needed in higher education.

The secondary modern curriculum was less demanding and more vocationally oriented. Secondary modern schools seldom offered any of the sixth-form courses (for those aged 16 to 18) needed to qualify for university attendance, and the great majority of secondary modern students left school at age 16. Although the introduction of the comprehensive school in the 1960s and 1970s altered this sharp bifurcation of secondary schooling, there are still schools that do not offer sixth-form courses (Kerckhoff, Fogelman, & Manlove, 1997).

The German educational system is perhaps the clearest current example of a highly stratified system, and its degree of stratification has changed very little since 1950 (Müller, Steinmann, & Ell, 1998). Students are separated early (usually in Grade 5, at about age 10) into three kinds of secondary schools that differ greatly in curricula and between which movement is quite rare. The elite school, the *Gymnasium*, usually serves students from Grade 5 through Grade 13. The successful *Gymnasium* student obtains the *Abitur*, a certificate entitling the student to enter university-level education. The *Realschule* offers an enriched general education in Grades 5 through 10. Successful students obtain a school-leaving certificate that entitles them to continue their education in an advanced vocational school. The lowest level of secondary school, the *Hauptschule*, provides a basic general education through Grade 9 or 10. *Hauptschule* students have only limited access to vocational schooling.

The probability of continuing to postsecondary schooling differs sharply according to the student's type of secondary school. The *Gymnasium* is prerequisite to university attendance. Although *Realschule* students may qualify for attendance at an advanced vocational school (*Fachoberschule*), that pathway is not open to *Hauptschule* students. The early tripartite separation of students essentially determines their potential level and kind of educational attainment. In turn, the level and kind of education obtained limits the students' later options in the labor force.

Although most European educational systems are more highly stratified than the American system, they are not all equally stratified, as the discussion of the British and the German systems suggests. The German system is much more rigidly stratified than the British one. There is also a sharp contrast between the German and the French systems.

The French system was nearly as highly stratified as the German until the 1970s when many new secondary school alternatives were introduced, providing additional opportunities and greater flexibility in obtaining various forms of postsecondary schooling (Lewis, 1985). Secondary education in France is in two stages, from age 11 to 15, and from age 15 to 18 or 19. The second stage leads to the award of the *baccalauréat*, which can be in general, in technical, or vocational studies. A *baccalauréat* in any of these provides access to higher education. The elite stream of higher education is in the *grandes écoles*, admission to which is often dependent on competitive examinations.

Both secondary and tertiary education are somewhat stratified in France, but it is a much more open system than that in Germany. Although secondary schools are specialized with different curricular emphases, all of the secondary schools provide access to higher education, and avenues exist for continued upward movement by successful students, whatever their secondary school origins. In that respect, the French system is much closer to the American than to the German system.

A distinctive feature of the American educational system, in contrast with almost all of those in Europe, is its low degree of stratification into different curricular and status streams. Turner (1960) referred to the American system as one that facilitated "contest mobility" through its open structure and its lack of irrevocable branching points. Neither the common school movement nor the early introduction of the comprehensive high school in the United States (Kaestle, 1983; Tyack, 1974) had parallels in Europe, although some European systems (e.g., the British and the French) have recently made some moves in that direction.

Rubinson (1986) emphasized the low degree of stratification in the United States by saying, "What tracking occurs is through the choice of a college-preparatory or general curriculum in high school . . . Much of the curriculum is common to all tracks, and students from any track can continue to higher education. No decision is irrevocable" (p.523). Not everyone has such a sanguine view of high school tracking (e.g., Oakes, 1985), but tracking within schools is a much less rigid form of stratification than separation into different types of schools. Additionally, high school tracks in the United States do not uniformly have sharply differentiated curricula (Vanfossen, Jones, & Spade, 1987).

Educational Standardization

The American educational system also differs from those in Europe by being highly decentralized. Each of the thousands of American school districts can devise its own programs, usually constrained to only a limited degree by state regulations. In sharp contrast, most European systems are much more subject to control by the national government, and major contributions to the funding of educational institutions are made by the national government.

The degree of control from outside the local community varies, however, both among countries and over time. One of the ongoing disputes in Great Britain since 1950 is between those who favor increased control and those who favor reduced control by the national government. The introduction of comprehensive high schools in the 1960s and the 1970s moved the system somewhat in the local control direction, but even that change was strongly influenced by an initiative by the national government. When Margaret Thatcher became Secretary of State for Education, she did all she could to reverse the trend. During Thatcher's time as

Prime Minister several actions were taken to strengthen the role of the national government and to weaken the local education authorities (see Kerckhoff, Fogelman, Crook, & Reeder, 1996).

Although the British educational system is controlled more than the American system by levels of government outside the local community, other European systems are subject to much more control from above. Despite their great difference in degree of stratification, the German and French educational systems are both subject to much more control from above than the American system. In France, the control is by the national government, whereas in Germany it is by a combination of the federal government and the 16 states (*Länder*). Two thirds of the country's entire expenditure on education comes from the national government in France, wheras in Germany the *Länder* are the major source of support for education (OECD, 1996).

Central control does not necessarily lead to standardization of the educational system, but there is a strong tendency for it to do so. Allmendinger (1989a) said,

> *Standardization* is the degree to which the quality of education meets the same standards nation-wide. Variables such as teachers' training, school budgets, curricula, and the uniformity of school-leaving examinations are relevant in measuring the standing of an educational system on this dimension. (p. 233)

If greater centralization leads to greater standardization, we would expect more consistency in the curricula to which students are exposed in more highly centralized systems. Stevenson & Baker (1991) reported that state control of the educational system is correlated with the uniformity of eighth-grade mathematics curricular offerings among 15 countries. As would be expected, the variation of the offerings is much larger in the decentralized American system than in the centralized French system.*

General and Vocational Educational Credentials

The educational systems of industrial societies also differ greatly in the nature of the educational credentials they award. The difference is most apparent at the secondary school level. Among the societies dealt with here, the most general credentials are awarded by the American system. Very few secondary school credentials have any direct relevance to positions in the labor force. Even the undergraduate credentials awarded by colleges and universities are mostly quite general and have only limited association with particular occupations. Degrees in such fields as engineering, accounting, and nursing are more the exception than the rule.

In contrast, most European school systems award secondary school credentials that have important occupational relevance. The credentials awarded in Germany are the most directly occupationally relevant. After completing compulsory schooling, the majority of young Germans enter what is called "the dual system," a combination of apprenticeship training and part-time schooling. This system prepares them for some 450 different occupations. A strong occupational orientation is also found at the tertiary level, especially in the *Fachschulen* and the *Fachhochschulen*. The latter provide higher education credentials, and it is possible to transfer from there to a university.

British credentials (called "qualifications") are also diverse, and many of them have direct relevance to access to labor-force positions. However, most of those with direct occupational relevance are obtained through part-time further education after leaving school and are

---

*England and Wales were included in the study and were classified as "decentralized." There was a great deal of variation in offerings there as well as in the United States. Germany was not included in the study.

awarded through such trade groups as City and Guilds and Royal Society of Arts. But the 30 or so types of British qualifications include many that are purely academic (e.g., O-level and A-level secondary school examinations). There is thus a mixture of academic and vocational credentials, and many fewer of them are as occupation specific as those in Germany.

The credentials awarded in France are among the most general awarded in European educational systems. There are three types of upper secondary school programs leading to the *baccalauréat*, but the majority of students obtain the general *baccalauréat*. Even the technical and vocational *baccalauréat* programs are very broad in scope. All students who obtain the *baccalauréat* are eligible to enter higher education. Universities offer diplomas at three levels of increasing specialization. However, the credentials awarded at the secondary and tertiary levels are seldom as specialized as those in Germany or even in Great Britain.

The vocational relevance of the credentials awarded by educational systems clearly affects the transition from school to work. The more specificity of the credentials, the greater the likelihood that a young person's entry into the labor force will be limited to particular occupations. The very general nature of American educational credentials makes them much less predictive than the highly specific vocationally relevant credentials awarded in Germany. The nature of the credentials awarded is thus central to any understanding of the transition process.

COMBINATIONS OF CHARACTERISTICS OF EDUCATIONAL SYSTEMS

The discussion thus far has dealt with variations in three characteristics of educational systems that might affect the nature of the transition from school to work. Although there is evidence of differences in these characteristics among the four societies dealt with here, it is not possible to make precise intersocietal comparisons of those differences. It is evident, however, that the four educational systems exhibit very different combinations of them.

Table 20.1 reports estimates of the relative levels of the four societies on the three characteristics. The reasons for these ratings can be most easily appreciated by first examining the characteristics of the two most extreme cases, Germany and the United States. Both France and Great Britain, in different ways, are more middle range on these characteristics when compared with Germany and the United States.

Germany

The German educational system is one of the most highly stratified systems in Europe. Not only is there a clearly differentiated tripartite organization of secondary schools, but access to

TABLE 20.1. **Estimates of Societal Differences in Characteristics of Educational Systems that Affect the Transition from School to Work.**

Society	Stratification	Standardization	General/ Vocational credentials
Britain	Mid	Mid	Gen/Voc
France	Mid	High	Gen/Voc
Germany	High	High	Vocational
United States	Low	Low	General

types of higher education institutions and to types of apprenticeships is dependent on having successfully completed programs in one of those types of secondary schools. The hierarchy of secondary and tertiary institutions is clearly linked with levels of adult placement in the labor force.

Although control of educational institutions is largely exercized by the individual *Länder*, they and the federal government cooperate to set common curriculum standards and to designate approved textbooks. The association of many school and apprenticeship programs with specific occupations also leads to a high degree of standardization of the materials offered in those programs.

The most striking feature of the German educational system is the strong linkage between its offerings and the occupational division of labor. Maurice, Sellier, & Silvestre (1986) referred to the German educational system's "capacity to structure" the flow of students from school to work. The German system is clearly organized around occupational differentiation. It is the most fully vocationally oriented of the four countries.

The United States

The American educational system is strikingly different from the German system in all of characteristics summarized in Table 20.1. Secondary schools are not stratified. With very few exceptions, they are general schools offering broad and diverse curricula. Although there are "tracks" within many of the schools, they tend to be loosely defined, and there is only a weak association between "being in" a track and taking any particular set of courses (Vanfossen et al., 1987). Tertiary institutions have varied reputations so far as the quality of their offerings is concerned, but most of them attempt to provide the same broad range of courses and programs.

The decentralization of control of schools at all levels reduces the possibility of standardization of offerings except at the broadest level. All secondary schools offer courses in American history, biological science, English literature, and so on, but there is no coordination of the decisions about the contents of such courses. Textbook choice is likely to be made at the district or even the state level, and that produces some limited standardization within subunits, but there is no basis for standardization at the national level.

American education credentials are very general at the secondary level. One either obtains a high school diploma or one does not. Even at the tertiary level, most college degrees have little or no specific vocational relevance. This is the most dramatic difference between the German and the American systems.

Great Britain

Until the late 1960s, British secondary schools were more clearly stratified than they are currently. The distinction between grammar schools and secondary modern schools and the separation of students at about age 11 created a stratified system. The introduction of comprehensive schools reduced the degree of stratification, but grammar schools continued to exist, and some of the comprehensive schools did not have sixth forms providing preparation for university attendance (Kerckhoff et al., 1997).

The British educational system is not centrally controlled, but it has always received significant funding from and has been subject to regulation by the national government. The move to comprehensive high schools was strongly influenced by the national government when the Labour Party was in power, and Margaret Thatcher's Conservative Party government introduced a number of regulations that slowed the process and changed some of its liberalizing effects. The national government has had more influence on the structuring of schools and the definition of kinds of credentials to be awarded, however, than on the specifics of the curriculum.

The traditional British system was wholly oriented toward academic courses rather than vocational preparation. Changes in the system since World War II have increased the vocational emphasis, but the changes have been largely at the postsecondary level. The increase in the number of polytechnics (and the elevation of many of them to university status) is one indication of this. Another indication, of even greater significance in the later discussion in this chapter, is the enlargement of the Colleges of Further Education that provided vocational courses, primarily on a part-time basis for those who have left full-time schooling.

Thus, the British system falls between the German and the American systems on all three dimensions. It is more stratified than the American system but much less stratified than the German system. There is somewhat more standardization than in the United States, but much less than in Germany. Additionally, the credentials it awards are a mixture of general and vocational in contrast to the heavy vocational emphasis in Germany and the emphasis on general credentials in the United States.

France

Although it does differentiate three kinds of secondary schools, the French educational system is much less rigidly stratified than the German system. All kinds of secondary schools award the *baccalauréat*, and any holder of the *baccalauréat* can enter higher education. At the same time, there are dominant linkages between types of secondary schools and types of tertiary institutions and programs. Like the British system, it is less stratified than the German system but more stratified than the American system.

France has the most standardized educational system of the four countries. The national Ministry of Education controls many more features of the system than in any of the other three countries. In Germany, the control is less by the federal government than by the coordinated *Länder*. Although both Germany and France are rated "high" in standardization in Table 20.1, that rating is appropriate for Germany only in comparison with Great Britain and, especially, the United States.

The differentiated French secondary schools and highly differentiated tertiary programs, as well as the credentials awarded at both levels, reflect both vocational and general academic definitions of educational attainment. That mix is nearer to the British system than to either the American or the German system.

Overview

There is a noteworthy consistency in Table 20.1 in the relative ratings of the countries' degrees of stratification and the awarding of vocational credentials. Overall, there is a strong tendency for highly stratified systems to emphasize vocational credentials, especially in the non-elite secondary schools. The differentiation between vocational and academic credentials has been the hallmark of most of the traditional European systems. In Germany, however, specialized vocational credentials are awarded by distinct types of schools and by the dual apprenticeship system at almost all occupational levels. Because most traditional European systems emphasized elite education that tended to be highly academic rather than vocational, as vocational programs were introduced they were viewed as "lower" than the academic programs. There is thus a strong tendency for systems that award vocational credentials to be defined as stratified systems.*

The clearest impression one obtains from Table 20.1, however, is that there is considerable variation among the four systems in the mix of these dimensions. To the extent that the three dimensions are associated with the nature of the transition from school to work, we should therefore expect variation in the nature of the transition process among these four societies.

Previous research and theorizing have established a basis for expecting systematic differences in the transition process based on these dimensions. Allmendinger (1989a) has argued that the combination of high stratification and high standardization forms the basis for a strong linkage between educational attainment and occupational positions. She used Germany and the United States as contrasting cases in point. Others (König & Müller, 1986; Maurice et al., 1986) have shown similar contrasts between Germany and France. In both of those contrasts it is clear that the societies with lower levels of stratification (the United States and France) also award less vocationally specific secondary school credentials.

Yet, although France and the United States both have less highly stratified systems than Germany, they are also different from each other in the degree of standardization of their educational programs. France's secondary school programs are much more standardized than those in the United States. Standardization can affect the association between educational credentials and labor force placements in ways that differ from the effects of stratification. More stratified systems award more hierarchically arrayed credentials that can match up with the hierarchically arrayed positions in the labor force. However, high degrees of standardization affect the linkage through the consistency of the educational experiences associated with any given credential. Credentials in a highly standardized system send clearer signals to those attempting to match credentials and jobs. The combination of a high level of stratification and a high level of standardization should thus produce a tighter credential–occupation linkage than a high level of either stratification or standardization alone.

More generally, it may be that particular combinations of stratification, standardization, and types of credentials can produce particular patterns of association between credentials and occupations. The next section is devoted to some observations about the nature of some of these patterns.

DO THE DIFFERENCES MATTER?

If the characteristics of the educational systems reviewed here do affect the early linkage between educational attainment and occupational placement, variations in and different combinations of those characteristics should help explain intersocietal differences in the transition from school to work. I consider three aspects of the transition from school to work and analyze their association with the three characteristics of the educational systems discussed previously.

The first aspect of the school-to-work transition to be discussed is the strength of the

* Müller & Shavit (1998) view stratification and an emphasis on vocational credentials as so closely correlated that they question whether it is possible to consider them as independent dimensions.

association between levels of educational attainment and occupational levels of first jobs. This is the most salient feature of the intersocietal differences in the transition process, and it has received the most systematic attention.

However, the comparative research has also brought to light other kinds of differences in the transition process. In particular, it has shown that there is more stability in the education–occupation relationship during the early labor force career in some societies than in others. It is important to recognize that the transition is a process that occurs over time. The initial education–occupation association is not necessarily equally meaningful in all cases. Variation in the stability of that association results from two other kinds of intersocietal differences.

The second aspect of the school-to-work transition to be examined is the extent to which workers return to school and change their levels of educational attainment during their early labor force careers. If many young workers alter their educational credentials soon after entering the labor force in some societies but that seldom happens in other societies, the education–occupation association at the moment of entry has very different early career implications in those two kinds of societies.

Finally, the third aspect of the transition from school to work is the amount of job changing and occupational mobility during workers' early careers in the labor force. Early job changes, especially if they involve changes in the levels of occupations, also have the potential for altering the career implications of the initial education–occupation association. If such changes are more common in some societies than in others, the transition from school to work will have different patterns in those two kinds of societies.

The second and third aspects of the transition from school to work discussed here make salient an issue faced by anyone studying the transition in Germany. Because the great majority of young Germans enter "the dual system" that combines an apprenticeship with some kind of formal schooling, a decision has to be made as to whether the period spent in the dual system is time in school or at work. That is, does the transition from school to work take place before or after the period in the dual system? Most analysts include the dual system as part of a person's educational experience. Allmendinger (1989b) was not wholly comfortable with that solution and chose to refer to three periods—school, a transition period in the dual system, and work. An important feature of the following discussion is its attempt to deal with the possibility of identifying a "transition period" in all four societies, not just in Germany.

Association between Educational Attainment and the Level of First Job

Societies that define many educational credentials in terms of positions in the labor force are likely to have a strong education–occupation association. The degree of vocational specificity of educational credentials has received a great deal of attention in studies of the transition from school to work, most of it using Germany as an example of high specificity. In their insightful comparison of the French and German educational systems, Maurice and associates (1986) referred to the German system's much greater "capacity to structure" the flow of young people from school into the labor force. The nature of German students' education and the credentials they obtain from it much more clearly define the specific occupations for which they are qualified and into which they will very probably move when they enter the labor force full-time.

An essential part of the German system's "capacity to structure" the move from school to work is the pervasiveness of apprenticeships and the dual system that serve to prepare the young person to take on a specific occupation. In 1990, 67% of the German men and 63% of the women 16 to 19 years of age entered vocational training in the dual system (Müller et al., 1998). There is nothing comparable in either France or the United States. Apprenticeships have become much less common in Great Britain since the 1960s, but many more British educational credentials have occupational relevance than do those in France and in the United States, although they are not as occupation-specific as those in Germany.

Educational systems that award general credentials pose serious problems for those making the transition from school to work as well as for the firms that may wish to employ them. Neither the student nor the employer has an adequate basis for judging the student's qualifications for any particular job. The association between level of educational attainment and level of occupation at entry into the labor force cannot be very strong if educational attainment is defined in only broad general terms. Labor-force entrants with a given level of educational attainment will necessarily be considered for a wide range of kinds of jobs.

A similar problem is posed by educational systems that are not highly standardized. Highly standardized educational systems produce relatively uniform products. Whatever the credentials they award, they provide more useful signals to prospective employers than are provided by credentials awarded in unstandardized systems. Systems that combine high stratification and high standardization should exhibit the strongest association between educational credentials and occupational levels.

There is more systematic evidence on this matter than on either of the other two features of the transition from school to work considered here, and it is mostly consistent with the view that both stratification and standardization increase the strength of association between educational attainment and occupational level of first job. Allmendinger (1989a) has shown a much stronger education–occupation linkage in Germany than in the United States; Maurice and associates (1986) have shown a stronger linkage in Germany than in France. One exception to the expected pattern, given the ratings in Table 20.1, is the finding reported by Winfield, Campbell, Kerckhoff, Everett, & Trott (1989) that there is a stronger linkage in the United States than in Great Britain.

Müller & Shavit (1998) conducted a meta-analysis of studies of the transition from school to work in 13 societies, including the 4 dealt with here. One part of their analysis examined the differences in occupational prestige between those with the highest and those with the lowest educational credentials awarded in each society. The magnitudes of those high–low differences were used as indicators of the strength of the association between educational attainment and occupational level. The order of the magnitude of the differences in the four societies dealt with here (ranged from largest to smallest) is as follows: Germany, France, the United States, Britain.

With the exception of the very low position of Britain, the order is what would be expected, given the ratings reported in Table 20.1. Germany has high levels of both stratification and standardization, and educational credentials in Germany have specific vocational relevance. The United States has low levels of both stratification and standardization, and few American educational credentials have vocational relevance. France and Britain have a mixture of these three characteristics.

The results of these several studies of the strength of association between educational attainment and the occupational level of the first job are generally consistent with the hypothesis that the association should be stronger in societies with high levels of stratification and standardization and a strong emphasis on vocationally relevant credentials. Yet, at least the case of Great Britain seems to deviate from the expected pattern. The British pattern, as well as some of the details reported in the other studies cited, lead to a consideration of the other two features of the transition from school to work. Both of them raise questions about a possible "transition period" in all of these societies that cannot be wholly represented by a single measure of the education–occupation association.

Changes in Educational Attainment after the First Job

Until recently, the implicit assumption about the transition from school to work has been that young people attended school until they had obtained whatever level of education they were going to obtain and then they entered the labor force. Making that assumption implies that the transition from school to work involves a single move from full-time schooling to full-time participation in the labor force.

It has become increasingly apparent that this view distorts the actual transition process, more so in some societies than in others. There are at least two important ways in which assuming a single move distorts the reality, and they are relevant to different degrees in the four societies discussed here.

One kind of deviation from a single transition event is for students to make more than one full transition. Some students enter the labor force full-time, go back to school full-time, and then reenter the labor force full-time. Multiple entries into the labor force have most often been recorded in studies of the transition from school to work in the United States (Coleman, 1984). Arum & Hout (1998) reported that 19% of the men and 21% of the women in the National Longitudinal Study of Youth had moved from school to work, back to school, and again back to work by the time they were 26 years old. Light (1995) also reported high rates of return, especially by white men. Such a pattern of moves is quite rare in Germany (Allmendinger, 1989b).

Return to full-time schooling also occurs in Great Britain, but a different pattern of improving one's credentials is much more common. Many British students leave secondary school at age 16 and enter the labor force. However, they often engage in part-time schooling in colleges of further education while working. This is frequently arranged and even paid for by their employers. Further education courses can improve a worker's credentials, which in turn can lead to job changing. Although part-time schooling after labor force entry can improve a worker's occupational attainment in both the United States and Great Britain, it is a more important factor in Great Britain (Kerckhoff, 1990).

Engaging in school and work activities simultaneously is extremely common in Germany. The majority of young Germans engage in the apprenticeship "dual system" that calls for a formal combination of schooling and work experience. It is difficult to identify a specific time of the transition from school to work for these apprentices, which was why Allmendinger (1989b) chose to refer to three periods: school, a transition period (during the apprenticeship), and work. Others who have analyzed data involving apprentices (e.g., Haller, König, Krause, & Kurz, 1985; Müller et al., 1998) have dealt with this problem by referring to the job entered after completion of an apprenticeship as the first job. In effect, this defines the apprenticeship as part of schooling and not as part of work.

Young people in Great Britain who combine work and school are treated in a very different way in most analyses. Once they enter the labor force, any part-time schooling is defined as occurring after the transition from school to work. Although there are many parallels between the "dual system" in Germany and further education in Great Britain, their effects on the early education–occupation association are treated quite differently.

Of the three examples just given, it is apparent that there is a greater likelihood that young people in Britain and in the United States than in Germany will increase their educational credentials after they have been defined as having taken their first job. The German system of formal occupationally relevant credentials also provides opportunities for higher level certification after completion of the apprenticeship, but such gains are not as common as gains through further education in Great Britain.

One study (Winfield et al., 1989) has shown that increases in educational credentials after labor force entry are even more common in Britain than in the United States. That study also shows an increasing strength of the association between educational credentials and occupational level during the early work career in Britain. By 20 years after entering the first job, the association between educational attainment and occupational attainment is much the same in the two societies, although that association was much weaker in Great Britain at the time of entry into the first job. These results present a different picture of the two educational systems than the "sponsored-contest" contrast suggested by Turner (1960). The difference is largely the result of the recent increase in the proportion of young Britains who obtain credentials through further education.

The situation in France is rather different from all of these. There is not a great deal of formal education after entering the labor force, but on-the-job training is widespread. Although that training increases job skills and can lead to advancement, it seldom leads to increases in formal educational credentials (Haller et al., 1985).

In their comparison of Germany and France, Maurice and associates (1986) analyzed this contrast between Germany and France in some detail. They pointed out that the very general French credentials posed an important employment problem. Not only does the employer face the need to provide additional training for new employees, but there is the real possibility that the new employee might use that additional training to qualify for a job elsewhere. This leads employers to narrow their training programs in such a way that the employees' new skills are firm-specific rather than nationally recognized and thus minimally useful elsewhere.

Job Changes and Early Career Mobility

Another unfortunate feature of educational systems that award only very general credentials is the likelihood that new employees will prove unsuitable for the position the employer needs to fill. Because of this, new entrants to the labor force often move from job to job several times before finding an appropriate position. Maurice and associates (1986) reported that the early years in the French labor force are thus often turbulant ones. König & Müller (1986) also reported much more job changing by young workers in France than in Germany.

Similar turbulance in the early years in the labor force has been observed in the United States, where secondary school credentials are more general than in any of the other three societies (Coleman, 1984; Coleman, Blum, Sørensen, & Rossi, 1972). Although there are many reasons for the turbulance, an important one is the lack of any clear linkage between educational credentials and occupational positions (Sørensen, 1975; Spilerman, 1977). Allmendinger (1989a) reported that 55.6% of the white American men and 43.5% of the black Americn men in her sample had had more than five job spells during their first 5 years in the labor force, compared with only 13.6% of German men.

Young workers move from job to job much more frequently in both France and the United States than in Germany. In the United States, much of that movement is due to returns to school and to reentries into the labor force (Coleman, 1984), but that is less true in France. The early career turbulance in both societies is the result of the general nature of the educational credentials young workers have at the time they enter the labor force, however. It often takes several job changes before a satisfactory fit between worker and job is found.

Haller and associates (1985) compared occupational career mobility patterns of men in France, in the United States, and in Austria. The Austrian educational system is very much like that in Germany (Ringer, 1979), and the pattern they reported for Austria is consistent with the pattern others have observed in Germany (Mayer & Carroll, 1987). Haller and associates found the most career mobility in the United States and the least in Austria, with France in between.

One of the reasons for the relatively high rates of occupational mobility in both France and the United States, Haller and associates (1985) noted, is the need for most skilled workers to work their way into those jobs rather than to enter them immediately after obtaining the necessary credentials through school or through apprenticeships. However, they also pointed to other factors in both France and Austria that limit job changes, including the stabilizing effects of nationalized industries and powerful labor organizations. They characterized the Austrian system as having "professionalized manual work" (an appropriate way to refer to the German system also), and they argued that nationalized industries tend to restrain personnel turnover in France more than private ownership does in the United States.

Job change and occupational mobility follow a different pattern in Great Britain than in any of the other three societies. There is more early occupational mobility there than in the United States (Winfield et al., 1989), largely as a result of part-time schooling after labor force entry (Kerckhoff, 1990). British students leave full-time schooling earlier, on average, than do American students. Fewer of the British have attained their final educational credentials by the time they enter the labor force, and more of them increase their credentials and their occupational level without leaving the labor force.

OVERVIEW OF THE EFFECTS OF DIFFERENCES IN EDUCATIONAL SYSTEMS

The research just reviewed provides considerable support for the general claim that the nature of the transition from school to work is related to the organization of a society's educational system. Differences in the educational systems are related to the strength of the association between the level of educational attainment and the level of the first job obtained. The differences are also associated with the degree to which young workers improve their educational credentials after entering the labor force. Finally, the differences are associated with the amount of job changing and career mobility in the early years in the labor force.

It is difficult to rate the four societies according to these three characteristics with complete confidence, but Table 20.2 summarizes the relationships to the extent possible, based on the evidence just reviewed. It is apparent from the earlier discussion that changes in educational credentials may be due to returns to full-time school, but they may occur in other ways also. It is also apparent that job changes may lead to social mobility in the early work career, but changes and mobility are not the same thing. Thus, Table 20.2 rates these four factors separately.

An examination of the ratings in Table 20.2 and the characteristics of the four societies' educational systems summarized in Table 20.1 shows some interesting associations. First, the society with the most highly stratified and standardized educational system (Germany) also strongly emphasizes vocational credentials. Second, that same society has the strongest association between educational attainment and the occupational level of first job. Correspondingly, the society with the lowest levels of both stratification and standardization and the most general educational credentials (the United States) has one of the weakest associations between educational attainment and occupational level of the first job. The United States also

TABLE 20.2. **Estimates of Societal Differences in Changes During the Early Years in the Labor Force**

Society	Return to school full-time	Increase in educational credentials	Number of early job changes	Early occupational mobility
Britain	Low	High	Mid	High
France	Low	Low	High	Mid
Germany	Low	Mid	Low	Low
United States	High	High	High	High

has a great deal of change in educational credentials after labor force entry and a great deal of early occupational mobility.

I have suggested previously (Kerckhoff, 1995) that there appear to be two general types of linkage between educational systems and labor force careers. The two types differ in the strength of the early education–occupation linkage, and they exhibit qualitatively different patterns in the transition from school to work. The four societies discussed here epitomize those types to varying degrees.

In Type One societies, the educational system is organized into highly stratified units that are consistently found throughout the society. Each of the stratified units is designed to specialize in awarding rather narrowly defined occupationally relevant credentials. During their educational careers, students are presented with branching career alternatives that establish the basis for increasingly delimited later opportunities and for obtaining increasingly specialized credentials. There is little opportunity to alter direction once a student has entered one of those career branches.

In Type Two societies, the educational system is organized into very general, unstratified units whose characteristics vary somewhat in different locales. These units award relatively undifferentiated credentials that have only very broad occupational relevance. Although students follow educational career lines in which later opportunities are dependent on earlier performances, the loose, unstratified structure of the educational units provides more opportunities to change course. The general nature of the credentials awarded means that there are only very limited bases on which to differentiate among those who leave school at any given age and enter the labor force.

In Type One societies, the educational system has the "capacity to structure" the flow of students into the labor force (Maurice et al., 1986) because students who leave the system are clearly differentiated according to highly stratified occupational qualifications. The association between educational attainment and the occupational level of first job is built into the way the educational system is organized, and the association is necessarily quite strong.

In sharp contrast, in Type Two societies, the general undifferentiated and unstandardized credentials that are awarded have very weak occupational relevance. Thus, the association between educational attainment and the level of the first job is bound to be quite weak. The global nature of the awarded credentials means there is little basis for them to be correlated with anything else, including the level of the first job. Additionally, the lack of occupational relevance of the credentials means that neither the students nor their prospective employers have much basis on which to decide which students are better qualified for which jobs. The distribution of students into first jobs is thus a fairly random process.

The weak education–occupation linkage in Type Two societies generates pressure to resort first job holders into different jobs. The resorting may be direct through job-to-job changes, but it may also occur through returns to full-time school and reentry into the labor force or through additional schooling obtained while working full-time. Given the stronger original association between educational attainment and occupational level in Type One societies, there is less pressure for change through any of these means. There is thus less change in educational credentials after entering the labor force and less early occupational mobility.

One major contributor to early occupational mobility in Type Two societies is the fact that those with relatively low educational credentials generally enter the labor force in unskilled jobs. Those who a few years later are found in skilled jobs had to move into them. In contrast, in Type One societies, workers enter directly into skilled jobs because of the certified job skills obtained in school or in apprenticeships.

Among the four societies discussed here, the two types are most clearly epitomized by Germany (Type One) and the United States (Type Two). Neither France nor Great Britain fits neatly into either type, however. Neither has a high level of stratification, and both provide a mix of general and vocational credentials. They differ from each other, though, because of the high level of standardization in France but only mid-range standardization in Britain.

The transition from school to work in France and Britain also differs from either of the types just described, although the two societies also differ from each other in the nature of the transition. In neither society is it common for workers to return to full-time schooling. However, the availability of colleges of further education encourages young British workers to improve their credentials after entering the labor force, but there is no comparable institution in France. Increased job skills are obtained through on-the-job training in France, but the training seldom serves to increase workers' formal credentials. The increased credentials provide a basis for more early career occupational mobility in Britain. At the same time, the support British employers give to their employees' further schooling helps to stabilize the employer–employee relationship. There is thus less early career "turbulance" in Britain than in France.

There is not adequate information available to rate many industrial societies on all of the factors considered in the ratings in Tables 20.1 and 20.2. It seems unlikely, however, that many other societies approach the degree of fit with the two types shown by Germany and the United States. The kinds of deviations from the two types found in France and Great Britain are probably more typical. The two types, viewed as ideal types, are significant reference points, however. If sufficient information can be obtained about enough other industrial societies, it may be possible to construct a more sensitive set of types and thereby increase our understanding of the role of the organization of educational systems in the social stratification process. Given that broader basis for comparison, it may also be possible to take systematic account for the other factors that affect the transition from school to work.

Even with the present limited information, Tables 20.1 and 20.2 show that the transition from school to work is a very different process in these four societies and that some of the variation in the transition process can be explained by the different ways in which the societies' educational systems are organized and operate. Although the available information on the educational systems and the effects they have on the transition process is far from complete, it is sufficient to reach that overall conclusion.

SOME REMAINING ISSUES

The discussion in this chapter has thus far ignored some serious limitations in the information used in the analyses reported and the conclusions reached based on them. What has been presented is, to the best of my knowledge, the most reasonable distillation of the available information. However, it is necessary, in closing, to acknowledge the limitations of that information and to suggest how those limitations may have distorted the picture derived from what has been reviewed.

Which First Job?

The whole purpose of the Shavit & Müller (1998) volume, as well as many earlier studies, is to examine the process by which young people leave school and enter their first jobs. Yet, it is apparent that those who study this process do not always agree about which job is the first job.

One question that is rather easily dealt with is the question of what constitutes a "job." Most analysts agree that it should be an activity for which one is paid, that it should be "full-time" (say, 30+ hours a week), that it should be held for at least some period of time (say, 3 months), and that it should not be held only during school vacations. The question of what qualifies as a first job is a more difficult one.

The case of the German apprentices (Allmendinger, 1989a; Müller et al., 1998) has received the most attention in this regard. Although an apprenticeship might be thought of as a first job, most scholars view that period of a young person's life as part of his or her education. So, the first job in most studies of Germany is the first job after completing an apprenticeship.

Assuming that this is a reasonable resolution in the case of Germany, how does one handle other parallel cases that are not exactly the same? Many young Britons enter first jobs that make it possible for the employee to take part-time courses at a college of further education facilitated by released time and even by payment of any costs by the employer. (The employer may even require the employee to take such courses.) These courses often lead to increased educational credentials which, in turn, can facilitate promotions.*

In such cases, should the "first job" be the one taken initially or the one made possible by the higher educational credential? Additionally, if the worker–employer arrangement continues for several years, at what point does one say the worker entered a first job? Most studies of Great Britain define the initial job as the "first job." It is apparent, however, that the very different definitions of the first job in Germany and in Great Britain are one reason scholars have reported a much stronger association between educational credentials and the occupational level of the first job in Germany than in Great Britain.

Multiple entries into the labor force, interspersed with periods in school, also occur in Britain, but they are more common in the United States (Arum & Hout, 1998). In such cases, should the "first job" be the job obtained on the initial entry into the labor force or the one obtained after all spells of full-time education have been completed?

If the first full-time job obtained on the initial entry into the American labor force is the reference point, the credential–occupation association is bound to be much weaker than if the reference point is the job obtained after the last spell of full-time schooling. Arum & Hout (1998) used the latter definition of first job. This has the merit of using a single definition for all cases, but it ignores the possible effects of multiple labor-force entries in some cases.

Although it is possible to criticize any of these ways of defining the first job, they all have the significant advantage of being clear and precise. That advantage often flows from the nature of the data sets used in the studies. Detailed longitudinal data sets provide full reports

---

* The definition of first job used by Heath & Cheung (1998) fails to consider many of these courses and the credentials obtained through them. This is why the ratings of Great Britain in Table 20.1 differ from those of Müller & Shavit (1998) that were based on the Heath & Cheung analysis.

of the education and the work histories of the participants. Because of that, they make it possible to define the first job in more than one way. This, in turn, forces the analyst to choose which definition to use.

However, such detailed longitudinal data sets are not always available. As a result, some of the studies of "first jobs" are not really studies of first jobs by any of these definitions. For instance, the excellent analyses of the Netherlands and of Sweden included in the Shavit and Müller (1998) volume (De Graaf & Ultee, 1998; Erikson & Jonsson, 1998) are not actually based on data on first jobs, whatever definition of the first job is preferred. The De Graaf and Ultee study analyzed data from a sample of young people who left school less than 10 years ago, and the Erikson and Jonsson study analyzed data from a sample of young people who were 25 to 35 years of age. So, both use data on early job rather than on the first job. Unfortunately, more refined longitudinal data were not available for their research.

The point here, however, is not to criticize these studies. It is to make it clear that the problem of defining the first job becomes the most troubling when studies are based on the very best possible longitudinal data. The more widely available such data sets become, the more important it will be to recognize and attempt to cope with the problem.

The Transition Period

The problem of defining the first job calls attention to the fact that it is not only Germany that has an awkward time in the life course that Allmendinger (1989b) referred to as the "transition period." All of the four societies discussed here have periods in which there is, or at least can be, a mix of education and labor force activity. The German case is quite clear because so many young people become apprentices and because apprenticeships have formal rules about combining schooling and work. However, young people in all of the other societies can experience a period during which there may be alternating or simultaneous school and work activities.

It is probably true that, given this commonly observed awkward period, the studies assembled in the Shavit & Müller (1998) volume treated the period in as uniform a fashion as possible. They generally skipped over that awkward period and adopted a definition of the first job as a job that comes after the period of mixed experiences is over. In one way or another, they used an early job as an index of the first job. There is merit in that rough uniformity when one is making inter-societal comparisons.

There remains the nagging possibility, however, that the differences in the transition period may be an important key to understanding the varied role of educational institutions in the societies' social stratification processes. Until we have adequate data from the transition period for a number of societies, and we can trace the patterns of change within that period, we cannot tell.

Credential and Class Distributions

Another very important remaining question can only be touched on here. This is the problem of defining the appropriate measures of educational attainment and occupational level of the first job. Some studies (e.g., Allmendinger, 1989a) have used ordinal scales for both: years of schooling and occupational prestige. These are not the most usual measures, however. The studies reported in the Shavit and Müller (1998) volume all conducted analyses using categories of both educational attainment and level of the first job. They adopted a revised version of a set of credential categories devised by Müller, Lüttinger, König, & Karle (1989), and the occupational class schema used in that volume and in many other comparative studies is one proposed by Erikson, Goldthorpe, & Portocarero (1979).

There are major societal differences in the distributions of both of those measures. For instance, a very large proportion of young French men (41.6%) have only the lowest level of educational credentials, whereas only a very small proportion (6.0%) of young German men have them. The societies also vary greatly in their distributions of occupational classes. In the United States, 40.7% of the young men are in the lowest class, and that is four times as many as in Germany.

These differences raise doubts about whether the credential and class categories are equally meaningful in all of these societies. They also raise questions about how well the categories lend themselves to intersocietal comparisons because of the effects the different distributions have on measures of association. As Müller and associates (1989) pointed out regarding the distributions of credentials, "The less concentrated the population is on the different certificates available in the educational system, the more easily can certificates be used for [job] selection purposes" (p. 9). Of course, the same can be said for the distributions of occupational classes. So, when we start comparing societies in terms of the association between those two highly varied distributions, important methodological questions need to be raised. The comparative analyses conducted by Müller and associates have shed some light on these questions, but there is much more to be done.

SUMMARY

This chapter has reviewed the nature of the educational systems in France, in Germany, in Great Britain, and in the United States to investigate how the characteristics of educational systems affect the process by which young people make the transition from school to work. The nature of the transition process varies greatly among those four societies, and the characteristics of their educational systems help to explain that variation.

From the review presented, it is possible to construct two ideal types of educational systems. Type One systems are highly standardized and stratified, and their educational credentials recognize vocational specialization. Type Two systems are relatively unstandardized and unstratified and their credentials have little vocational relevance. It appears that Type One societies have a stronger education–occupation association, lower rates of return to full-time school, fewer increases in educational credentials, fewer job changes, and lower rates of early occupational mobility. In effect, the transition from school to work is more orderly and stable in Type One societies.

Germany comes closest to having a Type One educational system, and the United States comes closest to having a Type Two educational system. France and Great Britain have mixtures of the characteristics used in this typology.

Difficult problems in studying the transition from school to work still remain. One is finding a definition of the first job that is wholly adequate for comparisons across societies. A related problem is the societal variation in the opportunities for increasing one's level of educational credentials while in the labor force rather than only while outside the labor force.

Two interrelated measurement problems also remain. One is the degree to which the measures used have comparable meaning in the societies being studied. The other is the great amount of societal variation in the distributions of individuals in the categories of educational credentials and occupational levels that are used.

ACKNOWLEDGMENTS: The preparation of this chapter was aided immeasurably by having access to a fine volume edited by Yossi Shavit and Walter Müller (1998) that was published as this chapter was nearing completion. The Shavit–Müller volume consists of a series of chapters analyzing the school-to-work transition in 13 societies using parallel methods of analysis, as well as a summary chapter by Müller and Shavit. Their chapter in this volume reports some observations based on that volume. I am grateful to them for providing me with the preliminary manuscript and an advance copy of the volume before it became available in this country.

Financial support during the period of preparation of this chapter from Statistics Canada, The U.S. National Center for Education Statistics, and the Spencer Foundation is gratefully acknowledged.

REFERENCES

Allmendinger, J. (1989a).*Career mobility dynamics: A general comparative analysis of the United States, Norway, and West Germany.* Berlin: Max-Planck Institut fur Bildungsforschung.

Allmendinger, J. (1989b). Educational systems and labor market outcomes. *European Sociological Review, 5,* 231–250.

Archer, M. (1979). *Social origins of educational systems.* Beverly Hills, CA: Sage.

Arum, R., & Hout, M. (1998). The early returns:The transition from school to work in the United States. In Y. Shavit & W. Müller (Eds.), *From school to work: A comparative study of educational qualifications and occupational destinations* (pp. 471–510). Oxford, England: Clarendon Press.

Coleman, J. S. (1984). The transition from school to work. *Research in Social Stratification and Mobility, 3,* 27–59.

Coleman, J. S., Blum, Z. D., Sørensen, A. B., & Rossi, P. H. (1972). White and black careers during the first decade of labor force experience. Part I: Occupational status. *Social Science Research, 1,* 243–270.

De Graaf, P. M., & Ultee, W. C. (1998). Education and early occupation in the Netherlands around 1990: Categorical and continuous scales and the details of a relationship. In Y. Shavit & W. Müller (Eds.), *From school to work: A comparative study of educational qualifications and occupational destinations* (pp. 337-367). Oxford, England: Clarendon Press.

Erikson, R., Goldthorpe, J. H., & Portocarero, L. (1979). Intergenerational class mobility in three European societies. *British Journal of Sociology, 30,* 415–441.

Erikson, R., & Jonsson, J. O. (1998). Allocation processes in the Swedish labour market. In Y. Shavit & W. Müller (Eds.), *From school to work: A comparative study of educational qualifications and occupational destinations* (pp.369–406). Oxford, England: Clarendon Press.

Furlong, A. (1992). *Growing up in a classless society? School to work transitions.* Edinburgh, Scotland: Edinburgh University Press.

Granovetter, M. (1974). *Getting a job.* Cambridge, MA: Harvard University Press.

Haller, M., König, K., Krause, P., & Kurz, K. (1985). Patterns of career mobility and structural positions in advanced capitalist societies: A comparison of men and women in Austria, France and the United States. *American Sociological Review, 50,* 579–603.

Heath, A., & Cheung, S.Y. (1998). Education and occupation in Britain. In Y. Shavit & W. Müller (Eds.), *From school to work: A comparative study of educational qualifications and occupational destinations* (pp. 71–101). Oxford, England: Clarendon Press.

Ishida, H., Müller, W., & Ridge, J. M. (1995). Class origin, class destination and education: A cross-national study of ten industrial nations. *American Journal of Sociology, 101,* 145–193.

Jacobs, J. A., & Lim, S. (1992) Trends in occupational and industrial sex segregation in fifty-six countries, 1960–80. *Work and Occupations, 19,* 450–486.

Kaestle, C. (1983). *Pillars of the republic: Common schools and American society, 1780–1960.* New York: Hill & Wang.

Kerckhoff, A. C. (1990). Educational pathways to early career mobility in Great Britain. *Research in Social Stratification and Mobility, 9,* 131–157.

Kerckhoff, A. C. (1995). Institutional arrangements and stratification processes in industrial societies. *Annual Review of Sociology, 21,* 323–347.

Kerckhoff, A. C., Fogelman, K., Crook, D., & Reeder, D. (1996). *Going comprehensive in England and Wales: A study of uneven change.* London: The Woburn Press.

Kerckhoff, A. C., Fogelman, K., & Manlove, J. (1997). Staying ahead: The middle class and school reform in England and Wales. *Sociology of Education, 70,* 19–35.

König, W., & Müller, W. (1986). Educational systems and labour markets as determinants of worklife mobility in France and West Germany: A comparison of men's career mobility, 1965–1970. *European Sociological Review, 2,* 73–96.

Lewis, H. D. (1985). *The French education system.* New York: St.Martin's Press.

Light, A. (1995). The effects of interrupted schooling on wages. *Journal of Human Resources, 30,* 472–502.

Maurice, M., Sellier, F., & Silvestre, J.-J. (1986). *The social foundations of industrial power: A comparison of France and Germany.* Cambridge, MA: MIT Press.

Mayer, K. U., & Carroll, G. R. (1987). Jobs and classes: Structural constraints on career mobility. *European Sociological Review, 3,* 14–38.

Müller, W. (1986) Women's labor force participation over the life course: A model case of social change. In P. B. Baltes, D. L. Featherman, & R. M. Lerner (Eds.), *Life-span development and behavior* (Vol.7, pp. 43–68. Hillsdale, NJ: Lawerence Erlbaum Associates.

Müller, W., Lüttinger, P., König, W., & Karle, W. (1989). Class and education in industrial nations. *International Journal of Sociology, 19,* 3–39.

Müller, W., & Shavit, Y. (1998). The institutional embededness of the stratification process: A comparative study of qualifications and occupations in thirteen countries. In Y. Shavit & W. Müller (Eds.), *From school to work: A comparative study of educational qualifications and occupational destinations* (pp. 1–48). Oxford, England: Clarendon Press.

Müller, W., Steinmann, S., & Ell, R. (1998). Education and labour market entry in Germany. In Y. Shavit & W. Müller (Eds.), *From school to work: A comparative study of educational qualifications and occupational destinations* (pp. 143–188). Oxford, England:Clarendon Press.

Oakes, J. (1985). *Keeping track: How schools structure inequality.* New Haven, CT: Yale University Press.

Organization for Economic Cooperation and Development (1996). *Education at a glance: OECD indicators.* Paris: Center for Educational Research and Innovation.

Ringer, F. (1979). *Education and society in modern Europe.* Bloomington, IN: Indiana University Press.

Rosenbaum, J. E., Kariya, T., Settersten, R., & Maier, T. (1990). Market and network theories of the transition from high school to work: Their application to industrialized societies. *Annual Review of Sociology, 16,* 263–299.

Rubinson, R. (1986). Class formation, politics, and institutions: Schooling in the United States. *American Journal of Sociology, 92,* 519–548.

Shavit, Y., & Müller, W. (1998). *From school to work: A comparative study of educational qualifications and occupational destinations.* Oxford, England: Clarendon Press.

Sørensen, A. B. (1975). The structure of intragenerational mobility. *American Sociological Review, 40,* 456–471.

Sørensen, A. B., & Blossfeld, H.-P. (1989). Socioeconomic opportunities in Germany in the post-war period. *Research in Social Stratification and Mobility, 1,* 67–94.

Spence, A. M. (1974). *Market signalling: Information transfer in hiring and related processes.* Cambridge, MA: Harvard University Press.

Spilerman, S. (1977). Careers, labor market structure, and socioeconomic achievement. *American Journal of Sociology, 83,* 551–593.

Spring, J. (1976). *The sorting machine.* New York: David McKay.

Stevenson, D. L., & Baker, D. P. (1991). State control of the curriculum and classroom instruction. *Sociology of Education, 64,* 1–10.

Treiman, D.J., & Yip, K.-B. (1989). Educational and occupational attainment in 21 countries. In M. L. Kohn (Ed.), *Cross-national research in sociology* (pp.373–394). Newbury Park, CA: Sage.

Turner, R. H. (1960). Sponsored and contest mobility and the school system. *American Sociological Review, 25,* 334–352.

Tyack, D. (1974). *The one best system: A history of American urban education.* Cambridge, MA: Harvard University Press.

Vanfossen, B., Jones, J., & Spade, J. (1987). Curriculum tracking and status maintenance. *Sociology of Education, 60,* 104–122.

Winfield, I., Campbell, R. T., Kerckhoff, A. C., Everett, D. D., & Trott, J. M. (1989). Career processes in Great Britain and the United States. *Social Forces, 68,* 284–308.

CHAPTER 21

Pathways from School to Work in Germany and the United States

JEYLAN T. MORTIMER
HELGA KRÜGER

Ever since Dreeben's now classic portrayal, *On What is Learned in School* (1968), sociologists have recognized that the institution of education has many diverse functions. However, its most clearly recognized and designated purpose is to prepare youths for adulthood, especially to provide the knowledge and skills that equip young people to adequately perform adult occupational roles. According to the modern life course regime, school is primarily preparation for adult work and for labor market positions. Once begun, the occupational career will define one's life chances even after retirement (Kohli, 1985). The linkage between years of education and adult occupational attainment in the United States, as well as in other modern countries, is well demonstrated (see, e.g., Blossfeld, 1987; Bridges, 1996; Di Prete & McManus, 1996; Kerckhoff, 1990, 1995). People who attain more formal education are able to enter occupations of higher prestige and to attain higher incomes throughout their working lives.

However, the educational arena is not the only domain in which young people prepare themselves for future work. Economists emphasize that both education and work experience are important for human capital formation (Becker, 1993). Sociologists also recognize that early occupational experience predicts subsequent attainment in the work career. However, in accord with the normative assumptions of the life course, investigators in the United States

JEYLAN T. MORTIMER • Department of Sociology, University of Minnesota, Minneapolis, Minnesota 55455
HELGA KRÜGER • Department of Sociology, University of Bremen, Bremen 28359, Germany

Handbook of the Sociology of Education, edited by Maureen T. Hallinan. Kluwer Academic/Plenum Publishers, New York, 2000.

have typically considered labor-force participation only after the completion of schooling as part of the process of socioeconomic attainment. In actuality, however, education and work experience in modern societies, especially in North America, tend to be increasingly overlapping, variable, and extended throughout life. Educational and work careers are becoming more like Buchmann's (1989) model of the destandardized and individualized life course, departing from Kohli's (1985) description of the biographical institutionalization of ordered life course sequences. Paid employment, initially of an informal character, typically begins in early adolescence; education often continues well into adulthood, simultaneously, or in alternation with paid jobs.

North American youths who are still in secondary school, and even before, want to work to earn extra spending money as well as to gain entry to a role that will be exceedingly important to them as adults. In fact, the vast majority of young people in the United States hold paid jobs while attending secondary school (Mortimer & Johnson, 1998; Steinberg & Cauffman, 1995). The situation is quite similar in Canada (Lowe & Krahn, 1992). For those who attend college or other institutions of postsecondary education, the combination of school and paid work is likewise customary. The frequent movement of American youths between school and work, even in prior decades, posed problems for status attainment researchers who have had to grapple with the operational definition of the first real job (see, e.g., Marini, 1987).

Confronted with the large number of employed high school students, U.S. educators have become critical of employment in adolescence, viewing this activity as competing with school achievement and educational commitment. Simply put, work is seen as drawing young people away from school (Bills, Helms, & Ozcan, 1995). Employment at this stage of life is thought to have little present or future benefit. Educators have been joined in their opposition to student employment by developmental psychologists (Greenberger & Steinberg, 1986; Steinberg & Cauffman, 1995), who are also concerned with the potential diversion of youth away from educational and other more developmentally beneficial activities. They point to the loss of a moratorium period in which young people can explore alternate interests and identities. It is argued that the kinds of jobs that young people can find in the free market economy—involving few skills and little advancement potential—are quite different from students' long-term career objectives and do little to further such goals. Relatively few employed students in the United States have jobs that are supervised by high school personnel or that are formally connected to the school curriculum.

However, some sociologists have viewed young people's connections to the labor force as providing useful socialization for the future. For example, although the Panel on Youth of the President's Science Advisory Committee (1974, chaired by James Coleman) noted the importance of formal education, it expressed concern that schools isolated youths from working adults other than their teachers. The panel members believed that this isolation contributed to the difficulties many young people have in finding jobs when they complete high school. Indicating the contemporary relevance of this concern, the central purpose of the Federal School to Work Opportunities Act of 1994 is to provide mechanisms to facilitate this transition.

American parents, likewise, value both formal schooling and work experience. Recognizing the significance of education for occupational and for income attainment, they tend to have high educational goals for their children. At the same time, they believe that certain attributes, promotive of achievement, are attained most readily through paid employment during the adolescent years. Parents in the United States see their children as acquiring increasing independence, responsibility, time management skills, and other virtues through paid jobs while they are attending high school (Aronson, Mortimer, Zierman, & Hacker, 1996; Phillips & Sandstrom, 1990). In fact, they attribute many of their own work competencies to the lessons they learned on the job when they were still teenagers (Aronson et al., 1996). Parents generally support their children in their efforts to attain and maintain jobs while they are still in school.

Thus the paradox exists: U.S. educators' widespread disapproval of youth employment, despite economists' recognition that human capital development occurs through employment as well as through formal education and training, and despite parents' hearty endorsement of their children working. A lively ensuing debate in the United States involves parents, educators, developmental psychologists, and other social scientists. This controversy has attracted the increasing attention of policymakers (Committee on the Health and Safety Implications of Child Labor, 1998).

Issues surrounding school and work in Germany are framed very differently. As in the United States, most youths experience formal schooling and paid work at the same time. However, unlike the United States, the combination of school and work receives virtually no criticism from educators or from others. There is little worry about whether working draws students away from educational pursuits. Instead, particularly during times of economic downturn, concern is directed to whether apprenticeship positions will be available for all youths who wish to obtain them. This is because the combination of education and work in Germany is formally structured and integrated by design. The apprenticeship provides a predictable set of educational and work experiences that have clear, well-recognized payoffs in occupational credentials for the future.

The strong connection between school and work, typical of Germany as well as of other European societies (Allmendinger, 1989; Kerckhoff, 1995), presents a strong contrast to the unregulated U.S. system. German youths select apprentice placements, which enable them to obtain specific career goals. German educators, employers, parents, and youths themselves agree that both school and work are necessary to prepare for the adult occupational role. This widespread consensus would appear to be quite in keeping with economists' dual focus on formal schooling and employment in the acquisition of human capital.

Awareness of structural differences—especially the varying linkages between youth jobs and adult jobs in the two systems—provides insight about why, in the American system, there is so much ambivalence about adolescent employment, whereas in the German system, there is near unanimous approval. Whereas macrostructural variations in the process of transition from school to work in Germany and in the United States have received much attention (see Hamilton, 1990, 1993), their social psychological consequences for youths themselves have been subject to less systematic scrutiny. Nonetheless, cross-national differences in the structure of the transition from school to work have critical implications for the ways young people think about and plan their futures and for the manner in which they typically exercise agency as they move into adulthood. This chapter focuses on these microlevel consequences and adaptations. In the absence of systematic comparative investigations of students' attitudes and orientations, we draw on empirical studies conducted within each country, as well as on pertinent observations and informed speculations. However, it is first necessary to describe in a more detailed manner the structural differences between the U.S. and the German systems: These constitute the social contexts for the formation of occupational preferences, attitudes about work and schooling, career planning, and other psychological and behavioral reactions.

DIFFERENCES IN THE TRANSITION FROM SCHOOL TO WORK

In the United States, formal education at the secondary level is usually quite general in nature. Students acquire high school diplomas, typically after completing 12 years of formal education, despite great diversity in the content of their educational experiences. Some students may have taken mostly college preparatory courses while in high school; others may have had more vocational or commercial coursework, sometimes accompanied by school-supervised work experience. Irrespective of stream or track, however, all students on completion of high school are granted the same degree. Similarly at the college level, 4-year B.A. or B.S. degrees are not typically occupationally specific. Although many young people acquire postsecondary vocational training, and a host of specific certificates and degrees, these generally lack widespread recognition, state legitimation, or enforcement (Kerckhoff & Bell, 1998).

As a result, there is little clarity about the relation between formal educational credentials (degrees) and occupational pathways for most positions below the professional level. Hamilton (1997) pointed out that if a teenager were to ask most American adults about how one becomes a doctor or a lawyer, fairly coherent and consistent answers would be forthcoming. In contrast, the same query about how to become a skilled craftsman (e.g., an air conditioning repairman) would probably yield rather vague and variable responses.

The nexus between formal educational preparation and the U.S. labor force is, in fact, quite unstructured in comparison to the German system. Outside of the professions, most occupations have few formal educational or degree requirements, and there are multiple educational and vocational routes through which the aspirant can gain entry to them. In consequence, youths must find their way from school to work without clear institutional bridges. Kerckhoff (1996), in his cross-national comparative analysis of the linkages between education and work, posited that school systems providing the more general credentials go hand-in-hand with relatively unstructured early employment trajectories.

Moreover, Kerckhoff (1996) noted that the more general the educational credential provided in a given national context, the longer the subsequent trial and testing period in the labor force. Youths in the United States spend a relatively long period of time moving from job to job, trying to establish a better fit between their own interests and abilities, and the experiences, challenges and rewards that may be gained through work. Prospective employers do not have access to formal educational credentials to provide them with information about what a given youthful job applicant can and cannot do. Consequently, they must rely on general signals in deciding whether to offer a job. These include high school diplomas and baccalaureate degrees, as well as age, dress, attitude and general comportment.

In such an unstructured situation, many youths do not succeed in their initial jobs, or, finding them unsatisfying, go on to try something else. Even if they have the requisite job skills, young people in their teens and early twenties are often not considered ready or sufficiently settled down to be worthy of organization-sponsored, in-house training or career development programs. Often they are restricted to low-level service jobs at or close to the minimum wage, much like those held on a part-time basis during high school.

Hence the long period of floundering (M. A. Hamilton, Hamilton, & Nichols, 1998; Osterman, 1980, 1989), particularly among the half of the U.S. youth population who do not go on to college (W.T. Grant Foundation, 1988). Young people who start but do not finish college are at a similar disadvantage in the labor market (Kerckhoff & Bell, 1998). Hamilton (1990) has lamented the loss of human capital development during these formative years when young people have left school but have not yet found productive stable employment.

In contrast, in Germany, both educational and occupational trajectories are highly structured, with an elaborate certification structure serving as bridge between them. The German educational system offers for the majority of youth a two-phase preparatory sequence for future occupational careers. The first phase is early general education; the second consists of occupationally specific learning. More than two thirds of German youths participate in the latter, skill-providing programs; only a minority of youths attain labor market qualifications via a university degree.

As in the United States, general schooling in Germany begins at age 6. After 4 years of primary school for all, German youths are distributed into three distinct streams. The most capable third of the cohort move directly from primary school into the *Gymnasium*, which offers 9 more years of general schooling and prepares youths for the university. About 70% are directed to the two other streams—to the *Hauptschule* (foundation school), where they will continue their general education for another 5 years, or to the *Realschule* (intermediate school), where they will attain their diploma in general education within 6 more years of schooling. After completing these general studies, *Hauptschule* and *Realschule* students move into a vocational education program.

German vocational education includes both occupationally specific training and formal education. The apprenticeship consists of 3 to 4 years of vocational training in an employment setting along with corresponding instruction in the school. In the apprentice position, the novice worker spends a day or two each week in the classroom, and 3 or 4 days per week in a firm. The state pays the vocational schooling costs; the employer pays a reduced wage to the apprentice during the duration of the training. Some vocational training, more frequently preparation for stereotypically female occupations, is almost exclusively school-based, but this also includes practical experiences in workplaces (see Culpepper & Finegold, 1999).

Though the German system may be thought of as rather definitive and inflexible, quite contrary to the modern vision of the destandardized and individualized life course, it does entail some flexibility and change in direction. For example, the formal education component of vocational education during the apprenticeship includes general education subjects. If pupils are sufficiently successful in these, they can move to a higher educational track, including University studies.

In combination, occupation-specific education and vocational training in the German system provide qualifications for a highly structured, hierarchical labor market consisting of five levels* (See Table 21.1). Only 3% to 6% of German youths will leave school without any certificate and will therefore be confined to the lowest (unqualified) employment rung. The remaining four levels of employment can be acquired only through possession of corresponding formal qualifications. The vocational education and training system, leading to the acquisition of a training certificate, absorbs the majority (about 70%) of German youths. Training certificates enable entry to 498 officially recognized qualified occupations. In 1996, 370 of these demanded apprenticeship experiences (Alex & Stooß, 1996) and 128 merely required school-based vocational education (Stooß, 1997).

A clear structure of educational–vocational qualification and a corresponding hierarchy of entrance positions in the labor market, from the unskilled worker to the university graduate, is thus established both in the private and the public sectors of employment. Even when there are company-sponsored internal training and promotion systems, workers rarely can progress beyond the ceiling of the occupational level for which they are formally qualified through their educational achievement and/or vocational training.

---

*This system is rooted historically in the merging of two regulatory systems, each of which controlled access to particular occupations and forms of employment. The first system was the artisan and craft guilds, producing the journeyman and master craftsman. In the modern industrial and service economy, these levels correspond to the skilled worker ("Facharbeiter"), and those possessing intermediate level specialist qualifications ("Meister"). The second system was the bureaucratic administrative organization for the four levels of civil service (lower, intermediate, upper intermediate and senior), each of which is attached to a corresponding level of educational qualification.

TABLE 21.1. Educational Qualifications and Occupational Destinations in the German System

Entry qualification	Occupational destinations
Academic Level University degree (Magister, Staatsexamen)	Professional scientist, top management, lawyer, pharmacist, senior civil service, teacher
Polytechnic Level Degree	Engineer, social worker, middle management, personal secretary, upper intermediate civil service
Technical College Graduate	Master craftsman, e.g., master artisan (painter, auto mechanic), secretary, technician, nurse, intermediate civil service
Vocational Training Certificate	Skilled worker, e.g., electrician, hairdresser, sales assistant, typist, office worker, receptionist, child care worker, medical/ dental assistant, lower civil service
No vocational education/training	Unskilled/semi-skilled worker, e.g., assembly line workers, construction workers, cleaners

The legal basis for this classificatory and regulatory scheme lies in the crafts tradition of formally guaranteed qualification security, both for the customer and the clients who are the recipients of products and services and for employers. This guarantee is linked to the German system of formal wage rates. That is, the possession of formal certification at a particular level gives individuals the legal right to a specified corresponding wage, given that they success-fully locate employment in the occupation for which they have been educated and trained (Blossfeld & Mayer, 1988; Drechsel, Görs, Gronwald, & Rabe-Kleberg, 1988; Heinz, 1995; Krüger, 1990). We therefore observe a highly regulated German system of stratification and standardization of pathways from school to work. In contrast to the United States, the educa-tional system clearly distributes the holders of qualifications into a labor market differentiated both horizontally and vertically.

Of course, for German youths there are risks in traversing the school-to-work transition. In periods of high unemployment in Germany, such as the present, employers have fewer positions for apprentices. Moreover, not all components of the vocational training system provide the same level of security. Exclusively school-based training systems, leading more frequently to sex-typed female occupations, induce greater susceptibility to unemployment or underemployment. This kind of training is therefore less valuable than that which offers both formal education and apprenticeship positions (Teubner, 1989). Completion of such dual prepa-ration, typically leading to male-typed occupations, is more likely to yield employment and earnings in accord with the acquired qualification. This differentiation between the training of male and female youths is rooted in the historical definition of males as breadwinners and females as homemakers. The resultant gender inequality in employment and in remuneration make it less advantageous for wives to pursue paid work and puts them at a disadvantage in negotiations with their husbands about labor market activity (Krüger, 1999).

THE ADOLESCENT AS ACTIVE AGENT

Now that we have considered the structural features of the school-to-work transition in the United States and in Germany, we turn to our central focus: the consequences of the two macrostructural regimes for the orientations and perspectives of youths moving through them.

Differences in the ways the bridges from school to work are constructed have manifold psychological implications. They mold the ways in which youths earn money, an activity having important symbolic meaning in becoming an adult. They influence the degree of confidence and certainty youths feel as they anticipate their educational and vocational futures. The cross-national differences in structure affect the sense of urgency in career planning, as well as the timing of this activity. They inflate or deflate youths' estimations of the opportunity that lies before them. They heighten or reduce anxieties as young people attempt to move toward their goals. Finally, they have important implications for youths' feelings of failure when they encounter obstructions in their paths.

These various psychological phenomena, including attributions, emotions and evaluations, all assume very different character in the two transitional contexts. Although there are variations within each country in the school-to-work transition (e.g., by gender, social class or region), because of space limitations these are given little attention here.

Balancing of School and Work

In considering work experience as part of the school-to-work transition for young people in the United States, we rely on data from the Youth Development Study. Since the late 1980s, a team of researchers has followed a cohort of youths in St. Paul, Minnesota. The study commenced when the pupils were in the ninth grade (the beginning of high school in St. Paul); most were 14–15 years old (in 1988). It has continued with annual surveys through the participants' mid-20s. Information to be presented in this chapter draws on questionnaires administered in high school classrooms, as well as on surveys obtained by mail through the ninth wave of data collection (1997). The initial panel included 1,000 young people, chosen randomly from a ninth-grade enrollment list. Of those who responded in the first wave, 93% were retained through the 4 years of high school; retention through the ninth wave was 78.6%. To obtain a perspective on youth employment, other than that of the teenagers themselves, we also surveyed parents by mail during the first and fourth years of the study.

Beginning the study as early as the ninth grade enabled observation of youths at a time when few had yet had any formal employment experience, though most had worked in the informal economy doing babysitting, yard work or other chores. Such informal work is often performed in the context of a family—for neighbors, relatives and adult friends of the youth's parents (but work performed in the context of the adolescent's own family, even if paid, is not considered as work here). The longitudinal data enabled us to examine subsequent paid work experience, in more formal adultlike workplaces, both during high school and subsequently.

In the United States, given the loose structuring of education and the labor market for most young people, youths must develop their own balancing acts. They themselves trade off and negotiate the time and energy directed to schooling and to working in their efforts to obtain advantages from both activities. Those who want to obtain higher educational degrees, as well as work-related knowledge and skills that may be difficult or impossible to obtain in school, must carve out their own pathways. This process of constructing one's own individualized amalgam of school and work begins as early as elementary school, as youngsters take on their first babysitting and grass-cutting jobs for neighboring families. It continues through the completion of formal education as they assume employment in retail stores, in restaurants, in gas stations, and in other contexts. The process includes youths from all socioeconomic strata—from high school dropouts to those who continue on to the highest professional and graduate degrees.

When American young people are asked why they have jobs, they typically do not say they are preparing for adult work. In fact, relatively few expect that they will continue in the same line of work as their high school jobs after they finish school. Instead, the foremost response to this question is "for the money"—to purchase immediately consumable items, such as stereos, music tapes, and concert tickets. Earnings also are used to buy cars and automobile insurance. Many youths pay for their own lunches at school, for clothes, for transportation and for other expenses. Youth employment may also be part of a broader strategy to acquire the postsecondary education that is necessary to achieve future occupational goals. Given the ubiquity of higher educational aspirations in the United States, saving for college is a more frequent use of students' earnings as they approach the end of high school. Whereas relatively few adolescent workers turn over their paychecks to their families, using earnings to help support familial objectives is more prevalent in rural settings than in urban areas. (Elsewhere [Shanahan, Elder, Burchinal, & Conger, 1996], earnings expenditures among the urban Youth Development Study participants and rural participants in the Iowa Youth and Families Project are compared.)

In the U.S. educational system, considerable importance is attached to secondary school achievement by the gatekeepers of higher education. A key measure of such success is grade point average (GPA). Obtaining high grades is thus of great importance for youth who aspire to graduate from college. In contrast, grades achieved in school bear no clearly recognizable relation to success for those youths who forego higher education and seek jobs immediately following high school (Rosenbaum, Takehiko, Settersten, & Maier, 1990). In fact, after high school graduation, many prospective employers do not even request high school transcripts or other indicators of academic performance. If they do want this information, high schools may not provide it (often due to a lack of requisite staffing).

In the absence of perceived vocational or other clear incentives to do well in school, many high school students may come to think that their school performance matters little for their futures. Those who become psychologically disengaged from school apparently find work more attractive than their more studious counterparts. We have found that young people who are disengaged from school early on tend to invest more time in paid work during the following years.

Whereas approximately 90% of Youth Development Study panel members had at least some paid work experience during high school (while school was in session), different employment patterns could be clearly discerned. Some youths worked almost continuously, at relatively high intensity (more than 20 hours per week on the average) while school was in session. Others were employed during most months of observation but their work intensity was restricted, on average, to 20 or fewer hours each week. Still others worked relatively few months (less than half the observed months, on the average), either at high or low intensity during the months they were employed.

Indicative of the exercise of individual agency in the school-to-work transition, psychological orientations as early as the ninth grade significantly predicted St. Paul youth's labor force activity during the 3 subsequent high school years (Mortimer & Johnson, 1998). That is, ninth-grade students who had lower educational aspirations, less interest in school, and lower levels of educational performance (as measured by ninth-grade GPA) subsequently pursued more highly intensive employment in Grades 10 through 12. These ninth graders were more strongly oriented to their peers, spending a greater amount of time with their friends, and engaging in more frequent drinking, smoking, and problem behavior at school. During the 10th through the 12 grades, they invested more than 20 hours per week on the average in paid work during the months they were employed.

In contrast, ninth graders who manifested a greater degree of psychological investment in the educational enterprise, who believed that they were learning things in school that would be useful to them in the future, and who expressed greater interest in school coursework, were more likely to pursue low-intensity employment that was limited, on the average, to 20 or fewer hours per week during high school. When work is restricted in this manner, the young person has more time to devote to school as well as to other activities. There was little difference, by gender, in this pattern of selection to work.

The distinguishable patterns of employment during secondary school are thus emergent phenomena resulting from youths' own time management strategies (Shanahan & Flaherty, 1998). American youths do not have a superimposed program of schooling and working, nor do they find clear linkages between jobs obtained during high school and adult occupational positions. In this unstructured transitional context, they negotiate with employers and parents in an attempt to balance working with schooling, extracurricular activities, and time with friends and family. Many youths curtail their work hours, or leave the labor force altogether, in response to changing circumstances in other domains of their lives—a difficult course in school or a highly demanding extracurricular activity. Though parents express approval of their children's employment, they may become concerned if job hours become excessive. Indicating negotiations surrounding work in the family context, job hours are a common source of disagreement between adolescents and their parents (Manning, 1990). As hours of work increase, more parent–child arguments in general ensue (Mortimer & Shanahan, 1994).

The emergent and unstructured character of youth employment in the United States does not mean that it is entirely random or that it has no predictable features. In fact, despite the absence of any superimposed framework, young people tend to move from job to job during high school in accord with their growing capacities. During this period, an aggregate occupational career can be discerned. That is, American teenagers start off doing informal paid work, typically at about the age of 12, for neighbors and for families in their communities. Fast-food enterprises and restaurants absorb a large portion of youth workers in the middle years of high school. As they approach secondary school completion, employed youths are spread across a wider variety of occupational locations. Along with these occupational trends during the high school years, young workers come to be assigned to more complex work tasks over time (as indicated by ratings constructed by the Department of Labor in the Dictionary of Occupational Titles) and to jobs requiring more training and greater supervisory responsibility (Mortimer, Finch, Dennehy, Lee, & Beebe, 1994). Indeed, there are many different employment options and settings for American teenagers (Bidwell, Schneider & Borman, 1998).

Highly intensive employment sets the stage for stronger engagement in the world of work. In fact, youths who work at higher intensity (generally more than 20 hours per week), when compared with those who have less temporal investment in the work role, describe their jobs during high school as providing them with greater responsibility, more learning opportunities and more challenging job tasks; they are also exposed to more frequent stressors in the work place (Mortimer, Harley, & Johnson, 1998). A pattern of high-intensity employment during high school, given its association with challenge and learning opportunities, would appear to be conducive to human capital development through work. Even though the experience of problems and tensions at work are immediately dissatisfying, such stressors could foster the acquisition of coping skills, promoting adaptation to work in the future (Shanahan & Mortimer, 1996).

The identified patterns of youth employment were found to have significant consequences for educational and vocational achievement during the years after high school. Consistent with the hypothesis that such early jobs can promote human capital, high-intensity employ-

Jeylan T. Mortimer and Helga Krüger

ment careers during high school were found to be associated with more rapid acquisition of full-time work following high school for males and for females, as well as higher earnings for males 4 years beyond (Mortimer & Johnson, 1998).

Young people who pursue lower intensity employment during high school achieve more months of postsecondary education. Whereas the differences by employment pattern in girls' educational attainment disappear when prior differences in ninth-grade attitudes and orientations (described earlier) are controlled, boys who followed a pattern of near-continuous, low-intensity employment achieved significantly more months of postsecondary schooling (Mortimer & Johnson, 1998).

Entwisle, Alexander, and Olson (1998) reported a similar pattern of findings based on a panel of largely poor, African–American youths. They observed that the elementary school students in Baltimore, Maryland who were less interested in school, and who came from poorer family backgrounds, subsequently obtained jobs that were of higher quality than those of their more academically engaged and advantaged peers. Such jobs would presumably enable greater human capital development. The authors viewed work experience during the junior high school and senior high school years as providing an alternate route to viable and stable employment for young people who are the least well equipped to benefit from regular formal education.

Other research linking high school work experience and early adult attainments in the United States, using indicators such as the time spent employed and unemployed after high school, earnings, and fringe benefits, have established clear associations between investment in paid work and positive labor market outcomes (Committee on the Health and Safety Implications of Child Labor, 1998; Ruhm, 1995, 1997). These extend up to a decade beyond high school.

Thus, both students in Germany and in the United States combine school and work prior to completing their formal education. However, German youths will be much more likely than American youths to recognize the connections between early work and the work they will pursue as adults. Clearly, the extent to which American and German adolescents increase their capacity to work in adulthood, as a result of their early work experiences, differs in degree. Still, there is evidence that through their early employment experiences, U.S. teenagers, as well as German youths, enhance their work readiness. However, in the United States the pattern of employment is individualized and emergent, constructed by youths themselves in a relatively uncertain school-to-work transition context. For them, school and work are for the most part institutionally disconnected. The vast majority of employed youths in the United States are not participants in school-sponsored internships or vocational programs.

It is pertinent to note that American educational ideology features the openness of the contest (Turner, 1960), for this configuration of beliefs and values surely influences the phenomenal experience of education as well as the transition from school to work. Highly valued are open doors allowing persons to move in and out of secondary and postsecondary schools, opportunities for late bloomers, and alternate routes to 4-year colleges and universities. Flexible and diverse pathways to adult occupations are consistent with this educational structure.

American parents and educators are highly averse to tracks or to other arrangements that could prematurely curtail a child's eventual educational chances. Groupings by ability or by achievement, where they do exist, are often camouflaged or denied (Rosenbaum, 1976). Such arrangements are actually quite common in U.S. schools, even at the elementary level where they are manifest in reading groups and other ability-based or achievement-based groupings (Alexander & Entwisle, 1996). Thus, sorting begins even earlier in the United States than in Germany (where elementary school grouping is unknown) and it is far subtler (S. F. Hamilton, personal communication, October 29, 1998).

However, the American educational ideology, and associated educational structures, make failure in the school setting less clearly visible and the consequences of such failure less foreseeable. Students who have widely disparate educational performance and preparation in secondary school plan to go to college (Clark, 1960; Dornbusch, 1994). The general American educational structure, loosely linked to particular occupational outcomes, does not encourage American youths who are initially less successful in school to scale down their high-level occupational aspirations. American high school students may perceive little necessity to seriously assess or reassess their career prospects even in the face of low grades or other indications of deficient progress. A clear message that one is not likely to succeed in attaining a high-level professional goal would likely foster redirection and accommodation to this reality, what Brandtstädter (1998, p. 847) called "flexible goal adjustment." However, it would seem that the open-ended American achievement ideology would be conducive to discounting such early negative feedback.

In general, the unstructured character of the U.S. school-to-work transition does not foster a high level of interest or engagement in career planning during adolescence. There may seemingly be little need to seriously consider the career at any particular time during this period, perhaps contributing to a subjective lack of direction. Students may perceive long-term opportunities to return to the educational system to achieve more advanced or specialized training if the need arises, and may perceive diverse portals for entry to desired occupational trajectories.

Lack of focused career planning in the educational context could be considered a rational response to change and to uncertainty in the labor market. Uncertainty about one's occupational future is amplified under conditions of rapid technological innovation, alternating economic expansion and contraction, firm mergers and downsizing, short-term employment contracts and other forms of contingent employment. In fact, in newly emerging and expanding fields, such as currently in computer science, work experience can become even more important than formal training, which lags behind technological innovations. American youths are told that they must learn to learn, that is, they have to make themselves ready for retraining and for major shifts in career track. This is predicted to occur several times over the course of their working lives.

Even after they complete high school, many American youths are in jobs that bear no clear relation to their long-term career goals. Among those in the Youth Development Study panel who were employed 4 years following high school (mostly 21 or 22 years of age), fully 38% of both boys and girls were not in jobs that they identified as their future work careers. Neither did they see these jobs as providing preparation that would lead them to, or foster their performance in, their chosen careers. Many of these young people held part-time jobs while they pursued postsecondary degrees. Six years after high school graduation (age 23 and 24), 27% of employed men and 25% of employed women still reported being in jobs that were not linked to their long-term career objectives.

The vague connections between schooling and working, combined with the American ideology of equal, rather unlimited, and ever-available opportunity, can stimulate quite unrealistic thinking about future work roles. Aronson's (1998) interviews with selected female participants in the Youth Development Study provide ample illustrations of such reactions. For example, one female interviewee in her mid-20s had graduated from college and had obtained a job in her major field. However, when queried about her future occupational objectives in an interview that took place 6 years after high school graduation, she responded in the following way:

> I don't know if it's because I'm still so young or what, but I'm not 100% [sure] that what I'm doing
> is what I want to be doing. . . . So I'm just kind of like in the thinking process of like, oh my God!
> What do I want to do? How do I want to go about this? . . . I can name like ten things off the top of
> my head that I would love to do. Ten careers, probably that have no relation to each other. And that's
> a hard thing. I haven't really narrowed it down. I'm kind of trying to keep my options open. (p. 90)

The following quote shows that the absence of career direction is not necessarily a negative subjective experience. For another young woman, uncertainty was coupled with a sense of great career openness and opportunity:

> I've been trying to figure out what I want to do when I grow up! If I'm not there already! I realize
> that, with my generation, we aren't doing one thing for the span of our lives. . . . I still haven't
> figured out where I want to end up. . . . I've considered pretty much the run of the gambit. I think
> I'm lucky to be in the United States in this era when I do have so many choices. . . . And I wouldn't
> give that up for anything in the world, but that makes it harder to figure out what it is you want
> when you can do anything in my talent range. I guess I probably won't be an astronaut or a nuclear
> physicist. [laughs] (Aronson, 1998, pp. 88–89)

Response to a Highly Structured Transition

German youths who are not on a path to the university encounter a very different kind of school-to-work transition. Whatever balance they obtain between schooling and employment is structured by their educational/vocational program, not by the youths themselves. Youths do not have to decide, nor do they have to negotiate with their parents or their employers, about how many hours to work in a given week or month; the system decides this for them. Connections between the school and work spheres are highly regulated, such that success in one sphere fosters success in the other. Once placement in the educational/career track has occurred, there is greater certainty and predictability with respect to future occupational options. This structure provides an exceedingly different context for the exercise of individual agency in adolescence.

From the German teenager's perspective, coping with uncertainty and with seemingly limitless opportunity is not the problem. Instead, the objective is to get the right entrance keys in the well-defined school-to-work transition structure. These keys provide entry to specific, predictable positions within the segmented labor market. At each point in the process, success will depend on being in the right place at the right time and on being the best among competing contenders for the same formal certificates. There are critical turning points in this process. First, within the general educational system at the age of 10 to 12, students are confronted with teachers' assessments of their intellectual capacities. Based on these evaluations, they are streamed into the *Hauptschule*, *Realschule*, and *Gymnasium*.* Second, at the time of entry to the vocational training system at the ages of 16 and 17, students in the first two streams have to decide which occupation for which to prepare themselves. Finally, those who pass through the *Gymnasium* at the age of 19 or 20 must choose what type of discipline within university studies to follow.

Some parents try to manipulate the system and to exercise agency in positioning their children. Knowing the importance of school success, these parents will opt to have their children prolong kindergarten so that they enter elementary school at age 7 instead of 6. More-

---

*Most parents follow this advice. If they object, the school must follow their wishes. However, if the pupils fail their yearly final examinations, they are required to shift into the earlier proposed stream.

over, in some schools the initial evaluation phase is prolonged. However, even in such situations, the German process remains more certain and less variable than the American process.

However, despite their greater certainty, German youths are not free from the need to cope with both short-term and long-term contingencies. There are three basic issues with which German youths must contend in their passage from school to work. The first is how to deal with the clearly visible and public manifestations of success and failure at the various decision points in the school-to-work transition. The second is how to meet economic needs during adolescence. The third is how to get a promising starting position following the acquisition of qualifications for the future career in the labor market.

In comparison to the United States, signs of failure are much more visible and clearly definitive as German youths move through the educational structure. The potential for erosion of opportunities in the labor market arises at structurally programmed educational crossroads. The first selection point occurs at age 10 to 12, when youths are divided into the three different schooling streams. The last occurs at the entry to the labor market—from the age of 19, 20, or 21 for those who enter skilled work, up to age 24 to 27 for those who enter positions requiring academic (university-level) qualifications.

After the first 4 years of schooling (age 10–12), the vast majority of students have to accept that they have not been selected for the *Gymnasium*. The very early awareness that school achievement is linked to adult occupational opportunity fosters a realistic view. Thus, at a very young age, *Hauptschule* and *Realschule* pupils become well aware that their chances to achieve a higher level professional or managerial position in the labor market are much diminished. For example, they may learn that their first career choice (e.g., to become a dentist) is not feasible, given their restriction to 498 occupations for which access can be gained via the apprenticeship route. Observing pupils who are not selected for the *Gymnasium*, teachers report the first signs of being fed up with schooling (*Schulmüdigkeit*).

Teachers also complain about the lack of discipline during the last two years of *Realschule* and *Hauptschule*, that is, during the search for an apprenticeship. This is the next important threshold for the majority of German youths. The apprentice placement has wide-ranging consequences for the youths' future placement in the stratification structure—earnings, lifestyle, and consumption possibilities are all at stake. Because of its significance for the ensuing career trajectory, seeking an apprentice position is usually accompanied by considerable anxiety.

Youths who are part of the dual (education and training) system are therefore urged to think quite specifically about their labor market futures at a relatively early stage (at the age of about 13–15 years, at which time American students are in the eighth through tenth grades). Students in the last 2 years of general schooling have access to considerable information about the 498 occupations obtainable via vocational education. They are supported in the search process by counselors, by teachers, by information books, and by detailed advisory pamphlets about each occupation. For each position, students are provided with skill profiles, entrance certificates needed for qualification, and career prospects.

Prior to assuming an apprentice assignment, all students must undergo two 6-week practical training experiences in occupations of their choice. The first occurs 2 years before finishing school; the second, in the last year of schooling. The pupils' evaluations of their initial experiences, as manifested by discussions in class, show that most become convinced not to enter the first trial occupation for many reasons (it is too demanding, the earnings are not high enough, the working conditions are too difficult, or the work is too repetitive, and so forth, see Schober, 1996). Following this first experience, all students have a second chance for a 6-week work experience in another occupation. They typically return with the same set of reactions.

These early work experiences provoke intense interest in knowing more about future occupations:

> On my way to school I looked around and started to interview everybody at work, and in the bank, and also the *Schornsteinfeger* (chimney sweeper) and the police at the corner, and I asked my parents and the neighbors. And then during summer holidays, I went to the clinic and jobbed there, and also next year in the big shop here. . . . And, naturally, I went to the official Works Councils, and what else did I do? I started to look in the papers . . . (quotation from in-depth interview with a student, age 14; Rettke & Kretzer, 1992: p. 125)

During the final 6 months of schooling, pupils begin to write apprentice applications; at this time they are confronted with the difficulties of getting the apprenticeship of their choice. It is not unusual for school-leavers to apply for up to 40 different positions. For occupations with the more promising labor market futures, the selection process includes three steps: a formal application presented for screening; a rather extensive test lasting one or two days (including personal/psychological screening and a written examination of general knowledge and occupation specific skills); and finally, a formal interview. This highly elaborated and extensive selection process is likely to have considerable psychological impact on the youthful career aspirant; clearly the selection process is important, and much depends on the outcome.

Much research has been conducted on the processes through which personal interests in specific occupations are adapted to labor market realities (for recent overviews, see Heinz, 1996; Schober, 1996). Step by step, students have to adapt to the fact that their occupational choices are restricted. Even as they leave the *Hauptschule* or the *Realschule*, many students console themselves (and others) by thinking that perhaps later on they will try to climb up the career ladder via the *Zweite Bildungsweg* (see the following paragraphs). Most applicants for apprentice positions have to change their preferences during a long series of failed attempts to obtain offers.

Thus, from a very early age when children are channeled into the three educational streams, to the time of apprenticeship placement, many German students have to come to terms with disappointment. Still, only a small fraction (3 to 6% per year) really give up and enter the labor market as unqualified workers. Undoubtedly, the small number of dropouts who enter the labor market without qualifications will be clearly aware of their limited employment options.

Applications for apprentice positions are more successful for those students who have had an opportunity to practice, while still in school, in the same occupational field. Social relationships and networks established during the practicum may also come into play. In the end, most youths become satisfied with any apprenticeship they can obtain, accommodating their self-concepts to the outcome.

Successful novice apprentices develop a clear identification with the obtained position, which establishes strong barriers against giving up during the next 3 to 4 years of training and learning (Heinz, Krüger, Rettke, Wachtveitl, & Witzel, 1987). However, some German youths continue to perceive their apprenticeships as dissatisfying. For those who are disappointed by their labor market opportunities and who are motivated toward a higher level of achievement, the special upgrading programs called *Zweiter Bildungsweg* provide a second chance, an alternate route to the university. Following this route necessitates that the apprentice manifest strong performance in the school-based portion of education/training. This level of achievement would require, for most aspirants, considerable effort during the apprenticeship period.

If, however, they have obtained an acceptable occupation after having finished the apprenticeship, no one will question their decision to remain in the labor market instead of reentering the educational system. This is because to become a qualified worker is completely normal and acceptable in Germany, worthy of striving and of youthful aspiration. This situation is quite unlike that in the United States where the vast majority of high school students plan to go to college and to enter professional and managerial careers, or at the least to gain entry to higher-level white-collar occupations. In Germany, vocational training is seen in a much more favorable light. In fact, those who have finished the *Gymnasium* often prefer to acquire an apprenticeship before entering the university in order to improve their labor market chances. A combination of academic study and apprenticeship is even expected in certain fields, such as banking and engineering-related occupations (H. Bertram, personal communication, September 30, 1998).

It should be noted that the process of apprentice assignment often works to the disadvantage of females. As Goldmann and Müller (1986) pointed out, only one fourth of all women in vocational training for sales personnel indicated this occupation as their preference when leaving school. Three fourths had tried in vain to enter other apprenticeships. A recent longitudinal study of selection processes in the German vocational training system (1988 to the present) shows that the 184 girls surveyed while still in school wished to enter 59 different occupations (Dietz, Mariak, Matt, Seus, & Schumann, 1997). Of these, only 20 were female-stereotyped. Their distribution in apprenticeships, 2 years later, showed that 60% were training in only four occupational certifications, all female stereotyped. The largest number were in sales personnel; only 6% had originally wished to enter this field (Dietz et al., 1997).

The disadvantage of women in the apprenticeship system is certainly not a new phenomenon. In the 60s, one woman reported, "And the last thing I wanted to become was a dressmaker. The work is too fiddly, too nervous. Dressmakers were all nervous in our eyes then. They were all so fidgety and jittery" (Born, Krüger, & Lorenz-Meyer, 1996, p. 89). Nonetheless, when offered work as an apprentice dressmaker, she immediately accepted, without even discussing the matter with her parents. A typical quote from one of the 128 females who were interviewed in 1984 follows:

> I wanted to be a police officer, and then, if not a police officer, a plumber. And I tried hard, and my applications always were in vain. And then I tried everywhere, as a baker, for an office job . . . I looked into the newspapers, and there they offered an apprenticeship for hotel service specialists (*Hotelfachfrau*). And immediately I applied, although in this case I didn't want to be a hotel service specialist. But I got the offer, and everything was o.k. (girl, age 16; Heinz et al., 1987, p. 207)

Women whose qualifications enable them to gain entry only to female-stereotypic jobs face highly constrained economic futures. As a result, many young women try to enhance their opportunities to enter their preferred occupations during the apprenticeship by participating much more frequently than their male peers in the special upgrading programs of the *Zweite Bildungsweg*.

It should be noted that job placements, outside of the apprenticeship, are much less attractive to youths than in the U.S. system. German youths who occupy apprentice positions have some of the same immediate consumption needs as their American counterparts, though they are less likely to be oriented to saving for college given the public financing of German higher education. However, in contrast to their American counterparts, German young people need not carve out an individually designed school and work program in the market economy to achieve their economic objectives. This is because being paid for one's labor is a constituent part of the apprenticeship system. Economic remuneration is therefore obtained as one acquires educational certification and work-relevant knowledge and skills. Furthermore, the apprentice must adhere to the usual full-time definition of the workday on those days assigned to employment in the firm; schooling days are also defined as full-time investments. Engagement in an additional job (other than the apprentice position) neither makes sense given the structured scheme of schooling and working, nor does time allow for it.

In the context of the highly regulated German occupational structure, the only jobs that youths can obtain without completing a formal apprenticeship are unqualified (that is, unskilled). Therefore, German youths who do not obtain apprentice positions have little opportunity to enhance their human capital through employment experience. Jobs available to them do not allow for obtaining very much in the way of work-relevant knowledge and skills not obtainable in school, nor do they enable advancement into skill-enhancing positions.

It is only amongst the small group of students at the *Gymnasium* that we witness the emergence of the U.S. youth work pattern: they are baby-sitting, delivering newspapers, doing night watch in clinics and holding other jobs. At the university level, given less constrained time schedules and greater student autonomy, there are similar balancing acts, characteristic of high school and college students in the United States, in which students negotiate and individually construct patterns of time and energy directed to schooling and working. In 1993, about 53% of German university students had some employment while enrolled (Griesbach & Leszczensky, 1993). Traditional students, who have come to the university through the *Gymnasium*, seek to improve their living standards through paid work.

Employment is especially necessary for those who arrived at the University through the *Zweite Bildungsweg*, the special upgrading program for those in apprenticeships. Students in this program are older than traditional students, are often married, and have responsibility for children. Given that the families of most of these students cannot provide them with economic support, their economic needs are great. Those who have pursued this alternate route to higher education often retain contacts with their prior employers, who had offered them jobs based on their prior qualifications. They continue to be employed in these contexts while pursuing their university studies.

For most German young people, as well as for the smaller proportion of students in the United States who pursue occupationally specific educational programs, the inability to find employment in the occupation for which they have prepared is a potential threat. Though many employers retain apprentices after the completion of their training in regular employment positions, this outcome is by no means assured. Securing appropriate employment is a particularly severe problem for youths who complete apprenticeships in periods of high unemployment and economic downturn.

The problem of occupational entry presents itself in somewhat different form to prospective university graduates in Germany. Whereas in prosperous times these labor market entrants have little difficulty, economic downswings foster motivation to prolong the status of student, sometimes seemingly indefinitely. Continuation of studies is fostered by the tuition-free character of university education in Germany. University students closely assess labor market fluctuations and try to match the dates of their final examinations to the most personally advantageous entry periods. They know that after completing their university studies, both unemployment and underemployment (which does not match their skills and credentials) will considerably diminish their future labor market prospects (Giddens, 1984).

With the growing scarcity in Germany of occupational openings requiring academic degrees, the situation of university students and graduates is coming to approximate the generally unstructured labor market in the United States. Because the connections between academic fields studied at the university and positions in the labor market are less strongly regulated than in fields at lower occupational levels, jobs held prior to the completion of formal schooling not only enrich the resumé, but they can also offer useful knowledge and skills. University students may find vocationally useful opportunities for networking, particularly in the service sector and in larger firms. These can be especially useful in information and computer science, in engineering, in administration, and in business management (Bundesministerium für Bildung, Wissenschaft, Forschung und Technologie, 1995). Thus, in these fields, there may be clearer linkage between academic program content and accompanying, usually part-time, work experience.

In recent years, increasing numbers of university leavers have become job creators, constructing new labor market niches. For example, they establish counseling bureaus for energy-efficient construction, for 'sustainable' nutrition, for healthful travel, for consumer information, for software development, and all types of marketing. Such small enterprises, sometimes successful, sometimes of short existence, are new within the German economy. Thus far, no systematic research has been conducted on the biographies, or subjective orientations, of the young people who establish them. A plausible hypothesis is that their prior work histories are characterized by more frequent side engagements in the labor market than typical of their counterparts who enter more traditional occupations.

CONCLUSIONS

Clearly, formal pathways matter. We have attempted to describe the process of transition from school to work from the standpoint of the person, by focusing on how the presence or absence of formal pathways can influence the subjective experience of transition. This comparison of highly structured and very loosely structured school-to-work transition regimes in Germany and in the United States suggests some tentative conclusions. First, the German structure provides highly visible, clearly interpretable, age-graded markers of success and of failure in movement between stages in school and in the passage from school to work. Because they have consequences for labor-market outcomes that are clearly understood by all concerned, they also influence personal identity.

Most obviously, as Turner (1960) noted long ago, the looser structure in the United States allows for, even promotes, a continuing sense of opportunity, despite initial failure. If opportunity is perceived as ever open, youths may feel that they can take advantage of it whenever it is convenient for them to do so. Thus, there is often relatively little perceived urgency, or need for focused, intensive efforts at any particular time during adolescence. During the process of transition, much time may be lost as the less highly motivated youths move between jobs, floundering until something better comes along, or until a decision is made to enter or to reenter college or to pursue other kinds of educational training. As a result, the transition to adulthood is extended, both psychologically and in terms of more tangible, structural markers of economic and residential independence (Aronson, 1998).

Our analysis suggests that the two systems promote quite different stances toward, and utilization of, both school and labor market opportunities to acquire human capital. In the German system, the approximately 70% of students who are to enter the apprenticeship system have a clear incentive to achieve in school so as to prepare for a desirable apprenticeship. For them, planful competence (Clausen, 1993) is manifest by studying official sources of information about jobs and careers; by seeking information from teachers and counselors; by trying out, at a relatively early age, a practicum in one of 498 vocational fields; and by gaining access to an apprentice position in a field of their choice. The structure encourages, one might even say, forces the student to become actively engaged in an intensive process of acquiring vocationally relevant information and planning for occupational entry. Once an apprenticeship is located, the task becomes one of preparing oneself to competently work in the same field, both through practical experience in on-the-job training and through formal instruction. At all points, the successful job aspirant will be oriented to the official agents and the experiences provided first by the formal educational system and second, by the formally integrated school and work system.

In the relative absence of occupational certification, and without the monopoly over employment that nationally recognized certification provides, youths in the United States are subject to very different incentives. For them, as well as for German youths, both practical experience in the workplace and contacts made there can matter for future labor market success. However, these are not structured for American youths; instead, they must construct their own balance between school and work. Youths embark on this path with very different resources. Some will be guided by the experiences and the active counsel of their parents, older siblings, and peers. Others must proceed more or less on their own. Additionally, precisely because the two systems of education and work are not integrated, attempts to obtain work experience come to be seen by educators (and by some developmental psychologists) as antagonistic to educational goals. They are even viewed as self-defeating to the youths themselves if employment diminishes their formal educational attainment. Thus, educators admonish youths to limit their investment in work so as not to interfere with their educational achievement.

However, youths in the United States are confronted with mixed messages and directives regarding school and work. Because both the secondary and the higher education that youths are encouraged to attain are quite general in nature, the occupationally ambitious young person still feels the need to acquire work experience. Through the grapevine of the advice network, and through their own experiences in the job market, youths learn that prospective employers are more likely to select job applicants who have had work experience. They learn that previous employers often provide necessary references. They also may be encouraged by their parents to find jobs that will develop their character, by fostering time-management skills and a sense of responsibility and independence. In short, they are advised to obtain paid work so as to ready themselves for adulthood, particularly for their adult occupational roles. Consistently, many studies have demonstrated the socioeconomic advantages of youths who do obtain work experience while they are still in school. Thus, the loose structuring of the school-to-work transition encourages an entrepreneurial and individualistic stance, as the young person tries to balance the requirements of each of the two spheres, obtaining relevant experience in the labor market while at the same time pursuing general educational credentials.

In view of these comparative observations, the situation of German school-leavers at the University level is particularly interesting. Because for them education and labor force positions are more loosely connected, their situation comes closer to that of American youths. Not surprisingly, they are also turning to side engagements in the labor force to obtain work experience and are developing a more entrepreneurial perspective, carving out new occupational niches for themselves.

Young people in both countries who are more disadvantaged in the official systems turn to alternate routes to mobility. For example, African–American youth participants in the Baltimore study may perceive that they have little chance of succeeding in the general system of primary, secondary and postsecondary education. They seek to acquire work experience and skills through early part-time jobs (Entwisle et al., 1998). Young German school pupils, facing a highly regulated apprenticeship structure, seek to gain entry to the more open, less tightly regulated occupational positions open to university leavers, through the *Zweite Bildungsweg*.

German women whose qualifications are through the less advantageous, exclusively school-based vocational training, will find themselves to be confined to gender-stereotyped female occupations. These jobs severely restrict their earnings prospects. Some women seek a second chance through the *Zweite Bildungsweg*. Others opt out of the occupational system altogether, seeking economic security in husbands' occupations. Whereas in the United States the labor-force participation rate of married women with children under age 6 was 64% in 1995, in the same year in Germany only 46% were in the work force (Han & Moen, 1998; Statistisches Bundesamt, 1996).

One might argue that the strengths and weaknesses of each system are altogether different. That is, the American, loosely coupled systems of school and occupation foster an active entrepreneurial orientation toward work from an early grade and a sense of opportunity and optimism about future prospects. American youths have a series of exploratory trial jobs, which increase their understanding of how the labor market operates. They gain skill in the use of contacts and networks as they move from job to job. Such early mobility could increase their attentiveness to new opportunities offered by change in technology and in the economy. The novice worker learns to operate in a dynamic shifting market of opportunities.

In contrast, the German system, as it orients students to formal school–labor market links, may be inadequate in the face of rapid technological and economic change. It usually takes years to change official educational programs in vocational training schemes, and the practicum in the work place will not always offer experience in the most up-to-date technologies of work. Young people in the German system will not be oriented to exploring diverse job opportunities beyond those that are offered by the education–training system, nor will they easily move back into the educational system to acquire new technical skills. The German system thus encourages stronger motivation to utilize and to succeed early on in the educational system. This is true for students who will enter the university, as well as for the much larger number of youths who are not geared toward higher educational attainment.

Though U.S. teachers and parents encourage all youths to think of themselves as college-bound, many American youths perceive themselves as lacking the capacity to achieve in formal education and have little interest in directing their efforts toward this goal. Lacking any clear vocational payoff, youths who are not college-bound often underutilize the educational resources that are available to them, underachieve, and become alienated from school. These are widely recognized problems for U.S. educators.

This discussion suggests important questions for educational policy-makers. How can educators in the United States learn from the German system, so as to better integrate schooling and working so that the individual student is not so much on his/her own in establishing an appropriate balance? Aside from obtaining further educational credentials, how can early schooling be made to seem more pertinent to the world of work, especially so that noncollege-oriented young people will have greater incentive for engagement in and participation in school? How can the perception of a conflict or of a tradeoff between the school and work spheres be lessened so as to facilitate effective planning?

For German educators and policymakers, we would ask, how can the German system loosen the tight regulation of school-to-work pathways so as to allow for change in occupational structure, recertification, or movement from one pathway to another? In what ways might the system be made more flexible, so as to encourage entrepreneurship and the creation of new economic opportunities? In both cases, there appears to be a need for institutional change in the school-to-work transition.

Clearly, formal pathways do matter for individual agency and action. Differences in the formality or the regulation of the school-to-work transition undoubtedly are rooted in cross-national differences in definitions and values regarding youth, educational and occupational attainments, and the stability versus the malleability of the life course. Evaluation of their implications for youths' subjective orientation and response will likewise be rooted in cultural differences.

ACKNOWLEDGMENT: The Youth Development Study, whose findings are featured in this chapter, is supported by the National Institute of Mental Health (MH 42843). The authors would like to thank Sabrina Oesterle for her assistance in the preparation of this chapter and for her valuable insights which contributed to its early development. This chapter was completed while Jeylan Mortimer was a Fellow at the Center for Advanced Study in the Behavioral Sciences. She is grateful for support provided by the Center, as well as by the Hewlett Foundation and the W.T. Grant Foundation (Grant 95167795) for the fellowship year. Helga Krüger's work on this chapter was partially supported by a Hill Visiting Professorship at the University of Minnesota. The authors would also like to thank Hans Bertram, Jochen Brandtstadter, Stephen Hamilton, Michael Shanahan and Annette Spellerberg for helpful comments on a previous manuscript.

REFERENCES

Alex, L., & Stooß, F. (1996). *Berufsreport. Daten, Fakten, Prognosen zu allen wichtigen Berufen. Der Arbeitsmarkt in Deutschland: Das aktuelle Handbuch.* Berlin: Argon Verlag.

Alexander, K. L., & Entwisle, D. R. (1996). Educational tracking during the early years: First grade placements and middle school constraints. In A. C. Kerckhoff (Ed.), *Generating social stratification: Toward new research agenda* (pp. 75–105). Boulder, CO: Westview Press.

Allmendinger, J. (1989). Career mobility dynamics. A comparative analysis of the United States, Norway, and West Germany. *Studien und Berichte 49.* Berlin: Max-Planck-Institut für Bildungsforschung.

Aronson, P. J. (1998). *Coming of age in the 1990s: Women's identities, life paths, and attitudes towards feminism.* Unpublished doctoral dissertation, University of Minnesota.

Aronson, P. J., Mortimer, J. T., Zierman, C. & Hacker, M. (1996). Generational differences in early work experiences and evaluations. In J. T. Mortimer & M. D. Finch (Eds.), *Adolescents, work, and family: An intergenerational developmental analysis* (pp. 25–62). Newbury Park, CA: Sage.

Becker, G. S. (1993). *Human capital: A theoretical and empirical analysis, with special reference to education* (3rd ed.). Chicago: University of Chicago Press.

Bidwell, C., Schneider, B. & Borman, K. (1998). Working: Perceptions and experiences of American teenagers. In K. Borman & B. Schneider (Eds.), *The adolescent years: Social influences and educational challenges. Part I* (pp. 160–182). Chicago: National Society for the Study of Education.

Bills, D. B., Helms, L. B. & Ozcan, M. (1995). The impact of student employment on teachers' attitudes and behaviors toward working students. *Youth and Society, 27*(2), 169–193.

Blossfeld, H. P. (1987). Entry into the labour market and occupational career in the federal republic: A comparison with American studies. *International Journal of Sociology, 17,* 86–115.

Blossfeld, H. P., & Mayer, K. U. (1988). Arbeitsmarktsegmentation in der Bundesrepublik Deutschland. Eine empirische Überprüfung von Segmentationstheorien aus der Perspektive des Lebenslaufs. *Kölner Zeitschrift für Soziologie und Sozialpsychologie, 40,* 245–261.

Born, C., Krüger, H., & Lorenz-Meyer, D. (1996). *Der unentdeckte Wandel. Annäherung an das Verhältnis von Struktur und Norm im weiblichen Lebenslauf.* Berlin: Sigma.

Brandtstädter, J. (1998). Action perspectives on human development. In R. M. Lerner (vol. ed.), *Handbook of child psychology. Vol. 1. Theoretical models of human development* (pp. 807–863). New York: Wiley.

Bridges, W. P. (1996). Educational credentials and the labor market: An inter-industry comparison. In A. C. Kerckhoff (Ed.), *Generating social stratification: Toward a new research agenda* (pp. 173–199). Boulder: Westview Press.

Buchmann, M. (1989). *The script of life in modern society*. Chicago: University of Chicago Press.

Bundesministerium für Bildung, Wissenschaft, Forschung und Technologie. (Ed., 1995). *Das soziale Bild der Studentenschaft in der Bundesrepublik Deutschland: 14. Sozialerhebung des Deutschen Studentenwerks*. Bonn: BMBF.

Clark, B. R. (1960). The "cooling out" function in higher education. *American Journal of Sociology, 65*, 569–576.

Clausen, J. A. (1993). *American lives: Looking back at the children of the great depression*. New York: The Free Press.

Committee on the Health and Safety Implications of Child Labor, National Research Council. (1998). *Protecting youth at work: Health, safety and development of working children and adolescents in the United States*. Washington DC: National Academy Press.

Culpepper, P. D., & Finegold, D. (Eds., 1999). *The German skills machine*. Oxford, UK/Providence, RI: Berghahn Books.

Dietz, G. U., Mariak, V., Matt, E., Seus, L., & Schumann, K. F. (1997). *Lehre tut viel . . .* Münster, Germany: Votum.

DiPrete, T. A., & McManus, P. A. (1996). Education, earnings gain, and earnings loss in loosely and tightly structured labor markets: A comparison between the United States and Germany. In Alan C. Kerckhoff (Ed.), *Generating social stratification: Toward a new research agenda* (pp. 201-221). Boulder, CO: Westview Press.

Dornbusch, S. M. (1994, February). *Off the track*. Presidential address at the annual meeting of the Society for Research on Adolesence, San Diego, California.

Drechsel, R., Görs, D. Gronwald, D., & Rabe-Kleberg, U. (Eds., 1988). *Berufspolitik und Gewerkschaften. Gewerkschaftliches Berufsverständnis und Entwicklung der Lohnarbeit*. Bremen, Germany: FSP Arbeit und Bildung.

Dreeben, R. (1968). *On what is learned in school*. Reading, MA: Addison-Wesley.

Entwisle, D. R., Alexander, K. L., & Olson, L. S. (1998, August). *The beginning of the work transition: Urban youth*. Paper presented at the annual meetings of the American Sociological Association, San Francisco, California.

Giddens, A. (1984). *The constitution of society: Outline of the theory of structuration*. Cambridge, England: Polity Press.

Goldmann, M., & Müller, U. (1986). *Junge Frauen im Verkaufsberuf*. Stuttgart, Germany: Enke.

Greenberger, E., & Steinberg, L. (1986). *When teenagers work: The psychological and social costs of adolescent employment*. New York: Basic Books.

Griesbach, H., & Leszczensky, M. (1993). *Studentische Zeitbudgets: Empirische Ergebnisse zur Diskussion über Aspekte des Teilzeitstudiums*. Hannover, Germany: HIS (Hochschul-Informations-System).

Hamilton, S. F. (1990). *Apprenticeship for adulthood: Preparing youth for the future*. New York: The Free Press.

Hamilton, S. F. (1993). Employment prospects as motivation for school achievement: Links and gaps between school and work in seven countries. In R. K. Silbereisen & E. Todt (Eds.), *Adolescence in context: The interplay of family, school, peers, and work in adjustment* (pp. 267–283). New York: Springer.

Hamilton, S. F. (1997). Commentary on "How do prior experiences in the workplace set the stage for transitions to adulthood?" *National Symposium on Transitions to Adulthood in a Changing Economy: No Work, No Family, No Future?* Pennsylvania State University, State College.

Hamilton, M. A., Hamilton, S. F., & Nichols, C. (1998). *Mapping early career paths: The impact of youth apprenticeship*. Unpublished manuscript. Ithaca, NY: Cornell University.

Han, S. K., & Moen, P. (1998). *Coupled careers: Men's and women's pathways through work and marriage in the United States*. Unpublished manuscript.

Heinz, W. R. (1995). *Arbeit, Beruf und Lebenslauf. Eine Einführung in die Berufliche Sozialisation*. München, Germany: Juventa.

Heinz, W. R. (1996). Youth transitions in cross-cultural perspective: School-to-work in Germany. In B. Gallaway & J. Hudson (Rds.), *Youth in transition: Perspectives on research and policy* (pp. 2–13). Toronto: Thompson Educational Publishing, Inc.

Heinz, W. R., Krüger, H., Rettke, U., Wachtveitl, E., & Witzel, A. (1987). *Hauptsache eine Lehrstelle. Jugendliche vor den Hürden des Arbeitsmarktes*. Weinheim, Germany: Deutscher Studien Verlag.

Kerckhoff, A. C. (1990). *Getting started: Transition to adulthood in Great Britain*. Boulder, CO: Westview Press.

Kerckhoff, A. C. (1995). Social stratification and mobility processes: Interaction between individuals and social structures. In K. S. Cook, G. A. Fine, & J. S. House (Eds.), *Sociological perspectives on social psychology* (pp. 476–496). Boston: Allyn and Bacon.

Kerckhoff, A. C. (1996). Building conceptual and empirical bridges between studies of educational and labor force careers. In A. C. Kerckhoff (Ed.), *Generating social stratification: Toward a new research agenda* (pp. 37–56). Boulder, CO: Westview Press.

Kerckhoff, A. C., & Bell, L. (1998). Hidden capital: Vocational credentials and attainment in the United States. *Sociology of Education, 71,* 152–174.

Kohli, M. (1985). The world we forgot: A historical review of the life course. In V. W. Marshall (Ed.), *Later life: The social psychology of aging* (pp. 271–303). Beverly Hills, CA: Sage.

Krüger, H. (1990). The shifting sands of a social contract: Young people in the transition between school and work. In L. Chisholm, P. Büchner, H. Krüger, & P. Brown (Eds.), *Childhood, youth and social change: A comparative perspective* (pp. 116–133). London/New York/Philadelphia: Falmer Press.

Krüger, H. (1999). Gender and skills: Distributive ramifications of the German skill system. In P. D. Culpepper & D. Finegold (Eds.), *The German skills machine.* Oxford, UK/Providence, RI: Berghahn Books.

Lowe, G. S., & Krahn, H. (1992). Do part-time jobs improve the labor market chances of high school graduates? In B. D. Warme, K. L. P. Lundy, & L. A. Lundy (Eds.), *Working part-time: Risks and opportunities* (pp. 131–148). New York: Praeger.

Manning, W. D. (1990). Parenting employed teenagers. *Youth and Society, 22*(2), 184–200.

Marini, M. M. (1987). Measuring the process of role change during the transition to adulthood. *Social Science Research, 16,* 1–38.

Mortimer, J. T., Finch, M. D., Dennehy, K., Lee, C., & Beebe, T. (1994). Work experience in adolescence. *Journal of Vocational Education Research, 19*(1), 39–70

Mortimer, J. T., Harley, C., & Johnson, M. K. (1998, February–March). *Adolescent work quality and the transition to adulthood.* Paper presented at the seventh Biennial Meeting of the Society for Research on Adolescence, San Diego, California.

Mortimer, J. T., & Johnson, M. K. (1998). New perspectives on adolescent work and the transition to adulthood. In R. Jessor (Ed.), *New perspectives on adolescent risk behavior* (pp. 425–496). New York: Cambridge University Press.

Mortimer, J. T., & Shanahan, M. (1994). Adolescent work experience and family relationships. *Work and Occupations, 21,* 369–384.

Osterman, P. (1980). *Getting started: The youth labor market.* Cambridge, MA: MIT Press.

Osterman, P. (1989). The job market for adolescents. In D. Stern & D. Eichorn (Eds.), *Adolescence and work: Influences of social structure, labor markets, and culture* (pp. 235–256). Hillsdale, NJ: Lawrence Erlbaum Associates.

Panel on Youth of the President's Science Advisory Committee. (1974). *Youth: Transition to adulthood.* Chicago: University of Chicago Press.

Phillips, S., & Sandstrom, K. (1990). Parental Attitudes toward "Youthwork." *Youth and Society, 22*(December), 160–183.

Rettke, U., & Kretzer, S. (1992). Analyse der Übergangsproblematik junger Frauen beim Übertritt vom Allgemeinbildenden in das Berufsbildende und das Beschaeftigungssystem. In H. Krüger (Ed.), *Frauen und Bildung: Wege der Aneignung und Verwertung von Qualifikationen in weiblichen Erwerbsbiographien* (pp. 87–142). Bielefeld, Germany: KT-Verlag.

Rosenbaum, J. E. (1976). *Making inequality: The hidden curriculum of high school tracking.* New York: Wiley.

Rosenbaum, J. E., Takehiko, K., Settersten, R., & Maier, T. (1990). Market and network theories of the transition from high school to work: Their application to industrialized societies. *Annual Review of Sociology, 16,* 263–299.

Ruhm, C. J. (1995). The extent and consequences of high school employment. *Journal of Labor Research, 16,* 293–303.

Ruhm, C. J. (1997). Is high school employment consumption or investment? *Journal of Labor Economics, 15,* 735–776.

Schober, K. (Ed., 1996). *Berufswahl: Sozialisations und Selektionsprozesse an der ersten Schwelle.* Dokumentation eines Workshops des Instituts für Arbeitsmarkt und Berufsforschung der Bundesanstalt für Arbeit in Zusammenarbeit mit dem Deutschen Jugendinstitut und dem Bundesinstitut für Berufliche Bildung. Nürnberg, Germany: IAB.

Shanahan, M. J., Elder, G. H., Jr., Burchinal, M., & Conger, R. D. (1996). Adolescent earnings and relationships with parents: The work-family nexus in urban and rural ecologies. In J. T. Mortimer & M. D. Finch (Eds.), *Adolescents, work, and family: An intergenerational developmental analysis* (pp. 97–128). Newbury Park, CA: Sage.

Shanahan, M. J., & Flaherty, B. (1998, February). Dynamic patterns of time use strategies in adolescence. Paper presented at the biennial meeting of the Society for Research on Adolescence, San Diego, California.

Shanahan, M. J., & Mortimer, J. T. (1996). Understanding the positive consequences of psychosocial stress. In B. Markovsky, M. Lovaglia, & R. Simon (Eds.), *Advances in group processes, Vol. 13* (pp. 189–209). Greenwich, CT: JAI Press.

Statistisches Bundesamt. (1996). *Ergebnisse des Microzensus.* Stuttgart, Germany: Metzler-Poeschel.

Steinberg, L., & Cauffman, E. (1995). The impact of employment on adolescent development. *Annals of Child Development, 11,* 131–166.

Stooß, F. (1997). *Reformbedarf in der beruflichen Bildung.* Expertise im Auftrag des Ministeriums für Arbeit, Gesundheit und Soziales des Landes Nordrhein-Westfalen.

Teubner, U. (1989). *Neue Berufe für Frauen. Modelle zur Überwindung der Geschlechterhierarchie im Erwerbsbereich.* Frankfurt/New York: Campus.

Turner, R. H. (1960). Sponsored and contest mobility and the school system. *American Sociological Review, 25,* 855–867.

W. T. Grant Foundation Commission on Work, Family, and Citizenship. (1988). *The forgotten half: Pathways to success for America's youth and young families.* Washington, DC: The William T. Grant Foundation.

CHAPTER 22

The Effects of Schooling
on Individual Lives

AARON M. PALLAS

INTRODUCTION

How does schooling shape the lives of adults? This question, posed in different ways, has been a central theme of the sociology of education in the United States and abroad. The varied responses to this question have been the basis for arbitrating among competing conceptions of how education and society are intertwined and for the implications of these conceptions for individual lives.

This chapter summarizes some of the evidence addressing the question of how schooling influences adult lives. Rather than focusing on the empirical associations between social origins, educational attainment, and adult socioeconomic outcomes, I look beyond the influential status attainment tradition, searching for evidence of the effects of schooling in multiple institutional domains, including the family, the workplace, and the polity. I operationalize these effects in terms of individuals' attitudes, beliefs, and behaviors.

The approach adopted in this chapter is necessarily selective. No review can cover the full spectrum of schooling's effects in a comprehensive and coherent way. Rather, I have chosen to summarize the evidence on schooling effects on individual lives in specific domains: effects on adult family life, on the workplace, on socioeconomic success, on knowledge and cognitive development, on political and social participation, on the development of values, on leisure time use, on psychological well-being, and on physical health and mortality. I further circumscribe the review by focusing almost exclusively on the United States in the

AARON M. PALLAS • Department of Counseling, Educational Psychology, and Special Education, Michigan State University, East Lansing, Michigan 48824-1034

Handbook of the Sociology of Education, edited by Maureen T. Hallinan. Kluwer Academic/Plenum Publishers, New York, 2000.

latter third of the 20th century. This emphasis does raise important concerns about the extent to which the inferences I draw are limited to this time and place, and it is important to recognize that the effects I summarize are observed in the context of a particular education system embedded in a particular set of cultural and historical conditions.

Explanations for Schooling Effects

There are three major types of explanations for schooling's effects on individual lives. The dominant account of such effects holds that schooling transforms the personal qualities of individuals. In this view, going to school confers knowledge about the world—for example, the labor market and the demands of specific jobs, the determinants of physical and mental health, the workings of government, and the nature of life in a modern society—and provides individuals with the cognitive tools to manipulate this knowledge so as to maximize their well-being, by solving problems, by adapting to new situations, and by selecting themselves into settings that are supportive of their ongoing development. Going to school also can transform individuals' values or preferences, shaping what they judge to be important enough to attend to in their social worlds. In both cases, the individual as social agent is in the foreground, and the social structure within which the individual is situated is in the background. This perspective might appropriately be labeled a *socialization theory* of schooling effects.

A second perspective reverses the emphasis accorded to structure and to agency, placing social structure in the foreground and individual agency in the background. In this view, educational attainment is an achieved status that grants individuals access to desired social positions that confer material and psychic rewards. Educational credentials open the door to well-paid and fulfilling jobs and to positions of social and political power that are not routinely available to the poorly educated, regardless of their personal qualities. Social institutions select and allocate individuals for such positions based on their educational attainments, although the underlying rationale for these selection processes is often unclear or in dispute. Following Kerckhoff (1976), this perspective might be called an *allocation theory* of schooling effects.

A third approach views the effects of schooling on individual lives as an artifact of the institutional authority of education. An *institutional theory* of schooling effects, typically associated with the work of John Meyer (1977; 1985), argues that the association between schooling and individual outcomes is observed not because schooling has produced these effects—via either a socialization or an allocation process—but rather because society has organized itself in such a way as to create this association. In this view, the fact that large bureaucracies reward highly educated workers more generously than less educated workers stems from a widely shared belief that college graduates have different, and more desirable, qualities than high school graduates—a belief that is rooted in an institutionalized account of how education works in modern societies, and not in the careful inspection of the qualities of individuals with differing amounts of schooling.

In practice, it is difficult to arbitrate among these competing accounts of the linkages between educational attainment and individual life outcomes. The dynamics of the relationship between structure and agency are complex, as structures shape cognition, motivation, and aspiration, and in turn individuals' thoughts and motives lead them to seek out and create structural contexts that can maximize the likelihood of positive outcomes. Moreover, particular representations of the process by which schooling affects adult outcomes may be consistent with more than one theoretical orientation. I nevertheless attempt to place the studies I summarize, and the explanations offered by their authors for the schooling effects they observe, into a suitable theoretical context.

The chapter is organized to reflect the causal imagery depicted in Figure 22.1. I first consider the effects of schooling on knowledge and cognitive development, on socioeconomic outcomes, and on workplace conditions. I then examine the influence of schooling on an array of other social, psychological, and physical outcomes, including social participation and support, psychological well-being, physical well-being and health, family, political participation, values,and leisure time. A recurring theme in the chapter is that schooling's effects on a variety of adult outcomes operate through the influence of schooling on the workplace. In this view, individuals who obtain more schooling succeed in finding employment that provides a rich array of economic and social–psychological resources. It is not just that schooling is a determinant of economic well-being. Schooling also influences the social and the psychological dimensions of work, which may or may not be correlated with its economic rewards. Nevertheless, there are numerous instances in which the effects of schooling on the lives of adults are not mediated by the workplace, and I will note these as well.

There are many other possible schemas for organizing this review. I have chosen this one to highlight the importance that researchers ascribe to knowledge and to cognitive development, to socioeconomic outcomes, and to workplace conditions as factors mediating the effects of schooling on the other outcomes I consider. In some cases, most of the observed association between schooling and individual outcomes can be explained by the role that schooling plays in determining work outcomes that reverberate throughout the subsequent life course. In other cases, schooling has a net association with social, psychological, and physical outcomes even when work outcomes are taken into account. In still others, there is a lack of high-quality evidence on the associations among schooling, mediating factors (i.e., knowledge and cognitive development, socioeconomic outcomes, and workplace conditions), and individual outcomes.

For this and for other reasons, Figure 22.1 is best seen as a heuristic for organizing the chapter, not as a meaningful model of the effects of schooling on any particular outcome. The causal imagery is not inviolable. It is not inevitable, for example, that workplace conditions and socioeconomic outcomes are antecedent to family outcomes or to psychological well-being; the former might be jointly determined with the latter or might even be consequences of them.

In the sections that follow, I strive to summarize some of the most compelling evidence on how schooling affects the lives of adults in contemporary American society. I begin by examining the evidence in the domains of adult life that I noted earlier. I then discuss how the design of research studies poses a threat to inferences based on that evidence. I conclude the chapter by discussing the implications of these findings for a sociological understanding of schooling's role in the lives of individuals.

THE EFFECTS OF SCHOOLING ON INTERVENING VARIABLES

In this section, I consider the effects of schooling on knowledge and on cognitive development, on socioeconomic outcomes, and on workplace conditions. Although these are important outcomes in their own right, I set them apart because researchers often treat them as key variables mediating the influence of schooling on a range of other outcomes considered later in the chapter.

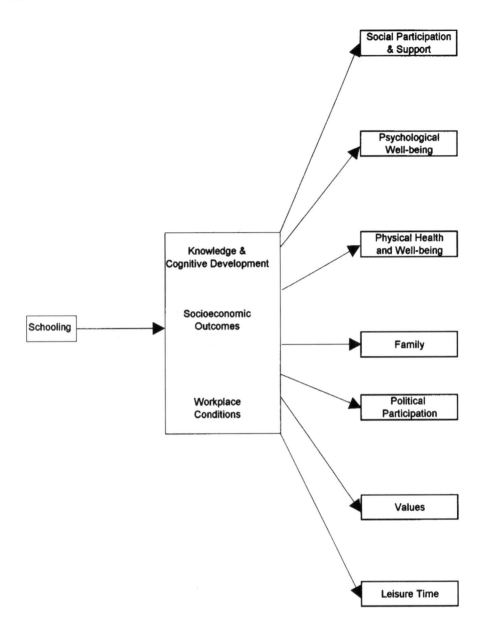

FIGURE 22.1. A heuristic model of schooling's effects on adult outcomes.

Knowledge and Cognitive Development

Individuals with more schooling have greater knowledge about a wide range of areas than their less educated peers, including current events and politics. Highly educated people also may display greater cognitive flexibility and problem-solving skills than poorly educated people. Moreover, individuals with high levels of schooling may create opportunities to learn by participation in and exposure to the media of mass communication.

There is considerable evidence that individuals who obtain more schooling are more knowledgeable about current events and public issues, both foreign and domestic, than individuals who get less schooling. Hyman, Wright, and Reed (1975) drew on 54 national surveys from the 1940s to the 1960s to demonstrate this for White men and women between the ages of 25 and 72. Analyses of more recent data sets show a similar pattern. Smith (1995) reported that the NORC General Social Surveys demonstrate a positive correlation between educational attainment and knowledge about the environment and about science and knowing the names of various political officials.

This last finding echoes Wolfinger and Rosenstone's (1980) earlier analyses of the 1972 National Election Study. In this study, the researchers asked respondents if they knew the six following political facts: the number of terms a president can serve, the length of a term for a U.S. Senator, the length of a term for a U.S. representative, the names of the House candidates in their district, the party controlling Congress before the election, and the party controlling Congress after the election. Wolfinger and Rosenstone judged individuals who knew five of these six facts to be well informed about politics. Their analyses showed a clear gradient in political knowledge across educational groups. Only 17% of high school graduates knew at least five of these six political facts, whereas 32% of those with some college had this much knowledge, as did 59% of those with 5 or more years of college.

In most of these cases, the mechanism by which schooling is presumed to impart this specific knowledge is not articulated. Hyman and associates (1975) ruled out the possibility that current-events knowledge was learned in school, arguing that knowledge of events that occurred after individuals had completed their schooling could not have been learned in school. However, their preferred explanation, that schooling creates an enduring receptivity to learning across the life course, is not founded on empirical evidence. Instead, Hyman and associates and the other scholars cited in this section, appeared to assume that schooling has a strong socializing influence on individuals' dispositions toward learning. Alternate explanations highlighting social structure receive less play. For example, it seems likely that the relationship between schooling and political knowledge is mediated by political participation. In this view, schooling functions more as a status characteristic associated with political power than as a transforming force.

In addition to their command of specific factual knowledge, highly educated people also display higher levels of literacy skills than those with less schooling. A recent national survey of American adults, the National Adult Literacy Survey (Kirsch, Jungeblut, Jenkins, & Kolstad, 1993), examined three forms of literacy: prose literacy, which pertains to the understanding of narrative prose; document literacy, which pertains to the understanding of documents one might encounter in everyday life; and quantitative literacy, which pertains to the understanding of basic mathematical skills in authentic contexts. Kirsch and associates (1993) reported a strong relationship between educational attainment and the level of literacy proficiency in this study. They classified literacy proficiency into five levels, ranging from low to high. Fewer than 10% of adults who did not complete high school scored at Level 4 or 5 in any of the three literacy domains. In contrast, approximately 25% of those who attended some college scored at Level 4 or 5, as did about one half of 4-year college graduates, as well as roughly 60% of individuals who attended graduate school.

Sensitive to the possibility that family background might affect both how far one goes through school and adult literacy proficiency, Kirsch and associates (1993) examined whether the relationship between education and literacy proficiency persisted when parental education was controlled. Even among individuals whose parents had similar levels of education, those who had completed more years of schooling had higher levels of proficiency than those with less schooling. Only about 15% to 20% of the association between education and literacy proficiency can be attributed to parental education.

More so than specific knowledge, adult literacy proficiency may reflect skills learned in school. Although the specific literacy tasks posed in the National Adult Literacy Survey (Kirsch et al., 1993) pertained to activities performed by adults more frequently than by children and youths, they nevertheless are straightforward extrapolations of basic reading and mathematics skills taught in elementary and secondary school. The association between schooling and adult literacy is taken as evidence that individuals who obtained more schooling had high levels of skill mastery and that their proficiency has simply persisted into adulthood. Little attention is paid to the possibility that the social contexts an individual encounters after leaving school might promote or retard literacy proficiency. For example, some workplaces might provide more opportunities to practice literacy skills than others. However, once one opens the door to this possibility, formulating meaningful models of how schooling might influence adult literacy poses a formidable challenge, as doing so requires detailed information on a host of social contexts and how they might support ongoing literacy acquisition (Pallas, 1995). It is much easier to assume that the only relevant context is the one that modern societies designate as the locus of literacy acquisition—the school.

Specific knowledge and adult literacy proficiency represent concrete manifestations of cognitive development. However, there also is evidence of schooling differences in abstract indicators of cognitive functioning, such as problem solving and adoption of innovation. People with more education are more likely to engage in problem solving in daily life than those who have less education. Ross and Mirowsky (1989) demonstrated this through analyses of the Illinois Survey of Well-Being, a study of individuals aged 18 to 85 in 1985. In this survey, respondents were asked questions such as "When faced with a problem, how often do you 1) try to figure out the cause and do something about it and 2) try to forget about it?" Ross and Mirowsky found that education has a sizeable total effect ($\beta = .20$) on problem-solving that is only modestly mediated by schooling's effects on potentially intervening variables such as perceived social support and perceived control over one's life

Ross and Mirowsky (1989) treated education as an indicator of socioeconomic status, not as a socializing agent. The causal chain they envisioned is that education, as a dimension of socioeconomic status, influences an individual's psychological well-being, such that highly educated individuals are likely to feel in control over their lives and in turn to try to understand problems and try to solve them. They do not consider the possibility that schooling might impart problem-solving skills directly, although the evidence they reported is that most of the effects of schooling on problem-solving are not mediated by psychological well-being.

Beyond schooling's association with problem solving, researchers also have found that individuals with more schooling are more open to new ideas, and and more likely to adopt innovations, than those with less schooling. The evidence for this is more idiosyncratic than for some of the other aspects of cognitive functioning I describe in this section, but the relevant study is widely cited. Wozniak (1987) reported an analysis from the Iowa Family Farm Research Project Survey that examined Iowa farmers' early adoption of an innovative technology—the cattle feed additive monensin sodium. He found that well-educated farmers were likely to adopt this new technology sooner than farmers with less schooling. Net of experience and other factors, each additional year of schooling increased the probability of early adoption by about one percentage point, or approximately 3% of the baseline probability of early adoption.

Wozniak (1989) did not state explicitly why he believed that schooling might increase the likelihood of early adoption, although he does state that better educated farmers may overcome resistance to early adoption more easily than less educated farmers. One source of resistance is the uncertainty about the production consequences of adopting an innovative technology. Better-educated farmers may, he suggested, have more information about agricultural innovations than less educated farmers, gleaning technical information from agricultural extension services and from private agricultural supply firms. In this sense, schooling serves as a source of human capital in the production process that generates more knowledge about productive technologies.

Both concrete and abstract indicators of knowledge and of cognitive development are responsive to individuals' opportunities for learning. For example, individuals with more schooling are exposed to mass media that may increase their knowledge. They are more likely to read newspapers, magazines, and books (Hyman et al., 1975). Moreover, whereas Hyman and associates (1975) found no differences among individuals with different levels of schooling in their daily television watching or radio listening, more recent evidence from the American's Use of Time Project surveys of 1965, 1975 and 1985 (Robinson & Godbey, 1997) show that college-educated people spend much less time watching television and listening to the radio or to recordings than do those with less schooling (Robinson & Godbey, 1997). If one accepts the premise that the print media convey more knowledge than these other media, then there is good reason to suppose that the differential exposure to the media is widening the knowledge gap among individuals with different amounts of schooling.

Formally, there are few socioeconomic barriers to access to print media, as these are often available at no charge in public libraries and at a modest cost elsewhere. It seems unlikely, therefore, that the effect of schooling on media exposure is mediated by economic factors. A more likely explanation is that schooling is an indicator of class cultures that differ in the value ascribed to "book" knowledge (Luttrell, 1998), and hence that variation in this value accounts for education-related differences in exposure to the mass media. Note that this explanation differs from Hyman and associates' (1975) contention that education by its very nature creates a receptivity to knowledge.

Exposure to the mass media is an informal indicator of one's opportunities to learn about current events and other contemporary lifestyle concerns. However, highly educated people also seek out and create additional opportunities to advance their learning. For example, college graduates have been more likely to participate in both formal and informal adult education than high school graduates, even controlling for social background (Hyman et al., 1975). This is not surprising, because well-educated people are both more likely to be aware of such opportunities for further education, and are more likely, by virtue of their earlier successes in school, to feel confident that they can benefit from them. In this view, schooling's effects on opportunities to learn are both structural and social–psychological: schooling grants access to knowledge about further education, and it imparts a motive to act on that knowledge.

In sum, individuals with more schooling have access to a richer array of information than those with less schooling. They know more about their social, cultural, and political worlds, and they can apply that knowledge to shape their futures. In this limited sense, knowledge is power, but it is a power that is very important to theories of how individuals make decisions. Economic theories of social action, for example, assume that individuals are rational decision-makers who make use of the available information when confronted with choice opportunities. Having more information can, they postulate, improve the quality of those decisions.

There are competing accounts of the mechanisms by which schooling leads to greater knowledge and cognitive development. Some researchers emphasize the direct socializing influence of schooling, whereas others see schooling as an indicator of a person's achieved socioeconomic status, which in turn locates individuals in positions in the social structure that provide greater opportunities to learn and that enmesh them in cultural groups that hold distinctive values about learning. In the next sections, I examine the evidence on schooling's effects on some of the socioeconomic outcomes and workplace conditions that are presumed to mediate schooling's influence on knowledge and on cognitive development.

Socioeconomic Outcomes

How much schooling one obtains affects a broad array of indicators of individual economic well-being. In this section, I briefly summarize the associations between schooling and labor-force participation, career transitions, occupational status, and wealth. I find that people who go further through school are more engaged in the workplace, have more orderly careers, earn more money, and hold jobs with higher levels of prestige and status.

I begin by examining schooling and labor-force participation. Individuals who are participating in the labor force are either working, looking for work while unemployed, or laid off from work. Educational attainment is related to labor-force participation. Bound, Schoenbaum, and Waidmann (1995) presented data from the Health and Retirement Survey on the labor-force attachment of middle-aged men. Men who had not completed high school were considerably less likely to participate in the labor force than men with at least a high school diploma. Only 73% of middle-aged men in this sample who lacked a high school diploma reported that they were in the labor force, whereas 82% of high school graduates and 87% of college graduates were in the labor force.

The effects of schooling on labor-force participation in midlife are foreshadowed much earlier in the life course. As young men and women enter the labor force, they may experience difficulty settling into a career, bouncing from one job to another as they seek a stable platform for moving into adult life. This period of instability is often referred to as the "floundering" phase of the life course (Namboodiri, 1987). Highly educated men are less likely to flounder than men with less schooling. Oppenheimer, Kalmijn, and Lim (1997), drawing on longitudinal data from the National Longitudinal Surveys of Youth, showed that college attendees and college graduates are able to move more quickly than high school graduates and high school dropouts into full-time work that lasts at least a year.

Beyond participation in the labor force, schooling has profound influences on the rewards that jobholders receive. The status attainment model pioneered by Blau and Duncan (1967), and then later elaborated by O. D. Duncan, Featherman, and Duncan (1972), by Sewell and Hauser (1975), and by others, postulated a direct effect of educational attainment on the status of one's first or current job. The national and regional surveys used to estimate various manifestations of this model invariably found large effects of education on occupational status (Featherman & Hauser, 1978; Grusky & DiPrete, 1990).

There also is a great deal of evidence that individuals who go further through school earn more than those who obtain less schooling (e.g., Jencks et al., 1979; Murnane, Willett, & Levy, 1995; Sewell & Hauser, 1980). Even the most sophisticated models of the determinants of wages and earnings found effects of schooling on earnings that persisted in the face of controls for family background and academic ability, which might influence both educational attainment and earnings. Moreover, the net wage gap between college graduates and high school graduates has been rising since the late 1970s (Murnane et al., 1995). This gap widens as the time elapsed since leaving school increases.

Beyond the immediate effects on earnings, educational attainment is also associated with household wealth. That is, households in which the head is highly educated have greater net worth, looking across a range of assets and debts, than households in which the head is poorly educated. Land and Russell (1996) demonstrated this finding using 7 years of panel data from the Survey of Income and Program Participation. They found that households with zero net worth are headed by householders with lower educational attainment than households with positive net worth. The effect of educational attainment on net worth presumably is mediated by occupational status and earnings.

In contrast, educational attainment does not distinguish effectively between households with negative net worth and those with positive net worth. Households with negative net worth do, however, have younger members, and also greater current debts, than households with positive net worth. Land and Russell (1996) suggested that this pattern may reflect the tendency for individuals to go into debt while investing in higher education, which mainly occurs at younger ages.

Economists and sociologists have developed differing explanations for the observed effects of schooling on socioeconomic rewards. The human capital tradition in economics (Becker, 1964; Schulz, 1961) assumes that individuals who have more schooling are paid more because the market is rewarding them for their greater productivity. In this view, schooling has multiple meanings. First, schooling imparts knowledge, skills, and values that employers view as resources in the production process. In this sense, schooling transforms the qualities of individuals, and it is a property of individual workers. Second, schooling serves to signal employers that individuals have the knowledge, skills, and values they desire, and it thus functions as an indirect measure of worker productivity that has a value in the market (Spence, 1974). In this view, schooling is a marker that the market uses to allocate individuals into positions in the occupational structure that have differing economic rewards associated with them. What matters is not whether schooling really does signal differences in worker productivity, but whether employers treat it as if it does.

In contrast, sociologists frequently have drawn attention to noneconomic forces shaping the process by which individuals are allocated to occupational positions. For example, Collins (1979) argued that employers may hire workers on the basis of the perceived similarity between the status group cultures of those doing the hiring and the status group cultures of prospective employees. That is, employers may reserve positions that carry the most rewards for those who are most like themselves. A prospective employee's level of education and the specific educational institution he or she attended can convey information about status group membership.

For both the modal economic and the sociological accounts of the relationship between schooling and socioeconomic outcomes, occupational positions are the key factors mediating schooling's effects. There is widespread recognition that different occupational positions carry different socioeconomic rewards and that individuals are selected into these different positions at least partly on the basis of their educational credentials. There are, however, sharp disagreements as to what those educational credentials represent.

In practice, it is difficult to arbitrate among competing accounts of why schooling affects the socioeconomic outcomes of individuals. To do so would require data on knowledge, skills, and values that could confidently be treated as an outcome of schooling and not as a possible determinant of educational attainment. In practice, it is all too common simply to assume that schooling differences represent differences in knowledge, in skills, and in values, rather than to develop independent measures of these presumed human capital inputs. In addition, it is practically impossible to develop comprehensive measures of the individual competencies required to carry out a range of occupational positions that are independent of the rewards associated with those positions.

Workplace Conditions

Schooling has diffuse effects on the conditions and contexts that individuals experience at work. The amount of schooling an individual obtains influences the tasks that one performs on the job, and it influences one's control over one's own work and the work of others. Schooling also shapes the satisfaction derived from work. In turn, workplace conditions mediate the effects of schooling on other outcomes.

A fundamental feature of work in the late 20th century is whether it is primarily manual or mental labor. Highly educated men are less likely than men with less schooling to have jobs that require physical effort. Recent evidence from the Health and Retirement Survey shows that 80% of middle-aged men who had not completed high school had jobs that involved physical effort, whereas only 36% of middle-aged men who had completed college held jobs requiring physical effort (Bound et al., 1995). A similar pattern has been observed for jobs that involve heavy lifting or stooping, two other attributes of one's work that might affect one's physical health. Conversely, individuals with more schooling are more likely than less educated persons to supervise others on the job (Ross & Reskin, 1992). In the Health and Retirement Survey data, 43% of middle-aged men with a college degree supervised others on the job, whereas only 19% of high school graduates were supervisors (Bound et al., 1995).

Schooling also is correlated with other attributes of work, such as the extent to which one has control over work and the routinization of work activities. Studies by Ross and her colleagues, as well as other recent investigations, have demonstrated that college-educated individuals are more likely to engage in nonroutine work (Ross & Reskin, 1992), to have more autonomy on the job (Lennon, 1994; Ross & Reskin, 1992), and to exercise more control over their work and the work of others (Link, Lennon, & Dohrenwend, 1993; Ross & Reskin, 1992), even when sociodemographic factors such as age, race, and sex are controlled. Link and associates (1993) also found that college graduates are three times more likely to have occupations involving direction, control, and planning than noncollege graduates (48% vs. 16%), which equates to a correlation of .30 between years of schooling and occupational control. Lennon (1994) also found that schooling was associated with other related workplace conditions, such as whether the job had time pressures associated with it, and with the amount of responsibility associated with the job.

Because poorly educated workers exercise relatively little control over the content and the conditions of their work, they probably are more alienated from work than highly educated workers. Drawing on national telephone surveys conducted in 1990 and in 1995, Ross and Van Willigen (1997) provided support for this view, demonstrating that the poorly educated are more likely to engage in alienated work than the well educated, even adjusting for social background differences among individuals with differing levels of schooling.

In view of the pervasive differences in the nature of the work done by well-educated people and by their less educated peers, one might expect that well-educated people would experience greater job satisfaction than less educated people. However Gruenberg (1980) pointed out that individuals who obtain different amounts of schooling may be socialized to have different expectations about what work might provide for them. If poorly educated individuals do not expect or value control over their work, for example, then they may be satisfied with relatively low levels of control. In contrast, if highly educated individuals are socialized to expect a great deal of control over their work, then even relatively high levels of control may feel unsatisfying.

Ross and Reskin (1992) examined these different predictions. They found that schooling does affect control over one's work, and that in turn, engaging in autonomous and nonroutine work is associated with greater job satisfaction. Thus, schooling has an indirect positive effect on job satisfaction that operates through these workplace conditions. However, Ross and Reskin (1992) also found a direct negative effect of schooling on job satisfaction. That is, once workplace conditions, earnings, and occupational prestige were controlled, highly educated people were less satisfied with their jobs than less educated people. They hypothesize that schooling raises one's expectations for control at work, so that at a given level of control at work, the highly educated will be less satisfied than the less educated.

In sum, there is a consistent association between schooling and workplace conditions, such that better educated workers engage in jobs that have different task structures and responsibilities than the work pursued by less educated workers. Workers with more schooling are more likely than less educated workers to engage in "white-collar" work that allows for considerable control over the nature and pace of the job. Conversely, workers with little formal schooling are much more likely to have "blue-collar" jobs that require manual, rather than mental, labor and that provide few opportunities for control.

Although the process by which individuals with differing levels of education are matched to particular occupational positions is central to understanding this literature, this process is rarely explored in studies of schooling and workplace conditions. Rather, a tacit technical–functional logic permeates these studies. With few exceptions, the implicit assumption is that schooling inculcates knowledge, skills, and values that employers either want or need in the individuals who are to fill high-status, white-collar jobs. On rare occasions (e.g., Ross & Van Willigen, 1997), there may be an acknowledgment that employers may seek credentials rather than knowledge, skills, and values. It is likely that the focus in this literature on the technical features of work accentuates a functionalist analysis.

THE EFFECTS OF SCHOOLING ON OTHER ADULT OUTCOMES

The next section of the chapter examines the remaining outcomes represented in Figure 22.1. These outcomes include social, psychological, and physical aspects of modern adult life. Though not exhaustive, they demonstrate the expanse of modern life that schooling may touch.

Social Participation/Support

Individuals with more schooling have stronger and more powerful social ties to their social worlds. They participate in cultural events and organizations at higher rates than those with less schooling. They also have more extensive social networks, and perceive greater levels of social support, than individuals with less schooling. For example, schooling is a strong predictor of participation in the arts. Robinson and Godbey (1997) reported that fewer than 10% of adults who have not completed high school attend at least one arts event a year, whereas more than three fourths of those with postgraduate degrees do so. Robinson and Godbey (1997) also found that college graduates spend more time going to cultural events than do those who obtained fewer years of schooling.

Schooling also is associated with participation in adult social life. Smith (1995) reported that in the 1987 General Social Survey, individuals with more schooling reported belonging to a larger number of voluntary groups, and engaging in a greater number of organizational activities, than those who obtained less schooling. There also is some evidence that individuals with limited schooling may be less likely to join self-help groups than those completing more years of schooling (Lorig et al., 1989).

Because individuals with more schooling have more ties to social groups, it is no surprise that schooling is related to *social support*, the perception that there are others on whom one can rely for advice and encouragement. Ross and Mirowsky (1989) found that individuals with more schooling reported higher levels of support than those with less schooling, but Ross's (Ross & Van Willigen, 1997) subsequent analyses of two national telephone surveys—the 1995 Aging, Status and the Sense of Control survey and the 1990 Work, Family and Well-Being survey—showed that the effect of schooling on social support was indirect. Ross and Mirowsky (1989) also found that schooling increases the likelihood of talking to others when faced with a problem by a modest amount, even when other factors are controlled.

The most common interpretation of schooling's effects on social support and participation is that schooling functions as an indicator of socioeconomic status, and individuals of higher status have broader and stronger social ties to their surroundings than lower status individuals. Were this the primary mechanism by which schooling influences social support and participation, the effects of schooling would be mediated by other status measures, such as occupational status and income. Yet in most cases, years of schooling has modest to sizeable direct effects on social support and participation even when these endogenous status measures are taken into account.

Because the literatures on social support and participation treat education primarily as a control variable, relatively little attention has been paid to other plausible explanations of why schooling has persistent direct effects on participation and support. In particular, there are few explorations of the implications of socialization theories of schooling (e.g., Dreeben, 1968) for understanding these schooling effects. This is an area that is ripe for further research.

Psychological Well-being

Individuals with more schooling report having more positive psychological health and well-being than those with less education. There are many aspects to psychological functioning, and in this review, I discuss only a subset: personal control, purpose in life, stress/distress, depression, and emotional health status. Although psychological well-being is often the province of psychologists, much of the relevant research has been conducted by sociologists.

For example, Ross and her colleagues (Bird & Ross, 1993; Ross & Mirowsky, 1989, 1992; Ross & Van Willigen, 1997) have examined the effects of education on a number of psychological outcomes, including one's sense of control over one's life. More educated people report more personal control than those with less education, even when a number of intervening variables are controlled. Ross and Van Willigen (1997) reported that the total standardized effect of education on personal control is .43. Although this association shrinks when background factors, such as age, sex, and minority status, and intervening factors, such as earnings and job autonomy, are controlled, it does persist (Ross & Mirowsky, 1989; Ross & Van Willigen, 1997).

Individuals with more education also tend to see greater purpose in life than do those with less schooling. Some evidence of this is provided by Carr's (1997) study of midlife women surveyed in follow-ups of the Wisconsin Longitudinal Study (Sewell & Hauser, 1992). By relying on items such as "I am an active person in carrying out plans I set for myself" and "I tend to focus on the present, because the future nearly always brings me problems" as indicators of purpose in life, Carr found a small effect of post-1975 education (i.e., education beyond approximately age 35) on purpose in life.

Recent research also has found an inverse relationship between educational attainment and psychological stress and distress (Kessler, 1982; Link et al., 1993; Ross & Van Willigen, 1997). Ross and Van Willigen examined a complex account of how schooling affects psychological distress. Part of the explanation, they argued, is that higher levels of schooling grant individuals access to work that is nonalienating and well paid. The substantive content of the work and its socioeconomic benefits produce a greater sense of personal control, which dampens the likelihood of psychological distress such as anxiety, anger, and malaise. At the same time, well-educated individuals are intellectually flexible and have high social status, both of which provide access to broad social networks that can provide supportive social relationships that buffer individuals from psychological distress. Ross and Van Willigen found that schooling's effects on psychological distress are entirely mediated by the characteristics of work, income, control, and support.

Kessler (1982) drew on data from eight epidemiological surveys to examine the relative importance of schooling, income, and occupational status in predicting psychological distress. Schooling was a stronger predictor of psychological distress than were either income or occupational status, and that was especially so for women who were not in the labor force. Kessler suggested that the relative importance of schooling in predicting psychological distress is contingent on the extent to which schooling is related to the social contexts in which individuals develop coping mechanisms that might buffer them from psychological distress.

Another construct tapping the affective domain of subjective experience is emotional health status. Bound and associates (1995) found a sizeable effect of educational attainment on emotional health status. In the Health and Retirement Survey, 32% of middle-aged men who had not completed high school described their emotional health status as "poor" or "fair," whereas only 6% of college graduates chose either of these two descriptors. This is, however, a very diffuse measure, and it does not reveal much about the meaning of emotional health.

Psychological distress and emotional health status differ from other indicators of psychological well-being, notably depression. Individuals who obtain more schooling generally score lower on measures of depression than those with less schooling (Link et al., 1993; Ross & Mirowsky, 1989; but see Carr, 1997). These effects are partially mediated by occupation, leading some to argue that education influences the risk of depression by placing individuals in occupational positions that have differing psychological characteristics. Link and associates, for example, suggested that individuals with more schooling gain access to jobs that involve more direction, control, and planning. In turn, working at such jobs increases a sense of control and mastery over daily life, which reduces the likelihood of depression. Ross and her colleagues also saw the link between schooling and occupation as critical, but they attended to other psychological consequences of work. In their view, personal control and social support are the key factors mediating the relationship between schooling and depression.

In summary, most studies examining the relationship between schooling and adult psychological stress or distress view work as the key factor mediating the effects of schooling. Psychological stress and distress are frequently viewed as responsive to an individual's material situation in life, which clearly is tied to socioeconomic conditions stemming from the nature of one's work. The linkage between educational attainment and access to occupations that provide social–psychological resources is taken for granted in much of this literature.

However, work is not the only intervening variable appearing in this literature. Ross and her colleagues pointed to the possibility that schooling can have an effect on the formation of social support networks that is not mediated by work. Education can, by virtue of the status it confers and the cognitive skills it promotes, enable individuals to enter into supportive social relationships with a range of others. In turn, this social support can mediate the possible psychological consequences of exposure to distressing life events. Thus, the accounts of how schooling might affect psychological stress and distress treat schooling as an achieved status, as a passport to nonalienating and rewarding work, and as a socializing agency.

Physical Health and Mortality

Schooling has remarkably broad influences on a range of indicators of physical health and well-being. Individuals who have obtained more schooling report better health outcomes and status than those who have obtained fewer years of schooling. For example, individuals who have obtained more years of schooling are considerably less likely to smoke than those who have obtained fewer years of schooling (Bound et al., 1995; Sander, 1995b). Among smokers, those with more schooling are more likely to quit smoking than those with less schooling (Sander, 1995a). These findings are obtained across multiple data sets and over different time periods.

As with many of the outcomes considered in this chapter, the most pronounced schooling differences pertain to the contrast of college graduates with noncollege graduates. Drawing on data reported by the U.S. Department of Health and Human Services, Sander (1995b) showed that, among adults age 20 and older in 1987, college graduates were much less likely to smoke than their less educated peers. Only about one in six college graduates over the age of 20 in 1987 smoked, compared to one third of high school graduates and to a similar fraction of nongraduates. The college graduation effect appears to have increased substantially over the two decades spanning from 1966 to 1987, as college graduates were only a few percentage points less likely than high school graduates and nongraduates to be smokers in 1966.

Beyond the effects of schooling on smoking behavior, there is modest evidence of schooling effects on blood pressure and cholesterol levels. Drawing on data from the Health and Nutrition Examination Survey I (HANES), Berger and Leigh (1989) found significant correlations between years of schooling completed and both systolic and diastolic blood pressure levels. In their analyses, each year of schooling reduces the systolic blood pressure by about 0.5 mm, and the diastolic blood pressure by about 0.2 mm. Similarly, Bound and associates (1995) found that poorly educated men surveyed in the Health and Retirement Survey were more likely to have hypertension than better educated men, although the differences were not dramatic. Approximately 46% of the men with less than a high school diploma had hypertension, whereas 36% of college graduates had this disease.

There is some conflicting evidence, however, in data from the Stanford Five City Project. Winkleby, Jatulis, Frank, and Fortmann (1992) did not find statistically significant differences in the mean systolic or diastolic blood pressures of men with various levels of schooling, and they found only small but significant differences in the diastolic blood pressure levels of women. Nor was there evidence in this study of schooling effects on the total or the high-density lipoprotein (HDL) cholesterol levels of men. Highly educated women in this study, however, had significantly lower total cholesterol counts than less educated women and had significantly higher HDL cholesterol levels.

Although the evidence for blood pressure and cholesterol levels is mixed, better educated men are less likely than less educated men to report specific medical conditions, such as severe chronic pain, arthritis, and hearing and vision problems. Bound and associates (1995) documented substantial differences across schooling levels in the risk of arthritis. Approximately 41% of men without high school diplomas reported suffering from arthritis, as did 34% of high school graduates. In contrast, only 28% of men with some college had arthritis, and only 22% of male college graduates reported this disease. Bound and associates (1995) also reported that men who are better educated report fewer hearing and vision problems than do men with less schooling. Approximately one fourth of the men lacking a high school diploma reported a vision problem, and a similar proportion described problems with their hearing. However only 5% of the college graduates reported a vision problem, and a similar fraction (9%) of these men indicated a problem with their hearing. Men with less than a high school education seemed particularly susceptible to vision problems, as only 11% of high school graduates reported such problems. In contrast, the relationship between schooling and the risk of hearing problems is approximately linear.

Educational attainment also is significantly related to functional limitations on daily activities. Bound and associates (1995) reported that among middle-aged men, those with more schooling find it less difficult than those with fewer years of schooling to shower, to eat, and to dress themselves. They also find it less difficult to engage in other light physical activities, such as climbing several flights of stairs, lifting ten pounds, stooping, picking up a dime, and raising their arms.

In this same study, Bound and associates (1995) found a strong association between educational attainment and general health status. Men with less than a high school diploma were six times more likely (19% vs. 3%) than male college graduates to report that their general health status is poor. The differences among high school graduates and college graduates were not as dramatic, although high school graduates were about twice as likely as college graduates to report poor general health. Even when a less stringent reporting standard was used, the differences across schooling levels still were substantial. Whereas 9% of college graduates reported their general health status to be either poor or fair, four times as many (39%) of the men who did not complete high school judged their general health to be at best fair.

Not surprisingly, in view of these consistent associations between schooling and functional limitations, schooling also is associated with limitations in one's ability to do paid work. This is shown in studies based on the National Longitudinal Study of Young Men (Berger & Leigh, 1989) and on the Health and Retirement Survey (Bound et al., 1995). The vast majority of middle-aged men do not report limitations in their ability to do paid work. However, a small fraction do, and these are disproportionately drawn from the less-educated ranks. Bound and associates (1995) reported that approximately 3 in 10 men who have not completed high school had a health problem that limits or prevents paid work. In contrast, only 2 in 10 with a high school diploma or with some college had such an employment disability, and only 1 in 10 college graduate had an employment limitation.

In addition to the consistent evidence of a relationship between schooling and these (relatively) tangible indicators of health status, researchers have found that education is associated with subjective health status. Better educated men and women also think that they are healthier than their less educated peers. Some of the evidence of this is drawn from the General Social Survey (David & Smith, 1992). Glenn and Weaver (1981) found that individuals with 4 or more years of college reported better subjective health than those with less schooling, and that this pattern is observed among White males, White females, and Black females (but not among Black males). Taubman and Rosen (1982) drew a similar conclusion for men and women participating in the Retirement History Survey (Social Security Administration, 1984), a panel of 11,000 individuals aged 58 to 63 surveyed in 1969, in 1971 and in 1973. They found that educational attainment was substantially related to individuals' reports of whether their health was better or worse than that of others of comparable ages.

In view of these effects, it is scarcely a surprise that better educated people live longer than those with less schooling. This finding originally achieved prominence in Kitagawa and Hauser's (1973) study of mortality in the United States. In that study, which drew on data from

1960, Kitagawa and Hauser observed a strong relationship, among those aged 25 to 64, between years of schooling and mortality; this relationship held for White men, for White women, for Black men, and for Black women. The differing mortality rates across educational levels resulted in a difference in life expectancy for highly educated and for poorly educated young adults of about 5 years.

More recently, Rogot, Sorlie, and Johnson (1992) have reported similar findings based on data from the National Longitudinal Mortality Study (National Heart, Lung, and Blood Institute, n.d.), a study of approximately 800,000 Whites participating in the Current Population Survey (U.S. Bureau of the Census, 1978) between 1979 and 1985. In the early 1980s, college-educated White men had a life expectancy at age 25 approximately 5 years greater than that of men who had not completed high school, and the life expectancy gap between White female college graduates and non-high school graduates was roughly 3 years. Similar gaps in life expectancy across these schooling levels were observed at age 45.

How might we explain the association between schooling and physical health and mortality? Much of the literature on the relationship between schooling and physical health outcomes treats schooling as an indicator of or a determinant of social class position. Once again, the material conditions of the workplace are held to mediate the influence of schooling on adult outcomes. Poorly educated men are much more likely to be engaged in work that involves physical labor, and the wear and tear on the body that this kind of work induces has both immediate and long-term health consequences.

Another possible explanation offered for schooling differences in health and mortality is that better educated people engage in healthier behaviors than less educated people. That is, it is likely that highly educated people have access to better information about managing their health and have resources that enable them to seek help when they need it. Although this is an important explanation for why schooling might be associated with health, there is not a great deal of research outside of the field of health education that bears on its plausibility.

There is, however, some evidence that schooling is associated with good health habits. For example, highly educated individuals are more likely to use seat belts than less educated persons. Leigh (1990) demonstrated this point with data from the Panel Study of Income Dynamics (Hill, 1992). Even correcting for various forms of selection bias, each additional year of schooling raised the probability of seat belt use by approximately five percentage points.

Family Effects

Schooling has a number of effects on adult family lives. How much schooling one obtains affects who one marries, which in turn influences the risk of marital disruption. Schooling also affects the timing of family events, including the timing of marriage and of childbearing. Moreover, education is associated with other aspects of family life as well. For example, schooling is associated with educational homogamy, the tendency for people to marry other people with similar levels of educational attainment. In recent years, individuals with at least a 4-year college education have become much less likely to marry people who either dropped out of high school or who did not persist in school beyond high school graduation (Kalmijn, 1991; Mare, 1991). One interpretation of this pattern is that schooling has increasingly become a marker for membership in status groups whose members share common values, interests, and social positions (Tzeng, 1992).

Yet educational homogamy is no guarantee of a happy marriage. There is little evidence of a consistent relationship between educational attainment and marital satisfaction or happiness for either men or women. Campbell, Converse, and Rodgers (1976) found that individuals who had completed college were less satisfied with their marriages than individuals who had not completed college. In contrast, Glenn and Weaver (1978) did not find a clear linkage between educational attainment and marital happiness. The relative lack of interest in this topic probably reflects two factors. First, there is more interest in marital disruption than in marital happiness, and in fact there is much more research on the determinants of marital disruption than on marital satisfaction, which has always been elusive to predict. Second, there are not strong, theoretically derived hypotheses about the nature of this relationship to drive research on this question.

Although schooling is not consistently related to marital satisfaction, it does affect the risk of divorce. Highly educated women are, in general, less likely to divorce than women with little schooling. The effect of education on divorce is not as large for men. Tzeng (1992) showed that women with at least a high school education are about 30% less likely to divorce than women with less than a high school education, and the effect is slightly larger for women who have attended some college.

Educational homogamy has important consequences for the risk of marital disruption. Couples where the wife has more schooling than her husband are about 28% more likely to divorce than couples with the same level of schooling (Tzeng, 1992). However, a similar pattern is observed when the husband has more schooling than his wife. Couples where the husband has more schooling than his wife are about 20% more likely to divorce than couples with the same level of schooling (Tzeng).

Increases in women's educational attainment have influenced fertility patterns as much as they have shaped marriage formation and dissolution. Since the 1960s, the rate at which women entered college increased rapidly, as did their participation in the labor force. The increased labor-force participation of women led to widespread predictions that their total fertility would fall. Instead, there is evidence that highly educated women have delayed childbearing (Lewis & Ventura, 1990; Rindfuss & Sweet, 1977). Although even less educated women have gradually delayed childbearing since the mid-1970s, the pattern is especially pronounced among highly educated women (Rindfuss, Morgan & Offutt, 1996). In the late 1960s, about 17% of the total fertility of women who had not completed high school occurred between the ages of 30 and 41, and about 33% of the total fertility of women who had completed 4 years or more of college occurred during this relatively late age range. However, by the late 1980s, there was a marked shift in the delaying of childbearing in this highly educated group and virtually no change in the group of less educated women. An estimated 47% of the total fertility of women who had completed 4 or more years of high school took place between the ages of 30 and 41 (Rindfuss et al., 1996).

The conventional explanation for this pattern is that women delay childbearing until after they have left school because they recognize the difficulty of combining the roles of student and mother. Rindfuss and associates (1996) also hypothesized that women's decision to delay childbearing may reflect their desire to place their children in organized childcare programs. Because high-quality childcare programs can be costly, women may delay childbearing until they can afford the expenses of such childcare. Rindfuss and associates did rule out the possibility that delayed childbearing is primarily the result of delayed marriage among the highly educated.

To recap, adult marriage and family outcomes are influenced by the amount of schooling that the respective partners have obtained. However, there are at least two ways in which marriage and family outcomes differ from most of the other outcomes in this chapter. First, marriage and family outcomes are not as likely to be mediated by work as other outcomes. Second, higher levels of schooling are not necessarily associated with more positive outcomes, as the most highly educated women have a higher risk of marital disruption than other well-educated women (Houseknecht & Spanier, 1980).

Most of the studies reviewed in this section treat schooling as an individual status characteristic or as an indicator of role performance. For example, Tzeng (1992) argued that schooling is treated as a resource in the marriage market, as it may signal membership in a desirable status group. Schooling may also signal future economic productivity, but such productivity is only realized if a marriage partner participates in the labor market. Moreover, the difficulties of combining advanced schooling with work and with childrearing suggests that schooling also conveys information about values, priorities, and foregone opportunities. What is, or might be, learned through prolonging one's schooling seems to be irrelevant to most accounts of how schooling might influence family outcomes.

Political Participation

People with more schooling are more involved in the political process than those with less schooling. They express a sense of civic duty and profess to be very interested in politics. They also are more likely to vote in local, in state, and in national elections than those with less education. Wolfinger and Rosenstone's (1980) tabulations from the 1972 National Election Study illustrate these findings. They demonstrated that highly educated people are more likely to express a high sense of citizen duty than less educated people. About 40% of those who had not completed high school felt a strong sense of citizen duty, compared to 50% for high school graduates and to 66% among those who had completed 5 or more years of college. Wolfinger and Rosenstone found an even stronger relationship between schooling and interest in politics. Fewer than one third of individuals with a high school degree or less said they are very interested in politics, whereas 55% of those completing college, and 75% of those obtaining 5 or more years of college, expressed such high interest.

Schooling affects voting behavior as well as political attitudes. Several studies have shown that individuals with more schooling are more likely to vote than those with less schooling. This relationship is a central finding of Wolfinger and Rosenstone's (1980) monograph on who votes, and it persists even when controlling for family income. More recent evidence from the Current Population Survey (U.S. Bureau of the Census, 1978) is cited by Levin and Kelley (1994), who showed that the likelihood that individuals aged 25 and older voted in the 1988 U.S. presidential election is highly responsive to their level of schooling. Fewer than one half of those lacking a high school diploma voted in that election, and a much smaller proportion of individuals with less than 8 years of schooling did so. Conversely, approximately 60% of high school graduates voted in the 1988 presidential election, as did three fourths of college graduates and more than four fifths of those with more than 16 years of schooling.

Wolfinger and Rosenstone (1980) interpreted the relationship between schooling and voting behavior as evidence of the socializing effects of schooling. They suggested that schooling increases individuals' capacities for working with the complexities and abstractions of political ideas, and that greater knowledge of the issues may lead to greater press for political participation. Schooling also may increase an individual's interest in the political process and the moral press to participate in the process. Schooling also reduces the costs of voting, Wolfinger and Rosenstone argued, by enabling individuals to navigate the bureaucratic aspects of registering to vote and of voting. They also speculated that by instilling a sense of citizen duty, schooling increases the expressive rewards of voting, in that voters feel that they have exercised an important civic responsibility.

Missing from this account is a view of schooling as a status characteristic associated with positions of privilege in society. A conflict orientation might see the association between schooling and political participation as evidence of the ability of superordinate groups to maintain their positions in democratic societies by using the political process in a way less available to the poorly educated.

Values

People who go farther through school often have different value orientations than those who obtain less schooling. This finding was the subject of a monograph by Hyman and Wright (1979). Davis (1979) found that years of schooling was significantly related to nine tenths of a set of 49 attitudes, even when other sociodemographic factors, such as age, sex, race, and religion were controlled. In fact, Davis reported that no other predictor had a significant effect on these attitudes as frequently as years of schooling. More recently, other scholars have documented the effect of education on a range of values, including the valuing of autonomy and conformity, self-direction, liberalism and attitudes toward equity, and misanthropy.

Over a period of several decades, sociologist Melvin Kohn and his colleagues have been studying the impact of location in the social class structure on personality and psychological functioning in the United States and in other Western and non-Western societies. In his best known work, Kohn (1969) explored the relationship between social class and values, particularly the valuing of conformity to external authority. Individuals who conform to external authorities can be distinguished from those who are self-directed. Kohn found a correlation between schooling and the valuing of self-direction versus conformity even when subsequent occupational position was controlled. Schooling also had an indirect effect on the values that parents held for their children.

Kohn (1969) speculated that the effects of schooling were primarily mediated by the substantive features of work, such that well-educated men were disproportionately likely to hold jobs that were complex and not closely supervised. However, he also hypothesized that education produced a level of intellectual flexibility and breadth of perspective necessary for the valuing of self-direction. More recently, Kohn, Naoi, Schoenbach, Schooler and Slomczynski (1990) contrasted the effects of education on psychological functioning in the United States, in Japan, and in Poland. Although they found strong effects of schooling on self-direction among U.S. men, there was no evidence of such effects in Japan and in Poland.

Schooling affects other values as well. For instance, individuals with more schooling are substantially more likely to hold liberal values than those with less schooling. Evidence of the effects of schooling on a range of liberal values is provided by Hyman and Wright (1979), who examined adults' responses to survey questions about civil liberties for nonconformists, freedom of information, due process of law for extremists and for deviants, liberty for public expression, and equality of opportunity for minorities. In general, there were large differences in the responses of college graduates and individuals who had not completed high school in the extent to which they supported these liberal positions.

A distant relative of liberalism is misanthropy, the extent to which individuals se others as conniving and as looking out for themselves, rather than as trustworthy and helpful. Smith (1997) showed that schooling is inversely related to misanthropy. Individuals with more schooling score lower on a three-item misanthropy scale that includes items such as "Do you think most people would try to take advantage of you if they got a chance, or would they try to be fair?" Years of schooling and misanthropy are correlated ($r = -.23$), and the net effect of education on misanthropy was only slightly reduced ($ß = -.17$) when a host of social background factors, including income, religiosity, gender, and exposure to traumatic events, were controlled. Smith (1997) argued that misanthropy is a function of material well-being. Because highly educated people are more advantaged than less educated people, he suggested, they are more likely to look favorably upon others. In contrast, less educated people may attribute their lesser social standing and resources to the machinations of others.

Explanations of the effects of schooling on values such as conformity, liberalism, or misanthropy emphasize either the socialization function of schooling or the connection between schooling and work, which may also have an important socializing effect. On the one hand, scholars such as Kohn (1969) have hypothesized that higher levels of schooling open the mind to considering a range of values orientations extending beyond those observed in one's family or in one's immediate surroundings. In this sense, schooling is a broadening activity. On the other hand, Smith (1997) emphasized the contribution schooling makes to material well-being by granting access to highly-rewarded jobs, but he paid little attention to the direct socializing influence of schooling in shaping values such as misanthropy.

Leisure Time

More educated people spend their time differently than individuals with less schooling. I have already cited evidence that highly educated people spend more time attending cultural and arts-related events. Robinson and Godbey's (1997) summary of data from three waves of the America's Use of Time Project documents other meaningful differences across schooling levels in leisure-time activities. In particular, Robinson and Godbey reported that

> College-educated people spend slightly more time working and commuting to work, and more time shopping and caring for children (even though they have fewer children) than the less educated. In contrast, they do less housework. They also sleep less and spend less time on grooming activities than those with a high school degree or less. While overall meal and eating times are the same by education level, college graduates spend more time eating out. (p. 192)

Robinson and Godbey (1997) also reported that college graduates spend more time engaged in fitness activities and organizational and educational activities than those with less schooling.

Robinson and Godbey (1997) attributed most of the schooling-related differences in leisure time use to the mediating influence of class cultures. College graduates spend more time working than less educated people and thus do not actually have more leisure time than the less educated. However, they use this time in ways that are consistent with the values of social elites, emphasizing activities that are slightly more altruistic and connected to a wider social organization.

Even though work is seen as the primary mediating factor, schooling has a stronger association with leisure time use than does either occupation or income. Thus, it is at least possible that a socialization explanation for schooling's association with leisure time use could be a useful adjunct to explanations emphasizing the connections between schooling and work.

THREATS TO VALIDITY

Most of the studies reported in this chapter imply causal relationships between schooling and adult outcomes, whether implicitly or explicitly. Some take into account potential threats to the validity of claims about education's effects on these various adult outcomes, whereas others do not. It is worth examining the most serious of these threats in some detail, as a means of sensitizing researchers and others to the risks involved in inferring the effects of education from associations between education and other variables. This section discusses the ways in which threats to the validity of causal claims are considered within the diverse literatures on which this chapter draws.

The most common threat to the validity of causal claims is the failure to take adequate account of antecedent factors that might explain the apparent association between a predictor, such as educational attainment, and an outcome. If such factors are not taken into consideration, the observed relationship might be spurious, and inferences about the predictor's influence on the outcome are thus erroneous. For example, there is a risk in inferring from the observed association between educational attainment and the valuing of independence versus conformity that schooling produces those values. Other research and theory indicate that one's social class background shapes both how far one goes through school and one's values. Perhaps an individual's social class origins account for the observed association between education and the valuing of independence versus conformity, rather than anything about education itself. Failing to take account of the fact that people who go farther through school begin their lives more socially advantaged would threaten the validity of claims about schooling's effects.

It is important, however, to distinguish between unobserved factors that precede both schooling and adult outcomes, and those that intervene between schooling and adult outcomes. In the latter case, such factors may identify the mechanisms by which schooling exerts an influence on a given adult outcome. For example, an individual's educational attainment is likely to influence his or her adult occupational status, and occupational status in turn may affect the values an adult holds. In this case, one might describe adult occupational status as an intervening or mediating factor that is associated both with schooling and the adult outcome. But adult occupational status at, say, age 40 would be unlikely to influence an individual's selection into a given level of schooling, whereas socioeconomic origins might well shape selection into higher levels of schooling.

There are a number of factors that plausibly might simultaneously influence selection into greater or fewer years of schooling and affect adult outcomes. Among the most important are socioeconomic status, academic ability and knowledge, physical and mental health, and psychological functioning. Each of these factors has been invoked as a potential explanation for the association between years of schooling and at least one, and sometimes several, of the adult outcomes considered in this chapter. No study provides suitable controls for all of these factors, and it would be a rare study that had such a panoramic view of social life. However, some studies do provide rough estimates of the extent of the bias incurred by failing to control for a given factor, typically by comparing estimates of the effects of educational attainment on an outcome when a particular selection factor is controlled with the estimates generated when that selection factor is not controlled. This section considers several such factors, including socioeconomic status, ability and knowledge, physical and mental health, and psychological functioning.

Socioeconomic Status

The socioeconomic status of a person's childhood home has been invoked as a possible explanation for the effects of schooling on socioeconomic outcomes (Leigh & Gill, 1997), on psychological well-being (Ross & Van Willigen, 1997), on knowledge and cognitive development (Hyman et al., 1975; Kirsch et al., 1993), and on political participation (Wolfinger &

Rosenstone, 1980), to name but a few of the outcomes considered herein. In particular, it is frequently argued that well-educated parents provide their children with better educational and health resources and information and are more likely to have high levels of social and political participation, and these advantages may be conveyed more or less directly to their children.

In some cases, family background controls are used as proxies for intelligence and academic ability. For example, Hyman and associates (1975) relied on social class as a proxy for intelligence, arguing that the correlation between class and intelligence made this a sensible thing to do. However, subsequent research (e.g., Alexander, Pallas, & Cook, 1981) showed that social background measures were not adequate proxies for academic ability when the outcomes themselves were cognitive in nature.

Studies that have incorporated measures of childhood family socioeconomic status provide some evidence on the possible consequences of failing to control for socioeconomic status when estimating the effects of schooling on adult outcomes. Hyman and associates' (1975) analyses suggest that social class origins explain about 10% to 33% of the relationship between schooling and knowledge. Similarly, Kirsch and associates (1993) found that about 15% to 20% of the schooling effect on adult prose, document, and quantitative literacy proficiency can be attributed to parental education, a measure of family socioeconomic status.

Ability and Knowledge

Because of the strong evidence of the effects of academic ability on how far individuals go through school, the failure to control for ability may seriously bias estimates of the effects of schooling on adult outcomes. This is most likely to be a problem when there is good reason to believe that ability is a potent influence on those outcomes. For example, the failure to control for ability when examining education's effects on knowledge and on cognitive development might be problematic because early ability is a powerful predictor both of educational attainment and adult cognitive functioning (Haveman & Wolfe, 1984; Pascarella & Terenzini, 1991). Hyman and associates (1975) argued, however, that certain kinds of "vulgar" knowledge about popular culture may not be as responsive to "schoolbookish" knowledge and ability.

For some outcomes, including socioeconomic outcomes, there are estimates of the consequences of failing to control for academic ability when estimating the effects of educational attainment. As was true for socieconomic status, unadjusted estimates may be much larger than estimates that adjust for selection effects. Blackburn and Neumark (1995) examined the consequences of omitting ability controls in models of the economic returns to years of schooling. Drawing on the National Longitudinal Survey of Youth (Center for Human Resource Research, 1992), they find that failing to control for ability leads to an upward bias of approximately 40% in the estimates of education's effects on wages.

Physical and Mental Health

Concerns about the role of prior physical and mental health in the association between schooling and adult physical and mental health frequently are represented in a contrast between what are referred to as social selection and social causation explanations of this association. The social selection hypothesis is that the association between educational attainment and adult physical or mental well-being is spurious, and its results from individuals with physical and/or mental disabilities selecting themselves, or being selected, into fewer years of schooling (Carr, 1997; Link et al., 1993). (The social causation hypothesis, in contrast, credits educational attainment with a causal influence on adult outcomes.) The social selection hypothesis, cast in this way, is a prominent hypothesis in the literature on the determinants of adult physical and mental health, but is not generally given serious consideration when other outcomes are at issue.

Psychological Functioning

Psychological attributes of individuals such as motivation and aspirations also are potentially confounding factors in the estimation of schooling's effects on adult outcomes (Pascarella & Terenzini, 1991). Whereas such factors often are moderately correlated with educational attainment, they typically are not highly correlated with adult outcomes of the variety considered here. Thus, it is unlikely that such controls could completely explain the relationships between schooling and adult outcomes. Few studies include such controls, largely because the requisite data are rarely available. Ideally, measures of aspiration and motivation should be causally prior to eventual educational attainment, which implies that the measures must be gathered relatively early in the life course. There are not very many longitudinal studies that meet this stringent requirement.

Two other psychological attributes have attained prominence as alternate explanations for the association between educational attainment and adult outcomes, particularly those that involve mental and physical health. Fuchs (Farrell & Fuchs, 1982; Fuchs, 1982, 1992) has posed an argument that a feature of individuals' decision making—typically referred to as "rate of time preference" or, more simply, "farsightedness," or the ability to delay gratification—may be an unobserved factor that influences both investments in education and investments in health. If this decision-making style is a stable personality trait, he argued, it may explain why individuals simultaneously invest in many years of schooling and in health-enhancing activities, supporting his contention that the relationship between schooling and healthy behaviors is spurious. The empirical evidence for this alternate explanation of the relationship between schooling and health is weak.

A closely related argument is that individual differences in willingness to take risks might explain the relationship between schooling and health outcomes. Leigh (1990) suggested that individuals who don't like taking risks may obtain more schooling than those who are bigger risk-takers, because schooling minimizes the risk of later unemployment. Similarly, individuals who don't like taking risks are more likely to engage in behaviors designed to minimize subsequent health risks, such as fastening their seat belts as a hedge against serious injury in an automobile accident. If willingness to take risks influences both educational attainment and engaging in healthy behaviors, then perhaps the association between schooling and health outcomes is due to their common dependence on risk preferences.

Leigh's (1990) study of the relationship between education and seat belt use does provide some support for these arguments regarding time and risk preferences. He found that the introduction of measures of time and risk preferences reduced the direct effect of schooling on seat belt use by 25% to 35%. However, these controls did not eliminate the effect of schooling, which continued to have a direct positive effect on seat belt use even in the presence of these controls.

Summary

Many factors affect both how far individuals go through school and their well-being as adults after they have left school. For this reason, it is essential to incorporate our understanding of these achievement processes, and their intersections, into our estimations of schooling's influences on adult outcomes. The evidence to date is that the failure to take account factors such as socioeconomic status, ability and knowledge, physical and mental health, and psychological functioning can lead to exaggerated claims about schooling's effects on adult outcomes of various types. However, schooling appears to be an important, although perhaps less potent, determinant of these outcomes even in the face of these controls.

CONCLUSION

The studies reported in this chapter demonstrate persuasively that schooling has pervasive effects on adult outcomes. Although there can be little doubt that the failure to take account of selection bias results in overly generous estimates of schooling effects, it is extremely unlikely that adding more stringent controls would completely eradicate the effects of schooling on adult well-being and functioning. Schooling, it seems, really does matter—at least at the intersection of time and space that this review considers, which is primarily the United States during the latter third of the 20th century. Educational attainment has become a kind of "social address" that locates individuals in the social structure, rivaling the importance of social class origins, race and ethnicity, and gender as shorthand summaries of who one is and what one is destined to become.

Yet the reasons why educational attainment is associated with variations in individuals' adult lives remain an enigma. Explanation of these effects that privilege one factor to the exclusion of all others fail to account for the full array of findings I have described. There is evidence in support of socialization explanations of schooling effects, as well as evidence consistent with allocation explanations of schooling effects. A great many studies report findings that are equally hospitable to each of these accounts of schooling's effects on individual lives.

These two major accounts of why schooling is associated with a range of adult outcomes make sense to a great many social scientists, and they are consistent with many of the most influential theoretical and methodological traditions in social scientific research on schooling, such as the human capital and the status attainment traditions. Yet the very plausibility of these accounts has had the unintended consequence of dissuading researchers from filling in the gaps that remain in this literature. Most social scientists are content to assume that schooling has these kinds of effects on individuals, even in the absence of a large aggregation of compelling evidence. Given the way that schooling has been institutionalized in the modern state, it is supposed both to produce changes in individuals and to function as a rational mechanism for sorting and selecting individuals for adult social positions. Small wonder, then, that social scientists might be as susceptible to prevailing myths about how schooling works as the naive person on the street.

Finally, the prevalence of these two institutionalized accounts of schooling's effects helps to explain the occasional failures of social scientists to contextualize their conclusions about educational effects. All research settings are characterized by particular cultural contexts and institutional arrangements, and the effects of schooling may be contingent on these contexts and arrangements (Featherman & Carter, 1976; Leigh & Gill, 1997; Levin & Kelley, 1994;

Patrinos, 1995). Increasingly, it is important to incorporate descriptions of historical and cultural conditions and institutional arrangements into research on the relationship between educational attainment and adult outcomes. Doing so may enable social scientists to be more successful in specifying the conditions under which particular relationships may be observed, and why.

ACKNOWLEDGMENTS: My thanks to Maureen Hallinan, Anna Neumann, James Rosenbaum, and an anonymous reviewer for their helpful comments on earlier drafts of this chapter.

REFERENCES

Alexander, K. L., Pallas, A. M., & Cook, M. A. (1981). Measure for measure: On the use of endogenous ability data in school process models. *American Sociological Review, 46,* 619–631.

Becker, G. S. (1964). *Human capital.* New York: National Bureau of Economic Research.

Berger, M. C., & Leigh, J. P. (1989). Schooling, self-selection, and health. *Journal of Human Resources, 24,* 433–455.

Bird, C. E., & Ross, C. E. (1993). Houseworkers and paid workers: Qualities of the work and effects on personal control. *Journal of Marriage and the Family, 55,* 913–925.

Blackburn, M. L., & Neumark, D. (1995). Are OLS estimates of the return to schooling biased downward? Another look. *The Review of Economics and Statistics, 77,* 217–229.

Blau, P. M., & Duncan, O. D. (1967). *The American occupational structure.* New York: The Free Press.

Bound, J., Schoenbaum, M., & Waidmann, T. (1995). Race and education differences in disability status and labor force attachment in the Health and Retirement Survey. *Journal of Human Resources, 30,* S227–S269.

Campbell, A., Converse, P. E., & Rodgers, W. L. (1976). *The quality of American life.* New York: Russell Sage Foundation.

Carr, D. (1997). The fulfillment of career dreams at midlife: Does it matter for women's mental health? *Journal of Health and Social Behavior, 38,* 331–344.

Collins, R. (1979). *The credential society: An historical sociology of education and stratification.* New York: Academic Press.

Davis, J. A. (1979). *Background variables and opinions in the 1972–1977 NORC General Social Surveys: Ten generalizations about age, education, occupational prestige, race, religion, and sex, and forty-nine opinion items* (GSS Topical Report No. 2). Chicago: National Opinion Research Center.

Dreeben, R. (1968). *On what is learned in school.* Reading, MA: Addison-Wesley.

Duncan, O. D., Featherman, D. L., & Duncan, B. (1972). *Socioeconomic background and achievement.* New York: Academic Press.

Farrell, P., & Fuchs, V. R. (1982). Schooling and health: The cigarette connection. *Journal of Health Economics, 1,* 217–230.

Featherman, D. L., & Carter, T. M. (1976). Discontinuities in schooling and the socioeconomic life cycle. In W. H. Sewell, R. M. Hauser, & D. L. Featherman (Eds.), *Schooling and achievement in American society* (pp. 133–160). New York: Academic Press.

Featherman, D.L., & Hauser, R.M. (1978). *Opportunity and change.* New York: Academic Press.

Fuchs, V. R. (1982). Time preference and health: An exploratory study. In V. R. Fuchs (Ed.), *Economic aspects of health* (pp. 93–120). Chicago: National Bureau of Economic Research, University of Chicago Press.

Fuchs, V. R. (1992). Poverty and health: Asking the right questions. *American Economist, 36*(2), 12–18.

Glenn, N. D., & Weaver, C. N. (1978). A multivariate, multisurvey study of marital happiness. *Journal of Marriage and the Family, 40,* 269–282.

Glenn, N. D., & Weaver, C. N. (1981). Education's effects on psychological well-being. *Public Opinion Quarterly, 45,* 22–39.

Gruenberg, B. (1980). The happy worker: An analysis of educational and occupational differences in determinants of job satisfaction. *American Journal of Sociology, 86,* 247–271.

Grusky, D.B., & DiPrete, T.A. (1990). Recent trends in the process of stratification. *Demography, 27,* 617-637.

Haveman, R. H., & Wolfe, B. L. (1984). Schooling and economic well-being: The role of nonmarket effects. *Journal of Human Resources, 19,* 3–33.

Houseknecht, S. K., & Spanier, G. B. (1980). Marital disruption and higher education among women in the United States. *The Sociological Quarterly, 21,* 375–389.

Hyman, H. H., & Wright, C. R. (1979). *Education's lasting influence on values*. Chicago: University of Chicago Press.

Hyman, H. H., Wright, C. R., & Reed, J. S. (1975). *The enduring effects of education*. Chicago: University of Chicago Press.

Jencks, C. S., Bartlett, S., Corcoran, M., Crouse, J., Eaglesfield, D., Jackson, G., McClelland, K., Mueser, P., Olneck, M., Schwartz, J., Ward, S., & Williams, J. (1979). *Who gets ahead? The determinants of economic success in America*. New York: Basic Books.

Kalmijn, M. (1991). Shifting boundaries: Trends in religious and educational homogamy. *American Sociological Review, 56,* 786–800.

Kerckhoff, A. C. (1976). The status attainment process: Socialization or allocation? *Social Forces, 55,* 368–381.

Kessler, R. C. (1982). A disaggregation of the relationship between socioeconomic status and psychological distress. *American Sociological Review, 47,* 752–764.

Kirsch, I. S., Jungeblut, A., Jenkins, L., & Kolstad, A. (1993). Adult literacy in America: A first look at the results of the National Adult Literacy Survey. Washington, DC: National Center for Education Statistics.

Kitagawa, E. M., & Hauser, P. M. (1973). *Differential mortality in the United States: A study in socioeconomic epidemiology*. Cambridge, MA: Harvard University Press.

Kohn, M. L. (1969). *Class and conformity: A study in values*. Chicago: University of Chicago Press.

Kohn, M. L., Naoi, A., Schoenbach, C., Schooler, C., & Slomczynski, K. M. (1990). Position in the class structure and psychological functioning in the United States, Japan, and Poland. *American Journal of Sociology, 95,* 964–1008.

Land, K. C., & Russell, S. T. (1996). Wealth accumulation across the adult life course: Stability and change in sociodemographic covariate structures of net worth data in the Survey of Income and Program Participation, 1984–1991. *Social Science Research, 25,* 423–462.

Leigh, J. P. (1990). Schooling and seat belt use. *Southern Economic Journal, 57,* 195–207.

Leigh, D. E., & Gill, A. M. (1997). Labor market returns to community colleges: Evidence for returning adults. *Journal of Human Resources 32,* 334–353.

Lennon, M. C. (1994). Women, work, and well-being: The importance of work conditions. *Journal of Health and Social Behavior, 35,* 235–247.

Levin, H. M., & Kelley, C. (1994). Can education do it alone? *Economics of Education Review, 13,* 97–108.

Lewis, C. & Ventura, S. (1990). Birth and fertility rates by education: 1980 and 1985. *Vital and Health Statistics, 21(49),* 1–40.

Link, B. G., Lennon, M. C., & Dohrenwend, B. P. (1993). Socioeconomic status and depression: The role of occupations involving direction, control, and planning. *American Journal of Sociology, 98,* 1351–1387.

Lorig, K., Seleznick, M., Lubeck, D., Ung, E., Chastain, R. L., & Holman, H. R. (1989). The beneficial outcomes of the arthritis self-management course were not adequately explained by behavioral change. *Arthritis and Rheumatology, 32,* 91–95.

Luttrell, W. (1998). *Schoolsmart and motherwise: Working-class women's identity and schooling*. New York: Routledge.

Mare, R. D. (1991). Five decades of educational assortative mating. *American Sociological Review, 56,* 15–32.

Meyer, J. W. (1977). The effects of education as an institution. *American Journal of Sociology, 83,* 53–77.

Meyer, J. W. (1985). Types of explanation in the sociology of education. In J. B. Richardson (Ed.), *Handbook of theory and research for the sociology of education* (pp. 341–359). New York: Greenwood.

Murnane, R. J., Willett, J. B., & Levy, F. (1995). The growing importance of cognitive skills in wage determination. *Review of Economics and Statistics, 77,* 251–266.

Namboodiri, N. K. (1987). The floundering phase of the life course. In R. G. Corwin (Ed.), *Research in sociology of education and socialization, Vol. 7* (pp. 59–86). Greenwich, CT: JAI.

Oppenheimer, V. K., Kalmijn, M., & Lim, N. (1997). Men's career development and marriage timing during a period of rising inequality. *Demography, 34,* 311–330.

Pallas, A. M. (1995). Federal data on educational attainment and the transition to work. In Board on Children and Families and the Committee on National Statistics (Eds.), *Integrating Federal Statistics on Children: Report of a Workshop* (pp. 122–155). Washington, DC: National Academy Press.

Pascarella, E. T., & Terenzini, P. T. (1991). *How college affects students: Findings and insights from twenty years of research*. San Francisco, CA: Jossey-Bass.

Patrinos, H. A. (1995). Socioeconomic background, schooling, experience, ability and monetary rewards in Greece. *Economics of Education Review, 14,* 85–91.

Rindfuss, R. R., Morgan, S. P., & Offutt, K. (1996). Education and the changing age pattern of American fertility: 1963–1989. *Demography, 33,* 277–290.

Rindfuss, R. R., & Sweet, J. A. (1977). *Postwar fertility trends and differentials in the United States*. New York: Academic Press.

Robinson, J. P., & Godbey, G. (1997). *Time for life: The surprising ways Americans use their time*. University Park, PA: Pennsylvania State University Press.

Rogot, E., Sorlie, P. D., & Johnson, N. J. (1992). Life expectancy by employment status, income, and education in the National Longitudinal Mortality Study. *Public Health Reports, 107,* 457–461.

Ross, C. E., & Mirowsky, J. (1989). Explaining the social patterns of depression: Control and problem solving—or support and talking? *Journal of Health and Social Behavior, 30,* 206–219.

Ross, C. E., & Mirowsky, J. (1992). Households, employment, and the sense of control. *Social Psychology Quarterly, 55,* 217–235.

Ross, C.E., & Reskin, B. (1992). Education, control at work, and job satisfaction. *Social Science Research, 21,* 134-148.

Ross, C. E., & Van Willigen, M. (1997). Education and the subjective quality of life. *Journal of Health and Social Behavior, 38,* 275–297.

Sander, W. (1995a). Schooling and quitting smoking. *The Review of Economics and Statistics, 77,* 191–199.

Sander, W. (1995b). Schooling and smoking. *Economics of Education Review, 14,* 23–33.

Schultz, T. W. (1961). Investment in human capital. *American Economic Review, 51,* 1–17.

Sewell, W. H., & Hauser, R. M. (1975). *Education, occupation, and earnings*. New York: Academic Press.

Sewell, W. H., & Hauser, R. M. (1980). The Wisconsin Longitudinal Study of social and psychological factors in aspirations and achievements. In A. C. Kerckhoff (Ed.), *Research in sociology of education and socialization, Vol. 1* (pp. 59–99). Greenwich, CT: JAI.

Smith, T. W. (1995). Some aspects of measuring education. *Social Science Research, 24,* 215–242.

Smith, T. W. (1997). Factors relating to misanthropy in contemporary American society. *Social Science Research, 26,* 170–196.

Spence, A. M. (1974). *Market signaling*. Cambridge, MA: Harvard University Press.

Taubman, P., & Rosen, S. (1982). Healthiness, education and marital status. In V. R. Fuchs (Ed.), *Economic aspects of health* (pp. 121–140). Chicago: University of Chicago Press.

Tzeng, M.-S. (1992). The effects of socioeconomic heterogamy and changes on marital dissolution for first marriages. *Journal of Marriage and the Family, 54,* 609–619.

Winkleby, M. A., Jatulis, D. E., Frank, E., & Fortmann, S. P. (1992). Socioeconomic status and health: How education, income, and occupation contribute to risk factors for cardiovascular disease. *American Journal of Public Health, 82,* 816–820.

Wolfinger, R. E., & Rosenstone, S. J. (1980). *Who votes?* New Haven, CT: Yale University Press.

Wozniak, G. D. (1987). Human capital, information, and the early adoption of new technology. *Journal of Human Resources, 22,* 101–112.

PART VI

POLICY IMPLICATIONS OF RESEARCH IN THE SOCIOLOGY OF EDUCATION

CHAPTER 23

Accountability in Education

Thomas B. Hoffer

The personal nature of many educational goals has always made the application of modern organizational theory a questionable tactic in both the study and the administration of schools and educational systems. Although few would question the standard of attaining measurable outcomes for capitalist enterprises and even for many government services, these notions can generate considerable ambivalence and even antipathy in the context of education. The scepticism notwithstanding, efforts to apply that standard to schools, to colleges, and to universities have rapidly grown.

Several aspects of this growth are of interest to sociologists. One is accounting for the growth itself: Why have efforts to formalize and expand accountability systems grown in recent years? Another concerns the implementation of accountability programs: What are the main lines along which educational institutions try to realize accountability, and what accounts for the differences among institutions? A third aspect of interest concerns the consequences—both intended and unintended—of accountability systems. This chapter provides an overview of the issues and research in these three areas of interest. The discussion is largely limited to public elementary and secondary school systems in the United States. To begin with, though, it is necessary to define more closely what is meant here by accountability and accountability systems.

INFORMAL AND FORMAL ACCOUNTABILITY

In its most general sense, accountability means giving a justification of what one has done. As such, schools and their staff have always had some form of accountability. Historical accounts

Thomas B. Hoffer • National Opinion Research Center, University of Chicago, Chicago, Illlinois 60637

Handbook of the Sociology of Education, edited by Maureen T. Hallinan. Kluwer Academic/Plenum Publishers, New York, 2000.

of school–community relationships often mention the responsiveness of school administrators and teachers to local community interests (see, e.g., Waller, 1932; for contemporary manifestations, see Lareau, 1989). The lack of boundaries and the resulting ability of local interests to control the schools was in fact an impetus to strengthen the power of educational professionals and bureaucracies vis-a-vis local political and business interests.

However, the key aspects of the ideal–typical traditional forms of accountability are that they are basically informal. Outcomes are not measured, performances are not gauged against codified standards, and organizational responses to acceptable or to unacceptable practices and results are not routinized. The focus of this chapter is specifically on the growth and consequences of formal accountability systems. As an ideal type, formal accountability systems consist of measured outcomes, codified outcome standards, and certain consequences for reaching or for not reaching the standards.

The focus on systems of accountability refers to linkages between schools and their environments. Public schools are typically embedded in formal organizational systems consisting of local districts and state educational systems. Accountability systems are devices for communicating information about the performance of schools to these higher levels of organization. As a system formalizes, the information is increasingly quantitative and methods of measurement are standardized. Educational accountability systems represent an example of what Espeland and Stevens (1998) referred to as commensuration, the comparison of different entities (e.g., students, schools, districts, or states) according to a common metric.

Accountability systems are intended to work as quality control mechanisms. In the current U.S. policy context, they can be viewed as an alternative to the kinds of market controls that an expanded system of school choice might provide (Ladd, 1996). The accountability system sends codified signals (e.g., test scores and dropout rates) about school effectiveness to education administrators and to external constituencies. A school choice system, in contrast, sends signals of client satisfaction in the form of enrollment decisions. Market systems may lead to signaling structures similar to those used in accountability systems, but this is not necessarily the case.

The idea of holding a school accountable for student outcomes immediately raises the question of how schools affect students. This is a question that sociologists of education have systematically worked on since the 1940s. The basic approach that has developed rests on a conception of the school as a purposive, goal-oriented organization. As such, the school is understood to transform inputs of various sorts into outputs through certain productive processes. Because outcomes are linked to inputs and to productive processes, it follows that accountability can be applied to all activities involved in the productive process, from the acquisition of resources to the teaching of particular concepts in a classroom.

The 1966 *Equality of Educational Opportunity* report, principally written by James Coleman, has likely been the single most important contributor to the conception of the school as a purposive, goal-oriented organization whose inputs and outputs can be quantified and compared. Coleman (1968) noted that school quality has historically been conceived mainly in terms of inputs. These include the number, experience, and training of teachers, and libraries, textbooks, computers, the school physical plant, and other material resources, as well as the skills and interests with which the students enter the school.

As Coleman (1968) argued, this conception of school quality has increasingly given way to the view that quality rests mainly in educational outcomes. Schooling outcomes are most commonly considered to consist primarily of students' academic skills and knowledge. To this, we can readily add course credits, degrees, and students' knowledge of the main postsecondary options available and their respective entry requirements. If one considers more closely what schools are most concerned with day-in and day-out, learning may be less than paramount and other outcomes may emerge as equally or as even more important. These additional goals include comportment (attendance, punctuality, and attentiveness) and students' health and safety during the school day.

A third class of variables, which we will call educational processes, is often added to the more familiar pair of inputs and outcomes. Processes refer to what Barr and Dreeben (1983) called the technology of schooling, and they include, most importantly, curriculum selection and sequencing, instructional grouping, and instructional practice or pedagogy. Policies related to educational processes focus mainly on curriculum, and they include required courses, topic coverage, and textbooks. The widely used concept of opportunity to learn (Dougherty, 1996; McPartland & Schneider, 1996) could alternately be used to describe most process variables.

The distinction between process and outcome variables often blurs, however, and indicators of these variables can be legitimately considered outcomes for many purposes. For example, the proportion of students completing eighth-grade algebra is a process indicator of middle-grade-level academic challenge, but it can also be treated as an outcome indicator of how far students have progressed in mathematics by the end of elementary school. Generally, the more that opportunity to learn overlaps with actual learning, the more blurred the distinction between mediating process variables and outcomes becomes. Despite the ambiguities, some recent proposals for accountability have advocated a focus on process variables, often under the rubrics of opportunity-to-learn, curriculum, and instruction standards (Smith, Scoll, & Link, 1996).

In one important respect, the conception of the school as a productive organization is limited. Students are legally obliged to attend school until (in most states) age 16, but they are not legally obliged to learn anything or to give evidence if they have learned something while there. In the final analysis, student outcomes are achieved by the students themselves, not by school systems, by schools, by curricula, or by their various agents. To claim that only these external factors are responsible for student outcomes is to underestimate the importance of students' choice and incentives (Bishop, 1996). As a practical matter, schools must engage in an array of activities to persuade students to cooperate with the organization's goal orientation. However, the dependence of school success on students' cooperation does not appear to be a factor that current accountability systems acknowledge beyond the attainment of minimal standards. Some economists have argued that the lack of attention to students' incentives is a serious limitation of current accountability efforts (Bishop, 1989).

In sum, accountability is not a new phenomenon in American education. The distinctive feature of current calls for greater accountability refer to formal accountability, typically involving quantification of student outcomes. The different sets of variables involved in producing student outcomes each point to different actors engaged in specific activities who are accountable for different things. Whereas accountability is most often discussed strictly in terms of measures of student outcomes, the concept of accountability can be equally applied to inputs and processes. Furthermore, formal accountability can be and increasingly is extended to the relationships of inputs to processes and to outcomes.

THE SCOPE OF CURRENT ACCOUNTABILITY SYSTEMS

The scope of an accountability system refers to who is held accountable by whom, for what, and with what practical consequences. The range of people involved in educational activities varies from one task or outcome to another, but it is potentially quite large. If an outcome such as academic achievement is considered, research supports the importance of school-level factors typically controlled by principals, class-level factors typically controlled by teachers, student-level factors of ability and effort, and family-level factors of parental support and encouragement (Darling-Hammond & Ascher, 1996). No current formal accountability systems include all of these relevant actors. Most include only the principal, some extend to teachers and students, and none include parents (Quality Counts, 1999).

Within formal accountability frameworks, principals are usually accountable for school average outcomes. These outcome variables include most prominently and commonly students' scores from select elementary and secondary grades on standardized achievement tests in mathematics, reading comprehension, science, and social studies. Other outcomes often measured include attendance, suspension, and high school dropout rates.

Formal standards on all of these outcomes vary from state to state, from district to district, and even from school to school within districts. In contrast to many other industrialized nations, the United States does not have national standards in any area of the elementary or the secondary school curriculum (Bishop, 1996). Nonetheless, considerable effort on the part of professional associations and foundations has gone into establishing national standards in recent years, and these have had considerable impact on state and on local standards.

The consequences of reaching or not reaching standards also vary considerably. In some cities, schools that fail to attain certain minimal levels of average student achievement are placed on probation. If a probationary school fails to surpass the minimum within a period of one or more years, the school is then dissolved and reconstituted with a new principal and new teaching staff. There are also numerous state and local data collection systems where data are placed in the public domain for whatever use or interpretation one might care to put to them. Sometimes these data are accompanied by evaluations that grade the school as a whole, as, for example, above average, average, or below average. In any case, these data may be widely publicized in newspapers and in other mass media and may be acted on by parents and businesses, but the consequences are largely of a market nature rather than formally organizational.

Standards and incentives for reaching them are rarely formalized for teachers. Teachers are rarely held responsible for student outcomes (Quality Counts, 1999). Exceptions are found in the localities where schools can be reconstituted. Some schools and districts have also attempted to establish merit pay systems tied to student outcomes in recent years, but these are few and hotly contested by the teachers' organizations.

Performance incentives for teachers are thus rare. Much more widespread have been efforts to standardize instructional practices, and particularly the curriculum. The subject-area professional teacher organizations of mathematics, science, English, and social studies have all issued comprehensive curriculum frameworks for grades K-12 since the late 1980s. These frameworks identify standards of concepts and skills that should be taught. Many state curriculum frameworks have borrowed heavily from the professional organizations. Teachers have little choice but to follow the curriculum frameworks established for their classes, because the texts the teachers must use are selected in terms of those frameworks.

Pedagogical technique is largely assessed by administrators during formal classroom observation sessions. The number of observations per year rarely number more than four classes per year for new teachers, and one or two per year for tenured faculty or, where tenure does not exist, for teachers with three or more years of experience. Observations usually are structured around checklists derived from popular conceptions of best practice.

At all levels of education, performance standards are most rigorously and systematically defined for students. Several states, including Texas and New York, have minimum competency test performance requirements for high school graduation. These and other states grant stratified diplomas, with the lowest being attendance and the highest indicating success in a college-preparatory curriculum. The Chicago Public Schools launched a system-wide policy of no social promotion in 1997, requiring eighth-grade students to score at least at the sixth-grade level on basic skills tests in reading and in mathematics. Students failing to attain that standard are required to attend summer school and to repeat the eighth grade if they fail the test after summer school.

System-wide student performance standards are usually, but not exclusively, defined for students at the low end of the achievement distribution. The New York State Regents system is the most comprehensive set of performance standards for higher achieving students. The Regents exams consist of end-of-course examinations that students must pass in order to attain high-level certification, and these certifications are required by the state university system. In all states, students also have incentives to achieve at higher levels because of university entrance requirements of high school course completions, preferences for students with higher college entrance exam scores, and preferences for students with higher class ranks.

How far that competition for selective college attendance extends, however, is not clear. Overall, the percentage of graduating seniors starting in a 4-year college or university in the year after high school is about 40%, whereas the percentage starting in nonselective 2-year community colleges is 22% (Smith, Young, Bae, Choy, & Alsalam, 1997). However, 4-year institutions themselves vary from relatively nonselective to highly selective, and the percentage of high school students who compete for places in the top tier is much less than 40%.

In sum, the scope of accountability systems in most contemporary American schools consists largely of informal feedback mechanisms whereby administrators', teachers', and students' performances are evaluated against commonsense conceptions of appropriate behavior. However, alongside and, to some extent, supplanting these informal arrangements is a significant formal apparatus of student assessments that is increasingly turned to for indications of system, school, and teacher effectiveness.

ACCOUNTING FOR THE GROWTH OF ACCOUNTABILITY SYSTEMS

The interest in formalizing accountability has been a regular feature of the American educational ideological landscape for most of the 20th century, and schools have routinely assessed the achievement levels of their students with standardized tests since the late 1950s. However, early interests in formalizing accountability systems made little headway, and tests scores were not used for measuring schools' effectiveness. Scores were instead used diagnostically to identify strengths and weaknesses of students, usually for the purposes of ability grouping and for college entrance. This changed dramatically in the 1980s, coinciding with the popularization of the idea that American schools were failing to provide adequate educations to many students. A principal vehicle of this view was the 1983 report of the National Commission on Excellence in Education, *A Nation at Risk*.

Why has the use of assessment data for accountability purposes grown? One line of explanation emphasizes how the culture of educational administration has promoted the growth of formalized accountability systems. Raymond Callahan, in his seminal *Education and the Cult of Efficiency* (1962), argued that much of the impetus toward systematic data collection and formal reporting mechanisms was the widespread belief among opinion leaders in the early decades of the 20th century that schools should be run like factories. Public school administrators were particularly vulnerable to external pressures to modernize schools, and thus adopted businesslike language and practices to legitimize themselves with the leaders.

Callahan (1962) argued that the formalizing and quantifying directions in education are fundamentally misguided and counterproductive. Callahan's main contentions are widely echoed in contemporary discourse. The argument is that education is not a mechanical activity, and efforts to make it mechanical undermine instruction and ultimately render it ineffective. School administrators should thus turn their attention fully toward the tasks of curriculum development and instructional leadership, and toward these ends the tools of quantification are largely useless. In short, educators need professional autonomy to be effective, and educational effectiveness is not a quantifiable entity.

The Callahan thesis identified the low power position of education administrators as a key factor in why they acquiesce to and even actively pursue external demands for quantification. A somewhat different perspective is suggested by Theodore Porter (1995) in *Trust in Numbers: The Pursuit of Objectivity in Science and Public Life*. Porter does not address education as a specific institutional case in his work, but his ideas are readily extended to education. His basic argument is that quantification is a way of resolving contested claims among parties separated by some social distance. As distance increases, trust becomes a more difficult and impersonal means of verifying performance claims that are sought. Formal accountability mechanisms are built on distrust, but they seek to re-establish trust on a new basis of objective evidence. Paradoxically, quantifying thus overcomes social distance and distrust, but it also creates distance by negating the force of personal testimony and other species of anecdotal and nonsystematic evidence (see Espeland, 1997, for an excellent exposition and elaboration of Porter's ideas).

How do these ideas apply to education? The transformation of primary and secondary education into mass institutions has had two important implications. One is that support of education has passed into the realm of municipal, state, and national governments and their respective taxation mechanisms. This has greatly expanded the constituencies of schools beyond the immediate sphere of families they serve, because money for operations comes from a much broader base of taxpayers and their elected representatives. Although the constituency of the schools has thus increased, most of those constituents have no immediate contact with the schools they are supporting. Education competes with other uses of tax dollars, and it thus needs to provide evidence that the public monies are being well used. This in turn leads to the growth of formal reporting mechanisms.

Other trends and developments have accelerated the movement toward formal accountability. The expansion and differentiation of higher education in the postwar era greatly increased the need for standardized information on the credentials of college applicants. As entrance testing rapidly grew, policy leaders turned to average SAT and ACT scores as indicators of assessing the quality of systems and of schools. The first nation's report card unveiled in the early 1980s used these data to compare state systems. The deficiencies of these scores for this purpose was readily apparent, and it was a strong impetus to expanding the National Assessment of Educational Progress (NAEP) to the state level in the late 1980s. However, the NAEP state assessments give little practical guidance to state and local officials, because the NAEP is a sample survey and does not report results for particular schools. The need for school-level information has fueled the great expansion of state testing programs.

The growth of regional and national labor markets also generates a need for efficient exchange of information about prospective employees. However, the kinds of information produced about individual students are rarely used by employers (Bishop, 1996; Miller, 1998; Rosenbaum & Binder, 1997). Probably more important to the expansion of accountability systems have been the effects of geographic mobility that modern labor markets encourage and require. Concretely, families typically want to know about the quality of public schools in communities in which they are considering residence. Without standardized forms of information, parents in that situation would face the alternatives of conducting time-consuming research or of risking even greater inefficiencies with trial-and-error methods. Similar information needs are faced by firms when deciding where to locate and recruit workers.

Recognizing the importance of such information, elected officials push for objective information about schools. If the information is favorable, it is a useful advertising tool for marketing the community. If the information is unfavorable, officials then have evidence of schools' shortcomings that can give them leverage over their school system.

Computer and information processing technology has made the compilation and distribution of data much easier and faster. The idea of annually compiling individual students' test scores for several grades and subject areas in a large school system was unthinkable in 1960. Internet technology has allowed most states and large local districts to make school-level and system-level performance reports readily available to private individuals and researchers.

To summarize, Porter's (1995) general argument about the growth of quantification strongly suggests that the movement to expand and improve accountability systems in education is not a passing fad instigated by wrong-headed elites. Whatever the shortcomings of past and current formal accountability systems, they can be traced back to informational needs of distant parties and to their inability to rely on informal and personal sources for that information. Where there is distance between the process of schooling and the constituencies of schools, trust will become problematic, and there will be pressure for quantification of the outcomes of the schooling processes. This points to two practical alternatives: formalize and quantify, or reduce the distance that calls them forth. There are clearly limits to the alternative of reducing distance, for the constituencies for information demand efficient forms of information and are unavoidably distributed over a wide geographic expanse in a modern society. The limits to formalization and quantification are less clear, but knowledge is growing as experience accumulates.

IMPLEMENTATION OF ACCOUNTIBILITY PROGRAMS

How do educational institutions try to realize accountability? The main instruments of accountability are the state assessments of student achievement. According to the most recent survey data, all but four states administered some form of statewide assessment during the 1995–1996 school year (Roeber, Bond, & Braskamp, 1997). Assessments generally are first made of students in the third or fourth grades and continue in most states through Grade 11.

Almost all student outcomes of interest are strongly correlated with family background variables of parental education, income, and socialization practices. Schools also affect the outcomes independently of family background, and the goal of an accountability system should be to identify the component of students' school outcomes that are attributable to their experiences in the school. This component is commonly referred to as the value added by the school, and its identification requires an initial stage of analysis. If one looks only at final results, then there are real risks that schools that have done a commendable job with initially low-achieving students will be overlooked, and schools that have done little with initially high-achieving students will be incorrectly labeled as successful (Meyer, 1996).

Ideally, schools would have measures of their students' knowledge and abilities when they start at a particular school and when they complete their studies at the school. If additional information on how much the students learned outside of school could also be obtained, then the value-added component could be directly estimated. The amount of learning outside of school is of course very difficult to measure, and researchers rely instead on factors presumed to be correlated with outside learning. These are typically parental education and income, and sometimes more subtle measures of parental support of learning are employed.

The ideal situation is currently very rare in American schools. Most schools have instead only single-time-point measures of performance and very limited information on their students' family backgrounds. The best that can be done in that case is to compare the single-time-point performance measures among schools that serve demographically similar kinds of students. Value added by the school is then estimated as the quantity above the average for schools enrolling similar students. The main problem with this method is that it is not possible to distinguish the portion of the value-added component that is due to the student's high school versus his or her elementary school, or to the elementary school versus the preschool.

Evidence on the validity and reliability of school performance assessments is notably absent from the research literature. Most states and localities have only cross-sectional school-level assessment data and a few measures of average student background. A few states and localities have longitudinal assessment data that allow for school-level analyses of test score gains. A very few localities have individual student-level data and longitudinal assessment programs, and these allow one to estimate models of school effects that are closest to current methodological ideals. However, it is unclear how likely inferences about relative school effectiveness will be in error under these different data regimes. This is a crucial practical question, because of increasing interest in using these data to judge job performances of administrators and of teachers, and because of the high costs of the methodological ideal.

Murnane (1996) suggested a useful strategy for addressing these issues, drawing on data from the small number of relatively complete databases. Using these data, one could first estimate the value-added component an outcome of interest for each school using the ideal model of matched samples with pretest and posttest scores and controls for social background variables. Schools would be ranked from highest to lowest on their estimated value-added components. Next, the value-added component would be estimated for the same set of schools using the overlapping but not fully matched pretest and posttest populations with background controls. The rank order of the schools from this estimation would then be compared with the rank ordering from the first estimation. To this comparison should be added a third, corresponding to the most common situation: value-added estimated with a cross-sectional measure of the student outcome, controlling only for students' social background. The rankings of the schools with respect to their value-added component may well differ under the different regimes, and it would be useful to not only document the differences but also try to identify specific conditions under which the rankings converge and diverge.

An initial effort in this direction is provided by Clotfelter and Ladd (1996), using data on the 1994 fifth-grade cohort from the entire state of South Carolina. Their analysis focused primarily on the correlations of various school performance measures with student demographic variables of percent minority and percent eligible for free or for reduced-cost lunch. They found that unadjusted, absolute test scores were most highly correlated with these measures of background. Scores measuring change from the fourth grade to the fifth grade, however, were also correlated positively with more advantaged backgrounds. This indicates that the most conservative strategy with respect to minimizing the chance of biases due to social background differences among schools is to adjust directly for background influences, rather than to rely on only pretest controls.

Identifying the relative value added by the schools allows one to assess the effectiveness of the schools, but it does not illuminate how the quality differences arise. Simply knowing how schools rank may be adequate for parents trying to choose a school, but is not very helpful to school administrators and teachers interested in improving their results (Willms, 1992). To gain an understanding of value-added differences among schools, it is necessary to identify characteristics of the schools that are associated with their effectiveness.

Reflecting the uncertainty that surrounds the mechanisms of school effectiveness, states and local school administrations generally do not systematically collect these kinds of explanatory data. Information about school characteristics can be obtained from surveys of principals, teachers, students, and parents. This kind of data collection has thus far been the dominion of outside researchers, and it is not yet a standard component of public accountability systems. The main sources of guidance for such data collection efforts are the national longitudinal studies conducted by the U.S. Department of Education. Exemplary efforts by researchers to collect systematic explanatory data that can be coupled with student assessment data in recent years are found in the work of the Consortium on Chicago School Research (Bryk, Sebring, Kerbow, Rollow, & Easton, 1998).

Important issues also surround the type of assessment instruments that are used to measure progress toward standards. The main controversy concerns the use of performance-based versus traditional assessments. The former refers to an assessment that calls for the actual performance of a skill and the creation of a response. Performance-based assessment systems may rely on cumulative portfolios of students' work, or they may require students to construct responses to questions in an examination context. It thus contrasts with what might be called traditional testing, whereby students are administered structured examinations that require selecting an answer from a list of provided response options.

Validity criteria are essential both to selection of individual items and to the whole set of items that make up an assessment. It is critical that assessments measure the full range of standards, rather than only the easiest or most difficult. In the United States, assessments designed to measure only the minimal standards have been employed by some states and localities in the past decades. These assessments may lead to a leveling-down of teaching and learning if only minima become the focus of these educational assessment systems. Comprehensive assessment systems avoid this danger.

The validity of an assessment can, and should be, evaluated in several ways. The most basic level of validity is face validity, whether the instrument in question appears to relevant parties as a reasonable measure of important standards. Researchers have developed several methods of gaining feedback from key groups on school assessments. Focus groups including teachers and experts involved in the articulation of standards can be helpful in screening the proposed assessment topics down to a manageable size that includes the most important topics. Other ways of gauging validity rely on data collected from the proposed items. Items and scales that are not correlated with relatively well-established outcomes or other factors are often found on closer scrutiny to be confusing or difficult to administer.

It is clear that validity issues lead directly to questions about what schools should be trying to teach and thus to an array of often contentious debates among social and political groups over the standards to be assessed. Much leeway is usually given to expert opinion by the public, but experts themselves often differ greatly in their views. Ultimately, political processes and organizational diversity (school choice) are turned to in order to adjudicate the conflicts.

In addition to being valid indicators, assessments must also be reliable. A reliable assessment consistently measures, across time and raters, what it is intended to measure. The reliability of items and of scales is normally assessed in terms of interrater agreement, internal consistency, and parallel form agreement. Reliability across raters is especially important and is problematic for assessment systems using portfolios and other forms of performance-based assessments (Koretz, 1996). As with the problems of validity, the problems of reliability are usually considered sufficiently important to warrant a pilot test of the instruments prior to the full implementation.

Even if the numerous measurement and analysis issues are resolved to the satisfaction of the various parties and the technical demands, it is not clear that the resulting accountability system would improve student outcomes. Coleman (1997) argued that American schools offer few incentives to teachers, to students, and to parents to realize higher levels of student achievement. He characterized the education system as often more concerned with fulfilling administrative procedural mandates rather than with improving student outcomes. Coleman traced this tendency to a general absence in American education of what he called external standards. External standards are established outside of classrooms instead of by the individual teachers within each class. They define what students should know and what they should be able to do at the end of levels of schooling (primary, middle, secondary) and at the end of courses within those levels. With outcome expectations unclear, teachers are placed in the untenable position of having to both establish standards and uphold them. This is untenable because standards are negotiated downward as teachers reduce demands in exchange for good behavior from the students.

Strong external standards are necessary but not sufficient to raise students' achievement levels. Coleman (1997) argued further that incentives for both attaining standards and for trying to attain them are also necessary. He proposes an output-driven model of school organization to implement the needed incentives as well as to provide the means for teachers and students to respond constructively to performance indications and thus attain the incentives. The output-driven school allocates rewards and punishments to teachers and to students at the end of each course and schooling level. These incentives are distributed on the basis of both absolute levels of achievement and value added from the previous course or schooling level.

The literature on the implementation of accountability systems indicates several general recommendations for the design of accountability systems. First, assessments should be built on specific outcome standards for each subject and grade level. Second, assessments should provide information both on the absolute levels of outcome attainment and on the students' growth. Third, the assessment system should provide sufficiently detailed feedback to school administrators and to teachers such that areas of success and failure can be clearly identified and acted upon at the school and the classroom levels. Fourth, the assessment system should provide the government and the public with valid and reliable summary information on outcomes for purposes of school evaluation. Fifth, incentives for schools, for teachers, and for students to attain educational goals should be identified and implemented. Sixth, the assessment system can be usefully strengthened with supplemental surveys of schools and of teachers to collect information on resource and practice differences associated with outcome differences.

These recommendations, it should be noted, are not fully implemented yet anywhere in the United States or elsewhere. They represent instead a summary of the recommendations that researchers and practitioners in the field have developed and are best viewed as a set of goals against which the available practical options in a given system can be defined.

CONSEQUENCES OF ACCOUNTABILITY SYSTEMS

Has the growth of accountability systems generally had a positive impact on American education? The expected positive consequences are that accountability for learning outcomes will lead to refined conceptions of goals; improved measures of goal attainment; greater attention to goals by administrators, by teachers, by parents, and by students; and higher outcomes. As we have seen, critics have noted deficiencies on each of these accounts, and they have argued further that the structure of incentives must change along with the information available.

The evidence on each of the assumed points is mixed. The point that seems most certain is that significant improvements have been realized in the conception of educational goals. Standards for outcomes and practice have been articulated by the main teaching professional associations in the subject domains, and these have worked their way in to the curriculum and the assessment programs of most states.

Measures of goal attainment have also generally improved. Most state departments of public education now have annual achievement testing programs for a subset of elementary and secondary grade levels, and the publicize school-average test scores. For the nation as a whole, the National Assessment of Education Progress (NAEP) has expanded to provide state-level reading and mathematics achievement scores that can be compared across states and over time.

The evidence is less clear whether administrators, teachers, parents, and students are paying more attention to goal attainments along the recommended lines of the accountability systems. In states and in localities with strong incentives for schools to realize minimally acceptable levels of average achievement scores, accountability systems have undoubtably served to focus principals' and teachers' attention on measured levels of goal attainment. Where students must attain certain levels of test scores to pass to the next grade or to graduate, standards and achievement are also of greater concern. However, these kinds of high-stakes situations are still relatively rare. Furthermore, the high stakes that have been implemented are not an issue for most principals, teachers, and students. This is because the minimal standards are not a challenge to any but the lowest achieving students. As we have seen, incentives for value-added improvements, which focus attention on the gains of all students, are only beginning to be implemented.

Finally, the evidence is even murkier concerning whether increased efforts to build accountability have had the ultimate desired effect of raising students' academic achievement. The most recent reports from the state-level NAEP assessments do show that mathematics achievement scores improved from 1990 to 1996 at all three grades assessed (Grades 4, 8, and 12). However, NAEP scores in reading did not improve over the same period (National Education Goals Panel, 1998).

The national-level evidence from the NAEP is inadequate for assessing the impacts of state and local accountability efforts. That is because these data cannot be analyzed in terms of variations among states in the nature and extent of accountability practices. It is thus possible that states with the strongest accountability programs are realizing substantial improvements in all subjects, and that further analysis of the extant data will show this. The state-level NAEP data that have begun to be collected in the 1990s should help to redress this problem as more data points become available. However, any effects of variations among districts within states are largely unknown and will remain so, because no comparable data were collected before and after the policy interventions.

It is also possible that an accountability system can have significant negative effects on school processes and outcomes. It should be noted that accountability systems are not neutral when no positive or negative effects on behavior are detectable, because the systems cost money to implement and to operate and would thus actually have a negative impact on the larger education system in which they are embedded. However, they can also have negative effects on behavior.

One way negative effects can occur is from the use of faulty tests. If unreliable or invalid identifications of school performance levels are made from a test, then the actual behavior of staff and students would not be measured by the test. This in turn could undermine beneficial efforts and reinforce ineffective practices. Similarly, if a test measures only a select subset of the standards set for the students, the test will encourage teaching to tests that are not good tests. This sort of bias is most likely to occur in the direction of encouraging rote memorization and recall versus teaching for understanding and for critical evaluation skills. This is simply because it is easier to write and grade tests of factual recall and recognition. In general, one can expect a leveling-down of teaching and learning when only minimal standards are established.

High standards and good tests may still have negative effects. Higher standards are intended to make school more difficult for most students. Whereas most students may respond with greater effort, some may find the challenges too great and higher dropout rates may result. Students who are especially challenged and unwilling to drop out may well need to spend more years in the school system, thus driving up educational costs.

Another set of potentially important consequences relate to the changing nature of teaching in schools with formal accountability systems. When standards are determined externally, teachers lose a measure of autonomy. As Coleman (1997) argued, this loss can be seen as the price of obtaining greater effort from students. In any case, the teacher who believes that he or she has a better set of standards or tests might not have the liberty to implement them as an individual agent. Although the use of external standards and the accompanying tests remove discretion and flexibility from individual teachers, systems can differ greatly in the extent to which they seek to gain and act on feedback from teachers. It is conceivable, for example, that mechanisms can be developed to obtain and to use feedback, thus encouraging a critical and innovative orientation among teachers. Coleman (1997) suggested that autonomy can be increased as an incentive for schools and for teachers to reach higher standards. Inability to develop such mechanisms could well lead to the diminished capacity of the teaching profession to attract talent.

CONCLUSIONS

School-level accountability for student achievement levels has grown rapidly in recent years and that trend is likely to continue. Despite the many shortcomings and even flaws in the current systems, the needs of parents, school administrators, and government agencies to have information on school performance are not going to disappear. Parents need to know whether a school is better or worse than the available alternatives for their children. School, district, and state administrators need diagnostic information to know whether their own schools are attaining standards expected by the communities they serve, and their jobs may well depend on that attainment. Elected officials need to know whether resources allocated to the schools are adequate and employed efficiently. The decisions made by these actors all involve value judgments and even political positions, but all involve matters of fact as well.

Formal accountability systems are developed to resolve distrust. They do not eliminate the need for trust of educators, but they instead change the terms on which trust is granted. As Porter (1995) noted, "The drive to eliminate trust and judgment from the public domain will never completely succeed. Possibly it is worse than futile" (p. 216).

Of all the main actors involved in education, teachers and students stand to benefit the least and bear the highest burdens from current assessment-based accountability systems. The main incentive currently available to students is the negative one of avoiding the sanctions of failing minimum-competency tests. For students not at risk of failure, there are no stakes on test performance. College entrance and curriculum tracking decisions are not made on the basis of accountability assessments, and students or their parents do not normally receive individual feedback on their assessed strengths and weaknesses.

One of the greatest challenges to formal accountability systems is to achieve a balance between good measurement and specificity of feedback to teachers. Insofar as good measurement entails samples of a comprehensive range of skills, the feedback to teachers becomes somewhat abstract. If the feedback is difficult to translate into specific lessons and concepts, then the test loses legitimacy because means of improvement are difficult to identify. On the other hand, if the feedback is specific and concrete, there is a risk that corrective actions will improve skills not sampled in the next assessment. There is also a risk that teaching and learning will become focused on the requirements of the tests as opposed to the subject matter more practically conceived. Neither alternative represents a benefit to teachers in their efforts to do their work more effectively.

School-average achievement test scores give little or no guidance to classroom teachers trying to assess and improve their effectiveness. School-level data aggregate information across classrooms and, unless a pretest–posttest design is used, they aggregate it across grades, as well. The contributions of individual teachers are thus thoroughly confounded with those of their colleagues and with out-of-school influences.

Standardized end-of-course examination systems such as the New York Regents system allow classroom-level assessments that can give teachers and administrators useful diagnostic information, while allowing for aggregation to the school level for external accountability. The main shortcoming of end-of-course scores is that the lack of a pretest makes it difficult to assess how much was learned from the class as opposed to previous classes, outside-of-school experiences, and ability differences among students. Pretests can of course be administered, but they are awkward because many—probably most—students will know little or nothing about a subject they have not yet taken. The pretest then becomes an empty formality.

A better control may be to use end-of-course exams from previous courses within a subject-area sequence. Unfortunately, those scores appear to be very rare. The current New York State data, for example, contain sequential data only in mathematics. However, even those scores are problematic because of incompleteness. The data have scores for Sequential Mathematics I and for Sequential Mathematics III, but none for the intermediate second level in the sequence. Controlling for the Course I score in an analysis of Course III outcomes would pick up initial differences due to the general ability factor but not those due to differences in success in Course II.

Coordinating courses into sequences of cumulative knowledge presents a major organizational challenge to schools with traditions of teacher autonomy. Teachers who feel their lessons are being scripted too closely by external agents may became less effective as their lessons become more mechanical and their resentment grows. Teacher buy-in to a coherent curriculum and accountability plan is thus important. However, most American schools now provide little or no time for teachers to coordinate and to plan as a group. An unanticipated result of efforts to rationalize the curriculum and to hold teachers accountable for it may be to promote the professionalism of teaching. The main alternative, to control teaching through bureaucratic mechanisms, may simply not be workable in the context of education.

The points made in this brief discussion of accountability should make it clear that, although probably unavoidable, summary accounts of what has been done with what results are necessarily complex and thus difficult to provide at levels of high quality in the context of education. Despite rapid advances, most state and local accountability systems are in their infancy and need considerable work in order to become more useful. Sociological analysis of accountability efforts has considerable potential to make positive contributions to understanding what kinds of information are needed by various actors and how best to obtain and disseminate it in terms of their various interests. This is not to pretend that there is one best way through the conflicting interests but rather to help the conflicting interests improve the factual bases of their claims.

REFERENCES

Barr, R., & Dreeben, R. (1983). *How schools work*. Chicago: University of Chicago Press.

Bishop, J. H. (1989). Why the apathy in American high schools? *Educational Researcher, 18*, 6–10.

Bishop, J. H. (1996). Signaling, incentives, and cchool organization in France, the Netherlands, Britain, and the United States. In E. A. Hanushek & D.W. Jorgenson (Eds.), *Improving America's schools: The role of incentives* (pp. 111–145). Washington, DC: National Academy Press.

Bryk, A. S., Sebring, P. B., Kerbow, D., Rollow, S., & Easton, J. Q. (1998). *Charting Chicago school reform: Democratic localism as a lever for change*. Boulder, CO: Westview Press.

Callahan, R. (1962). *Education and the cult of efficiency*. Chicago: University of Chicago Press.

Coleman, J. S. (1968). The concept of equality of educational opportunity. *Harvard Educational Review, 38*, 7–22.

Coleman, J. S. (1997). Output-driven schools: Principles of design. In J. S. Coleman, B. Schneider, S. Plank, K. S. Schiller, R. Shouse, & H. Wang (Eds.), *Redesigning American education*. Boulder, CO: Westview Press.

Coleman, J. S., Campbell, E. Q., Hobson, C. J., McPartland, J., Mood, A. M., Weinfeld, F. D., & York, R. L. (1966). *Equality of educational opportunity*. Washington, DC: U.S. Government Printing Office.

Clotfelter, C. T. & Ladd, H. F. (1996). Recognizing and rewarding success in public schools. In H. F. Ladd (Ed.), *Holding schools accountable: Performance-based reform in education*. Washington, DC: The Brookings Institution.

Darling-Hammond, L., & Ascher, C. (1996). *Creating accountability in big city schools*. New York: ERIC Clearinghouse of Urban Education at Teachers College, Columbia University.

Dougherty, K. J. (1996). Opportunity to learn standards: A sociological critique. *Sociology of Education (extra issue)*, 40–65.

Espeland, W. N. (1997). Authority by the numbers: Porter on quantification, discretion, and the legitimation of expertise. *Law & Social Inquiry, 22*, 1107–1133.

Espeland, W. N. & Stevens, M. L. (1998). Commensuration as a social process. *Annual Review of Sociology, 24*, 313–343.

Koretz, D. (1996). Using student assessments for educational accountability. In E. A. Hanushek & D. W. Jorgenson (Eds.), *Improving America's schools: The role of incentives*. Washington, DC: National Academy Press.

Ladd, H. F. (Ed., 1996). *Holding schools accountable: Performance-based reform in education*. Washington, DC: The Brookings Institution.

Lareau, A. (1989). *Home advantage*. New York: Falmer Press.

McPartland, J. M., & Schneider, B. (1996). Opportunities to learn and student diversity: Prospects and pitfalls of a common core curriculum. *Sociology of Education (extra issue)*, 66–81.

Meyer, R. H. (1996). Value-added indicators of school performance. In E. A. Hanushek & D. W. Jorgenson (Eds.), *Improving America's schools: The role of incentives*. Washington, DC: National Academy Press.

Miller, S. R. (1998). Shortcut: High school grades as an indicator of human capital. *Educational Evaluation and Policy Analysis, 20*, 299–312.

Murnane, R. J. (1996). Comments on chapters eight, nine, and ten. In H. F. Ladd (Ed.), *Holding Schools accountable: Performance-based reform in education*. Washington, DC: The Brookings Institution.

National Commission on Excellence in Education. (1983). *A nation at risk*. Washington, DC: U.S. Department of Education.

National Education Goals Panel. (1998). *Data volume for the National Education Goals report*. Washington, DC: U.S. Government Printing Office.

Porter, T. M. (1995) *Trust in numbers: The pursuit of objectivity in science and public life*. Princeton, NJ: Princeton University Press.

Quality Counts '99. (1999, January). Rewarding results, punishing failure (special issue). *Education Week, 18*.

Roeber, E., Bond, L., & Braskamp, D. (1997). *Annual survey of state student assessment programs fall 1996*. Washington, DC: Council of Chief State School Officers.

Rosenbaum, J. E., & Binder, A. (1997). Do employers really need more educated youths? *Sociology of Education, 70*, 68–85.

Smith, M. S., Scoll, B. W., & Link, J. (1996). Research-based school reform: The Clinton administration's agenda. In E. A. Hanushek & D. W. Jorgenson (Eds.), *Improving America's schools: The role of incentives*. Washington, DC: National Academy Press.

Smith, T. M., Young, B. A., Bae, Y., Choy, S. P., & Alsalam, N. (1997). *The condition of education 1997*. Washington, DC: National Center for Education Statistics.

Waller, W. (1932). *The sociology of t eaching*. Chicago: University of Chicago Press.

Willms, J. D. (1992). *Monitoring school performance: A guide for educators*. Washington, DC: Falmer Press.

Tribute to David Lee Stevenson

David Lee Stevenson died of heart disease on March 1, 1999 at the age of 47. David was a senior policy advisor to Acting U.S. Deputy Secretary of Education Marshall Smith, and most recently served as Assistant Director for Social and Behavioral Sciences in the Office of Science and Technology Policy in the Executive Office of the President. David's responsibilities included helping to develop legislation and policy for elementary and secondary education. He worked on numerous legislative proposals, including the Improving America's Schools Act, the Goals 2000 Act, and the Class Size Reduction Act, as well as the Department's education technology initiatives.

David also served as Deputy Executive Director of the congressionally established National Council for Education Standards and Testing which issued the report, "Raising Standards for American Education." This report developed the standards-based model of reform that was the framework for the reauthorization of the Elementary and Secondary Education Act and numerous state and local reform efforts.

David's many articles on the social development of youth, the social organization of schooling, and education policy appear in numerous books and journals. His most recent book, co-authored with Barbara Schneider, is *The Ambitious Generation, America's Teenagers: Motivated but Directionless* (April 1999, Yale University Press).

In commenting on David's impressive professional accomplishments, President Bill Clinton wrote, "As an educator, mentor, researcher, and policymaker, David made important and lasting contributions to the quality of education in our nation. . . . David's vision for American education, his dedication, and his leadership will have a lasting impact on the lives of students across our nation." U.S. Secretary of Education Richard W. Riley observed, "David made an important contribution in many different areas—teaching, legislation, policy, research, standards, and testing. He was a great friend of children and learning." Acting U.S. Deputy Secretary of Education Marshall Smith commented, "I have encountered few individuals as committed to helping children and improving education as David Stevenson—his professional accomplishments in policy development and research are truly remarkable."

David's death saddens his colleagues and friends, many of whom are authors of chapters in this Handbook. In a way, it is fitting that David's contribution appears as the final chapter. His work provides important guidelines to sociologists of education about how to increase the impact of their research on education policy. His intellectual contributions will be missed. Even more, he will be missed as a gifted, gentle, and loyal friend.

Maureen T. Hallinan

CHAPTER 24

The Fit and Misfit of Sociological Research and Educational Policy

David Lee Stevenson†

Sociologists studying education frequently ask how their research can be more influential in policymaking. This concern is reflected in the presidential address at a recent meeting of the American Educational Research Association: "I worry that current waves of education policy are neither informed by some educational research nor researchers" (Peterson, 1998, p. 4). My argument in this chapter is that social science research influences education policymaking often and in fundamental ways. This influence may be unnoticed by some researchers because it occurs in the less visible process of policy development rather than the more public debates of partisan legislative politics. By the time that policy initiatives become part of the grist of legislative politics, the importance of research findings in the policy debate often recedes and is replaced by political arguments and tradeoffs.

Although there are studies of how social science research influences the decision-making process (Weiss & Bucuvalas, 1980), less has been written about the role of social science research in education policy development, especially in comparison to the extensive literature on the implementation of policies and the consequences of education policies (McLauglin, 1985). In this chapter, I draw on over a decade of experience participating in and observing the development of federal educational policies. The chapter is divided into three parts. I begin with a brief description of the role of social science research in influencing both the public presentation of and the design of public policies. The second section, which is the main body of the chapter, is a description of four recent policy initiatives in education (comprehen-

†Deceased.

DAVID LEE STEVENSON • Office of Science and Technology Policy, Executive Office of the President, Washington, DC 20502

Handbook of the Sociology of Education, edited by Maureen T. Hallinan. Kluwer Academic/Plenum Publishers, New York, 2000.

sive school reform, standards-based reform, class-size reduction, and classroom technology), and an analysis of how the development of these four policies was influenced by research. In the third section, I suggest some reasons for why certain types of social science research are more influential than others in the policy development process.

POLICY AND SOCIAL SCIENCE RESEARCH

Social science research has been a foundational core for how policymakers view education, in particular its importance for the creation of human capital and the life chances of individuals (Becker, 1964; Jencks et al., 1972, 1979; Schultz, 1961; Sewell, Hauser, & Featherman, 1976). Findings from detailed empirical studies of the role of education in social mobility and for the system of occupational stratification are part of policymakers' fundamental understandings of the importance of education for individuals. These findings help sustain the interests of policymakers in equitable access to education and, increasingly, in access to quality education. Policymakers' understanding of how students pass through the educational system and how these passages are organized are based on broad sociological descriptions of the operation of the U.S. educational system. These include studies of ability grouping (Alexander & Entwisle, 1996; Dreeben & Barr, 1988; Hallinan & Sørenson, 1983, 1987), curricular differentiation (Alexander, Cook, & McDill, 1978; Gamoran, 1987; Stevenson, Schiller, & Schneider, 1994), college completion (Velez, 1985), and dropping out of high school (Natriello, 1987; Natriello, McDill, & Pallas, 1990). Such descriptive studies, which comprise much of the standard empirical work of sociologists of education, have become the background knowledge for policymakers. Their main effect on policymaking is to provide a research-based framework for policy formulations and to keep visible certain issues, such as differences in learning opportunities, and, thereby, to influence which topics are likely to be addressed. Social science research, however, can and sometimes does have a more direct effect on policymaking. To examine this topic, this chapter focuses on the development of policies rather than the legislative process (Jennings, 1998) or on issues of implementation (Elmore, 1980; McLaughlin, 1987; Pressman & Wildavsky, 1973). There are two major aspects of the policy development process that are influenced by research findings: the creation of a public rationale for the policy and the design of the policy.

The articulation of a persuasive public rationale is a key element in the development of an educational policy. Policies require an argument about their need and their potential effectiveness. Social science research can shape the vocabulary; the content, and the persuasiveness of the public rationale. As an illustration, I use the proposal of the Clinton Administration to develop voluntary national tests in fourth-grade reading and eighth-grade mathematics. A policy rationale is likely to include several elements: a description of what the policy is (voluntary national tests in reading and mathematics), an argument about why it is necessary (performance of students is too low), and a description of what the policy would accomplish (provide accurate information to teachers and parents that would lead to improvements in teaching and in learning).

Policymakers attempt to describe policies with a vocabulary that is easily understood and does not have narrow technical meanings. In the field of education, this can be surprisingly difficult—even terms such as "basic skills" are loaded with different and conflicting meanings to different audiences. The vision of what the policy would accomplish often identifies the policy levers of change. In the case of the voluntary national tests, the levers were setting clear standards of performance, providing detailed information to teachers and to parents about the performance of students (including students' performance on every test item), and making all of the test items publicly available so that teachers, parents, and students could see the content of what was being tested. The overall lever of change was detailed information that would lead teachers to reexamine their instructional practices and would enable parents and students to better understand the standards of performance and how students performed against these rigorous standards (Smith, Stevenson, & Li, 1998). Several elements of the rationale were based on empirical research findings: students' performance in reading has not improved in recent years (based on findings from the National Assessment of Educational Progress), early reading is an important predictor of later school success, performance of American students in middle school mathematics is poor compared to students in other countries (based on the results from the Third International Mathematics and Science Study), and the content and design of tests can influence instruction and learning.

A second aspect of policy development is the design of the policy. Policies vary in their degree of complexity. Some policies use rather simple levers. Examples of such policies are those designed to increase high school graduation requirements or to decrease class sizes in the early elementary grades. Policies with limited designs and a narrow focus are able to draw on a more discrete, limited research base and, as a result, can be more tightly tied to research evidence. The voluntary national tests, for example, relied on research on the current uses of assessments, on how assessments have influenced classroom instruction and learning, and the relationship between standards and assessments (Baker, 1994). More substantively complex policies, such as standards-based reform policies, are more likely to draw on a range of studies that address different aspects of the policy. Regardless of the complexity of the design of the policies, policies are rarely empirically based on the findings of a single study. Policies are more likely to be based on empirical evidence derived from numerous studies that provide a set of generally consistent findings with policy implications. Because policies are based on accumulated evidence rather than on findings of a specific study, they can be portrayed as loosely rather than tightly linked to specific pieces of social science research. This loose fit is an adaptive accommodation. Seldom are policies designed based on the findings of a single study, even a large-scale well-designed study. The generalizability and validity of the findings from any single study can be, and often are, challenged because of limitations of the sample, the design, or the methods of analysis. The standards of social science research for research used for policy purposes can be extraordinarily high, particularly if the policy is a politically contentious one. And, therefore, against such standards many excellent academic studies would be considered as flawed and inadequate. Consequently, there are strong incentives to draw on numerous studies and to base policies on results from a line of inquiry rather than on findings from a particular study.

Empirical Research, Public Rationales, and Policy Complexity

Differences in the relationship between empirical research and two aspects of policy the creation of a public rationale for the policy and the design of the policy—are illustrated in Figure 24.1 for four current educational reform policies: comprehensive school reform, standards-based reform, class-size reduction, and technology in classrooms.

These four policy initiatives differ in the strength of their empirical research base and their public rationale. Comprehensive school reform has a strong empirical research base and a less obvious public rationale. Standards-based reform has an average empirical research base and public rationale. Class-size reduction has both a strong research base and a strong

	Research Evidence	Public Rationale	Policy Complexity
Strong	Comprehensive School Reform Class Size Reduction	Technology Class Size Reduction	Standards Based Reform
Medium	Standards Based Reform Technology	Standards Based Reform	Comprehensive School Reform
Weak		Comprehensive School Reform	Class Size Reduction Technology

FIGURE 24.1. Research evidence and policy development for four educational reforms.

public rationale. Finally, technology in the classroom is the middle on its empirical base and high on its public rationale. What we do not have is a policy initiative that is weak in both its empirical basis as well as in its public rationale. Such policies are least likely to be seen as educationally and politically viable and, therefore, are unlikely to be proposed, and if proposed are not likely to exist for very long.

Figure 24.1 also displays the relationship between public rationales, empirical research, and the substantive complexity of the policy initiative. The most substantively complex policy initiative—standards-based reform—has neither strong public rationales nor a strong empirical research base. Substantively complex policies are likely to be more difficult to explain and are more likely to be loosely connected to a body of empirical research because it is less likely that a series of studies or a limited single line of inquiry is directly supportive of the policy. As these four cases illustrate, the relations of these three major components of a policy—the strength of its public rationale, the substantive complexity of the policy, and the strength of the research evidence—vary across policies. To provide insights into how these interrelationships play out in policy development, I describe the policy development process for each of these policies. The descriptions vary in their character and their length, which reflects the complexity and diversity of the policy development process.

FOUR POLICY INITIATIVES

Comprehensive School Reform

Since the late 1950s, the reform of American education primarily focused on schools as the unit of change. The large literature on school effectiveness has been built, at least in part, on the notion that schools are units of reform and that there is a model or models for how effective schools work (Glennan, 1998; Purkey & Smith, 1983). This research effort dramatized differences among schools and searched for pieces of evidence that some schools were more effective than others. When equity was a concern, it was expressed as either creating racially balanced schools (Coleman et al., 1966), equalizing funding across schools (Wise, 1968), or narrowing the gap in academic performance among schools (Newmann, 1989).

This long American tradition of reforming education one school at a time continues today. In 1991, the Bush Administration announced the creation of the New American Schools Development Corporation (NASDC), which would seek to develop new models of what high-performing schools could look like. With some initial funding from corporations, and later a $50 million gift from the Annenberg Foundation, NASDC funded the development of seven models of school reform. These models incorporate and expand existing models of school reform such as the School Development Program (Comer, 1997), Accelerated Schools Project (Levin, 1987), Success for All (Slavin, Madden, Dolan, & Wasik, 1996) and Coalition for Essential Schools (Sizer, 1991). Through the efforts of NASDC and others these school reform programs have been adopted in numerous elementary and secondary schools.

In 1997, Congress passed and President Clinton signed into law the Comprehensive School Reform Demonstration Project Act (CSRD). This initiative sought to promote school reform efforts built on the research base that had been established by detailed studies and evaluations of effective elementary and secondary schools. Financial incentives were provided to schools with low levels of student achievement, particularly schools in high-poverty areas. The improvement in students' achievement was to occur through comprehensive school reform that would involve virtually every aspect of teaching and learning, including professional development for school staff, the implementation of a coherent curriculum, and increased parental and community involvement. Like other federal programs, such as Title I, the goal for schools was to develop a comprehensive reform that would enable all children to meet challenging state content and performance standards. Comprehensive school reform was designed to replace a more limited piecemeal approach to school change.

The empirical research base for CSRD consisted of the cumulative findings of studies on effective schools and effective school programs. In the fall of 1990, the U.S. Department of Education awarded two contracts to study promising services funded under Chapter 1 (U.S. Department of Education, 1997b). These studies described alternatives to current Chapter 1 practices, compared promising alternatives to traditional practices, and assessed the replicability of programs. A major finding of the study was that students in schools involved in whole school reform were more likely to achieve greater academic gains than students in schools using pullout programs.

The CSRD legislation sought to put these and other research results on effective schools into widespread practice (Cohen, 1983). Schools could select from proven or promising whole school reform models and tailor them to the schools' individual needs. The comprehensive school reform models mentioned in the legislation included Authentic Teaching and Learning for All Students (ATLAS), Audrey Cohen College System of Education, Coalition of Essential Schools, Co-NECT Schools, Expeditionary Learning Outward Bound, Modern Red Schoolhouse, National Alliance for Restructuring Education, Roots and Wings, School Development Program, Talent Development Model for High Schools, and Urban Learning Centers (Department of Education Appropriations Act, 1998).

The design of CSRD demonstrates the difficulty of developing a strong public rationale for a policy based on the effective schools research. The research tradition has been responsible for the development of different methods of comprehensive school reform and each type of school reform has its own language that describes what it does. Often the language is not consistent across programs and similar terms can be used in very different ways. Also, the evaluations of the programs have revealed that small differences in the administration of the programs can create noticeable differences in their outcomes (Glennan, 1998). The sensitivity of the programs to issues of implementation pushes each program to use a vocabulary that becomes more precise and program specific. The lack of a strong common vocabulary makes it difficult to create strong and compelling language about what the comprehensive school reform would do and what kinds of reforms need to be undertaken. This is evident in a description of the seven comprehensive projects featured in the legislation and funded by NASDC: "The designs range from those that provide clear guidance for classroom organization and instructional materials to those that specify broad principles and key curricular and pedagogical practices but leave the specifics to the school" (Glennan, p. 22).

CSRD is an interesting example of how a strong research base did not generate a strong public rationale. In the absence of a strong common vocabulary, the policy does not focus on the general promotion of comprehensive school reform but rather on the adoption of specific research-based models of school reform. What is common about these programs is that they share the goal of helping all children reach higher levels of achievement and that they are research-based. The effective schools research literature is large and complex but has not generated a theoretical or conceptual framework that is widely shared. Without such a framework, it is difficult to explain policies and to create a school-based reform policy. The effective schools literature, however, has been the source for the development of school reform models and the policy, therefore, focuses on the adoption of developed models. The character of the research base directly influenced the public rationale for the policy as well as the content of the policy.

Standards-Based Reform

Standards-based reform is the dominant policy paradigm for improving elementary and secondary schooling. It also is an interesting example of the use of social science research in the development of policy. The placement of standards-based reform in Figure 24.1 indicates that the policy has neither a strong empirical research base nor a strong public rationale. Of all four policies, however, it is the most substantively complex. Despite this, it has become a reform policy that has led to the redesign of the federal elementary and secondary education programs and has become a stimulus for many state and district efforts.

Central to the standards-based model of reform is the idea of academic standards that define what students should know and be able to do and the alignment of other policies to help students reach these standards. The development of the standards-based model has a rich and complex history (Jennings, 1998; Ravitch, 1998; Riley, 1991). I can only attempt to provide a brief history that focuses on the public rationale for standards-based policies, how the standards-based model of reform policies developed, and its relationship to empirical research.

Most of the effective schools research was conducted on samples of public schools until Coleman and his colleagues (Coleman & Hoffer, 1987; Coleman, Hoffer, & Kilgore, 1982) began comparisons of private and public schools using the U.S. Department of Education's *High School & Beyond* data set (Calvin, Clarke, Mooney, McWilliams, Crawford, Stephenson, & Tournangeau, 1983). The debate began to shift from how public schools were different from each other to why private schools were different from public schools. The differences between the private and public sectors became sources for the explanations of the differences. The sources of such differences might exist in the social capital created by parents being able to choose their children's schools (Coleman, 1988) or in private schools' freedom from some forms of regulation (Chubb & Moe, 1990).

Most of the school effectiveness studies, whether on differences among public schools or between private and public schools, had been conducted by sociologists, by anthropologists, by political scientists, or by organizational theorists. The focus had been on explanations at the organizational level, and the measures of effectiveness had typically been standardized multiple-choice assessments that in most cases were not aligned with the content of instruction. Neither the types of assessment or the lack of alignment between the assessment and the content of classroom instruction were viewed as serious problems because standardized tests were widely used and were increasingly used for purposes of school accountability. Through private–public school comparisons, the effective school literature had opened the door to policy environment explanations for the poor performance of schools. However, the explanations tended to stop at the level of providing schools with regulatory relief, allowing school professionals greater autonomy in school-based decisions and permitting parents and students to choose their schools. The technical core of schooling—learning and instruction—remained beyond the bounds of the organizational critique of schools.

Whereas the effective school literature was growing, cognitive science had been developing very different understandings of how students learn and how instruction needed to be redesigned. The learning theory critique of current school practice was powerful because it, in essence, stated that the current methods of instruction and learning were seriously flawed (Resnick & Cropfer, 1989). Current practice went against research evidence about how students learn. Instruction needed to be radically overhauled from constant drill and practice instruction that focused on memorization and on the recitation of facts outside of their context to instruction for understanding that would help the student to think critically and to develop the capacity to solve complex problems.

Although such critiques of instruction and learning had been articulated previously, the theoretical developments and the empirical evidence were increasing, and the learning critique began to resonate with policy concerns about the productivity of schooling. First, the results from the National Assessment of Educational Progress continued to show little progress in students' performance between the 1970s and the early 1990s (National Center for Education Statistics, 1998). Second, the international assessments in mathematics and in science consistently showed U.S. students being outperformed by students in other countries, particularly economic competitors such as Japan (Keeves, 1992).

The learning critique of instructional practice was embodied, to a significant degree, in the curriculum evaluation standards of the National Council of Teachers of Mathematics (NCTM, National Council of Teachers of Mathematics, 1989). The NCTM Standards prescribed a radical overhaul of mathematics education and argued for the incorporation of new understandings of how students learn and how instruction should be organized. The ability to communicate about mathematics and to generate solutions to complex problems was seen as central to effective instruction and to students' learning. Such a change in mathematics education would require forms of assessment that were different from the traditional multiple-choice formats. The emphasis on students showing their work and on providing solutions to problems with multiple answers was beginning to change the dialogue about student assessment. The development of the NCTM standards was a significant achievement because it was not advocacy for change at the margins but, rather, it called for a dramatic change in mathematics education. The NCTM Standards became a model for standard setting that embodied an understanding of how students learn and the organization of the discipline of mathematics.

Although the research on why schools were not more effective had begun to include discussion of the policy environment and had begun to redefine how instruction and learning should take place within schools, there was not a policy framework with political support. To develop such a framework required a bipartisan setting where there was a need for building understandings across party lines and a need to produce policy documents that would articulate this consensus. The work of the Governors and the National Governors' Association (NGA) became central to this effort. In the fall of 1989, President Bush invited the nation's governors to an Education Summit at Charlottesville, Virginia. This was the beginning of the process of establishing a set of national education goals that were formally agreed to in January, 1990 (National Education Goals Panel, 1991). The six national education goals were stated in terms of outcomes, and the preamble of the document stressed how there would be many ways that states and local districts could reach the goals. The agreement that created the goals also called for the creation of a National Education Goals Panel, composed of governors and administrative officials, to monitor the progress of the nation and the states toward the goals.

Although the initial discussions of the Panel were about what constituted valid indicators of the nation's progress toward the national goals, the dominant issue in the Panel's discussion became how to measure and promote reaching the student achievement goals. To provide advice about the selection and development of indicators, the Panel created resource groups of national experts, many of whom were researchers. The papers from the resource group for the student achievement goal described the need to develop a set of national standards and a system of assessments that were aligned with these standards (National Education Goals Panel, 1991). Much of the public response to the Panel's conversation and to the national education goals focused on whether there should and would be national academic standards and a national test. National testing received a further push from the Bush Administration's America 2000 proposal that advocated the development of national standards and of American Achievement Tests, although the specifics of what these tests would be and how they would work were not described in the initial policy proposal (U.S. Department of Education, 1991).

Most of the discussion of national standards and assessments had occurred without the participation of Congress or legislative actions. An exception was the legislation that created the National Council on Education Standards and Testing. The Council was established to determine the feasibility and desirability of establishing voluntary national standards and a system of assessments. Established in June of 1991, the Council issued its report on January 24, 1992. (National Council on Education Standards and Testing, 1992) The report recommended that there be voluntary national standards and a national system of assessments tied to those standards. It also stressed the need for assessments to address important technical issues of reliability, validity, and fairness, particularly when the results of the assessments were used for high-stakes purposes for students or for educators.

The Council's report served as the policy formulation for standards-based reform and provided a blueprint for coherent policy changes across a range of areas. Its central purpose was not only to raise students' achievement but also to redefine the kind of student achievement that was desired. It was not possible to meet the purpose of standards-based reform without providing standards of what students should know and should be able to do without developing methods of assessing students' progress toward these standards. Other policies, such as professional development and accountability, were therefore evaluated in terms of their contribution to helping students reach the standards of achievement. In early 1993, the

Clinton Administration introduced Goals 2000: Educate America Act to promote standards-based reform in states and in local districts.

The standards-based model is essentially a systemic model for reforming state educational systems (Resnick & Tucker, 1992; Smith & O'Day, 1991). There is, however, an absence of strong empirical sociological research on state educational systems or on how state educational systems change. Sociological empirical research has tended to focus on schools as organizations or, descriptions of the national educational system. This pattern reflects the data collection of the National Center for Education Statistics of the U.S. Department of Education. The large longitudinal studies of high school and middle school students (National Longitudinal Study of 1972, High School & Beyond (Ricobson, Henderson, Burkeheimer, Place, & Levinsohn, 1981) and the National Educational Longitudinal Study of 1988–94) have been designed to provide data for school and for national analyses and have not had appropriate samples for analyses of state educational systems. The prospects for more systematic analyses of state educational systems, however, are improving. The redesign of the School and School Staffing Survey will yield better data on state representative samples of schools and teachers and the developing state NAEP data provides us with better information on the academic achievement of students. In addition, states are participating in the second data collection of the Third International Mathematics and Science Study, which will allow more detailed information on how states organize mathematics and science instruction.

The development of a standards-based reform model has stimulated research. For example, Coleman and his colleagues developed an argument for output-driven educational systems with implications for policy discussions of how to raise academic performance by providing flexibility in how schools can organize their work and accountability for results (Coleman, et al., 1997). This article outlines a model that includes the option for students to exit low-performing schools. Another set of empirical studies of standards-based reform by Bishop that examines the achievement of students in different Canadian provinces and the nature of the provincial assessment system (Bishop, 1997).

Standards-based reform is the most influential elementary and secondary education reform policy of the 1990s. It is an interesting policy case not only because of the breadth of the reforms it encourages and the breadth of the research evidence that it integrates, but also because it was developed and refined outside of a legislative context. The involvement of politicians including governors and members of Congress—in the work of the National Education Goals Panel and the National Council on Education Standards and Testing—permitted the development of a standards-based model that was substantively complex. The breadth and complexity of the standards-based reform policies drew on the work of researchers, whether it was setting standards for what students should know and should be able to do, changing professional development policies, or improving the nature and content of assessments.

The breadth and the complexity of the vision made it difficult to provide an easily understood public rationale for the reform efforts. The initial stumbling block was attempting to introduce the word "standard" into the public discourse about school reform. There was agreement that we should have standards, but there was less agreement as to how to define standards, who should set them, and why they might be important. The rationale that standards would lead to improvements in students' achievement and that they were necessary to bring coherence to policy goals was even more difficult to explain.

Although the standards-based model of reform drew on several different lines of research including cognition, teaching, policy, and sociology, there was no single study or set of studies of standards-based reform. In contrast to the examples of comprehensive school reform, there were no U.S. examples of standards-based reform to study. The absence of an easily understood public rationale and of strong empirical research studies of standards-based reform complicated efforts to incorporate standards-based reform into educational policies. The long policy incubation period provided an opportunity to build a deeper policy framework that was useful in the passage of federal legislation, such as Goals 2000: Educate America Act of 1994 and the Improving America's Schools Act of 1994. This federal legislation helped to institutionalize a standards-based model of state and local reform. Research played a fundamental role in defining the policy debate, but the development of standards-based reform policies could not be based on a single study or series of studies. The complexity of the policy required that it be based on a broad reading of the empirical research record.

Class-Size Reduction

A recent policy initiative adopted by numerous states and promoted by the U.S. Department of Education is to reduce the size of classes in the early elementary school grades. There is a large research literature on the effects of different class sizes on the academic achievement of students. In fact, the literature is sufficiently large to have generated a series of reviews and meta-analyses of previous studies (Glass, Cahen, Smith, & Filby, 1982; Glass & Smith, 1978; Hanushek, 1998; Mitchell, Carson, & Badarak, 1989; Odden, 1990; Robinson & Wittebols, 1986; Slavin, 1989; Tomlinson, 1988; Wenglinsky, 1997).

As in other areas of empirical education research, the effects of class size on students' achievement have been intensely debated. Unlike other research areas, however, there recently have been studies of large-scale implementations that have generated findings that have informed both the debate and the development of class-size reduction policies. One of the most rigorous of these studies is Tennessee's Project STAR (Student–Teachers Achievement Ratio). STAR was a 4-year longitudinal study of the effects of class-size reduction on students' achievement in kindergarten, in first grade, in second grade and in third grade. The study is notable for its size (over 7,000 students in 300 classrooms in 79 schools participated) and for the random assignment of teachers and students to reduced-sized or to regular-sized classes. The findings have been consistent with findings from other large-scale implementations (Center for School Assessment, 1986).

In the STAR study, students in smaller classes performed better on the reading achievement tests (Stanford Achievement Tests) and on curriculum-based tests (Basic Skills First) than students in regular-sized classrooms. These differences were found for White and for minority students as well for students in different geographical locations (urban, rural, and suburban). Students in smaller classes were less likely to be retained in the same grade at the end of the year and were more likely to be identified as having special educational needs. The gains in achievement for students in smaller classes were about double for minority students compared to majority students (Achilles, Nye, Zaharias, Fulton & Cain, 1996; Finn, 1998; Mosteller, 1995). These class-size reduction effects occurred without teachers of the small classes having any additional professional development in how to teach more effectively in smaller classes. At the end of third grade, students from smaller classes returned to regular-sized classrooms and the researchers continued to assess their academic achievement. The achievement differences between students in smaller classes and those in regular classes in the early grades were still evident in eighth grade although the size of the difference had diminished.

Part of the debate about smaller classes focuses on how small the classes have to be to show achievement gains for minority students and at what grade levels. From the research evidence, some have concluded that 15 to 18 students per class is the size needed to show achievement gains; these gains appear to be greatest in the early elementary school grades (U.S. Department of Education, 1998). The class-size debate has generated an additional line of argument that class-size reduction policies are not the best expenditure of additional funds and that the funds could be spent in other ways that would generate larger gains in students' achievement. Some of the alternatives suggested are wider support for comprehensive school reform, more investment in the training of teachers (Hanushek, 1998), and hiring classroom aides (Odden, 1990). The difficulty of each of these alternatives is that there is no strong empirical evidence from large-scale implementations that these initiatives will produce similar gains in students' achievement.

From a policy development perspective, it is not difficult to develop a strong public rationale for smaller classes. With children of the baby boom echo entering the school system in increasing numbers, there has been widespread crowding in elementary schools both in the cities as well as in the suburbs (U.S. Department of Education, 1997a). A policy for reducing class size in the first three grades of elementary school to boost the early achievement of students and to provide a better foundation in fundamental skills has a compelling rationale.

Despite the simplicity of class size initiatives, they can create unanticipated and undesired effects in their implementation. California was one of the first states to initiate a class-size reduction program in 1996–1997. The average elementary classroom in California had about 30 students, and the class size reduction initiative mandated a reduction to 20 students per class. California schools differed significantly in their physical capacity to create new classrooms to handle smaller classes with urban schools having problems finding space for new classrooms. The creation of smaller classes also increased the demand for early elementary school teachers and the urban schools were more likely to hire inexperienced and uncertified teachers to meet their demand. These schools were also experiencing an exodus of teachers (Bohrnstedt & Parrish, 1998; McRobbie, 1997).

The Clinton administration has proposed a Class-Size Reduction and Teacher Quality Act to reduce the national average class size in Grades 1 to 3 to 18 students. The goal of 18 students per class would be reached gradually over 7 years. The proposal also addresses the need for helping teachers learn how to more effectively teach in smaller classes and the need to help new teachers meet the state's certification requirements. It allows states to spend up to 15% of their funds an various forms of professional development so that the objective of having a well-prepared teacher in every reduced-size class can be met. Class-size policies are a good example of a narrow policy explicitly drawing on empirical research. The research literature supports the development of a compelling public rationale. Without high-quality studies like the STAR Study, it is unlikely the policy would have been promoted or enacted.

Technology in Classrooms

A fourth area of intense policy activity in the 1990s has involved efforts to increase the use of technology in classrooms. This is an interesting policy initiative because the empirical research literature on the use of computer technology to improve classroom instruction and students' achievement is limited and it is difficult to discern "clear and compelling conclusions" (Birman, Kirshstein, Levin, Matheson, & Stephens, 1997, p. 7). There are, however, schools that demonstrate those potential uses of computer technologies in improving teaching and learning, and there is a significant research literature on the use of computers in adult learning. Despite the weakness in the empirical research work, policymakers have been able to build a particularly strong public rationale for bringing more computer technology into classrooms in elementary and in secondary education. The public rationale for the widespread introduction of computer technology has two major arguments. The first focuses on preparing students for participation in an economy in which computer technology plays an increasingly prominent role. Computers are widely used in work settings, are readily available on college campuses, and are commonplace in many homes. If schools are going to prepare students with the skills and tools they need to be productive workers in an increasingly knowledge-based and technology-based economy, the schools need adequate computer technology. This rationale focuses on learning how to effectively use technology more than on how the use of technology will improve teaching and learning in basic subjects. The second argument is an equity argument. If technological literacy is so critical a skill for the labor market, then all students deserve access to computers and to computer technology in schools. The distribution of technological resources is broadly similar to the distribution of other resources with students attending suburban high schools more likely to have access to computers and to computer technology than students attending rural or urban schools (U.S. Department of Education, National Center for Education Statistics, 1995).

The two elements of this rationale are reflected in the education initiative of the U.S. Department of Education. This initiative has four components: connecting schools to the information superhighway, bringing multimedia computers into classrooms, the development and use of effective software, and preparing teachers to effectively use computer technology in classroom instruction. This initiative is being carried out through a combination of federal program activities and the work of grassroots nonprofit initiatives. The largest of the programs is designed to provide affordable access to the Internet. Schools and libraries will receive discounts on telecommunications services (such as phone service, internal connections, and Internet access) of more than $2 billion annually. The discounts range from 20% to 90% depending on the geographical location of the school and the percentage of students in the school who are poor. This special rate, called the E-rate, will help to assure that all schools can afford to be connected to the Internet. The E-rate initiative is designed to address the inequities in the availability of educational technology that is a central element of the public rationale for technology policies.

Another program initiative is designed to demonstrate how computer technology can be used to improve teaching and learning. The Technology Innovation Challenge Grant Program challenges schools to form partnerships with others (i.e., universities and businesses) to implement innovative programs on how computers and multimedia can be used throughout the curriculum. Some of these innovation projects will become the case studies of what can be accomplished with technology and will provide guidance for others. This hothouse program is complemented by a much larger program, which provides funds to states to support local schools. The Technology Literacy Challenge Fund provides funds that can be used by local schools to purchase computers, software, trained teachers and to pay for connections to the Internet. All 50 states are participating in the program, which is a 5-year, $2 billion program.

Technology is an area that lends itself to more grassroots and, nonprofit initiatives. Three major initiatives are well under way. States are organizing NetDays, which are community efforts to wire schools for computer technology. In 1996, more than 200,000 volunteers worked to wire over 3,000 schools in California for computers and for connections to the Internet. Similar NetDays have taken place in other states. Businesses also have come together to form a national nonprofit organization, U.S. Tech Corps, which is dedicated to helping schools use technology to improve teaching and learning. This volunteer effort encourages high-technology workers to work with local schools in setting and maintaining computer technology. Finally, there is an effort designed to help ensure that teachers are trained in the uses of new technologies. The McGuffy project, a nonprofit organization, is leading a movement to recruit and train half a million teachers in the use of technology in classrooms.

These policy initiatives reflect the strong public rationale for technology and the relatively weak research base. The initiatives focus on providing resources and stimulating innovation. They also draw on the deep public interest through a series of grassroots efforts.

DISCUSSION

The governance of elementary and secondary education in the United States is highly fragmented among federal, state, and local levels. Although every level of governance has particular domains of responsibility, the resulting patchwork of policies can create contradictions and tensions for local schools. Although research findings often play a major role in policy development at the federal level, they are less likely to have a major role in policy development at local levels. Local districts and schools are less likely to have the staff capacity to review and to incorporate research findings into the policy development process. Traditionally, state educational agencies have had a greater capacity to develop research-based policies. However, recent reductions in the staffing of state agencies may gradually erode their capacity and will probably reduce the likelihood of research findings playing a major role in the policy development process.

Another feature of policymaking that limits the incorporation of research findings is that most state and local policies are derivative of policies tried in other jurisdictions. The recent flurry of class-size reduction policies or charter school policies is a good example. In such cases, the policy development process is likely to be truncated and may begin with adapting the existing policies of others to fit local circumstances. The foreshortening of the policy development process may lessen the role of research and if research findings are not a significant part of the policy development process, they are unlikely to play even a minor role in the political debate about the policy. Whereas lack of capacity decreases the likelihood of the development of research-based policies, certain other features of policymaking enhance the chances that policymakers will be aware of and influenced by research findings. Because educational policies are usually politically contested, the potential costs of not knowing about studies that support or contradict a proposed policy can be very high. Consequently, there is a great demand for findings that have implications for the policies under development.

Policymakers work in an environment that gives more credence to certain types of research over others. They are more likely to pay attention to results that come from studies conducted by the federal or by state government agencies. One reason is that government agencies are more likely to defend reports or findings and, therefore, their views are more likely to be influential. In contrast, the work of academics is confined to the domain of experts. In the world of policymaking, the work of experts is often regarded as an excellent technical understanding of a subject but is also viewed as the work of a single individual or a group of collaborators. Most of the settings in which experts work, such as universities or think tanks, do not routinely defend or endorse the findings of their researchers. The quality and defensibility of the work of the researchers are seen as their responsibilities. Without a corporate actor wiling to endorse the results, the policy world can and does treat the claims of researchers as the claims of individuals.

The research of experts, however, is not all treated the same. There are certain characteristics of academic research that are likely to increase its legitimacy in the policy world. One is the use of government data, such as data from the Bureau of the Census or data from the National Center for Education Statistics. These data are used for many policy purposes by government officials and are viewed as highly credible. A second characteristic is if the research has been funded by a government agency. Usually such funding requires a peer review of the proposed work and a review of the reports by the agency but not agency endorsement. Finally, studies with relatively large samples and strong longitudinal designs, such as the Tennessee STAR study, are seen as methodologically more credible and more difficult to criticize.

Not all policies, however, are developed on the basis of such studies. Some policies, like the policies in the area of technology, draw on case studies of innovations. In these types of studies, the judgments regarding the strength of the research are based on how compelling the case story is. It is very seldom that the evidence from a case study is directly challenged because it is very unlikely that another researcher would collect data at the same site. The studies support policies designed, in essence, to produce similar case study results in other sites. There are seldom, however, studies of how policies can encourage similar results in different sites. An interesting feature of the NASDC projects featured in the comprehensive school reform policy is that they have attempted to address this issue (Glennan, 1998).

The relationship of social science research and policy development is complex and not adequately described. Within education, this relationship probably varies across the different levels of the educational system as well as between the executive and legislative branches. The four cases that I described were initiatives at the federal level, but there are many similar policies at the state and the district levels. Even among these four cases, there were significant differences in the social science research base for the policies as well as differences in how the research influenced the process of policy development.

The fragmentation of the governance of public elementary and of secondary education creates many actors with the responsibility to make policy decisions. Perhaps more than other institutional sectors, the high diffusion of public decisionmaking in education increases the chances that there will be numerous examples of policies that are inconsistent, if not contradictory, to a fair reading of the social science research evidence. To better understand the relationship of social science research to policy, it is necessary to examine the process of policy development separate from the partisan politics of legislative decision making. There is evidence that the policy development process incorporates research evidence, particularly policies developed in the executive branch. To expect the partisan political debate about educational policies to be silenced by the weight of social science evidence is to fail to understand the political process of policy debates.

REFERENCES

Achilles, C. M., Nye. B. A., Zaharias, J. B., Fulton, B. D., & Cain. C. (1996). Education's equivalent of medicine's Farmingham heart study. Washington, DC: ERIC Clearinghouse. ED 402677.

Alexander, K. L., Cook, M., & McDill, E. L. (1978). Curriculum tracking and educational stratification. *American Sociological Review, 43,* 47–66.

Alexander, K. L., & Entwisle, D. R. (1996). Educational tracking during the early years: First grade placements and middle school constraints. In A. C. Kerckhoff (Ed.), *Generating social stratification: Toward a new research agenda* (p. 83–113). Boulder. CO: Westview Press.

Baker, E. (1994). Researchers and assessment policy development: A cautionary tale. *American Journal of Education, 102,* 450–477.

Becker, G. (1964). *Human capital.* New York: National Bureau of Economic Research.
Birman, B. F., Kirshstein, R. J., Levin, D. A., Matheson, N., & Stephens, M. (1997). The effectiveness of using technology in K–12 education: A preliminary framework and review. Paper prepared by American Institutes for Research for U.S. Department of Education, Office of Educational Research and Improvement.
Bishop, J. H. (1997). The effect of national standards and curriculum-based exams on achievement. *American Economic Review, 87,* 260–264.
Bohrnstedt, G. W., & Parrish, T. B. (1998). *California's class size reduction initiative: Is it likely to reduce or create further inequities in California districts?* Paper presented at the American Sociological Association Meetings, San Francisco, California.
Center for School Assessment. (1986). *The relationship between class size and the achievement for first grade students in Indiana 1984–85.* Indianapolis, IN: Indiana Department of Education.
Chubb, J. E., & Moe, T. M. (1990). *Politics, markets, and America's schools.* Washington, DC: The Brookings Institute.
Cohen, D. K. (1983, March). Evaluation and reform. *New Directions for Program Evaluation, 17,* 73–81.
Coleman, J. S. (1988). Social capital in the creation of human capital. American *Journal of Sociology, 94,* S95–A120.
Coleman, J. S., Campbell, E. Q., Hobson, C. J., McPartland, J., Mood, A., Weinfeld, F. D., & York, R. L. (1966). *Equality of educational opportunity.* Washington: U.S. Government Printing Office.
Coleman, J. S., & Hoffer, T. (1987). *Public and private schools: The impact of communities.* New York: Basic Books.
Coleman, J. S., Hoffer, T., & Kilgore, S. (1982). *High school achievement: Public, Catholic and private school compared.* New York: Basic Books.
Coleman, J. S., Schneider, B., Plank, S., Schiller, K. S., Shouse, R., & Wang, H. (1997). *Redesigning American education.* Boulder, CO: Westview Press.
Comer, J. P. (1997). *Waiting for a miracle: Why schools can't solve our problems—and how we can.* New York: Dutton.
Department of Education Appropriations Act 1998, Title In of P. L. 105–78, November 13, 1997; 111 Stat. 1467.
Dreeben, R., & Barr, R. (1988). The formulation and instruction of ability groups. *American Journal of Education, 97,* 34–64.
Elmore, R. F. (1980). Backward mapping: Implementation research and policy decisions. *Political Science Quarterly, 94,* 601–616.
Finn, J. D. (1998). *Class size and students at risk: What is known? What is next?* Washington, DC: U.S. Department of Education, Office of Educational Research and Improvement.
Gamoran, A. (1987). The stratification of high school learning opportunities. *Sociology of Education, 60,* 135–155.
Glass, G. V., Cahen, L. S., Smith, M. L., & Filby, N. N. (1982). *School class size: Research and policy.* Beverly Hills, CA: Sage.
Glass, G. V., & Smith, M. L. (1978). *Meta-analysis of research on the relationship of class size and achievement.* San Francisco, CA: Far West Laboratory for Educational Research & Development
Glennan, T. K. (1998). *New American schools after six years.* Santa Monica, CA: Rand.
Hallinan, M. T, & Sørensen, A. B. (1983). The formation and stability of instructional groups. *American Sociological Review, 48,* 838–851.
Hallinan, M. T., & Sørensen, A. B. (1987). Ability grouping and sex differences in mathematics achievement. *Sociology of Education, 60,* 63–72.
Hanushek, E. A. (1998). The evidence on class size (Occasional paper number 98–1). Rochester, NY: W. Allen Wallis Institute of Political Economy.
Jencks, C., Bartlett, S., Corcoran, M., Crouse, J., Eaglesfield, D., Jackson, G., McClelland, K., Mueser, P., Olneck, M., Scwartz, J., Ward, S., & Williams, J. (1979). *Who gets ahead? The determinants of economic success in America.* New York: Basic Books.
Jencks, C., Smith, M., Acland, H., Bane, M. J., Cohen, D., Gintis, H., Heyns, B., & Michelson, S. (1972). *Inequality.* New York: Basic Books.
Jennings, J. F. (1998). *Why national standards and tests? Politics and the quest for better schools.* Thousand Oaks, CA: Sage.
Jones, C., Clarke, M., Mooney, G., McWilliams, H., Crawford, L. Stephenson, B., & Tournangeau (1983). *High school and beyond senior cohort, data file user's manual.* Chicago: National Opinion Research Center.
Keeves, J. P. (Ed., 1992). *The IEA study of mathematics III: Analysis of the mathematics curricula.* New York: Oxford University Press.
Levin, H. (1987). Accelerated schools for disadvantaged students. *Educational Leadership, 44,* 19–21.

McLaughlin, M. W. (1985). Implementation realities and evaluation design. In R. L. Shotland & M. M. (Eds.), *Social science and social policy* (pp. 96–120). Beverly Hills, CA: Sage.

McLaughlin, M. W. (1987). Learning from experience: Lessons from policy implementation. *Educational Evaluation & Policy Analysis, 9,* 171–178.

McRobbie, J. (1997, September). Class size reduction: Is it working? *Thrust for Educational Leadership.*

Mitchell, D., Carson, C., & Badarak, G. (1989). *How changing class size affects classrooms and students.* Riverside, CA: California Educational Research Cooperative.

Mosteller, F. (1995). The Tennessee study of class size in the early school grades. *The Future Children, 5,* 113–127.

National Academy of Education. (1987). *The nation's report card: Improving the assessment of student achievement.* Washington, DC: National Academy of Education.

National Center for Educational Statistics. (1998). *The condition of education 1998.* Washington, DC: U.S. Department of Education, Office of Educational Research and Improvement.

National Council on Education Standards and Testing. (1992). *Rising standards for American education: A report to Congress, the Secretary of Education, the National Education Goals Panel, and the American people.* Washington, DC: Author.

National Council of Teachers of Mathematics. (1989). *Curriculum and evaluation standards for school mathematics.* Reston, VA: Author.

National Education Goals Panel. (1991). *Measuring progress toward the national educational goals.* Washington, DC: Author.

Natriello, G. (Ed., 1987). *School dropouts.* New York: Teachers College Press.

Natriello, G., McDill, E. L., & Pallas, A. M. (1990). *Schooling disadvantaged children.* New York: Teachers College Press.

Newmann. F. M. (Ed., 1989). *Student engagement and achievement in American secondary schools.* New York: Teachers College Press.

Odden, A. (1990). Class size and student achievement: Research-based policy alternatives. *Educational Evaluation and Policy Analysis, 12,* 213–227.

Peterson, P. L. (1998). Why do educational research? Rethinking our roles and identities, our texts and contexts. *Educational Researcher, 27,* 4–10.

Pressman, J. L., & Wildavsky, A. B. (1973). *Implementation.* Berkeley, CA: University of California Press.

Purkey, S. C., & Smith, M. S. (1983). Effective schools: A review. *Elementary School Journal, 83,* 427–452.

Ravitch, D. (1998). *Brookings papers on education policy.* Washington, DC: The Brookings Institute.

Resnick, L., & Cropfer, B. (1989). *Toward the thinking curriculum: Current cognitive research.* Alexandria, VA: Association for Supervision and Curriculum Development.

Ricobson, J., Henderson, L., Burkeheimer, G., Place, C., & Levinsohn, J. (1981). *National longitudinal study: Base Year (1972) through fourth follow-up (1979).* Chapel Hill, NC: Center for Educational Research and Evaluation, Research Triangle Institute.

Riley, R. W. (1991). Reflections on Goals 2000. *Teachers College Record, 96,* 380–388.

Robinson, G. E., & Wittebols, J. H. (1986). *Class size research: A related cluster analysis for decision-making.* Arlington, VA: Education Research Service.

Schultz, T. (1961). Investment in human capital. *American Economic Review, 51,* 1–17.

Sewell, W. H., Hauser, R. M., & Featherman, D. L. (Eds., 1976). *Schooling and achievement in American society.* New York: Academic Press.

Sizer, T. R. (1991). *Horace's school: Redesigning the American high school.* Boston: Houghton Mifflin.

Slavin. R. E. (Ed., 1989). *School and classroom organization.* Hillsdale, NJ: Lawrence Erlbaum Associates.

Slavin, R. E., Madden, N. A., Dolan, L. J., & Wasik, B. A. (1996). *Every child, every school: Success for all.* Newbury Park, CA: Corwin.

Smith, M. S., & O'Day, J. A. (1991). Systemic school reform. In S. Furman & B. Malen (Eds.), *The politics of curriculum and testing.* Bristol, PA: Falmer Press.

Smith, M. S., Stevenson, D. L., & Li, C. P. (1998). Voluntary national tests would improve education. *Educational Leadership, 55,* 42–44.

Stevenson, D. L., Schiller, K., & Schneider, B. (1994). Sequences of opportunities for learning. *Sociology of Education, 67,* 184–198.

Tomlinson, T. M. (1988). *Class size and public policy: Politics and panaceas.* Washington, U.S. Department of Education, Office of Educational Research and Improvement.

U.S. Department of Education. (1991). *America 2000: An education strategy.* Washington, DC: Author.

U.S. Department of Education. (1997a). *A back to school special report on the baby boom echo: Here come the teenagers.* Washington, DC: National Center for Education Statistics.

U.S. Department of Education. (1997b). *Urban and suburban/rural special strategies for educating disadvantaged students studies, Final report*. Washington, DC: U.S. Government Printing Office.

U.S. Department of Education. (1998). *Reducing class size: What do we know?* Washington, DC: Office of Educational Research and Improvement.

U.S. Department of Education, Office of Research and Educational Improvement, National Center for Education Statistics. (1995). *Advanced telecommunications in U.S. public schools, K-12*. Washington, DC: U.S. Government Printing Office.

Velez, W. (1985). Finishing college: The effects of college type. *Sociology of Education, 58,* 191–200.

Weiss, C. H., & Bucuvalas, M. J. (1980). *Social science research and decision-making*. New York: Columbia University Press.

Wenglinsky, H. (1997). *When money matters: How educational expenditures improve student performance and when they don't*. Princeton, NJ: Educational Testing Service, Policy Information Center.

Wise, A. E. (1968). *Rich schools, poor schools: The promise of equal educational opportunity*. Chicago: University of Chicago Press.

Author Index

Subject Index

Ability grouping, 22, 61–62, 78, 152, 160, 266, 283, 315–316, 318, 322–323, 533, 548, 561
Academic organization, 125
Academic outcomes, 7, 115, 331–332, 359
Academic programs, 41, 123–124, 147–148, 403, 456, 462
Academic status
  in the classroom, 266–267, 272–276
Accelerated Schools Project, 551
Access to education, 7, 170, 242, 250, 253, 255–256, 548
Accountability in education,
  administrative, 398
  assessment-based, 537–542, 553–555
  formal system of, 10, 11, 529–535, 540–541
  market principles of, 395
  parental, 393–399
  political, 397
  teachers, 59, 93, 98, 398
Achievement
  academic, 3, 8, 10, 16, 22, 61, 72, 76, 79, 81, 105, 123, 135, 139, 140, 142–145, 147–148, 152–154, 156–160, 266, 268, 271, 274–275, 282, 294, 305, 314, 358–359, 362, 370, 375, 382–387, 399, 407, 532, 539, 555–556
  adolescent, 371
  in America, 485, 554, 565
  analysis, 270
  assessments, 357
  average, 146, 332, 433, 539, 541
  in Catholic schools, 122–123
  cognitive, 158, 345
  collective, 24
  comparisons of , 146
  cross-national, 352, 355, 358
  culture in, 357
  data, 352, 355, 358
  determinants of, 79, 115
  deviations, 155

Achievement (*cont.*)
  differences, 71, 76, 125, 275, 311–312, 348
  distribution of, 78, 122, 270, 279, 314
  dynamics, 358
  educational, 3, 105, 134, 142, 270–271, 276, 352, 356, 362, 479, 492, 572
  in English, 82, 148
  equality in, 76, 282, 363, 373, 384–385
  higher, 38, 76, 115, 123, 431
  individual, 115, 375
  international, 356–358, 363
  in Japan, 160, 355, 364
  in mathematics, 152, 167, 269–270, 278, 305, 337, 363, 404, 539
  measures of, 191, 279
  model of, 6
  outcomes of, 121, 191
  in public school, 22, 35, 42, 61, 115, 121–126, 131–132, 141, 147, 150–160,
  raising, 380
  in reading, 274, 280, 556
  in science, 270, 355
  social construction of, 358, 360
  socioeconomic, 134, 474
  standards, 202, 554
  stratification, 62, 269
  student, 8–9, 38–39, 41, 47, 60–63, 75–76, 78, 122, 131, 140, 146, 283, 296–297, 302–303, 305–306, 332, 343, 350, 358, 362, 369, 372, 375, 377, 381, 388–389, 403–404, 532, 535, 538, 540, 551, 554–557, 562
  variance in, 276, 279
  vocational, 483
Achievement gains, 62, 139, 143, 145, 147, 149, 156–157, 278, 344, 375, 556
Achievement gap, 280
Achievement growth, 150